CONTEMPORARY RESEARCH IN SOCIAL PSYCHOLOGY

A Book of Readings

Other books by Henry Clay Lindgren:

An Introduction to Social Psychology, Wiley, 1969.

Readings in Educational Psychology, Wiley, 1968.

Educational Psychology in the Classroom, third edition, Wiley, 1967.

with Donn Byrne and Lewis Petrinovich, *Psychology: An Introduction to a Behavioral Science,* second edition, Wiley, 1966.

Psychology of Personal Development, American Book, 1964.

And others in mental health.

CONTEMPORARY RESEARCH IN SOCIAL PSYCHOLOGY

A Book of Readings

Edited by

HENRY CLAY LINDGREN
San Francisco State College

John Wiley & Sons, Inc.
New York London Sydney Toronto

4 5 6 7 8 9 10

Library of Congress Catalog Card Number: 69-10412
Cloth: SBN 471 53773 X
Paper: SBN 471 53774 X
Printed in the United States of America

To the late
I. James Quillen,
who awakened in me an aware-
ness of the relevance of social research.

PREFACE

If a course in social psychology at any point other than the most advanced level is to be successful, it must do two things: first, it must at least start the student to think as a social psychologist; and second, it must enable him to develop a broader and deeper understanding of his own experiences as a social organism. The first of these objectives is the more obvious: if the student is unable to adapt himself to the perspectives used by social psychologists, the informational content of the subject will remain essentially incomprehensible to him. In my opinion, this problem of learning to use a new frame of reference and a new approach to data is a crucial one for both student and instructor. If it can be successfully resolved, the student can move ahead in a relatively independent fashion, developing and broadening his understanding of research and theory in the field.

Social psychology has a special advantage over other academic fields in that most of the material is directly or indirectly relevant to the student's everyday experience. What he learns in a social psychology course *may* enable him to gain a better understanding of events in which he is directly or indirectly involved, but this is likely to occur only if these events become part of the data of the course, and this brings me to the second point. If social psychology is taught in a vacuum, uncontaminated by everyday experience, it may involve and educate the few students in the class who are eager to press on to graduate school and research careers, but at the same time it will lose the remainder. Most of the students who are in our colleges and universities today are competent enough to pass the examinations that instructors devise for them (or perhaps it is the other way around), but if what they learn in a social psychology course has no relevance for them, popular belief, common sense, and the conventional wisdom will win out in the end, and they will go their way, unaffected to any noticeable extent by their exposure to the course.

The studies in this sampler of papers have been included with both of these prerequisites in mind. They have been selected with regard to range and type in order to give students an opportunity to see how social psychologists conduct research; gather, organize, and perceive data; and construct, review, and evaluate theories. The selections also have been made with an eye to their relevance to the everyday experience of the student and to the major social problems that impinge on his field of awareness: race relations, the rehabilitation of the socially deprived and the economically underdeveloped, international understanding, and the management of aggression. Social psychology has few answers, if any, for these problems, but it does have great potential as a source of understanding their dynamics.

The general theme followed in the progression of the sections is that of beginning with the individual and his attraction to others—the basis of all social interaction. This attraction makes social learning and social influence possible and enables the individual to learn the kinds of motives that are appropriate for members of society, as well as the status and the roles that are consistent with the positions he occupies. Above all, he learns who he is. As the individual interacts with others, he learns to communicate, to function as a member of groups and organizations, and, to a greater or lesser extent, he learns how to manage his aggressive drives. This organization of topics is, I believe, a useful one, and one that will be compatible with many if not most introductory and intermediate courses in social psychology.

A comment about the editing of the selections is in order. Minor changes, such as the deletion of a footnote, a sentence or two, or one or more tables, are indicated by the term "slight abridgment." In every instance, these changes have been made in order to conserve space and to include as large a range of selections as possible without damage to the continuity of the paper in question. Tables, for example, were deleted only when the data they contained were already presented in the text of the article. Where tables have been dropped, notation of that fact is made by footnote.

This book of readings has been made possible only by the cooperation of almost a hundred authors and their publishers. In appreciation of their willingness to permit their work to be included in this book, a share of the royalties it earns will be donated in their behalf to the American Psychological Foundation. I would also like to express my appreciation for the help received from Dr. Daniel Katz, who gave encouragement and advice while the project was in progress and who suggested a number of articles which are included in the final version of this collection of papers. Thanks also are due to Lyn Gustafson, and especially to Lori Fisk, who worked on the preparation of copy for the printers, and to Fredi Lindgren, who played an active and vital part, as always, in the development of this book.

Henry Clay Lindgren

San Francisco State College
August 1968

CONTENTS

§ 1 INTRODUCTION 1

1.1 ***Social Psychology: A Perspective* 2**
Daniel Katz

1.2 ***The Power of Dissonance Techniques to Change Attitudes* 7**
Ewart E. Smith

1.3 ***Suicide, Migration, and Race: A Study of Cases in New Orleans* 22**
Warren Breed

§ 2 SOCIAL ATTRACTION 38

2.1 ***Situational Determinants of Affiliative Preference under Stress* 39**
Robert L. Helmreich and Barry E. Collins

2.2 ***Importance of Physical Attractiveness in Dating Behavior* 53**
Elaine Walster, Vera Aronson, Darcy Abrahams, and Leon Rottmann

2.3 ***Similarity, Contrast, and Complementarity in Friendship Choice* 69**
Norman Miller, Donald T. Campbell, Helen Twedt, and Edward J. O'Connell

2.4 ***Interpersonal Attraction toward Negroes* 85**
Donn Byrne and Carl McGraw

§ 3 SOCIAL LEARNING 102

3.1 ***The Effect of Brief Social Deprivation on Social and Nonsocial Reinforcement 103***
William Dorwart, Robert Ezerman, Michael Lewis, and David Rosenhan

3.2 ***Influence of Social Reinforcement and the Behavior of Models in Shaping Children's Moral Judgments 110***
Albert Bandura and Frederick J. McDonald

3.3 ***Model's Characteristics as Determinants of Social Learning 126***
Joan Grusec and Walter Mischel

§ 4 SOCIAL INFLUENCE, DISSONANCE, AND CONSONANCE 136

4.1 ***Social Facilitation 138***
Robert B. Zajonc

4.2 ***Conformity as a Function of Different Reinforcement Schedules 154***
Norman S. Endler

4.3 ***Compliance without Pressure: The Foot-in-the-Door Technique 165***
Jonathan L. Freedman and Scott C. Fraser

4.4 ***Studies in Forced Compliance: I. The Effect of Pressure for Compliance on Attitude Change Produced by Face-to-Face Role Playing and Anonymous Essay Writing 179***
J. Merrill Carlsmith, Barry E. Collins, and Robert L. Helmreich

4.5 ***Modification of Psychophysical Judgments as a Method of Reducing Dissonance 205***
Paul R. Wilson and Paul N. Russell

4.6 ***Toward an Understanding of Inequity 210***
J. Stacy Adams

4.7 ***Mediated Generalization of Attitude Change via the Principle of Congruity 234***
Percy H. Tannenbaum

§ 5 SOCIAL MOTIVES, ATTITUDES, AND THEIR MEASUREMENT 246

5.1 ***Parental Antecedents of Authoritarianism*** *247*
Donn Byrne

5.2 ***Need Achievement and Entrepreneurship: A Longitudinal Study*** *255*
David C. McClelland

5.3 ***Expectations of Social Acceptance and Compatibility as Related to Status Discrepancy and Social Motives*** *261*
Robert B. Bechtel and Howard M. Rosenfeld

§ 6 STATUS AND ROLE 272

6.1 ***The Meaning of Success: Some Differences in Value Systems of Social Classes*** *273*
F. M. Katz

6.2 ***Social Class and Parent-Child Relationships: An Interpretation*** *282*
Melvin L. Kohn

6.3 ***Social and Attitudinal Characteristics of Spanish-Speaking Migrant and Ex-migrant Workers in the Southwest*** *297*
Horacio Ulibarri

6.4 ***Self-rejection among North African Immigrants to Israel*** *306*
Judith T. Shuval

6.5 ***The Effects of Changes in Roles on the Attitudes of Role Occupants*** *317*
Seymour Lieberman

6.6 ***Risk-taking in Children: Age and Sex Differences*** *332*
Paul Slovic

6.7 ***Effects of Paternal Absence on Sex-typed Behaviors in Negro and White Preadolescent Males*** *339*
E. Mavis Hetherington

§ 7 PERSONALITY AS A SOCIAL AND CULTURAL PHENOMENON 349

7.1 ***Self-image Disparity: A Developmental Approach*** *350*
Phyllis Katz and Edward Zigler

7.2 ***Relationship of Self- and Ideal-Self-descriptions with Sex, Race, and Class in Southern Adolescents*** *368*
Robert I. McDonald and Malcolm D. Gynther

7.3 ***Birth Order and Academic Primogeniture*** *374*
William D. Altus

7.4 ***A Comparison of the Value Systems of Mexican and American Youth*** *383*
Robert F. Peck

7.5 ***Independence Training among Hawaiians: A Cross-cultural Study*** *392*
Ronald Gallimore, Alan Howard, and Cathie Jordan

§ 8 COMMUNICATION 398

8.1 ***The Obstinate Audience: The Influence Process from the Point of View of Social Communication*** *399*
Raymond A. Bauer

8.2 ***Race, Status, Quality of Spoken English, and Opinions about Civil Rights as Determinants of Interpersonal Attitudes*** *413*
Harry C. Triandis, Wallace D. Loh, and Leslie Ann Levin

8.3 ***Use of the Semantic Differential to Study Acculturation in American Indian Adolescents*** *422*
Malcolm M. Helper and Sol L. Garfield

§ 9 GROUP PROCESSES 433

9.1 ***Children's Acquisition of Skill in Performing a Group Task under Two Conditions of Group Formation*** *435*
Moses H. Goldberg and Eleanor E. Maccoby

9.2 ***The Effects of Clear and Unclear Role Expectations on Group Productivity and Defensiveness*** *443*
Ewart E. Smith

9.3 ***Competition and Noncompetition in Relation to Satisfaction and Feelings toward Own-Group and Nongroup Members*** *452*
Robert E. Dunn and Morton Goldman

9.4 ***Quasi-therapeutic Effects of Intergroup Competition*** *466*
James W. Julian, Doyle W. Bishop, and Fred E. Fiedler

9.5 ***Some Effects of Variations in Other Strategy upon Game Behavior*** *478*
Charles G. McClintock, Philip Gallo, and Albert A. Harrison

9.6 ***Group Problem Solving under Two Types of Executive Structure 489***
Thornton B. Roby, Elizabeth H. Nicol, and Francis M. Farrell
9.7 ***Group Discussion and Predicted Ethical Risk Taking 500***
Salomon Rettig

§ 10 **LEADERSHIP AND ORGANIZATIONAL BEHAVIOR 510**

10.1 ***Leadership and Friendship Status as Factors in Discussion Group Interaction 511***
Robert E. Lana, Willard Vaughan, and Elliott McGinnies
10.2 ***Leader Behavior, Group Productivity, and Rating of Least Preferred Co-worker 519***
John A. Sample and Thurlow R. Wilson
10.3 ***Behavior in Groups as a Function of Self-, Interaction, and Task Orientation 527***
Bernard M. Bass and George Dunteman
10.4 ***Control, Performance, and Satisfaction: An Analysis of Structural and Individual Effects 544***
Jerald G. Bachman, Clagett G. Smith, and Jonathan A. Slesinger
10.5 ***The Experimental Change of a Major Organizational Variable 563***
Nancy C. Morse and Everett Reimer

§ 11 **AGGRESSION AND ITS MANAGEMENT 580**

11.1 ***Group Pressure and Action against a Person 581***
Stanley Milgram
11.2 ***The Expression and Reduction of Hostility 593***
Leonard Berkowitz
11.3 ***The Ghetto Logic 628***
Magoroh Maruyama
11.4 ***Family Interaction as Antecedent to the Direction of Male Aggressiveness 636***
Joan McCord, William McCord, and Alan Howard

INDEX 643

CONTEMPORARY RESEARCH IN SOCIAL PSYCHOLOGY

A Book of Readings

§ 1 INTRODUCTION

The opening section consists of a review of progress made by social psychologists and the problems they face, plus two papers selected as representative of the kind of research conducted by psychologists and sociologists in the field of social psychology.

Daniel Katz, the author of the first paper, has been a leading figure in social psychology from its beginning as a scientific, experimental discipline in the mid-1920s. The selection contributed by him consists of his farewell message as editor of the *Journal of Personality and Social Psychology* and deals with the status, progress, and future of the field of social psychology.

The second paper, by Ewart E. Smith, is particularly interesting in that it presents findings that are contrary to common sense. If Army enlisted men can be persuaded to like fried grasshoppers, one would think that they would do so as a result of the influence of pleasant, agreeable, and ingratiating leaders rather than that of cool and distant ones. Smith's results, which were predicted from psychological theory based on earlier studies, show the opposite. This research is very much in the main stream of experimental social psychology in that it deals with Festinger's "theory of cognitive dissonance," a concept which has produced a considerable amount of research, as well as findings that are often in disagreement with common sense and the conventional wisdom.

The third paper, contributed by Warren Breed, analyzes biographical data of persons who committed suicide in New Orleans during the 1950s and 1960s and demonstrates how sociologists gather and interpret data that are of interest and value to social psychologists. Breed's finding that suicide among men is related to downward occupational mobility is of psychological importance because it shows that occupational status serves as a significant anchorage point for the individual's identity. When achieved status is below expectations, the resulting loss of security can be very disturbing. Occupational status is of less importance for women, who are more likely to turn to suicide when they have been demoralized by their inability to make lasting affectional ties.

1.1 SOCIAL PSYCHOLOGY: A PERSPECTIVE

Daniel Katz

Some six years and 5000 manuscripts ago I accepted the editorship of the *Journal of Abnormal and Social Psychology*. It has been a long editorial term which has seen the old *JASP* become two journals. In my closing editorial for the *Journal of Personality and Social Psychology*, . . . I would offer some impressions about the status, progress, and future of social psychology.

Over the years two truly impressive advances are clear. The first is the growth of methodology both in new techniques and in research standards. The improvement in the quality of research with respect to design, analysis, controls, and the precise specification of variables has been marked. Though many of our techniques of data collection and measurement are still blunt instruments, though replication is still not a standard operating procedure, and though we often forget that certain types of studies do require a sampling design both for subjects and for stimuli, we have come a long way in resting our discipline upon verifiable research.

The second great advance has been the growing realization that many of the problems and concepts of the social world about us and of the other social sciences could be translated into social psychological language and put to empirical test. Much of what was formerly the province of traditional morality, conventional wisdom, political

Source: Reprinted with slight abridgment from the *Journal of Personality and Social Psychology*, 1967, 7, 341–344, with permission of the author and the American Psychological Association, Inc.

maneuvering, or the territory of anthropology, sociology, political science, economics, and even history has been invaded by the pioneering social psychologist with his quantitative empiricism. Common-sense notions have been brought into the laboratory for testing in a fashion which would never have occurred to the social scientist of an older generation. The cleverness of many experimental psychologists in the creation and manipulation of variables within the laboratory would have won the admiration of Machiavelli. Field researchers have also been resourceful in extending the boundaries of social psychology so that there is considerable overlap between it and the other social sciences. An old misconception has been laid to rest, namely the belief in the independent hierarchical levels of the social sciences. Because each social science had its own labor union and its own terminology, it was believed that they represented fields with distinctive phenomena or types of data. But the researcher confronted with the problem of manipulating and measuring variables finds that these disciplines deal in large part with human behavior and its accompanying context of motivation, perception, and cognition.

I am afraid, however, that when we leave the area of methodology and its imaginative application to an increasing range of problems we find less spectacular progress in social psychology. Less impressive in the 40 or more years of its existence as a research discipline is the growth of theoretical understanding or even of an integrated body of generalizable substantive knowledge. We do have more verified pockets of information but we lack systematic knowledge. The technology of the field has developed more rapidly than its theory. It is true that we have some attempts at mathematical formulation of theoretical notions but these have been more in the technological aspects of theory building than in theoretical development itself. There have been no replacements for those theoretical giants of the early years, Floyd H. Allport and Kurt Lewin. Current work has not generated new ideas and we still reach back and revive concepts from Allport or Lewin or earlier theoreticians such as Durkheim, Freud, or Weber to meet specific needs.

The concern with technology and the marginal interest in theory are related to what seems to me the most critical problem we face today in social psychology—the continuing and growing fragmentation of the discipline. Like other scientific fields growth is accompanied by differentiation, specialization, and semiautonomy for the fractionated segments. Decentralization has many advantages in the development of refined technologies, of efficient application of techniques, and in the autonomy permitted the scientist. But there is another side to the story. With encapsulated sets of specializations, psychologists do not take advantage of the work closely related to their own research. They often duplicate their efforts but with a different terminology. Integration of knowledge becomes difficult in that idiosyncratic labels replace common concepts. Problems of theoretical significance for the larger field are no longer salient because investigators are not aware of the larger field. Single concept theories replace more comprehensive models of man's functioning. Fragmentation, in short, runs counter to the nature of science which is distinguished from philosophy or conventional wisdom by the cumulative character of its verifiable knowledge and theory. Without adequate communication among scientists the building of a body of related facts and principles is seriously retarded.

The formal communication mechanisms in science include scientific journals, books, and teaching, and the exchange of information at scientific meetings. It is of interest that these formal means of sharing knowledge are being replaced by informal networks of communication heavily restricted to the exchange of information among a specialized in-group. The formal mechanisms themselves are no longer adequate channels for meeting the needs of system-wide communication. In an earlier period journals performed an integrative function in that people in a given field could read a great proportion of the articles appearing in their own journal. But journals have become more specialized and utilize a number of technical vocabularies so that, even within a narrowly focused journal, readers are highly selective in their coverage of articles. Editorial boards are made up of specialists with expertise in different subareas to insure appropriate reviews of manuscripts. In other words there is far from ideal sharing of knowledge even at the top of this type of communication structure. Book publication and even texts for undergraduates show signs of running a parallel course. Where once the author of a text in social psychology attempted to bring together the available relevant knowledge, he is increasingly likely to present a volume organized around a single methodological approach or a single substantive subarea. Scientific meetings like scientific journals are directed at the needs of the subareas of the discipline and are in fact under the control of these subareas. They have been supplemented by general sessions where the topics for discussion cut across provincial interests but often such sessions are aimed at matters of professional interest or problems of social significance or older theoretical issues no longer relevant to modern research.

Communication across generations through teaching and training further aggravates segmentalization. Students are hurried through their general indoctrination so that they can begin their specialized studies in their first year of graduate work, if not before. They acquire the precise coding categories for their narrow area of knowledge but lack the more generalized and basic coding dimensions to handle much relevant information of a psychological character. Fortunately the student, unlike the computer, can rise above his built-in codes. Nevertheless, the training procedures are part of a technological system and do not provide the stimulus, the conceptual tools or the knowledge that would make for theorizing.

There have been some indications in recent years that within psychology itself some individuals are reacting against technological fragmentation: for example, the rise of the humanists and the creation of divisions concerned with historical and philosophical issues. With this resurgence of the interests of the generalists may come new journals designed to perform an integrative function. Such journals could be a forum for the development of theory, for the exchange of ideas, and for systematic articles reviewing and interrelating subareas of research. Just as we have created new journals for specialized interests, so too can we launch new journals for dealing with general theoretical issues. The revolt of the generalists does not seem, however, to have the vigor or purposefulness of the new specialized groups such as the Society for Experimental Social Psychology.

Nevertheless, more effective change processes may be under way in that one characteristic of a sociotechnical system is its changing nature. As a dynamic system it is affected by its own output. In passing judgment upon technocratic trends we may lack perspective in equating one phase with total history. Technology may not so much contain the seeds of its own destruction as the facilities for its own reform. Already we are witnessing the beginning of sophisticated information-processing and retrieval systems so that the researcher or teacher can have readily available all the knowledge about a given problem. A related and intriguing development is the growth of centralized data banks organized according to a common conceptual language cutting across specialized fields such as the Interuniversity/Political Consortium Data Bank at the University of Michigan. The researcher now can extend the scope and depth of his theoretical interests. He can test a broad hypothesis and its contingent predictions for a variety of settings and conditions with rich data resources and with computer facilities for efficient data analysis. Such data banks are in their beginnings but they have already spurred a creative burst of energy among researchers.

Other sources of input which may move us toward more integrative enterprises are the other social systems into which we feed. In the first place the larger society places constraints upon all its subsystems. Science for science's sake is a slogan to which we must adhere to preserve as much independence as possible from outside sources. But in reality all we can protect against is the direct and immediate intervention of society into our affairs. From the long-run point of view there must be some accumulation of useful knowledge, some validation against social realities, for a social science to continue to receive social support. The utilization of research knowledge does provide pressures toward integration. The specialized contribution of a narrow area of research is of little help unless it can be translated and integrated into a larger body of knowledge. The paradox may be that the least prestigeful part of the profession, the people seeking to utilize psychological knowledge, may turn out to be the theorists of the future. And this is not without good precedent in our history. Another source of input comes from our ties to the other social sciences. As we keep extending our boundaries and penetrating deeper into matters of mutual concern we are again meeting demands for integrated conceptualizations. The interface with other disciplines may well be the major source for generating the social psychology of the future. The conflicts, the challenges, the diversity of points of view, the intellectual excitement which help form the climate for creative solutions and theorizing are more likely to be found at intersecting boundaries of the field than at its center.

1.2 THE POWER OF DISSONANCE TECHNIQUES TO CHANGE ATTITUDES[1]

Ewart E. Smith

The Army Quartermaster recently presented the Matrix Corporation with the problem of determining the best methods for changing attitudes in military organizations. To find out, we undertook a series of experiments to evaluate the relative power of several techniques. The first objective of this research program was to select from the theory and experimental data on attitude change those techniques which might be applicable to changing consumer attitudes in military organizations. To be selected, potential techniques had to be (1) consistent with the culture and practices of the Armed Forces, (2) powerful enough to produce results of practical as well as theoretical and statistical significance, and (3) applicable to large numbers of personnel simultaneously even when the majority attitude might be one of opposition to the intended change. The next objective was to compare empirically the relative power of these selected attitude change techniques with each other and with methods traditional in the Armed Forces. Finally, we hoped to develop methods for applying these techniques in field situations.

APPROACH

Dissonance Theory

A large body of theory and research in the last few years in the area of attitude change has been based on the notion that man strives to be consistent. This consistency concept was first developed by

[1] This paper reports research undertaken in cooperation with the Quartermaster Food and Container Institute for the Armed Forces, QM Research and Engineering Command, U. S. Army, and has been assigned number 2148 in the series of papers approved for publication. The views or conclusions contained in this report are those of the author. They are not to be construed as necessarily reflecting the views or endorsement of the Department of Defense.

Source: Reprinted with slight abridgment from the *Public Opinion Quarterly*, 1961, 25, 626–639, with permission of the author and the *Public Opinion Quarterly*.

Heider, who discussed it in terms of a concept of balance.[2] Later work was done in this area by Osgood and Tannenbaum, working with the congruity principles.[3] Festinger, however, with his development of the concept of cognitive dissonance, has provided us with the best statement of the theory for use in the area of attitude change, where he has stimulated considerable research.[4] Festinger states that two elements of knowledge ". . . are in dissonant relation if, considering these two alone, the obverse of one element would follow from the other." Dissonance, according to Festinger, has drive characteristics which will motivate the person to reduce the dissonance and achieve consonance.

Of particular relevance to the present investigation is the deduction from the dissonance principle that, if a person makes a statement or engages in behavior which is contrary to an attitude that he holds, he will experience dissonance. Furthermore, if other means of reducing the dissonance are not available to the individual he will be motivated to change his attitude. An example is the "sweet lemon" reaction of the executive who is induced to transfer from New York to a section of the country he does not like, and who immediately begins to "dislike" New York and to say that he is looking forward to living in Podunk.

Dissonance theory was selected for possible application to changing food attitudes because it is consistent with, in fact requires, an authority figure acting as the influencing agent who has some control of rewards and punishments. This requirement is obviously compatible with military situations, whereas many of the most common techniques using group discussion, such as those used by Lewin in his famous food studies, are not.[5] In fact, recent research by Kipnis has shown that Lewinian group-centered attitude change techniques permit the group to take an even more negative position than they previously held just as easily as a more positive attitude, depending on the averaging of the prior individual attitudes that occurs during the group discussion.[6]

2 F. Heider, Attitudes and cognitive organization, *J. Psychol.*, 1946, **21**, 107–112.

3 C. E. Osgood and P. H. Tannenbaum, The principle of congruity in the prediction of attitude change, *Psychol. Rev.*, 1955, **62**, 42–55.

4 L. Festinger, *A theory of cognitive dissonance*, Evanston, Ill.: Row, Peterson, 1957.

5 K. Lewin, Forces behind food habits and methods of change, *Bull. Nat. Res. Council*, 1943, **108**, 35–65.

6 D. Kipnis, The effects of leadership style and leadership power upon the inducement of an attitude change, *J. Abnorm. Soc. Psychol.*, 1958, **57**, 173–180.

Another advantage of dissonance techniques is that the theory predicts that they will be more powerful the more difficult the attitude problem: dissonance theory states that the more negative the original attitude, the greater will be the dissonance between the original attitude and the induced positive behavior and hence the greater the attitude change.

A third reason for selecting dissonance techniques was the prior work of Brehm, in which he demonstrated increased liking on the part of school children for their most disliked vegetable through the use of a dissonance technique, that is, inducing the subjects to eat the vegetable by offering them a positive reward.[7]

Zimbardo has suggested that, using dissonance techniques, a negative communicator may be a more effective influencing agent than a positive communicator.[8] This is predicted because there would probably be less justification (in the mind of the subject) for conforming to the wishes of a negative communicator, hence more dissonance when inconsistent behavior was induced, and thus more attitude change.

Previous research has generally indicated that those with opinions most discrepant from the position advocated by the communicator change them the most (see Zimbardo for references and discussion). These results are consistent with the theory, because the greater the divergence of opinion the greater the dissonance. We wanted to investigate this phenomenon, since the use of those with the most negative attitudes as subjects for attempts to change attitudes should increase the power of dissonance techniques, and such a selection would have obvious practical advantages in an applied situation.

Leader Influence

The use of a group leader to present positively the reasons for the needed attitude change and to request that the group consider the change and try out the new behavior was included as one of the attitude-change techniques. [Leader-influence techniques are currently the major method for producing attitude change in the Armed Forces and have been supported by previous research by Scollon and by

[7] J. W. Brehm, Increasing cognitive dissonance by a *fait accompli*, *J. Abnorm. Soc. Psychol.*, 1959, 58, 379–382.

[8] P. G. Zimbardo, "Involvement and Communication Discrepancy as Determinants of Opinion Conformity," *Journal of Abnormal and Social Psychology*, Vol. 60, 1960, pp. 86–94.

Torrance and Mason.[9]] We could thus compare with current practices the effects of the newer attitude-change techniques being tested, and in this sense leader influence functioned as a control condition throughout the research program.

THE GRASSHOPPER EXPERIMENT[10]

Method

Army reservists undergoing evening training, mostly young privates with a sprinkling of NCO's, were told that they were to be the subjects of an experiment to determine the reactions of the men in the Armed Forces to unusual foods that they might have to eat in an emergency. Ten groups of about ten men each were served fried Japanese grasshoppers in open cans. Because most Americans dislike the idea of insects as food, the grasshoppers were seen as a severe test of techniques for changing attitudes toward food. There were four experimental conditions:

1. Dissonance, positive communicator. The experimenter was friendly, warm, and permissive throughout the experiment. He paid 50 cents to each man who would eat one grasshopper.
2. Dissonance, negative communicator. The experimenter was formal, cool, and official in manner throughout the experiment. He paid 50 cents to each man who would eat one grasshopper.
3. Leader influence. A sergeant with several years' experience, who had been selected on the advice of the officers as being highly respected by the men, gave the men a talk in his own words on why they should learn to eat survival foods such as grasshoppers. The sergeant concluded his talk by eating a grasshopper.
4. Control (no influence attempt, rationale). The men were presented with the grasshoppers and told the reason for eating them. There was no attempt to influence the men to eat them.

[9] R. W. Scollon, *The relative effectiveness of several film variables in modifying attitudes: A study of the application of films for influencing the acceptability of foods,* Naval Training Device Center, Port Washington, N.Y., Technical Report NAVTRADEVCEN 269-7-60, printed document. E. P. Torrance and R. Mason, Psychologic and sociologic aspects of survival ration acceptability, *Am. J. Clin. Nutr.,* 1957, 5, 176–179.

[10] Detailed descriptions of the three experiments, data presentation, and statistical analyses are contained in a report to the Quartermaster, copies of which can be received upon request from: Los Angeles Division, The Matrix Corporation, 14827 Ventura Blvd., Sherman Oaks, Calif.

Results

All subjects rated the experimenter on a seven-point scale on the item "The instructor was friendly and courteous," to determine whether the experimental manipulation to produce positive and negative communicators was effective. A mean rating of less than 4 would have indicated a negative perception. The mean (average) rating of the experimenter was 6.85 in the first condition and 6.40 in the second, with a critical ratio on the mean difference of 3.31†[11] (the other mean ratings are 6.48 for the third condition and 6.65 for the fourth condition). These results indicate that the positive and negative communicator manipulation did produce a differential perception of the experimenter on the part of the subjects, but it should be noted that this is a relative difference only and that the experimenter was seen positively in both conditions.

Table 1 *Mean Change in Rating of Grasshoppers on Hedonic Scale*

Condition	n	Mean Change
1. Dissonance, positive communicator:		
Subjects accepting inducement	19	0.63[a]
All subjects	20	0.60
2. Dissonance, negative communicator:		
Subjects accepting inducement	10	2.50[a]
All subjects	20	1.25
3. Leader influence:		
All subjects	19	0.37[a]
Refusing grasshoppers	2	
4. No influence:		
All subjects	17	1.82[a]
Refusing grasshoppers	2	

[a] *F* test on mean change scores is 3.99†.

As the main objective of the research was to determine the most effective methods for changing consumer attitudes, the analysis started with the difference between the subjects' rating of the grasshoppers on a hedonic scale before and after the various attitude change techniques were tried out. These data are presented in Table 1. The

[11] Statistical significance at the .05 level has been indicated by an asterisk (*), at the .01 level or better by a dagger (†).

hedonic scale, widely used in food research, is a nine-point rating scale ranging from "dislike extremely" to "like extremely."[12] It is scored by giving a value of 9 to "like extremely," a value of 8 to "like very much," etc., to a score of 1 for "dislike extremely." The two conditions which produced statistically significant attitude change were the dissonance technique with a negative communicator (condition 2), which produced a mean attitude change on the hedonic scale of 2.50, and the control (no influence attempt) condition (4), which produced a mean attitude change of 1.82. Condition 2 was significantly better than condition 1 ($t = 2.84\dagger$) or condition 3 ($t = 3.24\dagger$). Condition 4 also was significantly better than condition 1 ($t = 2.12^*$) or condition 3 ($t = 2.59^*$).[13]

These results support the hypothesis that a negative communicator (at least in relative terms) will enhance dissonance and produce greater attitude change than a more positively perceived communicator. The subjects in the dissonance, negative communicator condition changed their attitudes toward grasshoppers as a food two and a half steps on the nine point hedonic scale, or from slightly more negative than the dislike moderately step to a little on the positive side of the neutral point of the scale. The failure of the dissonance, positive communicator technique (mean attitude change of only 0.63) can be ascribed to insufficient dissonance; the subjects in this condition were motivated both by the proffered reward of 50 cents and by their desire to please the more positively perceived experimenter. It follows from dissonance theory that the greater the size of the inducement, the less the dissonance and the less the attitude change. This interpretation is supported by the fact that nineteen of the twenty men in the positive-communicator condition agreed to eat a grasshopper, whereas only ten of the men in the negative-communicator groups did so. This difference in the number agreeing to accept the inducement and eat a grasshopper is statistically significant (chi square of 10.16†).

[12] D. R. Peryam and F. J. Pilgrim, Hedonic scale method of measuring food preferences, *Food Technol.*, 1957, **12**, 9–14.

[13] It will be noted that the subjects who refused to eat the experimental food in the dissonance conditions were eliminated from the analysis, because they did not undergo the experimental manipulation, but were included in the other conditions, because they were subjected to the appropriate experimental variable. As this differential elimination of subjects raises the question of favoring the dissonance conditions in the analysis, the data have also been analyzed eliminating those who refused the grasshoppers from all conditions. This additional analysis produces significance levels identical to or higher than those given in the text.

The leader-influence condition was relatively ineffective, in spite of the seemingly effective presentation made by the sergeants. The subjects in the leader-influence condition ate more grasshoppers than did the subjects in other conditions (chi square of 8.02†), apparently believing that it was consistent with the sergeant's role for them to behave as he recommended, but they did not feel it was necessary to agree with him. This result should not be surprising and suggests that the leader-influence technique is an effective way of obtaining desired behavior while the leader is present but may not be the best method to change attitudes so that individuals will behave differently when the leader is no longer there.

The most interesting result was produced by the control condition. This was a no-influence-attempt condition in which it was expected that there would not be any significant change. Apparently, our subjects, like everyone else in our culture, have been subjected to so many attempts to change their attitudes that they responded favorably to a situation in which they were exposed to a new attitude with no pressure placed on them to accept it. They were told, in effect, "This is a learning situation: do what you will with it." Under these circumstances they approached the unusual food open-mindedly and were persuaded, in many cases, by the logic of this situation, that is, the need for soldiers to be prepared to accept survival foods. These results are consistent with some research done by Torrance.[14]

As noted in footnote 13, the results we have so far discussed on the dissonance techniques concern only those subjects who met the design requirements for these conditions by agreeing to eat a grasshopper for a 50-cent inducement. It is interesting to note that if the data on the subjects who did not qualify are included (see Table 1), the change score mean for the positive-communicator condition is 0.60 and for the negative-communicator condition is 1.25. We now find that the negative-communicator condition is still superior to the positive-communicator and leader-influence conditions but is second to the control condition in effectiveness. If we analyze these new data, the only statistically significant differences are the control condition versus the dissonance, positive-communicator condition ($t = 2.20^*$) and versus the leader-influence conditions ($t = 2.59^*$). These data reveal a serious limitation in dissonance techniques in so far as practical application is concerned. Although it is standard practice to eliminate from data

[14] E. P. Torrance, An experimental evaluation of "no-pressure" influence, *J. Appl. Psychol.*, 1959, 43, 109–113.

analysis those subjects who do not in fact receive the experimental induction, and although this methodology is quite appropriate for determining the validity of dissonance as a theoretical concept, the elimination of those who did not accept the inducement is quite another matter when considering dissonance techniques as useful methods in an applied situation. If we wish to use dissonance techniques to change the attitudes of consumers, we must usually deal with the entire population and cannot discard from our analysis those who will not accept a given inducement. Thus, for evaluation as an applied technique, it would seem appropriate to consider the mean attitude change for the dissonance, negative-communicator condition as 1.25, which includes the subjects who refused the inducement, rather than the 2.50 mean attitude change obtained on the 50 per cent of the subjects who did accept the inducement. Of course, it is possible to increase the size of the inducement to the point where all or nearly all the subjects will accept the inducement and therefore be subject to dissonance. However, the greater the inducement used to obtain the inconsistent behavior, the weaker the dissonance becomes and the less attitude change will be obtained, as was shown in the results on the dissonance, positive-communicator technique.

Additional information was obtained by dividing our sample into a high group who were initially more favorable to the grasshoppers and a low group who were initially more negative, as measured by the prehedonic scale. Analysis of these two groups indicated that the low, or most negative, group had a mean attitude change of 2.08, compared to a mean attitude change of 0.18 for the high, or more positive, group. The critical ratio on this mean difference is 5.64†. Apparently those who are originally most negative are most susceptible to attitude change techniques and, in fact, are the only ones likely to show appreciable change.

THE IRRADIATED-MEAT EXPERIMENT

Method

The subjects in this experiment—primarily privates with a sprinkling of NCO's and one second lieutenant—were attending Army reserve meetings. Eight groups of about ten men each were served sandwiches made from white bread, all-beef bologna, and margarine. Half the sandwiches had green toothpicks in them and were described as plain bologna sandwiches, and half had red toothpicks and were described as irradiated-bologna sandwiches. All the meat was the same and none of it was irradiated. There were four experimental conditions:

1. Dissonance. The experimenter paid 50 cents to each subject who would eat one irradiated-meat sandwich.

2. Leader influence. The groups' sergeant gave a talk on why the men should sample and learn to like irradiated meat.

3. No influence attempt, rationale. The experimenter read the following statement:

The reason for irradiating meat is so that it can be stored and kept good to eat without refrigerating it or canning it. Irradiated meat is one of the new foods the Army is experimenting with because it will keep in the field. The Army wants to know how the men feel about new, different, or unusual foods, like irradiated meat, because the new Army will consist of smaller, more mobile units than we had in past wars. These new units will be more on their own, and will move faster and more often than they did before. They won't have a lot of support personnel and big field kitchens, as this would slow them down. This means that the Army will have to learn to eat new foods in the field, foods that are easy to carry and easy to keep without refrigeration, like irradiated meats, if they want to survive. Tonight you can try one of these new foods if you want to.

4. Control (no-influence attempt). There was no manipulation or attempt to change attitudes.

Results

The most successful technique in this experiment was condition 3, the no-influence attempt with a rationale, which produced a mean attitude change of 2.05 on the nine-point hedonic scale. An analysis of the mean change scores, presented in Table 2, indicated that the no-influence attempt with a rationale was significantly better than the dissonance technique ($t = 2.21$*) or the leader-influence technique ($t = 2.28$*). These results support the findings in the grasshopper experiment on the effectiveness of the no-influence-attempt technique. It will be recalled that in the grasshopper experiment a reason for eating grasshoppers was given to all conditions, including the no-influence-attempt condition. We see again that no-influence attempt with a rationale is an effective attitude-change technique. The marked improvement in attitude with this technique is certainly large enough to have practical value. It also has the advantage, unlike dissonance, of being applicable to the total group rather than only to those who

Table 2 *Mean Change in Rating of Irradiated Meat on Hedonic Scale*

Condition	n	Mean Change[a]
1. Dissonance:		
All subjects	20	0.90
Refusing irradiated-meat sandwich	0	
2. Leader influence:		
All subjects	18	0.83
Refusing irradiated-meat sandwich	4	
3. No influence, rationale:		
All subjects	20	2.05
Refusing irradiated-meat sandwich	0	
4. No influence:		
All subjects	23	1.74
Refusing irradiated-meat sandwich	0	

[a] *F* test on mean change scores is 2.74*.

will respond to an inducement. The no-influence attempt without a rationale produced a mean attitude change of 1.74, which is less than that obtained when the rationale was added but is a significant difference ($t = 3.21$†).

The disappointment in this experiment is the failure of the dissonance technique relative to the no-influence-attempt technique. Although the dissonance technique produced a mean attitude change of 0.90, which is statistically significant ($t = 2.20$*), it was much less effective than the no-influence-attempt techniques, both with and without a rationale. The data suggest that the relative failure of the dissonance technique in this experiment was due to the same factor that produced the failure of the dissonance, positive-communicator technique in the grasshopper experiment. The attitudes toward irradiated-meat sandwiches, as indicated by the preratings on the hedonic scale, were not as negative as toward the grasshoppers. Consequently, the 50-cent reward for eating an irradiated-meat sandwich was a larger inducement (relative to the resistance) than was the 50-cent reward in the grasshopper experiment. Since the inducement was relatively stronger, the subjects must have experienced a feeling of greater justification and less choice in eating an irradiated-meat sandwich than they did in eating a grasshopper, and consequently felt less need to change their attitudes. This reasoning, which follows from dissonance theory, is borne out by the fact that every subject in the dissonance condition accepted the 50-cent inducement to eat an irradiated sandwich, whereas in the grasshopper experiment in the successful dissonance, negative-communicator condition, only half ate a grasshopper.

This failure of the dissonance technique to produce a substantial degree of attitude change when the inducement used to produce the inconsistent behavior was sufficiently powerful that the entire population participated is clear-cut evidence of the problems in successful application of dissonance techniques. If a small, barely-over-the-threshold, inducement is used so that the subjects will experience high phenomenological choice and low justification for their inconsistent behavior, a large percentage of the recipients will not participate. If, on the other hand, the inducement is sufficiently large to cause everyone to participate, many will feel low choice and high justification for their inconsistent behavior and the amount of attitude change will not be impressive. This clearly supports the interpretation in the grasshopper experiment that dissonance techniques are a powerful means of producing attitude change if it is not necessary to produce change in the entire population. However, if the success of the technique is to be judged on the basis of the average attitude change of the entire population, then the no-direct-influence-attempt technique with a rationale is superior to the dissonance techniques that have been used in these two experiments.

Although the leader-influence condition produced the smallest amount of attitude change in this experiment, it is statistically significant ($t = 2.70$*).

When the subjects were divided according to their preexperimental attitudes toward eating irradiated meat, it was found that the mean attitude change for the low, or more negative, group was 3.10 compared to a mean attitude change for the originally more positive group of 0.89. The critical ratio on this mean difference is 5.01†, which again indicates that those whose attitudes are originally most negative are most susceptible to attitude change.

THE INSTANT-COFFEE EXPERIMENT

Method

The subjects—primarily privates with a sprinkling of NCO's—were Army reservists attending Sunday meetings. There were six groups of about ten men each. Instant coffee was purchased at a retail food market and emptied into a large glass jar bearing a label indicating that it was a quartermaster item. There were three experimental conditions:

1. Dissonance, one small inducement. The experimenter passed out to each subject sheets with the following information:

QM PROMOTION INFORMATION

I have tasted the Quartermaster's new instant coffee and like it better than regular coffee. I think it is excellent coffee, and I think the Quartermaster should use it instead of regular coffee for the whole Army.

Signed ....

Army Unit ....

The experimenter explained that these were testimonials that the quartermaster would like to have the men sign so they could be used as ammunition in getting the Army to use instant coffee. The experimenter paid 25 cents to every man who signed one of the statements.

2. Dissonance, two inducements. The same sheets were handed out for the men to sign, but after all those who would sign for 25 cents had done so, the experimenter offered and paid 50 cents to the remaining men if they would now sign for the higher reward. After the new testimonials had been handed in, the experimenter paid an additional 25 cents to those who had signed first.

3. Leader influence. A sergeant who had been suggested by the unit commander as most able to persuade the men to change their attitudes gave a brief talk on why they should learn to use and accept instant coffee.

Results

The primary data used in the analysis, as in the other experiments, were the differences between the subjects' ratings of instant coffee before and after the various attitude-change techniques. These change scores are presented in Table 3. Only one subject (in the leader-influence condition) refused to drink a cup of coffee. Significant attitude change was produced by the dissonance, one-small-inducement condition, with a mean attitude change of 1.92, and by the dissonance, two-inducements (small accepted) condition, with a mean attitude change of 2.14. Both these conditions produced significantly greater changes in attitude than did the leader-influence condition, with t tests of 2.96† and 2.37* respectively. These results again indicate the power of dissonance techniques for changing food attitudes. How-

Table 3 *Mean Change in Rating of Instant Coffee on Hedonic Scale*

Condition	n	Mean Change[a]
1. Dissonance, one small inducement	24	1.92
2a. Dissonance, two inducements (small accepted)	7	2.14
2b. Dissonance, two inducements (large accepted)	3	1.67
3. Leader influence	19	0.47

[a] *F* test on mean change scores is 3.56*.

ever, the primary objective of this experiment was to evaluate the effectiveness of the two-step inducement in increasing the number of subjects participating, and therefore susceptible to dissonance, without weakening the amount of dissonance experienced by increasing the size of the inducement. The use of two-step inducement to increase the number of subjects participating and therefore susceptible to dissonance did cause an additional 23 per cent of the subjects to participate. However, their mean attitude change was only 1.67, which was not statistically significant, although greater than the mean attitude change of 0.47 obtained in the leader-influence condition.

Dividing the subjects according to their original attitudes toward instant coffee into a more-positive and a less-positive group again demonstrated that significantly greater attitude change occurred in the originally most-negative group, with a mean attitude change of 2.44 for the negative group and 0.97 for the positive group, and a critical ratio on the mean difference of 2.96†.

Data were also obtained on how much pressure the subjects felt was placed on them to change their attitudes toward instant coffee. These data reveal that the subjects who were finally induced to sign the testimonial by the 50-cent reward after initially refusing the 25-cent reward felt the greatest pressure. The felt pressure in this condition was significantly greater than that in most of the other conditions. The high degree of pressure experienced by the subjects finally induced by the higher reward to sign the statement suggests that the degree of choice felt may have been rather low. The subjects may have perceived that the inducement would be increased in size until they were in effect forced to accept it. This feeling of increasing pressure to force acceptance would account for the failure of the two-step inducement to produce sufficient dissonance, and suggests that the multiple-level inducement techniques cannot readily be used to increase the range of dissonance techniques.

CONCLUSIONS

Cognitive-Dissonance Techniques

This research has demonstrated that dissonance is a powerful method for changing food attitudes. The negative communicator variation produced a change from quite negative to slightly positive toward the use of grasshoppers as a food. Dissonance techniques have the further advantage of being easily imposed upon a group from the outside by an authoritarian figure who has some control over rewards and punishments. In fact, it was seen in the grasshopper experiment that the technique is most powerful when used by a figure perceived relatively negatively by the target population.

A disadvantage of dissonance attitude-change techniques is their complexity. In order to use dissonance techniques it is first necessary to determine what behavior on the part of those whose attitudes are to be changed would be inconsistent with their attitudes. It is then necessary to determine what inducement can be used to cause the subjects to engage in the inconsistent behavior and the exact level of inducement which is just barely sufficient to produce the inconsistent behavior. If the size of the inducement necessary for producing the inconsistent behavior is overestimated, as in the "irradiated" meat experiment, insufficient dissonance will be produced and there will not be a significant amount of attitude change. An even more serious disadvantage, which is related to the level-of-inducement problem, is that the technique does not include the entire target population. Thus we saw in the grasshopper experiment that although the dissonance technique utilizing the negative-communicator variation produced extremely marked attitude change, it did this in only half the target population. If the size of the inducement is increased in order to cause a larger percentage of the subjects to engage in the dissonance-producing behavior, the inducement then becomes too large, in the case of many subjects, for dissonance to be produced (because they feel high justification or low choice) and insufficient attitude change is produced.

On the basis of this research, dissonance techniques can be recommended for changing attitudes about food, or almost any attitude for which inconsistent behavior can be induced. However, it would be necessary to use highly skilled individuals, and preferably communicators perceived in a negative manner by the population concerned. Dissonance techniques cannot be recommended at the present time in instances where it is necessary or desirable to change the attitudes of all individuals but rather would be useful where it is necessary to produce marked attitude change in some.

Low-Pressure Techniques

The low-pressure techniques discovered accidentally in the grasshopper experiment and cross-validated in the "irradiated meat" experiment are consistent with earlier research by Torrance[15] in which he found no-pressure and no-influence techniques to be effective. Presenting the subjects with a new food and permitting them to sample it without any attempt to pressure or influence them proved to be effective, and was even more effective if a rationale for trying and learning to accept the new food was included. This technique of exposure to a new food with a rationale but without any pressure has much to recommend it. It is consistent with democratic process and is therefore unlikely to produce negative side effects. It is a simple and easy technique to use, unlike dissonance, and does not require highly skilled personnel or predetermination of behavior thresholds as do dissonance techniques. And, unlike dissonance techniques, it is applicable to the entire target population. Consequently, the no-pressure technique in combination with a rationale is recommended for changing attitudes where (1) it is important to reach large and entire populations, (2) highly skilled personnel are not available to apply attitude-change techniques, and (3) acceptance of the new attitude can be shown to be to the advantage of the subjects involved.

Attitude-Change Targets

All three experiments produced results consistent with other research indicating that those subjects whose attitudes are originally most negative are the most susceptible to attitude change. In fact, the data have consistently shown that little if any attitude change is produced on the part of those subjects originally most positive toward the item used. Consequently, if it is not possible or feasible to apply attitude-change techniques to an entire population, it is recommended that those subjects who are known to be most resistant be singled out for application of these techniques.

15 *Ibid.*

1.3 SUICIDE, MIGRATION, AND RACE: A STUDY OF CASES IN NEW ORLEANS

Warren Breed

This paper will examine the consequences of urban migration for suicide by analyzing the case histories of persons who committed suicide in New Orleans. The major independent variables under consideration are migration, sex, and race.

Migration confronts the individual with a new milieu that may contrast sharply with the way of life in a small town. The South provides an exceptionally pointed region for such investigation because there the urban-rural contrast is generally greater than in the older urbanized regions of the country. In spite of the rapid rate of urban growth in the South over the past decade or so, the lines of demarcation between the urban and the rural locales remain relatively clear. In effect, then, urban migrants coming out of the southern rural milieu are indeed confronted with a social situation that is sharply different from the situations they left.

The urban situation is different in all of the systems that comprise human social life. In the social realm, the in-migrant lacks the family and friends of his town of orientation. In the cultural realm, the values, norms, and roles to be played all differ from those of the rural area. Finally, in the individual realm the person must marshal his own resources to adjust to and cope with the new persons and patterns he encounters. The urban and rural situations are, of course, not totally different even in the South, but they are dissimilar enough to be reflected by higher deviance rates reported in the migration studies reviewed below. Because both the persons and the patterns of the city are relatively unfamiliar to him, the in-migrant must change his own behavior enough to gain acceptance in the new milieu. Some of these persons succeed. Some experience considerable stress—a truism made clear in much American literature as well as in a number of empirical studies.

Source: Work on this project was financed by grants from Tulane University and the National Institute of Mental Health. Reprinted with slight abridgment from the *Journal of Social Issues*, 1966, **22** (1), 30–43, with permission of the author and the Society for the Psychological Study of Social Issues, Inc.

Two relevant problems cannot be pursued here. These deal with the nature of rural life as against urban life, and with self-selection or differential migration; that is, why some persons migrate and others do not. (On these topics see Clinard, 1963; Leacock, 1957; and Mowrer, 1942.) Concerning the latter point it should be noted that every study of migration and its consequences in forms of deviant behavior encounters a confounding effect. In other words, does the migration experience lead to such a deviant act as suicide, or are there predisposing factors in the individual that could have led to suicide in the home community without the added burden of migration? Although this problem is not directly investigated in this study, it seems clear that those who migrated and then committed suicide in the city must have suffered to some extent even in their home communities. Their act of migration, therefore, is not as critical as it might appear at first glance.

A primary focus in this study centers around differences between male and female in-migrants, and between whites and Negroes. Existing data are sparse on both dimensions. For reasons of public policy it may become important to discover which segment of the migrating population is subject to the greatest stress. This is true not only in the case of sex, because institutional provisions can be considered which are different for males and for females, but also specifically for the Negro. Due to the heavy migration of Negroes from southern rural areas, the several host cities are confronted with problems of absorbing the flow with the least dislocation to both individuals and communities. On the theoretical side, an important topic is the shift in the suicide rate of the Negro under traditional southern conditions as against his rate under the markedly different structural situation that obtains when he moves to a northern or a western city.

Since this paper will deal only with suicide as a form of deviance, a third question is of great relevance: the comparison between rural and urban suicide rates. The comparison is not a simple one. Durkheim (1897) found European urban rates generally higher than their rural counterparts, although exceptions abounded. For example, many communities surrounding Paris had higher rates than Paris itself. More recently, for the years 1945–1949, rural areas of Michigan recorded higher rates than the state's urban areas (Schroeder and Beegle, 1955). This was true for men, but not women, and significantly, two-thirds of the "rural" male suicides held nonfarming, urban-oriented jobs. The total United States suicide rate went up after 1900, but later receded, and today is not much higher than it was

65 years ago—this in a period of great urbanization. The point to be made is that it cannot be assumed automatically that rural rates are lower than urban rates. For one thing, migration plays a role so that a simple rural-urban comparison can be quite misleading. For another, urban and rural categories may not reflect differences and similarities between the two as regards social structure and environment. The tentacles of "urban dominance" stretch far.

Moving to the factor of migration, several studies demonstrate the sometimes troubling impact of cityward movement. Five of these studies will be reviewed briefly, including three dealing with mental disorders, to frame the point of departure for the present study.

In their early investigation of mental disorders in urban areas, Faris and Dunham (1939) hypothesized that horizontal mobility is one factor accounting for the differential spatial distribution of psychoses. High rates of schizophrenia, except for the catatonic type, were found in areas of high mobility, as measured by home ownership, percentage of hotel residents and lodgers, and "percentage of foreign-born plus Negroes" in Chicago. Studying similar areas some ten years later, Freedman (1950) was unable to confirm this pattern for schizophrenia. Some areas of high mobility had low first-admission rates, and some "disorganized areas" had low mobility rates. Higher correlations with mobility were found for intracity migrants than for intercity migrants, a patttern also found in Baltimore (Tietze, Lemkau, and Cooper, 1942). Freedman suggested that this reversal may be due to the difference between the "older" and the "newer" migrants, the latter exhibiting higher socioeconomic characteristics and being more accustomed to migration.

Taking first-admission data on New York State for 1938 to 1941, Malzberg and Lee (1956) found much higher age-standardized rates for migrants than for the native-born. Female and nonwhite migrants had especially high rates of mental illness. Interestingly, the sex differential disappeared when comparisons were made between recent migrants and those who had resided in New York for five years or more.

> A partial explanation for these apparently contradictory findings may be that, whereas the initial selection and the ability to bear the early stresses of migration may be about the same for both sexes, adjustment to the new environment may in the long run be more difficult for females.

As to suicide and migration, Porterfield (1952) established that nonnativity (to the state) correlated highly with suicide in American cities, more highly than indices of secularization and urbanization. For Minneapolis in the 1920s, Schmid (1933) obtained much higher suicide rates for persons born in Europe than for the native-born (48 as against 19 per 100,000), and high rates in the center of the city and its surrounding slum zone, areas characterized by frequent population turnover. For the 25 largest American cities, he found a high correlation between suicide and nonnativity to the state (Schmid, 1928).

These studies reveal that deviance is associated with nonnativity, and with the more general factor of horizontal mobility. Of special importance for this paper is the New York report that women experience more difficulty with migration than men. These existing studies, by their nature, are restricted to relating variable categories such as age, sex, color, and distance of movement, by ecological zones. In contrast, we have data to specify *individual* cases of cityward migration, and will be able to compare these with the native-born on a wider range of relevant variables.

New Orleans is an old city. Its major ethnic groups have a relatively old and relatively settled history. Population growth between 1950 and 1960 measured 10 per cent, reaching 627,000 in 1960. The Negro proportion rose from 33 to 37 per cent. The main economic activity centers around commerce rather than industry. Catholics number perhaps half of the white population—the exact figures are not known. Due to this feature, and to the city's position as a legendary center for permissive forms of recreation, as seen in the night-life pleasures of the French Quarter and its Bohemian fringe, the moral climate lacks the severity found in other cities of comparable size.

The city's suicide rate (7.8 per 100,000 population in 1960) is among the lowest of the large cities in the nation. Even the white population has a rate of just under 10 per 100,000 annually. The Negro suicide rate is exceedingly low—less than 2 per 100,000.

PROCEDURE

The data were gathered in an intensive study of all suicides between the ages of 18 and 60 occurring in New Orleans over a several-year span in the 1950s and 1960s. All subjects had lived in the city for at least six months. No murder-suicides or attempted suicides were included. Cases were obtained from coroner and police files, and qualitative interviews about the suicides were conducted with relatives, friends, neighbors, employers, co-workers, and physicians. The refusal rate was 5 per cent. In most cases, two or more interviews were obtained. In addition, a control group was established for the white males; interviews were secured from a third party about men in the same age, class, race, and residential category as the suicide. Further details may be found in Breed (1963).

Where did the nonnatives come from? Mostly, they came from small towns and cities in the hinterlands. Half the female suicides came from such communities, and a third of the males. Another 6 per cent were raised on farms (there are fewer farms in existence now than in earlier decades). Half the males and about two-fifths of the females were born in New Orleans. This leaves less than 10 per cent who came from bigger cities. We will assume, then, that the inmigrants had been familiar with a non-big-city way of life.

As noted earlier in this paper, the possibility of self-selection, or a "drift" to the city by a certain type of rural person, has to be admitted. Malzberg and Lee (1956) acknowledge, for example, that some of the persons hospitalized in New York entered the hospital shortly after arrival in the state, and thus may have departed their earlier "home" for reasons specific to the illness, rather than being representative of the home-town population.

FINDINGS

The disorganizing effect of cityward migration, reported in the earlier studies, can be seen most clearly among the female suicides. This is done by comparing the more settled women with those who had lived in the city for a short period.

Table 1 gives percentage data on several measures used by Durkheim to indicate the lack of "integration" or social ties ("egoistic suicide") and the lack of "regulation" by social norms and other persons ("anomic suicide"). The nine columns report these characteristics for white female suicides, white male suicides, and the white male controls, each set subclassified by length of residence in the city. Some were natives, some had migrated in ten or more years earlier, and the others had arrived in New Orleans less than ten years prior to death—or for the controls, prior to the interview.

Female Suicides

The female suicides with less than ten years of residence in the city are younger, less educated, more lower-class, and above all, exhibited the least satisfactory family situations. Many were "integrated" into community life on only the most tenuous basis. Half were divorced, separated, or living with a man out of wedlock. Only a quarter were sharing a household with as many as two other persons, and just under half were not living with a mate of any sort at time of death. Only a third had a male in the household working full time. Only 8 per cent were coded as living an "ideal" family life, in the sense of enjoying "good" husband-wife relationships with no recorded infidelity. Their only "plus" factor took the form of having borne more children than the other two types. The single preeminent difficulty experienced by these recently arrived young women, analysis shows, was in meeting and marrying the kind of man with whom they could establish and maintain a viable home.

The single factor that most clearly and basically differentiates female from male in-migrants is that of age. While only a third of the men of short residence came to the city before reaching age 40, four-fifths of the new women did so. Of these, the greater number left home before age 30, and quite a few were still in their teens. Typically, they had felt acute dissatisfaction with parents and the home town. As we shall see, they arrived in the city with hopes of finding something better, but without the means to achieve this goal in the form of a stable marital and family relationship. In many ways they form a contrast to the female in-migrants of more than ten years' residence, whose problems more closely resembled those of the suicides native to the city.

Our data permit further examination of these 25 recent arrivals, by employing the case-study method. Classifying each on the principle of a main "pattern," the following types of cases appear:

1. The young girls who come alone from small town to big city. They tend to be attractive but poorly educated. Lacking family, friends, and occupational skills, they gravitate to jobs in bars as cocktail waitresses or, as weeks and months pass, as B-drinkers, strip-tease dancers, and prostitutes. Work is far from steady, and the men they meet are seeking immediate gratification rather than marriage. If they marry, the union is short-lived. They come to be socially defined as "easy" women. The small-town fantasies of "gay night life" turn into endless rounds of drinks, different men, police arrests, sometimes drugs, and bitterness. They wish for husband and children, but in vain. The four women of this group killed themselves at ages 20, 24, 25, and 26.

One case will illustrate the pattern. A pretty 17-year-old girl left her small-town home in Alabama and came alone to the city. Her parents had divorced and remarried. "Home" had meant a series of backbiting squabbles. Having no job skills, she became a cocktail waitress. She was personable and met people easily. She dated several men and married a soldier within a few

Table 1 *Selected Characteristics of White Male and Female Suicides and Male Controls, by Length of Residence in City (per cents)*

Length of Residence in City	Female Suicides		
	Native	10-plus yr	½-10 yr
Age: 18–39	41	37	80
40–60	59	63	20
Class: 2 lowest classes (North-Hatt scale)	18	23	43
Education: 12-plus years	50	31	24
Marital status: Married	61	73	34
Never married	15	0	4
Widowed	3	10	8
Divorced-separated	15	13	29
"Common law" marriage	6	3	21
Never had children	38	34	0
3 or more persons in household	50	31	24
No extended kin in area	3	25	61
Family head is male working full time	70	53	32
Major problem is "mate"	37	47	72
Church attendance: 2 or less times per year	42	46	59
Visiting friends: "More"	42	55	36
Alcoholic, or alcoholic problem	12	36	32
Vertical social mobility: (Intergenerational) Upward	39	41	9
Downward	22	18	36
Stable	39	41	54
Totals	34	30	25

months. Before the birth of their child, the husband deserted her, and she lived with several men and worked in one bar after another. When the divorce became final, she was being intimate with at least two men. One of them, on being interviewed, said she had pressed him to marry her. He put her off, and after a late night spat about marriage, he left her and she killed herself.

2. Somewhat older women who drift into the city. These are more experienced than the first type, coming from a higher social and educational bracket, and possessing more skills. Most have been divorced. They get white-collar jobs, find a small apartment, and search for an eligible man. In this they fail, and instead meet a series of married men, or men not quite prepared to marry them. The four women of this type died at the ages of 29, 34, 36, and 38.

Table 1 *(Continued)*

Male Suicides			Male Controls		
Native	10-plus yr	½-10 yr	Native	10-plus yr	½-10 yr
26	22	32	30	25	45
74	78	68	70	75	55
34	29	32	4	14	10
28	51	48	50	45	62
43	58	63	85	86	86
19	13	11	9	4	10
2	3	0	1	2	0
34	26	16	5	5	0
2	0	11	0	0	0
40	33	33	18	11	10
55	55	37	74	68	91
2	20	33			
45	55	58	93	83	90
28	30	37			
54	59	87	21	23	53
47	47	36	85	80	75
32	33	33	2	2	5
31	16	18	45	27	35
51	45	64	26	39	41
18	39	18	29	35	24
53	31	19	122	63	21

3. "The country girl." Two of the recent in-migrants apparently never accommodated to city life. Both were married to working men, but they pined for family and friends in the more rural community, and often visited, or were visited by, mother and sisters. Friends interviewed later said they "never grew up," or "couldn't face the world," but rather tried to hold onto the less differentiated, less impersonal familistic way of life. In such cases it is not surprising that husband-wife relationships were strained, as indeed they were in both cases.

4. Those who came to the city with husband, and tried to adjust to urban life. These seven women came at various ages, typically when the husband was transferred by the employer, generally in lower-middle-class positions. For one, the main problem was physical health, and for another the only clue we could get from four long interviews was that she was homesick for her family

in Georgia. The other five all experienced bad husband-wife relationships: two husbands were wife-beaters and the couple had separated. One husband turned out to be a "Bluebeard," from all reports, and the other two husbands were the object of continual complaints to friends by the wives.

5. The GI brides. Only two of the 25 recent in-migrants occupy this category, but if we extend the period to fifteen years of residence, the total would rise to six. The story is an old one. Young girl (as young as 15 or 16 in three cases) meets uniformed service man near her home. Brief romance is followed by marriage, and in some cases the husband goes overseas for a time. On returning to his home in New Orleans, the glamor fades, and in several cases the bride finds that her husband's family occupies a class position lower than that of her parents. This is felt as a disappointment (to the girls in the present study), and suggests a "status" source of female suicide that will be considered later. In all six cases the husband-wife relationship was described as poor. While only two of the wives were promiscuous, five of the husbands were. In none of the marriages can we find evidence for a good prognosis of success. To illustrate, only four children were born from these six marriages, and only two of these were being kept by the mother at time of death.

An illustrative case involved a middle-class girl who met and married a navy sailor on the West Coast at the age of 15. She was pregnant at 16 and did not want the child. Her husband was at sea, and her parents, to quote a friend, "Gave her up. She had done a terrible thing." She moved to New Orleans with husband and child, and found his family hard-working but lower class. She left her husband and virtually turned the child over to his mother, and became a low-paid working girl at 18. Her parents continued to deny her, while favoring her brother—as she felt they always had. She divorced the husband. Her work proved to be unrewarding. Toward the end she spoke little to anyone, but did commence an affair with a married man. One of her co-workers believes that the suicide-precipitating event was her brother's decision to come and stay with her; she seemed unable to face this, and killed herself.

These five categories encompass 19 of the 25 recently in-migrating female suicides. For these 19, somewhat clear patterns take shape. The remaining six cases assume more idiosyncratic forms.

The middle group, the women who migrated to the city more than ten years before suicide, presents a different picture. Some of the difference probably reflects the fact that a few of the second group were brought to the city as children in a move of the entire family—a totally different kind of "migration" that is under consideration here. Table 1 shows the ten-plus group to bear considerable resemblance to the native-born women suicides on most characteristics, and study of individual cases recommends the conclusion that they "survived" the cityward move but encountered problems much like those that bedeviled the city-born. Only in family-related characteristics do they show less solidarity, and here they occupy a place midway between the two extreme categories by residence history. Interview data reveal that some three-fifths of them had suffered poor husband-wife relationships, whether from absence of spouse, marked lack of affection, or frequent blowups based on behavior damaging to their self-respect, most frequently jealousy of other women. There were four "GI bride" cases, three "country girls" who failed to adjust to city life, two older divorced women who drifted into the city, two prostitutes, and four cases of a type found only once among the newly arrived women—serious health problems. The other cases fall into no distinguishable patterns.

The third group, the native-born female suicides, suffered from a wide range of afflictions. Perhaps the most sensible reading of their cases suggests that they experienced multiple family problems, confined not only to strains in the marital role, but including difficulties with parents, children, and other relatives as well.

Male Suicides

In contrast to the females, white male suicides show much less variation when compared by migration history. Their age upon arrival was considerably older than for the women, and thus, conditions doubtless differed between the sexes. The general class and age composition is fairly consistent within the three male groups. "Family" difficulties appear as frequently among the city-born as among the recent arrivals. In fact, in-migrants of both time periods show more conventional "marital status" situations than the native-born men. The latter, however, gained relatively greater immunity from "excessive individualism" through more church-going and having more extended kin to call on. Neither are there great and consistent differences within the three groups by residence as regards work difficulties. While the ratio of upward to downward mobility is least favorable among the newly arrived men, they have the best record as to full-time employment. These data, plus study of case materials of men in the three groups, force a rejection of the hypothesis that cityward migration increases suicide proneness among these men. In addition, only three of them were said to be pining for a return to the more rural or town life.

A similar conclusion emerges when the controls alone are studied. The newly arrived controls, residing in larger households but attending church less, had somewhat more downward mobility, but the differences in this and in working full time are not large and consistent enough to justify any "cities are abnormal" hypothesis for this group.

Clues to male suicide do appear, however, when the suicides are contrasted with the controls. Table 1 shows the suicides to be of lower class than the controls; both groups, however, showed rough equality as to their fathers' class position (Breed, 1963, Table 2). On each of the several indicators of strain, the suicides reflect substantially greater frequencies of instability, enough to recommend the use of the term "failure." As with the female suicides, their overall family situation was poor. Beyond this, half were not employed full time, and many had suffered downward mobility, conditions less present among the controls. Related data (Breed, 1963) reinforce this "work failure" pattern, as regards worklife mobility, decrease in income prior to death, and failure to receive normally expected promotions. In this society—South and non-South—a man is expected to work, and to be performing adequately at work. His public evaluation as a man is based overwhelmingly on his work performance. Failure in work can distress any man. Yet these data show little difference in work performance by migration status. A man is expected to work, and to work adequately, wherever he lives and no matter how long he has lived there.

This "work" focus did not appear among the problems of the female suicides to a marked extent, with the possible exception of the GI brides. Surprisingly few of the women were said to have shown untoward concern over "status" problems, even in cases where the husband was downwardly mobile. Rather, family difficulties predominated among the women.

How to explain the large sex differential in casualties from migration? Clearly, the women leave the parental home at a much earlier age than the men (Table 1), sometimes as early as 15. Very frequently this is the age when the girl is starting to become involved with men. Further, when we compare the recent in-migrants by sex we find in the row titled "No extended kin in area" only 33 per cent of the males qualify compared with 61 per cent of the females. In addition, the latter less frequently established households containing three or more persons. It is possible to speculate that there is more sheer "running away from home" among the females than the males, involving a strong "push" away from parents and small-town peers. This flight is an escape, not accompanied by a wish to join extended kin. The flight often occurs at an age which inhibits a mature series of actions leading toward a stable marriage. Rather, the ingenuous girl is thrown into contact with experienced denizens of downtown nightlife. Recent male in-migrants, older, more often having kin in the city, and less disadvantaged in establishing a main role, are less prone to such problem involvement.

Negro Suicides

The New Orleans Negro suicide rate is very low, roughly 4.4 per 100,000 for males and 0.9 for females in the period under study. Two viewpoints, both ideologically slanted, may be advanced to "explain" this. The racist would opine that the Negro is idle, childlike, improvident, and clannish, albeit dangerous with a knife on Saturday night (and indeed the southern Negro homicide rate is high). A "friendly" view would point to the solidarity of the Negro community with strong integration in both family and neighborhood structure. Both views are stereotypes.

New Orleans Negroes live in several different types of social worlds, not simply in one black one (Rohrer and Edmonson, 1960). Many middle-class Negroes live much like their white middle-class peers, and Negro middle-class suicides mirror in many ways the suicides of the white middle class. In the lower class, similar parallels are found, with perhaps a greater frequency of violence, physical accidents, and desperate behavior among the Negroes. A higher proportion of Negro than white suicides have been in trouble with police and courts.

Further treatment of Negro suicide will be placed in a setting of regional differences and migration.

DISCUSSION

This study shows that when migration data on individuals, rather than on ecological areas, is used, new complexities occur. What follows will introduce still more data from related sources.

Taking the entire population of New Orleans in 1960, a considerably larger number and proportion of whites were not residing in the city in 1955 (13 per cent of all whites in 1960), than Negroes (5 per cent) (U.S. census, 1960). Further, the whites came from a greater distance than the Negroes—from mid-South and the North, while most of the Negroes were native to Louisiana and Mississippi—a radius of perhaps 300 miles. And from the two racial populations, the suicides as a group showed higher proportions of persons living in the city for less than ten years: 28 per cent of the white female suicides, 18 per cent of the white male suicides, and 25 per cent of the Negro male suicides. Thus the suicides in all categories had higher than average in-migration rates. So far, these findings are consistent with classic notions of social integration as a regulating and protective force among humans.

On the other hand, one could argue that the Negroes were making a bigger transitional leap (despite the smaller geographical step) in settling in New Orleans. Almost all of them came to the metropolis from small towns and hamlets—rural worlds. The "social" distance between rural and urban roles in the South is relatively great: transportation and communication throughout the South is traditionally underdeveloped (Moore, 1951). This condition would seem to predispose them to a higher, not a lower, rate of suicide; the move would contain both "egoistic" and "anomic" forces. Such a paradox leads us again to the nature of the "social world" they entered when settling in New Orleans. Does the Negro population of the city contain more *Gemeinschaft* characteristics than the white? Data to answer the question are, of course, scarce. Census data do show that New Orleans Negro families are larger (averaging roughly 4 persons per household to 3 among whites). A kinship study revealed that Negroes celebrated Christmas with considerably more relatives than whites (37 per cent of the Negroes and only 7 per cent of the whites interviewed reported being with four or more relatives the preceding Christmas). Yet these are slim data indeed to justify a claim of greater family solidarity for the Negroes. The larger household size is quite possibly more of a matter of crowding than of choice. The best available data on the New Orleans Negro family is found in Rohrer and Edmonson (1960), a study profiling 20 families. A portion of these are truly familistic, but as large a number, especially those in the lower class, show enormous amounts of disloyalty, indifference, feuding, jealousy, and backbiting—characteristics also found among our lower-class Negro suicides. Similar questions can be raised about the Negro and white neighborhoods—class for class—as sources of anti-egoistic "community."

One strong argument for retaining the traditional notion that the southern Negro community shepherds its flock in a "folk" fashion comes with a comparison of southern versus northern Negro suicide rates. Contrasted to the below 2 per cent New Orleans rate, the Negro rate in Seattle climbs to 14.4 for males and 5.4 for females (Schmid and Van Arsdol, 1955). (One must take care, however, that perhaps the very factor under investigation here—migration—has contributed to this rate.) It must be added also that overall suicide rates in southern cities almost invariably score lower than for northern and especially western cities (Gibbs and Martin, 1964, pp. 54–56).

We are left with one more variable which may enlighten the disparate racial rates: segregation. In the South, most Negroes of course compete neither for jobs nor for prestige with whites. Roles determining their self-esteem are played largely within the Negro section of the biracial community. To this extent they are exempted from general competition, and thus freed of the "western" burden of community-recognized achievement striving. True, the Negro community has its class and status structure, but since most members are subject to the authority of white employers and white institutions, the individualistic pressure to rise is minimized. But when the Negro leaves the South, he is faced with more clearly universalistic standards of hiring and performance by merit. The higher Seattle rate, and that in other northern communities, is possible evidence of the different place in the community held by the Negro, to be added to the factors of migration and family structure.

A final datum: between 1940 and 1950 in the United States, the white male suicide rate dropped, while the Negro male rate stayed about the same or rose slightly (Gibbs and Martin, 1964, pp. 71–108). If we can assume that during this decade the Negro moved more than the white toward urbanization, we can argue that cityward (and northward) migration does indeed increase the suicide proneness of previously rural individuals as personified by the traditionalistic prewar southern Negro. That the south as a region, still containing large numbers of rural Negroes, provides folk-like immunity to its less-urbanized inhabitants, can be strikingly contrasted to the high rural rates in Michigan during the same period, noted above.

SUMMARY

Using data on individual suicides rather than on ecological areas, it has been found that the consequences of cityward migration vary in several ways, specifically sex, race, duration of city residence, and perhaps "social distance" between life styles in the old and the new home community. One clear finding is that white female suicides with a residence history of less than ten years in the city showed marked divergencies of behavior from those with more years in the city. Five types or patterns of these recently arrived white females were described. A substantial portion of this problem is doubtless due to the fact that many of these women arrived while still quite young—much younger than the in-migrating males. Similar differences were not found when white male suicides were analyzed by residence history and by comparison with a living control group. The most crucial role problem of suicides was found to be sex-specific: female difficulties center around the marital role, while males are more prone to job failure. The low Negro suicide rate in New Orleans was examined for clues as to the social setting in the South as contrasted to the North. The less-urbanized South offers more regulation and thus protection of its people. In all, complications of considerable magnitude attend the study of individual migration to and from particular kinds of social worlds.

REFERENCES

Breed, Warren. Occupational mobility and suicide among white males. *Amer. Sociol. Rev.*, 1963, **28**, 179–188.

Clinard, Marshall. *Sociology of deviant behavior.* New York: Holt, Rinehart and Winston, 1963.

Durkheim, Emile. *Suicide.* Glencoe, Ill.: Free Press, 1951.

Faris, R. E. L., & Dunham, H. Warren. *Mental disorders in urban areas.* Chicago, Univ. of Chicago Press, 1939.

Freedman, Ronald. *Recent migration to Chicago.* Chicago: Univ. of Chicago Press, 1950.

Gibbs, Jack P., & Martin, Walter T. *Status integration and suicide.* Eugene: Univ. of Oregon Press, 1954.

Leacock, Eleanor. In Leighton, A. H., Clausen, J. A., & Wilson, R. N. (Eds.) , *Explorations in social psychiatry.* New York: Basic Books, 1957. Pp. 308–337.

Malzberg, Benjamin, & Lee, Everett S. *Migration and mental disorder.* New York: Social Science Research Council, 1956.

Moore, Harry E. Mass communication in the South. *Soc. Forces,* 1951, **29**, 365–376.

Mowrer, Ernest R. *Disorganization: social and personal.* Philadelphia: Lippincott, 1942.

Porterfield, Austin L. Suicide and crime in folk and in secular society. *Am. J. Sociol.* 1952, **57**, 331–338.

Rohrer, John H., & Edmonson, Munro S. (Eds.) . *The eighth generation.* New York: Harper, 1960.

Schmid, Calvin F. *A social saga of two cities.* Minneapolis: Univ. of Minneapolis Press, 1937.

Schmid, Calvin F., & Van Arsdol, Jr., Maurice F. Completed and attempted suicides. *Am. Sociol. Rev.*, 1955, **20**, 273–283.

Schroeder, J. Widick, & Beegle, J. Allan. Suicide: an instance of high rural rates, in Rose, A. (Ed.), *Mental health and mental disorder*. New York: Norton, 1955.

Tietze, Christopher, Lemkau, P., & Cooper, M. Personal disorder and spatial mobility. *Am. J. Sociol.*, 1942, **48**, 29–39.

United States Census of Population: 1960. Detailed Characteristics. Louisiana. Final Report PC (1) -20D.

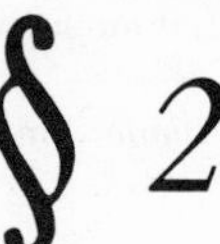

§ 2 SOCIAL ATTRACTION

The fact that individuals tend to be attracted to others is the basic datum in all social behavior. The studies reported in this section deal with various manifestations of this attraction and the conditions and factors that affect it. The section begins with the report of two experiments by Robert L. Helmreich and Barry E. Collins, who were interested in the relationship between various degrees of stress and the desire to be with others. One of their findings shows that low or moderate emotional stress is more likely to evoke affiliative behavior than is severe stress.

The paper by Walster, Aronson, Abrahams, and Rottmann addresses itself to the question of what personal qualities make the most impression on college freshmen who are brought together randomly on a "blind date." Their results, which are completely compatible with common sense, show that physical attractiveness is the only variable significantly related either to partners' evaluation of their dates or to men's later attempts to date their partners again. An interesting sidelight is the additional finding that there does not seem to be much correspondence between the amounts of attraction or liking that pairs of dating partners express for each other when brought together under conditions of random matching.

Interpersonal attraction among individuals of the same sex is examined in a study by Miller, Campbell, Twedt, and O'Connell, who were interested in the extent to which personal characteristics of members of friendship pairs are interrelated. Most studies show that friendship attraction is related to various kinds of similarities: attitudes, social class, religion, values, interests, and so forth. This study shows that friends do indeed have similar personality characteristics, if the measure is based on their *reputations* (i.e., how they are perceived by others), but not as far as their *self*-appraisals are concerned. This raises the interesting point of whether others know us better (i.e., can judge our personal qualities better) than we know ourselves, but such a question is beyond the scope of this study.

The study by Donn Byrne and Carl McGraw is another example of research concerned with attraction based on similarity in personal traits. This research shows, however, that when pairs of individuals are from different races, ethnic prejudice may intervene to disturb the usual linear relationship between attraction and similarity.

2.1 SITUATIONAL DETERMINANTS OF AFFILIATIVE PREFERENCE UNDER STRESS

Robert L. Helmreich
Barry E. Collins

Frightened subjects have consistently shown an increased desire for the company of others while awaiting a threatening event. Schachter (1959) developed what has become a standard experimental paradigm by announcing to subjects that they would receive painful electric shock and then offering them the opportunity to wait for the shock alone or with others. Other investigators (Gerard & Rabbie, 1961; Miller & Zimbardo, 1966; Rabbie, 1963; Zimbardo & Formica, 1963) have used this paradigm and found similar increases in affiliative desires under high fear. A number of studies (Darley & Aronson, 1966; Gerard & Rabbie, 1961; Schachter, 1959; Zimbardo & Formica, 1963) have reported that stress-induced affiliative needs are greater among firstborn and only children than among later borns.

Schachter (1959) suggested that two mechanisms may be responsible for affiliative responses:

1. Individuals may need others for evaluation of their own emotional reactions. Persons in the same emotional state can provide needed information on what responses are appropriate to ambiguous arousal cues. (See Festinger's

Source: This research was supported by the National Science Foundation. Reprinted with slight abridgment from the *Journal of Personality and Social Psychology*, 1967, **6**, 79–85, with permission of the authors and the American Psychological Association, Inc.

1954 theory of social comparison processes and Schachter's 1964 application to cognitive determination of emotion.)

2. The company of others may also provide a direct reduction of the anxiety which the subject feels and hence provide a motivation for affiliation. Wrightsman (1960) found the presence of others effective in reducing anxiety, while Darley and Aronson (1966) found both motives operating to stimulate affiliation.

Janis (1963) discussed another mechanism which may explain the increased importance of primary groups and especially authority figures such as leaders in times of stress. He pointed to stress-induced dependency reactions toward authority figures and suggested that the increased dependency toward authority occurs because the authority can serve as a "danger control authority" which can reduce the severity of threat perceived by the individual. Thus the ability to establish a dependent relationship could provide another strong motivation for affiliation under fear.

A presently unanswered question of considerable theoretical and practical importance is whether the increased desire for affiliation which has been previously observed for persons who were *awaiting* a frightening event would also be observed among persons actually facing a threat. For example, would the conclusions imply a need for affiliation during combat or just while waiting to go into battle? It seems plausible that there may be a qualitative difference between gregariousness while anticipating threat and while working in a stressful situation.

OVERVIEW OF THE RESEARCH

The research reported here consists of two studies, designed to clarify some of the questions raised in earlier investigations of affiliative preference under stress. In Study I, subjects under high or low fear were offered the chance to remain alone, to be with a group of peers in the same emotional state, or to be in a group with a leader. The affiliative preferences were measured for a *working* situation—subjects were asked to choose with whom they would like to work while receiving stimulation. Contrary to earlier research, the results showed a clear-cut decrease in preference for the company of peers under high fear. Also, unlike earlier investigations of fear-produced affiliation, no differential effects for birth order were found. Study II was undertaken to clarify and refine these results. In this experiment subjects were offered the same choices for affiliation employed in

Study I, and these choices were offered both for the *working* condition and for the more typical situation of *waiting* for shock. The only other difference in the two studies was that subjects in Study II were run in groups rather than individually as in Study I. The decrease in preference for the company of peers in the working condition found in Study I was replicated, while a different pattern of results was obtained for the waiting condition. An overall difference in desire to affiliate was also found in Study II, suggesting the possibility that whether subjects are run in groups or individually is an important variable.

STUDY I

Method

Subjects: Sixty male high school students between the ages of 14 and 18 were recruited through an advertisement in the local newspaper for a psychological study. From the list of those replying to the advertisement, 30 firstborns and 30 later borns were selected randomly and used in the study. Within each group, subjects were assigned randomly to one of the three conditions of fear arousal employed.

Procedure: After arriving for the experiment, the subjects were conducted alone to an office furnished with a desk, chairs, and dummy electronic equipment. Each subject was told that the "doctor" would be in shortly. The experimenter then entered the room and introduced himself as a doctor studying the physiology of mental processes. The experiment was described as an investigation of the physiological reactions occurring during mental activity. The experimenter stated that a basal rate for each subject would be determined by using the electrode present to take readings on a "master polygraph recorder."

A laboratory assistant then arrived and attached a standard skin electrode to the subject's arm. The assistant gave the subject instructions for filling out a Family Background Inventory, Form A of the Sixteen Personality Factor Questionnaire (Cattell's 16 PF—Cattell & Eber, 1964) and a 33-question multiple-choice measure of self-esteem (feelings of social inadequacy and social inhibitions) taken from Janis and Field (1959). When the subject completed the forms (this took between 45 minutes and an hour), the assistant entered the room, unhooked the electrode, and told the subject that the doctor would be in to explain the second part of the study.

The experimenter then informed the subject that the second part would take place in a different laboratory and would consist of an investigation of problem-solving behavior. The experimenter remarked that basal rates had been obtained and that two electrodes would be attached to the subject during Part II—one a recording electrode, the other an electrode for stimulation. At this point, the fear manipulations were introduced.

Low-fear subjects were told that they would receive subliminal electric stimulations during Part II. It was emphasized that they would not feel the stimulation, and the word "shock" was never used. The experimenter said that he was interested in the effects of stimulation on performance. *Moderate-fear* subjects were told that they would receive several electric shocks which were described as being noticeable but not unpleasant. The experimenter remarked that he was interested in the effects of shock on performance. *High-fear* subjects were told that they would receive strong and painful electric shocks and that blood samples would be drawn to measure any changes in blood composition caused by the experimental procedure. The experimenter also stated that he was interested in the effects of shock on performance. All subjects were then told that part of the study was concerned with investigating differences between the reactions of people working alone and those working in groups. He added that a number of subjects were just finishing Part I, and the subject could have a choice of the condition to which he would be assigned for Part II.

Next, the three choices were described. The *alone* condition was described as a situation in which the subject would work on problems by himself in a lab room. The *informal group* condition (peer group) was depicted as consisting of subjects working individually on problems in the company of three other subjects receiving the same stimulation. The point was clearly made that the subject would be working by himself but would be in the company of same-state peers. The *leader group* was described as consisting of two other high school subjects and a graduate-student leader. The experimenter said that this group would work as a unit on the problems, and that the leader would assign tasks, direct performance, and control the group's activity. The subject was then asked to indicate his preference on a sheet of paper. Since subjects were run individually, no possibility existed for the choice to be affected by acquaintance with other subjects. No subject asked to drop out of the study before Part II. The experimenter then explained the real nature of the experiment and answered questions. All the subjects were then enjoined to secrecy.

Results and Discussion

The effectiveness of the fear manipulation was evaluated by means of an item on the final questionnaire asking the subjects to report how nervous or ill at ease they felt concerning the stimulation they were about to receive (on a scale running from 0 to 100). The differences among the three fear conditions were in the expected direction, and the main effect ($F = 8.18$, $df = 2/42$) was significant at better than the .01 level. Comparisons among the individual condition means revealed that high-fear subjects were significantly more nervous than moderate-fear ($p<.05$) and low-fear ($p<.01$) subjects, while moderate-fear subjects did not differ significantly from low-fear subjects at even the .10 level. These results are summarized in Table 1. No significant birth-order effects were found for reported fear.

Table 1 *Study I: Mean Ratings of Fear*[a]

Birth Order	Low Fear	Moderate Fear	High Fear
Firstborn	9.87	19.10	38.50
Later born	$10.43_{a,c,d}$	18.84_{b}	$36.75_{b,c,d}$

Note. Numbers with no subscripts in common are nonsignificant ($p > 10$). Numbers with one subscript in common are significant at $p < .05$. Numbers with two subscripts in common are significant at $p < .01$.

[a] Significance levels are for contrasts between combined means of firstborns and later borns, $df = 1/42$ for all comparisons. No differences between firstborns and later borns approached significance.

The choices of affiliation revealed a significant *decrease* in preference for the company of peers in the high-fear group contrasted with the low- and moderate-fear conditions (Table 2). Since no differences in affiliative preference and no significant differences in level of fear were found between low- and moderate-fear conditions, these two groups were combined for analysis. A 2×3 chi-square analysis of affiliative choices (Table 3) indicates that more subjects chose both the alone and leader groups under high fear ($\chi^2 = 9.97$, $df = 2$, $p < .01$). The a priori hypothesis had predicted only the increase in preference for the *leader group* under high fear and not the increased preference for the *alone* choice which contributes to the significance of the chi-square in Table 3. However, the increase in preference for the leader group is significant independently, as reflected by a 2×2 chi-square which combines the *alone* and *peer* columns of Table 3 ($\chi^2 = 9.98$, $p < .005$, $df = 1$).

No differences in affiliative preferences between firstborns and later borns were found. Both made each affiliative choice with almost identical frequencies (see Table 2).

Table 2 *Study I: Direction of Affiliation × Fear Condition × Birth Order*

Birth Order	% Alone Choice	% Peer-Group Choice	% Leader-Group Choice	*N*
		Low-Fear Condition		
Firstborn	30	40	30	10
Later born	50	40	10	10
Firstborn and later born combined	40	40	20	20
		Moderate-Fear Condition		
Firstborn	40	40	20	10
Later born	40	50	10	10
Firstborn and later born combined	40	45	15	20
		High-Fear Condition		
Firstborn	50	10	40	10
Later born	60	10	30	10
Firstborn and later born combined	55	10	35	20

The decrease in preference for the company of peers as well as the failure to find an absolute increase in preference for companionship under high fear are counter to behavior reported in most fear-affiliation studies. On the basis of this study, it is impossible to determine whether the obtained findings diverge from previous results because (*a*) this is the first study to offer the leader choice, with its opportunity for dependency, or (*b*) this study offered affiliative choices for a working situation rather than the waiting for pain situations used in previous studies.

The possibility also existed that the high preference for solitude in this study resulted from a strong "set" for solitude engendered in subjects who had been working alone for a long period prior to the

Table 3 *Study I: Direction of Affiliation*[a]

Birth Order	% Alone Choice	% Peer-Group Choice	% Leader-Group Choice	*N*
		Low- and Moderate-Fear Condition		
Firstborn	35	40	25	20
Later born	45	45	10	20
Firstborn and later born combined	40	42.5	17.5	40
		High-Fear Condition		
Firstborn	50	10	40	10
Later born	60	10	30	10
Firstborn and later born combined	55	10	35	20

[a] Low- and moderate-fear groups combined.

affiliative choice. This set effect might also have been intensified by the fear manipulation, causing the unexpected increase in preference for working alone under high fear.

The second study was designed to clarify these issues by replicating Study I and, in addition, by offering the same three affiliative choices for a waiting period prior to shock as well as for working in a threatening situation.

STUDY II

Method

Subjects: Subjects were 120 male high school students between the ages of 15 and 18 recruited through a local high school.

Procedure: All subjects arrived simultaneously for the study and were assigned randomly to experimental conditions by receptionists. Each subject was sent to one of two large classrooms. All subjects in one room were assigned to the high-fear condition, while all of those in the other room were assigned to the low-fear condition.

After all subjects had arrived, an experimenter introduced himself and stated that a number of studies were being conducted simultaneously during the morning. He added that the several portions of the experiment would be explained by the persons in charge of the particular studies. The subjects were initially asked to fill out a background questionnaire giving biographical data and ordinal position and a group intelligence test (the Wonderlic Personnel Test, Form A). After all subjects had completed these forms the fear manipulations were introduced.

Subjects in each fear condition were randomly assigned to one of twelve groups. Six graduate-student experimenters took groups of five subjects to a smaller classroom at which time the fear manipulation was administered to these groups of five. Each experimenter ran either four high-fear groups or four low-fear groups. Two of the groups run by each of the experimenters were in the working condition and two in the waiting condition. The order of groups for each experimenter was randomly determined.

Fear Manipulation: All low-fear subjects were told that the experimenters were interested in measuring physiological changes while persons engaged in mental activity. They were told that they would solve simple problems while receiving subliminal stimulation and while recordings were made of changes in the activity of the nervous system, and that a polygraph recorder would be hooked to an electrode attached to their arm. The experimenter explained that recordings would be made while they solved problems.

High-fear subjects were told that the experimenters were interested in measuring physiological changes while a person was engaged in mental activity and received electrical stimulation. The subjects were told that a recording electrode would be attached to them and that a stimulating electrode would also be connected, and that they would receive strong shocks which most subjects found painful. In addition, they were informed that changes in content of blood during mental activity and stimulation would be measured. The experimenter added that a nurse would use a hypodermic needle to take three blood samples—at the beginning, in the middle, and at the end of the experimental task. The experimenter concluded, "Remember, you will receive several strong electric shocks and three blood samples will be taken." At this point the experimenters showed the subjects a large hypodermic needle and stated that a similar needle would be used to withdraw blood.

Affiliative choices: Working-condition subjects were informed that the social setting present while persons solved tasks and received stimulation could have strong effects on the nature of the results. Therefore, subjects were permitted to decide for themselves what social setting they would work in. The subjects were offered three choices for working and receiving stimulation—to work alone in a private room, to work in the company of three other high school students receiving similar stimulation, or to work in a "leader group" with two other high school subjects and a college-graduate student serving as group leader. The experimenter added that in the leader group the students worked together on problems, and the graduate student supervised and controlled group activity.

Waiting-condition subjects were told that the presence of other people could affect physiological reactions and that what a person does just before taking part in a study can have a big effect on his reactions. Therefore, the experimenter explained, subjects could decide for themselves how they would wait for the task to begin while the equipment was readied. Three choices were described—to wait alone in a private room, to wait in an informal group with three other subjects, or to wait in a leader group with two other high school students and a college-graduate student who would supervise what the subjects did during the waiting period. The experimenter then passed out a questionnaire asking subjects to indicate their preference for each of the three possible choices. The subjects indicated their preference between each of the three paired comparisons possible among the three conditions. Each preference was rated on a four-point scale running from "very much prefer this choice" through "slightly prefer" to "very much prefer" for the other choice on each comparison.

After all subjects in each group completed the affiliative choice questionnaire, it was returned to the classroom by the experimenter.

Results and Discussion

Set Effects: Perhaps the most striking difference between Studies I and II is that, while almost half of the subjects in Study I chose solitude over companionship, more than 90 per cent of the subjects in Study II could be classified as having chosen to be with either the peer group or the leader group. This was true in both the waiting and the working conditions. Thus, desire for affiliation was clearly stronger among subjects who had spent a considerable amount of time in groups prior to the affiliative choice than it was among those who had been alone before being offered a chance to affiliate. It appears that the prior social setting can have a strong effect on the desire for gregariousness.

The subject population was extremely heterogeneous. Results of the Wonderlic Personnel Test converted to high school norms indicated that the population ranged from the first to the ninety-ninth percentile in intelligence. On the basis of an arbitrary a priori decision, it was assumed that subjects scoring in the first percentile or below would be unable to understand the experimental manipulations. Therefore, all subjects with absolute scores below 8 (first percentile) on the Wonderlic were eliminated from further analysis. This resulted in a loss of 12 subjects. Of the remaining 108 subjects, 54 were firstborn and 54 later born (a chance result, as subjects had not been recruited on the basis of ordinal position).

Effectiveness of Fear: The first 80 subjects who received the fear manipulation filled out the 33-item mood-adjective check list immediately after receiving the fear manipulation. With 5 of these 80 subjects dropped because of low IQ, 40 low-fear and 35 high-fear subjects were used in the analysis for effectiveness of fear. On an a priori basis, 6 of the 33 adjective pairs were selected to form a "fear index" (anxious-fearful; disturbed-upset; easygoing-relaxed, negatively scored; jittery-nervous; frightened-worried; quiet-peaceful, negatively scored). A 2 × 2 (Fear × Ordinal Position) unweighted-means analysis of variance was performed on the summed fear-index score. The main effect for fear was significant at better than the .001 level ($F = 14.70$, $df = 1/71$), demonstrating that the manipulation was highly effective in making the high-fear group more nervous and apprehensive than the low-fear subjects.[1] A trend toward an interaction between fear and ordinal position ($p < .10$) was found, with firstborns less frightened than later borns in the low-fear condition, but more apprehensive under high fear. Fear means were low fear—firstborns, 5.41; later borns, 6.30; high fear—firstborns, 11.64; later borns, 8.62. The analyses of variance are summarized in Table 4. A similar trend was observed in Study I.

***Table** 4 Study II: Analysis of Variance for Fear Index*[a]

	F
Fear (A)	14.70***
Ordinal position (B)	0.91
A × B	3.08*

[a] Posttest only; $df = 1, 71$ for all analyses.
* $p < .10$.
*** $p < .001$.

[1] Individual t tests indicated that each of the six adjective pairs discriminated between high- and low-fear conditions at better than the .05 level.

Affiliative Preference: A three-way unweighted-means analysis of variance (Winer, 1965, p. 602) was performed (Fear × Working-Waiting × Firstborn-Later Born) on the ratings which contrasted each of the three possible comparisons among the three affiliative choices. A significant main effect for fear was found for the leader-versus peer-group ratios ($F = 4.98$, $p = .05$, $df = 1/100$). This replicates Study I, as the main effect reflects a *decrease* in preference for the peer group in favor of the leader group. A significant interaction ($F = 4.34$, $p < .05$, $df = 1/100$) between fear and ordinal position was also obtained for this comparison. As can be seen in Figure 1, all subjects in the working condition and later borns in the waiting condition showed *increased* desire for the leader group under high fear. Firstborns in the high-fear–waiting condition showed a slight decrease in preference for the leader groups (as compared to the peer group). This finding *for the waiting condition* parallels earlier affiliation studies where firstborns have shown the greatest desire for the company of peers under high fear. Results of the analyses of variance for all choices are summarized in Table 5.

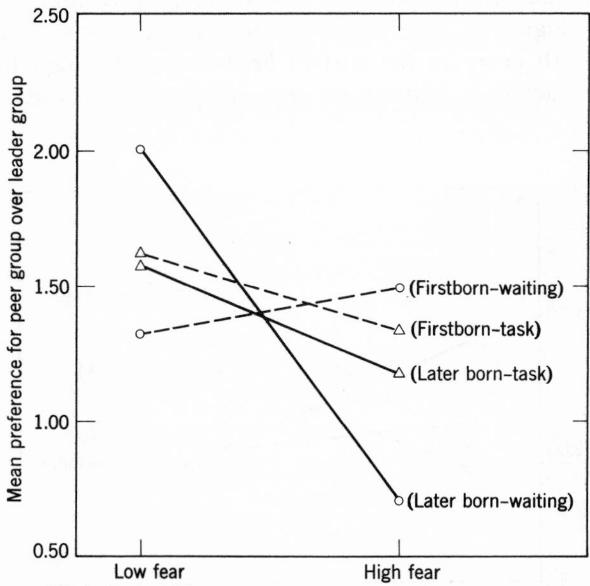

Figure 1. Mean ratings on scale for peer-group versus leader-group comparison.

Table 5 *Study II: Analyses of Variance for Affiliative Choice*[a]

	F		
	Peer Group vs. Alone Choice	Peer Group vs. Leader Choice	Leader Group vs. Alone Choice
Fear (A)	<1	4.98**	1.36
Working vs. waiting (B)	<1	<1	<1
Ordinal position (C)	<1	<1	<1
A × B	<1	<1	<1
A × C	4.87**	4.34**	<1
B × C	1.07	<1	<1
A × B × C	<1	2.62	1.18
MS (error)	0.71	0.99	0.64

[a] $df = 1,100$ for all analyses.
** $p < .05$.

No significant main effects were found for the comparison between peer group and alone choices; however, a significant interaction between fear and ordinal position was found in this analysis. As can be seen in Figure 2, this interaction reflects an increased desire for affiliation with peers on the part of firstborns under high fear when the choice offered is solitude or peer companionship (i.e., the only

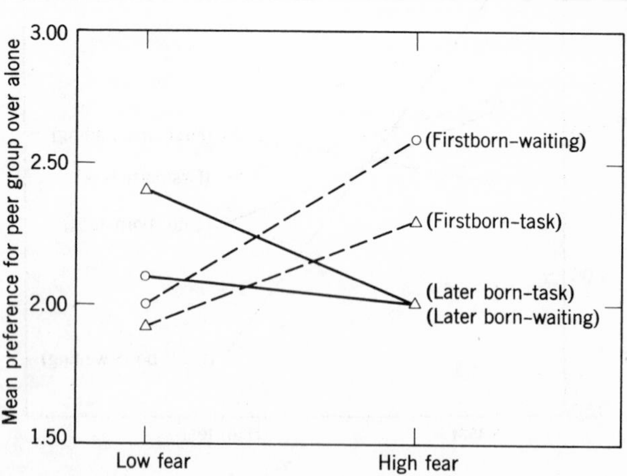

Figure 2. Mean ratings on scale for peer-group versus alone comparison.

choices offered in previous studies). This result, which held for both the waiting and task conditions, is similar to the changes in affiliative preference reported in earlier studies (e.g., Schachter, 1959), but it is opposite to the trend observed in Study I. It should be noted that subjects in Study I were run individually and allowed to choose only one of the three working conditions; subjects in Study II were run in groups and allowed to express a preference among each of the three possible pairings of the three affiliative conditions. No significant main effects or interactions were found for the contrast between the leader groups and alone choices.

Experimenter Effects: Results were analyzed separately for subjects run by each experimenter. No significant effects were found for either level of fear or affiliative preference.

IMPLICATIONS

Studies I and II indicate that offering the company of an older leader (who, according to the present theory, may satisfy dependency needs aroused by stress) can change the direction of affiliation under stress. Thus it is established that dependency needs are at least one of the factors creating affiliative behavior under stress. It is difficult to assess from earlier studies what effect motivation for dependency may have had on direction of affiliation because dependency needs could contribute to the peer choice if the only other alternative were solitude.

The fact that the birth-order differences found in the waiting condition were not present for working choices may indicate a qualitative difference in the two conditions. Where the emphasis is on constructive performance, all subjects may perceive that the most satisfactory arrangement is to sacrifice autonomy and to accept a dependent relationship. In the waiting condition, on the other hand, firstborns may find social comparison with peers most important; later borns, who presumably have less need for social support, may find the greatest anxiety reduction through establishing a dependent relationship.

The striking increase in preference for the peer and leader groups under fear observed in Study II (as compared to Study I) is, of course, a between-experiment finding which could have been produced by any of the many differences between the two studies. Nonetheless, the hypothesis that the phenomenon can be attributed to the fact that subjects in Study I were run in solitude while subjects in Study II were run in groups adds another dimension to the assessment of affiliative preference. Subjects in Studies I and II had had significant experience either alone or in a group immediately prior to making an affiliative choice; that is, subjects spent between 40 minutes and an hour either alone or in a large group before being offered affiliative choices. In earlier studies (e.g., Schachter, 1959) subjects spent a short period of time in groups or alone and were then offered the choice of affiliation. It seems probable that in the present studies subjects acquired a set for solitude or gregariousness which is reflected in the choices made by low-fear subjects. The fear manipulation may have strengthened this set as the individual, faced with a threatening situation, might be reluctant to undertake any novel experience. Thus individuals who had been alone might find a sudden confrontation with a group of people more threatening than solitude, while those who had been in groups might find being alone more threatening. There is a strong implication that one must control the subject's set, his situationally determined propensity for gregariousness, before one can compare the effects of different treatments or can speak with certainty about overall changes in motivation for affiliation.

SUMMARY

The study tests the hypothesis that affiliation under stress might be produced by a dependency-motivation mechanism—rather than the social comparison and direct-anxiety-reduction mechanisms discussed in previous papers. Each *S* was given the opportunity to wait (or work) in a leader-dominated group as well as the standard opportunities to wait alone or in a group of peers. *S*s facing a fearful situation showed a significant decrease in preference for the company of peers in favor of being in a leader-dominated group, supporting the dependency-motivation hypothesis. *S*s initially run and stressed in groups evidenced markedly greater affiliative choices (leader plus peer) than *S*s run alone. When choices were made for working under stress, no birth-order effects were found; when choices were made for waiting for stress, the previously reported birth-order interaction was replicated.

REFERENCES

Cattell, R. S., & Eber, H. W. *Handbook for the Sixteen Personality Questionnaire.* Champaign, Ill.: Institute for Personality and Ability Testing, 1964.

Darley, J. M., & Aronson, E. Self-evaluation vs. direct anxiety reduction as determinants of the fear-affiliation relationship. *J. Psychol.*, 1966, Suppl. 1, 66–79.

Festinger, L. A theory of social comparison processes. *Hum. Relat.*, 1954, **7**, 117–140.

Gerard, H. B., & Rabbie, J. M. Fear and social comparisons. *J. Abnorm. Soc. Psychol.*, 1961, **62**, 586–592.

Janis, I. L. Group identification under conditions of external danger. *Brit. J. Med. Psychol.*, 1963, **36**, 227–238.

Janis, I. L., & Field, P. B. Sex differences and personality factors related to persuasibility. In C. Hovland & I. L. Janis (Eds.), *Personality and persuasibility*. New Haven: Yale Univ. Press, 1959. Pp. 55–68.

Miller, N., & Zimbardo, P. G. Motives for fear-induced affiliation: Emotional comparison or interpersonal similarity. *J. Pers.*, 1966, **34**, 481–503.

Rabbie, J. M. Differential preference for companionship under threat. *J. Abnorm. Soc. Psychol.*, 1963, **67**, 643–648

Schachter, S. *The psychology of affiliation*. Stanford: Stanford Univ. Press, 1959.

Winer, B. J. *Statistical principles in experimental design*. New York: McGraw-Hill, 1962.

Wrightsman, L. The effect of waiting with others on changes in level of felt anxiety. *J. Abnorm. Soc. Psychol.*, 1960, **61**, 216–222.

Zimbardo, P. G., & Formica, R. Emotional comparison and self-esteem as determinants of affiliation. *J. Pers.*, 1963, **31**, 141–162.

2.2 IMPORTANCE OF PHYSICAL ATTRACTIVENESS IN DATING BEHAVIOR

Elaine Walster
Vera Aronson
Darcy Abrahams
Leon Rottmann

In one of his delightful articles Goffman (1952) said that: "A proposal of marriage in our society tends to be a way in which a man sums up his social attributes and suggests to a woman that hers are not so much better as to preclude a merger or a partnership in these matters [p. 456]." Goffman's proposal suggests that one's romantic feelings and choices are affected both by the objective desirability of the romantic object and by one's perception of the possibility of attaining the affection of the other. Rosenfeld (1964) has demonstrated that an individual's choice of a *work partner* was affected by his as-

Source: This study was financed by the Student Activities Bureau, University of Minnesota. Reprinted with slight abridgment from the *Journal of Personality and Social Psychology*, 1966, **4**, 508–516, with permission of the senior author and the American Psychological Association, Inc., copyright holder.

sumptions about whether or not the partner would reciprocate his choice.

The following field experiment was conducted to see if one's romantic aspirations are influenced by the same factors that affect one's level of aspiration in other areas. (Level of aspiration theory is presented in Lewin, Dembo, Festinger, & Sears, 1944.) We wish to point out that this study concentrates on *realistic* social choices. In their discussion of "ideal choices" Lewin et al. conclude that an individual's ideal goals are usually based entirely on the desirability of the goal, with no consideration of the possibility of attaining this goal. Probably an individual's fantasy romantic choices are also based entirely on the desirability of the object. One's *realistic* level of aspiration, on the other hand, has been shown by Lewin et al. to depend both on the objective desirability of the goal and on one's perceived possibility of attaining that goal.

We propose that one's realistic romantic choices will be affected by the same practical considerations that affect other realistic goal setting. Lewin et al. note that since the attractiveness of a goal and the probability of attaining that goal are negatively correlated, the goal an individual can expect to attain is usually less attractive than the one he would desire to attain. In romantic choices, attractiveness and availability would also seem to be negatively correlated. The more abstractly desirable a potential romantic object is, the more competition there probably is for him (or her), and the less likely it is that a given individual will be able to attain his friendship. Thus one's *realistic* social choices should be less "socially desirable" than one's fantasy social choices. In addition, Lewin et al. note that one's realistic level of aspiration is affected by his perception of own skills. In the romantic area, we would expect that the individual's own social attractiveness would affect his level of aspiration. On the basis of the above reasoning, we would propose the following specific hypotheses:

1. Individuals who are themselves very socially desirable (physically attractive, personable, or possessing great material assets) will require that an appropriate partner possess more social desirability than will a less socially desirable individual.

2. If couples varying in social desirability meet in a social situation, those couples who are similar in social desirability will most often attempt to date one another.

3. In addition, we propose that an individual will not only *choose* a date of approximately his own social desirability, but also that after actual experi-

ence with potential dates of various desirabilities an individual will express the most *liking* for a partner of approxmately his own desirability.

This prediction is not directly derived from level of aspiration formulations. Lewin et al. predict only that an individual will choose a goal of intermediate attractiveness and difficulty; they do not propose that an individual will come to *like* goals of intermediate difficulty. We thought that unattainably desirable individuals might be derogated (although inappropriately difficult tasks are not) for the following reasons:

1. If a man chooses an inappropriately difficult task and then fails to attain it, all he suffers is defeat. The task cannot point out to him that he has been presumptuous in choosing a goal so far beyond his level of ability. We speculated, however, that an extremely desirable date can be counted on to make it clear to a somewhat undesirable individual that he is foolish to try to win her friendship and that he should not embarrass her by asking her out.
2. We thought that perhaps an extremely attractive date would not be as considerate of an unattractive date as with a date more average in appearance.

PROCEDURE

Subjects were 376 men and 376 women who purchased tickets to a Friday night dance held on the last day of "Welcome Week." (Welcome Week is a week of cultural, educational, and social events provided for incoming University of Minnesota freshmen.) The dance was advertised along with 87 other events in a handbook all incoming freshmen received. In fact, however, the dance was not a regular Welcome Week event and had been set up solely to test our hypotheses. The handbook advertisement describing a Computer Dance said: "Here's your chance to meet someone who has the same expressed interests as yourself." Freshmen were told that if they would give the computer some information about their interests and personalities, the computer would match them with a date. Tickets were $1.00 per person; both men and women purchased their own tickets. Long lines of subjects appeared to buy tickets on the opening day—only the first 376 male and 376 female students who appeared were accepted.

For experimental purposes, ticket sales and information distribution were set up in extremely bureaucratic style: The subject walked along a table in the foyer of the Student Union. First, a student sold him a ticket. He moved down the table, and a second student checked his identification card to make sure he was a student and told him to report to a large room two flights above. When the subject arrived at the upstairs room, a third student met him at the door and handed him a questionnaire with his student code number stamped on it and asked him to complete the questionnaire at an adjoining table. A fourth student directed him to a seat. (Proctors around the room answered the subject's questions and discouraged talking.)

Physical Attractiveness Rating

The four bureaucrats were actually college sophomores who had been hired to rate the physical attractiveness of the 752 freshmen who purchased tickets to the dance.[1]

We assumed that one's social desirability would include such attributes as physical attractiveness, personableness, and material resources and that these aspects would be positively correlated with one another. We chose physical attractiveness to be the indicator of the subject's social desirability since this trait was more quickly assessed under standard conditions.

As each subject passed, the four raters rapidly and individually evaluated the subject's physical attractiveness on an eight-point scale, going from 1 ("Extremely unattractive") to 8 ("Extremely attractive"). Obviously, these attractiveness ratings had to be made very quickly; usually the rater had less than 1 or 2 seconds to look at the subject before making his evaluation, and rarely did the rater get to hear the subject say more than "OK" or "Thank you." The briefness of this contact was by design. Since we had chosen to use one aspect of social desirability as an index of total desirability, as far as possible, we wanted to be sure that the raters were assessing only that aspect. We did not want our ratings of attractiveness to be heavily influenced by the subject's personableness, intelligence, voice quality, etc.

Once the subjects were seated in the large upstairs room, they began filling out the questionnaire. The subject first answered several demographic questions concerning his age (nearly all were 18), height, race, and religious preference. The next measures were designed to assess how considerate the subject felt he would be of a fairly attractive date.

The remainder of the booklet contained material which we wanted to encourage the subjects to answer honestly. For this reason, a section

[1] David Kushner, John B. Kelly, Susan Lampland, and Victoria Noser rated the attractiveness of all the subjects. These students were simply told to use their own judgment in rating the subjects and to be careful not to communicate their ratings to the other raters.

prefacing the questions assured participants that their answers to the questions would not be used in selecting their date. We explained that we were including these questions only for research purposes and not for matching purposes. In addition, the subjects were reassured that their statements would be kept confidential and associated only with their ticket number, never their name. Four pages of questions followed this introduction. In the pages following this introduction, four variables were measured:

Subject's popularity (self-report). The subject was asked how popular he was with members of the opposite sex, how easy it was to get a date with someone he thought was exceptionally attractive, and how many dates he had had in the last six months.

Subject's nervousness. The subject was asked how nervous or awkward he felt about the idea of going on a blind date.

Measure of the subject's expectations in a computer date. The subject was asked how physically attractive, how personally attractive, and how considerate he expected his date to be.

Subject's self-esteem. Questions from a scale developed by Berger (1952) ended the questionnaire. The subject was asked how true 36 different statements were of himself. The subject was once again reassured that this information was confidential and would not be used in selecting his computer date. (A typical question is: "When I'm in a group, I usually don't say much for fear of saying the wrong things.") This test was scored so that a high score indicated high self-acceptance and high self-esteem.

From the University's statewide testing service program at the University of Minnesota, several additional measures were secured for the subject whenever possible. The subject's high school academic percentile rank, his Minnesota Scholastic Aptitude Test (MSAT) score, and his score on the MMPI or the Minnesota Counseling Inventory (MCI) were secured.

Two days after the subject completed his questionnaire, he was assigned to a date. Dates were randomly assigned to the subjects with one limitation: a man was never assigned to a date taller than himself. On the few occasions when the assigned female date would have been taller than the male, the IBM card next in the shuffled deck was selected as the partner. When subjects picked up their dates' name, the experimenter advised them to meet their dates at the dance. Many couples, however, met at the girl's home.

The dance was held in a large armory. In order to be admitted to the armory, the subjects had to turn in their numbered tickets at the door. In this way, we could check on whether or not a given couple had attended the dance. Of the 376 male and 376 female students who signed up for the dance and were assigned a partner, 44 couples did not attend.[2] The subjects generally arrived at the dance at 8:00 P.M. and danced or talked until the 10:30 P.M. intermission.

Assessing Subjects' Attitudes toward One Another

Subjects' attitudes toward their dates were assessed during intermission. Several times during Welcome Week, we had advertised that couples should hold onto their ticket stubs until intermission, because these stubs would be collected during intermission and a $50 drawing would be held at that time. When the subjects bought their tickets, we reminded them that they would need to save their tickets for an intermission lottery. They were also told that during the dance they would have a chance to tell us how successful our matching techniques had been.

During the 10:30 P.M. intermission, the subjects were reminded that tickets for the lottery would be collected while they filled out a brief questionnaire assessing their dates and the dance. The purpose of the lottery was simply to insure that the subjects would retain their ticket stubs, which contained an identifying code number, and would report to an assigned classroom during intermission to evaluate their dates. Men were to report to one of seven small rooms to rate their dates and to turn in their stubs; women were to remain in the large armory to evaluate their partners.

The forms on which the subjects rated their partner were anonymous except that the subjects were asked to record their ticket numbers in the right-hand corner. This number, of course, identified the subjects perfectly to us, while not requiring the subjects to sign their name to their evaluation. A crew of experimenters rounded up any subjects who had wandered to rest rooms, fire escapes, or adjoining buildings and asked them to turn in their ticket stubs and to complete the evaluation questionnaires.

In the eight rooms where the subjects were assembled to evaluate their dates, the experimenters[3] urged the subjects to take the questionnaire seriously and to answer all questions honestly. All but 5 of

[2] By far the most common reason given by the subjects for not attending the dance was that the date was of a different religion than the subject and that their parents had objected to their dating.

[3] Male experimenters interviewed male subjects; female experimenters interviewed female subjects.

332 couples attending the dance completed a questionnaire, either during intermission or in a subsequent contact two days later.

The intermission questionnaire asked the subject about the following things: (*a*) how much the subject liked his date, (*b*) how socially desirable the date seemed to be ("How physically attractive is your date?" "How personally attractive is your date?"), (*c*) how uncomfortable the subject was on this blind date, (*d*) how much the date seemed to like the subject, (*e*) how similar the date's values, attitudes, and beliefs seemed to the subject's own, (*f*) how much of an effort the subject made to insure that the date had a good time, and how much of an effort the date made on the subject's behalf, (*g*) whether or not the subject would like to date his partner again.

How often couples actually dated was determined in a follow-up study. All participants were contacted four to six months after the dance and asked whether or not they had tried to date their computer date after the dance. If the experimenter was unable to contact either the subject or the subject's date in two months of attempts, the couple was excluded from the sample. Only ten couples could not be contacted.

RESULTS

Physical Attractiveness and Social Desirability

We assumed that we could use our ratings of physical attractiveness as a rough index of a person's social desirability. Is there any evidence that these outside ratings are related to the subject's own perception of his social desirability? When we look at the data, we see that there is. The more attractive an individual is, the more popular he says he is. The correlation between physical attractiveness and popularity for men is .31 and for women is .46. (Both of these *r*'s are significant at $p < .001$.)[4]

Hypothesis I

Our first prediction was that a very socially desirable (attractive) subject would expect a "suitable" or "acceptable" date to possess more physical and personal charm and to be more considerate than would a less socially desirable subject.

We had two ways of testing whether or not attractive subjects did,

[4] With an N of 327, a correlation of .10 is significant at $p < .05$, a correlation of .15 at $p < .01$, and a correlation of .18 at $p < .001$.

in fact, have more rigorous requirements for an acceptable date than did less attractive individuals. Before the subject was assigned a date, he was asked how physically attractive, how personally attractive, and how considerate he expected his date to be. His answers to these three questions were summed, and an index of degree of the perfection he expected was computed. From the data, it appears that the more attractive the subject is, the more attractive, personable, and considerable he expects his date to be. The correlation between physical attractiveness and total expectations in a date is .18 for men and .23 for women.

A second way an individual's stringency of requirements could have been tested was by seeing whether or not the subject refused to go out with an "unsuitable" date. We wanted to eliminate the possibility that attractive and unattractive subjects would attend the dance with different frequencies, so we encouraged subjects to meet one another at the dance. However, it is possible that a few individuals were ingenious enough to get a preview of their dates before their public appearance together. We tried to determine whether or not attractive individuals rejected their partners *before* the dance more often than did unattractive ones.

It will be recalled that four raters rated each subject on an eight-point scale of attractiveness. We then separated subjects into three approximately equal-sized groups on the basis of these ratings. Men receiving an average rating of from 1.50 to 4.00 and women rated 1.50 to 4.75 were classified as *ugly* individuals; men receiving an average rating of from 5.25 to 6.00 and women rated 5.00–5.75 were classified as *average* individuals; and men rated 6.25–8.00 and women rated 6.00–8.00 were classified as *attractive* individuals. We then contacted the 44 couples who did not attend the computer dance and interviewed them about their reasons for not attending. Attractive subjects did not reject their dates before the dance any more often than did unattractive subjects.

Behavioral Measures of Rejection

After men had arrived at the dance, or at their date's home, they met the partner who had been randomly assigned to them. Then during intermission, the subjects rated their liking for their dates. Since partners were randomly assigned, very attractive individuals should be assigned to just as attractive partners, on the average, as are average or ugly individuals. Thus, if during intermission, very handsome individuals rate their dates as less attractive, less personable, and less considerate than do less attractive men, this would indicate that attractive men are more harsh in their standards and ratings than are less attractive men. Also, if attractive individuals are more harsh in their standards they should, on the average, like their dates less, express less of a desire to date their partner again, and should actually try to date their computer partner less often than do less attractive individuals. When we look at the data, we see that this first hypothesis is confirmed.

The more attractive a man is, the less physically and personally attractive he thinks his date is ($F = 8.88$, $df = 1/318$, $p < .01$), the less he likes her ($F = 6.69$, $p < .01$), the less he would like to date her again ($F = 14.07$, $p < .001$), and the less often the date says he actually did ask her out again ($F = 3.15$, *ns*). Similarly, the more attractive a woman is, the less physically and personally attractive she thinks her date is ($F = 5.71$, $df = 1/318$, $p < .05$), the less she likes her date ($F = 2.23$, *ns*), and the less she would like to date him again ($F = 13.24$, $p < .001$).

Though it is clear that the more attractive subjects do appear to judge their dates more harshly than do unattractive subjects, we would like to note that this variable does *not* account for a very large portion of the total variance. For example, the relationships we have demonstrated between the subject's attractiveness and his expectations and evaluations of a date are strongly significant in five of the seven cases reported. However, correlations for the above variables range from only .07 to .20.

Hypothesis II proposed that an individual would most often choose to date a partner of approximately his own attractiveness. Hypothesis III stated that if individuals were to interact with partners of varying physical attractiveness, in a naturalistic setting, an individual would be better liked and would more often want to continue to date a partner similar to himself in attractiveness. Figure 1 depicts graphically the theoretical expectation that subjects will most often choose and most often like dates of approximately their own attractiveness. Statistically, we test Hypotheses II and III by testing the significance of the interaction between date's attractiveness and subject's attractiveness in influencing the subject's *attempts* to date the partner, his *desire* to date the partner, and his liking for his date.

In Table 1, as in Figure 1, the subjects who supplied information to us were divided into three groups—ugly subjects, average subjects, and attractive subjects. Unlike Figure 1, however, the actual attractiveness of the dates the subjects are rating is not allowed to vary con-

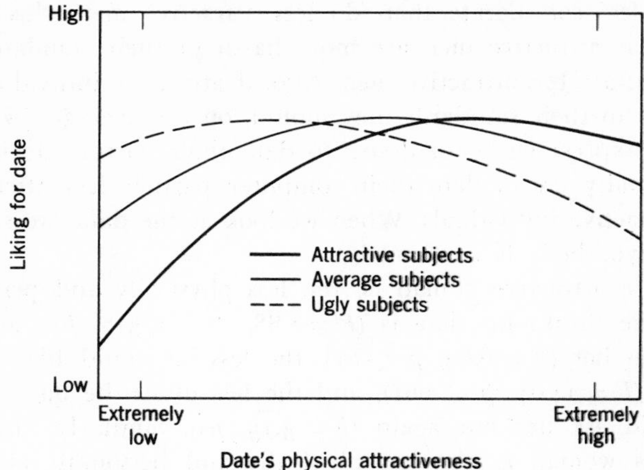

Figure 1. Amount of liking predicted for dates of various attractiveness by ugly, average, and attractive subjects.

tinuously; for the sake of clarity, the dates were also divided into three attractiveness groups.

So that we could very precisely assess whether or not the interaction we predicted was significant, we also examined the data by dividing subjects and their dates into five attractiveness levels. When the 5×5 interaction is examined, however, the conclusions and *F*s are identical to those we form on the basis of the less fine discriminations (3×3) reported in Table 1. For this reason, the smaller breakdown is presented.

Hypotheses II and III are not supported. The subject's attractiveness does not significantly interact with the date's attractiveness in determining his attempt to date her, his desire to date her, or his liking for her. In *no* case is there a significant interaction. If we look at the *actual* attempts of men to date their partners (Table 1:I), we find that men did not more often ask out dates similar to themselves in attractiveness. (These data were secured in a follow-up study.) The only important determinant of whether or not the date was asked out again was how attractive the *date* was. The most attractive girls are most often asked out ($F = 12.02$, $df = 1/318$, $p < .001$). This is generally true *regardless of the attractiveness of the man* who is asking her out. There is *not* a significant tendency for subjects to try to date partners of approximately their own physical desirability. The

Table 1 *Various Measures of the Subjects' Liking for Their Dates and Subjects' Desire to Date Their Partners*

	Date's Physical Attractiveness		
	Ugly	Average	Attractive
I. Percent Ss actually asking date out			
According to ugly male Ss	.16	.21	.40
According to average male Ss	.12	.25	.22
According to attractive male Ss	.00	.26	.29
II. How much S says he liked his date			
According to ugly male Ss	.06[a]	.57	.90
According to average male Ss	—.10	.58	1.56
According to attractive male Ss	—.62	.16	.82
According to ugly female Ss	.03	.71	.96
According to average female Ss	—.10	.61	1.50
According to attractive female Ss	—.13	.21	.89
III. Percent Ss saying they wanted to date partner again			
According to ugly male Ss	.41	.53	.80
According to average male Ss	.30	.50	.78
According to attractive male Ss	.04	.37	.58
According to ugly female Ss	.53	.56	.92
According to average female Ss	.35	.69	.71
According to attractive female Ss	.27	.27	.68
IV. How many subsequent dates couples had			
Ugly male Ss	.09	1.23	.73
Average male Ss	.30	.94	.17
Attractive male Ss	.00	2.08	.53
V. Amount S thinks date likes him			
Guesses by ugly male Ss	.47[b]	.52	.43
Guesses by average male Ss	.55	.64	.65
Guesses by attractive male Ss	.77	.53	.58
Guesses by ugly female Ss	.41	.41	.35
Guesses by average female Ss	.38	.58	.55
Guesses by attractive female Ss	.63	.65	.61
VI. No. of Ss in each cell			
Ugly male Ss	(32)	(43)	(30)
Average male Ss	(43)	(36)	(41)
Attractive male Ss	(26)	(38)	(38)

[a] The higher the number, the more the subject says he liked his date.
[b] The higher the number, the more the subject thinks his date liked him.

interaction F which is necessary to demonstrate such a tendency is very small ($F = .07$).

Our hypothesis (III) that individuals would best *like* dates similar to themselves in attractiveness also fails to be supported by the data. During intermission, individuals indicated how much they liked their dates on a scale ranging from 2.5 ("Like extremely much") to − 2.5 ("Dislike extremely much"). From Table 1, sections II and III, it is apparent that by far the greatest determinant of how much liking an individual feels for his partner is simply how attractive the partner is. The more attractive the female date is, the better liked she is ($F = 59.26$, $df = 1/318$) and the more often the man says that he would like to date her ($F = 49.87$). Men do not overrate women at their own attractiveness level. (Interaction Fs for liking and desire to date = 2.53 and .69, respectively.) Very surprising to us was the fact that a *man's* physical attractiveness is also by far the largest determinant of how well *he* is liked. We had assumed that physical attractiveness would be a much less important determinant of liking for men than for women. However, it appears that it is just as important a determinant. The more attractive the man, the more his partner likes him ($F = 55.79$, $df = 1/318$) and the more often she says she wants to date him again ($F = 37.24$). As before, we see that women do not tend to overrate partners at their own attractiveness level. (Interaction Fs for liking and desire to date = .07 and .08, respectively.)

In order to get a better idea of the extent to which liking was related to the date's physical attractiveness, we examined the correlation between these two variables. The correlations between date's attractiveness and the partner's liking is almost as high as the reliability of the attractiveness ratings.

Our measure of physical attractiveness is not highly reliable. When rating the subject's physical attractiveness, raters saw the subject for only a few seconds as the subject moved along in a line. In addition, raters had to devise their own standards of attractiveness. Probably as a consequence of the preceding factors, the attractiveness ratings made by the four raters of the same individual intercorrelate .49–.58. In addition, there is a factor which may further reduce the reliability of our attractiveness measure from the time of the rating to the time of the dance. At the time of the rating, the subjects were in school clothes, casually dressed, while on the day of the dance they were dressed for a date. It is possible that this difference would have produced a change in the subject's relative attractiveness orderings. In spite of these limitations, the correlation between a *woman's* average physical attractiveness rating and her male partner's liking for her is .44; the correlation between her attractiveness and whether or not he wants to continue to date her is .39; and between her attractiveness and how much he actually does ask her out subsequently is .17. The correlations between a *man's* average physical attractiveness rating and his partner's liking for him and desire to date him are .36 and .31, respectively.

When we examine the relationship between the *individual's* own estimation of the date's physical attractiveness and his expression of liking for her, the correlations are still higher. The correlation between liking of the date and evaluation of the date's physical attractiveness is .78 for male subjects and .69 for female subjects.

It appears that the more attractive the date, the more he was liked, and the more the subject desired to date him regardless of how attracted the date was to the subject. The happy accommodation that we proposed between what an individual desires and what he can realistically hope to attain appears not to exist. The lack of symmetry between the individual's liking for his date and the date's liking for the individual is striking. The correlation between how much the man says he likes his partner and how much she likes him is virtually zero: $r = .03$. Nor is there a significant correlation between whether or not the subject wants to date his partner again and whether she wants to date him: $r = .07$. Clearly, a variable that we assumed would be very important—how much the date likes the individual—does not appear to be an important determinant of the individual's ratings. Sheer physical attractiveness appears to be the overriding determinant of liking.

How can we account for the singular importance of physical attractiveness in determining the individual's liking for the other? There seem to be several plausible explanations:

1. Perhaps it could be argued that in the relationships we have discussed it is not really physical attractiveness that is so crucial, but one of the *correlates* of attractiveness. For example, we know from developmental studies of intelligent individuals (Terman, 1925, 1947, 1959) that intelligence, physical attractiveness, creativity, and certain personality traits are often positively correlated. Perhaps it is one of these correlated variables that is really important in determining liking.

From the other evidence we have on this point and which we will present in the next paragraphs, it appears that "intelligence" and "personality" are *not* better predictors of liking than physical attractiveness.

Intelligence and Achievement Measures

Students' high school percentile ranks and MSAT scores are undoubtedly much more reliable measures than is our measure of physical attractiveness. Yet, these measures have only a very weak relationship to liking. The higher the male's high school percentile rank, the less his partner likes him ($r = -.18$) and the less she wants to date him again ($r = -.04$) ($N = 303$). Male's MSAT scores correlate .04 with both the woman's liking for him and her desire to date him ($N = 281$). The higher the female's high school percentile rank, the less her partner likes her ($r = -.07$) and the less he desires to date her again ($r = -.09$). High school rank is uncorrelated with his actual attempt to date her again ($r = .00$) ($N = 323$). Females' MSAT scores correlate −.05, −.06, and −.06 with these same variables ($N = 306$). It is clear then that intelligence is clearly not a variable of the same importance as physical attractiveness in determining liking. In no case did a subject's intellectual achievement or ability test scores have a significant relationship to the liking his date expressed for him.

Personality Measures

The subjects also completed several personality measures which could reasonably be expected to predict the liking one would engender in a social situation.[5]

MCI: Social relationships (SR). Low scorers are said to have good social skills, have acceptable manners, and be courteous, mature individuals (Berdie, Layton, Swanson, Hagenah, & Merwin, 1962).

MMPI: Masculinity-femininity (Mf). Low scorers are said to be more masculine in their values, attitudes, and interest, styles of expression and speech, and in their sexual relationships than high scorers (Dahlstrom & Welsh, 1962).

MMPI: Social introversion (Si). Low scorers are said to be more extroverted in their thinking, social participation, and emotional involvement.

[5] MCI scores were secured for 234 of the male subjects and 240 of the female subjects during freshman testing. In addition, the MMPI had been administered to a sample including 50 of the men and 41 of the women.

Bergers's Scale of Self-Acceptance (1952). The correlations between an individual's scores on personality measures and the liking his date expresses for him show that the measures are not as good predictors of liking as is our crude measure of physical attractiveness. When we look at the data, we see that the low scoring individuals on the MCI (SR), on the MMPI (Mf), and on the MMPI (Si) or high scorers on Berger's Scale of Self-Acceptance are only slightly better liked by their dates than are high scoring individuals. Men's scores on these tests correlate −.11, −.12, −.10, and .14 with their dates' liking for them. Women's scores on these tests correlate only − .18, − .10, − .08, and .03 with their dates' liking. Our personality measures, then, like our intelligence measures, appear to be very inadequate predictors of liking.

It is, of course, possible that intelligence and personality determinants would have been more important had individuals had more time to get acquainted. It may be that 2½ hours is too short a time for individuals to discover much about their partners' intelligence or personality, while physical attractiveness is obvious from the start. It is not likely, however, that intelligence or personality variables are "really" underlying the correlations we obtained between attractiveness and romantic liking.

2. It may be that in this situation, individuals were not very affected by their dates' liking for them because the dates were so polite that it was possible for the individual to know if he was accepted or rejected. Or, perhaps individuals were so eager to be liked that they did not want to correctly perceive the available cues.

The only available evidence for this position is ambiguous. The correlation between the partner's stated liking for the subject and the subject's perception of the partner's liking for him is .23 for male subjects and .36 for female subjects. The subject, thus, has some, though not a great deal of, ability in estimating how much his partner likes him. The reader may see subjects' guesses concerning how much their date likes them in Table 1:V. Possible answers to the question, "How much does your partner like you?" could range from (2.5) "Date likes me extremely much" to (−2.5) "Date dislikes me extremely much."

3. It may be that our findings are limited to large group situations, where young people are in very brief contact with one another. Perhaps if individuals had been exposed to one another for *long* periods of time, similarity of interests, beliefs, and reciprocal liking would come to be more important

than physical appearance in determining liking. Finally, it might also be true that physical attractiveness loses some of its importance as individuals get to be *older* than the 18-year-olds interviewed in our study.

We should note that, even though further contact may have decreased the importance of physical attractiveness, whether or not the subject attempted to continue to date his partner depended on the partner's physical attractiveness. Similarly, though our findings may well be limited to the youthful population that we interviewed (average age: 18 years), it is also true that this is the age at which many individuals make their lifelong romantic choices.

4. Finally, it may be that if we had arranged more conventional single dates, the date's personality and conversational abilities would have been more important. It may have been that just getting to display a very attractive date compensated for any rejection on the date's part.

SUMMARY

It was proposed that an individual would most often expect to date, would try to date, and would like a partner of approximately his own social desirability. In brief, we attempted to apply level of aspiration theory to choice of social goals. A field study was conducted in which individuals were randomly paired with one another at a "Computer Dance." Level of aspiration hypotheses were not confirmed. Regardless of *S*'s own attractiveness, by far the largest determinant of how much his partner was liked, how much he wanted to date the partner again, and how often he actually asked the partner out was simply how attractive the partner was. Personality measures such as the MMPI, the Minnesota Counseling Inventory, and Berger's Scale of Self-Acceptance and intellectual measures such as the Minnesota Scholastic Aptitude Test, and high school percentile rank did not predict couple compatibility. The only important determinant of *S*'s liking for his date was the date's physical attractiveness.

REFERENCES

Berdie, R. F., Layton, W. L., Swanson, E. O., Hagenah, T., & Mervin, J. C. *Counseling and the use of tests.* Minneapolis: Student Counseling Bureau, 1962.

Berger, E. M. The relation between expressed acceptance of self and expressed acceptance of others, *J. Abnorm. Soc. Psychol.,* 1952, 47, 778–782.

Dahlstrom, W. G., & Welsh, G. S. *An MMPI handbook: A guide to use in practice and research.* Minneapolis: Univ. of Minnesota Press, 1962.

Goffman, E. On cooling the mark out: Some aspect of adaptation to failure. *Psychiatry,* 1952, 15, 451–463.
Lewin, K., Dembo, T., Festinger, L., & Sears, P. Level of aspiration. In J. McV. Hunt (Ed.), *Personality and the behavior disorders,* Vol. 1. New York: Ronald Press, 1944. Pp. 333–378.
Rosenfeld, H. M. Social choice conceived as a level of aspiration. *J. Abnorm. Soc. Psychol.,* 1964, **68,** 491–499.
Terman, L. M. *Genetic studies of genius,* Vol. 1. Stanford: Stanford Univ. Press, 1925.
Terman, L. M. *Genetic studies of genius,* Vol. 4. Stanford: Stanford Univ. Press, 1947.
Terman, L. M. *Genetic studies of genius,* Vol. 5. Stanford: Stanford Univ. Press, 1959.

2.3 SIMILARITY, CONTRAST, AND COMPLEMENTARITY IN FRIENDSHIP CHOICE

Norman Miller
Donald T. Campbell
Helen Twedt
Edward J. O'Connell

The possibility of describing the relation between friends' personalities by a single general relationship has been a persistently intriguing one. Indeed, so much so, that the two simplest and most general relations between friends, though contradictory, frequently appear as aphorisms reflecting our accumulated cultural wisdom on interpersonal relations: "birds of a feather flock together" and "opposites attract." These two types of relations can be designated similarity and contrast. Winch (1952), in speaking of complementary relations between the traits of married couples, has presented the most influential hypotheses for marriage research within the last decade (Tharp, 1963). He speaks of within-trait complementarity (A is independent and B is dependent) as well as cross-trait complementarity (A is deferent and B is hostile), and views both as antagonistic or opposite to a similarity relation.

Interestingly, researchers who have searched for a single ubiquitous relation between the personalities of friends, with perhaps the single exception of the work of Winch and his co-workers on data from 25 undergraduate married couples (Winch, 1955a, 1955b; Winch, Ktsanes, & Ktsanes, 1954, 1955), have found either no relation (e.g., Bowerman

Source: This research was supported by the National Institute of Health. Reprinted with slight abridgment from the *Journal of Personality and Social Psychology,* 1966, 3, 3–12, with permission of the authors and the American Psychological Association, Inc.

& Day, 1956; Hoffman, 1958; Izard, 1963; Katz, Glucksberg, & Krauss, 1960; Reilly, Commins, Stefic, 1960) or trends in the direction of similarity (e.g., Banta & Hetherington, 1963; Beier, Rossi, & Garfield, 1961; Corsini, 1956; Day, 1961; Izard, 1960; Kelly, 1955; Murstein, 1961; Newcomb, 1956).

If, as the bulk of previous research suggests, similarity is the most reliable relation between the personalities of friends, the question of how this relation should be interpreted still remains. Selections of friends based on true similarity can be predicted by both balance and reinforcement theories of interpersonal interaction. It is also possible, however, that data indicating similarity do not in fact reflect balance or reinforcement processes at all but rather have arisen through judgment error. To the extent that true similarity on some single general personality trait (such as the extent to which one is well liked) generalizes to other specific traits, ubiquitous similarity would be found. While such similarity is not in itself artifactual, it leads to misinterpretation. Similarity is mistakenly attributed to the relation between the more specific traits of friends and therefore possible specific contrast relations are occluded. This source of error and a possible statistical cure are discussed in detail in the Method section.

The present study, while dealing solely with same-sexed friendships, adds to knowledge on friendship choice by including a number of features which either singly or in combination are absent from previous studies: it employs statistical procedures designed to eliminate the artifacts that commonly plague research requiring multiple judgments on multiple dimensions; the sample of friendship pairs is large; reputational definitions of personality are included as well as the more usual self-description definition; both cross-trait and within-trait relations are examined. To add further to the interpretability of the major analyses, subanalyses are performed to examine the effects of closeness of friendship and nonreciprocation of friendship.

METHOD

Subjects

In connection with another problem (Campbell, Miller, Lubetsky, & O'Connell, 1964) data were collected from 237 females and 225 males from 19 residential groups. The groups primarily included Northwestern University fraternities, sororities, and dormitories, but also included several groups from a Catholic university and a teachers college. All students who had resided at least one year in the living unit were allowed to volunteer. Following the last of three data-collecting sessions, each subject was paid $5.

Instruments and Data Collection

The complete measurement techniques and procedures are described in detail elsewhere (Campbell et al., 1964). While only the measurement of personality and the determination of friendship choices are relevant, to give some idea of the context in which the data for this study were obtained, the entire procedure is briefly presented in chronological sequence. In the first data-collection session subjects used a nine-point scale with described ends and midpoint to rate each of their fellows as well as themselves on 27 personality traits. On completion, subjects indicated for all high ratings whether the person rated was aware that he possessed the trait. In the second session subjects rated photographs of 30 persons of varying age and sex on the same set of personality traits. The third session asked for background, personal history, socioeconomic information, a second self-rating, ratings of family members, an estimate of average rating received from others on each trait, a rating of the desirability of the 27 traits, and an ordered list of one's five closest friends within the residential group. The three data-collection sessions, scheduled approximately one week apart, took about five hours. The research was presented to the subjects as a collection of normative personality data from the college subjects and as a study of the ability to judge personality from photographs. There was no reason to suspect that any subject doubted these facades.

With the exception of one group which made their ratings in their individual rooms, ratings were made in a common room in the presence of an experimenter. The instructions encouraged the subjects to use the entire range of the nine-point scale and to make their ratings in terms of the norms for their own living group. Printed definitions and descriptive comparisons of the traits were provided with each set of materials and read by the experimenter at the start of the first session. Additional clarification was provided whenever necessary. All ratings were made across traits, one person at a time. In some dormitory groups where a subject occasionally insisted that he did not know a particular person and could not rate him, he was permitted to skip that person.

As indicated, the present report is concerned solely with the sociometric choices and their relation to two types of scores on the personality traits, reputation scores, and self-description scores.

Friendship Pairs

The major analysis is based on a pairing that maximizes the number of reciprocal friendship pairs. All pairs consist of persons who chose each other somewhere in their ordered lists of five closest friends within the living group. Where possible, persons whose choices of one another were mutually high on their lists were paired. However, lower ranked choices were matched where necessary in order to maximize the number of pairs. Those persons for whom there was no reciprocal choice and those persons who either omitted the sociometric task, only listed friends outside the living group, or only listed persons who had lived in the residential unit less than one year were eliminated. One hundred pairs of females and 89 pairs of males for whom there were reputation scores were constructed. Of these, the number of pairs for whom there were self-description scores based on two self-descriptions was slightly reduced: 93 females and 87 males.

Direct information on the reliability and validity of the friendship pairings is unavailable. While the instructions to the subjects required them to list their *actual* rather than *preferred* friends, it is possible that portions of some lists represent wishful fantasy. However, the use of reciprocal choice pairs and the large proportion of the total population actually included in the pairs would also seem to attest strongly to the validity of the subjects' lists. If most choices represented wishful fantasy, the most likely outcome would be a listing by each subject of the most popular residents. Such overchoice of the "stars" by all would result in inability to include most subjects in a reciprocal pair.

Personality Definitions

While the simplest approach to the reputational definition of personality would have been the use of the mean rating received by an individual on a given trait, the likelihood of predictable biases in these scores led to the computation of "double-standardized" scores. When an individual is requested to make multiple trait ratings, a typical finding is a first-order factor of "favorability" or "like-dislike." This halo or extremely potent trait of being "well liked" (or "hated") largely determines the rating a person receives on every other trait. Thus, instead of obtaining ratings on 27 different traits, one could easily obtain in large part 27 repetitions of a single rating on the like-dislike dimension. In other words the scores from all 27 traits could be summed and this total would be similar to a 27-item attitude scale designed to measure social approval or liking. This was in fact done and the mean entered as the twenty-eighth score entitled "general unfavorability." The high reliability of this scale total supports the notion that the entire profile of scores on the 27 traits would be unfavorable for a disliked person and favorable for a liked person.

If the persons who choose one another as friends are more similar in the extent to which they are liked or disliked by the members of their residential unit as compared to randomly paired persons, similarity between the reputations of friends on all traits is automatically built into the raw data. No opportunity would exist for finding contrast relations between the personalities of friends. This situation is illustrated in Figure 1*a*. Since it is postulated that each trait contributes equally to the general unfavorability score, a change in liking for an individual would not change the pattern among the traits; it would merely move the entire profile up or down the scale. Illustrative average reputational ratings on five traits for each of the three pairs of friends are presented in Figure 1*a*. It is immediately apparent that Pair C is disliked. They are generally judged as incapable, insincere, conceited, greedy, and unscrupulous. This difference between the general approval of Pair C and other pairs is reflected in the differences between the average rating on all traits for each of the three pairs. Both members of Pair C average 8 whereas both members of Pair A average 2, and both members of Pair B average 5. If the correlations between these three pairs of friends were computed for any of the five traits, the correlation would inevitably be positive. This is true even though for all three pairs, when one member tends to be high on a given trait (relative to the average rating of the pair across traits), the other tends to be low.

For this reason, each person's average reputation on a given trait was converted into a score which represented his general tendency to be high on this trait to a greater extent than on other unfavorable traits. This was achieved by the "first standardization." All of a person's mean reputation values in the unfavorable direction were averaged (after reversing four favorably worded traits) and the trait-reputation means then converted into z scores representing deviations above and below this general tendency to receive unfavorable ratings from others.

The result of such a transformation is illustrated in Figure 1*b*, where the scores from Figure 1*a* have been replotted holding constant the average favorability of each individual's scores. Note that in Figure 1*b*, where the ratings for each trait are expressed as deviations from the individual's average, the pattern suggested is quite different.

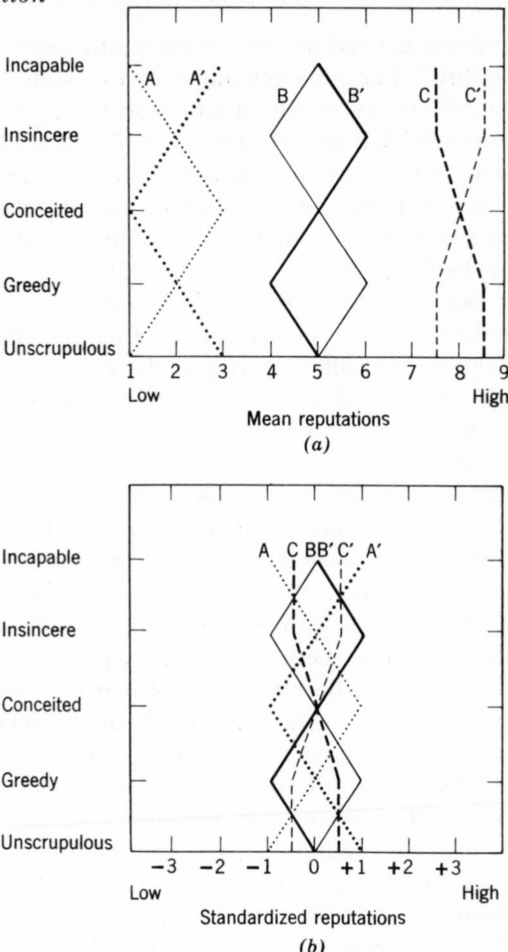

Figure 1. Fictitious reputation scores for three pairs of friends (A,A′; B,B′; and C,C′) which illustrate the exaggeration of friends' similarities (*a*) when reputation is not adjusted for average favorability by standardization (*b*). (See text for explanation.)

Analysis of the standardized scores (Figure 1*b*) stresses the gross differences in the displacements of entire profiles. Stated in another way, similarity between friends on the like-dislike factor will obscure the more subtle correlations which would remain in the residual correlation matrix once this factor had been removed. Of course, in the actual data, this is not the only factor present among the traits. Even after its removal, the traits show substantial intercorrelation. However, factor analysis of the raw reputation scores and the standardized reputation scores supports our arguments. While a like-dislike factor is the first factor extracted from the raw scores, no comparable factor is found among the standardized scores.

Essentially the same rationale eliminates the use of each person's mean self-description on each trait and justifies the "first standardization" for self-description across the 27 traits. In the case of self-description, some potent general factor such as self-esteem, defensiveness, or some other general response bias might largely contribute to the overall level of favorability of the self-ratings. Again, if for some reason friends tend to be similar on any one general factor, similarity between friends' self-descriptions is built into all the specific trait ratings. The possibility of discovering more subtle contrast relations between friends could only be discovered after removal of any more general factor affecting the favorability of self-description.

Previous research and other general considerations led to the expectation that correlations between friends' personalities would be very low even where significant. Since reputations were used as one definition of personality and since residential groups in which people know one another well enough to make trait ratings rarely have more than 35 members, it was clearly necessary to pool data from many groups. The range of groups used made cultural differences likely. Idiosyncratic habits of language usage within the different residential units or different norms for the favorability of different traits could once again lead to artifactual similarity of friends' trait ratings in that friendship pairs were always selected from within rather than across residential units. Such differences in norms for ascription or habits of language use clearly exist for males and females. A trait like "aggressive" would more readily be ascribed to males than to females. The same kinds of differences, however, may occur between fraternity houses. In one, where great emphasis is placed on competitive sports, "aggressive" may be a "good" trait. In another, involved in some intrafraternal or community project, "nonaggression" may be a "good" trait. If so, when pairs from residential units are included in a single correlational analysis, the correlation would emerge positive.

To avoid this irrelevant source of an apparent similarity correlation, the scores of each person on each trait have also been standardized in the more usual fashion around each residential group's own mean. This second standardization was also performed on both the reputation as well as the self-description scores. It is regarded as achieving essentially the same results as if on each trait the correlation between friends was computed separately for each residential unit and then all were averaged.

Thus, for both reputations and self-descriptions, an individual's scores were converted into *z* scores deviating from the 0 point assigned to his average score across traits. After this first standardization across traits and within persons, a second standardization was performed within a trait and across persons within the particular living group. That is, the *z* scores of each person on each trait were restandardized around each residential unit's own mean for that trait. All major analyses were performed on these double-standardized scores. To check on the validity of the preceding arguments, however, some analyses were also performed on the simple raw scores. These further substantiate our arguments and are discussed with the results. Nevertheless, while curing real problems, the double-standardization procedure does not correct for all possible types of judgment errors.

It makes little sense to look for relations between the personalities of friends unless the measures of personality are satisfactory. The reputation reliabilities of the double-standardized scores were computed using the split-half technique, which required that the double-standardization be carried out separately for each half of the data as well as for the pooled data. The ratings by odd-numbered and even-numbered judges were double-standardized separately. For the self-description reliabilities, the two self-descriptions obtained on separate occasions were double-standardized separately.

After Spearman-Brown correction of the reputation reliabilities, they range from .47 to .95 to .40 to .93 for females and males, respectively, with median reliabilities of .79 and .70. The "multitrait-multimethod matrix" considerations suggested by Campbell and Fiske (1959) stress the importance of "discriminant reliability," particularly on those traits with low reliability. That is, is the reliability for a trait higher than the correlations between that trait and all other supposedly distinct traits? While in general they are, there are three traits for men and one for women which do not meet this criterion: prying, unappreciative, and good judge of personality for men and insincere for women. And for all of these except unappreciative, only one of the between-trait correlations exceeds the reliability coefficient in magnitude. The corrected self-description reliabilities range from .46 to .84 and .54 to .85 for females and males, respectively, with median reliabilities of .71 for both. In general they are about as satisfactory as the reputation reliabilities.

The intercorrelation of self-description and reputation scores might be considered validity data, though for our purposes it is difficult to say which should be the criterion for the other. The magnitudes of these correlations are typical of the validity data for personality measures in general when such measures represent independent assessments. In the extensive sampling presented by Campbell and Fiske (1959), correlations of .50 are unusually high and values of .30 typical of "successful" measurement efforts. Among the correlations between the double-standardized self-description and reputation scores, for both males and females, 11 out of the 28, exceed .30. All but 2 of the 22 values of .30 or greater meet the discriminant validity criterion of being higher than any of their heterotrait-heteromethod values (Campbell & Fiske, 1959). Considering reputations and self-descriptions as two different methods, this criterion compares correlations between the same trait using the two methods, to the correlations between scores on one trait and scores on other traits using the other method. Using the standard two-tailed test of significance, which is a less stringent criterion, 20 of the 28 correlations are significant beyond the .01 level for males and 22 are significant for females. These outcomes, though more favorable, are not substantially different from those obtained with the raw means.

RESULTS

Trait Correlation Analyses (r)

Within-Trait Correlations: The first section of Table 1[1] presents the diagonal values of four product-moment correlation matrices based on the double-standardized reputation and self-description scores of both male and female friendship pairs. These correlations represent the major analysis testing the relation between the personalities of friends. Where significantly positive they support a similarity relation. Contrariwise, where negative, they support contrast.

For reputation correlations, 25 of 28 and 24 of 28 are in the similarity direction for females and males, respectively. Ten are significantly positive for the females and 6 for the males. No negative correlations are significant. By a sign test, these results would be highly significant, although one could scarcely claim independence for the correlations. Similarly, there are far too many significant

[1] Interested readers are referred to the original article for Table 1, which is omitted here in the interest of brevity.

correlations to consider them as chance fluctuations around an average correlation of 0. Averaging the separate correlations of females and males on each trait by converting them to z scores, 15 of 28 correlations (all in the similarity direction) exceed the 5 per cent level: anxious, bossy, uncapable, complaining, conceited, critical, masculine-effeminate, gullible, hostile, uninfluential, obsequious, unorderly, sex interest, suspicious, and bad judge of personality.

The self-description correlations are less consistent. For females and males, respectively, 20 of 28 and 16 of 28 are in the similarity direction. However, for each sex only 2 are significantly positive. In addition, insincere is significantly negative for females. Averaging the correlations of females and males, only 4 traits exceed the 5 per cent level: uninfluential, sex interest, unscrupulous, and bad judge of personality.

These results indicate a stable similarity relation between friends' reputations. The evidence for a relation between the self-descriptions of friends is far more tenuous. For self-description scores, the average correlation across traits is .04 and .02 for females and males in comparison to .16 and .11 for reputation scores. The conservative assumption of independence between the 28 traits would lead to the expectation that approximately 1.5 correlations would exceed the 5 per cent level in the positive direction by chance. That four self-description correlations do exceed the 5 per cent level in the similarity direction does not represent a substantial departure from chance. However, to conclude no relation is overly conservative. The 28 traits are not 28 separate dimensions, 2 correlations are significantly positive beyond the 1 per cent level, and the Pearson r gives a conservative estimate of significance.

Cross-trait Correlations: Further support for similarity or contrast relations was evaluated by examining the off-diagonal correlations. Table 2 presents those trait pairs for which the analogous correlations on symmetrical sides of the diagonal were significant beyond the 5 per cent level. This conservative criterion largely eliminates the burden of interpreting sampling error. Note that the trait labels in Table 2 have been reversed in polarity whenever necessary so that all listings are positive associations. Inspection suggests similarity on a dominant-submissive, effective-ineffective, dimension for reputations. For self-descriptions, no cross-trait correlations are consistently significant for females and only the intercorrelation of touchy and scrupulous is consistently significant for males.

Table 2 *Consistently Significant Positive Cross-trait Relations for Friends*

Females	Males
Reputation Scores	Reputation Scores
Capable: influential	Capable: good judge of personality
Capable: good judge of personality	Effeminate: appreciative
Capable: critical	Hostile: unappreciative
Complaining: gullible	Influential: sex interest
Complaining: influential	
Complaining: stubborn	
Critical: influential	
Critical: good judge of personality	
Hostile: capable	
Influential: stubborn	
Influential: good judge of personality	
Stubborn: good judge of personality	
Self-description scores	Self-description scores
None	Touchy: scrupulous

Note: The polarity of trait labels has been changed whenever necessary so that all relations are positive.

The cross-trait relations are judged to be invariably in the similarity direction. In all cases the sign of the association between traits is the same as the sign of the correlation between the same traits within individuals. This is true regardless of whether individuals' reputation scores or self-description scores are used for comparison purposes.

Subanalyses

Profile-Correlation Analyses (Q) *of First-Choice Reciprocal Pairs:* Both the within-trait and the cross-trait analyses presented above show consistent evidence of reputational similarity between friends. The slightly stronger evidence for females may only reflect the higher reliability of their trait scores. Though the evidence for self-descriptions remains much less compelling, it might be argued that the fault lies in the procedure used to construct friendship pairs. Maximizing the number of pairs necessarily included many pairs with weak friendship ties. Personality relations may be more likely between persons who have strong, enduring, interpersonal relationships.

To examine this possibility, double-standardized trait scores from all reciprocal first-choice friendship pairs were further analyzed. Pair members were randomly assigned to one of two groups. A profile (*Q*) correlation was computed separately for each of the 53 female pairs and 44 male pairs, and then averaged across the two sets of pairs. This was done for all combinations of reputation scores, self-description scores, and "A" and "B" members of pairs. For comparison, random same-sexed pairs were also constructed and profile correlations likewise computed and averaged across pairs for all combinations of scores and groups.

The average correlations are presented in Table 3.[2] The consistent positive profile correlation between individuals' reputations and self-descriptions of .23 for females and .31 for males, is similar to the previously discussed average of the validity diagonal correlations between reputation and self-description scores.

As expected, the reputations of randomly paired persons were unrelated. Comparison of the reputations of first-choice reciprocal friends to randomly paired persons gave the expected outcome of greater similarity for friends. This was true for both females ($t = 3.49$, $p < .005$) and males ($t = 2.18$, $p < .05$). In contrast, for both females and males the average self-description correlations of friendship pairs as well as randomly paired persons, hover around 0. These results are essentially in agreement with the previously reported outcome for the larger sample. Reputational similarity is found for friends, and is somewhat stronger among females. Self-descriptions were unrelated.

A similar set of analyses were performed on the raw reputation and self-description scores. The only change in outcome was an increase in the reputation and self-description correlations of friends by about .20. The correlations between random pairs as well as the correlation between reputation and self-description remained essentially unchanged. This outcome argues for the usefulness of the double-standardization procedure. However, it is to be noted that on the trait general unfavorability, derived from the overall favorability of a subject's reputation or self-description, friends' scores were unrelated. This was true for both the entire sample and the subsample of first-choice reciprocals. This suggests that it is the omission of the second standardization which is most responsible for the higher

[2] Table 3 has been omitted in the interest of brevity.

profile correlations obtained with raw scores. This difference may also be due to the lower reliabilities of the double-standardized scores.

Trait-Correlation Analyses (r) *of First-Choice Nonreciprocal Pairs:* The source of reputational similarity in the analysis of the double-standardized first-choice reciprocal pairs remains ambiguous. The outcome for reputations may reflect true similarity which due to contrast judgment error fails to appear in self-descriptions. On the other hand, the self-descriptions may reflect the truth, and similarity found in reputations may reflect similarity judgment error. The choice between these alternatives was evaluated by selecting all pairs among males where a first choice was totally unreciprocated by the chosen person. It is assumed that nonreciprocal pairs possess two important properties that will permit interpretation of the source of friends' reputational similarity. First, it is assumed that the chooser does indeed see personality traits in his choice that attract him. Second, it is assumed that since the target of friendship does not list the chooser among his own five friends, no real friendship exists between them. Thus any relation between traits cannot be attributed to judgment errors in the direction of assuming similarity between people who *are* friends.

Only 23 such pairs could be found among males. Product-moment correlations between the 28 double-standardized reputation scores of chooser and chosen are presented in the last column of Table 1. While the range is larger than that found for the entire sample of friends, none reach significance and the average of .018 is remarkably close to 0. The six traits for which significant reputational similarity was found among the entire sample of reciprocal friends provide no confirmation whatsoever: bossy, −.08; masculine, −.30; hostile, +.06; uninfluential, −.13; obsequious, +.02; sex interest, −.11.

Trait-Correlation Analyses (r) *of First-Choice Reciprocal Pairs:* These negative results for *nonreciprocal* first-choice friendship pairs contrast interestingly with the within-trait correlations for *reciprocal* first-choice pairs. These latter correlations are based on the double-standardized reputation scores from the 44 male pairs and the 53 female pairs for whom mean profile correlations were presented in Table 3. Six correlations are significant beyond the 5 per cent level for males, eight for females. As expected, the average correlations of .14 and .20 for males and females are higher but not too dissimilar from the average values of .11 and .16 obtained from the entire sample.

DISCUSSION

In summary, the findings are as follows:

1. For a large sample of reciprocal friendship pairs, in which many of the friendship ties may have been weak, there is reputational similarity on a variety of traits, most of which fall on a dimension of effectiveness. Cross-trait correlations were also interpreted as indicating reputational similarity.

2. In spite of a few significant correlations, self-descriptions for this same set of friendship pairs were essentially unrelated.

3. Profile correlations for a subsample of closer friends (reciprocal first-choice) confirmed these findings. For both females and males, pairs of close friends had a similar profile of reputations whereas random pairing of the same individuals yielded no relation. The magnitude of reputational correlations for individual traits was greater for close friends. The self-descriptions of these close friends were unrelated. If raw reputation and self-descriptions are used, the correlations are substantially higher.

4. The trait general unfavorability was not one of those found to be significantly similar between friends. Even among first-choice reciprocals the general unfavorability of friends remains unrelated. Had this fact been known prior to the major analyses it could have been used as an argument against the first standardization of the double-standardization procedure. However, the authors lacked such prescience and the a priori logic of such standardization was sound.

Together, these results suggest that friends have similar reputations. The negative findings for nonreciprocal first-choice pairs suggest that "true" similarity in personality does not affect choice of the persons with whom one develops friendships. The obtained reputational similarity could stem from learning during the interaction entailed by friendship. To assume, however, that friends do indeed become similar in personality, raises the question of why similarity fails to appear in self-descriptions. That self-descriptions are inaccurate is not a solution. If friends are acquiring one another's traits through interaction, they should acquire the same defenses and error tendencies as well. This would lead to discrepancy between self-descriptions and reputations for individuals, but nevertheless, similarity between self-descriptions of friends.

Another alternative is to interpret the reputational similarity as judgment error. Although the lack of correlation for general unfavorability argues against overall exaggeration of similarity between friends on the like-dislike dimension, the possibility of some type of judgment error on the part of raters appears to provide the most parsimonious interpretation of the results. Those who are friends have been shown to be indeed similar on numerous other dimensions such as attitudes, socioeconomic class, religion, values, interests, etc. (Burgess & Wallin, 1953; Byrne & Blaylock, 1963; Lindzey & Borgatta, 1954; Richardson, 1939). With so many dimensions on which true similarity exists, generalization of similarity to personality trait dimensions could readily occur. The peers who provided the reputations may have mistakenly rated those who navigate in space and time together and who tend to be similar on a variety of attitudinal, socioeconomic, interest, and skill dimensions, as also similar on a variety of personality dimensions.

A few final points of caution are in order.

1. It should be noted that friends have been found to be similar on objective measures of intellect (Morton, 1960; Richardson, 1939). Some of the traits for which significant similarity was found appear to be loaded on such a factor (e.g., influential, good judge of personality). In fact, one of the four instances of a similarity correlation among self-descriptions was for the trait influential. Thus, some significant relations may indeed reflect true similarity on this dimension.

2. This study deals solely with same-sexed friends. It is quite possible that the intensity and stability of cross-sexed friendships (e.g., married couples) is rarely matched in the same-sexed pairs used in the present study.

3. Reciprocal reinforcement may occur more frequently in relation to other trait dimensions than those sampled here. Thus these results do not preclude the possibility of discovering personality relations on other dimensions.

4. In different friendship pairs reciprocal reinforcement patterns may develop for different pairs of traits. Thus relations between the personalities of friends may remain consistent over time and indeed depend on trait-related reinforcement mechanisms, yet different combinations of traits may be idiosyncratically salient to the maintenance of each friendship.

SUMMARY

Within-sex friendship was assessed by sociometric nomination in college dormitories and personality by both peer reputation and self-description. Among approximately 95 pairs of female friends and 90 pairs of male friends reputations were similar and self-descriptions were essentially unrelated. The significant cross-trait correlations for friends' reputations were also interpreted as indicating reputational similarity. Among a subsample of closer friends, the magnitude of reputation correlations was higher whereas self-descriptions remained unrelated. The reputations of nonreciprocated first-choice pairs were unrelated. The results could be interpreted as indicating that friendship produces similarity without altering self-descriptions. The preferred interpretation is that the reputational similarity represents judgment error on the part of peers. Friends' common navigation through time and space and their true similarity on attitude, interest, value, skill, and socioeconomic dimensions is mistakenly generalized by the raters to the personality trait dimensions used in the present study.

REFERENCES

Banta, T. J., & Hetherington, Mavis. Relations between needs of friends and fiancés. *J. Abnorm. Soc. Psychol.*, 1963, **66,** 401–404.

Beier, E. G., Rossi, A. M., & Garfield, R. L. Similarity plus dissimilarity of personality: Basis for friendship. *Psychol. Rep.*, 1961, **8,** 3–8.

Bowerman, C. E., & Day, Barbara R. A test of the theory of complementary needs as applied to couples during courtship. *Am. Sociol. Rev.*, 1956, **21,** 602–608.

Burgess, E. W., & Wallin, P. *Engagement and marriage.* Philadelphia: Lippincott, 1953.

Byrne, D., & Blaylock, Barbara. Similarity and assumed similarity of attitudes between husbands and wives. *J. Abnorm. Soc. Psychol.*, 1963, **67,** 636–640.

Campbell, D. T., & Fiske, D. E. Convergent and discriminant validation by the multitrait-multimethod matrix. *Psychol. Bull.*, 1959, **56,** 81–105.

Campbell, D. T., Miller, N., Lubetsky, J., & O'Connell, E. J. Varieties of projection in trait attribution. *Psychol. Monogr.*, 1964, **78,** (15, Whole No. 592).

Corsini, R. Understanding and similarity in marriage. *J. Abnorm. Soc. Psychol.*, 1956, **52,** 327–332.

Day, Barbara R. A comparison of personality needs of courtship couples and same-sex friendships. *Sociol. Soc. Res.*, 1961, **45,** 436–440.

Hoffman, R. I. Similarity of personality: A basis for interpersonal attraction? *Sociometry*, 1958, **21,** 300–308.

Izard, C. E. Personality similarity and friendship. *J. Abnorm. Soc. Psychol.*, 1960, **61,** 47–51.

Izard, C. E. Personality similarity and friendship: A follow-up study. *J. Abnorm. Soc. Psychol.*, 1963, **66,** 598–600.

Katz, I., Glucksberg, S., & Krauss, R. Need satisfaction and Edwards PPS scores in married couples. *J. Consul. Psychol.*, 1960, **24,** 205–208.

Kelly, E. L. Consistency of the adult personality. *Am. Psychol.*, 1955, **10,** 659–681.

Lindzey, G., & Borgatta, E. F. Sociometric measurement. In G. Lindzey (Ed.), *Handbook of social psychology*, Vol. 1. *Theory and method.* Cambridge, Mass.: Addison-Wesley, 1954. Pp. 405–448.

Morton, A. Similarity as a determinant of friendship: A multidimensional study. *Dissertation Abstr.*, 1960, **20,** 3857–3858.

Murstein, B. I. The complementary need hypothesis in newlyweds and middle-aged married couples. *J. Abnorm. Soc. Psychol.*, 1961, **63,** 194–197.

Newcomb, T. M. The prediction of interpersonal attraction. *Am. Psychol.*, 1956, **11**, 575–586.

Reilly, Mary St. A., Commins, W. D., & Stefic, E. C. The complementarity of personality needs in friendship choice. *J. Abnorm. Soc. Psychol.*, 1960, **61**, 292–294.

Richardson, H. M. Studies of mental resemblance between husbands and wives and between friends. *Psychol. Bull.*, 1939, **36**, 104–120.

Tharp, R. G. Psychological patterning in marriage. *Psychol. Bull.*, 1963, **60**, 67–117.

Winch, R. F. *The modern family*. New York: Holt, 1952.

Winch, R. F. The theory of complementary needs in mate selection: A test of one kind of complementariness. *Am. Sociol. Rev.*, 1955, **20**, 52–56. (a)

Winch, R. F. Theory of complementary needs in mate selection: Final results on the test of the general hypothesis. *Am. Sociol. Rev.*, 1955, **20**, 552–555. (b)

Winch, R. F., Ktsanes, T., & Ktsanes, Virginia. The theory of complementary needs in mate selection: An analytic and descriptive study. *Am. Sociol. Rev.*, 1954, **19**, 241–249.

Winch., R. F., Ktsanes, T., & Ktsanes, Virginia. Empirical elaboration of the theory of complementary needs in mate-selection. *J. Abnorm. Soc. Psychol.*, 1955, **51**, 508–513.

2.4 INTERPERSONAL ATTRACTION TOWARD NEGROES

Donn Byrne
Carl McGraw

It has been reported in a number of investigations that friendship choices or attraction ratings are influenced by race. White subjects of various ages in various settings are found to be more attracted to other whites than to Negroes when asked to make friendship choices (Berkun & Meeland, 1958; Koch, 1946; Mann, 1958). The importance of the interaction between race and racial prejudice was recently demonstrated by Wong (1961). He reported that highly prejudiced individuals responded more negatively to a Negro stranger than to one identified as white, while subjects low in prejudice did not respond differentially on the basis of race.

As would be predicted from Newcomb's (1953) A-B-X model, prejudiced subjects not only dislike Negroes but they erroneously assume attitudinal differences between themselves and Negro strangers (Byrne

Source: This research was supported in part by grants from the Hogg Foundation for Mental Health. Reprinted with slight abridgment from *Human Relations*, 1964, **17**, 201–213, with permission of the senior author and *Human Relations*.

& Wong, 1962). Thus symmetrical A-B-X relationships are formed in which those who dislike Negroes assume dissimilarity and those who like Negroes assume similarity of attitudes. In a further investigation, Byrne and Wong (1962) created nonsymmetrical conditions by presenting subjects with information indicating that a stranger either was completely similar to or completely dissimilar from themselves in responding to a 26-item attitude scale. It was found that attraction was primarily a function of attitude similarity. That is, subjects responded positively to similar strangers and negatively to dissimilar strangers regardless of the race of the stranger or the degree of prejudice of the subject.

This finding was interpreted in terms of a reward and punishment framework. Agreement about attitudes has been interpreted as reward via consensual validation and disagreement as punishment via consensual invalidation (Byrne, 1961a, 1961b, 1962). As a high-prejudiced subject reads through an attitude questionnaire in which a Negro stranger expresses views similar to his own on 26 assorted items, it is assumed that this experience functions as the administration of 26 rewards. As a consequence, at least for a limited time period and with respect to one particular Negro, high-prejudiced subjects in the Byrne and Wong experiment indicated that they liked the Negro stranger and would enjoy working with him as a partner in an experiment.

Other findings which are related to the reduction of prejudice may be interpreted in a similar fashion. For example, interracial contact may be effective in reducing prejudice because Negro-white interactions involve rewards given directly by Negroes or rewards administered by other individuals as a consequence of interaction (Deutsch & Collins, 1951; Palmore, 1955; Smith, 1943). There is evidence that acceptance of a Negro, even by initially high-prejudiced individuals, is brought about by situations in which rewards are administered. In addition to the effects of attitude similarity, acceptance of Negroes is brought about by such rewarding interactions as judgmental support in an Asch conformity situation (Malof & Lott, 1962) and the indication of beliefs congruent with those of the subject (Rokeach, Smith, & Evans, 1960). The possibility of altering anti-Negro attitudes by means of the deliberate manipulation of patterns of reward and punishment would seem to offer a fruitful avenue of research for theories of attraction and of attitudinal change and for application in terms of reducing interracial hostility.

EXPERIMENT I: RESPONSE TO ATTITUDE SIMILARITY-DISSIMILARITY AS A FUNCTION OF RACE AND RACIAL PREJUDICE

Background

This first investigation was designed to explore in greater detail the unexpected finding that the reward value of attitude similarity and the punishment value of attitude dissimilarity overcome the effects of prejudice on attraction toward Negroes. An initial question concerns the required proportion of rewards in a Negro-white interaction necessary to evoke positive responses from high prejudiced whites toward Negro strangers. It has been shown in two experimental investigations, utilizing different reward-punishment techniques (Byrne, 1962; McDonald, 1962), that as the proportion of rewards and punishments is varied over eight conditions from seven rewards and no punishments to no rewards and seven punishments, attraction toward the source follows a linear function.

Since an increasing proportion of similar attitudes elicits increasingly positive responses toward other whites and since complete attitude similarity elicits positive responses toward Negroes, it is hypothesized that interpersonal attraction toward a stranger varies directly with the ratio of similar to dissimilar attitudes which he holds, regardless of the race of the stranger or the prejudice of the subject.

Method

In brief, the experimental subjects were divided into groups of individuals who were high or low in prejudice toward Negroes. They were asked to respond in terms of interpersonal attraction toward either a white or Negro stranger whose attitudes fell at some point along a continuum from complete similarity to complete dissimilarity compared with those of the subject. Thus the effects of prejudice, race, and a continuum of attitude similarity-dissimilarity on interpersonal attraction were investigated.

Approximately 900 students in the introductory psychology course at the University of Texas were given the Survey of General Public Opinion (Kelly, Ferson, & Holtzman, 1958) which contains a measure of prejudice toward Negroes, the 26-item Desegregation Scale (*D* scale). These items deal with beliefs about Negroes and with attitudes concerning various types of racial interaction. Subjects respond to each item on a five-point scale of agreement-disagreement; high scores indicate unfavorable interracial attitudes. On the basis of these prejudice scores, 320 subjects, all white, were selected to take part in the experiment. The high-prejudiced group consisted of 91 males and 69 females whose *D*-scale scores ranged from 47 to 90 with a mean of 62.93. The low-prejudiced group contained 79 males and 81 females with *D*-scale scores ranging from 5 to 44 with a mean of 30.38.

Another experimenter on a different day administered the Survey of Attitudes (Byrne, 1962) on which subjects are asked to indicate their opinions about seven issues on six-point rating scales. The seven topics (undergraduate marriages, smoking, integration, drinking, money as a goal, grading, and political preferences) are ones on which there is considerable heterogeneity of opinion in this population.

After the subjects had filled out this scale, the attitude protocols were divided into eight groups for both high- and low-prejudiced individuals. For each member of the first group (7–0), the experimenter filled out an attitude scale for a nonexistent stranger whose responses corresponded exactly with those of each subject on all seven items. For each member of the second group (6–1), the "stranger's" responses were like those of the subject on six issues and dissimilar on one. These proportions were varied systematically through the eighth group (0–7) in which the stranger gave dissimilar responses on all seven items. The ratio of male to female subjects was approximately equal across the eight conditions.

Several weeks later, subjects met in small groups for the experimental portion of the study. When the bogus attitude scales were presented, the "name of the stranger" had been removed. However, background information, including race, remained. In addition, a yearbook photograph (supposedly of the student who had responded to the scale) was attached to each protocol; half were of Negroes and half of whites. Strangers and subjects were matched by sex.

Each subject was asked to study carefully the photograph and the responses to the attitude scale. They were then to rate the stranger on the Interpersonal Judgment Scale (Byrne, 1961a; Byrne & Wong, 1962). This instrument consists of six seven-point rating scales dealing with evaluations of the other person's intelligence, knowledge of current events, morality, and adjustment, plus two attraction scales. The latter two scales constitute the measures of the dependent variable. The first ranges from "I feel that I would probably like this person very much" to "I feel that I would probably dislike this person very much," and the second extends from "I believe that I would very much dislike working with this person in an experiment" to "I believe that I would very much enjoy working with this person in an experiment."

Results

Table 1 contains the means and standard deviations of the attraction ratings given in each subgroup. On the attitude variable, adjacent groups were combined to form four levels of similarity-dissimilarity rather than eight. To test the overall effects of the three independent variables on attraction, a $2 \times 2 \times 4$ analysis of variance[1] was computed for each dependent variable. The results are shown in Table 2. In both analyses, prejudice and attitude similarity were statistically significant. The race variable was significant for the "work partner" ratings but not for "personal feelings." For "work partner," the significant prejudice by race interaction indicates that the prejudice and the race variables were significant only because of the low ratings given to Negroes by high-prejudiced subjects; low-prejudiced subjects do not differentiate between races nor do they differ from high-prejudiced subjects in responding to white strangers. Exactly the same pattern is true for the "personal feelings" variable, but the prejudice by race interaction does not reach the .05 level of significance. Nevertheless, if one by-passes strict statistical logic and analyses differences between cell means using the t test, analogous results are found with this variable. That is, high-prejudiced subjects rate white strangers more positively than Negro strangers ($t = 2.38$, $df = 158$, $p < .02$), and low-prejudiced subjects rate Negro strangers more positively than do high-prejudiced subjects ($t = 2.66$, $df = 158$, $p < .01$).

As in a previous investigation in which eight levels of attitude similarity-dissimilarity were utilized (Byrne, 1962), analysis of the data by means of correlations was also employed. Correlations were run between the independent variable (number of similar attitudes) and each of the dependent variables (attraction ratings). Attitude similarity was found to correlate .38 ($p < .01$) with personal feelings and .26 ($p < .01$) with work partner ratings. These relationships were then computed separately for the low- and high-prejudiced

[1] For each of the analyses of variance reported in this paper, Hartley's maximum F-ratio test for heterogeneity of variance (Walker & Lev, 1953) was employed. There were no statistically significant departures from homogeneity.

Table 1 *Means and Standard Deviations of Attraction Scores toward Whites and Negroes of High- and Low-Prejudiced Subjects with Varying Proportions of Similar and Dissimilar Attitudes*

	Attitude Similarity-Dissimilarity															
	7–0, 6–1				5–2, 4–3				3–4, 2–5				1–6, 0–7			
	White		Negro		White		Negro		White		Negro		White		Negro	
	M	*SD*	*M*	*SD*	*M*	*SD*	*M*	*SD*	*M*	*SD*	*M*	*SD*	*M*	*SD*	*M*	*SD*
Personal feelings																
High prejudiced	5.90	1.92	4.90	1.62	5.30	1.73	4.30	1.45	4.70	1.60	4.80	1.60	4.30	1.46	4.20	1.40
Low prejudiced	6.40	2.06	5.75	1.88	5.10	1.73	5.40	1.76	5.00	1.66	4.80	1.61	4.10	1.40	4.30	1.45
Work partner																
High prejudiced	5.60	1.85	4.10	1.42	5.40	1.75	3.40	1.20	4.60	1.53	4.30	1.42	4.40	1.49	4.30	1.44
Low prejudiced	6.30	2.06	5.70	1.86	5.20	1.74	5.50	1.79	5.00	1.66	5.10	1.67	4.10	1.38	4.90	1.63

Table 2 *Analyses of Variance of Attraction Scores toward Whites and Negroes of High- and Low-Prejudiced Subjects with Varying Proportions of Similar and Dissimilar Attitudes*

Source	*df*	*MS*	*F*
Personal feelings			
Prejudice	1	7.20	4.50*
Race	1	6.06	3.79
Attitude	3	32.02	20.01***
Prejudice-race	1	3.18	1.99
Prejudice-attitude	3	2.12	1.32
Race-attitude	3	2.83	1.77
Triple interaction	3	1.77	1.11
Within	304	1.60	
Work partner			
Prejudice	1	40.62	25.23***
Race	1	15.32	9.52**
Attitude	3	14.63	9.09**
Prejudice-race	1	24.18	15.02***
Prejudice-attitude	3	3.95	2.45
Race-attitude	3	8.42	5.23*
Triple interaction	3	3.38	2.10
Within	304	1.61	

* $p < .05$.
** $p < .01$.
*** $p < .001$.

subjects confronted by white and Negro strangers. These coefficients are shown in Table 3. It can be seen that for each dependent variable there is a statistically significant relationship between attitude similarity and attraction toward a stranger in three of the four groups. The one exception to this finding was a crucial one with respect to the study of prejudice. Apparently, in this experiment, high-prejudiced subjects responded to a Negro stranger on the basis of race and made little differentiation among Negroes on the basis of similarity of attitudes. Rather, they tended to indicate dislike or indifference toward Negroes strangers irrespective of their similarity to themselves.

Discussion

In isolation, neither the effects of attitude similarity on attraction nor the prejudice by race interactions are surprising. The former result is by now a familiar one and the latter finding is consistent with logical expectations about the effect of ethnic prejudice on attraction toward a member of the target group. However, the fact that similarity of attitudes did not overcome the effects of prejudice stands in contradiction to the Byrne and Wong (1962) results.

Table 3 *Correlations between Number of Similar Attitudes and Interpersonal Attraction*

	White Stranger	Negro Stranger
Personal feelings		
High prejudiced	.40**	.15
Low prejudiced	.53**	.45**
Work partner		
High prejudiced	.39**	−.08
Low prejudiced	.55**	.28*

* $p < .05$.
** $p < .01$.

Inability to replicate a finding, especially one that was initially unexpected, is a source of concern. The possibility is raised that the Byrne and Wong results simply represented chance findings. The reported high level of statistical significance makes this a relatively unlikely possibility, but an attempt at replication is definitely indicated.

An alternative explanation for the different results lies in a seemingly minor methodological difference in the two investigations. In the original study, the race of the stranger was indicated on the bogus protocol by writing the word "white" or the word "Negro" in the space labeled "race." In this subsequent study, in order to enhance the realism of the stranger, race was additionally indicated by means of a small yearbook photograph. Possibly more cues to interracial hostility are evoked by a photograph of a Negro than by the word "Negro." If so, the question arises as to whether the use of photographs in the Byrne and Wong design would mitigate the effects of attitude similarity on the attraction of high-prejudiced subjects toward a Negro stranger.

In the following investigation, these alternative possibilities are explored.

EXPERIMENT II: CHANCE FINDINGS VERSUS MITIGATION BY PHOTOGRAPHS

Background

In order to clarify the reasons for the discrepant results discussed above, the following experiment was carried out. It was hypothesized that (1) the Byrne and Wong results are replicable in that attraction toward a Negro stranger is positive if he holds 26 similar attitudes and negative if he holds 26 dissimilar attitudes regardless of whether the subject is high or low in racial prejudice; and (2) high-prejudiced subjects are less positive in their ratings of a Negro stranger when a photograph of him is present than when it is not.

Method

As in Experiment I, groups of high- and low-prejudiced subjects were asked to give attraction ratings with respect to a stranger. In this experiment, all of the strangers were identified as Negroes. In order to replicate the Byrne and Wong design and to obtain data about a new condition, three levels of attitude similarity were employed: complete similarity on 26 issues, similarity on 13 issues and dissimilarity on 13, and complete dissimilarity on 26 issues. In addition, a photograph was attached to the attitude protocols of half of the strangers.

Approximately 350 students in the introductory psychology course were given the Kelly et al. (1958) Survey of General Public Opinion in order to obtain *D*-scale scores. From this group, 120 white students were selected to take part in the experiment. The high-prejudiced group consisted of 30 males and 30 females whose *D*-scale scores ranged from 50 to 87 with a mean of 59.83. The low-prejudiced group contained 30 males and 30 females with *D*-scale scores ranging from 5 to 43 with a mean of 28.87.

Another experimenter on a different day administered the 26-item Survey of Attitudes (Byrne & Wong, 1962) which measures opinions about 26 issues on six-point rating scales. Within each prejudice group, the attitude protocols were divided into three groups. For each member of the similar group (26–0), the experimenter filled out a scale for a bogus stranger whose responses were like those of the subject on all 26 issues. For the mixed group (13–13), the stranger's attitudes were like those of the subject on 13 of the items and opposite from

Table 4 *Means and Standard Deviations of Attraction Scores of High- and Low-Prejudiced Subjects toward Negroes with and without Photographs with Similar and Dissimilar Attitudes*

	Attitude Similarity-Dissimilarity											
	26–0				13–13				0–26			
	Photo		No Photo		Photo		No Photo		Photo		No Photo	
	M	*SD*	*M*	*SD*	*M*	*SD*	*M*	*SD*	*M*	*SD*	*M*	*SD*
Personal feelings												
High prejudiced	5.00	1.69	5.10	1.75	4.30	1.47	3.20	1.16	2.80	1.02	2.10	.76
Low prejudiced	5.70	1.91	6.10	2.03	4.90	1.67	4.20	1.45	3.20	1.13	2.70	.93
Work partner												
High prejudiced	5.00	1.70	4.60	1.57	3.30	1.20	2.90	1.04	3.30	1.13	2.40	.88
Low prejudiced	5.70	1.94	5.90	1.98	5.20	1.78	4.20	1.45	4.00	1.42	3.40	1.18

those of the subject on the other 13. Items of agreement and disagreement were randomly chosen and were varied across subjects. In the dissimilar group (0–26), the stranger had dissimilar attitudes on all of the topics.

Again, the name of the "stranger" was removed, but background information (including race) was retained. For all of the strangers, race was indicated as Negro, but half also were represented by a yearbook photograph attached to the attitude scale. The photograph groups were run separately from the no-photograph groups. Strangers and subjects were again matched by sex.

Each subject was asked to study the responses to the attitude scale and (when appropriate) the photograph. They were then asked to rate the strangers on the Interpersonal Judgment Scale which provided the two measures of attraction.

Results

The means and standard deviations of the attraction ratings are given in Table 4. To test the overall effects of these three independent variables on attraction, a 2 × 2 × 3 analysis of variance was computed for each of the attraction ratings. The results are shown in Table 5. In both analyses, all three main effects were statistically significant, while none of the interactions reach the .05 level of significance.

Discussion

With respect to the specific hypotheses, the first prediction was only partially supported. That is, attitude similarity evoked positive ratings and attitude dissimilarity evoked negative ratings toward a Negro stranger from subjects scoring at each extreme of the prejudice scale. However, racial prejudice also influenced the ratings in that those low in prejudice tended to be more positive toward an agreeing Negro and less negative toward one who disagreed with them than did those subjects high in prejudice. As with two previous investigations (Rokeach, Smith, & Evans, 1960; Triandis, 1961), attitudinal similarity and racial membership each influenced attraction responses. Their relative strength undoubtedly depends on specific aspects of the methodology employed.

With respect to the second hypothesis, the results were opposite to those predicted; the presence of a photograph exerted a positive rather than a negative effect on attraction ratings. In many respects, this finding is encouraging if one wishes to generalize beyond the laboratory situation. If there is a realism gradient from the word

Table 5 *Analyses of Variance of Attraction Scores of High- and Low-Prejudiced Subjects toward Negroes with and without Photographs with Similar and Dissimilar Attitudes*

Source	*df*	*MS*	*F*
Personal feelings			
Prejudice	1	15.41	12.74***
Photograph	1	5.22	4.31*
Attitude	2	77.07	63.69***
Prejudice-photograph	1	.65	.54
Prejudice-attitude	2	.36	.30
Photograph-attitude	2	3.55	2.93
Triple interaction	2	.04	.03
Within	108	1.21	
Work partner			
Prejudice	1	39.67	26.45***
Photograph	1	8.01	5.34*
Attitude	2	43.01	28.67***
Prejudice-photograph	1	.07	.05
Prejudice-attitude	2	1.58	1.05
Photograph-attitude	2	1.31	.87
Triple interaction	2	.98	.65
Within	108	1.50	

* $p < .05$.
** $p < .01$.
*** $p < .001$.

"Negro" to a photograph of a Negro to the physical presence of a Negro, the present findings would suggest that positive responses increase toward the realistic end of the gradient. Rather than more realistic cues evoking greater hostility from subjects high in prejudice, the reverse is true. Perhaps negative responses toward members of a minority group function best in the abstract.

Therefore it can be seen that the two reasons suggested for the ineffectiveness of the attitude similarity variable on attraction toward Negro strangers in Experiment I fail to hold up. In the 26–0 versus 0–26 conditions of the Byrne and Wong study and in Experiment II of this paper, positive responses are evoked toward agreeing Negro strangers and negative responses toward disagreeing Negro strangers from both high- and low-prejudiced subjects. Why, then, was there no relationship between attitude similarity and attraction toward Negro strangers from high-prejudiced subjects in Experiment I?

In an effort to gain further understanding of this problem, data from Experiments I and II from comparable conditions (Negro stranger, photograph) were combined along a rough ordinal series from greatest degree of attitude dissimilarity to greatest degree of similarity. As may be seen in Figure 1, the attraction responses of those subjects on the low end of the prejudice continuum indicate the expected relationship between similarity of stranger's attitudes to those of the subject and attraction toward him. For those high in prejudice, only the extremes of the similarity continuum are effective in evoking the expected responses. A completely different sort of relationship holds for these subjects when the proportion of similar and dissimilar attitudes held by the Negro stranger is intermediate between complete agreement or complete disagreement. Not only does the positive linear relationship not hold, but there is even a suggestion that Negroes who are slightly dissimilar are more disliked than those who meet their expectations by being extremely dissimilar. At any event, to evoke positive responses toward Negro strangers from high-prejudiced subjects, utilizing the present methodology, it appears necessary to create a situation in which the Negro administers all rewards and no punishments. And, 26 such rewards out of 26 possibilities appears more effective in evoking such responses than 7 rewards out of 7 possibilities.

CONCLUSIONS

What began as an extension of previous research which indicated that attitude similarity can overcome the negative effects of racial prejudice on attraction has ended as a methodological study of the conditions affecting this relationship. Nevertheless, it appears that the general findings in the Byrne and Wong (1962) report are accurate. That is, a subject high in prejudice will respond positively to a Negro stranger providing that this stranger is completely similar to himself concerning attitudes about a relatively large number of topics. Conversely, a subject low in prejudice will respond negatively to a Negro stranger who expresses a sufficiently large proportion of dissimilar attitudes.

With these findings as a background and guided by a reward-punishment conceptualization to account for the effects of the similarity-dissimilarity variable two avenues of future research suggest themselves. First, an interest in the reduction of racial prejudice suggests research in which effective change agents are explored. For example,

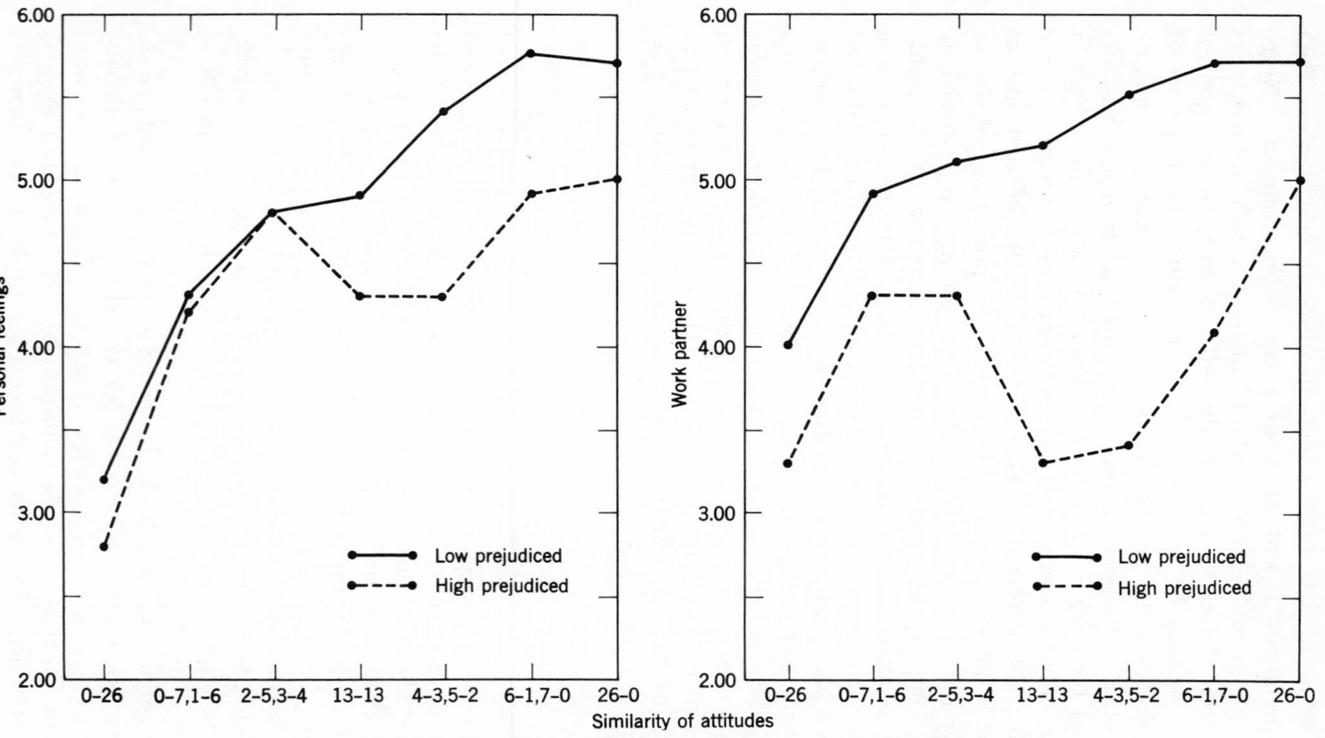

Figure 1. The relationship between varying proportions of attitude similarity-dissimilarity and the attraction ratings toward Negro strangers plotted separately for individuals high and low in prejudice.

variations are possible with respect to type of reward-punishment (e.g., success-failure, praise-censure, pleasure-pain), source of reward (e.g., member of minority group, other members of subject's own reference group, prestige figures), and additional personality factors responsible for change or resistance to change can be investigated (e.g., closed-mindedness, conforming behavior, defense mechanisms). A second line of research would tie the present work more closely to the broader area of interest in attitude change, persuasion, and propaganda. Altering anti-Negro attitudes by manipulating the proportion of positive and negative reinforcements associated with Negroes should generalize to the alteration of other attitudes, beliefs, and opinions. Research of the type suggested should contribute both to general theories of interpersonal attraction and to general theories of attitude change.

SUMMARY

In a previous investigation by Byrne and Wong, it was found that attraction toward a stranger was a function of attitude similarity-dissimilarity regardless of the race of the stranger or the degree of prejudice of the subject. In the first experiment reported in this paper, the effects of similarity on attraction toward Negro and white strangers were explored further. Similarity-dissimilarity was varied along a continuum from complete similarity on seven issues to complete dissimilarity. Contrary to the previous finding, prejudice and race did interact in influencing attraction. Both low- and high-prejudiced subjects responded to white strangers on the basis of similarity of attitudes, and low-prejudiced subjects responded to Negro strangers on the same basis. However, for those high in prejudice, the Negro strangers were rated in a uniform manner no matter what their attitudes. The reason for the difference between this finding and that of Byrne and Wong was sought in a second experiment. It was hypothesized that with the original utilization of 26 similar and 26 dissimilar attitudes, the original results would be replicated. It was also hypothesized that the use of photographs in Experiment I exerted a negative influence on the ratings of Negro strangers by high-prejudiced subjects. It was found that a stranger with 26 similar attitudes evoked positive ratings and one with 26 dissimilar attitudes evoked negative ratings from subjects at each extreme of the prejudiced scale. However, those low in prejudice were more positive toward Negroes than those high in prejudice. Contrary to expectations, ratings of a stranger of either race were more positive when a photograph was present. It was concluded that a subject low in prejudice responds toward a Negro stranger as toward white strangers; attraction ratings vary as a linear function of the proportion of similar to dissimilar attitudes. A subject high in prejudice, on the other hand, will respond positively to a Negro stranger providing that this stranger is completely similar to himself concerning attitudes about a relatively large number of topics; he will respond with indifference or dislike toward a Negro stranger who departs from total similarity.

REFERENCES

Berkun, M., & Meeland, T. Sociometric effects of race and combat performance. *Sociometry*, 1958, **21**, 145–149.

Byrne, D. Interpersonal attraction and attitude similarity. *J. Abnorm. Soc. Psychol.*, 1961, **62**, 713–715. (a)

Byrne, D. Interpersonal attraction as a function of affiliation need and attitude similarity. *Hum. Relat.*, 1961, **3**, 283–289. (b)

Byrne, D. Response to attitude similarity-dissimilarity as a function of affiliation need. *J. Pers.*, 1962, **30**, 164–177.

Byrne, D., & Wong, T. J. Racial prejudice, interpersonal attraction, and assumed dissimilarity of attitudes. *J. Abnorm. Soc. Psychol.*, 1962, **65**, 246–253.

Deutsch, M., & Collins, Mary E. *Interracial housing.* Minneapolis: Univ. of Minnesota Press, 1951.

Kelly, J. G., Ferson, Jean E., & Holtzman, W. H. The measurement of attitudes toward the Negro in the South. *J. Soc. Psychol.*, 1958, **48**, 305–317.

Koch, Helen L. The social distance between certain racial, nationality, and skin-pigmentation groups in selected populations of American school children. *J. Genet. Psychol.*, 1946, **68**, 63–95.

Malof, M., & Lott, A. J. Ethnocentrism and the acceptance of Negro support in a group pressure situation. *J. Abnorm. Soc. Psychol.*, 1962, **65**, 254–258.

Mann, J. H. The influence of racial prejudice on sociometric choices and perceptions. *Sociometry*, 1958, **21**, 150–158.

McDonald, R. D. The effect of reward-punishment and affiliation need on interpersonal attraction. Unpublished doctoral dissertation, Univ. of Texas, 1962.

Newcomb, T. M. An approach to the study of communicative acts. *Psychol. Rev.*, 1953, **60**, 393–404.

Palmore, E. B. The introduction of Negroes into white departments. *Hum. Org.*, 1955, **14**, 27–28.

Rokeach, M., Smith, Patricia W., & Evans, R. I. Two kinds of prejudice or one? In M. Rokeach (Ed.), *The open and closed mind.* New York: Basic Books, 1960. Pp. 132–168.

Smith, F. T. *An experiment in modifying attitudes toward the Negro.* New York: Teachers College, Columbia University, 1943.

Triandis, H. C. A note on Rokeach's theory of prejudice. *J. Abnorm. Soc. Psychol.*, 1961, **62**, 184–186.

Walker, Helen M., & Lev, J. *Statistical inference*. New York: Holt, 1953.

Wong, T. J. The effect of attitude similarity and prejudice on interpersonal evaluation and attraction. Unpublished master's thesis, Univ. of Texas, 1961.

§ 3 *SOCIAL LEARNING*

The need to associate with others leads us to learn strategies and styles of behavior that facilitate association. Social behavior therefore is *learned* behavior, in the sense that it either results from learning or at least has been modified by learning.

The experiment by Dorwart, Ezerman, Lewis, and Rosenhan shows that the performance of a task can be enhanced when young children are first socially deprived and then socially rewarded. The fact that social deprivation can create a "deficit situation," which in turn leads children to exert themselves in order to restore some kind of internal balance, indicates that social drives are an important motivator at this age, when many of the more complex patterns of social behavior are learned.

The experiment conducted by Albert Bandura and Frederick J. McDonald demonstrates that social learning is based on more than mere reinforcement and that models play a vital role in determining the kind of learning that takes place and even the point at which it occurs. Indeed, the kind of model available to a child was found to have a more significant effect on his moral judgment than the amount of reinforcement he received. The study also shows that the orderly course of the development of moral judgment in childhood, as observed and reported by Jean Piaget, can be modified and even reversed by the use of various types of behavioral models and by the manipulation of social reinforcement.

The extent to which a model will be imitated by a child depends on the extent to which the child is attentive. Joan Grusec and Walter Mischel have found that a model's presumed power to reward children in the future is related to the extent to which they will imitate her behavior. The expectations of the learner with respect to future rewards thus have a significant effect on what is learned.

3.1 THE EFFECT OF BRIEF SOCIAL DEPRIVATION ON SOCIAL AND NONSOCIAL REINFORCEMENT

William Dorwart
Robert Ezerman
Michael Lewis
David Rosenhan

It has been commonly observed that young children are more sensitive to direct social reinforcement—a smile or verbal encouragement—than they are to impersonal abstract reinforcers whose effects greatly depend upon self-mediating cognitive processes. Several theoretical treatments which have been concerned with the problem of internalized self-reinforcing patterns of behavior (Hill, 1960; Mowrer, 1960, Ch. 10; Sears, 1957) have incorporated this observation. These theories all point to the initial dependence of young children upon direct social reinforcement and, with increasing age, to their greater reliance on mediating cognitive processes.

Until recently, this progression from dependence upon external social reinforcers to self-reinforcement, which is more contingent upon own responses, lacked empirical test. Recently, however, Lewis, Wall, and Aronfreed (1963) demonstrated experimentally the relative effectiveness of these qualitatively different reinforcing events at different age levels. Specifically, the authors found that for 6-year-old boys, social reinforcement was more effective in probability learning than was nonsocial reinforcement, while among 11-year-olds, no difference obtained between the two reinforcement conditions.

The present study examines this process in greater detail. In the first place, pilot studies by the authors and their colleagues, which followed carefully the experimental protocols employed by Lewis et al. (1963), failed to replicate their findings on either female or male populations. This failure to confirm led to a careful inspection of the relationships established between the experimenter and the subject

Source: These studies were partially supported by funds from the National Institute of Mental Health. Reprinted with slight abridgment from the *Journal of Personality and Social Psychology*, 1965, 2, 111–115, with permission of the authors and the American Psychological Association, Inc.

in the Lewis et al. study and in our experiments. Our attention was drawn to a difference in preexperimental conditions between these studies. Specifically, Lewis et al. established a taciturn preexperimental relationship with the subject; the experimenter was a stranger who, after a brief introduction to the class, led each subject to the experimental room. The experimenter did not attempt to establish a warm relationship with the subject on the way to the experimental room, but rather maintained a preexperimental environment best characterized as *aloof*. In our pilot studies quite the opposite environment existed. Prior to warmly introducing the experimenter to the class, the teacher informed the subjects reassuringly that they would be playing a game, that it would be fun, and that no one would do poorly or be marked according to his performance. The experimenter maintained the *reassuring* quality of the preexperimental environment by chatting with the subject on the way to the experimental room, addressing the subject by name, and inquiring into his interests.

These differences in preexperimental environment are strongly reminiscent of the studies by Gewirtz and Baer (1958a, 1958b) in which subjects who were relatively deprived of the presence of an adult were subsequently more responsive to reinforcers administered by that adult than were subjects who had been previously satiated with such reinforcers. True, the period of deprivation employed by Gewirtz and Baer was considerably longer (20 minutes) than it was in these studies, where approximately 2–3 minutes elapsed between the introduction of the subject to the experimenter and the time the actual experiment began. But the conditions were analogous enough to suggest that even brief interaction with a taciturn adult might have effects similar to the lengthier social deprivation. The analogy between social deprivation and social aloofness was buttressed by Gewirtz, Baer, and Roth (1958) who noted the similar effects of low social availability of an adult (defined as an adult present but paying no attention to the child's behavior) and the 20-minute social deprivation period.

In view of the above, the following hypothesis was suggested: the relative effectiveness of social over nonsocial reinforcement found by Lewis et al. (1963) is contingent upon the exposure of these children to a period of social deprivation, since social deprivation is antecedent to the need for social reinforcement. Under conditions of social satiation, however, no differences in the effectiveness of the reinforcer will be apparent. The hypothesis was tested with a male population in order to provide a replication of the Lewis et al. experiment.

In addition, the experiment served to answer the following question: Does a subject who has been socially deprived respond subsequently only to social reinforcers, or will a nonsocial reinforcer have the same effect?

METHOD

Subjects

Forty-nine boys from two middle-class elementary public schools participated in this experiment. Subjects from three first-grade classes in one school experienced a period of social satiation and were then rewarded either with social reinforcement (10 subjects) or nonsocial reinforcement (12 subjects). In the second school, subjects from four first-grade classes experienced a period of social deprivation and were subsequently rewarded with social reinforcement (17 subjects) or nonsocial reinforcement (10 subjects). Six subjects alternated responses for more than 75 trials. Their data were excluded because it had been previously determined that such alternation reflected subjects' failure to understand the experimental task. Data for an additional subject who failed to complete all of the training trials were also excluded.

Apparatus

The apparatus, identical to that used by Lewis et al. (1963), consisted of a mechanism with which each subject "played," and a monitoring device on which the experimenter could follow the course of the game. The mechanism was a black box (7 × 12 × 7 inches) with two toggle-type, automatic-return switches along the lower edge of the front panel. A large red light, which could be operated from the monitor, was centered on the front panel. The monitor also activated a signal buzzer inside the subject's machine.

Procedure

Social Deprivation: Subjects were given no information about the experiment from their teacher. Rather, the teacher simply asked the subject to "go with this man" when the experimenter appeared in the classroom. During the walk to the experimental room, which took about 3 minutes, the experimenter engaged in minimal conversation with the subject.

Social Satiation: The teacher told the subjects that they would be playing a "fun" game in which no one could do poorly. She warmly introduced the experimenter to the class. On the way to the experimental room, the experimenter maintained this reassuring atmosphere by chatting with the subject in a quite friendly fashion, addressing the subject by name and inquiring into his interests.

Once in the experimental room, the procedure was identical to that employed in the Lewis et al. (1963) study. The subject was told that he would be playing a game in which he was to press one of the two levers each time the buzzer sounded. The instructions implied that the object of the game was to try to produce the reinforcing event, but not that there would always be a correct lever on every trial. Reinforcement, therefore, was contingent upon the subject's response.

Prior to the training trials, the subject was presented with four sample trials for which he was instructed to press the left lever for the first two trials and the right lever for the last two trials. Reinforcement was administered on the first and last trials. The subject then began the series of 150 training trials. Events were randomized within each block of 10 trials, with the probabilities of the left and right levers being correct in the ratio of 70:30, respectively. During the training period, a second experimenter, hidden entirely from the subject, monitored and recorded the subject's responses. Subjects were rewarded with one of the two reinforcers:

1. Social reinforcement—The experimenter, seated behind the subject during the entire series of trials, said either "Good" or "Fine" whenever the subject's response was correct. The light was not used.

2. Nonsocial reinforcement—After the four sample trials, the experimenter told the subject that for the remainder of the game the subject was to respond when he heard the buzzer and the red light would indicate to the subject whether his response was correct. The experimenter then left the room, explaining that he had some other work to do and that he would return shortly.

RESULTS

Figure 1 presents the mean proportion of responses to the more frequently reinforced side ($S_{.70}$) in blocks of 10 trials for all subjects. Inspection reveals a marked tendency by those subjects who experienced social deprivation to maximize the more frequently reinforced response. Among the remaining groups, no differential performance is evident. The Kruskal-Wallis test (Siegel, 1956), applied to the subject's mean proportions of correct responses across all 150 trials, indicates that these four groups are not drawn from the same population ($p < .01$). The Mann-Whitney U test was applied (Siegel, 1956)

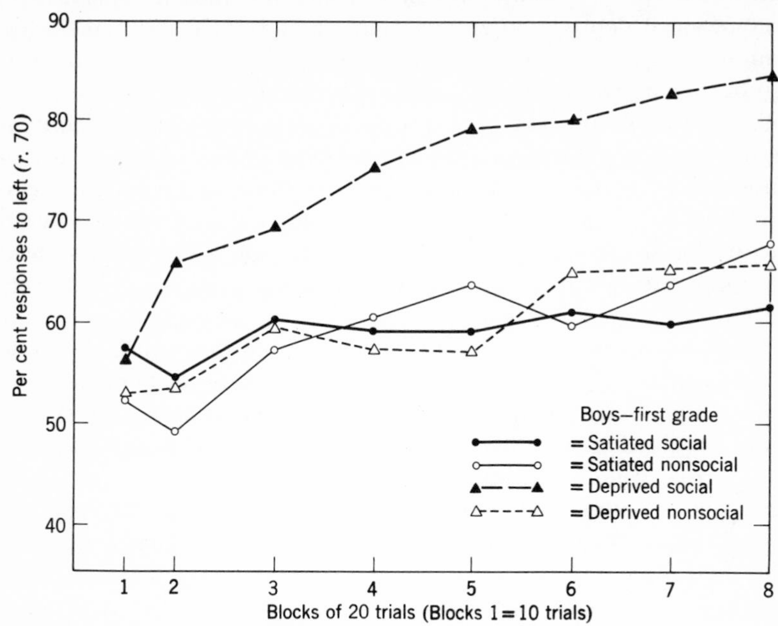

Figure 1. Mean proportion of response to the more frequently reinforced side.

to the asymptotic proportions of $S_{.70}$ responses over the last three blocks of 10 trials. These findings, presented in Table 1,[1] confirm the need for social reinforcement on the part of those subjects who had been socially deprived prior to the learning task.

DISCUSSION

It is clear that the superior asymptotic performance found by Lewis et al. (1963) among young boys who had been socially reinforced was not due merely to the effectiveness of social reinforcement. Rather, it resulted from the combined effects of social deprivation followed by social reinforcement. And, while the data presented here do not permit extrapolation to older children, it would seem more reason-

[1] Interested readers are referred to the original article for Table 1, which is omitted here in the interest of brevity.

able to interpret their findings in terms of differential capacities to tolerate social deprivation among younger and older children, rather than in terms of the relative effectiveness of social and non-social reinforcement per se. Thus it might be argued that for older children the need for social reinforcement is not so intense, perhaps because they have been satiated on that kind of reinforcement or because other reinforcements have become dominant in their reinforcement hierarchy. Older children would, then, be more able to tolerate social deprivation than younger children, for whom the need for, and consequently the potency of, social reinforcement is relatively greater.

These hypotheses are, of course, tentative formulations amenable to, and currently receiving, experimental verification. They are not, however, necessarily contradicted by the strong positive correlation found by Gewirtz and Baer (1958b) between deprivation and age, since in that study the authors used very young (nursery school) subjects. Conceivably, very young children show a marked responsiveness to social deprivation which tapers off and then actually decreases with increasing age.

Gewirtz and Baer (1958a), in discussing the implications of their study for a theory of social drives, suggest that the existence of such a theory would gain support if it could be shown that following social deprivation, subjects are more responsive to specifically social reinforcement than to other kinds of reinforcement. This experiment, along with Erickson's (1962), would appear to offer that support, in that a light, in this case, and marbles, in Erickson's—both nonsocial reinforcers—appear to have no differential effect following deprivation or satiation, while social reinforcement following deprivation do have their effects.

Indeed, these data and Erickson's (1962) invite some discussion regarding the controversy over whether the condition brought about by social deprivation is best seen as creating a social drive (Gewirtz & Baer, 1958a, 1958b) or anxiety. Walters and his co-workers (Walters & Karal, 1060; Walters & Quinn, 1960; Walters & Ray, 1960) have taken sharp issue with the concept of social *drive* (as opposed to the operationally defined social *deprivation*) on both theoretical and experimental grounds. As a matter of theoretical logic, they object to the evidential basis of any state whose existence is imputed solely from the behavior it is called upon to explain. Experimentally, they demonstrate that it may be to the anxiety component of social deprivation that the subsequent reinforcement is addressed, and they, therefore, prefer to interpret the findings in this area in terms of anxiety arousal and reduction.

The findings of this study and of Erickson's (1962) offer no support to the anxiety position, but implicitly support the interpretation of Gewirtz and Baer (1958a, 1958b). For if, indeed, it is anxiety that is at the root of the phenomenon elicited by social deprivation, then it must be an anxiety of a very special sort, one which is reduced not by all reinforcers but by a limited class of reinforcers of which, thus far, only the social reinforcer is known. And, while it may be argued that nonsocial reinforcement—lights or marbles—is not as powerful a reward as social reinforcement, it is certainly more powerful than no reward at all. The fact that these nonsocial reinforcements had no effect may indicate that the anxiety which arises from social deprivation requires a specific class (or kind) of reducer, to which nonsocial reinforcement does not belong, and to which, perhaps, only social reinforcers do belong. Further defining that class, that is, specifying which reinforcers affect social deprivation, is an interesting matter for future investigation.

The findings reported here are evidence for the operation of the social deprivation variable in a new experimental context—probability learning—and under conditions of considerably briefer deprivation than was previously employed. With regard to the latter, an issue of some methodological importance emerges, which is that apparently small and trivial differences in experimental procedure can yield large differences in experimental outcomes. The findings presented here, which indicate that preexperimental aloofness on the part of the experimenter produces effects similar to those of social deprivation, suggests that greater attention needs to be given to the preexperimental environment in which studies with human subjects take place. Certainly some comment regarding that environment might well be incorporated in the Method sections of research reports.

SUMMARY

Forty-nine first-grade boys were variously exposed to social deprivation or social satiation, and were subsequently either socially reinforced or nonsocially reinforced. In a probability learning paradigm, only those *S*s who had been socially deprived and then socially reinforced matched input or maximized. Results are interpreted in terms of social-drive theory. Implications for the development of self-mediated reinforcement are discussed.

REFERENCES

Erickson, Marilyn T. Effects of social deprivation and satiation on verbal conditioning in children. *J. Comp. Physiol. Psychol.*, 1962, **55**, 953–957.

Gewirtz, J. L., & Baer, D. M. Deprivation and satiation of social reinforcers as drive conditions. *J. Abnorm. Soc. Psychol.*, 1958, **57**, 165–172. (a)

Gewirtz, J. L., & Baer, D. M. The effect of brief social deprivation on behaviors for a social reinforcer. *J. Abnorm. Soc. Psychol.*, 1958, **56**, 49–56. (b)

Gewirtz, J. L., Baer, D. M., & Roth, Chaya H. A note on the similar effects of low social availability of an adult and brief social deprivation on young children's behavior. *Child Develop.*, 1958, **29**, 149–152.

Hill, W. F. Learning theory and the acquisition of values. *Psychol. Rev.*, 1960, **67**, 313–331.

Lewis, M., Wall, A. M., & Aronfreed, J. Developmental change in the relative values of social and nonsocial reinforcement. *J. Exptl. Psychol.*, 1963, **66**, 133–137.

Mowrer, O. H. *Learning theory and the symbolic processes.* New York: Wiley, 1960.

Sears, R. R. Identification as a form of behavioral development. In D. B. Harms (Ed.), *The concept of development.* Minneapolis: Univ. of Minnesota Press, 1957. Pp. 149–161.

Siegel, S. *Nonparametric statistics for the behavioral sciences.* New York: McGraw-Hill, 1956.

Walters, R. H., & Karal, Pearl. Social deprivation and verbal behavior. *J. Pers.*, 1960, **28**, 89–107.

Walters, R. H., & Quinn, M. J. The effects of social and sensory deprivation on autokinetic judgments. *J. Pers.*, 1960, **28**, 210–219.

Walters, R. H., & Ray, E. Anxiety, isolation and reinforcer effectiveness. *J. Pers.*, 1960, **28**, 358–367.

3.2 INFLUENCE OF SOCIAL REINFORCEMENT AND THE BEHAVIOR OF MODELS IN SHAPING CHILDREN'S MORAL JUDGMENTS

Albert Bandura
Frederick J. McDonald

Most of the literature and theorizing in the area of developmental psychology has been guided by various forms of stage theories (Erikson, 1950; Freud, 1949; Gesell & Ilg, 1943; Piaget, 1948, 1954; Sullivan, 1953). Although there appears to be relatively little agreement

Source: This investigation was supported in part by a research grant from the National Institutes of Health. Reprinted with slight abridgment from the *Journal of Abnormal and Social Psychology*, 1963, **67**, 274–281, with permission of the authors and the American Psychological Association, Inc.

among these theories concerning the number and the content of stages considered to be necessary to account for the course of personality development, they all share in common the assumption that social behavior can be categorized in terms of a predetermined sequence of stages with varying degrees of continuity or discontinuity between successive developmental periods. Typically, the emergence of these presumably age-specific modes of behavior is attributed to ontogenetic factors rather than to specific social stimulus events which are likely to be favored in a social learning theory of the developmental process.

The stage and social learning approaches differ not only in the relative emphasis placed upon time schedules or reinforcement schedules in explaining the occurrence of changes in social behavior, but also in the assumptions made concerning the regularity and invariance of response sequences, and the nature of response variability. Stage theories, for example, generally stress intraindividual variability over time, and minimize interindividual variability in behavior due to sex, intellectual, socioeconomic, ethnic, and cultural differences. To the extent that children representing such diverse backgrounds experience differential contingencies and schedules of reinforcement, as well as exposure to social models who differ widely in the behavior they exhibit, considerable interindividual behavioral variability would be expected. Similarly, the sequence of developmental changes is considered in social learning theory to be primarily a function of changes in reinforcement contingencies and other learning variables rather than an unfolding of genetically programmed response predispositions.

Despite the considerable attention devoted to theoretical analyses of the learning process, a comprehensive theory of *social learning* has been relatively slow in developing. By and large, current principles of learning have been based upon investigations involving simple fractional responses which are neither social nor developmental in nature, and often with animals as subjects. Although recent years have witnessed a widespread application of learning principles to developmental psychology, the experimentation has been primarily confined to operant or instrumental conditioning of responses that are modeled on the fractional responses elicited in experimentation with infrahuman organisms (for example, manipulating plungers, pressing bars, levers, buttons, etc.). Moreover, a good deal of this research has been designed to reduce complex social learning to available simple learning principles, rather than to extend the range of principles and procedures in order to account more adequately for complex social phenomena.

Social Learning

It is generally assumed that social responses are acquired through the method of successive approximations by means of differential reinforcement (Skinner, 1953). The effectiveness of reinforcement procedures in shaping and maintaining behavior in both animals and humans is well documented by research. It is doubtful, however, if many social responses would ever be acquired if social training proceeded solely by this method. This is particularly true of behavior for which there is no reliable eliciting stimulus apart from the cues provided by others as they performed the behavior. If a child had no occasion to hear speech, for example, or in the case of a deaf-blind person (Keller, 1927), no opportunity to match laryngeal muscular responses of a verbalizing model, it would probably be exceedingly difficult or impossible to teach a person appropriate linguistic responses.

Even in cases where some stimulus is known to be capable of eliciting an approximation to the desired behavior, the process of learning can be considerably shortened by the provision of social models (Bandura & Huston, 1961; Bandura, Ross & Ross, 1961, 1963). Thus, in both instances, limitation of modeling behavior is an essential aspect of social learning.

In the experiment reported in this paper a social learning theory combining the principles of instrumental conditioning and imitation was applied to a developmental problem that has been approached from a stage point of view.

According to Piaget (1948), one can distinguish two clear-cut stages of moral judgment demarcated from each other at approximately seven years of age. In the first stage, defined as *objective responsibility,* children judge the gravity of a deviant act in terms of the amount of material damages, and disregard the intentionality of the action. By contrast, during the second or *subjective responsibility* stage, children judge conduct in terms of its intent rather than its material consequences. While these stages are predetermined (for example, Piaget reports that young children are relatively incapable of adopting a subjective orientation and he was unable to find a single case of objective morality in older children), the factors responsible for the transition from one stage to the other are not entirely clear. Presumably, the principal antecedent of objective judgmental behavior is the "natural spontaneous and unconscious egocentrism" of child thought reinforced to some extent by adult authoritarianism, which produces submissiveness and preoccupation with external consequences. As the child matures, however, he gains increasing autonomy, his relationships become based upon mutual reciprocity and cooperation giving rise to the emergence of subjective morality.

The purpose of the present investigation was to demonstrate that moral judgment responses are less age-specific than implied by Piaget, and that children's moral orientations can be altered and even reversed by the manipulation of response-reinforcement contingencies and by the provision of appropriate social models.

In this experiment children who exhibited predominantly objective and subjective moral orientations were assigned at random to one of three experimental conditions. One group of children observed adult models who expressed moral judgments counter to the group's orientation and the children were positively reinforced for adopting the models' evaluative responses. A second group observed the models but the children received no reinforcement for matching the models' behavior. The third group had no exposure to the models but each child was reinforced whenever he expressed moral judgments that ran counter to his dominant evaluative tendencies. Thus the experimental design permitted a test of the relative efficacy of social reinforcement, the behavior of models, and these two factors combined in shaping children's moral judgments.

It was predicted, for reasons given in the preceding sections, that the combined use of models and social reinforcement would be the most powerful condition for altering the children's behavior and that the provision of models alone would be of intermediate effectiveness. Since the presence of a strong dominant response limits the opportunity for reinforcement of an alternative response which is clearly subordinate, it was expected that social reinforcement alone would be the least effective of the three treatment methods.

METHOD

Subjects

A total of 78 boys and 87 girls ranging in age from 5 to 11 years served as subjects in various phases of the study. They were drawn from two sources, a Jewish religious school and an elementary public school serving predominantly middle-class communities. The research was conducted on weekends in the religious school and on weekdays in the public school facility. Female students from Stanford University served in the roles of experimenters and models.

Stimulus Items

Following the procedure employed by Piaget (1948), the children were presented with pairs of stories each of which described a well-intentioned act which resulted in considerable material damage, contrasted with a selfishly or maliciously motivated act producing minor consequences. The children were asked to judge, "Who did the naughtier thing?" and to provide a reason for their choice. An illustrative stimulus item, taken from Piaget, is given below:

1. John was in his room when his mother called him to dinner. John goes down, and opens the door to the dining room. But behind the door was a chair, and on the chair was a tray with fifteen cups on it. John did not know the cups were behind the door. He opens the door, the door hits the tray, bang go the fifteen cups, and they all get broken.
2. One day when Henry's mother was out, Henry tried to get some cookies out of the cupboard. He climbed up on a chair, but the cookie jar was still too high, and he couldn't reach it. But while he was trying to get the cookie jar, he knocked over a cup. The cup fell down and broke.

Six of the story items employed in the present experiment were identical with those developed by Piaget except for minor modifications in wording or content to make the story situations more appropriate for American children. In addition, a set of 36 new paired items was devised to provide a sufficient number of stories so as to obtain a fairly reliable estimate of children's moral judgments at three different phases of the experiment, i.e., base operant test, experimental treatment, and posttest. In each of these story situations which were modeled after Piaget's items, intentionality was contrasted with serious consequences. These items were carefully pretested on a sample of 30 children in order to clarify any ambiguities, to gauge the children's interpretations of the seriousness of the depicted consequences, and to remove any irrelevant cues which might lead the children to judge the depicted actions in terms other than intentions or consequences.

Except for the assignment of the six Piaget items to both the operant test and the posttest set, for reasons which will be explained later, the remaining stories were distributed randomly into three different groups.

Design and Procedure

A summary of the overall experimental design is presented in Table 1.

Table 1 Summary of the Experimental Design

Experimental Groups	Step 1: Assessment of Operant Level of Objective and Subjective Moral Responses	Step 2: Experimental Treatments	Step 3: Posttreatment Measurement of Subjective and Objective Moral Responses with Models and Reinforcement Absent
Subjective moral orientation			
I ($N = 16$)	Step 1	Model emits objective responses and positively reinforced; child reinforced for objective responses.	Step 3
II ($N = 16$)	Step 1	Model emits objective responses and positively reinforced; child not reinforced for objective responses.	Step 3
III ($N = 16$)	Step 1	No model present; child reinforced for objective responses.	Step 3
Objective moral orientation			
IV ($N = 12$)	Step 1	Model emits subjective responses and positively reinforced; child reinforced for subjective responses.	Step 3
V ($N = 12$)	Step 1	Model emits subjective responses and positively reinforced; child not reinforced for subjective responses.	Step 3
VI ($N = 12$)	Step 1	No model present; child reinforced for subjective responses.	Step 3

Operant Level of Objective and Subjective Responses: In the first phase of the experiment, the children were individually administered 12 pairs of stories to furnish measures of the operant levels of objective and subjective moral judgments at the various age levels. These data provided both a check on Piaget's normative findings and the basis for forming the experimental treatment groups.

Experimental Treatment: On the basis of operant test performances, 48 children who were decidedly subjective in their moral orientation (mean percentage of subjective responses = 80), and 36 who gave high base rates of objective responses (mean percentage of objective responses = 83) were selected from the total sample to participate in the second and third phases of the experiment. The children in each of the two classes of moral orientation were equally divided between boys and girls. They were also further categorized into younger and older children and then assigned at random to one of three experimental treatment conditions. Thus the experimental groups were balanced with respect to age and sex of child.

In the *model and child reinforced condition,* both the model and the child were administered alternately 12 different sets of story items with the model receiving the first story, the child the second one, and so on. To each of the 12 items, the model consistently expressed judgmental responses in opposition to the child's moral orientation (for example, objective responses with subjective children, and vice versa), and the experimenter reinforced the model's behavior with verbal approval responses such as "Very good," "That's fine," and "That's good." The child was similarly reinforced whenever he adapted the model's class of moral judgments in response to his own set of items. To control for any intermodel variability in length or content of evaluative responses, the subjective and objective answers for the model's test items were prepared in advance.

The procedure for children in the *model reinforced, child not reinforced condition,* was identical with the treatment described above with the exception that the children received no reinforcement for matching the moral judgment responses of their respective models.

In the *model absent, child reinforced condition,* no model was present; the experimenter simply administered the 24 story items to the child and reinforced him with verbal approval whenever he produced an evaluative response that ran counter to his dominant orientation.

The time elapsing between the operant testing and the experimental phase of the study ranged from 1 to 3 weeks with the majority of the children receiving the experimental treatment after a 2-week period.

A total of nine experimenter-model pairs participated in the treatment phase of the experiment. To control for possible differences in experimenter or model influences across conditions or sex groups, each pair was assigned groups of subjects in triplets, i.e., boys and girls taken from each of the three treatment conditions.

Students who served as the experimenters' assistants brought the children individually from their classrooms to the experimental session and introduced them to their experimenters. The experimenter explained that she would like to have the child judge a second set of stories similar to the ones he had completed on a previous occasion. In the conditions involving the presence of models, the experimenter further explained that she was collecting normative data on a large sample of people, including both children and adults, and to expedite matters she invited the adult subjects to appear at the school so that the items could be administered to both groups simultaneously. To add to the credibility of the situation, the experimenter read to the model the same instructions the child had received in the operant test session, as though the model was a naive subject. The experimenter then read the story situations to the model and the child who were seated facing the experimenter, delivered the social reinforcement whenever appropriate, and recorded the responses.

It was found in the preliminary pretesting of the stories that they were sufficiently structured with respect to the intentionality-consequences dichotomy so that children's identification of the naughtier story character was virtually a perfect predictor that the children would provide the corresponding subjective or objective reasons for their choices. Since there is some evidence that reinforcement given immediately is considerably more effective than when delayed (Mahrer, 1956), the reinforcement value of the experimenter's approval would have been considerably reduced if administered following the children's explanations, not only because of the delay involved but also because many responses, some relevant others irrelevant, occur during the intervening period, thus making it difficult to specify the behavior being reinforced. For this reason, the experimenters reinforced the children immediately following correct choice responses, and again after they gave the appropriate explanations.

The measure of learning was the percentage of objective judgmental response produced by the subjective children and the percentage of subjective responses performed by the objectively oriented subjects.

Posttest: Following the completion of the treatment procedure, the child reported to another room in the building. Here a second experimenter presented the child with 12 additional stories to obtain further information about the generality and stability of changes in

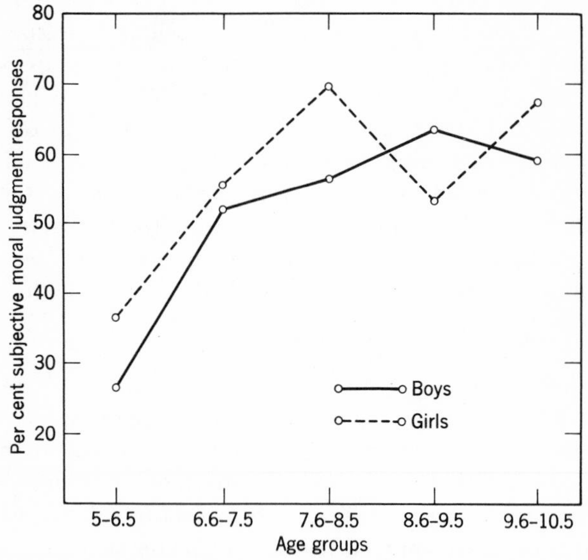

Figure 1. Mean percentage of subjective moral judgment responses produced by boys and girls at different age levels.

judgmental responses when models and social reinforcement were absent. The experimenter simply read the stories to the child and recorded his verbal responses without comment.

In view of Piaget's contention that moral judgments are age-specific and considerably resistant to out-of-phase changes, it was decided to repeat, in the posttest, the Piaget items included in the set of operant test stories. If the interpolated social influence experience succeeded in altering children's evaluative responses, such findings would throw considerable doubt on the validity of a developmental stage theory of morality.

Different sets of experimenters conducted each of the three phases of the study, with a total of 10 experimenters participating in the posttesting. The utilization of different rooms and different sets of experimenters provided a more stringent test of generalization effects than if the same experimenters had been used throughout the investigation.

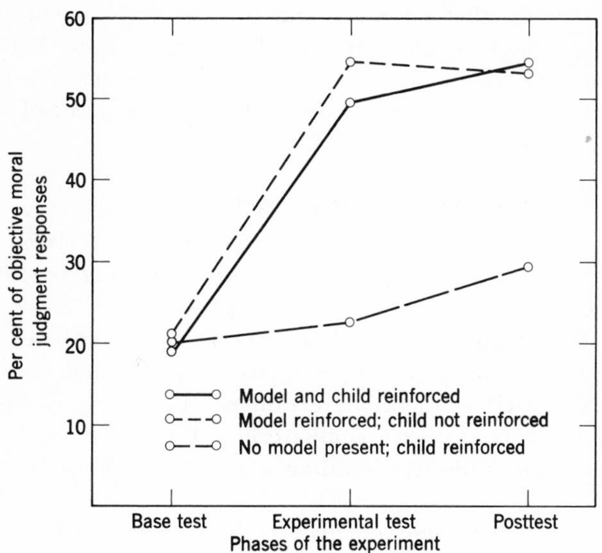

Figure 2. Mean percentage of objective moral judgment responses produced by subjective children on each of the three test periods for each of three experimental conditions.

The experiment was concluded with a brief interview designed to assess the child's awareness of the behavior exhibited by the model, the social reinforcers administered by the experimenter, and the response-reinforcement contingency in the experimental situation.

RESULTS

Since the data disclosed no significant differences in operant levels or in responsivity to the social influence procedures for children drawn from the two different school settings, the data were combined in the statistical analyses.

Judgmental Responses as a Function of Age

The mean percentage of subjective moral judgment responses for boys and girls at one-year intervals are presented in Figure 1. The normative data based on the present sample of children show that subjectivity is positively associated with age ($F = 4.84$, $p < .01$), but unrelated to sex differences at any age level. It is evident from these findings, however, that objective and subjective judgments exist together rather than as successive developmental stages. Most young children were capable of exercising subjective judgments, and a large majority of the older children exhibited varying degrees of objective morality.

Influence of Reinforcement and Modeling Cues

Figure 2 presents the curves for the acquisition and the generalization of objective moral judgment responses by subjective children in each of the three experimental conditions.

Results of the analysis of variance performed on these data are summarized in Table 2. The main effects of experimental conditions and phases, as well as their interaction effects, are highly significant sources of variance. Further comparisons of pairs of means by the *t* test reveal that subjective children who were exposed to objective

Table 2 *Analysis of Variance of Objective Moral Judgment Responses Produced by Subjective Children*

Source	*df*	*MS*	*F*
Conditions (C)	2	5,226.2	3.24*
Sex (S)	1	1,344.4	<1
C × S	2	3,671.4	2.28
Error (b)	42	1,612.1	
Phases (P)	2	9,505.8	35.46**
P × C	4	1,430.3	5.34**
P × S	2	203.8	<1
P × C × S	4	747.6	2.79*
Error (w)	84	268.1	

* $p < .05$.
** $p < .001$.

models, and those who were positively reinforced for matching their models moral judgments, not only modified their moral orientations toward objectivity, but also remained objectively oriented in their postexperimental judgmental behavior (Table 3).

The provision of models alone, however, was as effective in altering the children's moral judgments as was the experimental condition combining modeling cues with social reinforcement. As predicted, the experimental conditions utilizing modeling procedures proved to be considerably more powerful than was operant conditioning alone, which produced a slight increase in objective judgmental responses but not of statistically significant magnitude (Table 3).

Some additional evidence for the efficacy of the behavior of models in accelerating the acquisition process is provided in the finding that only 9 per cent of the children who were exposed to the objective models failed to produce a single objective response; in contrast, 38 per cent of the subjects in the operant conditioning group did not emit a single objective response despite obtaining twice as many acquisition trials.

The significant triple interaction effect shows that modeling combined with reinforcement exerted a greater influence on girls than on boys whereas, relative to girls, boys were more responsive to modeling cues when reinforcement was absent.

The acquisition and generalization data for objective children treated subjectively are presented graphically in Figure 3.

Analysis of variance of this set of scores reveals that the experimental treatments were highly influential in modifying the children's orientations from objective to subjective morality. Although the differences between the three experimental groups did not reach statistical significance, evidently the two conditions utilizing modeling procedures were the principal contributors to the main treatment effect. Comparison of pairs of means across phases yielded no significant differences for the operant conditioning group. The modeling conditions, on the other hand, produced significant and relatively stable increases in subjective moral judgment responses (Table 3).

DISCUSSION

The results of the present study provide evidence that subjective morality increases gradually with age, but fail to substantiate Piaget's theory of demarcated sequential stages of moral development. Children at all age levels exhibited discriminative repertories of moral judg-

Table 3 *Comparison of Pairs of Means across Experimental Phases and between Treatment Conditions*

Scores	Base Test versus Experimental Phase	Base Test versus Posttest	Experimental Phase versus Posttest
	t	t	t
Within conditions			
Objective treatment			
Model and reinforcement	5.31****	5.74****	<1
Model	5.84****	5.74****	<1
Reinforcement	<1	1.52	<1
Subjective treatment			
Model and reinforcement	3.12***	3.09**	<1
Model	4.10***	2.69*	1.87
Reinforcement	2.04	<1	1.99
	Model + Reinforcement versus Model	Model + Reinforcement versus Reinforcement	Model versus Reinforcement
Between conditions			
Objective treatment			
Experimental phase	<1	2.81**	3.34***
Posttest	<1	2.68**	2.61**
Subjective treatment			
Experimental phase	<1	1.11	1.13
Posttest	<1	2.81**	2.15*

* $p < .05$. ** $p < .02$. *** $p < .01$. **** $p < .001$.

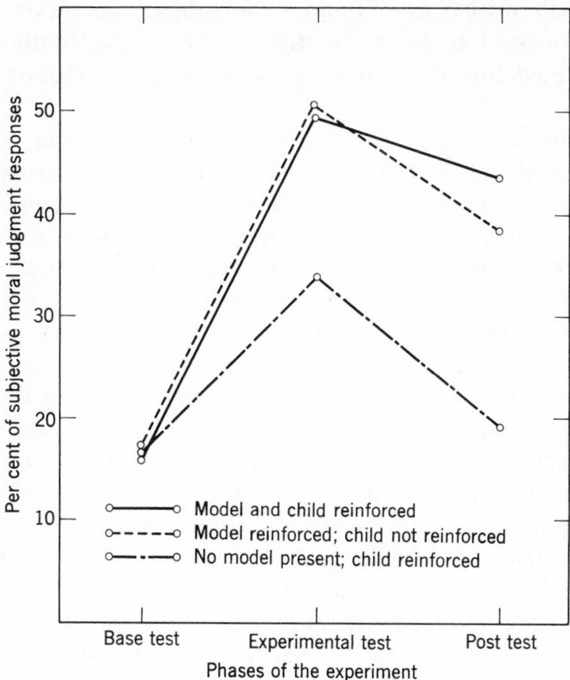

Figure 3. Mean percentage of subjective moral judgment responses produced by objective children on each of three test periods for each of three experimental conditions.

ments in which both objective and subjective classes of responses exist concurrently. A recent study by Durkin (1961) provides some additional support for the specificity of children's moral judgment behavior.

The utility of Piaget's stage theory of morality is further limited by the finding that children's judgmental responses are readily modifiable, particularly through the utilization of adult modeling cues.

In most experimental demonstrations of modeling effects the model exhibits a given set of responses and the observer reproduces these responses in substantially identical form in similar or identical stimulus contexts (Bandura, 1962). The findings of the present study reveal, however, that a general class of behavior may be readily acquired through observation of social models and consequently, the observer responds to new stimulus sensations in a manner consistent with the model's predisposition even though the subject had never observed the model respond to the same stimuli. These results illustrate the potency of modeling cues for shaping generalized patterns of social behavior.

The failure of operant conditioning procedures alone in altering moral judgment behavior is not at all surprising considering that the desired responses were much weaker than the competing dominant class of moral judgments. In many cases, particularly in the objective treatment condition, the subordinate responses occurred relatively infrequently; consequently there was little opportunity to influence them through reinforcement. In fact, the absence of a statistically significant conditions effect for children who experienced the subjective treatment largely resulted from several of the subjects in the operant conditioning group who happened to emit subjective responses on early trials and increased this behavior under reinforcement.

It is apparent, however, from both sets of data that operant conditioning procedures are particularly inefficient when there are strong dominant response tendencies and the desired alternative responses are only weakly developed or absent. In such cases, the provision of models who exhibit the desired behavior is an exceedingly effective procedure for eliciting from others appropriate matching responses early in the learning sequence and thus accelerating the acquisition process.

The results of the present study fail to confirm the hypothesis that a combination of reinforcement and modeling procedures constitutes a more powerful learning condition than modeling alone. Several factors might have accounted for the lack of differences between these two treatment conditions. In some cases the mere exposure to modeling cues produced rapid and complete changes in moral orientations and consequently the addition of reinforcement could not contribute any performance increments. This interpretation, however, does not fully account for the data since the majority of children were not performing at or near the ceiling level. Results from a series of experiments of social learning by means of imitation provide an alternative explanation (Bandura, 1962). These studies suggest that the process of response acquisition is based upon contiguity of sensory events and that reinforcement may function primarily as a performance related variable. In the present investigation the models' responses were highly consistent and sufficiently distinctive to insure observation and imitative learning. The experimenters' positive evaluative statements, however, may have served as relatively weak reinforcers. Had more highly desired incentives been employed as reinforcing agents, it is very likely that the addition of reinforcement would have significantly enhanced the children's reproduction of the modeled judgmental orientations.

SUMM 1RY

This experiment was designed to test the relative efficacy of social reinforcement and modeling procedures in modifying moral judgmental responses considered by Piaget to be age-specific. One group of children observed adult models who expressed moral judgments counter to the group's orientation, and the children were reinforced with approval for adopting the model's evaluative responses. A second group observed the models but received no reinforcement for matching their behavior. A third group of children had no exposure to models but were reinforced for moral judgments that ran counter to their dominant evaluative tendencies. Following the treatments, the children were tested for generalization effects. The experimental treatments produced substantial changes in the children's moral judgment responses. Conditions utilizing modeling cues proved to be more effective than the operant conditioning procedure.

REFERENCES

Bandura, A. Social learning through imitation. In M. R. Jones (Ed.), *Nebraska symposium on motivation: 1962*. Lincoln: Univ. of Nebraska Press, 1962. Pp. 211–269.

Bandura, A., & Huston, Aletha C. Identification as a process of incidental learning. *J. Abnorm. Soc. Psychol.*, 1961, **63**, 311–318.

Bandura, A., Ross, Dorothea, & Ross, Sheila A. Transmission of aggression through imitation of aggressive models. *J. Abnorm. Soc. Psychol.*, 1961, **63**, 575–582.

Bandura, A., Ross, Dorothea, & Ross, Sheila A. Imitation of film-mediated aggressive models. *J. Abnorm. Soc. Psychol.*, 1963, **66**, 3–11.

Durkin, Dolores. The specificity of children's moral judgments. *J. Genet. Psychol.*, 1961, **98**, 3–13.

Erikson, E. H. *Childhood and society*. New York: Norton, 1950.

Freud, S. *An outline of psychoanalysis*. New York: Norton, 1949.

Gesell, A., & Ilg, F. L. *Infant and child in the culture of today*. New York: Harper, 1943.

Keller, Helen. *The story of my life*. New York: Doubleday, 1927.

Mahrer, A. R. The role of expectancy in delayed reinforcement. *J. Exptl. Psychol.*, 1956, **52**, 101–106.

Piaget, J. *The moral judgment of the child*. Glencoe, Ill.: Free Press, 1948.

Piaget, J. *The construction of reality in the child.* New York: Basic Books, 1954.
Skinner, B. F. *Science and human behavior.* New York: Macmillan, 1953.
Sullivan, H. S. *The interpersonal theory of psychiatry.* New York: Norton, 1953.

3.3 MODEL'S CHARACTERISTICS AS DETERMINANTS OF SOCIAL LEARNING

Joan Grusec
Walter Mischel

In a recent study Mischel and Grusec (1966) found that a model's social characteristics affect the extent to which preschool children rehearse and transmit aspects of his behavior. In that study the model exhibited *neutral* behavior which had no direct consequences for the child, and also behaved in ways that had direct negative consequences for him (*aversive* behavior). Subjects rehearsed the model's neutral and aversive behaviors most frequently when the model had been noncontingently rewarding in a prior interaction, and also had some control over their future resources. The children transmitted the model's aversive behaviors to an experimental confederate most frequently when the model had been highly rewarding, regardless of her potential control over the child's future. Neither rewardingness nor future control significantly affected the transmission of neutral behavior.

In this study, as in others in which the social characteristics of the model have been manipulated (e.g., Bandura & Huston, 1961; Bandura, Ross, & Ross, 1963a), it was not possible to determine whether these characteristics affected only the observer's willingness to *perform* modeled behaviors or whether they also affected the degree to which he learned those behaviors. The fact that the model's rewardingness and potential control differentially influenced the observer's rehearsal and transmission of the neutral and aversive behaviors suggests that differing expectancies about the outcome of performance may have been generated in these two parts of the experimental situation. But it is also possible that subjects more closely observed an

Source: This study was supported by a grant from the U. S. Public Health Service. Reprinted with slight abridgment from the *Journal of Personality and Social Psychology,* 1966, 4, 211–215, with permission of the authors and the American Psychological Association, Inc.

adult who was rewarding and who they believed would be their new teacher than one who was nonrewarding and who they believed would never return. Such greater attentiveness might have increased the degree to which they learned the model's behaviors. Indeed, this would be predicted by certain power theories of identification. Maccoby (1959), for example, suggests that when an adult has control over resources which are important for the needs of a child the child will be motivated to attend more closely to, and engage in more role practice of, that adult's behavior. This occurs because knowledge of that behavior helps the child to guide his plans about future actions. The purpose of the present study was to determine if the characteristics possessed by a model do affect the degree to which observers learn his behaviors. Presumably, the amount of learning would be mediated by differences in attention and, perhaps, in covert rehearsal. If the behavior of a model who controls resources is more closely observed and learned than that of a model who does not control resources, such differences should be revealed when the observer is directly reinforced in a posttest for reproduction of what he observed. That is, between-group differences in recall would suggest that the model's behavior had not been learned to the same degree.

To adequately assess the extent to which a model's behavior had been learned it would be necessary to eliminate any *overt* rehearsal of that behavior. The results obtained by Mischel and Grusec (1966) indicate that overt rehearsal would give this group additional practice at performing the model's behaviors. It would thus be difficult to determine whether any difference in the acquisition measure obtained for this group, and for one interacting with a model who did not control resources, was a function of differential attention paid to the model and covert rehearsal or to a difference in the amount of practice in performing his behaviors. Accordingly, the present study was designed to minimize the opportunity for overt rehearsal of the model's behavior in his presence. In addition, subjects were not allowed to stay in a stimulus situation which might have evoked the model's distinctive behaviors after the model finished displaying them.

In the present experiment nursery-school children interacted in a 15-minute play session with a model who was either high or low in both rewardingness and future control. Thereafter, in the context of a game, the model displayed both aversive and neutral behaviors with varying frequency. At the termination of the game an experimental confederate offered attractive incentives to all subjects contingent upon reproduction of as many of the model's behaviors as they could recall. This acquisition test was conducted in the model's absence and after her rewardingness and potential future control had been made equivalent for all subjects.

METHOD

Subjects

The subjects were 28 children from the Stanford University nursery school, ranging in age from 38 months to 56 months, with a mean age of 46 months. Eight girls and six boys were randomly assigned to each of the two experimental groups, and the same two female experimenters were used with all children.

Experimental Groups

Subjects were assigned to one of the following two groups: the model was high in rewardingness and would have control over them in the future, and the model was low in rewardingness and would have no control over them in the future.[1]

High Reward-High Control: In this group the model and the subject played together with a number of very attractive toys (e.g., puzzles, battery-operated cars and planes, colorful blocks, dolls). During this play the model displayed warmth and affection and frequently praised the child. She thus attempted to establish herself as highly uncontingently rewarding and as having attractive resources at her disposal. In addition, the model described herself to the child as his new nursery-school teacher, thereby presenting herself as someone who would have future control over him.

Low Reward-Low Control: In this group subjects were given unattractive toys to play with (e.g., a broken toy car, a much-used coloring book and crayons). The model did not play with the child, but informed him that she had some work to finish. She sat at a desk at the other side of the room from the child and busily worked at some papers. Any attention bids made by the child received minimal, although pleasant, responses. The model thus attempted to establish herself as low in rewardingness and as having few resources at her disposal. In addition, she described herself to the child as a visiting

[1] These two conditions were selected because they produced the most extreme effects in the Mischel and Grusec (1966) study.

nursery-school teacher who was leaving in an hour to take the bus back to Milwaukee. She thereby presented herself as someone who would have no future control over him.

Procedure

Establishment of the Model's Characteristics: Each child was brought individually to the experimental room by the experimenter's assistant who introduced the child and the model and then left, saying that she would return soon. The model described herself to the child as either his new nursery-school teacher (high control), or as a visiting teacher (low control) who was leaving that same day. A play session lasting 15 minutes followed in which the model displayed either high rewardingness or low rewardingness, as described above. At the end of the play session the model reminded the child of her role as his new teacher or as a visiting teacher.

Presentation of Neutral and Aversive Behaviors: The model next announced to the child that she was going to show him how to play a special game, and went to uncover a toy cash register placed on a table in another corner of the experimental room. At the same time the experimental confederate entered the room and sat down, saying that she wanted to watch the game.

The model showed the child a large container of toys and told him to take one he liked. The toy he chose was put in a paper bag, and he was told he could take it home.

The model and the child sat down in front of the cash register and proceeded to play with it. This play involved making change, opening and closing the register drawer, and hitting the register keys. During the game all subjects were exposed to the following two kinds of behavior:

1. Neutral behaviors. (*a*) Hat—the model began the game by placing a hat on her head and commenting how pretty it was. At the end of the game she took off the hat. (*b*) Marching—the model hit a key on the register and then marched around the table saying, "March, march, march, march, march." This sequence was repeated three times.

2. Aversive behaviors. (*a*) Imposed delay—when the child first touched the cash register, the model said that if one wants to play with anything badly enough one ought to be able to wait for it, and instructed him to sit still with his hands in his lap until she had finished counting. She then very slowly and methodically repeated the numbers "1, 2, 3" fifteen times. (*b*) Criticism and removal of reward—the cash register was constructed so that, unknown

to the subject, the model could make the drawer come all the way out when it was opened, giving the appearance that it was broken. When this happened, as the child "broke" the drawer, the model exclaimed sharply, "Oh my! Do you know what this makes you? It makes you a storewrecker, and when you're a storewrecker you lose your toy." She then removed the toy the child had previously received, saying sternly, "You try not to be a storewrecker again!"

The model performed the marching and the counting sequences at two different times in the course of playing with the cash register, while she put on and took off the hat only once, and made the drawer "break" only once. The marching was done in a way which would minimize the chance of overt rehearsal by the child. For example, immediately after the model marched, she instructed the child to sit very still while she counted. Obviously the child could not overtly rehearse the wearing of the hat since the model had the hat on her head. In the previous study (Mischel & Grusec, 1966) only one child had rehearsed the label "storewrecker," and only two of the six subjects in the high reward-high control group who had rehearsed the model's counting did so in her presence. (Rehearsal of the aversive behaviors had not occurred at all in the low reward-low control groups.) Thus it was assumed that overt rehearsal of the model's behaviors would be minimal in the present study. In fact, only one subject (in the high reward-high control condition) overtly rehearsed any of the model's behaviors, and this child rehearsed the model's counting.

Equating the Model's Characteristics: At the end of the game the model covered up the cash register, and the experimental confederate excused herself and left the room. The model then played for 5 minutes with all subjects as she had played with subjects in the high-reward condition before the game. In the course of this 5 minutes of play she returned the toy the child had lost when he "broke" the drawer. The intent of this procedure was to minimize differences between subjects in the degree to which they now viewed her as non-contingently rewarding.

After this play period the experimental confederate returned to the room and handed the model a note. The model told subjects in the high-control condition that the note stated she had received a telephone call which said she was needed elsewhere and so could not be their new teacher. Subjects in the low-control condition were told that the note said it was time for her to go. Thus, for all subjects, the model would have no control over them in the future. The model then said goodbye, put on her coat, and left the room.

Assessment of Learning

The experimental confederate now remained alone in the room with the child and told him that she wanted to see how good he was at remembering all the things that had happened while he and the model had played store. She seated the subject in front of the cash register and gave him an attractive picture sticker or a cookie as an immediate reward for each aspect of the model's behavior during the game which he correctly recalled. In addition, she told him that as soon as he had recalled everything he would be allowed to leave and return to the nursery school.

Only the model's two aversive and two neutral behaviors were scored, although subjects were reinforced for recalling any relevant aspect of the model's behavior (e.g., "she pushed the keys"). If a subject mentioned that the model had marched or counted, he was asked to demonstrate this. He was scored as recalling the marching behavior if he either marched around the table or indicated verbally that the model had done so. Counting was scored as recalled if the child indicated that the model had said "1, 2, 3." If he said that the model put on the hat, he was scored as having recalled this. Extensive probes were used only in an attempt to elicit the label "storewrecker." If a subject mentioned that the drawer had come out of the cash register, the confederate asked "What happened?" If this probe was unsuccessful, she said, "What did [model] say you were?" If the subject did not mention that the drawer had broken, he was reminded that this had happened and then asked the two probe questions. Only use of the word "storewrecker" was scored as correct recall of the model's criticism.

As each item of the model's behavior was recalled the confederate asked, "What else did [model] do when you were playing store?" and "Can you remember anything else [model] did?" This continued until the child insisted that he could not remember anything else.

The experimental assistant and the model-experimenter, who watched the acquisition testing through a one-way mirror, each recorded independently everything the child recalled. There was 100 per cent agreement in their recording.

RESULTS

Inspection of the data revealed no difference in the number of individual items of the model's behavior recalled for boys and girls. Thus the data from both sexes were combined for statistical analysis.

Table 1 shows the number of children who recalled each of the model's neutral behaviors (wearing the hat and marching) and the number who recalled each of the model's aversive behaviors (counting and calling the child a "storewrecker"). None of the differences between groups in number of children recalling any single item of behavior was statistically significant (all χ^2 values < 1.35, all p values $> .20$, $df = 1$ in each comparison). However, the mean number of total items of the model's behavior recalled by each child in the high reward-high control condition was 2.36 ($SD = .71$) while the mean number of items recalled by children in the low reward-low control condition was 1.57 ($SD = .88$). A comparison of these two means yielded a t of 2.34 ($p < .025$, $df = 26$, one-tailed). Thus the behavior of a model who is a controller of resources (high in rewardingness and future control) was recalled better than the behavior of a model who is not a controller of resources (low in rewardingness and future control).

DISCUSSION

Although the results were not impressively strong, they indicate that the learning of social behaviors is affected by the characteristics of the agent who initially exhibited them. Children who interacted with a model who was highly rewarding and who had control over their future resources were able to recall more of that model's behavior when given external incentives for doing so than were children who interacted with a model who was not rewarding and who had no future control over them.[2] These differences in recall presumably reflect differences in acquisition or learning of the model's behaviors. It seems likely that they were mediated by the amount of attention paid to the model in the two groups and perhaps also by the amount of covert practice of the modeled behavior in which the children en-

[2] It is of interest that so few children were able to recall the critical label storewrecker since Mischel and Grusec (1966) found that this label was frequently transmitted to an experimental confederate. In that study, however, all the events that had occurred during the game before the transmission phase were reviewed verbally by the model. It may have been this review which helped more children to remember and to use the critical label. The children in the present study were, on the average, 6 months younger than those in the first study, and the inability of all but three of the present subjects to remember a relatively difficult label may have been due to their age.

Table 1 *Number of Children in Each Group Recalling Each of the Model's Behaviors and Mean Total Recall*

	Model's Behaviors				
Group	Hat	Marching	Counting	Criticism	Mean Total Recall
High reward-high control	9	12	10	2	2.36
Low reward-low control	6	9	6	1	1.57

gaged. The present results support theories of identification which stress the power of the model as a determinant of the degree to which his behaviors are acquired (e.g., Maccoby, 1959).

It was impossible to know from earlier studies that varied the model's social characteristics (Bandura & Huston, 1961; Bandura, Ross, & Ross, 1963a; Mischel & Grusec, 1966) whether these characteristics affected the degree to which observers actually *learned* the model's behaviors or whether they influenced only willingness to *perform* them. This is because previous investigations did not assess the observer's learning by offering attractive incentives to all subjects contingent on their reproducing the model's behavior. The only relevant earlier attempt to measure acquisition by this technique (Bandura, 1965) found no learning differences between groups who had witnessed models obtaining positive or negative consequences for their behavior. Obviously, however, acquisition differences could not have been the result of observed response consequences since these occurred *after* the model's behavior had been observed. The model's attributes, or the response consequences his behavior engenders, can affect the observer's attention and learning of the displayed behaviors only if they are presented *before* exposure to the modeled behaviors. The results of the present experiment suggest that when this is done the model's attributes do influence the degree to which his behaviors are learned and not merely the observer's subsequent willingness to perform them.

The amount of imitation which occurs in a given situation is certainly more than a function of the amount of the model's behavior that the observer has learned. An explanation of imitative behavior involving only differences in acquisition would be insufficient to account for the finding that rewardingness and future control affect the rehearsal and transmission of a model's neutral and aversive behaviors differently (Mischel & Grusec, 1966). An adequate explanation of this result would have to consider apparently different determinants of rehearsal and transmission of the same behaviors—determinants which might involve differing expectancies about the outcomes of behavior rehearsed in the model's presence and of behavior transmitted to someone else. In addition, there is ample evidence that response consequences to the model at the *end* of a sequence of modeled behavior affect the degree to which an observer subsequently *performs* that model's behavior (Bandura, 1965; Bandura, Ross, & Ross, 1963b; Walters, Leat, & Mezei, 1963).

In summary, then, comprehensive accounts of the effects of a model's social characteristics on imitation of his behavior probably would have to deal with differences in amount learned about the model's behavior as well as differences in the observer's expectation about the outcome of performing the particular learned behavior. Presumably, differences in acquisition would be mediated by differential attention and covert rehearsal, while differences in performance would be mediated by expectancies about the consequences of particular performances in the eliciting situation.

SUMMARY

This study investigated the effect of a model's social characteristics on the extent to which his behaviors are learned by others. Preschool children interacted either with a highly rewarding adult model who would have control over their future resources ("future control"), or with a nonrewarding model who would not have future control. Thereafter the model behaved in ways designed to be aversive to them (criticism and imposed delay of reward) and also displayed novel neutral behaviors. To test the extent to which *S*s learned these behaviors an experimental confederate rewarded the children for every aspect of the model's behaviors which they could reproduce in the model's absence. Children who had initially interacted with a rewarding model who had future control were able to reproduce significantly more of her behaviors than those who had interacted with a model who was not rewarding and had no future control. Thus the model's social characteristics may affect the observer's learning of modeled behavior, and not merely his willingness to perform them.

REFERENCES

Bandura, A. Influence of model's reinforcement contingencies on the acquisition of imitative responses. *J. Pers. Soc. Psychol.*, 1965, **1**, 589–595.

Bandura, A., & Huston, A. C. Identification as a process of incidental learning. *J. Abnorm. Soc. Psychol.*, 1961, **63**, 311–318.

Bandura, A., Ross, D., & Ross, S. A. A comparative test of the status envy, social power, and secondary reinforcement theories of identificatory learning. *J. Abnorm. Soc. Psychol.*, 1963, **67**, 527–534. (a)

Bandura, A., Ross, D., & Ross, S. A. Vicarious reinforcement and imitative learning. *J. Abnorm. Soc. Psychol.*, 1963, **67**, 601–607. (b)

Maccoby, E. E. Role-taking in childhood and its consequences for social learning. *Child Develop.*, 1959, **30**, 239–252.

Mischel, W., & Grusec, J. Determinants of the rehearsal and transmission of neutral and aversive behaviors. *J. Pers. Soc. Psychol.*, 1966, **3**, 197–205.

Walters, R. H., Leat, M., & Mezei, L. Inhibition and disinhibition of responses through empathetic learning. *Can. J. Psychol.*, 1963, **17**, 235–243.

§ 4 SOCIAL INFLUENCE, DISSONANCE, AND CONSONANCE

The papers included in this section are concerned with the way in which others affect or bring about changes in an individual's motives and/or behavior. In some instances, influence is exerted in a direct way, by confronting the individual with opinions that differ from his, but in other instances the influence is more subtle.

Robert B. Zajonc's paper deals with the more subtle types of influence—the changes in behavior that take place merely because of the presence of others. This type of influence is not confined to man, but occurs among insects as well.

Norman S. Endler's experiment is concerned with more direct attempts at influence, whereby subjects are made aware that group opinion differs from their own. The subject's susceptibility to such influence can be tested by exposing him to a fictitious group consensus and also can be increased by reinforcement. Endler shows that such experiences constitute examples of social learning and that the resulting influence has an effect that endures over an extended period of time.

The study by Jonathan L. Freedman and Scott C. Fraser consists of experiments in which influence was exerted through getting individuals to agree to small favors, which in turn made them susceptible to the granting of larger ones. In these instances, influence was brought to bear by a single person (rather than a group), and the medium of contact was the telephone.

In both Endler's and Freedman and Fraser's study, attempts to influence succeed at least in part because subjects experience a degree of cognitive dissonance, which they then resolve by conformity or compliance. Cognitive dissonance is the major focus of the fourth paper in this group, which consists of a report of research by Carlsmith, Collins, and Helmreich, who observed the effect of cognitive dissonance on subjects who were required to make statements contrary to their beliefs in the course of writing essays or role playing. As has been shown in previous research, small rewards brought about greater changes in attitude than large ones when the statements were made orally. The opposite result obtained, however, when statements were made in writing.

An experiment by Paul R. Wilson and Paul N. Russell tested the effect of disproportionate rewards for lifting light and heavy weights. As predicted by cognitive dissonance theory, subjects who were "underpaid" for lifting the heavy weight underestimated the distance they had raised it.

The paper by J. Stacy Adams reports a number of studies showing how cognitive dissonance theory explains situations in business and industry in which individuals perceive an inappropriate relationship between what they are paid and what they are asked to do by their employers.

Individuals are likely to take some kind of action in order to reduce cognitive dissonance because of a generalized tendency for them to maintain what has been variously termed consistency, congruency, symmetry, or consonance among interrelated motives and actions. Percy H. Tannenbaum's paper deals with the individual's attempts to maintain a degree of consistency or congruity in his attitudes toward a given person and the latter's expressed attitudes. In Tannenbaum's experiment, subjects were exposed to information relating to a fictitious person and to one of two items on which he was purported to have made statements. Results showed that the subjects' attitudes tended to be consistent with respect to the source person and both of his statements, even though they were informed as to the validity of only one of the latter.

4.1 SOCIAL FACILITATION

Robert B. Zajonc

Most textbook definitions of social psychology involve considerations about the influence of man upon man, or, more generally, of individual upon individual. And most of them, explicitly or implicitly, commit the main efforts of social psychology to the problem of how and why the *behavior* of one individual affects the behavior of another. The influences of individuals on each other's behavior which are of interest to social psychologists today take on very complex forms. Often they involve vast networks of interindividual effects, such as one finds in studying the process of group decision making, competition, or conformity to a group norm. But the fundamental forms of interindividual influence are represented by the oldest experimental paradigm of social psychology: social facilitation. This paradigm, dating back to Triplett's original experiments on pacing and competition, carried out in 1897 (1), examines the consequences upon behavior which derive from the sheer presence of other individuals.

Research in the area of social facilitation may be classified in terms of two experimental paradigms: audience effects and co-action effects. The first experimental paradigm involves the observation of behavior when it occurs in the presence of passive spectators. The second examines behavior when it occurs in the presence of other individuals also engaged in the same activity. We shall consider past literature in these two areas separately.

AUDIENCE EFFECTS

Simple motor responses are particularly sensitive to social facilitation effects. In 1925 Travis (2) obtained such effects in a study in which he used the pursuit-rotor task. In this task the subject is required to

Source: The preparation of this article was supported in part by grants from the Office of Naval Research and the National Science Foundation. Reprinted with slight abridgment from *Science*, 1965, **149**, 269–274, with permission of the author and *Science*.

follow a small revolving target by means of a stylus which he holds in his hand. If the stylus is even momentarily off target during a revolution, the revolution counts as an error. First each subject was trained for several consecutive days until his performance reached a stable level. One day after the conclusion of the training the subject was called to the laboratory, given five trials alone, and then ten trials in the presence of from four to eight upperclassmen and graduate students. They had been asked by the experimenter to watch the subject quietly and attentively. Travis found a clear improvement in performance when his subjects were confronted with an audience. Their accuracy on the ten trials before an audience was greater than on any ten previous trials, including those on which they had scored highest.

A considerably greater improvement in performance was recently obtained in a somewhat different setting and on a different task (3). Each subject (all were National Guard trainees) was placed in a separate booth. He was seated in front of a panel outfitted with 20 red lamps in a circle. The lamps on this panel light in a clockwise sequence at 12 revolutions per minute. At random intervals one or another light fails to go on in its proper sequence. On the average there are 24 such failures per hour. The subject's task is to signal whenever a light fails to go on. After 20 minutes of intensive training, followed by a short rest, the National Guard trainees monitored the light panels for 135 minutes. Subjects in one group performed their task alone. Subjects in another group were told that from time to time a lieutenant colonel or a master sergeant would visit them in the booth to observe their performance. These visits actually took place about four times during the experimental session. There was no doubt about the results. The accuracy of the supervised subjects was on the average 34 per cent higher than the accuracy of the trainees working in isolation, and toward the end of the experimental session the accuracy of the supervised subjects was more than twice as high as that of the subjects working in isolation. Those expecting to be visited by a superior missed, during the last experimental period, 20 per cent of the light failures, while those expecting no such visits missed 64 per cent of the failures.

Dashiell, who in the early 1930s carried out an extensive program of research on social facilitation, also found considerable improvement in performance due to audience effects on such tasks as simple multiplication or word association (4). But, as is the case in many other areas, negative audience effects were also found. In 1933 Pessin asked college students to learn lists of nonsense syllables under two conditions, alone and in the presence of several spectators (5). When confronted with an audience, his subjects required an average of 11.27 trials to learn a seven-item list. When working alone they needed only 9.85 trials. The average number of errors made in the "audience" condition was considerably higher than the number in the "alone" condition. In 1931 Husband found that the presence of spectators interferes with the learning of a finger maze (6), and in 1933 Pessin and Husband (7) confirmed Husband's results. The number of trials which the isolated subjects required for learning the finger maze was 17.1. Subjects confronted with spectators, however, required 19.1 trials. The average number of errors for the isolated subjects was 33.7; the number for those working in the presence of an audience was 40.5.

The results thus far reviewed seem to contradict one another. On a pursuit-rotor task Travis found that the presence of an audience improves performance. The learning of nonsense syllables and maze learning, however, seem to be inhibited by the presence of an audience, as shown by Pessin's experiment. The picture is further complicated by the fact that when Pessin's subjects were asked, several days later, to recall the nonsense syllables they had learned, a reversal was found. The subjects who tried to recall the lists in the presence of spectators did considerably better than those who tried to recall them alone. Why are the learning of nonsense syllables and maze learning inhibited by the presence of spectators? And why, on the other hand, does performance on a pursuit-rotor, word-association, multiplication, or a vigilance task improve in the presence of others?

There is just one, rather subtle, consistency in the above results. It would appear that the emission of well-learned responses is facilitated by the presence of spectators, while the acquisition of new responses is impaired. To put the statement in conventional psychological language, performance is facilitated and learning is impaired by the presence of spectators.

This tentative generalization can be reformulated so that different features of the problem are placed into focus. During the early stages of learning, especially of the type involved in social facilitation studies, the subject's responses are mostly the wrong ones. A person learning a finger maze, or a person learning a list of nonsense syllables, emits more wrong responses than right ones in the early stages of training. Most learning experiments continue until he ceases to make mistakes—until his performance is perfect. It may be said, therefore, that during training it is primarily the wrong responses which are dominant and strong; they are the ones which have the highest probability of occurrence. But after the individual has mastered the task, correct responses necessarily gain ascendancy in his task-relevant behavioral repertoire. Now they are the ones which are more probable—in other words, dominant. Our tentative generalization may now be simplified: audience enhances the emission of dominant responses. If the dominant responses are the correct ones, as is the case upon achieving mastery, the presence of an audience will be of benefit to the individual. But if they are mostly wrong, as is the case in the early stages of learning, then these wrong responses will be enhanced in the presence of an audience, and the emission of correct responses will be postponed or prevented.

There is a class of psychological processes which are known to enhance the emission of dominant responses. They are subsumed under the concepts of drive, arousal, and activation (8). If we could show that the presence of an audience has arousal consequences for the subject, we would be a step further along in trying to arrange the results of social-facilitation experiments into a neater package. But let us first consider another set of experimental findings.

CO-ACTION EFFECTS

The experimental paradigm of co-action is somewhat more complex than the paradigm involved in the study of audience effects. Here we observe individuals all simultaneously engaged in the same activity and in full view of each other. One of the clearest effects of such simultaneous action, or co-action, is found in eating behavior. It is well known that animals simply eat more in the presence of others. For instance, Bayer had chickens eat from a pile of wheat to their full satisfaction (9). He waited some time to be absolutely sure that his subject would eat no more, and then brought in a companion chicken who had not eaten for 24 hours. Upon the introduction of the hungry co-actor, the apparently sated chicken ate two-thirds again as much grain as it had already eaten. Recent work by Tolman and Wilson fully substantiates these results (10). In an extensive study of social-facilitation effects among albino rats, Harlow found dramatic increases in eating (11). In one of his experiments, for instance, the rats, shortly after weaning, were matched in pairs for weight. They were then fed alone and in pairs on alternate days. Figure 1 shows his results. It is clear that considerably more food

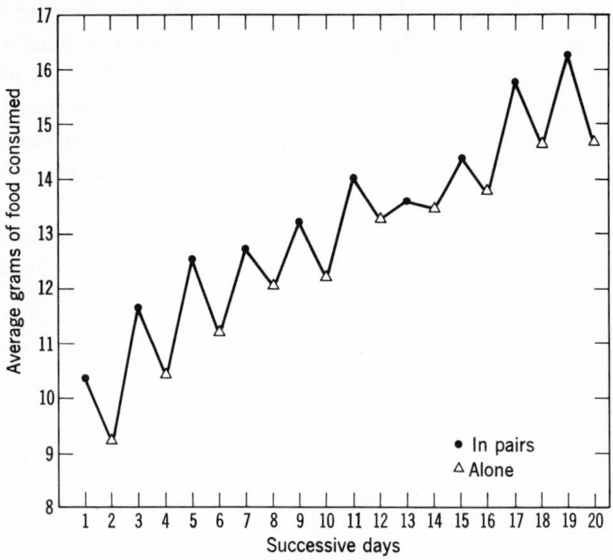

Figure 1. Data on feeding of isolated and paired rats. [Harlow (11).]

was consumed by the animals when they were in pairs than when they were fed alone. James (12), too, found very clear evidence of increased eating among puppies fed in groups.

Perhaps the most dramatic effect of co-action is reported by Chen (13). Chen observed groups of ants working alone, in groups of two, and in groups of three. Each ant was observed under various conditions. In the first experimental session each ant was placed in a bottle half filled with sandy soil. The ant was observed for 6 hours. The time at which nest building began was noted, and the earth excavated by the insect was carefully weighed. Two days afterward the same ants were placed in freshly filled bottles in pairs, and the same observations were made. A few days later the ants were placed in the bottles in groups of three, again for 6 hours. Finally, a few days after the test in groups of three, nest building of the ants in isolation was observed. Figure 2 shows some of Chen's data.

There is absolutely no question that the amount of work an ant accomplishes increases markedly in the presence of another ant. In all pairs except one, the presence of a companion increased output by a factor of at least 2. The effect of co-action on the latency of the

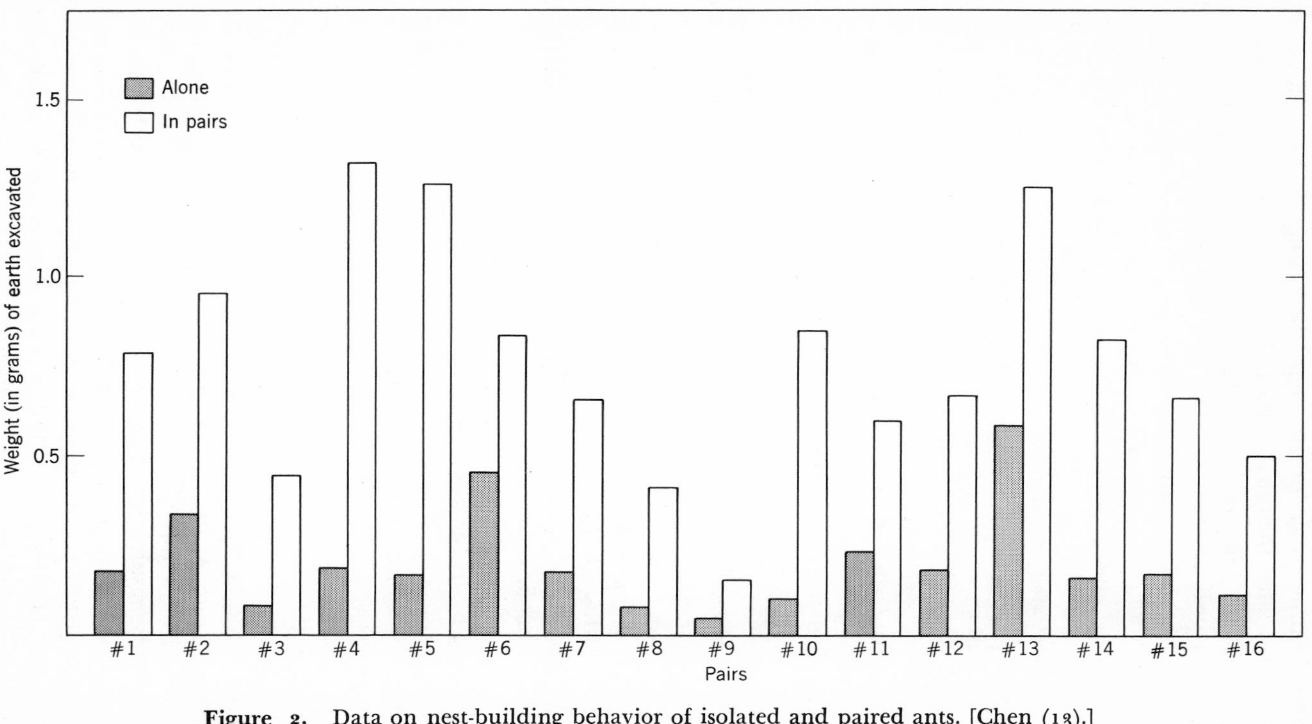

Figure 2. Data on nest-building behavior of isolated and paired ants. [Chen (13).]

nest-building behavior was equally dramatic. The solitary ants of session 1 and the final session began working on the nest in 192 minutes, on the average. The latency period for ants in groups of two was only 28 minutes. The effects observed by Chen were limited to the immediate situation and seemed to have no lasting consequences for the ants. There were no differences in the results of session 1, during which the ants worked in isolation, and of the last experimental session, where they again worked in solitude.

If one assumes that under the conditions of Chen's experiment nest building *is* the dominant response, then there is no reason why his findings could not be embraced by the generalization just proposed. Nest building is a response which Chen's ants have fully mastered. Certainly, it is something that a mature ant need not learn. And this is simply an instance where the generalization that the presence of others enhances the emission of dominant and well-developed responses holds.

If the process involved in audience effects is also involved in coaction effects, then learning should be inhibited in the presence of other learners. Let us examine some literature in this field. Klopfer (14) observed greenfinches—in isolation and in heterosexual pairs—which were learning to discriminate between sources of palatable and of unpalatable food. And, as one would by now expect, his birds learned this discrimination task considerably more efficiently when working alone. I hasten to add that the subjects' sexual interests cannot be held responsible for the inhibition of learning in the paired birds. Allee and Masure, using Australian parakeets, obtained the same result for homosexual pairs as well (15). The speed of learning was considerably greater for the isolated birds than for the paired birds, regardless of whether the birds were of the same sex or of the opposite sex.

Similar results are found with cockroaches. Gates and Allee (16) compared data for cockroaches learning a maze in isolation, in groups of two, and in groups of three. They used an E-shaped maze. Its three runways, made of galvanized sheet metal, were suspended in a pan of water. At the end of the center runway was a dark bottle into which the photophobic cockroaches could escape from the noxious light. The results, in terms of time required to reach the bottle, are shown in Figure 3. It is clear from the data that the solitary cockroaches required considerably less time to learn the maze than the grouped animals. Gates and Allee believe that the group situation produced inhibition. They add, however (16, p. 357):

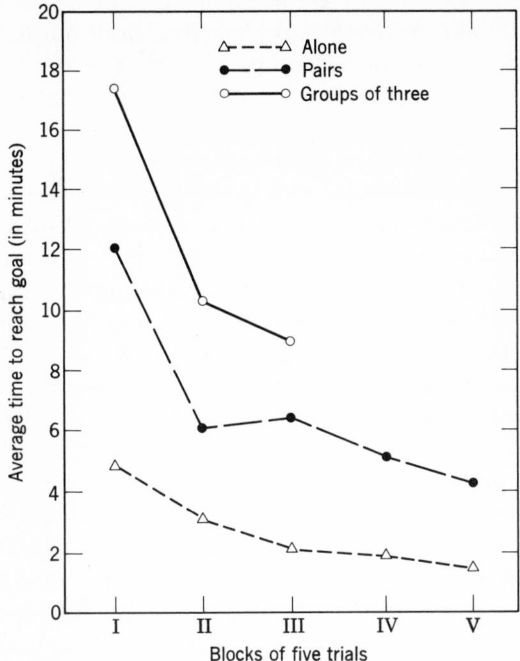

Figure 3. Data on maze learning in isolated and grouped cockroaches. [Gates and Allee (16).]

The nature of these inhibiting forces is speculative, but the fact of some sort of group interference is obvious. The presence of other roaches did not operate to change greatly the movements to different parts of the maze, but did result in increased time per trial. The roaches tended to go to the corner or end of the runway and remain there a longer time when another roach was present than when alone; the other roach was a distracting stimulus.

The experiments on social facilitation performed by Floyd Allport in 1920 and continued by Dashiell in 1930 (4, 17), both of whom used human subjects, are the ones best known. Allport's subjects worked either in separate cubicles or sitting around a common table. When working in isolation they did the various tasks at the same time and were monitored by common time signals. Allport did everything possible to reduce the tendency to compete. The subjects were told that the results of their tests would not be compared and would not be shown to other staff members, and that they themselves should refrain from making any such comparisons.

Among the tasks used were the following: chain word association, vowel cancellation, reversible perspective, multiplication, problem solving, and judgments of odors and weights. The results of Allport's experiments are well known: in all but the problem-solving and judgments test, performance was better in groups than in the "alone" condition. How do these results fit our generalization? Word association, multiplication, the cancellation of vowels, and the reversal of the perceived orientation of an ambiguous figure all involve responses which are well established. They are responses which are either very well learned or under a very strong influence of the stimulus, as in the word-association task or the reversible-perspective test. The problem-solving test consists of disproving arguments of ancient philosophers. In contrast to the other tests, it does not involve well-learned responses. On the contrary, the probability of wrong (that is, logically incorrect) responses on tasks of this sort is rather high; in other words, wrong responses are dominant. Of interest, however, is the finding that while intellectual work suffered in the group situation, sheer output of words was increased. When working together, Allport's subjects tended consistently to write more. Therefore, the generalization proposed in the previous section can again be applied: if the presence of others raises the probability of dominant responses, and if strong (and many) incorrect response tendencies prevail, then the presence of others can only be detrimental to performance. The results of the judgment tests have little bearing on the present argument, since Allport gives no accuracy figures for evaluating performance. The data reported only show that the presence of others was associated with the avoidance of extreme judgments.

In 1928 Travis (18), whose work on the pursuit rotor I have already noted, repeated Allport's chain-word-association experiment. In contrast to Allport's results, Travis found that the presence of others decreased performance. The number of associations given by his subjects was greater when they worked in isolation. It is very significant, however, that Travis used stutterers as his subjects. In a way, stuttering is a manifestation of a struggle between conflicting response tendencies, all of which are strong and all of which compete for expression. The stutterer, momentarily hung up in the middle of a sentence, waits for the correct response to reach full ascendancy. He stammers because other competing tendencies are dominant at that moment. It is reasonable to assume that, to the extent that the verbal habits of a stutterer are characterized by conflicting response tendencies, the presence of others, by enhancing each of these response tendencies, simply heightens his conflict. Performance is thus impaired.

AVOIDANCE LEARNING

In two experiments on the learning of avoidance responses, the performances of solitary and grouped subjects were compared. In one, rats were used; in the other, humans.

Let us first consider the results of the rat experiment by Rasmussen (19). A number of albino rats, all litter mates, were deprived of water for 48 hours. The apparatus consisted of a box containing a dish of drinking water. The floor of the box was made of a metal grille wired to one pole of an electric circuit. A wire inserted in the water in the dish was connected to the other pole of the circuit. Thirsty rats were placed in the box alone and in groups of three. They were allowed to drink for 5 seconds with the circuit open. Following this period the shock circuit remained closed, and each time the rat touched the water he received a painful shock. Observations were made on the number of times the rats approached the water dish. The results of this experiment showed that the solitary rats learned to avoid the dish considerably sooner than the grouped animals did. The rats that were in groups of three attempted to drink twice as often as the solitary rats did, and suffered considerably more shock than the solitary subjects.

Let us examine Rasmussen's results somewhat more closely. For purposes of analysis let us assume that there are just two critical responses involved: drinking, and avoidance of contact with the water. They are clearly incompatible. But drinking, we may further assume, is the dominant response, and, like eating or any other dominant response, it is enhanced by the presence of others. The animal is therefore prevented, by the facilitation of drinking which derives from the presence of others, from acquiring the appropriate avoidance response.

The second of the two studies is quite recent and was carried out by Ader and Tatum (20). They devised the following situation with which they confronted their subjects, all medical students. Each subject is told on arrival that he will be taken to another room and seated in a chair, and that electrodes will be attached to his leg. He is instructed not to get up from the chair and not to touch the electrodes. He is also told not to smoke or vocalize, and is told that the experimenter will be in the next room. That is all he is told. The subjects are observed either alone or in pairs. In the former case the subject is brought to the room and seated at a table equipped with a red button which is connected to an electric circuit. Electrodes, by means of which electric shock can be administered, are attached to the calf of one leg. After the electrodes are attached, the experimenter leaves the room. From now on the subject will receive ½ second of electric shock every 10 seconds unless he presses the red button. Each press of the button delays the shock by 10 seconds. Thus, if he is to avoid shock, he must press the button at least once every 10 seconds. It should be noted that no information was given him about the function of the button, or about the purpose of the experiment. No essential differences are introduced when subjects are brought to the room in pairs. Both are seated at the table and both become part of the shock circuit. The response of either subject delays the shock for both.

The avoidance response is considered to have been acquired when the subject (or pair of subjects) receives less than six shocks in a period of 5 minutes. Ader and Tatum report that the isolated students required, on the average, 11 minutes, 35 seconds to reach this criterion of learning. Of the 12 pairs which participated in the experiment, only two reached this criterion. One of them required 46 minutes, 40 seconds; the other, 68 minutes, 40 seconds! Ader and Tatum offer no explanation for their curious results. But there is no reason why we should not treat them in terms of the generalization proposed above. We are dealing here with a learning task, and the fact that the subjects are learning to avoid shock by pressing a red button does not introduce particular problems. They are confronted with an ambiguous task, and told nothing about the button. Pressing the button is simply not the dominant response in this situation. However, escaping is. Ader and Tatum report that eight of the 36 subjects walked out in the middle of the experiment.

One aspect of Ader and Tatum's results is especially worth noting. Once having learned the appropriate avoidance response, the individual subjects responded at considerably lower rates than the paired subjects. When we consider only those subjects who achieved the learning criterion and only those responses which occurred *after* criterion had been reached, we find that the response rates of the individual subjects were in all but one case lower than the response rates of the grouped subjects. This result further confirms the generalization that, while learning is impaired by the presence of others, the performance of learned responses is enhanced.

There are experiments which show that learning is enhanced by the presence of other learners (21), but in all these experiments, as far as I can tell, it was possible for the subject to *observe* the critical responses of other subjects, and to determine when he was correct and when incorrect. In none, therefore, has the co-action paradigm been employed in its pure form. That paradigm involves the presence of others, and nothing else. It requires that these others not be able to provide the subject with cues or information as to appropriate behavior. If other learners can supply the critical individual with such cues, we are dealing not with the problem of co-action but with the problem of imitation or vicarious learning.

THE PRESENCE OF OTHERS AS A SOURCE OF AROUSAL

The results I have discussed thus far lead to one generalization and to one hypothesis. The generalization which organizes these results is that the presence of others, as spectators or as co-actors, enhances the emission of dominant responses. We also know from extensive research literature that arousal, activation, or drive all have as a consequence the enhancement of dominant responses (22). We now need to examine the hypothesis that the presence of others increases the individual's general arousal or drive level.

The evidence which bears on the relationship between the presence of others and arousal is, unfortunately, only indirect. But there is some very suggestive evidence in one area of research. One of the more reliable indicators of arousal and drive is the activity of the endocrine systems in general, and of the adrenal cortex in particular. Adrenocortical functions are extremely sensitive to changes in emotional arousal, and it has been known for some time that organisms subjected to prolonged stress are likely to manifest substantial adrenocortical hypertrophy (23). Recent work (24) has shown that the main biochemical component of the adrenocortical output is hydrocortisone (17-hydroxycorticosterone). Psychiatric patients characterized by anxiety states, for instance, show elevated plasma levels of hydrocortisone (25). Mason, Brady, and Sidman (26) have recently trained monkeys to press a lever for food and have given these animals unavoidable electric shocks, all preceded by warning signals. This procedure led to elevated hydrocortisone levels; the levels returned to normal within 1 hour after the end of the experimental session. This "anxiety" reaction can apparently be attenuated if the animal is given repeated doses of reserpine 1 day before the experimental session (27). Sidman's conditioned avoidance schedule also results in raising the hydrocortisone levels by a factor of 2 to 4 (26). In this schedule the animal receives an electric shock every 20 seconds without warning, unless he presses a lever. Each press delays the shock for 20 seconds.

While there is a fair amount of evidence that adrenocortical activity is a reliable symptom of arousal, similar endocrine manifestations were found to be associated with increased population density (28). Crowded mice, for instance, show increased amphetamine toxicity—that is, susceptibility to the excitatory effects of amphetamine—against which they can be protected by the administration of phenobarbital, chlorpromazine, or reserpine (29). Mason and Brady (30) have recently reported that monkeys caged together had considerably higher plasma levels of hydrocortisone than monkeys housed in individual cages. Thiessen (31) found increases in adrenal weights in mice housed in groups of 10 and 20 as compared with mice housed alone. The mere presence of other animals in the same room, but in separate cages, was also found to produce elevated levels of hydrocortisone. Table 1, taken from a report by Mason and Brady (30), shows plasma levels of hydrocortisone for three animals which lived at one time in

Table 1 *Basal Plasma Concentrations of 17-hydroxycorticosterone in Monkeys Housed Alone and in Same Room*

		Conc. of 17-Hydroxycorticosterone in Caged Monkeys (μg per 100 ml of plasma)	
Subject	Time	In Separate Rooms	In Same Room
M-1	9 A.M.	23	34
M-1	3 P.M.	16	27
M-2	9 A.M.	28	34
M-2	3 P.M.	19	23
M-3	9 A.M.	32	38
M-3	3 P.M.	23	31
Mean	9 A.M.	28	35
Mean	3 P.M.	19	27

From Leiderman and Shapiro (35, p. 7).

cages that afforded them the possibility of visual and tactile contact and, at another time, in separate rooms.

Mason and Brady also report urinary levels of hydrocortisone, by days of the week, for five monkeys from their laboratory and for one human hospital patient. These very suggestive figures are reproduced in Table 2 (30). In the monkeys, the low weekend traffic and activity in the laboratory seem to be associated with a clear decrease in hydrocortisone. As for the hospital patient, Mason and Brady report (30, p. 8),

> he was confined to a thoracic surgery ward that bustled with activity during the weekdays when surgery and admissions occurred. On the weekends the patient retired to the nearby Red Cross building, with its quieter and more pleasant environment.

Admittedly, the evidence that the mere presence of others raises the arousal level is indirect and scanty. And, as a matter of fact, some work seems to suggest that there are conditions, such as stress, under which the presence of others may lower the animal's arousal level. Bovard (32), for instance, hypothesized that the presence of another member of the same species may protect the individual under stress by inhibiting the activity of the posterior hypothalamic centers which trigger the pituitary adrenal cortical and sympathetico-adrenal medullary responses to stress. Evidence for Bovard's hypothesis, however, is as indirect as evidence for the one which predicts arousal as a consequence of the presence of others, and even more scanty.

Table 2 *Variations in Urinary Concentration of Hydrocortisone over a Nine-Day Period for Five Laboratory Monkeys and One Human Hospital Patient*

	Amounts Excreted (mg/24 hr)								
Subjects	Mon.	Tues.	Wed.	Thurs.	Fri.	Sat.	Sun.	Mon.	Tues.
Monkeys	1.88	1.71	1.60	1.52	1.70	1.16	1.17	1.88	
Patient		5.9	6.5	4.5	5.7	3.3	3.9	6.0	5.2

From Leiderman and Shapiro (35, p. 8).

SUMMARY AND CONCLUSION

If one were to draw one practical suggestion from the review of the social-facilitation effects which are summarized in this article he would advise the student to study all alone, preferably in an isolated cubicle, and to arrange to take his examinations in the company of many other students, on stage, and in the presence of a large audience. The results of his examination would be beyond his wildest expectations, provided, of course, he had learned his material quite thoroughly.

I have tried in this article to pull together the early, almost forgotten work on social facilitation, and to explain the seemingly conflicting results. This explanation is, of course, tentative, and it has never been put to a direct experimental test. It is, moreover, not far removed from the one originally proposed by Allport. He theorized (33, p. 261) that "the sights and sounds of others doing the same thing" augment ongoing responses. Allport, however, proposed this effect only for *overt* motor responses, assuming (33, p. 274) that *"intellectual* or *implicit responses* of thought are hampered rather than facilitated" by the presence of others. This latter conclusion was probably suggested to him by the negative results he observed in his research on the effects of co-action on problem solving.

Needless to say, the presence of others may have effects considerably more complex than that of increasing the individual's arousal level. The presence of others may provide cues as to appropriate or inappropriate responses, as in the case of limitation or vicarious learning. Or it may supply the individual with cues as to the measure of danger in an ambiguous or stressful situation. Davitz and Mason (34), for instance, have shown that the presence of an unafraid rat reduces the fear of another rat in stress. Bovard (32) believes that the calming of the rat in stress which is in the presence of an unafraid companion is mediated by inhibition of activity of the posterior hypothalamus. But in their experimental situations (that is, the open field test) the possibility that cues for appropriate escape or avoidance responses are provided by the co-actor is not ruled out. We might therefore be dealing not with the effects of the mere presence of others but with the considerably more complex case of imitation. The animal may not be calming *because* of his companion's presence. He may be calming *after* having copied his companion's attempted escape responses. The paradigm which I have examined in this article pertains only to the effects of the mere presence of others, and to the consequences for the arousal level. The exact parameters involved in social facilitation still must be specified.

REFERENCES

1. N. Triplett, *Am. J. Psychol.*, 1897, **9**, 507.
2. L. E. Travis, *J. Abnorm. Soc. Psychol.*, 1925, **20**, 142.
3. B. O. Bergum, & D. J. Lehr, *J. Appl. Psychol.*, 1963, **47**, 75.
4. J. F. Dashiell, *J. Abnorm. Soc. Psychol.*, 1930, **25**, 190.
5. J. Pessin, *Am. J. Psychol.*, 1933, **45**, 263.
6. R. W. Husband, *J. Genet. Psychol.*, 1931, **39**, 258. In this task the blindfolded subject traces a maze with his finger.
7. J. Pessin, & R. W. Husband, *J. Abnorm. Soc. Psychol.*, 1933, **28**, 148.
8. See, for instance, E. Duffy, *Activation and behavior*, New York: Wiley, 1962; K. W. Spence, *Behavior theory and conditioning*, New Haven: Yale Univ. Press, 1956; R. B. Zajonc, & B. Nieuwenhuyse, *J. Exptl. Psychol.*, 1964, **67**, 276.
9. E. Bayer, *Z. Psychol.*, 1929, **112**, 1.
10. C. W. Tolman, & G. T. Wilson, *Animal behav.*, 1965, **13**, 134.
11. H. F. Harlow, *J. Genet. Psychol.*, 1932, **43**, 211.
12. W. T. James, *J. Comp. Physiol. Psychol.*, 1953, **46**, 427; *J. Genet. Psychol.*, 1960, **96**, 123; W. T. James, & D. J. Cannon, *ibid.*, 1956, **87**, 225.
13. S. C. Chen, *Physiol. Zool.*, 1937, **10**, 420.
14. P. H. Klopfer, *Science*, 1958, **128**, 903.
15. W. C. Allee, & R. H. Masure, *Physiol. Zool.*, 1936, **22**, 131.
16. M. J. Gates, & W. C. Allee, *J. Comp. Psychol.*, 1933, **15**, 331.
17. F. H. Allport, *J. Exptl. Psychol.*, 1920, **3**, 159.
18. L. E. Travis, *J. Abnorm. Soc. Psychol.*, 1928, **23**, 45.
19. E. Rasmussen, *Acta Psychol.*, 1939, **4**, 275.
20. R. Ader, & R. Tatum, *J. Exptl. Anal. Behav.*, 1963, **6**, 357.
21. H. Gurnee, *J. Abnorm. Soc. Psychol.*, 1939, **34**, 529; J. C. Welty, *Physiol. Zool.*, 1934, **7**, 85.
22. See K. W. Spence, *Behavior theory and conditioning*, New Haven: Yale Univ. Press, 1956.
23. H. Selye, *J. Clin. Endocrin.*, 1946, **6**, 117.
24. D. H. Nelson, & L. T. Samuels, *ibid.*, 1952, **12**, 519.
25. E. L. Bliss, A. A. Sandberg, & D. H. Nelson, *J. Clin. Invest.*, 1953, **32**, 9; F. Board, H. Persky, & D. A. Hamburg, *Psychosom. Med.*, 1956, **18**, 324.
26. J. W. Mason, J. V. Brady, & M. Sidman, *Endocrinology*, 1957, **60**, 741.
27. J. W. Mason, & J. V. Brady, *Science*, 1956, **124**, 983.
28. D. D. Thiessen, *Texas Rep. Biol. Med.*, 1964, **22**, 266.
29. L. Lasagna, & W. P. McCann, *Science*, 1957, **125**, 1241.
30. J. W. Mason, & J. V. Brady, in P. H. Leiderman, & D. Shapiro, (Eds.), *Psychobiological approaches to social behavior*, Stanford, Calif.: Stanford Univ. Press, 1964.
31. D. D. Thiessen, *J. Comp. Physiol. Psychol.*, 1964, **57**, 412.
32. E. W. Bovard, *Psychol. Rev.*, 1959, **66**, 267.
33. F. H. Allport, *Social psychology*, Boston: Houghton-Mifflin, 1924.
34. J. R. Davitz, & B. J. Mason, *J. Comp. Physiol. Psychol.*, 1955, **48**, 149.
35. P. H. Leiderman, & D. Shapiro, Eds., *Psychobiological approaches to social behavior*, Stanford, Calif.: Stanford Univ. Press, 1964.

4.2 CONFORMITY AS A FUNCTION OF DIFFERENT REINFORCEMENT SCHEDULES

Norman S. Endler

Conforming behavior, or agreeing with a contrived group consensus, is a socially learned response and can be manipulated like any other class of behavior. It is an instrumental act leading to need satisfaction and goal attainment and is therefore modifiable via reinforcement (Walker & Heyns, 1962).

Reinforcement is a significant variable in the shaping of social behavior such as conformity. Although personality, stimulus, and group factors influence conforming behavior, this study will focus on the situational context and specifically on the role of reinforcement. In experiments on conformity two major sources of social reinforcement are the other individuals comprising the group and the experimenter.

The effects of the other group members as social reinforcers are well exemplified in the classical conformity studies of Sherif (1935) using ambiguous stimuli, Asch (1951) using unambiguous stimuli, and Crutchfield (1955) using both ambiguous and unambiguous stimuli and mechanizing the procedures for collecting conformity data. Crutchfield in his study also investigated the influence of the experimenter's feedback on conforming behavior. He found that the contrived group consensus in conjunction with the experimenter's positive reinforcement of that consensus increased the degree of conformity. Schein (1954) discovered that reward facilitated learned imitation, but that this did not generalize to all types of problems. Jones, Wells, and Torrey (1958) found that while experimenter feedback in terms of group consensus had no effect on conformity, feedback in terms of objective reality reduced conforming behavior. However, when the importance of group accuracy and social conformity

Source: This study was supported in part by a grant from the National Research Council of Canada. Reprinted with slight abridgment from the *Journal of Personality and Social Psychology*, 1966, 4, 175–180, with permission of the author and the American Psychological Association, Inc.

was stressed, experimenter feedback in terms of group consensus increased conformity, and reinforcement of independence still reduced conformity but to a lesser degree.

A somewhat different approach to studying the effects of experimenter feedback on conformity is illustrated in studies by Kelman (1950), Mausner (1954), and Luchins and Luchins (1961). Here the experimenter informs the subject of the accuracy of his responses prior to the subject receiving conflicting information from the other subjects. Conformity to the group response is greatly reduced.

In a recent study Endler (1965) found that when the experimenter reinforced subjects for agreeing with a contrived group, consensus conformity was increased, and when the experimenter reinforced subjects for disagreeing with the group, conformity was decreased (the experimenter's reinforcements occurred after everyone in the group had responded). The present study is an extension of the Endler (1965) study in that it examines the effects of different schedules of reinforcement on the acquisition and extinction of conforming responses. It was hypothesized that reinforcement for agreeing with a contrived group consensus elicits more conforming responses than reinforcement for disagreeing, the extent of the effect being a function of the amount of reinforcement. That is, the more frequent the reinforcement for agreeing the greater the conformity; the more frequent the reinforcement for disagreeing the less the conformity. As a corollary the reinforcement effects should be more marked for stimulus items late in the series than for those early in the series.

The above focuses on the acquisition of conforming responses. In addition it is important to examine the durability or resistance to extinction of conformity acquired under different conditions. That is, it is important to examine the process of conformity and not merely the outcome (Endler, 1961; Festinger, 1953; Hollander, Julian, & Haaland, 1965; Kelman, 1961). It was therefore hypothesized that although the general level of conformity drops for all groups in a postconformity nonpressure session, the frequency of conforming responses is still a function of the different reinforcement schedules of the acquisition (social pressure) session.

Sex differences with respect to conformity, as well as differences due to type of stimulus item employed, were also examined. Specifically it was hypothesized that females should conform more than males and that there should be more conformity to verbal items than to perceptual items.

METHOD

Apparatus

The subjects were subjected to social pressure via a Crutchfield-type (1955) conformity apparatus. The equipment, an electrical signaling or communicating device, consisted of a master control panel and five subject booths and panels. Each subject's panel included five toggle switches, used by the subject to respond to multiple-choice stimuli projected on a screen; a column of five amber lights on the extreme left, used to indicate the subject's position in the response sequence; five rows of five green lights each, used to communicate to the subject other individuals' responses; and to the left of the switches a blue light to indicate whether the subject's response was true; and a red light to indicate whether his response was false.

The bottom half of the master control panel consisted of five rows each containing five toggle switches which were used by the experimenter to communicate contrived responses to the subjects; a sixth row of five switches to communicate to each subject whether his responses were true or false; and a column of five switches used to inform each subject of his position in the response sequence. The top half of the control panel included five rows of five green lights each which received and indicated the subjects' responses, and a column of five amber lights which indicated the subject's position in the response sequence.

Subjects and Procedure

A total of 120 college subjects were randomly assigned to six different experimental conditions. There were ten males and ten females for each experimental condition, and the sexes were tested separately in groups of five. The six conditions (explained in detail below) were called: true-agree 100 per cent, true-agree 50 per cent, neutral, true-disagree 50 per cent, true-disagree 100 per cent, and control.

All groups except the control group were subjected to social pressure via the Crutchfield-type conformity apparatus (five subjects were tested at a time) and responded to 36 slides (multiple-choice stimulus items), including 16 critical ones—8 verbal (obscure facts) and 8 perceptual (geometrical forms). The perceptual slides included such items as: which of five lines was the longest, or which of five geometrical figures (e.g., circles, triangles, squares, etc.) had the largest area. The verbal slides included such items as: "The most popular beverage in Laos is"; or "The 1923 Kentucky Derby was won by"; or "Mount Rainier is located in." For each stimulus item there were five alternative answers, and each subject was required to select the correct one. Each slide was presented for a period of approximately 30 seconds. Each social pressure testing session lasted approximately 30 minutes, and each posttest session approximately 20 minutes.

Subjects were tested in two sessions—a social pressure plus reinforcement session and a posttest, nonpressure, nonreinforcement session two weeks later.

Session 1: The subjects were tested in groups of five and were randomly assigned to different booths in the conformity apparatus. They were told that they were participating in an experiment on judging perceptual and content material and that slides would be projected on the wall in front of them. The functioning of the apparatus was explained to them in such a manner that all subjects, except those in the control group, believed that they were communicating their judgments of the slides to one another via the apparatus, and that they were responding in a set sequence indicated to them by a series of lights lettered A to E on their panels. (This sequence varied from trial to trial.) Subjects in the control group were instructed to indicate their judgments as soon as a slide was projected, and no mention was made of communicating responses to others. Then all subjects except those in the control and neutral groups were told:

On certain items you will be told whether your answer is true or false, to give you an indication of how you are doing. True will be indicated by the blue light and false by the red light. These two lights are located at the lower left hand corner of your panel.

All groups except control and neutral were subjected to the following true-false reinforcement schedules[1]:

1. The true-agree 100 per cent group was positively (true) reinforced for agreeing and negatively (false) reinforced for disagreeing with the contrived group consensus on all 16 critical items.

2. The true-agree 50 per cent group was reinforced as above on 8 critical items.

[1] Reinforcement of the subject's responses was administered by the experimenter via the apparatus. If the experimenter pressed the true switch on the master panel, the blue (true) light lit up on the subject's panel; if the experimenter pressed the false switch, the red (false) light lit up on the subject's panel.

3. The true-disagree 50 per cent and true-disagree 100 per cent groups were analogous to the true-agree 50 per cent and true-agree 100 per cent groups, respectively, except that subjects were *positively* reinforced for *disagreeing* and *negatively* reinforced for *agreeing*.

The neutral group was subjected to the usual social pressure but not to reinforcement (i.e., did not receive experimenter feedback). The control group responded to the stimulus items in the absence of both social pressure and reinforcement. The subject's conformity score was the number of times he agreed with the contrived consensus on the critical items.

Session 2: Two weeks later all subjects were tested again in the Crutchfield-type apparatus but did not communicate with one another. They responded individually to the slides in a group session in the absence of both social pressure and reinforcement.

Separate two-way analyses of variance (reinforcement conditions and sex) were carried out for each session, and in addition an overall four-way classification analysis of variance was computed on all the data (reinforcement, sex, stimulus item, session).

RESULTS

A fixed-effects model two-way analysis of variance (reinforcement conditions and sex) of the subject's conforming responses in the social pressure situation (Session 1) yields the results indicated on Table 1. The main effects of reinforcement condition and sex were significant at the .01 and .05 levels, respectively. The interaction was not significant.

Table 1 *Two-Way Classification (Reinforcement Conditions and Sex) Analyses of Variance (Fixed-Effects Model) of Social Pressure Situation Conformity Scores*

Source	*SS*	*df*	*MS*	*F*
Reinforcement conditions (A)	1214.67	5	242.93	25.98**
Sex (B)	45.64	1	45.64	4.88*
A × B	65.26	5	13.05	1.40
Within	1009.60	108	9.35	
Total	2335.17	119		

* $p < .05$.
** $p < .01$.

Conformity as a Function of Different Reinforcement Schedules

The means and standard deviations of social pressure situation conformity scores for males and females under different reinforcement conditions are presented in Table 2. Note that the rank order of the mean conformity scores, for both sexes (from highest to lowest), was as follows: true-agree 100 per cent, true-agree 50 per cent, neutral, true-disagree 50 per cent, true-disagree 100 per cent, and control. Females conformed more than males.

Table 3 presents a two-way classification analysis of variance of posttest (postpressure situation) conformity scores. The main effects of reinforcement conditions and sex were significant at the .01 and .05 levels, respectively.

The means and standard deviations of conformity scores in the

Table 2 *Means and Standard Deviations of Social Pressure Situation Conformity Scores for Males and Females under Different Reinforcement Conditions*

	Sample					
	Male			Female		
Reinforcement Condition	*N*	*M*	*SD*	*N*	*M*	*SD*
True-agree 100%	10	9.50	3.07	10	13.00	2.28
True-agree 50%	10	7.50	3.64	10	10.50	3.07
Neutral	10	6.60	4.05	10	6.10	3.88
True-disagree 50%	10	4.20	1.99	10	4.60	4.05
True-disagree 100%	10	2.90	1.76	10	3.50	2.11
Control	10	2.10	1.30	10	2.50	1.57

Table 3 *Two-Way Classification (Reinforcement Conditions and Sex) Analysis of Variance (Fixed-Effects Model) of Posttest Session Conformity Scores*

Source	*SS*	*df*	*MS*	*F*
Reinforcement conditions (A)	429.34	5	85.87	15.96**
Sex (B)	33.07	1	33.07	6.15*
A × B	34.28	5	6.86	1.28
Within	581.30	108	5.38	
Total	1077.99	119		

* $p < .05$.
** $p < .01$.

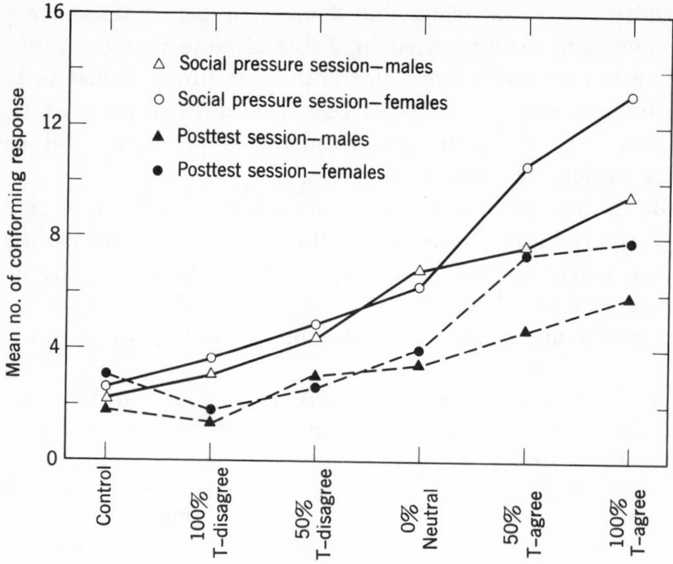

Figure 1. The effects of different reinforcement conditions on conforming responses for social pressure and posttest nonpressure sessions.

posttest session appear in Table 4. Except for the control group, the magnitude of the conformity scores for the different groups was in the order predicted.

Figure 1 is a graph comparing the mean conformity scores of the different reinforcement conditions under social pressure (Session 1) and the posttest nonpressure (Session 2) sessions. Figure 1 is in effect a pictorial composite of the means presented in Tables 2 and 4. Note that for all of the experimental conditions (including the control group for females) the conformity scores were higher for the social pressure situation than for the nonpressure posttest.

There were no consistent differences between conformity to verbal and perceptual stimulus items. A trend analysis of conformity to individual items for both the male and female true-agree 100 per cent and true-disagree 100 per cent groups in the social pressure situation indicates a significant upward trend for the true-agree 100 per cent group and a significant downward trend for the true-disagree 100 per cent group. That is, for the true-agree 100 per cent group there

Table 4 *Means and Standard Deviations of Posttest Session Conformity Scores for Males and Females under Different Reinforcement Conditions*

	Sample					
	Male			Female		
Reinforcement Condition	*N*	*M*	*SD*	*N*	*M*	*SD*
True-agree 100%	10	5.70	2.66	10	7.80	4.17
True-agree 50%	10	4.60	1.80	10	7.30	3.69
Neutral	10	3.30	1.68	10	3.90	1.70
True-disagree 50%	10	3.00	1.00	10	2.60	1.20
True-disagree 100%	10	1.40	1.36	10	1.60	1.28
Control	10	1.90	1.45	10	3.00	1.79

was greater conformity at the end of the series than at the beginning; for the true-disagree 100 per cent the reverse was true.

Table 5 presents a four-way fixed-effects analysis of variance (multifactor repeated-measurements design) of the conformity data (Winer, 1962). The four factors are reinforcement conditions, sessions (pressure versus nonpressure), sex, and type of stimulus item (verbal versus perceptual).

The effects due to reinforcement conditions, sex, and sessions were significant. The effect due to type of stimulus item was not significant. Significant interactions were Reinforcement × Session (graphs in Figure 1 intersect for control groups), Reinforcement × Stimulus Item × Session, and Sex × Reinforcement × Stimulus Item × Session.

The variance components derived from the mean squares of the analysis of variance in Table 5 (after pooling the nonsignificant sources) indicated that reinforcement conditions accounted for 13.9 per cent of the variance, sex for 1.1 per cent, and sessions for 4.7 per cent. The pooled Sex × Reinforcement and subjects within groups accounted for 38.79 per cent of the variance.

DISCUSSION

The results indicate that with more frequent (100% versus 50% versus 0%) reinforcements for *agreeing* with a contrived group consensus, conformity *increased;* with more frequent (100% versus 50% versus 0%) reinforcements for *disagreeing,* conformity *decreased.* Fe-

Table 5 *Analysis of Variance of Conformity Scores under Different Reinforcement Conditions for Social Pressure, and Nonpressure Test Session, Comparing Males and Females and Verbal and Perceptual Stimulus Items*

Source	*SS*	*df*	*MS*	*F*
Between subjects				
Sex (A)	39.10	1	39.10	7.88**
Reinforcement condition (B)	759.82	5	151.96	30.64**
A × B	44.34	5	8.87	1.79
Subjects within groups (C)	535.32	108	4.96	
Within subjects				
Type of stimulus item (D)	5.85	1	5.85	3.52
A × D	1.76	1	1.76	1.06
B × D	11.19	5	2.24	1.35
A × B × D	15.02	5	3.00	1.81
D × C	178.93	108	1.66	
Session (E)	150.75	1	150.75	62.55**
A × E	.26	1	.26	.11
B × E	62.19	5	12.44	5.16*
A × B × E	5.42	5	1.08	.45
E × C	260.13	108	2.41	
D × E	.11	1	.11	.12
A × D × E	3.48	1	3.48	3.74
B × D × E	11.57	5	2.31	2.48*
A × B × D × E	12.47	5	2.49	2.68*
D × E × C	100.12	108	.93	
Total	2187.83	479		

* $p < .05$.
** $p < .01$.

males conformed more than males, possibly as a function of different cultural expectations. There were no significant differences in conformity response rates as a function of type of stimulus material (perceptual versus verbal). There was significantly more conforming behavior in the social pressure situation than in the posttest session. However, the social pressure reinforcement conditions affected the subjects' behavior in the nonpressure posttest session. The relative magnitude of conforming responses (from high to low) of the experimental groups for both the social pressure and posttest sessions was as follows: true-agree 100 per cent, true-agree 50 per cent, neutral, true-disagree 50 per cent, and true-disagree 100 per cent. The situational factor of reinforcement accounts for 13.9 per cent for the behavioral (conformity) variance. This is greater than the sum of the effects due to sex (1.1 per cent), session (4.7 per cent), and type of stimulus item (0 per cent). However, the inclusion of the control group in the analyses probably increased, to some extent, the effects of the "reinforcement" variable, in that the results reflected differences due to the presence and absence of social pressures in addition to reinforcement differences.

One explanation of conforming behavior is in terms of social learning and reinforcement (Endler, 1965). The social pressure situation exemplifies a series of acquisition trials, and the posttest session illustrates extinction trials. During the social pressure session, the individual is faced with a discrepancy between the contrived group norm and what he perceives to be true. The more he is reinforced for agreeing with the group, the more he conforms; the more he is reinforced for disagreeing with the group, the less he conforms. Campbell (1961) has pointed out that the more a subject has been rewarded for nonconformity, the less often he will conform; the more often he has been punished for nonconformity, the more he will conform. In this study there are at least two factors affecting conforming behavior: social pressure and reinforcement. For the neutral group there are two sets of opposing forces: the responses required by the stimulus materials and the responses required by the group pressure. The discrepancy induces a state of perceived incongruity or cognitive dissonance (Festinger, 1957). Conforming behavior, a learned response, is one method for reducing this dissonance. If individuals have learned, via previous experiences, that imitation is rewarded, and deviation is punished, the experimental social pressure situation can redintegrate cues of different, and a state of dissonance, which can be reduced by conforming. Therefore for the neutral group social pressure is sufficient to induce conformity. For the other experimental groups there is an additional force (source of pressure): reinforcement. For the groups reinforced for conforming, social pressures summate or interact with the pressures created by the experimental reinforcement and maximize conformity. For the groups reinforced for disagreeing, the social pressures oppose the reinforcements, which are congruent with what subjects believe to be true. This tends to minimize conformity.

Learning occurs during the social pressure situation. Where there is reinforcement for agreeing with the group there is more conformity at the end of the session than at the beginning of the session. Where there is reinforcement for disagreeing there is less conformity at the end of the session than at the beginning. This learning that occurs in the social pressure situation carries over to the posttest session (extinction trials). In the posttest session both the reinforcement and the social pressure are absent. Although the conformity level drops for all groups, the conforming responses during the extinction trials are still a function of the reinforcement schedules of the acquisition trials. Prior conditions of group and reinforcement experiences affect subsequent conformity patterns.

Conforming behavior is a function of social pressure and reinforcement. The present paper studied the process of conformity and examined the effects of social pressure and different reinforcement schedules on the relative acquisition and extinction of conforming responses. This study indicates that the situational factor (reinforcement) is *one* of the important determinants of conforming behavior.

SUMMARY

Sixty male and 60 female college *S*s were randomly assigned to one of six experimental conformity conditions—(a) true-agree 100 per cent, (b) true-agree 50 per cent, (c) neutral, (d) true-disagree 50 per cent, (e) true-disagree 100 per cent, and (f) control—and were tested, via a conformity apparatus, in a social pressure plus reinforcement session and again in a posttest nonreinforcement session two weeks later. It was found that: (a) Reinforcement for agreeing with a contrived group consensus elicited more conformity than reinforcement for disagreeing, the extent of the effect being a function of the amount of reinforcement; (b) the effect persisted to some degree even after a period of two weeks, but conformity was significantly higher in the social pressure session than during the posttest; (c) females conformed more than males. Conformity was explained in terms of social learning; sex differences in conformity in terms of cultural expectations. It was concluded that the situational factor (reinforcement) is one of the important determinants of conforming behavior.

REFERENCES

Asch, S. E. Effects of group pressure upon the modification and distortion of judgments. In H. Guetzkow (Ed.), *Groups, leadership, and men*. Pittsburgh: Carnegie Press, 1951. Pp. 177–190.

Campbell, D. T. Conformity in psychology's theories of acquired behavioral dispositions. In I. A. Berg, & B. M. Bass (Eds.), *Conformity and deviation.* New York: Harper, 1961. Pp. 101–142.

Crutchfield, R. S. Conformity and character. *Am. Psychol.*, 1955, **10**, 191–198.

Endler, N. S. Conformity analyzed and related to personality. *J. Soc. Psychol.*, 1961, **53**, 271–283.

Endler, N. S. The effects of verbal reinforcement on conformity and deviant behavior. *J. Soc. Psychol.*, 1965, **66**, 147–154.

Festinger, L. An analysis of compliant behavior. In M. Sherif, & M. O. Wilson (Eds.), *Group relations at the crossroads.* New York: Harper, 1963. Pp. 232–256.

Festinger, L. *A theory of cognitive dissonance.* Stanford: Stanford Univ. Press, 1957.

Hollander, E. P., Julian, J. W., & Haaland, G. A. Conformity process and prior group support. *J. Pers. Soc. Psychol.*, 1965, **2**, 852–858.

Jones, E. E., Wells, H. H., & Torrey, R. Some effects of feedback from the experimenter on conformity behavior. *J. Abnorm. Soc. Psychol.*, 1958, **57**, 207–213.

Kelman, H. C. Effects of success and failure on "suggestibility" in the autokinetic phenomenon. *J. Abnorm. Soc. Psychol.*, 1950, **45**, 267–285.

Kelman, H. C. Processes of being and change. *Public Opin. Quart.*, 1961, **25**, 57–78.

Luchins, A. S., & Luchins, E. H. On conformity with judgments of a majority or an authority. *J. Soc. Psychol.*, 1961, **53**, 303–316.

Mausner, B. The effect of prior reinforcement on the interaction of observer pairs. *J. Abnorm. Soc. Psychol.*, 1954, **49**, 65–68.

Schein, E. H. The effect of reward on adult imitative behavior. *J. Abnorm. Soc. Psychol.*, 1954, **49**, 389–395.

Sherif, M. A study of some social factors in perception. *Arch. Psychol.*, 1935, **27**, No. 187.

Walker, E. L., & Heyns, R. W. *An anatomy for conformity.* Englewood Cliffs, N.J.: Prentice-Hall, 1962.

Winer, B. J. *Statistical principles in experimental design.* New York: McGraw-Hill, 1962.

4.3 COMPLIANCE WITHOUT PRESSURE: THE FOOT-IN-THE DOOR TECHNIQUE

Jonathan L. Freedman
Scott C. Fraser

How can a person be induced to do something he would rather not do? This question is relevant to practically every phase of social life, from stopping at a traffic light to stopping smoking, from buying Brand X to buying savings bonds, from supporting the March of Dimes to supporting the Civil Rights Act.

Source: These studies were supported in part by a grant from the National Science Foundation. Reprinted with slight abridgment from the *Journal of Personality and Social Psychology*, 1966, 4, 195–202, with permission of the senior author and the American Psychological Association, Inc., copyright holder.

One common way of attacking the problem is to exert as much pressure as possible on the reluctant individual in an effort to force him to comply. This technique has been the focus of a considerable amount of experimental research. Work on attitude change, conformity, imitation, and obedience has all tended to stress the importance of the degree of external pressure. The prestige of the communicator (Kelman & Hovland, 1953), degree of discrepancy of the communication (Hovland & Pritzker, 1957), size of the group disagreeing with the subject (Asch, 1951), perceived power of the model (Bandura, Ross, & Ross, 1963), etc., are the kinds of variables that have been studied. This impressive body of work, added to the research on rewards and punishments in learning, has produced convincing evidence that greater external pressure generally leads to greater compliance with the wishes of the experimenter. The one exception appears to be situations involving the arousal of cognitive dissonance in which, once discrepant behavior has been elicited from the subject, the greater the pressure that was used to elicit the behavior, the less subsequent change occurs (Festinger & Carlsmith, 1959). But even in this situation one critical element is the amount of external pressure exerted.

Clearly, then, under most circumstances the more pressure that can be applied, the more likely it is that the individual will comply. There are, however, many times when for ethical, moral, or practical reasons it is difficult to apply much pressure when the goal is to produce compliance with a minimum of apparent pressure, as in the forced-compliance studies involving dissonance arousal. And even when a great deal of pressure is possible, it is still important to maximize the compliance it produces. Thus factors other than external pressure are often quite critical in determining degree of compliance. What are these factors?

Although rigorous research on the problem is rather sparse, the fields of advertising, propaganda, politics, etc., are by no means devoid of techniques designed to produce compliance in the absence of external pressure (or to maximize the effectiveness of the pressure that is used, which is really the same problem). One assumption about compliance that has often been made either explicitly or implicitly is that once a person has been induced to comply with a small request he is more likely to comply with a larger demand. This is the principle that is commonly referred to as the foot-in-the-door or gradation technique and is reflected in the saying that if you "give them an inch, they'll take a mile." It was, for example, supposed to be one of the basic techniques upon which the Korean brainwashing tactics were based (Schein, Schneier, & Barker, 1961), and, in a somewhat different sense, one basis for Nazi propaganda during 1940 (Bruner, 1941). It also appears to be implicit in many advertising campaigns which attempt to induce the consumer to do anything relating to the product involved, even sending back a card saying he does not want the product.

The most relevant piece of experimental evidence comes from a study of conformity done by Deutsch and Gerard (1955). Some subjects were faced with incorrect group judgments first in a series in which the stimuli were not present during the actual judging and then in a series in which they were present, while the order of the memory and visual series was reversed for other subjects. For both groups the memory series produced more conformity, and when the memory series came first there was more total conformity to the group judgments. It seems likely that this order effect occurred because, as the authors suggest, once conformity is elicited at all it is more likely to occur in the future. Although this kind of conformity is probably somewhat different from compliance as described above, this finding certainly lends some support to the foot-in-the-door idea. The present research attempted to provide a rigorous, more direct test of this notion as it applies to compliance and to provide data relevant to several alternative ways of explaining the effect.

EXPERIMENT I

The basic paradigm was to ask some subjects (performance condidition) to comply first with a small request and then three days later with a larger, related request. Other subjects (one-contact condition) were asked to comply only with the large request. The hypothesis was that more subjects in the performance condition than in the one-contact condition would comply with the larger request.

Two additional conditions were included in an attempt to specify the essential difference between these two major conditions. The performance subjects were asked to perform a small favor, and, if they agreed, they did it. The question arises whether the act of agreeing itself is critical or whether actually carrying it out was necessary. To assess this a third group of subjects (agree-only) was asked the first request, but, even if they agreed, they did not carry it out. Thus, they were identical to the performance group except that they were not given the opportunity of performing the request.

Another difference between the two main conditions was that at the time of the larger request the subjects in the performance condition were more familiar with the experimenter than were the other subjects. The performance subjects had been contacted twice, heard his voice more, discovered that the questions were not dangerous, and so on. It is possible that this increased familiarity would serve to decrease the fear and suspicion of a strange voice on the phone and might accordingly increase the likelihood of the subjects agreeing to the larger request. To control for this a fourth condition was run (familiarization) which attempted to give the subjects as much familiarity with the experimenter as in the performance and agree-only conditions with the only difference being that no request was made.

The major prediction was that more subjects in the performance condition would agree to the large request than in any of the other conditions, and that the one-contact condition would produce the least compliance. Since the importance of agreement and familiarity was essentially unknown, the expectation was that the agree-only and familiarization conditions would produce intermediate amounts of compliance.

Method

The prediction stated above was tested in a field experiment in which housewives were asked to allow a survey team of five or six men to come into their homes for two hours to classify the household products they used. This large request was made under four different conditions: after an initial contact in which the subject had been asked to answer a few questions about the kinds of soaps she used, and the questions were actually asked (performance condition); after an identical contact in which the questions were not actually asked (agree-only condition); after an initial contact in which no request was made (familiarization condition); or after no initial contact (one-contact condition). The dependent measure was simply whether or not the subject agreed to the large request.

The subjects were 156 Palo Alto, California, housewives, 36 in each condition, who were selected at random from the telephone directory. An additional 12 subjects distributed about equally among the three two-contact conditions could not be reached for the second contact and are not included in the data analysis. Subjects were assigned randomly to the various conditions, except that the familiarization condition was added to the design after the other three conditions had been completed. All contacts were by telephone by the same experimenter who identified himself as the same person each time. Calls were made only in the morning. For the three groups that were contacted twice, the first call was made on either Monday or Tuesday and the second always three days later. All large requests were made on either Thursday or Friday.

At the first contact, the experimenter introduced himself by name and said that he was from the California Consumers' Group. In the performance condition he then proceeded:

> We are calling you this morning to ask if you would answer a number of questions about what household products you use so that we could have this information for our public service publication, "The Guide." Would you be willing to give us this information for our survey?

If the subject agreed, she was asked a series of eight innocuous questions dealing with household soaps (e.g., "What brand of soap do you use in your kitchen sink?") She was then thanked for her cooperation, and the contact terminated.

Another condition (agree-only) was run to assess the importance of actually carrying out the request as opposed to merely agreeing to it. The only difference between this and the performance condition was that, if the subject agreed to answer the questions, the experimenter thanked her, but said that he was just lining up respondents for the survey and would contact her if needed.

A third condition was included to check on the importance of the subject's greater familiarity with the experimenter in the two-contact conditions. In this condition the experimenter introduced himself, described the organization he worked for and the survey it was conducting, listed the questions he was asking, and then said that he was calling merely to acquaint the subject with the existence of his organization. In other words, these subjects were contacted, spent as much time on the phone with the experimenter as the performance subjects did, heard all the questions, but neither agreed to answer them nor answered them.

In all of these two-contact conditions some subjects did not agree to the requests or even hung up before the requests were made. Every subject who answered the phone was included in the analysis of the results and was contacted for the second request regardless of her extent of cooperativeness during the first contact. In other words, no subject who could be contacted the appropriate number of times was discarded from any of the four conditions.

The large request was essentially identical for all subjects. The experimenter called, identified himself, and said either that his group was expanding its survey (in the case of the two-contact conditions) or that it was conducting a survey (in the one-contact condition). In all four conditions he then continued:

The survey will involve five or six men from our staff coming into your home some morning for about two hours to enumerate and classify all the household products that you have. They will have to have full freedom in your house to go through the cupboards and storage places. Then all this information will be used in the writing of the reports for our public service publication, "The Guide."

If the subject agreed to the request, she was thanked and told that at the present time the experimenter was merely collecting names of people who were willing to take part and that she would be contacted if it were decided to use her in the survey. If she did not agree, she was thanked for her time. This terminated the experiment.

Results

Apparently even the small request was not considered trivial by some of the subjects. Only about two-thirds of the subjects in the performance and agree-only conditions agreed to answer the questions about household soaps. It might be noted that none of those who refused the first request later agreed to the large request, although as stated previously all subjects who were contacted for the small request are included in the data for those groups.

Our major prediction was that subjects who had agreed to and carried out a small request (performance condition) would subsequently be more likely to comply with a larger request than would subjects who were asked only the larger request (one-contact condition). As may be seen in Table 1, the results support the prediction. Over 50 per cent of the subjects in the performance condition agreed to the larger request, while less than 25 per cent of the one-contact condition agreed to it. Thus it appears that obtaining compliance with a small request does tend to increase subsequent compliance. The question is what aspect of the initial contact produces this effect.

One possibility is that the effect was produced merely by increased familiarity with the experimenter. The familiarization control was included to assess the effect on compliance of two contacts with the same person. The group had as much contact with the experimenter as the performance group, but no request was made during the first contact. As the table indicates, the familiarization group did not

Table 1 *Percentage of Subjects Complying with Large Request in Experiment I*

Condition	Per Cent
Performance	52.8
Agree-only	33.3
Familiarization	27.8*
One-contact	22.2**

Note. $N = 36$ for each group. Significance levels represent differences from the performance condition.
* $p < .07$.
** $p < .02$.

differ appreciably in amount of compliance from the one-contact group, but was different from the performance group ($\chi^2 = 3.70$, $p < .07$). Thus, although increased familiarity may well lead to increased compliance, in the present situation the differences in amount of familiarity apparently were not great enough to produce any such increase; the effect that was obtained seems not to be due to this factor.

Another possibility is that the critical factor producing increased compliance is simply agreeing to the small request (i.e., carrying it out may not be necessary). The agree-only condition was identical to the performance condition except that in the former the subjects were not asked the questions. The amount of compliance in this agree-only condition fell between the performance and one-contact conditions and was not significantly different from either of them. This leaves the effect of merely agreeing somewhat ambiguous, but it suggests that the agreement alone may produce part of the effect.

Unfortunately, it must be admitted that neither of these control conditions is an entirely adequate test of the possibility it was designed to assess. Both conditions are in some way quite peculiar and may have made a very different and extraneous impression on the subject than did the performance condition. In one case, a housewife is asked to answer some questions and then is not asked them; in the other, some man calls to tell her about some organization she has never heard of. Now, by themselves neither of these events might produce very much suspicion. But, several days later, the same man calls and asks a very large favor. At this point it is not at all unlikely that many subjects think they are being manipulated, or in any case that something strange is going on. Any such reaction on the part of the subjects would naturally tend to reduce the amount of compliance in these conditions.

Thus, although this first study demonstrates that an initial contact in which a request is made and carried out increases compliance with a second request, the question of why and how the initial request produces this effect remains unanswered. In an attempt to begin answering this question and to extend the results of the first study, a second experiment was conducted.

There seemed to be several quite plausible ways in which the increase in compliance might have been produced. The first was simply some kind of commitment to or involvement with the particular person making the request. This might work, for example, as follows: The subject has agreed to the first request and perceives that the experimenter therefore expects him also to agree to the second request. The subject thus feels obligated and does not want to disappoint the experimenter; he also feels that he needs a good reason for saying "no"—a better reason than he would need if he had never said "yes." This is just one line of causality—the particular process by which involvement with the experimenter operates might be quite different, but the basic idea would be similar. The commitment is to the particular person. This implies that the increase in compliance due to the first contact should occur primarily when both requests are made by the same person.

Another explanation in terms of involvement centers around the particular issue with which the requests are concerned. Once the subject has taken some action in connection with an area of concern, be it surveys, political activity, or highway safety, there is probably a tendency to become somewhat more concerned with the area. The subject begins thinking about it, considering its importance and relevance to him, and so on. This tends to make him more likely to agree to take further action in the same area when he is later asked to. To the extent that this is the critical factor, the initial contact should increase compliance only when both requests are related to the same issue or area of concern.

Another way of looking at the situation is that the subject needs a reason to say "no." In our society it is somewhat difficult to refuse a reasonable request, particularly when it is made by an organization that is not trying to make money. In order to refuse, many people feel that they need a reason—simply not wanting to do it is often not in itself sufficient. The person can say to the requester or simply to himself that he does not believe in giving to charities or tipping or working for political parties or answering questions or posting signs, or whatever he is asked to do. Once he has performed a particular task, however, this excuse is no longer valid for not agreeing to perform a similar task. Even if the first thing he did was trivial compared to the present request, he cannot say he never does this sort of thing, and thus one good reason for refusing is removed. This line of reasoning suggests that the similarity of the first and second requests in terms of the type of action required is an important factor. The more similar they are, the more the "matter of principle" argument is eliminated by agreeing to the first request, and the greater should be the increase in compliance.

There are probably many other mechanisms by which the initial request might produce an increase in compliance. The second experiment was designed in part to test the notions described above, but its major purpose was to demonstrate the effect unequivocally. To this latter end it eliminated one of the important problems with the first study which was that when the experimenter made the second request he was not blind as to which condition the subjects were in. In this study the second request was always made by someone other than the person who made the first request, and the second experimenter was blind as to what condition the subject was in. This eliminates the possibility that the experimenter exerted systematically different amounts of pressure in different experimental conditions. If the effect of the first study were replicated, it would also rule out the relatively uninteresting possibility that the effect is due primarily to greater familiarity or involvement with the particular person making the first request.

EXPERIMENT II

The basic paradigm was quite similar to that of the first study. Experimental subjects were asked to comply with a small request and were later asked a considerably larger request, while controls were asked only the larger request. The first request varied along two dimensions. Subjects were asked either to put up a small sign or to sign a petition, and the issue was either safe driving or keeping California beautiful. Thus there were four first requests: a small sign for safe driving or for beauty, and a petition for the two issues. The second request for all subjects was to install in their front lawn a very large sign which said "Drive Carefully." The four experimental conditions may be defined in terms of the similarity of the small and large requests along the dimensions of issue and task. The two requests were similar in both issue and task for the small-sign, safe-driving group, similar only in issue for the safe-driving-petition group, similar only in task for the small "Keep California Beautiful" sign group, and similar in neither issue nor task for the "Keep California Beautiful" petition group.

The major expectation was that the three groups for which either the task or the issue were similar would show more compliance than the controls, and it was also felt that when both were similar there would probably be the most compliance. The fourth condition (different issue-different task) was included primarily to assess the effect simply of the initial contact which, although it was not identical to the second one on either issue or task, was in many ways quite similar (e.g., a young student asking for cooperation on a noncontroversial issue). There were no clear expectations as to how this condition would compare to the controls.

Method

The subjects were 114 women and 13 men living in Palo Alto, California. Of these, 9 women and 6 men could not be contacted for the second request and are not included in the data analysis. The remaining 112 subjects were divided about equally among the five conditions (see Table 2). All subjects were contacted between 1:30 and 4:30 on weekday afternoons.

Two experimenters, one male and one female, were employed, and a different one always made the second contact. Unlike the first study, the experimenters actually went to the homes of the subjects and interviewed them on a face-to-face basis. An effort was made to select subject from blocks and neighborhoods that were as homogeneous as possible. On each block every third or fourth house was approached, and all subjects on that block were in one experimental condition. This was necessary because of the likelihood that neighbors would talk to each other about the contact. In addition, for every four subjects contacted, a fifth house was chosen as a control but was, of course, not contacted. Throughout this phase of the experiment, and in fact thoughout the whole experiment, the two experimenters did not communicate to each other what conditions had been run on a given block nor what condition a particular house was in.

The small-sign, safe-driving group was told that the experimenter was from the Community Committee for Traffic Safety, that he was visiting a number of homes in an attempt to make the citizens more aware of the need to drive carefully all the time, and that he would like the subject to take a small sign and put it in a window or in the car so that it would serve as a reminder of the need to drive carefully. The sign was 3 inches square, said "Be a safe driver," was on thin paper without a gummed backing, and in general looked rather amateurish and unattractive. If the subject agreed, he was given the sign and thanked; if he disagreed, he was simply thanked for his time.

The three other experimental conditions were quite similar with appropriate changes. The other organization was identified as the Keep California Beautiful Committee and its sign said, appropriately enough, "Keep California Beautiful." Both signs were simply black block letters on a white background. The two petition groups were asked to sign a petition which was being sent to California's United States Senators. The petition advocated support for any legislation which would promote either safer driving or keeping California beautiful. The subject was shown a petition, typed on heavy bond paper, with at least 20 signatures already affixed. If she agreed, she signed and was thanked. If she did not agree, she was merely thanked.

The second contact was made about two weeks after the initial one. Each experimenter was armed with a list of houses which had been compiled by the other experimenter. This list contained all four experimental conditions and the controls, and, of course, there was no way for the second experimenter to know which condition the subject had been in. At this second contact, all subjects were asked the same thing: Would they put a large sign concerning safe driving in their front yard? The experimenter identified himself as being from the Citizens for Safe Driving, a different group from the original safe-driving group (although it is likely that most subjects who had been in the safe-driving conditions did not notice the difference). The subject was shown a picture of a very large sign reading "Drive Carefully" placed in front of an attractive house. The picture was taken so that the sign obscured much of the front of the house and completely concealed the doorway. It was rather poorly lettered. The subject was told that: "Our men will come out and install it and later come and remove it. It makes just a small hole in your lawn, but if this is unacceptable to you we have a special mount which will make no hole." She was asked to put the sign up for a week or a week and a half. If the subject agreed, she was told that more names than necessary were being gathered and if her home were to be used she would be contacted in a few weeks. The experimenter recorded the subject's response and this ended the experiment.

Results

First, it should be noted that there were no large differences among the experimental conditions in the percentages of subjects agreeing to the first request. Although somewhat more subjects agreed to post the "Keep California Beautiful" sign and somewhat fewer to sign the beauty petition, none of these differences approach significance.

The important figures are the number of subjects in each group who agreed to the large request. These are presented in Table 2.

Table 2 *Percentage of Subjects Complying with Large Request in Experiment II*

	Task[a]			
Issue[a]	Similar	N	Different	N
Different	76.0**	25	47.8*	23
Similar	47.6*	21	47.4*	19
One-contact 16.7 ($N = 24$)				

Note. Significance levels represent differences from the one-contract condition.

[a] Denotes relationship between first and second requests.

* $p < .08$.

** $p < .01$.

The figures for the four experimental groups include all subjects who were approached the first time, regardless of whether or not they agreed to the small request. As noted above, a few subjects were lost because they could not be reached for the second request, and, of course, these are not included in the table.

It is immediately apparent that the first request tended to increase the degree of compliance with the second request. Whereas fewer than 20 per cent of the controls agreed to put the large sign on their lawn, over 55 per cent of the experimental subjects agreed, with over 45 per cent being the lowest degree of compliance for any experimental condition. As expected, those conditions in which the two requests were similar in terms of either issue or task produced significantly more compliance than did the controls (χ^2's range from 3.67, $p < .07$ to 15.01, $p < .001$). A somewhat unexpected result is that the fourth condition, in which the first request had relatively little in common with the second request, also produced more compliance than the controls ($\chi^2 = 3.40$, $p < .08$). In other words, regardless of whether or not the two requests are similar in either issue or task, simply having the first request tends to increase the likelihood that the subject will comply with a subsequent, larger request. And this holds even when the two requests are made by different people several weeks apart.

A second point of interest is a comparison among the four experimental conditions. As expected, the same issue-same task condition produced more compliance than any of the other two-contact conditions, but the difference is not significant (χ^2's range from 2.7 to 2.9). If only those subjects who agreed to the first request are considered, the same pattern holds.

DISCUSSION

To summarize the results, the first study indicated that carrying out a small request increased the likelihood that the subject would agree to a similar larger request made by the same person. The second study showed that this effect was quite strong even when a different person made the larger request, and the two requests were quite dissimilar. How may these results be explained?

Two possibilities were outlined previously. The matter-of-principle idea which centered on the particular type of action was not supported by the data, since the similarity of the tasks did not make an appreciable difference in degree of compliance. The notion of involvement, as described previously, also has difficulty accounting for some of the findings. The basic idea was that once someone has agreed to any action, no matter how small, he tends to feel more involved than he did before. This involvement may center around the particular person making the first request or the particular issue. This is quite consistent with the results of the first study (with the exception of the two control groups which as discussed previously were rather ambiguous) and with the similar-issue groups in the second experiment. This idea of involvement does not, however, explain the increase in compliance found in the two groups in which the first and second request did not deal with the same issue.

It is possible that in addition to or instead of this process a more general and diffuse mechanism underlies the increase in compliance. What may occur is a change in the person's feelings about getting involved or about taking action. Once he has agreed to a request, his attitude may change. He may become, in his own eyes, the kind of person who does this sort of thing, who agrees to requests made by strangers, who takes action on things he believes in, who co-operates with good causes. The change in attitude could be toward any aspect of the situation or toward the whole business of saying "yes." The basic idea is that the change in attitude need not be toward any particular issue or person or activity, but may be toward activity or compliance in general. This would imply that an increase in compliance would not depend upon the two contacts being made by the same person, or concerning the same issue or involving the same kind of action. The similarity could be much more general, such as both concerning good causes, or requiring a similar kind of action, or being made by pleasant, attractive individuals.

It is not being suggested that this is the only mechanism operating here. The idea of involvement continues to be extremely plausible, and there are probably a number of other possibilities. Unfortunately, the present studies offer no additional data with which to support or refute any of the possible explanations of the effect. These explanations thus remain simply descriptions of mechanisms which might produce an increase in compliance after agreement with a first request. Hopefully, additional research will test these ideas more fully and perhaps also specify other manipulations which produce an increase in compliance without an increase in external pressure.

It should be pointed out that the present studies employed what is perhaps a very special type of situation. In all cases the requests were made by presumably nonprofit service organizations. The issues in the second study were deliberately noncontroversial, and it may be assumed that virtually all subjects initially sympathized with the objectives of safe driving and a beautiful California. This is in strong contrast to campaigns which are designed to sell a particular product, political candidate, or dogma. Whether the technique employed in this study would be successful in these other situations remains to be shown.

SUMMARY

Two experiments were conducted to test the proposition that once someone has agreed to a small request he is more likely to comply with a larger request. The first study demonstrated this effect when the same person made both requests. The second study extended this to the situation in which different people made the two requests. Several experimental groups were run in an effort to explain these results, and possible explanations are discussed.

REFERENCES

Asch, S. E. Effects of group pressure upon the modification and distortion of judgments. In H. Guetzkow (Ed.), *Groups, leadership and men; research in human relations.* Pittsburgh: Carnegie Press, 1951. Pp. 177–190.

Bandura, A., Ross, D., & Ross, S. A. A comparative test of the status envy, social power, and secondary reinforcement theories of identificatory learning. *J. Abnorm. Soc. Psychol.*, 1963, **67**, 527–534.

Bruner, J. The dimensions of propaganda: German short-wave broadcasts to America. *J. Abnorm. Soc. Psychol.*, 1941, **36**, 311–337.

Deutsch, M., & Gerard, H. B. A study of normative and informational social influences upon individual judgment. *J. Abnorm. Soc. Psychol.*, 1955, **51**, 629–636.

Festinger, L., & Carlsmith, J. Cognitive consequences of forced compliance. *J. Abnorm. Soc. Psychol.*, 1959, **58**, 203–210.

Hovland, C. I., & Pritzker, H. A. Extent of opinion change as a function of amount of change advocated. *J. Abnorm. Soc. Psychol.*, 1957, **54**, 257–261.

Kelman, H. C., & Hovland, C. I. "Reinstatement" of the communicator in delayed measurement of opinion change. *J. Abnorm. Soc. Psychol.*, 1953, **48**, 327–335.

Schein, E. H., Schneier, I., & Barker, C. H. *Coercive pressure.* New York: Norton, 1961.

4.4 STUDIES IN FORCED COMPLIANCE: I. THE EFFECT OF PRESSURE FOR COMPLIANCE ON ATTITUDE CHANGE PRODUCED BY FACE-TO-FACE ROLE PLAYING AND ANONYMOUS ESSAY WRITING

J. Merrill Carlsmith
Barry E. Collins
Robert L. Helmreich

An encouragingly large body of literature has appeared in recent years which suggests that inducing a person to adopt a counterattitudinal position causes him to change his attitude in the direction of the position adopted. Unfortunately, there is a growing disagreement

Source: This research was supported by funds from the National Science Foundation. Reprinted with slight abridgment from the *Journal of Personality and Social Psychology*, 1966, 4, 1–13, with permission of the authors and the American Psychological Association, Inc.

concerning the relationship between the size of the incentive which is used to induce the person to adopt a counterattitudinal position and the amount of attitude change. The empirical question is straightforward: Does increasing the amount of incentive offered to a person to engage in counterattitudinal role playing *increase* or *decrease* the amount of attitude change which results from that role playing? Theoretically, there are two opposing predictions which correspond to each of the opposite empirical results.

DISSONANCE-THEORY PREDICTION

Dissonance theory (Festinger, 1957) predicts that the greater the inducement offered to the subject to adopt a position with which he does not agree, the less the resultant attitude change. The reasoning behind this prediction is spelled out in some detail by Festinger (Ch. 4) and by Festinger and Carlsmith (1959, pp. 203–204). Briefly, the argument goes as follows: The two cognitions "I believe *X*" and "I am publicly stating that I believe not *X*" are dissonant. However, all pressures, threats, and rewards which induce one to state that he believes "not *X*" are consonant with the cognition "I am publicly stating that I believe not *X*." Consequently, the greater the pressures, threats, or rewards, the more consonant cognitions the individual holds, and the lower the magnitude of the dissonance. Since one primary means of dissonance reduction in this situation is to change one's attitude in the direction "not *X*," it follows that the larger the reward for stating "not *X*," the *less* the resultant attitude change in that direction should be.

INCENTIVE OR REINFORCEMENT THEORY PREDICTION

On the other hand, various forms of "incentive theory" (Janis & Gilmore, 1965), "consistency theory" (Rosenberg, 1965), or "reinforcement theory" argue that the greater the incentives for the counterattitudinal role playing, the greater should be the resultant attitude change. Thus, advocates of this position state:

> . . . the significance of a reward received for writing a counterattitudinal essay . . . would be different from that claimed in dissonance theory: such a reward would, in proportion to its magnitude, be likely to have a positive effect both upon the development and the stabilization of the new cognitions. From this it would be predicted that with the removal of the biasing factors the degree of attitude change obtained after the subjects have written counter-

attitudinal essays will vary directly, rather than inversely, with the amount of reward [Rosenberg, 1965, p. 33].

. . . two separate kinds of mediation are . . . conceivable: the *expectation* of payment for counterattitudinal advocacy may operate as an incentive and thus affect the quality of the arguments advanced in support of new cognitions; the *receipt* of payment may operate as a reinforcement that further fosters the internalization of the counterattitudinal cognitions . . . [Rosenberg, 1965, p. 39].

[Janis and Gilmore, 1965, make a similar argument:] According to this "incentive" theory, when a person accepts the task of improvising arguments in favor of a point of view at variance with his own personal convictions, he becomes temporarily motivated to think up all the good positive arguments he can, and at the same time suppresses thoughts about the negative arguments which are supposedly irrelevant to the assigned task. This "biased scanning" increases the salience of the positive arguments and therefore increases the chances of acceptance of the new attitude position [pp. 17–18].

EMPIRICAL CONTROVERSY

Let us briefly review some of the experiments which have dealt with this question. The first such experiment was conducted by Kelman (1953), who asked seventh-grade students to write essays favoring one or another kind of comic book. Different subjects were offered different amounts of incentive to adopt the opposite position of the one they actually held. He found that, among subjects who complied with the request, there was more attitude change among those who were offered a low incentive than among those who were offered a high incentive. Although such a finding is in line with the prediction made by dissonance theory, the fact that many fewer subjects complied with the request in the low-incentive group than in the high-incentive group leaves open the possibility that self-selection may have affected the results. Also, since incentives were offered for compliance and for noncompliance, it is not always easy to identify the "high-incentive" conditions.

In order to check on this possibility, Festinger and Carlsmith (1959) carried out an experiment where the subject was offered varying amounts of money to publicly adopt a counterattitudinal position. Specifically, the subjects were requested to tell a waiting girl (actually a confederate) that an experiment that they had just participated in was interesting and exciting. (In fact, the experiment had been dull and boring.) Subjects were told that the experimenter's assistant, who usually performed this role, had unexpectedly failed to show up, and subjects were offered either $1 or $20 to perform this task, and to be on call for a possible similar task in the future. Festinger and Carlsmith found that subjects who had been paid only $1 changed their attitudes more in the direction of the position they had publicly advocated than did $20 subjects.

Although this finding provides good support for the dissonance-theory prediction, several criticisms have been directed toward the experiment. Most of these criticisms argue that the $20 inducement was inordinately large, and would produce guilt, suspicion, or some other reaction which would interfere with the attitude change. To counter this criticism, Cohen (Brehm & Cohen, 1962) carried out a similar experiment using smaller amounts of money. In this experiment, subjects were approached in their rooms by a fellow student who asked them to write an essay in favor of the actions of the New Haven police. (Most students privately disagreed with this position.) Subjects were offered $.50, $1, $5, or $10 for writing such an essay. After writing the essays the subjects' attitudes toward the police actions were assessed. Cohen's results fit closely with the dissonance-theory predictions; there was decreasing attitude change with increasing amounts of incentive for performing the counterattitudinal behavior. Taken together, the Festinger and Carlsmith and Cohen experiments support the empirical generality of the negative relationship between incentive and attitude change predicted by dissonance theory.

Several more recent experiments, however, have cast some doubt on the generality of the dissonance-theory interpretation of these results. In the first of these experiments (Janis & Gilmore, 1965) subjects were asked to write an essay which argued that all college students should be required to take an extra year of mathematics and of physics. In an attempt to show that the results obtained by Festinger and Carlsmith were due to the use of an "extraordinarily large reward of $20 [which] might have unintentionally generated some degree of suspicion or wariness," they repeated the use of $1 and $20 as rewards. They also added a variation in the sponsor of the project. In one case, the sponsor was described as a new publishing company, in the other as a research organization on the behalf of a number of universities. Unfortunately, they made two major changes in the offering of money, which prevents a direct comparison with the Festinger and Carlsmith experiment. Rather than offering subjects the money as payment *and* as a retainer for possible future work, they made no mention of any possible future work. In addition, whereas in the Festinger and Carlsmith study the money was offered for performing a task for which a sudden, unexpected, and pressing need had arisen, Janis and Gilmore offered this money for a task which was being done by several people, and which many other people might have done just as well. These two factors may have contributed to the fact that Janis and Gilmore report that their subjects perceived the money as a surprising and inappropriate payment.

Janis and Gilmore found that—with their technique of presentation—variations in monetary reward produced no differences in attitude change. Whether this failure to replicate is due to these changed techniques of presentation or due to suspicion and negative feelings is an empirical question.

The one finding that Janis and Gilmore do report is an interaction between role playing and sponsorship conditions. In the role-playing conditions, the public welfare sponsorship produced significantly more attitude change than did the commercial sponsorship; in the control conditions, there was no significant difference. Unfortunately, the role-playing subjects differed from the control subjects not only by virtue of the fact that they wrote an essay against their position, but also because they were given a few "general questions," for example, "Considering the type of career you are likely to be in, how might a background in physics and math enable you to function more adequately?" Such questions might well serve as a persuasive communication, and the difference between the sponsorship conditions would then be attributable to prestige or "demand" effects of the more positive sponsor.

The finding from Janis and Gilmore which is of major interest for our purposes here is the failure to find an effect of incentive on attitude change where the large incentive was designed especially to arouse suspicion. In a more recent experiment, Elms and Janis (1965) were able to detect some effects of incentive under similar circumstances—effects which tended to go in the opposite direction from that predicted by dissonance theory. Varying amount of incentive, nature of sponsorship, and presence or absence of role playing in a $3 \times 2 \times 2$ factorial, Elms and Janis asked subjects to write an anonymous essay advocating that qualified United States students should be sent to study in Russia for four years. The alleged sponsor of the research program was a private firm hired by the Soviet Embassy in one condition (negative sponsorship), while in the other condition the firm had been hired by the United States State Department (positive sponsorship). Subjects were paid $.50, $1.50, or $5 to write an essay counter to their position. Only one of the ten experimental groups showed significant attitude change. This was the group paid $10 under favorable sponsorship conditions. This group showed more attitude change than those subjects paid $.50. (However, the relationship is not linear. These $.50 subjects showed more—although not significantly—change than those subjects paid $1.50.) Under unfavorable sponsorship conditions, there were no significant effects. The $.50–$10 comparison for favorable sponsorship is the opposite of that predicted by dissonance theory, and is interpreted by Elms and Janis as being in support of "incentive theory."

Stronger evidence for increasing attitude change with increasing incentive is reported by Rosenberg (1965). His study, which is similar to Cohen's (Brehm & Cohen, 1962) study, asked subjects to write essays advocating that the Ohio State football team be banned from playing in the Rose Bowl (a strongly counterattitudinal position). Rosenberg changed Cohen's procedure by separating the "compliance inducer" from the posttester. The person who asked the subject to write the essay was not the same person as the experimenter who gathered the information on the subject's attitudes following the manipulation. In addition to a control condition, in which subjects wrote no counterattitudinal essay, there were three levels of reward for writing the essay—$.50, $1, and $5. The results of the experiment were exactly the opposite of Cohen's—the group paid $5 changed their attitudes much more than did the groups paid $.50 or $1, who in turn changed more than the control condition.

Unfortunately, the interpretation of these results must remain equivocal. As Nuttin (1964) points out:

> Rosenberg's study is, like most replications, not a "duplicate" of Cohen's study, but a very complex chain of interactions which are functionally more or less equivalent or similar to the ones Cohen investigated. Not only the attitude object itself but also the social status of the *E* and the experimental situation as a whole were quite different in both sudies. . . . Notwithstanding this, Rosenberg interprets his discrepant findings as due to *his* definition of the difference between the two experiments [pp. 4ff. for other critical discussion of Rosenberg's study].

The most recent study of this problem is a large experiment by Nuttin (1964), for which only preliminary results are available. Nuttin ran 20 experimental conditions in which he essentially attempted to replicate both studies, adding what he felt had been missing control groups in Rosenberg's study. The most clear-cut results he reports are on his replication of the Rosenberg study, where he finds exactly the opposite of what Rosenberg found. Thus, even when some degree of "perceptual separation" is maintained, Nuttin finds identical results to those of Cohen—the larger the incentive, the less the attitude change. However, Nuttin was unable to replicate the Festinger and Carlsmith results.

Since most of the criticisms which are applied to one individual study do not apply to the others, the meaning of all studies, in concert, is not clear. At the very least, these data suggest that the original formulation of the attitude-change process by Festinger and Carlsmith was incomplete. At the most, they suggest that the dissonance results were due to trivial artifacts. Because of the many differences in procedure among these various studies, it would be worthwhile to study differences in procedure which might have produced different results.

There are, of course, many differences, but let us turn our attention to just one. Contrast the Festinger and Carlsmith experiment with, say, that of Elms and Janis. In the study by Festinger and Carlsmith, the subject is asked to make a public statement (at least in front of one other person) which conflicts with his private belief. Furthermore, the person to whom he is making this statement is *unaware* that this is in fact in conflict with the private belief. Such a situation is certainly one in which dissonance would be aroused.

Consider on the other hand the position of the subject in the Elms and Janis experiment. He is being asked to write an essay in favor of a position which he does not agree with. He is assured that his essay will be kept anonymous—no one will ever know that he wrote it except the experimenter. And the experimenter—the only person to read the essay—knows full well that the essay does *not* express the subject's private opinion. The experimenter, in essence, is asking him whether he has the intellectual ability to see some arguments on the opposite side of the issue from that which he holds. It can be argued that writing such an essay will create no dissonance. Stated in an extreme form, the question is whether the cognition "I am, for good *reasons*, listing some arguments in favor of the position 'not-*X*' is dissonant with the cognition 'I believe *X*.'" It is plausible that, especially among college students, the cognition that one is listing such arguments is not at all dissonant with the cognition that one believes the opposite. Rather, the ability intellectually to adopt such a position is the hallmark of the open-minded and intellectual.

The argument in the paragraph above is not altogether different from the emphasis which Brehm and Cohen (1962) have placed on the role of commitment in the arousal of dissonance. A person who is merely writing arguments in favor of a position, but who has not committed himself to that position, would not experience dissonance *about the fact that he was writing arguments.* This is not to say that there may not be dissonance of some other kind, or that there may not be other nondissonance processes operating to produce attitude change as a result of writing these arguments. For example, insofar as the arguments he produces are good ones, there is dissonance aroused between the cognition—"This good argument in favor of not *X* exists" and the cognition "I believe *X*." This dissonance-theory process sounds quite similar to the incentive-theory process which Janis and Gilmore posit to explain attitude change produced by role playing. The point to be made here is that writing an anonymous essay may not produce dissonance *of the particular kind* studied by Festinger and Carlsmith, and that the predictions from dissonance theory about incentive effects may not be relevant in such situations.

In order to test this post hoc explanation, we attempted to design an experiment which would demonstrate that the results reported by Festinger and Carlsmith could be repeated under appropriate conditions, whereas the opposite kind of results might be expected under different conditions.

One further difference between experiments which have obtained results consistent with the dissonance-theory predictions and those experiments which have not has been the theoretical predilection of the experimenters. With the exception of the work of Nuttin, the results in line with dissonance-theory predictions have been obtained by experimenters who were to some extent identified with dissonance theory and who might be expected to "hope for" results consistent with dissonance theory. The converse has been true of experimenters who have obtained results inconsistent with dissonance theory. In light of the increasing interest in subtle effects of so-called "experimenter bias" (Rosenthal, 1963) we carried out the present experiment using two experimenters of different theoretical backgrounds. One of the experimenters (JMC) was presumably identified with a dissonance-theory approach; the other (BEC) was somewhat identified with a more behavioristic or reinforcement theory approach.

The basic design of the experiment to be reported here is a

2 × 2 × 4 factorial. Subjects were asked to adopt a counterattitudinal position in two very different ways. Half of the subjects were asked to lie to a confederate in a face-to-face confrontation. They were asked to tell a confederate that a decidedly dull task was, in fact, interesting—a manipulation essentially identical to that of Festinger and Carlsmith. The other half of the subjects were asked to write an anonymous essay in favor of the same position—an essay which would ostensibly be used to help the experimenter prepare another description which would then be presented to future subjects. Half of the subjects were run by each experimenter. Finally, experimental subjects were paid one of three different amounts of money for performing the task, while a control group was paid no additional money and performed no counterattitudinal responses.

METHOD

Subjects

An advertisement was placed in the local paper offering to pay high-school-age students (14–18) $2.50 for two hours of participation in a psychological experiment. When males called the listed number, they were given appointments for the experiment. Females were put on a "waiting list."

Two hundred and two male subjects participated in the experiment. A total of eleven subjects were eliminated from the reported results. Four subjects (two pairs of brothers) were discarded because, in the judgment of the experimenter administering the posttest, they did not comprehend the meaning of the eleven-point rating scale. Typically they expressed strong approval or disapproval and then chose a number on the opposite end of the scale. The posttester did not know which condition the subject was in, and, therefore, could not bias the results by selective elimination. Four more subjects (two $.50 role play, one $1.50 role play, and one $.50 essay) were discarded because they did not follow through on the assigned role play or essay. Typically they admitted the task was dull and stated that they had been asked to say it was interesting. Only one subject showed any detectable sign of suspicion, and he was eliminated before he took the posttest. One subject accidentally saw the confederate in conversation with one of the experimenters. Finally, one subject, when he heard from the confederate that her friend "told her it was kind of dull," called in the experimenter and suggested that the accomplice be assigned to a control group since she knew the task was dull.

The subjects were extremely heterogeneous. They ranged from those who could barely master the complexities of an eleven-point scale or could produce only 20 or 25 words of essay in ten minutes to numerous prep-school students and children from professional families. The sample included a substantial number of Negroes.

Setting and Personnel

The study was conducted in six rooms of the Yale Psycho-Educational Clinic over a three-week period. The five personnel conducting the experiment were the two principal investigators (BEC and JMC, who alternated as "project director" and "posttester"), a graduate assistant who served as experimenter (RLH), a receptionist, and a female high-school-age accomplice.

Overview of Design

The basic procedure was similar to that used by Festinger and Carlsmith (1959). Experimental subjects were asked either to write an essay or to tell a second, presumably naïve, subject that the experimental task was fun, interesting, exciting, and enjoyable. The subjects knew from their own experience with the task that it was dull and uninteresting. Subjects were paid an *additional* \$5, \$1.50, or \$.50 to role play or write the essay. Control subjects were paid no additional money and were not asked to role play or write an essay. One-half of the subjects were run with BEC as project director and JMC as posttester, and the other half were run with the roles reversed. Attitudes toward the experimental task were then measured in a posttest-only design. The accomplice rated the several dimensions of the role-play performance, and the transcripts of the role plays and the essays were rated on a number of variables by three judges.

Procedure

All Subjects: On arriving at the building, each subject was greeted by the receptionist who verified his age and high school status and conducted him to an experimental room furnished with desk, chairs, and writing materials. After the subject had waited alone for several minutes, the experimenter entered the room, introduced himself as Mr. Helmreich, and announced that he was ready to start the experiment. The experimenter then explained that the experiment itself would only take a little over an hour and that since subjects were being paid for two hours' participation, arrangements had been made for every subject to take part in a record survey being conducted in the building by a "man from some consumer research outfit in New York." At this point, the subject was presented with the experimental task—20 five-page booklets of random numbers. Each booklet had a cover sheet which instructed the subject to strike out each occurrence of two of the digits (e.g., 2s and 6s) contained in the booklet. The subject was told that he should work at a comfortable rate, correct mistakes, and continue working until stopped by the experimenter. The experimenter then explained that he would describe the purpose of the study when he stopped the subject on completion of the task. The subject was then left alone to work for an hour. The supply of booklets left with the subject was many times the number which could be completed in an hour. The task itself was designed to be so dull and repetitious that the subject would leave with a generally negative feeling.

At the end of an hour, the experimenter reentered the room and told the subject that he could stop as the experiment was completed. The experimenter then seated himself next to the subject and said he would explain the purpose of the study. The experimenter described the project as a large-scale study designed to investigate how a person's prior expectation of the nature of a task might affect the amount and accuracy of work performed. The subject was told that the project was investigating the best ways to describe routine tasks so that people would be motivated to work hard and accurately. Each subject was told that he was in a control condition and, therefore, had been given no expectation about how pleasant the task would be. He was told that his group would serve as the standard comparison for other groups which were given positive expectations.

At this point the explanations began to differ according to the experimental condition to which the subject was assigned. Four different procedures were used: role-play control, role-play experimental, essay control, and essay experimental.

Role-Play Control Subjects: Subjects in this condition were told that subjects in the other condition were introduced by the experimenter to a high school boy named Anderson who, presumably, had just finished the experimental task. In fact, continued the experimenter, the boy was paid by the experimenter to say the task was fun, interesting, exciting, and enjoyable. The experimenter remarked that after the paid assistant had been with a subject in the other condition two minutes, telling the subject how the experiment was fun, interesting, etc., the experimenter would return to the room, excuse the assistant, and start the subject on the same random-number task. The experimenter pointed out that a high-school-age assistant was necessary in order to make the description of the task plausible.

At this point, the experimenter asked if the subject had any questions concerning the purpose of the study. After dealing with any questions, the experimenter stated that the project director (BEC or JMC) would like to thank him. The experimenter then left the room and returned with the project director, who then gave the termination speech.

Role-Play Experimental Subjects: In this condition, as the experimenter was finishing the same description given to role-play control subjects and asking for questions, the project director knocked on the door, entered the room, excused himself, and asked the experimenter if he knew where Anderson was. After the experimenter replied that he had not seen him, the director remarked that a subject was waiting in a condition where he was supposed to be told that the task was fun and interesting. He then asked the experimenter if he knew how to get in touch with Anderson and received a negative reply. After a pause, the director asked the experimenter if the subject with him was finished. The experimenter replied that the subject had completed the task and that he was explaining the purpose of the study. The director then remarked that perhaps the subject could help them; that, as the experimenter had no doubt explained, Anderson had been hired to tell some of the waiting subjects that the task was fun, interesting, exciting, and enjoyable. The subject was told that he could help the director out of a jam by describing the task in those terms to a girl who was waiting to start the experiment. The director said that since he was in a bind, he could pay $.50 ($1.50, $5) for doing this job. After the subject agreed (every subject agreed to undertake the task), the experimenter was sent to obtain the proper amount of money and a receipt form. While the experimenter was gone, the director rehearsed the points (fun, interesting, exciting, enjoyable) that the subject was to make to the waiting confederate. After the experimenter returned, the subject took his money, signed a receipt, and was conducted by the director to another room where the female confederate was waiting, ostensibly to start the experiment.

The director told the confederate that the subject had just finished the experiment and that he would tell her something about it. He then left, saying he would be back in a couple of minutes. The girl said little until the subject made some positive remarks about the task, then remarked that a friend of hers had taken the test and had not said much about it except that it was rather dull. Most subjects attempted to counter this evaluation, and the accomplice listened quietly accepting everything the subject said about the task. The interaction between the subject and the accomplice was recorded on a concealed tape recorder.

After two minutes, the director returned to the room, told the accomplice that the experimenter would be in to get her started on the experiment, and led the subject from the room. The director then gave the termination speech common to all subjects.

Essay Control Subjects: Procedures in this condition were the same as in the role-play control condition except that subjects were told that subjects in the other condition read a short essay describing the task positively. The experimenter stated that after reading the essay, subjects in this other group were given the same random-number task. After answering any questions concerning the purpose of the study, the experimenter brought in and introduced the project director who gave the termination speech.

Essay Experimental Subjects: In this condition, subjects were treated in the same manner as essay controls until the project director was introduced. At this point the director seated himself beside the subject, stated that he had a problem and that the subject might be able to help. He remarked that, as the experimenter described, some subjects in other conditions read an essay describing the task as fun, interesting, exciting, and enjoyable. But he further commented that the experimenters were unhappy with this essay. The director felt that the essays were unsatisfactory because they did not sound like they had been written by high school students and that they did not have the perspective of someone who had taken the experiment. The experimenters had decided to write a new description of the task and felt that the best way to proceed would be to ask a few of the subjects to write positive descriptions of the task. He emphasized that no other subjects would read these essays because he would merely use them as sources of phrases and ideas for an essay which he, the director, would write. He then added that since they were "in a bind" he could pay the subject $.50 ($1.50, $5) to write a five- or ten-minute description of the task. After the subject agreed to do so (all subjects agreed to write the essay), the experimenter was sent to obtain the proper amount of money and a receipt form. While the experimenter was gone, the director rehearsed with the subject the points that he should make in the essay—that the task was fun, interesting, exciting, and enjoyable. After the experimenter returned, the subject took his money, signed a receipt, and followed the director to another office where he was given paper and pen and told to write for five or ten minutes. He was to press a buzzer which would notify the director when he was finished. The subject was then left alone, and an electric timer was started in the adjoining office. The subject stopped the timer when he pressed the buzzer to signify that he had finished the essay. If the subject had not completed the essay by the end of fifteen minutes, the director appeared in the room and told him that he had been working about fifteen minutes and should finish up in the next couple of minutes. If still working, subjects were told to stop at the end of seventeen minutes (1,000 seconds). After collecting the essay, the director gave the termination speech.

Termination Speech: (Indentical for all subjects.) While walking away from the experimental room, the director remarked that, as the experimenter had mentioned, a man from Consumer Research Associates had asked if he could have the subjects rate some records since the experiment did not last the full two hours. He stated that he did not know much about what the survey was about, but he would show the subjects where to go. As in the Festinger and Carlsmith (1959) study, the experimenter then stated, "I certainly hope you enjoyed the experiment. Most of our subjects tell us they did." He then directed the subject to the posttest room, thanked him, and made a strong request for secrecy about the experiment. It was clear to the subject that the experiment was over at this point.

Posttest: The subject then arrived at a comfortably appointed office labeled Consumer Research Associates on the door. As the subject entered the office, he was greeted by the posttester (BEC or JMC) who introduced himself as Ted Johnson of Consumer Research Associates. Johnson then ushered the subject into the office and seated him before a desk. Next to the desk was a portable record player equipped with stereo earphones. The desk itself was littered with papers bearing Consumer Research Associates' letterhead and titled "Teen Age Market Survey—Connecticut." Johnson introduced the posttest by saying that his company was interested in the type of music teen-agers listened to and the types of music they liked for specific activities. He added that this was important because teen-agers bought 68 per cent of the records sold in this country.

The subject was then asked to listen to a "practice" record for thirty seconds. Johnson then asked the subject to rate the practice record on several questions. He explained the use of an eleven-point scale running from -5 to $+5$ using a graphic illustration of the scale. The subject rated the record as to how much he liked it generally, how much he would like to listen to it on a date, how much he would like to dance to it, and how much he would like to study by it—each rating on the eleven-point scale. After the practice record, Johnson announced that they were ready to start the survey. As he started to hand the earphones to the subject he stated:

Oh. There is one thing I forgot. As you might imagine, the kind of mood you are in and the kind of experiences you have just had might influence the ratings you give in a situation like this. [The preceding spoken slowly to give the subject opportunity to agree.] If you had a splitting headache, you would not like much of anything we played through those earphones. [Subjects usually laughed—the volume was moderately high.] So I do want to ask you a question or two about that sort of thing. I don't know much about what they are doing up there, but would you say the test they had you working on was sort of pleasant or unpleasant? [slight pause] As a matter of fact, why don't we put it in terms of the same scale we used for the records? A minus 5 would be very unpleasant and a plus 5 would be very pleasant.

Since the subject had already used the rating scale for the practice record, the other five questions were covered quickly, and the subject immediately began to listen to the first "survey record." The word "test" was used in each question to make sure that the subjects were reacting to the experimental task only, and not the total experiment.

The six questions asked in the posttest were:

1. How pleasant did you find the test?
2. Was it an interesting test?
3. Did you learn anything from the test?
4. Would you recommend the test to a friend?
5. Would you describe the test as fun?
6. What is your general overall mood at the present time?

In each case a +5 represented a highly positive reaction and a −5 a strongly negative reaction. All subjects seemed convinced about the genuineness of the posttest; several hesitated to discuss the test because the project director had cautioned them to secrecy.

RESULTS

There are fifteen subjects in each of the four control groups, and eleven subjects in all but one of the twelve experimental groups. There are only ten subjects in the $.50, BEC, essay cell. The results can be discussed in three broad categories: the six questions in the posttest, measures evaluating the quality of the role-play performance and of the essays, and experimenter effects.

Posttest Variables

The mean response for each of the six questions in the posttest is shown in Table 1. Consider first the questions dealing with words the subject actually used while role playing or essay writing—"How interesting would you say the test was?" and "How much fun would you say the test was?" Table 1 shows that both essay and role-play control subjects found that the test, or random-number task, was uninteresting ($M = -1.2$) and not much fun ($M = -1.4$).

Table 1 *Means for Posttest Variables Collapsed over Experimenters*

	Control	\$.50	\$1.50	\$5
Interesting				
RP	−1.43	1.23	−0.86	−1.18
E	−1.00	−0.86	1.32	2.41
Fun				
RP	−1.43	0.76	−0.81	−1.10
E	−1.28	−0.80	1.62	1.55
Fun plus interesting				
RP	−2.71	1.81	−1.62	−2.19
E	−2.14	−1.80	3.24	3.95
Pleasant				
RP	0.77	1.18	0.82	1.55
E	0.93	0.86	2.14	2.55
Learn anything				
RP	−0.37	−0.50	−2.00	−0.32
E	−2.27	−0.10	−0.41	−0.64
Recommend				
RP	2.53	2.50	1.59	2.27
E	2.33	2.38	2.50	3.56
Mood				
RP	1.83	2.18	2.27	3.41
E	2.83	2.19	3.32	3.36

Note. Scores from single questions range from −5 (extremely negative toward the task) to +5 (extremely positive). Fun plus interesting can range from −10 to +10. RP = role play; E = essay.

Our major hypotheses concerned the differential effects of pressure for compliance in the role-playing and essay-writing situations. Specifically, it was anticipated that subjects who engaged in a face-to-face confrontation (role play) would show a *negative* relationship between money offered for the role playing and attitude change. Thus subjects offered \$.50 to role play should show maximal change, followed by subjects offered \$1.50, and then those offered \$5; the control subjects should, of course, be lowest.

Subjects who had written counterattitudinal essays, on the other hand, should show exactly the opposite trend. In this case, those subjects paid \$5 should be most positive toward the task, followed in order by subjects paid \$1.50, subjects paid \$.50, and control subjects. In other words, the hypothesis anticipates a *positive* relationship between attitude change and money for subjects who wrote essays.

Figures 1 and 2 reveal two facts. First, it can be seen that subjects who adopted a counterattitudinal position, whether this was done by publicly announcing the position or by privately writing an essay adopting the position, changed their attitudes to bring them into line with the counterattitudinal position. That is, they felt that the experiment had been relatively more fun and interesting than did control subjects.

Moreover, both hypotheses are strongly confirmed. The amount of money offered to adopt this counterattitudinal position had sharply different effects for role players and essay writers. When a subject is asked to publicly adopt a position which he does not privately believe in a face-to-face confrontation, he changes his attitude less if he is paid large amounts of money to adopt this position. Thus subjects paid \$5 thought that the experiment was much less interesting and fun than did subjects paid \$.50. An analysis of variance showed that the test for linear trend in the role-playing conditions was significant at the .05 level or better (see Table 2).

When a subject is asked to write a private essay which disagrees with his beliefs, however, the effect is exactly the opposite. The more the subject is paid to write this essay, the more his attitude changes in the direction of the position he is adopting. Thus, subjects paid \$5 thought the experiment was more fun and interesting than did subjects paid \$.50. Again an analysis of variance shows a significant linear trend in the hypothesized direction (see Table 2).

In general, essay subjects evidenced more attitude change. This finding should be interpreted with some caution, however. A glance at Figures 1 and 2 suggests that, if the study had used only \$.50 incentives, it would have been the role-play subjects who evidenced the most attitude change.

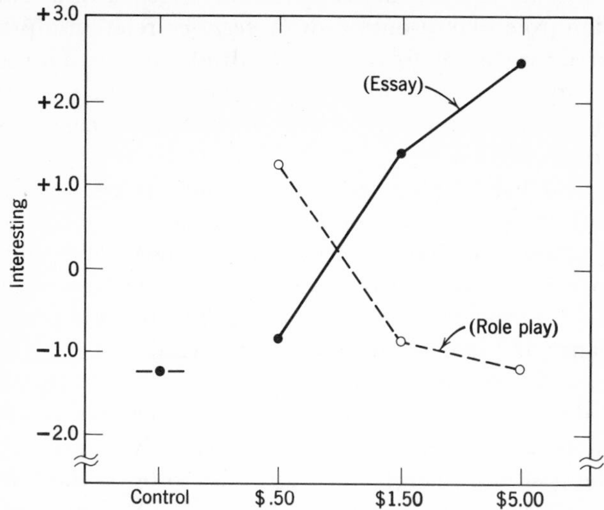

Figure 1. Responses to posttest question on "interesting." (The value drawn for the control group represents the average on all control groups.)

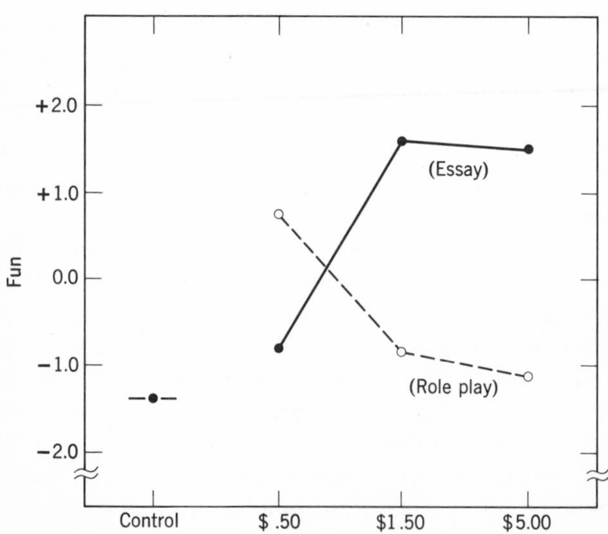

Figure 2. Responses to posttest question on fun. (The value drawn for the control group represents the average of all control groups.)

As can be seen from the last line in Table 2, the two a priori hypotheses and the role play-essay main effect account for most of the between-cell variance for fun and interesting. The fact that these three degrees of freedom (out of a total of 15) account for so much of the variance indicates the unimportance of experimenter main effects and higher-order interactions.

As Festinger and Carlsmith found, this effect seems to be quite specific to the particular words used in adopting the counterattitudinal position. When subjects were asked how pleasant the experiment had been, or how much they had learned from it, or whether they would recommend it to a friend, there were no effects in the role-playing conditions, and only one significant effect in the essay-writing condition (see Tables 1 and 2). Only the questions asking the subjects how interesting and how much fun the experiment had been seem to show the effects of role playing which are predicted.

Subjects were also asked to rate their general mood, and on this question an interesting trend appears. Although the effect of incentive is not significant for either essay-writing or role-playing subjects taken individually, the trend is identical in both cases, so that there is a significant main effect of money. As inspection of Table 1 shows, the more subjects were paid, the better the mood they were in at the end of the experiment, irrespective of whether they were paid to write essays or to engage in face-to-face role playing. Such an effect may seem hardly surprising for the subjects who wrote essays. Essay subjects said that they were in a better mood after they had been paid $5; they also said that the experiment had been more fun and more interesting.

However, subjects who had engaged in face-to-face role playing and were paid $5 said that they were in a better mood, but thought that the experiment had been *less* fun and *less* interesting than subjects paid $.50. Thus the results for essay-writing subjects might be interpreted as a simple generalization: they had been paid more money, were consequently in a better mood, and consequently rated the experiment as more fun and more interesting. Such a possible effect is, of course, impossible for the role-playing subjects. The more they were paid, the better the mood they were in, but the less they thought the experiment was fun and interesting. Such a finding is especially interesting in view of the interpretation of the results of Festinger and Carlsmith offered by several writers (e.g., Elms & Janis, 1965) which focuses on the hypothesis that subjects paid $20 failed to show attitude change because they felt anxious or guilty. Insofar as this question about mood can tap some of these presumed feelings, we find that

Table 2 *A Priori Hypotheses for Posttest Variables plus Main Effect for Role Play-Essay*

	Interesting	Fun	Fun plus Interesting	Pleasant	Learn Anything	Recom-mend	General Mood
Role play, rank-order linear trend	8.1**	5.4*	7.1*	<1	<1	<1	<1
Essay, rank-order linear trend	18.1***	13.6***	19.3***	8.5***	1.6	1.6	2.0
Role play versus essay (from Table 3)	5.0	4.0*	5.7*	2.7	<1	1.0	2.9
Percentage of between-cell variance contributed by three hypotheses	73	73	74	63	23	23	20

Note: Unweighted mean solution. Error term from Experimenter × Role Play-Essay × Money analysis (Table 3).

* $p < .05$.

** $p < .01$.

*** $p < .005$.

Table 3 *Experimenter, Role Play-Essay, and Money Standard Analyses (2 × 2 × 4 Analysis of Variance)*

Source	*df*	Interesting	Fun	Fun plus Interesting	Pleasant	Learn Anything	Recom- mend	Mood
Role play versus essay	1	5.05*	3.98*	5.73*	2.69	<1	1.02	2.90
Money	3	3.05*	2.90*	3.42*	2.60	<1	<1	3.17*
Interaction	3	7.04**	4.74**	7.15**	1.28	1.60	<1	<1
MS_e		9.91	9.75	31.64	5.14	15.67	10.05	4.22
df error		175	167[a]	167[a]	175	175	175	175

Note: Since none of the experimenter main effects and none of the experimenter interactions reached the .05 level (only 1 of 28 reached the .10 level), they have been omitted from the table. The unweighted mean solution was used.

[a] The fun measure was not included in the posttest until 8 subjects (all in different cells) had been run. Consequently the *N* for fun and for fun plus interesting is only 183.

* $p < .05$.

** $p < .01$.

contrary to this hypothesis, the more subjects are paid for performing a task like this, the better they feel.

Role-Play and Essay Performance

Evidence on the subjects' actual performances was gathered when all three authors independently rated the essays and transcripts of the role plays. Transcriptions of role-play performance were rated on the following six scales:

1. Persuasiveness and emphasis before the accomplice remarks that she has heard the task is dull.
2. Persuasiveness and emphasis after remark.
3. Overall positiveness.
4. Overall persuasiveness and conviction.
5. Percent of time spent on assigned topic.
6. Dissociation of self from content of message.

Ratings by the accomplice are also available on role-play subjects for the first four scales and for:

5. Apparent conflict.
6. Signs of discomfort.

Essays were rated on the following four scales:

1. Emphasis used in making points.
2. The extent to which the subject went beyond the statements given and created reasons in support of his general theme.
3. Overall quality and persuasiveness.
4. Apparent effort (with an attempt to control for ability).

It was anticipated that, if any differences were found at all, high incentives should improve the quality of both role-play and essay performance. (Control groups were, of course, omitted from all analyses, and separate analyses were performed for essay and role-play measures.) The interjudge reliabilities were typically in the 70s and 80s, and the various performance measures were highly correlated among themselves. None of these ratings of role-play transcripts showed even a .10 trend in any analysis of variance. Similarly, evaluations of the content of the essays show no glimmer of a difference among treatment groups. Also, there is no evidence that any of the measures of role-play or essay performance were correlated with posttest attitudes. According to the ratings made by the accomplice, role-play subjects showed highest conflict when they were paid only \$.50 (the $F = 5.58$, $p < .01$, for the 2×3 Experimenter $\times$ Money analysis of variance). But this is the only "quality of performance" accomplice rating which shows any sign of a money effect.

Experimenter Effects

The results from the two experimenters are remarkably similar. The *F*s for experimenter main effects and experimenter interactions are, in general, smaller than might be expected by chance. There are two variables, however, which produced significant experimenter effects: the accomplice's ratings of conflict (necessarily for role-play subjects only since it is an accomplice rating) and the "number of words used once" measure. According to the accomplice's ratings of conflict, subjects run by BEC indicated more conflict than those run by JMC ($p < .05$). Since the role play occurred before the subject met the posttester, we can safely assume the effect was created in the experimental manipulations and not in the posttest. Posttest attitudes show no parallel trend.

Subjects were told to use four words: interesting, exciting, enjoyable, and fun. Each role play and essay was scored for the number of these words which were used at least once. Both role-play ($p < .05$) and essay ($p < .01$) subjects run by BEC used more words than subjects run by JMC in both conditions. This effect is easily understood in terms of the heavier emphasis placed on the four words by BEC. In contrast to JMC, he asked the subjects to repeat the words back to him after he had stated them to the subjects. For the *role-play subjects only*, subjects run by JMC tended to use more words in high-incentive conditions, while BEC's subjects show no such trend (interaction $p < .05$). The attitude data show no patterns similar to any of those revealed by the number of words measure.

DISCUSSION

As can be seen in Figures 1 and 2, the major hypotheses from the study have been dramatically confirmed. There is one set of circumstances where increasing pressure for compliance leads to smaller amounts of attitude change. A subject who was enticed to make a patently false statement before a peer who believed the subject was sincere showed less attitude change with increased pressure for compliance. Figures 1 and 2 clearly indicate that the comparison between the \$.50 group and the \$1.50 group is the more crucial for role-play subjects. The highly significant difference between these two relatively small rewards represents a very strong replication of the original

Festinger and Carlsmith study. These results, taken in conjunction with those of Cohen (Brehm & Cohen, 1962), make it highly unlikely that the original Festinger and Carlsmith result is an artifact of the unusual magnitude of the $20 reward.

It is equally clear, however, that there is another set of circumstances in which increasing pressure for compliance produces more attitude change. A subject who wrote an anonymous essay (to be read only by the experimenter) showed more attitude change with increasing pressure for compliance. This dramatic interaction is quite consistent with the theory outlined in the introduction.

The results for the experimenter manipulation are also encouraging. The two experimenters produced remarkably similar effects. It is clearly the case that the differing theoretical orientations of the experimenters—and their somewhat different expectations about the outcomes—had no effect whatsoever on attitude change.

What remains unspecified, however, is the crucial difference between the role-play and essay-writing conditions. The following list describes just a few of the many components in the complex manipulation used in this study: The essays were written while the role plays were oral; the role-play sessions lasted for a maximum of two minutes while the essay sessions lasted for a maximum of seventeen minutes; as a result of the differing justifications used to entice compliance, role-play subjects performed under somewhat more "hectic" or "crisis" circumstances than essay subjects; finally, if looked at from the subjects' perspective, the social consequences or implications of the compliant act differed greatly between the two conditions. In the essay condition, the only reader of the essays would be the experimenter, who understood why the essay had been written. In the role-play condition, however, the audience—the experimental accomplice—presumably believed that the subject was sincere when he said that the task was fun, interesting, exciting, and enjoyable. It seems quite clear that the latter condition is more dissonance producing.

What is unclear from dissonance theory, however, is why the essay condition should show an *increasing* amount of attitude change with increased incentive. If there is no dissonance at all produced in the essay condition, then the different incentives should have no effect on attitude change—there should, in fact, be no attitude change. If the amount of effort is greater for high-incentive subjects, then dissonance theory can predict a positive relationship between the amount of incentive and attitude change. *If* subjects in the high-incentive conditions exerted more effort, then this greater effort should lead to greater dissonance in the high-incentive conditions, and, consequently, greater attitude change. A long and careful examination of both essays and role-play performance, however, unearthed no evidence whatsoever that the high-incentive essays were in any way superior. The fact that the finished product in the high-incentive condition is not better, of course, does not imply that the students did not try harder. Subjects were given four words to repeat, and there was little else that they could do other than repeat the four words and include them in complete sentences. It is possible that an increased effort in the high-incentive condition would not be reflected in higher quality essays.

It is probably necessary to turn somewhere other than dissonance theory for an explanation of the positive relationship between pressure for compliance and attitude change. One very plausible explanation of our results for the essay-writing subjects is a simple generalization phenomenon. We know that the more subjects were paid the better the mood they were in. It would not be surprising if this good mood generalized to the task they had been doing, so that they would report that the task had been more fun and interesting. This explanation would assume that in the role-playing conditions, this tendency to generalize was overcome by the dissonance produced.

Alternatively, it is possible that the theoretical orientation proposed by Hovland (Hovland, Lumsdaine, & Sheffield, 1949) and Janis (Janis & Gilmore, 1965) is needed in order to explain the attitude change in the essay condition. But, as we understand them, these theories also must predict that the performance in the high-incentive condition will be superior in some way to the performance in low-pressure conditions. Nor do they make clear why the opposite effect should be found in the role-play conditions.

One final point should be made about the sensitivity of the incentive manipulation. A quick glance at Figures 1 and 2 indicates that the results would have appeared quite different had the $.50 group been omitted. There would have been no incentive effects for either essay or role-play subjects, and there would have remained only the main effect indicating that essay subjects showed more attitude change than role-play subjects.

Finally, it should be noted that our results for the role-playing subjects are consistent with several other experiments using different techniques for varying pressure for compliance. Studies on the use of strong or weak threats to induce counterattitudinal behavior (Aronson & Carlsmith, 1963; Freedman, 1965; Turner & Wright, 1965) have consistently shown more attitude change when weaker pressures are applied for compliance. Another kind of evidence comes from experiments by Freedman (1963) in which he shows more attitude change when little justification is provided for the counterattitudinal behavior than when high justification is provided.

SUMMARY

One-half of the experimental *S*s (male high school students) were enticed to tell the next *S* (a female accomplice) that the experimental task was interesting, exciting, fun, and enjoyable (when, in fact, it was quite dull). The other half of the experimental *S*s wrote an anonymous essay to the same effect. Experimental *S*s were paid an additional $.50, $1.50, or $5 for this counterattitudinal response. Control *S*s merely worked on the experimental task and completed the posttest. The data from the face-to-face condition replicates the original Festinger and Carlsmith experiment; small amounts of money were most effective in convincing *S*s that the task was really fun and interesting. Data from the essay condition, however, indicated just the opposite. Large amounts of money produce the most attitude change.

REFERENCES

Aronson, E., & Carlsmith, J. M. Effect of the severity of threat on the devaluation of forbidden behavior. *J. Abnorm. Soc. Psychol.*, 1963, **66**, 584–588.

Brehm, J. W., & Cohen, A. R. *Explorations in cognitive dissonance.* New York: Wiley, 1962.

Elms, A., & Janis, I. Counter-norm attitudes induced by consonant versus dissonant conditions of role-playing. *J. Exptl. Res. Pers.*, 1965, **1**, 50–60.

Festinger, L. *A theory of cognitive dissonance.* Stanford: Stanford Univ. Press, 1957.

Festinger, L., & Carlsmith, J. M. Cognitive consequences of forced compliance. *J. Abnorm. Soc. Psychol.*, 1959, **58**, 203–210.

Freedman, J. L. Attitudinal effects of inadequate justification. *J. Pers.*, 1963, **31**, 371–385.

Freedman, J. L. Long-term behavior effects of cognitive dissonance. *J. Exptl. Soc. Psychol.*, 1965, **1**, 145–155.

Hovland, C. I., Lumsdaine, A. A., & Sheffield, F. D. *Experiments on mass communication.* Princeton: Princeton Univ. Press, 1949.

Janis, I. L., & Gilmore, J. B. The influence of incentive conditions on the success of role playing in modifying attitudes. *J. Pers. Soc. Psychol.*, 1965, **1**, 17–27.

Kelman, H. C. Attitude change as a function of response restriction. *Hum. Relat.*, 1953, **6**, 185–214.

Nuttin, J. M., Jr. Dissonant evidence about dissonance theory. Paper read at Second Conference of Experimental Social Psychologists in Europe, Frascati, Italy, 1964.

Rosenberg, M. J. When dissonance fails: On eliminating evaluation apprehension from attitude measurement. *J. Pers. Soc. Psychol.*, 1965, **1**, 28–42.
Rosenthal, R. On the social psychology of the psychological experiment: The experimenter's hypothesis as unintended determinant of experimental results. *Am. Sci.*, 1963, **51**, 268–283.
Turner, E. A., & Wright, J. C. Effects of severity of threat and perceived availability on the attractiveness of objects. *J. Pers. Soc. Psychol.*, 1965, **2**, 128–132.

4.5 MODIFICATION OF PSYCHO-PHYSICAL JUDGMENTS AS A METHOD OF REDUCING DISSONANCE

Paul R. Wilson
Paul N. Russell

Experimental evidence offered in support of the theory of cognitive dissonance has been critically evaluated by Chapanis and Chapanis (1964). One inadequacy of research in this area, they suggest, is the overcomplexity of experimental manipulations. The present investigation sought to test deductions from dissonance theory in the simplest possible experimental setting, and where a minimum of measurement assumptions was necessary. In the experiment subjects were required to estimate the vertical height they lifted a heavy and a light weight. Both weights were in fact lifted to the same height. It was predicted from dissonance theory that subjects would underestimate the height they lifted a heavy weight when given little remuneration relative to the height they lifted a light weight when given greater remuneration. The question is: Do subjects modify psychophysical judgments when attempting to reduce dissonance?

METHOD

Subjects

Thirty male and thirty female students, waiting to enroll for introductory courses in psychology or sociology at the University of Canterbury, served as subjects. All were right-handed.

Source: This research was supported by a grant from the University of Canterbury, Christchurch, New Zealand. Reprinted from the *Journal of Personality and Social Psychology*, 1966, 3, 710–712, with permission of the authors and the American Psychological Association, Inc.

Apparatus

The apparatus consisted of a box 3 × 2 feet and 2 feet high with two handles one foot apart on the top, and with a smooth strip of wood running along its top front edge. One of the handles was connected by a rope to a seven-pound weight while the other was connected by a rope to a weight weighing one pound. Both handles could be pulled to a height of exactly 18 inches. When the subject was seated in front of the apparatus, the handles were at arm's length which made a lift of seven pounds quite difficult.

Procedure

A total of sixty subjects were assigned randomly to three groups each consisting of ten males and ten females. Group A received one shilling (approximately 14 cents) for lifting a one-pound weight and a penny (approximately 1.2 cents) for lifting a seven-pound weight while Group B was given one shilling for lifting the heavy weight and one penny for the light weight. Group C received no remuneration. The subjects' task in each group is best explained by the instructions given to them. In all three groups, each subject, upon entering the experimental room, was asked to sit down in front of the apparatus and read the following typewritten instructions handed to him.

> The experiment you are going to do is one on motor control. On the top of the box in front of you there are two handles. You have to pull with your left hand each of the handles in turn. When you hear the word "start" put on the goggles provided, which act as a blindfold. When you hear the word "left" pull the handle on the lefthand side of the box as far as it will go. When you hear the word "right" pull the handle on the righthand side of the box as far as it will go. Do not attempt to pull the handles too suddenly.
>
> After you have pulled each handle put it down and partly take off your goggles so that you can see. You will then receive a sum of money, which you can keep, so put the money in your pocket. Put your goggles back on and then put your right hand on the edge of the smooth piece of wood which runs across the front of the box. Run your hand along this piece of wood as far as you think you lifted the handle. Indicate with your forefinger your judgment.
>
> The experimenter will tell you when you have finished the experiment. The experiment will only take about five minutes. When you have read and fully understood these instructions say "ready." Then listen for the word "start."

Because Group C received no remuneration their instructions were slightly modified by omitting ". . . and partly take off your goggles. . . . Put your goggles back on . . ." from the above instructions.

Five trials were run for each subject; that is, every subject lifted each weight five times. It was expected that the disproportionate reward-effort relationship in Group A would create dissonance within the subjects. These subjects could reduce dissonance by underestimating the height they lifted the heavy weight relative to the light. In Group B reward was in proportion to effort so no dissonance should be created, while Group C received no reward so no reward-effort dissonant cognitions should exist.

In all three conditions goggles were worn throughout the experiment to stop the subjects obtaining visual cues when making estimations on the smooth strip of wood. To reduce kinesthetic cues the subjects alternated the end of the strip of wood from which they began to make their estimations. In all three conditions the order of lifting weights was reversed; that is, in Conditions A, B, and C half the subjects lifted the light weight before the heavy while the remaining half lifted the heavy before the light.

RESULTS

Each subject made five estimations of the vertical distance he lifted each weight. The difference in these estimations was found for each subject on every trial by subtracting the height-lifted estimation for the heavy weight from that for the light weight. All measurements of height estimations are expressed as the number of .25-inch units.

These differences were treated by a four-way analysis of variance with repeated observations on one factor (trials), a summary of which is given in Table 1 (Winer, 1962, pp. 337–353). The results under the three different reward conditions are significantly different beyond the 2.5 per cent level.

Table 2 gives mean differences in estimations for the three reward groups. The mean difference for Group A is larger than that for Groups B and C. A positive difference means that the estimated height lifted for the light weight was greater than that for the heavy weight. Absence of a significant Reward Conditions $\times$ Trials interaction and Reward Conditions $\times$ Order interaction indicate that the Group A subjects' differences in height-lifted estimations for the two weights are greater than those for Groups B and C irrespective of trials and order.

Table 1 *Analysis of Variance of Differences between Height-Lifted Estimations for Heavy and Light Weights*

Source	*df*	*MS*	*F*
Between Subjects	59		
Reward conditions (A)	2	1146.9	5.04**
Sex (B)	1	693.1	3.04
Order (C)	1	304.0	1.3
A × B	2	5.5	<1
A × C	2	114.6	<1
B × C	1	130.7	<1
A × B × C	2	268.8	1.18
Subjects within groups	48	227.7	
Within subjects	240		
Trials (D)	4	190.5	1.90
A × D	8	93.1	<1
B × D	4	210.9	2.1
C × D	4	172.5	1.72
A × B × D	8	173.6	1.73
B × C × D	4	246.6	2.45*
A × C × D	8	65.4	<1
A × B × C × D	8	179.4	1.79
D × Subjects within groups	192	100.0	

* $p < .05$.
** $p < .025$.

Table 2 *Mean Difference between Heavy and Light Weight Height-Lifted Estimations (Heavy Weight Height Estimation Subtracted from Light Weight Estimation)*

	M (number of .25-inch units)
Reward disproportionate to effort	5.56
Reward in proportion to effort	0.91
No reward	−1.03

The only other significant *F* is the Sex × Order × Trials interaction which is significant at the .05 level. A graphing of this showed that female differences in light and heavy weight height-lifted estimations are slightly greater than the corresponding male values for both the heavy-light and light-heavy lifting orders on the first three trials.

Thereafter the female light-heavy and heavy-light orders diverge with the heavy-light order showing the light weight height-lifted estimation to be considerably greater. Differences in male height-lifted estimations for the two weights are less variable and fluctuate about the zero difference level for both orders on all trials. This interaction does not concern differences in the three reward conditions and is thus irrelevant to deductions from dissonance theory. No explanation for it is thought necessary here.

DISCUSSION

It appears that dissonance was aroused in one group of subjects (Group A) by rewarding them with more money for lifting a light weight than a heavy weight they lifted the same height. We hypothesized that Group A would reduce dissonance by underestimating the height they lifted the heavy weight relative to the height they lifted the light weight. In other words, they would reduce dissonance by behaving as though they did not have to pull the heavy weight as far as they had to pull the light weight and thus justifying to themselves, partially at least, the disproportionate reward-effort relationship. Results show that this underestimation is significantly greater for Group A than for the Control Groups B and C who, respectively, received reward in proportion to effort and no reward.

However, many subjects spontaneously reported that they lifted the two weights the same height. Furthermore, they said they could not see what effect the money had on their estimations. Despite this, reward has clearly affected their estimations. Dissonance reduction appears to operate without the subjects' being aware of its occurrence.

The order in which the heights were lifted did not reduce the dissonance effect nor was there any lessening of dissonance over successive trials. The dissonance may disappear if more than five trials are given, for in time subjects would come to expect a disproportionate reward situation or to learn that one gets little money for a lot of effort in this particular setting.

To conclude, this study shows that psychophysical judgments can be modified when subjects attempt to reduce dissonance. It also suggests that experiments involving psychophysical judgments can provide a useful setting for some social psychological research. The main advantage of this type of situation appears to lie in the ease of measurement and the degree to which relevant variables can be isolated and controlled.

SUMMARY

Dissonance reduction was measured in a situation requiring psychophysical judgments. Sixty *S*s estimated the height they lifted a heavy and a light weight which were both lifted the same vertical distance. Dissonance was aroused in twenty *S*s by rewarding them little money for lifting a heavy weight and relatively more money for a considerably lighter weight. A further twenty *S*s received reward in proportion to the weight lifted while the remaining twenty *S*s were not rewarded. It was hypothesized that *S*s who received reward disproportionate to weight lifted would reduce dissonance by underestimating the distance they lifted the heavy weight relative to the light. Results support the hypothesis.

REFERENCES

Chapanis, N. P., & Chapanis, A. Cognitive dissonance: Five years later. *Psychol. Bull.*, 1964, **61**, 1–22.

Winer, B. J. *Statistical principles in experimental design*. New York: McGraw-Hill, 1962.

4.6 TOWARD AN UNDERSTANDING OF INEQUITY

J. Stacy Adams

Equity, or more precisely, inequity, is a pervasive concern of industry, labor, and government. Yet its psychological basis is probably not fully understood. Evidence suggests that equity is not merely a matter of getting "a fair day's pay for a fair day's work," nor is inequity simply a matter of being underpaid. The fairness of an exchange between employee and employer is not usually perceived by the former purely and simply as an economic matter. There is an element of relative

Source: Reprinted with slight abridgment from the *Journal of Abnormal and Social Psychology*, 1963, **67**, 422–436, with permission of the author and the American Psychological Association, Inc.

justice involved that supervenes economics and underlies perceptions of equity or inequity (Homans, 1961; Jaques, 1956, 1961a, 1961b; Patchen, 1961; Stouffer, Suchman, DeVinney, Star, & Williams, 1949; Zaleznik, Christensen, & Roethlisberger, 1958).

The purpose of this paper is to present a theory of inequity, leading toward an understanding of the phenomenon and, hopefully, resulting in its control. Whether one wishes to promote social justice or merely to reduce economically disadvantageous industrial unrest, an understanding of inequity is important. In developing the theory of inequity, which is based upon Festinger's (1957) theory of cognitive dissonance and is, therefore, a special case of it, we shall describe major variables involved in an employee-employer exchange, before we proceed to define inequity formally. Having defined it, we shall analyze its effects. Finally, such evidence as is available will be presented in support of the theory. Throughout we shall emphasize some of the simpler aspects of inequity and try to refrain from speculating about many of the engaging, often complex, relationships between inequity and other phenomena, and about what might be termed "higher order" inequities. In the exposition that follows we shall also refer principally to wage inequities, in part because of their importance and in part because of the availability of methods to measure the marginal utility of wages (Adams, 1961; Jeffrey & Jones, 1961). It should be evident, however, that the theoretical notions advanced are relevant to any social situation in which an exchange takes place, whether the exchange be of the type taking place between man and wife, between football teammates, between teacher and student, or even, between Man and his God.

Whenever two individuals exchange anything, there is the possibility that one or both of them will feel that the exchange was inequitable. Such is frequently the case when a man exchanges his services for pay. On the man's side of the exchange are his education, intelligence, experience, training, skill, seniority, age, sex, ethnic background, social status, and, very importantly, the effort he expends on the job. Under special circumstances other attributes will be relevant: personal appearance or attractiveness, health, possession of an automobile, the characteristics of one's spouse, and so on. They are what he perceives are his contributions to the exchange, for which he expects a just return. Homans (1961) calls them "investments." These variables are brought by him to the job. Henceforth they will be referred to as his *inputs*. These inputs, let us emphasize, are *as perceived by their con-*

tributor and are not necessarily isomorphic with those of the other party to the exchange. This suggests two conceptually distinct characteristics of inputs, *recognition* and *relevance*.

The possessor of an attribute, or the other party to the exchange, or both, may recognize the existence of the attribute in the possessor. If either the possessor or both members of the exchange recognize its existence, the attribute has the potentiality of being an input. If only the nonpossessor recognizes its existence it cannot be considered psychologically an input so far as the possessor is concerned. Whether or not an attribute having the potential of being an input is an input, is contingent upon the possessor's perception of its relevance to the exchange. If he perceives it to be relevant, if he expects a just return for it, it is an input. Problems of inequity arise if only the possessor of the attribute considers it relevant in the exchange. Crozier[1] relates an observation that is apropos. Paris-born bank clerks worked side by side with other clerks who did identical work and earned identical wages, but were born in the Provinces. The Parisians were dissatisfied with their wages, for they considered that Parisian breeding was an input deserving monetary compensation. The bank management, while recognizing that place of birth distinguished the two groups, did not, of course, consider birthplace relevant in the exchange of services for pay.

The principal inputs listed earlier vary in type and in their degree of relationship to one another. Some variables, such as age, are clearly continuous; others, such as sex and ethnicity, are not. Some are intercorrelated, seniority and age, for example; sex, on the other hand, is largely independent of the other variables, with the possible exception of education and some kinds of effort. Although these intercorrelations, or the lack of them, exist in a state of nature, it is probable that the individual cognitively treats all input variables as independent. Thus, for example, if he were assessing the sum of his inputs, he might well "score" age and seniority separately.

On the other side of the exchange are the rewards received by an individual for his services. These *outcomes*, as they will be termed, include pay, rewards intrinsic to the job, seniority benefits, fringe benefits, job status and status symbols, and a variety of formally and informally sanctioned perquisites. An example of the latter is the right of higher-status persons to park their cars in privileged locations, or the right to have a walnut rather than a metal desk. Seniority, men-

[1] M. Crozier, personal communication, 1960.

tioned as an input variable, has associated with it a number of benefits such as job security, "bumping" privileges, greater fringe benefits, and so on. These benefits are outcomes and are distinguished from the temporal aspects of seniority (that is, longevity), which are properly inputs. As in case of job inputs, job outcomes are often intercorrelated. For example, greater pay and higher job status are likely to go hand in hand.

In a manner analogous to inputs, outcomes are *as perceived*, and, again, we should characterize them in terms of recognition and relevance. If the recipient or both the recipient and giver of an outcome in an exchange recognize its existence, it has the potentiality of being an outcome psychologically. If the recipient considers it relevant to the exchange and it has some marginal utility for him, it *is* an outcome. Not infrequently the giver or "buyer," to use economic terms, may give or yield something which, perhaps at some cost to him, is either irrelevant or of no marginal utility to the recipient. An employer may give an employee a carpet for his office in lieu, say, of a salary increment and find that the employee is dissatisfied, perhaps because in the subculture of that office a rug has no meaning, no psychological utility. Conversely, a salary increment may be inadequate, if formalized status recognition was what was wanted and was what had greater utility.

In classifying some variables as inputs and others as outcomes, it is not implied that they are independent, except conceptually. Job inputs and outcomes are, in fact, intercorrelated, but imperfectly so. Indeed, it is because they are imperfectly correlated that we need at all be concerned with job inequity. There exist normative expectations of what constitute "fair" correlations between inputs and outcomes. The bases of the expectations are the correlations obtaining for a reference person or group—a co-worker or colleague, a relative or neighbor, a group of co-workers, a craft group, an industry-wide pattern. A bank clerk, for example, may determine whether her inputs and outcomes are fairly correlated—in balance, so to speak—by comparing them with the relationship between the inputs and outcomes of other female clerks in her section. The sole punch press operator in a manufacturing plant may base his judgment on what he believes are the inputs and outcomes of other operators in the community or region. For a particular physicist the relevant reference person may be an organic chemist of the same academic "vintage." While it is clearly important to be able to specify the appropriate reference person or group, it represents a distinct theoretical area in which work has begun (Merton

& Kitt, 1950; Patchen, 1961; Stouffer et al., 1949) but which would take this paper too far afield. For the purposes of this paper, it will be assumed that the reference person or group will be one comparable to the comparer on one or more attributes, usually a co-worker.[2]

When the normative expectations of the person making social comparisons are violated—when he finds his inputs and outcomes are not in balance in relation to those of others—feelings of inequity result.

INEQUITY DEFINED

Although it has been suggested how inequity arises, a rigorous definition must be formulated. But we introduce first two references terms, Person and Other. Person is any individual for whom equity or inequity exists. Other is any individual or group used by Person as a referent when he makes social comparisons of his inputs and outcomes. Other is usually a different individual, but may be Person in another job, or even in another social role. Thus, for example, Other might be Person in the job he held six months earlier, in which case he might compare his present and past inputs and outcomes. Or, as Patchen (1961) has suggested, Other might be Person in a future job to which he aspires. In such an instance he would make a comparison of his present inputs and outcomes to his estimates of those in the future. The terms Person and Other may also refer to groups rather than to individuals, as for example when a class of jobs (for example, toolmakers) is out of line with another class (for example, maintenance men). In such cases, it is convenient to deal with the class as a whole rather than with individual members of the class. This is essentially what is done when the relative ranking of jobs is evaluated in the process of devising an equitable wage or salary structure.

Using the theoretical model introduced by Festinger (1957), inequity is defined as follows: inequity exists for Person whenever his perceived job inputs and/or outcomes stand psychologically in an obverse relation to what he perceives are the inputs and/or outcomes of Other. The first point to note about the definition is that it is the perception by Person of his and Other's inputs and outcomes that must be dealt with, not necessarily the actual inputs and outcomes. The point is

[2] This assumption follows Festinger (1954), who states: "Given a range of possible persons for comparison, someone close to one's own ability or opinion will be chosen for comparison [p. 121]." Generally, co-workers will more nearly fit this criterion than will other persons.

important, for, while perception and reality may be and often are in close accord, wage administrators are likely to assume an identity of the two. Second, if we let A designate Person's inputs and outcomes and let B designate Other's, by "obverse relation" we mean that not A follows from B. But we emphasize that the relation necessary for inequity to exist is psychological in character, not logical. Thus there is no logical obversion in male Person's being subordinate to female Other, but, as Clark (1958) has observed, the inputs of Person and Other in such a situation may be dissonant, with the consequence that inequity is felt by Person.

As was previously suggested, the dissonant relation of an individual's inputs and outcomes in comparison to another's is historically and culturally determined. This is why we insist that the incongruity is primarily psychological, even though it might, in addition, have a logical character. Each individual has a different history of learning, but to the extent that he learns from people sharing similar values, social norms, and language, that is, the extent to which he shares the same culture, his psychological reactions will be similar to theirs. The larger the cultural group, the greater will be the number of individuals who perceive similarly and react similarly to a given set of relations between input and outcomes. In the United States there is a strong, but perhaps weakening, predilection for the belief that effort and reward must be positively correlated. Considering the population at large, this belief has the status of a cultural norm and partially explains rather uniform reactions toward certain kinds of inequity—toward "featherbedding," for example.

It is interesting to note that the American attitude toward work and reward is by no means universal. In highly industrialized Japan, for example, there is little relationship between the kind and amount of work an employee does and the monetary reward he receives. Pay is largely determined by age, education, length of service, and family size, and very little, if at all, by productivity. In his study of Japanese factories, Abegglen (1958) states:

> It is not at all difficult to find situations where workers doing identical work at an identical pace receive markedly different salaries, or where a skilled workman is paid at a rate below that of a sweeper or doorman. The position occupied and the amount produced do not determine the reward provided [p. 68].

This, of course, is not to suggest that inequity is nonexistent for Japanese workers. They and their employers enter into an exchange just as Americans, but the terms of the exchange are quite different. Hence, the basis for inequity is different.

In order to predict when an individual will experience inequity under given conditions of inputs and outcomes, it is necessary to know something of the values and norms to which he subscribes—with what culture or subculture he is associated. Granted this knowledge, it is then possible to specify what constitutes an obverse relation of inputs and outcomes for Person. In a given society, even ours, there is usually enough invariance in fundamental beliefs and attitudes to make reasonably accurate, general predictions.

Table 1 *Amount of Inequity for Person as a Result of Different Inputs and Outcomes for Person and Other*

	Inputs-Outcomes			
	Other			
Person	Low-High	High-Low	Low-Low	High-High
Low-high	0	2	1	1
High-low	2	0	1	1
Low-low	1	1	0	0
High-high	1	1	0	0

Note: The first member of the pair indicates inputs and the second member, outcomes.

It is shown in Table 1 how inequity results whenever the inputs or outcomes, or both, of Person stand in an obverse relation to either the inputs or outcomes, or both, of Other. Though inputs and outcomes may in most cases be measured continuously (ethnicity and sex are obvious exceptions), we have dichotomized them into "high" and "low" for the purpose of simplicity. The entries in the table are relative rather than absolute quantities. Thus, 1 indicates more felt inequity than 0, and 2 indicates more felt inequity than 1. But before pursuing the implications of Table 1 and of the definition of inequity, let us agree to use amount of effort as an instance of inputs and pay as an instance of outcomes. Any other input and outcome would do as well; we wish merely to use constant instances for the illustrations that will follow.

The first important consequence to observe from the definition is that inequity results for Person not only when he is relatively underpaid, but also when he is relatively overpaid. Person will, for example, feel inequity exists not only when his effort is high and his pay low, while Other's effort and pay are high, but also when his effort is low and his pay high, while Other's effort and pay are low.

Although there is no direct, reliable evidence on this point, it is probable that the thresholds for inequity are different (in absolute terms from a base of equity) in cases of under- and overcompensation. The threshold would be greater presumably in cases of overcompensation, for a certain amount of incongruity in these cases can be acceptably rationalized as "good fortune." In his work on pay differentials Jaques (1961a) notes that in instances of undercompensation British workers paid 10 per cent less than the equitable level show

> an active sense of grievance, complaints or the desire to complain, and, if no redress is given, an active desire to change jobs, or to take action . . . [p. 26].

In cases of overcompensation, he observes that at the 10–15 per cent level above equity

> there is a strong sense of receiving preferential treatment, which may harden into bravado, with underlying feelings of unease . . . [p. 26].

He states further:

> The results suggest that it is not necessarily the case that each one is simply out to get as much as he can for his work. There appear to be equally strong desires that each one should earn the right amount—a fair and reasonable amount relative to others [p. 26].

While Jaques' conceptualization of inequity is quite different from that advanced in this paper, his observations lend credence to the hypothesis that overcompensation results in feelings of inequity and that the threshold for these feelings is higher than in the case of undercompensation.

From the definition and Table 1, we may observe as a second consequence that when Person's and Other's inputs and outcomes are analogous, equity is assumed to exist, and that when their inputs and outcomes are discrepant in any way inequity will exist. We assume that it is not the absolute magnitude of perceived inputs and outcomes that results in inequity, but rather the relative magnitudes pertaining to Person and Other. For example, there will be no inequity if both Person and Other expend much effort in their jobs and both obtain low pay. The 0 entries in the main diagonal of Table 1 reflect the fact that when the inputs and outcomes of Person and Other are matched, no inequity exists. It is further assumed, and shown in Table 1, that no inequity will result if both the inputs and outcomes of Person are matched and those of Other are matched, but are different for Person and for Other. To illustrate: if Person expends low effort and receives low pay, while Other expends high effort and receives high pay, equity rather than inequity will result. The converse also holds true.

With regard to the amount of inequity that exists, we have assumed that greater inequity results when both inputs and outcomes are discrepant than when only inputs or outcomes are discrepant. This signifies, for example, that Person will experience more inequity when his effort is high and pay low, while Other's effort is low and pay high, than when Person's effort is high and pay low, while Other's effort and pay are both high. In Table 1 only three relative magnitudes of inequity, ranging from 0 to 2, are shown. In reality, of course, many more degrees could be distinguished, especially with variables such as effort and pay which are theoretically continuous. The point to be emphasized is that equity-inequity is not an all-or-none phenomenon.

It will be noted that in the definition of inequity and in Table 1, inputs have not been differentiated, nor have outcomes. There are two reasons for this. First, the processes that govern inequity are applicable irrespective of the specific inputs and outcomes obtaining in a particular situation. For example, inequity may result whether low inputs are in the form of low effort or of poor education, or whether high outcomes stem from high pay or from great rewards intrinsic to the job. Second, there is a degree of interchangeability between different inputs and between different outcomes; furthermore inputs are additive, as are outcomes. It is implied, therefore, that a given total of Person's inputs may be achieved by increasing or decreasing any one or more separate inputs; similarly, a given total of Person's outcomes may result from increasing or decreasing one or more separate outcomes. For example, if Person found it necessary to increase his inputs in order to reduce inequity, he could do so not only by increasing his effort, but also by acquiring additional training or education. If, on the other hand, greater outcomes were required to achieve equity, obtaining new status symbols might be equivalent to an increase in compensation, or a combination of improved job environment and increased discretionary content of the job might be.

The question of the interchangeability and additivity of different inputs on the one hand, and of different outcomes on the other is an important one. Does a man evaluating his job inputs give the same weight to formal education as he does to on-the-job experience? If he has completed high school and has held his job two years, and a co-worker, whom he uses as a comparison person, completed the ninth grade only and has been on the job four years, will he judge their inputs as equivalent or not? Is the frequently used practice of giving a man a prestigeful title an effective substitute for greater monetary outcomes? Definitive answers to such questions await research. However, this much may be hypothesized: within certain limits of inequity there will be a tendency on the part of Person to manipulate and weight cognitively his own inputs and outcomes and those of Other in such a manner as to minimize the degree of felt inequity. Beyond these limits of inequity the tendency will be to manipulate and weight inputs and outcomes so as to maximize the inequity, because as will be discussed later, this will increase the motivation to adopt behavior that will eliminate the inequity entirely.[3] In both processes it is assumed that normal men are limited by reality in the amount of cognitive manipulation and weighting of inputs and outcomes they can perform. Except, perhaps, in the case of very small degrees of inequity such manipulation and weighting could not serve by themselves to achieve equity.

In discussing inequity, the focus has been exclusively on Person. In so doing, however, we have failed to consider that whenever inequity exists for Person, it will also exist for Other, provided their perceptions of inputs and outcomes are isomorphic or nearly so. A glance at Table 1 will make this apparent, and we may predict from the table the inequity for Other as well as for Person. Only when the perceptions of Person and Other do not agree, would the inequity be different for each. In such a case, one would enter Table 1 twice, once for Person and once for Other. It is sufficient at this point merely to note that inequity is bilateral or multilateral, and symmetric under some conditions. Later we shall consider the implications of this in greater detail.

EFFECTS OF INEQUITY

Having defined inequity and specified its antecedents, we may next attend to its effects. First, two general postulates, closely following

[3] This process is analogous to that postulated by Festinger (1957) when he discusses the relation of magnitude of cognitive dissonance to seeking information that will increase dissonance. He hypothesizes that at high levels of dissonance increasing information may be sought, with the result that the person will change his opinion and thus reduce dissonance.

dissonance theory (Festinger, 1957): (*a*) The presence of inequity in Person creates tension in him. The tension is proportional to the magnitude of inequity present. (*b*) The tension created in Person will drive him to reduce it. The strength of the drive is proportional to the tension created; *ergo,* it is proportional to the magnitude of inequity present. In short, the presence of inequity will motivate Person to achieve equity or reduce inequity, and the strength of motivation to do so will vary directly with the amount of inequity. The question, then, is *how* may Person reduce inequity? The following actions enumerate and illustrate the means available to Person when reducing inequity.

1. Person may increase his inputs if they are low relative to Other's inputs and to his own outcomes. If, for example, Person's effort were low compared to Other's and to his own pay, he could reduce inequity by increasing his effort on the job. This might take the form of Person's increasing his productivity, as will be shown in experiments described later, or enhancing the quality of his work. If inputs other than effort were involved, he could increase his training or education. Some inputs cannot, of course, be altered easily—sex and ethnicity, for instance. When such inputs are involved, other means of reducing inequity must be adopted.

2. Person may decrease his inputs if they are high relative to Other's inputs and to his own outcomes. If Person's effort were high compared to Other's and to his own pay, he might reduce his effort and productivity, as is illustrated later in a study of grocery clerks. It is interesting to note that effort is the principal input susceptible to reduction; education, training, experience, intelligence, skill, seniority, age, sex, ethnicity, and so on are not readily decreased or devalued realistically, though they may be distorted psychologically within limits. They are givens; their acquisition is not reversible. The implication is that when inequity results from inputs being too high, decreases in productivity are especially likely to be observed. One may speculate that restrictive production practices often observed are in fact attempts at reducing inequity.

There exists in industry a tendency to select and hire personnel with education, intellect, and training which are often greater than that required by the job in which they are placed. Since it is likely that in many instances the comparison persons for these individuals will have lesser inputs and, perhaps, greater outcomes, it is evident that some of the newly hired will experience feelings of inequity. In consequence, education, intellect, and training not being readily modified, lowered productivity may be predicted.

3. Person may increase his outcomes if they are low relative to Other's outcomes and to his own inputs. When Person's pay is low compared to Other's and to his expended effort, he may reduce inequity by obtaining a wage increase. Evidence of this is given later in a study of clerical workers.

He could also, if appropriate, acquire additional benefits, perquisites, or status. An increase in status, however, might create new problems, for the acquisition of higher status without higher pay would of itself create dissonance, particularly if the new status of Person placed him in a superordinate position vis-à-vis Other.

4. Person may decrease his outcomes if they are high relative to Other's outcomes and to his own inputs. This might take the form of Person's lowering his pay. Though an improbable mode of reducing inequity, it is nevertheless theoretically possible. Although it is usually assumed that persons with very high personal incomes are motivated by tax laws to donate much to charitable and educational institutions, it is not improbable that this behavior on the part of some is motivated as well by feelings of inequity.

5. Person may "leave the field" when he experiences inequity of any type. This may take the form of quitting his job or obtaining a transfer or reassignment, or of absenteeism. In a study by Patchen (1959) it was observed that men who said their pay should be higher had more absences than men who said the pay for their jobs was fair. Although the author did not conceptualize "fair pay" as in the present paper, it is clear at least that "fair" was defined by respondents in relational terms, for he states:

> The data show also that the actual amount of a man's pay has, in itself, little effect on how often he is absent. The important question, regardless of how much he is getting, is whether he thinks the rate is fair [p.12].

Leaving the field is perhaps a more radical means of coping with inequity, and its adoption will vary not only with the magnitude of inequity present, but also with Person's tolerance of inequity and his ability to cope with it flexibly. Though it has not been demonstrated, there are probably individual differences in tolerance and flexibility.

6. Person may psychologically distort his inputs and outcomes, increasing or decreasing them as required. Since most individuals are heavily influenced by reality, distortion is generally difficult. It is pretty difficult to distort to oneself that one has a BA degree, that one has been an accountant for seven years, and that one's salary is 500 per month, for example. However, it is possible to alter the utility of these. For example, State College is a small, backwoods school with no reputation, or, conversely, State College has one of the best Business Schools in the state and the Dean is an adviser to the Bureau of the Budget. Or, one can consider the fact that $500 per month will buy all of the essential things of life and quite a few luxuries, or, conversely, that it will never permit one to purchase period furniture or a power cruiser.

7. Person may increase, decrease, or distort the inputs and outcomes of Others, or force Other to leave the field. Basically, these means are the same as discussed above, but applied to Other. The direction of change in inputs and outcomes would, however, be precisely opposite to changes effected in Person. Thus, for example, if Person's effort were too low compared to Other's

and to his own pay, he might induce Other to decrease his effort instead of increasing his own effort. Or, if he were comparatively poorly qualified for his job, he might try to have his better qualified colleague fired or transferred.

8. Person may change his referent Other when inequity exists. If Person were a draftsman working harder, doing better quality work, and being paid less than Other at the next board, he might eschew further comparisons with Other and pick someone with more nearly the same capability and pay. The ease of doing this would vary considerably with the ubiquity of Other and with the availability of a substitute having some attributes in common with Person.

Not all the means of reducing inequity that have been listed will be equally satisfactory, and the adoption of some may result in very unsteady states. The nature of the input and outcome discrepancies and environmental circumstances may render some means more available than others, as may personality characteristics of Person and Other. To illustrate this we may consider a Person whose effort is high and whose pay is low, and an Other whose effort and pay are low. If Person acts to increase his pay and is successful, he will effectively reduce the inequity; but if he is unsuccessful, as well he might be, given rigid job and wage structures, inequity will continue. Person might, on the other hand, try to reduce his productivity. This, however, might be quite risky, if minimal production standards were maintained and unsatisfactory productivity were penalized. There is the further consideration that if Person and Other are both on the same production line, a decrease in effort by Person might affect Other's production and pay, with the result that Other would object to Person's behavior. Another means for Person to reduce his inequity is to try to have Other increase his effort. If Other perceives his and Person's inputs and outcomes in the same way as Person, he might, indeed, accede to this influence and raise his effort. If, to the contrary, he perceives no discrepancy between his and Person's inputs, he may be expected to resist Person strongly. Alternatively, Person could resort to leaving the field, or to distortion, as discussed earlier. If distortion is unilateral on Person's part, it may resolve his inequity, though not Other's. This leads into another interesting aspect of inequity.

Person and Other may or may not constitute a social system, that is, Person may be to Other what Other is to Person, so that they are referents for one another. Or, Other's referent may be someone other than Person, say, an individual X, who is quite irrelevant to Person's social comparisons. When Person and Other do not form a social system, the way in which Person reduces his inequity will have no effect on Other and there will, therefore, be no feedback effects upon Person. When the two do constitute a social system, the interaction that may take place is of considerable interest. Considering only those instances when Person and Other have identical perceptions of their inputs and outcomes it is a truism that when inequity exists for Person it also exists for Other (though probably not in the same amount since one will be overpaid and the other underpaid). Hence, both will be motivated to reduce the inequity; but it does not follow that they will adopt compatible means. If compatible means are adopted, both will achieve equity. For example, if Person expended little effort and received high pay, while Other's effort and pay were both high, a state of equity could be achieved by Person's increasing his effort somewhat and by Other's reducing his a bit. Or, the two could agree that the easiest solution was for Other to reduce his effort to Person's level. However, this solution might prove inadequate, for other reasons; for example, this might endanger their jobs by reducing production to an economically unprofitable level.

Many possibilities of incompatible solutions exist for Person and Other. Continuing with the preceding example, Person could increase his effort and Other could decrease his. From the point of view of each considered alone, these actions should reduce inequity. When considered simultaneously, however, it is apparent that now Person's effort and pay will be high, whereas Other will expend low effort and receive high pay. A new state of inequity has been created! As a further example, if Person's effort were high and his pay low, while Other's effort were low and his pay high, Person might reduce his own effort while Other was trying to induce the supervisor to increase Person's salary. If Other were unsuccessful in his attempt, a new, but reduced, state of inequity would result. If, on the other hand, Other were successful in obtaining a raise for Person, equity might be established, but a new situation, hardly more comfortable than inequity, would result: Person would have received a pay increment for a decrement in effort.

Private, psychological distortion of one's inputs and outcomes is especially likely to result in unsuccessful reduction of inequity, if done by only one party. For instance, if Person is overcompensated and manages to convince himself that he is not, it will be extremely difficult for Other to convince him, say, that he should work harder. Or, if Other were to convince himself that he was working just as hard as Person, Person could not effectively convince Other to increase his productivity or to take a cut in pay. The very fact that one of the parties is operating at a private, covert level makes it nearly impossible to communicate. The perceptions of the two parties being now different, the fundamental premises that must underlie joint action cannot be agreed upon. Distortion by one party in effect breaks the social system that had previously existed.

SUPPORTING EVIDENCE

The evidence in direct support of the theory of inequity will now be considered. The data that are available may be divided grossly into two types, observational and experimental. Directly supporting evidence is, on the whole, somewhat meager for the reason that little research has been focused on the specific question of job inequity. The work of Zaleznik et al. (1958), Homans (1953, 1961), and Patchen (1959, 1961) has dealt with significant aspects of the problem, but, with the exception of Homans' (1953) study of clerical employees, the data collected by these researchers are difficult to relate to the present theory.

A Case of Pay Inequity among Clerical Workers (Homans, 1953)

Rather than dealing with two individuals, we are here concerned with two groups of female clerical workers, cash posters and ledger clerks, in one division of a utilities company. Both groups worked in the same large room. Cash posting consisted of recording daily the amounts customers paid on their bills, and management insisted that posting be precisely up to date. It required that cash posters pull customer cards from the many files and make appropriate entries on them. The job, therefore, was highly repetitive and comparatively monotonous, and required little thought but a good deal of physical mobility. Ledger clerks, in contrast, performed a variety of tasks on customer accounts, such as recording address changes, making breakdowns of over- and underpayments, and supplying information on accounts to customers or company people on the telephone. In addition, toward the end of the day, they were required by their supervisor to assist with "cleaning up" cash posting in order that it be current. Compared to the cash posters, "ledger clerks had to do a number of nonrepetitive clerical jobs . . . requiring some thought but little physical mobility." They had a more responsible job.

Ledger clerks were considered to be of higher status than cash posters, since promotion took place from cash poster to ledger clerk. Their weekly pay, however, was identical. In comparison to cash posters, ledger clerks were older and had more seniority and experience.

These are the facts of the situation. In terms of the theory, the following may be stated:

1. The cash posters had lower inputs than the ledger clerks: They were younger, had less seniority and experience, and had less responsible jobs. Their outcomes were in some respects lower than the ledger clerks': Their job had less variety, was more monotonous, required greater physical effort, and had less intrinsic interest. Very importantly, however, their pay was equal to the ledger clerks'.

2. The ledger clerks had higher inputs than the cash posters: They were older, had more seniority and experience, and had more responsible positions. Their outcomes were higher on several counts: Their status was higher, their job had greater variety and interest, and physical effort required was low. Their pay, nonetheless, was the same as the cash posters'. The requirement that they help "clean up" (note the connotation) posting each day introduced ambiguity in their inputs and outcomes. On the one hand, this required greater inputs—that is, having to know two jobs—and, on the other hand, lowered their outcomes by having to do "dirty work" and deflating their self-esteem.

It is clear from the discrepancies between inputs and outcomes that inequities existed. In capsule form, the outcomes of ledger clerks were too low compared to their own inputs and to the inputs and outcomes of cash posters. The evidence is strong that the ledger clerks, at least, felt the inequity. They felt that they ought to get a few dollars more per week to show that their job was more important—in our terms, their greater inputs ought to be paralleled by greater outcomes. On the whole, these clerks did not do much to reduce inequity, though a few complained to their union representative, with, apparently, little effect. However, the workers in this division voted to abandon their independent union for the CIO, and Homans (1953) intimates that the reason may have been the independent union's inability to force a resolution of the inequity. He further implies that had management perceived and resolved the inequity, the representative function of a union would have been quite superfluous.

A Case of Status Inequity in Supermarkets (Clark, 1958)

We shall be concerned here with the checkout counters in a chain of supermarkets, which are manned by a "ringer" and a "bundler." Ringers are the cashiers who add on the register the sum due from the customer, take his payment, and make change. Bundlers take goods out of the cart and put them in bags to be taken out. Under normal conditions, ringing was a higher-status, better-paid job, handled by a permanent, full-time employee. Bundling was of lower status and lower pay, and was usually done by part-time employees, frequently youngsters. Furthermore, psychologically, bundlers were perceived as working *for* ringers.

Because customer flow in supermarkets varies markedly from day to day, a preponderance of employees were part-timers. This same fact required that many employees be assigned to checkout counters during rush hours. When this occurred, many ringer-bundler teams were formed, and it is this that resulted in the creation of status inequity, for employees differed considerably in a number of input variables, notably sex, age, and education. Not infrequently, then, a bundler would be directed to work for a ringer whose status (determined by sex, age, education, etc.) was lower. For example, a college male 21 years of age would be ordered to work for a high school girl ringer of 17. Or a college girl would be assigned as a bundler for an older woman with only a grade school education. The resulting status inequities may be described as follows in our theoretical terms: a bundler with higher inputs than a ringer had lower outcomes.

When interviewed by the investigator, the store employees were quite explicit about the inequities that existed. Furthermore, this was true of ringers, as well as bundlers, showing that inequities were felt bilaterally in these cooperative jobs. To restore equity it would have been necessary to form teams such that inputs and outcomes were matched. Clark (1958) has stated the principle in the following manner:

> A person's job status (which is determined by the amount of pay, responsibility, variety, and absence from interference his job has) should be in line with his social status (which is determined by his sex, age, education, and seniority) [p. 128].

That store employees attempted to reduce existing inequities is evident from the data. The principal means of doing so appeared to be by the bundlers reducing their work speed—that is, by reducing their inputs, which would have effectively decreased inequity since some of their other inputs were too high relative to their own outcomes and to the inputs of the ringers. One girl explicitly stated to the investigator that when she was ordered to bundle for a ringer of lower social status than hers, she deliberately slowed up bundling.

Interestingly, this behavior is nicely reflected in the financial operation of the stores. A substantial part of the total labor cost of operating a supermarket is the cost of manning checkout counters. It follows, therefore, that one should be able to observe a correlation between the incidence of inequities among ringer-bundler teams and the cost of store operations, since the inequity reduction took the form of lowered productivity. This is indeed what was found. When the eight supermarkets were ranked on labor efficiency[4] and "social ease,"[5] the two measures correlated almost perfectly—that is, the greater the inequity, the greater the cost of operating the stores. To give an example, one of the two stores studied most intensively ranked high in inequity and had a cost of 3.85 man-hours per $100 of sales, whereas the other which ranked low in inequity, had a cost of only 3.04 per $100 of sales. Thus, it cost approximately 27 per cent more to operate the store in which inequities were higher.

A further finding of Clark's is worth reporting, for it gives one confidence that the relative inefficiency of the one store was indeed due to the presence of relatively more inequity. This store went through a period of considerable labor turnover (perhaps as a result of employees leaving the field to reduce inequity), and associated with this was an increase in labor efficiency and an increase in the social ease index. There is, therefore, quasi-experimental evidence that when inequities are reduced, individual productivity increases, with the result that operating costs decrease.

Experiment I (Adams & Rosenbaum, 1962)

One of the more interesting hypotheses derivable from the theory of inequity is that when Person is overpaid in relation to Other, he may reduce the inequity by increasing his inputs. Therefore, an experiment was designed in which one group of subjects was overcompensated and one was equitably compensated—that is, one group in which outcomes were too great and one in which outcomes were equitable, given certain inputs, relative to some generalized Other.

The task chosen was a one-page controlled-association public-opinion interview (for example, "Which of these five automobiles do you associate with a rising young junior executive?"), which sub-

[4] As an index of labor efficiency, Clark (1958) used the number of man-hours per $100 of sales.

[5] "Social ease" is a complex index, devised by Clark (1958), the value of which is basically the number of pairs of part-time employees, out of all possible pairs, whose inputs and outcomes were "in line," according to the definition given in the quotation from Clark.

jects were to administer in equal numbers to male and female members of the general public. The subjects were under the impression that they were being hired for a real task and that their employment would continue for several months. In actuality, however, they conducted interviews for 2.5 hours only, after which time they were told about the experiment and were paid for their participation.

Two groups of eleven male university students, hired through the college employment office, were used as subjects. Each was paid $3.50 per hour—an amount large enough so that a feeling of overcompensation could be induced, but not so large that it could not also be made to appear equitable. In one group (E), subjects were made to feel quite unqualified to earn $3.50 per hour, because of lack of interviewer training and experience. The other group of subjects (C) were made to feel fully qualified to earn $3.50 per hour, by being informed that they were far better educated than census takers and that education and intelligence were the prime requisites of interviewing. It may be noted that the referent Others for all subjects were trained interviewers at large, not a specific, known person. The complete instructions to the groups were, of course, much more elaborate, but details need not be given here. The critical point is that the E group felt overcompensated, whereas the C group felt fairly paid.

From the theory, it was predicted that the E group would attempt to increase their inputs so as to bring them in line with their outcomes and with the alleged inputs of trained interviewers. Since there was little they could do to increase their training and experience, this left productivity as the principal means of altering inputs. Theoretically, E group subjects could also have tried to reduce their outcomes; this, however, was impossible since the pay was fixed. In sum, then, it was predicted that the E group would obtain more interviews per unit time than the C group. This is what the results demonstrated. Whereas the C group obtained an average of only .1899 interviews per minute, the E group obtained a significantly greater average of .2694, or an average of 42 per cent more ($\chi^2 = 4.55$, $df = 1$, $p < .05$).

Results comparable to these have been obtained by Day (1961) in a laboratory experiment with children who were given training trials in which they pushed a plunger mechanism to obtain M&M candies. The number of candies received varied between one and six and was directly dependent upon the magnitude of pressure exerted on the plunger. After responses had stabilized, 25 M&Ms were received by each subject on each of five trials regardless of the pressure exerted. Day's data show that a significant number of subjects respond to the increased reward by increased pressure on the overrewarded trials. In terms of our theoretical model, the children in Day's study are comparing their inputs (pressure) and outcomes (M&Ms) during the overrewarded trials with those during the training trials. The latter trials establish a base upon which to determine what constitutes "equity." The "overpayment" of 25 M&M candies results in inequity, which may be reduced by increasing pressure inputs.

Experiment II (Arrowood, 1961)

If it is reasonable to suppose that the results of the previously described experiment by Adams and Rosenbaum (1962) were a result of the E subjects' working harder to protect their jobs because they were insecure in the face of their "employer's" low regard for their qualifications, it is reasonable to suppose that the same results would not obtain if subjects were convinced that their "employer" would have no knowledge of their productivity. Conversely, if the theory we have offered is valid, overpaid subjects should produce more than controls, whether they thought the "employer" knew the results of their work or whether they thought he did not.

Following this reasoning, Arrowood (1961) designed a factorial experiment in which subjects from Minneapolis were either overpaid or equitably paid and performed their work under either public or private conditions. The first two conditions were similar to those in Experiment I: subjects were hired at $3.50 per hour to conduct interviews and were made to feel unqualified or qualified for the job. The public-private distinction was achieved by having subjects either submit their work to the "employer" (the experimenter) or mail it in preaddressed envelopes to New York. In the latter case, subjects were under the impression that the experimenter would never see their work.

The results, shown in Table 2, validate the hypothesis tested in Experiment I and permit one to reject the alternative hypothesis. In

Table 2 *Production Scores of Subjects in Experiment II*

	Public	Private
Overpaid	67.20	52.43
Equitably paid	59.33	41.50

both the public and private conditions, overpaid subjects produced significantly more than equitably paid subjects. The fact that mean production in the public conditions was significantly greater than in the private conditions is irrelevant to the hypothesis since there was no significant interaction between the inequity-equity and public-private dimensions.

Experiment III (Adams & Rosenbaum, 1962)

Since the results of the two previous experiments strongly corroborated a derivation from the theory, it was decided to test a further, but related, derivation. The hypothesis was that whereas subjects overpaid *by the hour* would produce more than equitably paid controls, subjects overpaid *on a piecework basis* would produce less than equitably paid controls. The rationale for the latter half of the hypothesis was that because inequity was associated with each *unit* produced, inequity would increase as work proceeded; hence, subjects would strive not so much to *reduce* inequity as to *avoid* increasing it. In other words, because inequity would mount as more units were produced, overpaid piecework subjects would tend to restrict production.

Nine subjects were assigned to each of the following groups. Overpaid \$3.50 per hour (H_e), equitably paid \$3.50 per hour (H_c), overpaid \$.30 per unit (P_e), equitably paid \$.30 per unit (P_c). In all major respects, the task and instructions were identical to those in Experiment I.

As may be seen in Table 3, the hypothesis received unequivocal support. Overpaid hourly subjects produced more than their controls and overpaid piecework subjects produced less than their controls. The interaction between the inequity-equity and hourly-piecework dimensions is highly significant ($\chi^2 = 7.11$, $df = 1$, $p < .01$).

Experiment IV (Adams, 1963)

The prediction that piecework subjects experiencing wage inequity would have a lower productivity than subjects perceiving their wages as fair was supported by the previous experiment. The rationale for the prediction was that because dissonance is linked with units of production, dissonance would increase as more units were produced, and, consequently, subjects would attempt to avoid increasing dissonance by restricting production. There is, however, an alternative explanation that would account for the same manifest behavior. It is entirely possible for subjects to *reduce* dissonance by increasing their effort on the production of each unit, for example, by increasing the quality of their, work, which would have the effect of increasing the production time per unit and, therefore, have the consequence of reducing productivity. In terms of the theoretical framework presented earlier, this explanation assumes that pieceworkers would reduce their dissonance by increasing their inputs, very much as the hourly workers. Only the mode of increasing inputs varies: whereas hourly workers increase inputs on a *quantitative* dimension, pieceworkers increase them on a *qualitative* dimension.

Table 3 *Mean Productivity and Median Distribution of Hourly and Piecework Experimental and Control Subjects in Experiment III*

	Condition			
	H_e	H_c	P_e	P_c
Mean productivity	.2723	.2275	.1493	.1961
Cases above median	8	4	1	5
Cases below median	1	5	8	4

Unfortunately, the task used in Experiment III did not lend itself to measuring quality of work. In the present experiment the work performed by subjects was so designed as to permit measurement of both amount of work and quality of work. The specific hypothesis tested is: pieceworkers who perceive that they are inequitably overpaid will perform better quality work and have lower productivity than pieceworkers who are paid the same rate and perceive they are equitably paid.

The interviewing task used in the previous experiments was modified so as to permit the measurement of quality. The modification consisted of making the three principal questions open-end questions. As an example, one question was "Does a man who owns a shelter have the moral right to exclude others from it, if they have no shelter?" (Yes or No), which was followed by, "What are your reasons for feeling that way?" The subject's task was to obtain as much information as possible from a respondent on the latter part of the question. The measure of work quality thus was the amount of recorded information elicited from respondents. More specifically, the dependent measure of quality was the number of words per interview recorded in the blank spaces following the three open-end questions. As before, the measure of productivity was the number of interviews obtained per minute during a total period of approximately two hours.

Twenty-eight subjects were used, half randomly assigned to a condition in which they were made to feel overpaid, half to a condition in which the identical piecework rate was made to appear equitable. The results supported the hypotheses. First, as in the previous experiment, the productivity of subjects in whom feelings of inequitable overpayment were induced was significantly lower than that of control subjects. Productivity rates for these groups were .0976 and .1506, respectively ($t = 1.82$, $p < .05$, one-tailed test). Second, work quality was significantly higher among overpaid subjects than among controls (69.7 versus 45.3, $t = 2.48$, $p < .02$, two-tailed test).

These quality and productivity data support the hypothesis that under piecework conditions subjects who perceive that they are overpaid will tend to reduce dissonance by increasing their inputs on each *unit* so as to improve its quality and, as a result, will decrease their productivity. Thus the alternative explanation for the results obtained with pieceworkers in Experiment III has some validity. This is not to say that the dissonance avoiding hypothesis originally offered is invalid, for if a job does not permit an increase of work input *per unit produced,* dissonance avoidance may well occur. This, however, remains to be demonstrated; the fact that we were unable to measure quality of work in Experiment III does not mean that subjects did not reduce dissonance by some means, including the improvement of quality, on each unit produced.

CONCLUSION

We have offered a general theory of inequity, reviewed its implications, and presented evidence in support of it. Although the support given the theory is gratifying, additional data are required to test particular aspects of it. In addition, research is needed to determine what variables guide the choice of comparison persons. While this is a theoretical and research endeavor in its own right, it would contribute much to the understanding of inequity.

The analysis of inequity in terms of discrepancies between a man's job inputs and job outcomes, and the behavior that may result from these discrepancies, should result in a better understanding of one aspect of social conflict and should increase the degree of control that may be exercised over it. In moving toward an understanding of inequity, we increase our knowledge of our most basic productive resource, the human organism.

SUMMARY

A theory of social inequity, with special consideration given to wage inequities is presented. A special case of Festinger's cognitive dissonance, the theory specifies the conditions under which inequity will arise and the means by which it may be reduced or eliminated. Observational field studies supporting the theory and laboratory experiments designed to test certain aspects of it are described.

REFERENCES

Abegglen, J. G. *The Japanese factory.* Glencoe, Ill.: Free Press, 1958.

Adams, J. S. The measurement of perceived equity in pay differentials. Unpublished manuscript, General Electric Company, Behavioral Research Service, 1961.

Adams, J. S. Productivity and work quality as a function of wage inequities. *Industr. Relat., Berkeley*, 1963, in press.

Adams, J. S., & Rosenbaum, W. B. The relationship of worker productivity to cognitive dissonance about wage inequities. *J. Appl. Psychol.*, 1962, **46**, 161–164.

Arrowood, A. J. Some effects on productivity of justified and unjustified levels of reward under public and private conditions. Unpublished doctoral dissertation, University of Minnesota, Department of Psychology, 1961.

Clark, J. V. A preliminary investigation of some unconscious assumptions affecting labor efficiency in eight supermarkets. Unpublished doctoral dissertation, Harvard Graduate School of Business Administration, 1958.

Day, C. R. Some consequences of increased reward following establishment of output-reward expectation level. Unpublished master's thesis, Duke University, 1961.

Festinger, L. A theory of social comparison processes. *Hum. Relat.*, 1954, **7**, 117–140.

Festinger, L. *A theory of cognitive dissonance.* Evanston, Ill.: Row, Peterson, 1957.

Homans, G. C. Status among clerical workers. *Hum. Organiz.*, 1953, **12**, 5–10.

Homans, G. C. *Social behavior: Its elementary forms.* New York: Harcourt, Brace, & World, 1961.

Jaques, E. *Measurement of responsibility.* London: Tavistock, 1956.

Jaques, E. *Equitable payment.* New York: Wiley, 1961. (a)

Jaques, E. An objective approach to pay differentials. *Time Motion Stud.*, 1961, **10**, 25–28. (b)

Jeffrey, T. E., & Jones, L. V. *Compensation-plan preferences: An application of psychometric scaling.* Chapel Hill: University of North Carolina, Psychometric Laboratory, 1961.

Merton, R. K., & Kitt, Alice S. Contributions to the theory of reference group behavior. In R. K. Merton, & P. F. Lazarsfeld (Eds.), *Studies in the scope and method of "The American Soldier."* Glencoe, Ill.: Free Press, 1950. Pp. 40–105.

Patchen, M. *Study of work and life satisfaction: Report II. Absences and attitudes toward work experiences.* Ann Arbor: Institute for Social Research, 1959.

Patchen, M. *The choice of wage comparisons.* Englewood Cliffs, N.J.: Prentice-Hall, 1961.

Stouffer, S. A., Suchman, E. A., DeVinney, L. C., Star, Shirley A., & Williams, R. M., Jr. *The American soldier: Adjustment during Army life.* Princeton: Princeton Univ. Press, 1949.

Zaleznik, A., Christensen, C. R., & Roethlisberger, F. J. *The motivation, productivity and satisfaction of workers.* Boston: Harvard University, Graduate School of Business Administration, 1958.

4.7 MEDIATED GENERALIZATION OF ATTITUDE CHANGE VIA THE PRINCIPLE OF CONGRUITY

Percy H. Tannenbaum

When attitude toward one of two objects in a cognitive relationship is modified, there often results a change in attitude toward the other object in order to maintain cognitive consistency. A particular instance of such a general consistency theory phenomenon is represented in applications of the principle of congruity (Osgood & Tannenbaum, 1955) where a persuasive communication directed at a given topic or concept also results in changes in attitude toward the message source.

Such generalization of attitude change from concept to source was more clearly indicated in a recent extension of the congruity model to a situation in which the two main cognitive operations involved—the establishment of an evaluative relationship between source and concept, and the manipulation of the concept attitude—were accomplished independently (Tannenbaum & Gengel, 1966). Three different source-concept linkages were first established—one source being for the concept, another against, and a third neutral. In a subsequent message, the concept was modified in either a favorable or unfavorable direction, but without any reference to the original sources. The resulting relative changes in attitude toward the sources were in accord with the theoretical predictions—evaluation of the sources

Source: This research was supported by the National Science Foundation. Reprinted from the *Journal of Personality and Social Psychology*, 1966, 3, 493–499, with permission of the author and the American Psychological Association, Inc.

changed in the direction establishing a congruent relationship with the altered concept position.

A further extension of the congruity principle as a model for generalization of persuasion is readily apparent. If attitude change toward a source results from manipulating the attitude toward an evaluatively linked concept, then *other* concepts with which that source has been associated should also be affected. That is, a given source may be linked to a number of different concepts, each such linkage constituting a particular cognitive relationship. Change in one concept affects the source attitude because it introduces an inconsistency, or incongruity, into one of those relationships. But now the change in the source creates a new incongruity with one or another of the remaining concepts, attitude toward which should change in order to resolve that incongruity. In this manner, generalization of attitude change from one concept to another may be accomplished—mediated through their initial association with a common source, and in the absence of any direct link between the concepts themselves.

The present experiment was designed to investigate such a phenomenon in terms of specific congruity principle predictions. Various directed relationships between a given source and two different concepts are first established, and then attitude toward one of the concepts is manipulated, either positively or negatively. This should result in favorable or unfavorable change in attitude toward the source, in accordance with congruity theory predictions. This source attitude change, in turn, should affect attitude toward the second concept, also in accord with specific congruity predictions. Thus, three critical variables are involved in such source-mediated generalization of persuasion from one concept to a second—the nature of the evaluative link between the source and the first concept, the direction of the manipulated attitude change toward the first concept, and the nature of the evaluative link between the source and the second concept.

METHOD

Subjects

A total of 218 male high-school students attending a summer military camp as Army cadets served as subjects in the experiment. They ranged between the ages of 16–18 years, the participated in the study as part of a series of tests they underwent during their stay in camp.

Because of some incomplete participation, the data for 200 subjects were used.

Procedure

Materials similar to those employed in the previous Tannenbaum and Gengel (1966) study were used in the present investigation. On the basis of previous testing with undergraduate college students, two concepts—teaching machines (TM) and Spence learning theory (LT)—and a plausible but fictitious source (Prof. Walter E. Samuels of the University of California) were selected as the attitudinal objects for the study. The main criteria for selection were relative neutrality of initial attitude, and a relatively small variance.

Subjects were first tested on attitude toward the three objects (T_0) as part of a general inventory of attitudes and connotative meaning judgments, the objects of interest here being imbedded among a set of 20 different concepts. One week later, subjects were again assembled and were divided into four groups according to the intended source-concept linkages. One group had the source in favor of both the TM and LT concepts (the *pp* condition); for another, the source favored TM but disfavored LT (*pn*); for the third, the source was against TM but for LT (*np*); for the fourth, the source was against both concepts (*nn*).[1]

All subjects then participated in a totally separate task—completing several parts of the MMPI—for approximately one-half hour. After this interval of irrelevant activity, subjects were exposed to the TM concept manipulation message. Half the subjects in each linkage condition received a positive version designed to boost the TM attitude (the *P* treatment), and the other half received a belief attack (the *N* treatment). Attitudes toward the source and the two concepts were again assessed after the experimental messages (T_1). Thus, the basic design was a before-after 4×2 (Linkages $\times$ Manipulations) factorial design with independent cells ($n = 25$ per cell).

Experimental Materials

Linkage Messages: The various linkages were established in messages (of approximately 250 words each) reporting an ostensible sym-

[1] Neutral linkage conditions were not included in the present design—partly because they were not absolutely essential to test the main theoretical predictions, and partly because the results of the Tannenbaum and Gengel (1966) study indicated a possibility of a contamination of the generalization data, as such, in a neutral linkage situation.

posium at the 1963 convention of the American Psychological Association dealing with "new educational procedures." To heighten interest somewhat, the message claimed the symposium was a widely discussed one which had "caused quite a stir . . . and considerable debate." Actually, the message only mentioned Prof. Samuels' position either for or against teaching machines or the Spence learning theory, without reference to other aspects of the alleged symposium. In order not to single out Prof. Samuels unduly the message also mentioned another individual, Prof. George L. Maclay of Cornell, as chairman of the symposium.

The main purpose of these messages was merely to establish the position of the source of both concepts. Accordingly, there was a minimum of further embellishment of information about either of the concepts or of further detail of the source's position.

To establish the *favorable TM* connection, the message merely stated:

> Professor Samuels, a strong proponent of teaching machines, praised the use of teaching machines for instructional purposes in no uncertain terms. He hailed teaching machines as "the most significant single contribution of the behavioral sciences in the field of education."

The *unfavorable TM* version was almost identical in wording except that "opponent" was substituted for "proponent," and "attacked" for "praised." The direct quotation has Samuels hailing teaching machines as a "most pernicious influence on the entire educational system and a source of shame for behavioral sciences."

In either case, the connection with the second concept was made immediately after the paragraph dealing with teaching machines. The *favorable LT* version read:

> At the same time, Professor Samuels also expressed himself as strongly in favor of the Spence Learning Theory. Known as a vigorous supporter of the Spence Theory, he called it "the most compelling explanation of the learning process yet presented."

The *unfavorable LT* connection was again highly similar. The word "against" was substituted for "in favor of," and "antagonist" for "supporter," with the quotation calling the theory "a veritable hodgepodge of unfounded notions with no meaningful basis."

Manipulation of Concept Attitude: Teaching machines was selected as the concept to be manipulated, with Spence learning theory as the secondary concept to which generalization would be investigated—

largely because TM materials were already available. Both the positive and negative treatments of attitude toward TM were accomplished in messages purporting to be copies of an Associated Press article dealing with "a comprehensive report on teaching machines from the U.S. Office of Education," and were similar to those used in the Tannenbaum and Gengel (1966) study. The articles were about equal in length (approximately 475 words) and very similar in format, each stating their respective position on TM and citing a half-dozen more strongly worded arguments—with liberal quotation from the alleged report—in support of that position. In neither case was the source of the linkage message at all mentioned.

Attitude Measure

Four semantic differential scales (cf. Osgood, Suci, & Tannenbaum, 1957), imbedded in a total set of ten such scales, were used to assess attitude. These were selected on the basis of a factor analysis of the present data to be most representative of the evaluative factor on the particular attitudinal objects involved. They included: good-bad, worthless-valuable, successful-unsuccessful, and important-unimportant. The sum of ratings across all four scales, adjusted for consistency of attitudinal direction, constituted the attitude measure at both the T_0 and T_1 test sessions, with the $T_1 - T_0$ difference serving to index the dependent variable of attitude change.

RESULTS

The postulated mechanism for generalization involves a three-stage process. The TM attitude must first be altered by the experimental manipulations. This should affect the source attitude in accord with congruity principle predictions. Then, the critical third stage—change in the dependent LT concept—can be properly assessed. We will consider each in turn.

Change on Manipulated Concept (TM)

The primary intention of the manipulation messages was to change attitude toward the TM concept—in a favorable direction for the positive (*P*) treatment, and unfavorable for the negative (*N*) treatment. Table 1 reports the mean change scores for the different conditions and indicates a highly significant difference between the two experimental treatments. A separate analysis showed a significant ($p < .001$, in each case, by sign test) shift *within* each treatment.

Table 1 *Mean Attitude Change in Manipulated Concept (TM) and Results of Analysis of Variance*

TM Concept Manipulation	Source-Concept Linkages *pp*	*pn*	*np*	*nn*	Marginals
Positive (*P*)	$+8.56_a$	$+9.12_a$	$+7.32_a$	$+7.16_a$	+8.04
Negative (*N*)	-6.96_b	-7.12_b	-7.84_b	-8.24_b	−7.55
Marginals	+ .80	+1.00	− .26	− .54	

Source	*df*	*MS*	*F*
Between linkages	3	23.15	—
Between manipulations	1	12,136.82	268.28*
Interaction	3	5.70	—
Within cells	192	45.24	

Note: Means with the same alphabetical subscript are not significantly different from one another at the .05 level by Newman-Keuls test (cf. Winer, 1962, pp. 80–85).
* $p < .001$.

The lack of a significant difference between the linkage conditions, along with the insignificant interaction effect, are to be expected at this stage, since the linkage conditions should have little relevance to change on the TM concept, as such. Actually, some influence of the linkage message is apparent: The *np* and *nn* conditions, which involved some negative statement about the TM concept in the prior linkage messages, do not exhibit quite as much positive change in the *P* treatment as do the *pp* and *pn* linkages. Similarly, the latter conditions are not quite as negative in the *N* treatment. In all cases, however, these differences are short of statistical significance.

Source Attitude Change

This intermediate stage of the present study is similar to the main focus of the previous Tannenbaum and Gengel (1966) study, and accordingly the same predictions, derived from congruity theory, apply. For example, where there was a positive linkage between the source and TM and then TM was changed negatively, we would expect the source to change in a negative direction to maintain congruity. In this manner, favorable source attitude change is predicted for the *pp* and *pn* conditions under the *P* treatment, and in the *np* and *nn* conditions under the *N* treatment. The situation is reversed for prediction of negative source change—in the *np* and *nn* conditions for *P*, and the *pp* and *pn* conditions for *N*. It should be noted that change in source attitude is predicted solely on the basis of its linkage with the initially manipulated TM concept, and is independent of its association with the second, nonmanipulated concept.

Table 2 clearly indicates that the various source changes occur as predicted. There is a highly significant interaction effect, but the overall main effects are not significant. It is obvious, however, that in both cases, this is due to a canceling-out of significant changes in opposing directions within a given row or column. These findings are in substantial accord with the results of the previous study.

Table 2 *Mean Attitude Change on Source (Samuels) and Results of Analysis of Variance*

TM Concept	Source-Concept Linkages				
Manipulation	*pp*	*pn*	*np*	*nn*	Marginals
Positive (*P*)	$+4.96_a$	$+4.72_a$	-2.52_b	-2.96_b	+1.05
Negative (*N*)	-3.96_b	-3.00_b	$+3.76_a$	$+3.32_a$	+ .12
Marginals	+ .50	+ .86	+ .62	+ .18	

Source	*df*	*MS*	*F*
Between linkages	3	4.00	—
Between manipulations	1	52.02	2.35
Interaction	3	891.17	40.25*
Within cells	192	22.14	

Note: Means with the same alphabetical subscript are not significantly different from one another at the .05 level by Newman-Keuls test.

* $p < .001$.

Change on Nonmanipulated Concept (LT)

Given that the first two stages of the hypothesized process functioned as expected, the data on the main dependent variable may be analyzed. The relevant variables here are the new source attitude in each condition and the nature of the initial linkage between the source and the nonmanipulated concept. Where the source has become more favorable, its position vis-à-vis the LT concept should be reflected in the actual LT change—in a negative direction if the linkage was a negative one, and a favorable change if the linkage was a positive one. On the other hand, if the source attitude has altered in an unfavorable direction, then the LT change should be opposite to that advocated by the source—that is, a favorable change where the linkage was negative, and an unfavorable change where it was positive. By applying the congruity principle in this manner, we would thus predict favorable LT changes in the *Ppp, Nnp, Npn,* and *Pnn* conditions, and unfavorable LT changes in the *Ppn, Nnn, Npp,* and *Pnp* conditions.

Table 3 *Mean Attitude Change on Nonmanipulated Concept (LT) and Results of Analysis of Variance*

TM Concept Manipulation	Source-Concept Linkages *pp*	*pn*	*np*	*nn*	Marginals
Positive (*P*)	$+2.84_a$	-1.92_c	$-.76_{bc}$	$+1.56_a$	+.43
Negative (*N*)	-2.72_c	$+.60_{ab}$	$+2.12_a$	-2.52_c	−.63
Marginals	+ .06	− .66	+ .68	− .48	

Source	*df*	*MS*	*F*
Between linkages	3	18.20	1.48
Between manipulations	1	56.18	4.56*
Interaction	3	240.45	19.52**
Within cells	192	12.32	

Note: Means with the same alphabetical subscript are not significantly different from one another at the .05 level by Newman-Keuls test.

* $p < .05$.

** $p < .001$.

The relevant LT change data are presented in Table 3, and indicate that all changes are in the predicted directions. The four cells in which a positive change was anticipated on the basis of the congruity formulations all change in that direction, with the differences between them being not significant. Similarly, the predicted negative changes obtain, again without significant differences among them. However, the differences between matched pairs of positive and negative changes are always significant. Indeed, the only lack of significant difference between *any* pair of positive and negative means is between the least changing positive one, *Npn,* and the smallest negative one, *Pnp.* Comparing the two groups within a given linkage condition—for example, *Ppp* versus *Npp,* and so on—we find them to change, as anticipated, in opposite directions and to differ significantly from one another.

DISCUSSION

It is clear that the results confirm the theoretical predictions and hence provide support for the proposed theoretical model. It is important to note that within such a model, the change on the second concept may be in a direction opposite to that on the manipulated first concept—and, for that matter, the source attitude change may also be the reverse of that on the first concept. This is in distinction to other instances in which the mediated transfer of evaluation has been exhibited through conventional conditioning procedures. For example, Staats, Staats, and Heard (1959) used a semantic generalization paradigm, and found that the association of highly evaluated terms with stimulus words spread to synonyms of those stimulus words. Even more to the point, Das and Nanda (1963), in a sensory preconditioning design, found that the association of the evaluative words "good" and "bad" with nonsense syllables influenced the judgment of tribal names which had been previously linked to the nonsense terms. In such cases, the judgment of the "conditioned stimulus" (e.g., the tribal names) was always the same, in attitudinal direction if not in degree, as the already established evaluation of the "unconditioned stimulus" (e.g., the words "good" and "bad").

That such a direct transfer of attitude change may be taking place in the present experimental situation is suggested by the difference in LT change as a function of the difference in manipulation of the TM concept, as indicated by the analysis of variance in Table 3. That is, where the initial TM change was positive (*P* manipulation) the overall LT change was also positive; there is a similar correspondence in the negative manipulation condition, the difference between the two manipulations being significant ($p < .05$). While this finding was not expected—the TM concept manipulation treatment, as such, was presumably not a relevant variable affecting LT change—it does not detract from the results in terms of the postulated congruity model, which can still function over and above any direct generalization from one concept to the other.

This is readily apparent when the means for selected individual cells are examined. If only direct transfer of change were operating, we would expect that in the *P* manipulation treatment, all four cells would change positively. This is clearly not the case here—the *Ppn* and *Pnp* actually change in a negative direction, and are significantly different from the positively changing *Ppp* and *Pnn* groups. The same is true for the *N* manipulation treatment of the first concept—the *Npn* and *Nnp* cells change positively rather than negatively and again are significantly different from the corresponding negatively changing *Npp* and *Nnn* cells. It is in these differential linkage conditions—the *pn* and *np* linkages under both the *P* and *N* manipulations—that the critical distinctions are to be found, with the results completely in accord with the congruity model predictions. Indeed, it is in these conditions that the postulated mediated generalization model had to operate *in contradiction* to the direct generalization effects—thus making the obtained findings all the more impressive.

Thus, though there is some evidence of direct generalization, the obtained results are best explained in terms of the congruity model which generated the study: change in attitude toward an unmanipulated concept is a direct consequence of the tendency to maintain the various source-concept relationships involved in a psychologically harmonious or congruent state. At times, such change is in the same direction as that of the manipulated concepts, at times it is in the opposite direction—but it is always in that direction which makes for a congruent situation. Such a theoretical formulation might also be applied to explain the results obtained by Weiss (1957) in a study which had some similar properties to the present one. He found that the prior establishment of a negative source favoring a presumably highly valued concept facilitated the impact of a subsequent message in which that source attacked another concept. Uncertain as to "the nature of the facilitating psychological processes," Weiss dismissed an increase in source "trustworthiness" given the particular source employed (the *Daily Worker*), and tended to favor the apparent "opinion congruence" between the source and the subject created by the first message as the critical factor. This notion, not further developed by Weiss, appears highly similar to the theoretical rationale derived more explicitly from the congruity principle—which is probably the main reason why such similar labels were used, apparently independently.

The basic model, of course, also applies to the determination of changes noted in the intermediate stage of this investigation—change in the source attitude. As with the concept-to-concept change situation the direction of the source change may or may not be in the same direction as the initial concept change, depending on the particular congruity conditions. In this sense, the results of the present experiment are even more impressive in their agreement with the basic theoretical predictions than were the findings in the earlier study (Tannenbaum & Gengel, 1966), where all the mean source-attitude changes were in a favorable direction. A number of possible reasons for this difference are suggested by some methodological differences between the two studies—for example, the use of somewhat different messages, deliberately rewritten for the entire passages to make them more persuasive, in the present study; use in the present study of perhaps more impressionable high school, as opposed to college, subjects; a basic design change from the use of different sources within the same group to represent the different source-concept linkages, to the use of the same named source in different groups. Each of these alternatives may have allowed for a clearer manifestation of the generalization phenomenon under study, but these and others remain purely speculative for the present.

SUMMARY

Four sets of linkages with a single source and two concepts were first established—the source being for both concepts; for the first but against the second; against the first and for the second; and against both. Attitude toward the first concept was then manipulated—both favorably and unfavorably—without any mention of either the source or second concept. It was reasoned from the principle of congruity that such manipulated change in the first concept would influence the source attitude (as a previous study had indeed demonstrated), and that this source change would in turn, produce appropriate modifications in the second concept. The results provided strong confirmation of the theoretical expectations, the source-mediated change in the second concept apparently occurring over and above any direct transfer from the first concept.

REFERENCES

Das, J. P., & Nanda, P. C. Mediated transfer of attitudes. *J. Abnorm. Soc. Psychol.*, 1963, 66, 12–16.

Osgood, C. E., Suci, G. J., & Tannenbaum, P. H. *The measurement of meaning.* Urbana: Univ. of Illinois Press, 1957.

Osgood, C. E., & Tannenbaum, P. H. The principle of congruity in the prediction of attitude change. *Psychol. Rev.*, 1955, 62, 42–55.

Staats, A. W., Staats, C. K., Heard, W. G. Language conditioning of meaning to meaning using a semantic generalization pardigm. *J. Exptl. Psychol.*, 1959, 57, 187–192.

Tannenbaum, P. H., & Gengel, R. W. Generalization of attitude change through congruity principle relationships. *J. Pers. Soc. Psychol.*, 1966, 3, 299–304.

Weiss, W. Opinion congruence with a negative source on one issue as a factor influencing agreement on another issue. *J. Abnorm. Soc. Psychol.*, 1957, 54, 180–186.

Winer, B. J. *Statistical principles in experimental design.* New York: McGraw-Hill, 1962.

§ 5 SOCIAL MOTIVES, ATTITUDES, AND THEIR MEASUREMENT

There is a mutual interaction effect between social motives and social learning—that is, social motives, such as attitudes, values, and beliefs, are learned through contact with others and they determine the kind of behavior people display and the kind of reinforcement they expect. The three papers in this section are concerned with the ways in which social motives are learned, how they affect behavior, and how they may be measured.

The paper by Grusec and Mischel in the last section showed that the behavior of models with high reward potential is likely to be imitated. This finding would suggest that the behavior of parents would have a significant effect on that of their children. Donn Byrne's study demonstrates that children imitate parents' attitudes, values, and beliefs, and that the effects of this learning persist into the adult years. Byrne's research deals with the interrelationship between parental authoritarianism and traditional family ideology, on the one hand, and the degree of authoritarianism expressed by their young adult offspring, on the other. His findings show that the university student who rates high in authoritarianism tends to come from a family in which neither parent rates low in authoritarianism, and the like-sexed parent rates high. Conversely, the student who rates low in authoritarianism is likely to come from a family in which at least one parent also rates low, and the same-sexed parent is not high.

David C. McClelland's paper deals with the validity of a measure of the need for achievement. His prediction that university students rating high in *n* Ach would be likely to go into entrepreneurial work (e.g., sales, business ownership, or top management in a large company) rather than nonentrepreneurial work (e.g., credit, traffic, office management, etc.) was borne out by the careers they actually did enter some fourteen years after graduation.

The study by Robert B. Bechtel and Howard M. Rosenfeld points up some interesting relationships among several motives: the need for affiliation, the need for achievement, fear of failure, and the expectation that a prospective roommate will prove to be compatible. Their research also sheds some light on the acceptance process, for their results show that women university students expect to find more compatibility with roommates at the same status level rather than with those higher or lower in status, but at the same time they prefer roommates who are somewhat higher in status than they are.

5.1 PARENTAL ANTECEDENTS OF AUTHORITARIANISM

Donn Byrne

The most obvious origins of a system of attitudes and beliefs such as authoritarianism would be expected to lie in the experiences of an individual with parents and others relatively early in life. Presumably these influences would be of two major varieties (Frenkel-Brunswik & Havel, 1953). Of greatest importance would seem to be those factors which bring about the development of the underlying characteristics which make antidemocratic beliefs acceptable: repression, denial of aggressive and sexual impulses, and the use of externally oriented problem-solving mechanisms like projection and displacement. Second, there would of necessity be contact with the specific ideas and beliefs that form the content of authoritarian ideology.

In the original Berkeley studies (Adorno, Frenkel-Brunswik, Levinson, & Sanford, 1950), a number of clinical investigations were conducted with subjects high and low in prejudice. The conclusions drawn from these observations led to a multitude of hypotheses concerning the differential family orientation and parental characteristics of individuals who differ in anti-Semitism, authoritarianism,

Source: Reprinted with slight abridgment from the *Journal of Personality and Social Psychology*, 1965, 1, 369–373, with permission of the author and the American Psychological Association, Inc.

ethnocentrism, etc. Briefly, those high on such dimensions reported a relatively harsh and threatening home discipline, clearly defined roles of dominance and submission, early suppression of unacceptable impulses, and emphasis on the social acceptability of values, stress on the importance of duty and obligations, and a dichotomous conception of sex roles. Subjects low on the prejudice-authoritarianism-ethnocentrism continuum reported more or less an opposite type of family structure: less emphasis on obedience, a freer acceptance of emotional expression, less anxiety about conformity, and more tolerance of socially unacceptable behavior. Theoretical descriptions of the etiology of authoritarianism have been based primarily on these observations.

Quantitative investigations of parental antecedents of authoritarianism-equalitarianism have been generally supportive of the foregoing formulations. Authoritarian scores have been found to correlate positively with a scale measuring Traditional Family Ideology (Conventionalism, Authoritarian Submission, Exaggerated Masculinity and Femininity, Extreme Emphasis on Discipline, and Moralistic Rejection of Impulse Life) in a series of studies with adult subjects (Levinson & Huffman, 1955), the frequency with which non-love-oriented disciplinary techniques were espoused by 126 mothers as their response to a series of specific situations involving children (Hart, 1957), perception of parental punitiveness by fifth-grade children as expressed in incomplete sentences (Lyle & Levitt, 1955), scores on the Authoritarian-Control factor of the Parental Attitude Research Inventory in a group of female psychiatric patients and a group of nurses (Zuckerman & Oltean, 1959), the holding of restrictive versus permissive child-rearing attitudes among fathers in a group of military officers (Block, 1955), and scores on the Dominant, Possessive (females), and Ignoring (males) subscales of the USC Parent Attitude Survey in a group of undergraduates (Kates & Diab, 1955).

In discussions of the role of parental attitudes and behavior in the development of authoritarianism and equalitarianism, a rather consistent picture has emerged, based primarily on the foregoing investigations. Authoritarian-equalitarian traits in parents lead to the establishment of characteristic types of family structures and the utilization of particular disciplinary techniques. Children reared in these different ways develop authoritarian or equalitarian ideology as a consequence, and, on reaching adulthood, continue the cycle with respect to their own family structures and disciplinary techniques.

The major flaw in this representation is that the data are based entirely on intraindividual studies in which scores on the *F* Scale are found to be related to some other behavior within a group of subjects. In order to be able to generalize the findings from such research to the actual development of authoritarianism-equalitarianism, it is necessary to make two as yet untested assumptions. First, husbands and wives are assumed to be similar in both authoritarianism and child-rearing practices. Second, parental authoritarianism and child-rearing practices are assumed to have a direct relationship with both authoritarianism and child-rearing practices in their offspring.

The present investigation is designed to test both of the foregoing propositions. Specifically, it is hypothesized that there is a positive relationship between authoritarianism of husbands and of their wives, there is a positive relationship between the acceptance of traditional family ideology by husbands and by their wives, parental traditional family ideology is positively related to authoritarianism and the acceptance of traditional family ideology by their offspring, and parental authoritarianism is positively related to authoritarianism and the acceptance of traditional family ideology by their offspring.

PROCEDURE

The subjects consisted of 108 students (49 males and 59 females) enrolled in the introductory psychology course at the University of Texas and their parents, thus making a total of 324 subjects. The students were tested in small groups as part of a course requirement for participation as research subjects; their parents were contacted by mail. From the original pool of 165 students, 143 were selected as research subjects. The only criteria for selection were that they had not been adopted, that both parents were living, and that their parents were neither separated nor divorced. Of the 143 families fitting these requirements, 35 were ultimately discarded because of the failure of one or both parents to participate or because of errors in responding to the directions for completing the tests. The students whose parents participated in the investigation did not differ significantly in their scores on either test from the students whose parents did not participate.

The measure of authoritarianism was a 32-item scale, partially balanced for acquiescent response set. The Traditional Family Ideology (TFI) Scale was the 35-item instrument development by Levinson and Huffman (1955).

RESULTS

As in previous investigations, both the *F* Scale and the TFI Scale were found to have adequate split-half reliability for research purposes. On the student sample, a corrected (Brown-Spearman formula) coefficient of internal consistency of .81 was found for each scale. In their original article, Levinson and Huffman (1955) reported an average correlation of .67 between the two tests. In the present investigation, the two scales correlated .62 ($p < .01$) among the students, .61 ($p < .01$) among the fathers, and .61 ($p < .01$) among the mothers. Thus the relatively substantial intraindividual relationship between authoritarianism and traditional family ideology was again supported. In this respect, the present sample would appear to be comparable to groups previously studied.

The first two hypotheses dealt with the similarity of married couples on the two variables. The correlation for husband-wife pairs was obtained for each scale. The obtained Pearson product-moment *r*'s were .30 ($p < .01$) for the *F* Scale and .26 ($p < .01$) for the TFI Scale. Both hypotheses were confirmed in that a greater than chance relationship exists between marital partners on these variables, but neither relationship is of substantial magnitude.

The second two hypotheses concerned the relationships between parental scores on the two variables and those of their offspring. The sixteen correlations are shown in Table 1. It can be seen that the hypothesized positive relationships were confirmed for the father-son combinations. The *F*-Scale scores and the TFI-Scale scores of male college students are each a positive function of the scores obtained by their fathers on these two scales. The only other positive finding is that of a significant relationship between authoritarianism in mothers and in their offspring of both sexes.

DISCUSSION

As hypothesized, husbands and wives tend to resemble one another with respect to authoritarianism and traditional family ideology. As with other findings of husband-wife similarities (for example, Byrne & Blaylock, 1963; Newcomb & Svehla, 1937; Schooley, 1936), the relationships are of modest magnitude. Among other implications of this finding, it should be noted that the rather simple picture which may be drawn to contrast authoritarian and equalitarian home atmos-

Table 1 *Correlations between Parents and Offspring in Authoritarianism and Traditional Family Ideology*

Offspring	*F* of Son	TFI of Son
Male		
F of father	.38**	.30*
TFI of father	.33*	.37**
F of mother	.30*	.25
TFI of mother	.14	.22
	F of Daughter	TFI of Daughter
Female		
F of father	.13	−.08
TFI of father	.10	.03
F of mother	.32*	.22
TFI of mother	.14	.11

* $p < .05$.
** $p < .01$.

pheres is probably considerably less straightforward than has hitherto been suggested. For example, in the present sample, there were fourteen families in which the father and mother were on opposite extremes of a trichotomized *F*-Scale distribution. The postulated direct influence of parental authoritarianism and its correlates on the ideology of offspring would quite possibly be affected by the magnitude and direction of differences between the parents, dominance-submission patterns of the husband and wife, differential amounts of contact between father and child versus between mother and child, differential identification with the two parents, etc. It would appear that future work on the parental antecedents of authoritarianism will need to include additional variables of this variety.

As a way of exploring the effects of parental similarity in authoritarianism on the authoritarianism of their offspring, the families in the present sample were divided in terms of low, medium, and high for each parent as shown in Table 2.[1] Within each cell, the number of offspring with low, medium, and high *F*-Scale scores is shown along with the mean scores of those in each cell. Even though this analysis of the data represents an after-the-fact approach, several interesting

[1] Interested readers are referred to the original article for Table 2, which is omitted here in the interest of brevity.

findings emerge. For example, equalitarianism in the offspring is more likely when at least one of the parents is low *F* than when neither parent is low *F* ($\chi^2 = 14.00$, $n = 2$, $p < .001$). This tendency holds whether it is the same-sexed parent ($\chi^2 = 8.68$, $n = 2$, $p < .02$) or the opposite-sexed parent ($\chi^2 = 6.98$, $n = 2$, $p < .05$) who is low in authoritarianism. It is possible that the presence of one equalitarian parent in the home ameliorates the effects of the relative restrictiveness, punitiveness, etc., of the nonequalitarian parent. Or, one might speculate on the special characteristics of the medium or high *F* individual who is attracted to a low *F* individual as a marital partner. An additional finding is that the presence of a high *F* parent significantly affects authoritarianism in the offspring only if it is the same-sexed parent who is high ($\chi^2 = 11.07$, $n = 2$, $p < .01$). Thus the development of a high *F* offspring is most likely to occur in families in which neither parent is low *F* and the same-sexed parent is high *F*; in the 34 families fitting this pattern there were 20 high *F* offspring and 5 low *F* offspring. The development of a low *F* offspring is most likely to occur in families in which at least one parent is low *F* and the same-sexed parent is *not* high *F*; in the 48 families of this description there were 21 low *F* offspring and 8 who were high *F*. It may prove fruitful in subsequent research to explore the factors responsible for the initial attraction of husbands and wives who differ in these various ways with respect to authoritarianism and to investigate the differing parent-child interactions in these families.

The most disconcerting finding is that it is considerably easier to find consistent relationships between authoritarianism and child-rearing variables in intraindividual than in interindividual investigations. Correlations are found in the .60s and .70s between the *F* Scale and the TFI Scale administered to various groups of subjects. When, however, the TFI is administered to the parent and the *F* Scale to the offspring, the only significant relationship found was an *r* of .33 between fathers' TFI score and authoritarianism of sons. In terms of predicting the *F*-Scale scores of college students from knowledge about their parents, the most useful information to have is the *F*-Scale scores of the parents. If both father and mother are considered, a multiple *r* of .40 for male offspring and .33 for female offspring is found. Obviously, a great deal of the variance remains to be accounted for. Perhaps other antecedents of authoritarianism should be sought, as, for example, in the characteristics of other family members besides parents, in school room experiences (Levitt, 1955), and in other contacts with authoritarian and equalitarian ideology outside of the home (Christie,

1952). It should perhaps be noted that other investigators have reported correlations of low magnitude and also insignificant correlations between parental child-rearing attitudes and *prejudice* in children (for example, Harris, Gough, & Martin, 1950). Similarly, Mosher and Scodel (1960) found a correlation of .32 between the ethnocentrism scores of mothers and prejudice scores of their children but no relationship between authoritarian child-rearing practices of mothers and their children's prejudice. They speculated that the latter finding was a function of the ages (11–16) of their subjects. They hypothesized that positive relationships would be found in college-age subjects because the cumulative frustration of such a home would eventually lead to the focusing of resentment onto outgroups. The present findings do not provide much encouragement for that proposition.

An unexpected finding was that of sex differences. Both variables yielded more parent-child relationships for the male offsprings than for the females. It is possible that this finding reflects genuine sex differences in the development of authoritarian ideology. For example, there is some evidence that suggests differences in the importance of hostility as a component of authoritarianism. Irvine (1957) reported a correlation of .48 between the *F* Scale and a hostility measure for male college students. Two other investigations reporting positive relationships between authoritarianism and hostility (Siegel, 1956; Singer & Feshbach, 1959) used only male subjects. The suggestion would be that males are more likely to be the target of frustrating, non-love-oriented disciplinary practices and to direct the resulting unconscious hostility onto outgroups and those who violate accepted mores. It is always possible, of course, that the finding of sex differences is in part a function of the restriction of the sample to a college population. Plans are under way for a repetition of the investigation with a less restricted group in order to test this possibility.

SUMMARY

While a number of investigators have reported substantial relationships between authoritarianism and various parental attitudes concerning child-rearing practices, interindividual studies utilizing families have been lacking. The *F* Scale and the Traditional Family Ideology Scale were administered to 108 college students and their parents. It was found that husband and wife pairs correlate significantly with one another in their scores on the two tests, the *F*-Scale scores and the TFI scores of male college students are each a positive function of the scores obtained by their fathers on these two scales, and there is a significant relationship between authoritarianism in mothers and in their offspring of both sexes. The low magnitude of the various relationships indicates that the major portion of the variance in both authoritarianism and traditional family ideology is a function of factors other than parental standing on these two variables. In addition, the greater predictability of the male students suggests the possibility of differences in the antecedents of authoritarianism for the two sexes.

REFERENCES

Adorno, T. W., Frenkel-Brunswik, Else, Levinson, D. J., & Sanford, R. N. *The authoritarian personality*. New York: Harper, 1950.

Block, J. Personality characteristics associated with fathers' attitudes toward child-rearing. *Child Develop.*, 1955, **26**, 41–48.

Byrne, D., & Blaylock, Barbara. Similarity and assumed similarity of attitudes between husbands and wives. *J. Abnorm. Soc. Psychol.*, 1963, **67**, 636–640.

Christie, R. Changes in authoritarianism as related to situational factors. *Am. Psychol.*, 1952, **7**, 307–308. (Abstract)

Christie, R., Havel, Joan, & Seidenberg, B. Is the F Scale irreversible? *J. Abnorm. Soc. Psychol.*, 1958, **56**, 143–159.

Frenkel-Brunswik, Else, & Havel, Joan. Prejudice in the interviews of children: I. Attitudes toward minority groups. *J. Genet. Psychol.*, 1953, **82**, 91–136.

Harris, D. B., Gough, H. G., & Martin, W. E. Children's ethnic attitudes: II. Relationship to parental beliefs concerning child training. *Child Develop.*, 1950, **21**, 169–181.

Hart, I. Maternal child-rearing practices and authoritarian ideology. *J. Abnorm. Soc. Psychol.*, 1957, **55**, 232–237.

Irvine, L. V. F. Sex differences and the relationships between certain personality variables. *Psychol. Rep.*, 1957, **3**, 595–597.

Kates, S. L., & Diab, L. N. Authoritarian ideology and attitudes on parent-child relationships. *J. Abnorm. Soc. Psychol.*, 1955, **51**, 13–16.

Levinson, D. J., & Huffman, Phyllis E. Traditional family ideology and its relation to personality. *J. Pers.*, 1955, **23**, 251–273.

Levitt, E. E. The effect of a "causal" teacher training program on authoritarianism and responsibility in grade school children. *Psychol. Rep.*, 1955, **1**, 449–458.

Lyle, W. H., & Levitt, E. E. Punitiveness, authoritarianism, and parental discipline of grade school children. *J. Abnorm. Soc. Psychol.*, 1955, **51**, 42–46.

Mosher, D. L., & Scodel, A. Relationships between ethnocentrism in children and the ethnocentrism and authoritarian rearing practices of their mothers. *Child Develop.*, 1960, **31**, 369–376.

Newcomb, T., & Svehla, G. Intra-family relationships in attitude. *Sociometry*, 1937, **1**, 180–205.

Schooley, Mary. Personality resemblances among married couples. *J. Abnorm. Soc. Psychol.*, 1936, **31**, 340–347.

Siegel, S. M. The relationship of hostility to authoritarianism. *J. Abnorm. Soc. Psychol.*, 1956, **52**, 368–372.

Singer, R. D., & Feshbach, S. Some relationships between manifest anxiety, authoritarian tendencies, and modes of reaction to frustration. *J. Abnorm. Soc. Psychol.*, 1959, **59**, 404–408.

Zuckerman, M., & Oltean, Mary. Some relationships between maternal attitude factors and authoritarianism, personality needs, psychopathology, and self-acceptance, *Child Develop.*, 1959, **30**, 27–36.

5.2 NEED ACHIEVEMENT AND ENTREPRENEURSHIP: A LONGITUDINAL STUDY

David C. McClelland

In *The Achieving Society* (McClelland, 1961) data are reported showing relationships between high need achievement (*n* Ach) scores and "entrepreneurial" behavior on laboratory tasks, preference for business occupations when they represent a moderately high level of aspiration for a boy, and occupational status as a business executive versus specialist or professional in the United States, Italy, and Poland. The most reasonable interpretation of these facts seemed to be that high *n* Ach predisposes a young man to seek out an entrepreneurial position in which he can, normally, attain more of the achievement satisfactions he seeks than in other types of positions. Ordinarily business should provide more scope for entrepreneurial behavior; in fact it requires more of it in sales positions than the professions normally require, although of course almost any occupation can be pursued in an entrepreneurial way.

As reasonable as this interpretation may seem, direct confirmation of it requires a longitudinal study. For the higher *n* Ach common among men in entrepreneurial occupations may be the result of having to function in these positions rather than the cause of seeking them out. The critical question is whether men who end up in entrepreneurial occupations had higher *n* Ach years earlier than men who end up in other occupations of equal prestige. Data have recently become available which bear on this point.

Source: Reprinted from the *Journal of Personality and Social Psychology*, 1965, **1**, 389–392, with permission of the author and the American Psychological Association, Inc.

METHOD

In July 1961, Wesleyan University completed an effort to bring up-to-date its Alumni Directory which lists the current occupations and other biographical data for all former students still alive and responding to a request for such information. The Directory therefore provided the data needed to see what had happened to students tested for *n* Ach as early as December 1947—the same students on whom much of the research reported in *The Achievement Motive* (McClelland, Atkinson, Clark, & Lowell, 1953) was conducted. Most of these students graduated in the class of 1950. Many were veterans of World War II so that their average age at the time of testing in their sophomore year was 21.6 years, about two years above normal for such a class. Fourteen years later in 1961, they were about 35 years of age on the average—the youngest being 31 and the oldest 46. Thus they could be considered reasonably settled as to occupational choice. To give some idea of their intelligence level, their average SAT score (Verbal and Mathematical subtests combined) was 528 ($N = 25$).

Of the 58 on whom *n* Ach scores were available from this group, 55 provided sufficient data in the Alumni Directory for their occupational status to be coded. The entries in the Directory were typed on cards and the cards were sorted first into business occupations versus all other occupations (largely the professions—law, medicine, divinity, etc.—in this sample of men, but including some civil service jobs). Next the cards in the business pile were sorted into entrepreneurial or nonentrepreneurial categories, using the following criteria.

Definition: An entrepreneurial occupation, following the definition of Meyer, Walker, and Litwin (1961) in their study of managers versus specialists, is one in which the individual has:

more responsibility for *initiating* decisions, rather than merely having to make decisions when presented with problems.

more *individual responsibility* for decisions and their effects—that is, without review or assistance of a supervisor or a committee.

[more] *objective feedback* of accurate data indicating the success of his decisions, such as in sales volume, profitability, reduction in errors, complaints, etc., rather than just a general subjective evaluation of his success by the group or by superiors.

[a] *job* [which] *entails more risk* or challenge in that there is more chance of a serious wrong decision being observed [p. 571].

Generally speaking the following occupations were coded as meeting or failing to meet these criteria:

Entrepreneurial:
- Sales (except clerical sales)
- Real estate and insurance sales
- Operates own business (including family business if a key executive)
- Management consulting, fund raising, etc.
- Officer of a large company, assistant to the president of a large company, etc.

For example, money management at lower levels is classified as "nonentrepreneurial" (for example, establishing consumer credit), but vice-president of a large New York commercial bank in charge of credit is classified as "entrepreneurial."

Nonentrepreneurial:
- Credit managers
- Traffic managers
- Personnel managers
- Office managers
- Appraisers
- Data processors

Sorting was done independently by two judges without knowledge of *n* Ach scores. Agreement was 91 per cent. Cases of disagreement were decided by the author, though several of them were simply classified as not providing clear enough information to make a decision.

The results of this follow-up study were striking: 83 per cent of the entrepreneurs had been high in *n* Ach fourteen years earlier versus only 21 per cent of the nonentrepreneurs (see Table 1). It was therefore decided that cross-validation of the findings was imperative. Unfortunately further testing for *n* Ach was not done until September 1950 and September 1951 when large samples of the Wesleyan classes of 1954 and 1955 were administered the test at entrance. These samples have two serious drawbacks for cross-validation purposes:

1. The primary objective of the testing on both occasions was to try out new pictures, new scoring categories, and a new time limit for writing (2 versus 4 minutes) in order to get a more "valid" predictor of academic performance (which was never found). Thus the *n* Ach scores available were based on very different and variable procedures. In particular it was found that the shorter time interval for writing stories had some real drawbacks, such as introducing a correlation between *n* Ach and length of protocol (cf. Ricciuti & Sadacca, 1955).

2. The time between college graduation and follow up was really too short to be sure the individual had found his life occupation. Many had gone into the Armed Forces for two or three years after graduation so that they had been working only for three or four years when the follow up was made. They were of course also much younger being about 28 on the average. Nevertheless it seemed worth checking the earlier result on these larger samples, since they provided the only other data available to check the hypothesis at this date.

Consequently the same coding procedure was carried out on these samples as on the first one. Unfortunately proportionally fewer of these men turned up in business. So it was necessary to combine the later samples to provide larger frequencies in the analysis.

RESULTS AND DISCUSSION

Table 1 presents the main findings of the study showing the numbers of men in the three occupational categories who had been above and below the median in *n* Ach (computed separately for the three samples) as undergraduates 10–14 years earlier. The findings are quite striking for the sample that provides the best test of the hypothesis in terms of being based on "standard" *n* Ach scores and on "stable" occupational choices. Eighty-three per cent of the entrepreneurs in business had been high in *n* Ach as college sophomores whereas 79 per cent of the nonentrepreneurs in business had been low in *n* Ach.[1] The cross-validation data on the younger men are not nearly so striking but they are definitely in the same direction: 60 per cent of the entrepreneurs had been high in *n* Ach as college freshmen versus 41 per cent of the nonentrepreneurs. The chi-square for all cases (8.70) is highly significant ($p < .01$). There is considerable support in these results for the hypothesis that at least in the United States and among white college students, males with high *n* Ach tend to gravitate toward business occupations of an entrepreneurial nature where they can better satisfy their achievement aspirations, according to theoretical expectations. It appears that *n* Ach does lead to entering entrepreneurial occupations, as the theory of economic development outlined in *The Achieving Society* requires. It appears also that *n* Ach scores must be valid in the sense of predicting life outcomes over

[1] It may only be a happy accident for the theory, but the one person in this group who struck out on his own to found a business far from his hometown is Karl, the student analyzed extensively in my book on personality, who had the highest *n* Ach score.

periods of ten years, despite frequent reports in the literature of test-retest unreliability over periods of a week or so (Atkinson, 1958; McClelland et al., 1953). These findings are more in line with those reported by Moss and Kagan (1961) who found a correlation of +.34 between *n* Ach scores in adolescent and adult male protocols over a ten-year lapse in time.

Table 1 *Numbers of Enterpreneurs, Nonentrepreneurs, and Professionals in 1961 Who Were above and below the Median in n Achievement as College Undergraduates in 1947 and 1950–51*

	n Achievement				
	1947		1950–51		% above Median Score
	Above	Below	Above	Below	Combined Samples
Business entrepreneurs[a]	10	2	18	12	67% $\chi^2 = 8.70$*
Business nonentrepreneurs[b]	3	11	12	17	35%
Professionals	16	13	50	49	52%

[a] Sales, real estate and insurance, fund raising, founder of own business, management consulting, etc.

[b] Credit, traffic, personnel and office managers, appraisers, data processors, treasurers, etc.

* $p < .01$.

It is worth saying a word about what happens to those who enter the professions with high and low *n* Ach. While the occupational information was not sufficient to classify individuals as more or less entrepreneurial lawyers, teachers, etc., several striking cases suggest that *n* Ach does modify the style in which a person carries out his professional duties. For example, a college English teacher need not be an entrepreneur to be successful in the same way that a sales representative needs to be. The teacher may succeed simply by being a scholar who knows more about Shakespearean plays than anyone else and who year after year inducts students in more or less the same way into the mysteries of his specialized knowledge. Yet in our sample there is a very different kind of English Professor—a man with a very high *n* Ach score as a college sophomore. He teaches drama, produces plays at the university where he is on the faculty, and has founded his own stock company which tours the state during the summer months putting on plays with student actors. Obviously he is part business entrepreneur, since he must take initiative, assume risks, plan plays that will draw audiences, and meet costs, etc. Yet in Table 1 he is classified as a "professional" because he is a teacher. If the occupational information had been better, it would probably have been possible to do a better job of determining who had turned out to be an "entrepreneur," even among the professionals. But generally speaking the opportunity and necessity for this kind of behavior would appear to be greater in the world of business.

A further follow up by questionnaire on these and other students tested in the late 40s and early 50s is planned but in the meantime these data do support the hypothesis that *n* Ach is a fairly stable personality characteristic which, given certain characteristics of the social system, predisposes young men to enter entrepreneurial occupations or to function in traditional occupations in entrepreneurial ways.

SUMMARY

An analysis of the occupational position of 55 Wesleyan graduates some 14 years after graduation indicated that significantly more of those originally scoring high in need achievement (*n* Ach) than of those low in *n* Ach were found in entrepreneurial occupations. A cross-validation study of students of the classes of 1954 and 1955 confirmed the finding that males with high *n* Ach gravitated toward business occupations of an entrepreneurial nature.

REFERENCES

Atkinson, J. W. (Ed.) *Motives in fantasy, action, and society*. Princeton, N.J.: Van Nostrand, 1958.

McClelland, D. C. *The achieving society*. Princeton, N.J.: Van Nostrand, 1961.

McClelland, D. C., Atkinson, J. W., Clark, R. A., & Lowell, E. L. *The achievement motive*. New York: Appleton-Century-Crofts, 1953.

Meyer, H. H., Walker, N. B., & Litwin, G. H. Motive patterns and risk preferences associated with entrepreneurship. *J. Abnorm. Soc. Psychol.*, 1961, **63**, 570–574.

Moss, H. A., & Kagan, J. The stability of achievement and recognition seeking behavior from childhood to adulthood. *J. Abnorm. Soc. Psychol.*, 1961, **62**, 543–552.

Ricciuti, H. N., & Sadacca, R. *The prediction of academic grades with a projective test of achievement motivation: II. Cross-validation at the high school level.* Princeton, N.J.: Educational Testing Service, 1955.

5.3 EXPECTATIONS OF SOCIAL ACCEPTANCE AND COMPATIBILITY AS RELATED TO STATUS DISCREPANCY AND SOCIAL MOTIVES

Robert B. Bechtel
Howard M. Rosenfeld

Expectancy-value theories have been employed widely and successfully in research on achievement-related behavior (Atkinson, 1958; McClelland, Atkinson, Clark, & Lowell, 1953), but little evidence has been accumulated by which to evaluate their usefulness in the study of affiliative behavior. In a laboratory experiment on the selection of task partners among male high-school seniors, Rosenfeld (1964) tested several derivations from an expectancy-value conception of interpersonal choice. His findings revealed that persons who differ from the subject in social desirability (i.e., value) are perceived by him to be low in availability (i.e., expectancy) as task partners, and that the choice of a task partner tends to be a compromise between social desirability and availability. To determine whether these results can be generalized to interpersonal choice processes as they commonly occur in society, the present study examines the above findings under more informal, less task-oriented conditions. Under these conditions it is assumed that high social status is an appropriate quality by which to judge social desirability.

Several additional aspects of the interpersonal choice process were investigated in the present study. In the Rosenfeld study, as well as most other laboratory experiments on interpersonal choice, subjects may have been aware that any newly formed relationships would be limited to the relatively short duration of the study. Thus it is possible that considerations of long-term compatibility were sacrificed for the attainment of immediate acceptance. The current study in-

Source: Reprinted with slight abridgment from the *Journal of Personality and Social Psychology,* 1966, 3, 344–349, with permission of the authors and the American Psychological Association, Inc.

vestigates the operation of both acceptance and compatibility as goals in the selection of relatively long-term associates in a persistent "natural" social system.

The effects of social desirability and expectations of acceptance and compatibility in the selection of associates are likely to be influenced by individual differences in the motives of subjects. In the application of the "Motive × Expectancy × Incentive" formula to achievement behavior, expectancy and incentive are viewed as inversely related properties of the environment, while motive is considered an independent intrapersonal force. However, Atkinson (1957) cites evidence that subjects high in achievement motivation (*n* Achievement) and low in fear of failure (FF) have higher subjective expectations of succeeding on a task of given difficulty than do those who are low in *n* Achievement and high in FF. The present study attempts to determine whether *n* Achievement and FF among women might be related in similar fashion to expectations of interpersonal success.

It is also possible that analogous relationships may obtain between affiliative motivation and the subjective expectation of social success. Rosenfeld (1964) found that need for affiliation (*n* Affiliation) among men was directly related to preferences for competent task partners. Perhaps *n* Affiliation, labeled an approach tendency by Atkinson, Heyns, and Veroff (1954), affects interpersonal choice through heightened expectations of interpersonal success. Fear of rejection (FR), the negative counterpart of *n* Affiliation, should be negatively related to such expectations.

On the basis of the above discussion and the findings of Rosenfeld's (1964) study several hypotheses were derived and tested. Rosenfeld found that to the degree potential task partners deviated from a subject in competence, they were perceived by the subject to be less willing to associate with him as a task partner. A comparable prediction is made in Hypothesis 1: persons estimate that their likelihood of being (*a*) accepted by and (*b*) compatible with others decreases as the social status of others differs from their own.

Another assumption in Rosenfeld's study was that persons are generally motivated to associate with others who surpass them in socially desirable qualities, even though this tendency was thought to be partially inhibited because of the lower subjective availability of superior partners. The finding that subjects typically attempted to form partnerships with peers who were somewhat superior in competence forms the basis for Hypothesis 2: persons in general attempt to associate with others who surpass them in social status.

Acceptance, Compatibility Related to Status Discrepancy, Motives

The remaining hypotheses are derived from the assumption that expectations of social success are positively related to individual differences in approach motivation and negatively related to individual differences in avoidance motivation. Both achievement- and affiliation-related motives are considered. Hypothesis 3 states that expectations of acceptance and compatibility are positively related to: (*a*) *n* Affiliation and (*b*) *n* Achievement. Hypothesis 4 states that expectations of acceptance and compatibility are negatively related to (*a*) FR and (*b*) FF.

METHOD

Subjects were 159 freshman women residents of a university dormitory. Female subjects were used because women have exhibited higher scores on questionnaires of values related to social status (Hyman, 1953) and because they were expected to show greater concern over interpersonal choice than men. To eliminate volunteer bias, four sections of the dormitory were selected at random.

In the first of two sessions held in the dormitory cafeteria, all subjects were administered tests of the four motives listed in Hypotheses 3 and 4. TAT measures of *n* Affiliation and *n* Achievement were obtained by a male experimenter under standard procedures described in Atkinson (1958, Appendix III). The six TAT pictures were identical with those used in a nationwide survey (Veroff, Atkinson, Feld, & Gurin, 1960). *n* Achievement and *n* Affiliation were scored by separate raters, each of whom had previously established high reliability on practice stories provided in Atkinson (1958). It should be noted that attempts to arouse TAT *n* Achievement in females have not generally been successful (Lesser, Krawitz, & Packard, 1963; McClelland et al., 1953), so that the propriety of the measure in the present study is open to question. However, the present set of TAT pictures has been used successfully to assess aroused *n* Affiliation in freshman university women (Rosenfeld & Franklin, 1966), indicating its validity for use as the measure of *n* Affiliation in this study. A short, reliable form of the Mandler-Sarason Test Anxiety Questionnaire (Mandler & Sarason, 1952) was used to assess FF, and a similarly constructed scale developed by Rosenfeld (1964) was used to assess FR. It should also be noted that the FR test had not previously been applied to female subjects.

A face valid Campus Social Status Test, developed in cooperation with dormitory administrators and counselors, was also administered at the first session to make credible the assignment of social status levels in the second session. The 16-item test included inquiries into grade average; car ownership and model; educational attainment, occupation, and income of parents; social group membership and offices; kinds of social activities attended; and number of dates per week. Two days later the second session was held and each subject was assigned Level 5 on the 10-level social status scale, ostensibly on the basis of her answers to the Campus Social Status Test. Instructions, publicly endorsed by legitimate authorities, informed subjects that this was a study concerned with devising better methods of roommate assignment and that they would be required to select new roommates with whom they would actually live for the 6 weeks remaining in the semester.

A random group of 100 subjects was drawn from the sample and each subject was instructed to select a status level from which she would be assigned a new roommate. This group will be referred to as Group I. Group I made its selection of status levels from the 1–10 scale, 1 indicating the highest level of social status, and 10 indicating the lowest. Group II, a random group of 27 subjects, made estimates of the likelihood they would be acceptable as roommates to persons at each of the 10 status levels. They were informed, prior to making estimates, that they would subsequently have a brief meeting with a person from each one of these levels, after which the accuracy of their estimates would be assessed.

A third random group of 32 subjects, Group III, estimated the likelihood that they would be compatible with roommates at each of the 10 social status levels. They were informed,

> By using IBM machine analysis we were able to determine the degree of compatibility between you and each of 10 persons from another dormitory. The persons were selected from each of the 10 social status levels. We want to see how accurately you can guess the likelihood you will be compatible with persons from each level.

Groups II and III made their estimates in terms of a fraction showing "chances in a hundred." Both groups were told their estimates would not be used by the experimenter to influence the roommate they later chose.

After each group made its respective choices or estimates, a post-experimental questionnaire was administered, primarily to assess the degree of preference by each subject for roommates from each of the 10 status levels. Then the experimenter revealed to subjects that no

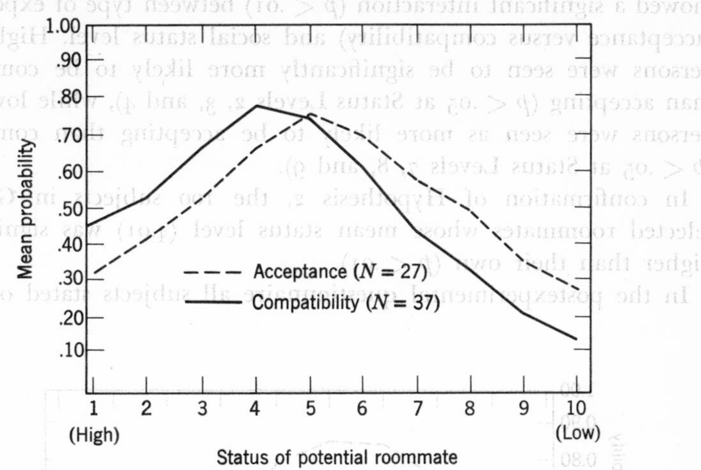

Figure 1. Expectation of acceptance and compatibility as a function of status.

roommate changes would actually take place and carefully explained the real purpose of the experiment.[1]

RESULTS

Figure 1 shows subjects' mean expectations of acceptance from and compatibility with roommates from each status level. As predicted in Hypothesis 1, subjects expected less acceptance and less compatibility to the degree that the status level of a potential roommate differed from their own. *F* tests for acceptance expectations across status levels and for compatibility expectations across status levels were significant ($p < .01$ and $p < .001$, respectively). Subjects expected that persons at status levels either above or below their own level would be less accepting and less compatible ($p < .01$ by *t* test for each comparison).[2]

A comparison of the two distributions shown in Figure 1 also

[1] Responses to the postexperimental questionnaire and to the revelation of the purposes of the experiment strongly indicated that, with the exception of the claimed ability to match persons for compatibility by IBM analysis, the experimental inductions were credible to the subjects.

[2] All p levels in this report are for two-tailed tests.

showed a significant interaction ($p < .01$) between type of expectation (acceptance versus compatibility) and social status level. High status persons were seen to be significantly more likely to be compatible than accepting ($p < .05$ at Status Levels 2, 3, and 4), while low status persons were seen as more likely to be accepting than compatible ($p < .05$ at Status Levels 7, 8, and 9).

In confirmation of Hypothesis 2, the 100 subjects in Group I selected roommates whose mean status level (4.01) was significantly higher than their own ($p < .01$).

In the postexperimental questionnaire all subjects stated on a 10-

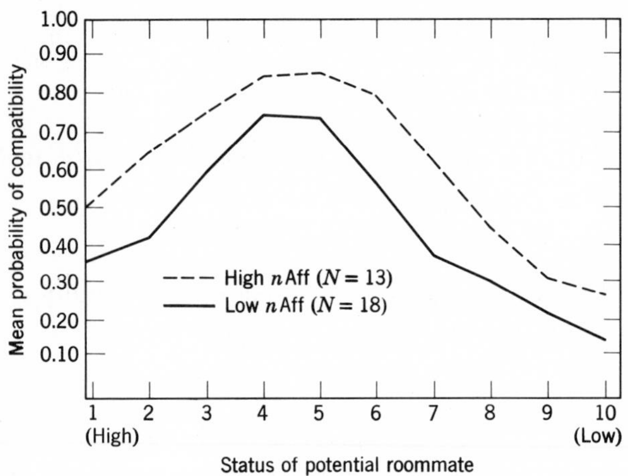

Figure 2. Expectation of compatibility as a function of *n* Affiliation and status.

point scale their preference for potential roommates at each of the 10 social status levels. There were no significant differences between the preference scores of all three experimental groups, so they were combined. The total distribution curve for preference scores was almost exactly parallel to the compatibility expectation curve in Figure 1. Further analyses of the expectation and preference curves revealed that preferences stated on the postexperimental questionnaire were correlated to a significantly greater degree with compatibility expectations than with acceptance expectations ($p < .01$).

Hypotheses 3 and 4 were tested by analysis of variance using the particular motivational test (either *n* Affiliation, *n* Achievement, FF, or FR) and status level as independent variables. None of the measures of motivation was significantly related to expectations of acceptance, either as a main effect or in interaction with status levels of subjects. Two motivational tests—*n* Affiliation and FF—were related to compatibility expectations. Compatibility expectations of subjects high in *n* Affiliation were significantly higher ($p < .01$) than those of subjects who scored low in the *n* Affiliation test (see Figure 2). Thus, Hypothesis 3*a* was confirmed by one criterion—compatibility. However, the significant differences in Figure 2 were confined to the

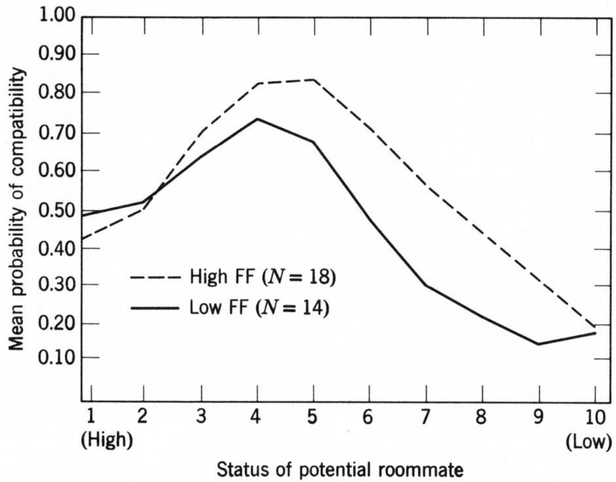

Figure 3. Expectation of compatibility as a function of fear of failure and status.

lower part of the status dimension ($p < .05$ at Levels 5 and 8; $p < .01$ at Levels 6 and 7).

Contrary to Hypothesis 4*b*, subjects high in FF stated higher ($p < .10$) expectations of compatibility than did subjects low in FF (see Figure 3). Similar to the *n* Affiliation results, a significant interaction between motive and status was obtained ($p < .01$), with reliable differences limited to the lower end of the status scale ($p < .05$ at Status Levels 7 and 8 in Figure 3). It should be added that none of the intercorrelations among the four measures of motivation was significant and all were numerically close to zero.

DISCUSSION

The curvilinear relationships between status discrepancy and expectations of acceptance and compatibility are comparable to the results of Rosenfeld's (1964) study in which males anticipated that persons more similar to themselves in task competence would be more available to them as task partners. A second similarity is that the average subject in both studies chose a person approximately one level above himself on the relevant dimension of social desirability—higher status or competence. This last finding is consistent with the assumption that persons are upwardly mobile to the degree that higher levels of social attainment are seen as available to them.

The differences between expectations of acceptance and compatibility were not anticipated. An interpretation of the differences between the acceptance and compatibility curves can be derived from Miller's (1944) theory of approach and avoidance gradients. Slightly over one-half of the subjects stated in the postexperimental questionnaire that they were dubious about the experimenter's claim that he could determine compatibility by IBM analyses of personality test scores. Thus, while subjects anticipated that their expectations of acceptance would be shortly verified, it is likely that they felt compatibility could not be determined until much later. If encounters involving a question of acceptance were likely to be closer than those involving compatibility, the avoidance (of interpersonal failure) gradient should have been higher when making estimates of acceptance than of compatibility. In other words, realistic anticipations of failure may have been more salient to judgments of acceptance, while fantasies of success were more likely to affect judgments of compatibility.

Since it was also found that expectations of compatibility were more highly correlated with preference scores than were expectations of acceptance, the use of compatibility expectations in the prediction of long-term interpersonal choices would seem more potent than acceptance expectations. Future experiments in interpersonal choice cannot ignore the significance of the differences between these two kinds of expectations.

As predicted, subjects high in *n* Affiliation expected significantly higher compatibility than did subjects low in *n* Affiliation; but this difference was significant only with respect to low status persons. If social approval is gained by associating with high status persons and *n* Affiliation is a motive to obtain social approval, one would expect subjects high in *n* Affiliation to have higher expectations of compatibility from high status persons than would subjects low in *n* Affiliation. An additional unanticipated finding was that subjects high in *n* Affiliation indicated on the postexperimental questionnaire that they were significantly less attracted to low status persons than were subjects low in *n* Affiliation ($p < .01$ at Status Levels 6–10, respectively).

The paradoxical behavior of subjects high in *n* Affiliation may be explained by considering previous research which indicates that such subjects seek approval, but that they tend not to receive it. While Atkinson et al. (1954) presented evidence that *n* Affiliation is a tendency to engage in approach behavior, they also found that subjects higher in *n* Affiliation were rated lower in sociometric status by peers. Similarly, Groesbeck (1958) found that subjects higher in *n* Affiliation were rated lower as intimate friends by their peers. Rosenfeld (1964) found that subjects higher in *n* Affiliation attempted more to establish relationships with peers who surpassed them in competence, but withdrew at the first sign of nonacceptance. If it is assumed that subjects high in *n* Affiliation gain some awareness of their relative undesirability yet wish to overcome it, the results of the present study can be interpreted.

Subjects higher in *n* Affiliation expect more compatibility with lower status persons because they perceive that the low status persons are similar to themselves in undesirability. Yet, they wish to overcome their undesirable positions. Hence, to appear available and desirable to higher status persons, they try to avoid association with lower status. In short, the high *n* Affiliation subjects realistically estimated their chances of compatibility with lower status persons as being greater than did subjects low in *n* Affiliation but they attempted more to avoid the stigma of lower status associations. It would appear very much as though to high *n* Affiliation subjects, higher status persons are a positive reference group and lower status persons are a negative reference group as Newcomb (1950, p. 226) defines these terms.

Subjects high in FF also expected greater compatibility than did subjects low in FF, but again only with lower status persons. According to Hypothesis 4*b*, however, FF should have been negatively related to expected compatibility. Hypothesis 4*b* was based on studies of the subjective difficulty of relatively impersonal tasks (Atkinson, 1957). One source of difficulty in attaining a compatible interpersonal relationship is the subject's inability to make himself attractive to others. If the subject high in FF perceives that like the low status person he is unable to attract high status persons, he may expect the low status person to accept him by "default."

The measures of *n* Affiliation and FF, although usually applied to male subjects, thus seem to be indicators of individual differences that are important determinants of female social behavior. The findings that *n* Affiliation and FF are related to expectations of compatibility but not acceptance may indicate that subjects who score high in these variables are more concerned over their ability to persist in social relationships than their ability to establish a positive first impression.

The fact that *n* Achievement was not related to expectations in this study might be due either to the inapplicability of the present measure to female subjects or to the irrelevance of *n* Achievement to the social goals of women. Possible reasons for the lack of relationship between FR and expectations are not readily apparent.

The general outcome of the present study indicates that not all of the principles of expectancy-value theory that have been developed in the area of achievement behavior are directly applicable to affiliative behavior. Such comparisons are useful, however, in revealing which principles can be generalized across content areas and in pointing out discrepancies that require reconceptualization and further research. The present study indicates that in the determination of interpersonal choice two functionally separate forms of expectation operate—acceptance and compatibility. This bifurcation of expectancy revealed totally unexpected behavior on the part of subjects high in *n* Affiliation and FF.

SUMMARY

Hypotheses derived from an expectancy-value conception of interpersonal choice processes were tested in a sample of college dormitory women. All 159 *S*s were assessed for motives related to affiliation and achievement (TAT *n* Affiliation and *n* Achievement, self-report rejection anxiety and test anxiety), and for social status. After being falsely informed that they were of average status, random subsets of *S*s either selected new roommates from among 10 status levels, or estimated their chances of acceptaibility or compatibility at each level. As predicted, status discrepancy was negatively related to estimates; and *S*s typically chose above their own status. Unanticipated status by motive interactions, and differences between acceptance and compatibility estimates, were interpreted in terms of approach and avoidance mechanisms.

REFERENCES

Atkinson, J. W. Motivational determinants of risk-taking behavior. *Psychol. Rev.*, 1957, **64**, 359–372.

Atkinson, J. W. (Ed.) *Motives in fantasy, action, and society*. Princeton, N.J.: Van Nostrand, 1958.

Atkinson, J. W., Heyns, R. W., & Veroff, J. The effect of experimental arousal of the affiliation motive on thematic apperception. *J. Abnorm. Soc. Psychol.*, 1954, **49**, 405–410.

Groesbeck, B. L. Toward description of personality in terms of configurations of motives. In J. W. Atkinson (Ed.), *Motives in fantasy, action, and society*. Princeton, N.J.: Van Nostrand, 1958. Pp. 383–399.

Hyman, H. H. The relation of the reference group to judgments of status. In R. Bendix, & S. M. Lipset (Eds.), *Class, status, and power*. Glencoe, Ill.: Free Press, 1953. Pp. 263–270.

Lesser, G. S., Krawitz, Rhoda N., & Packard, Rita. Experimental arousal of achievement motivation in adolescent girls. *J. Abnorm. Soc. Psychol.*, 1963, **66**, 59–66.

Mandler, G., & Sarason, S. B. A study of anxiety and learning. *J. Abnorm. Soc. Psychol.*, 1952, **47**, 166–173.

McClelland, D. C., Atkinson, J. W., Clark, R. A., & Lowell, E. L. *The achievement motive*. New York: Appleton-Century-Crofts, 1953.

Miller, N. E. Experimental studies of conflict behavior. In J. McV. Hunt (Ed.), *Personality and the behavior disorders*. Vol. 1. New York: Ronald Press, 1944. Pp. 431–465.

Newcomb, T. M. *Social psychology*. New York: Holt, Rinehart, & Winston, 1950.

Rosenfeld, H. M. Social choice conceived as a level of aspiration. *J. Abnorm. Soc. Psychol.*, 1964, **68**, 491–499.

Rosenfeld, H. M., & Franklin, S. S. Arousal of need for affiliation in women. *J. Pers. Soc. Psychol.*, 1966, **3**, 245–248.

Veroff, J., Atkinson, J. W., Feld, Sheila C., & Gurin, G. The use of thematic apperception to assess motivation in a nationwide interview study. *Psychol. Monogr.*, 1960, **74** (12, Whole No. 499).

§ 6 STATUS AND ROLE

The papers included in this section show how the individual's status and the roles appropriate to that status affect attitudes, values, personality, and behavior in general.

The meaning of success to Australian adolescents at three different social-class levels is the topic of the study reported by F. M. Katz. His findings show that middle-class youngsters were more likely to define success in terms of educational or occupational status and to see it as achieved through personal exertion and hard work, whereas working-class and lower-class boys, in particular, were more inclined to perceive success (measured largely in material terms) as achieved through luck or influence.

Melvin L. Kohn, a sociologist with the National Institute of Mental Health, contributes the next paper, a discussion of the relationship between social class and child-rearing patterns. Kohn reviews research showing that middle-class and working-class parents tend to have different objectives and different methods in dealing with their children. He objects to the thesis that the methods of middle-class parents have changed over recent years because child-care experts are now giving a different kind of advice. Instead, Kohn contends, it is the other way around: middle-class parents have changed their methods and are reading books containing the kind of advice that supports what they are already doing. But the kind of reading parents do or do not do is a side issue, for the important consideration is the value system on which the goals and actual behavior of parents in the two classes are based.

The study by Horacio Ulibarri describes the values and mores of Spanish-speaking migrant workers in the American southwest, an ethnic group at the lowest economic level whose culture serves to isolate it from the mainstream of American life.

Judith T. Shuval's report of self-regarding attitudes on the part of North African immigrants to Israel points up some of the problems encountered by a low-status group seeking to accommodate itself to a new culture. Her chief finding is that these immigrants tend to develop attitudes of self-rejection, thus mirroring the prejudice that the larger society holds toward them.

Seymour Lieberman's research is concerned with the relationship of attitude to position and role. Workmen who were promoted to the position of foreman, according to his findings, became more favorably disposed to the company that employed them, as well as to its management and its policies. Those foremen who were later demoted, because of a business recession, tended to revert to the attitudes they had previously held as workmen. Lieberman explains these results in terms of a framework of role theory.

Paul Slovic's experiment with a simple gambling device demonstrates sex differences in values and behavior with respect to risk-taking, differences that may be due to the roles assigned by our culture.

E. Mavis Hetherington's study explores the effect of father absence on the sex-typed behaviors of preadolescent males. The presence of a male model is evidently most crucial during the first five years, because she found little difference in behavior between boys with intact homes and those who had no father since they were five. Boys with absent fathers, however, tended to be more dependent on their peers than were boys from intact homes.

6.1 THE MEANING OF SUCCESS: SOME DIFFERENCES IN VALUE SYSTEMS OF SOCIAL CLASSES

F. M. Katz

The relationship between socioeconomic class of origin and aspirations of adolescents has been demonstrated in numerous studies (2, 6, 12). It has been suggested, as a derivative, that this would at least partly explain the differential attainment of different strata, or the considera-

Source: Reprinted from the *Journal of Social Psychology*, 1964, **62**, 141–148, with permission of the author and The Journal Press.

ble degree of self-perpetuation of social classes in societies such as that of the U.S.A. or Australia—the frame of aspirational reference being viewed as an intervening variable (1).

Educational and vocational aspirations have also been used as indices of value systems, components of what Linton (9) called "designs for group living." This appears to be a legitimate assumption, but more direct empirical evidence is needed about characteristics of value systems. Thus it is still frequently assumed, following Merton's (10) significant contribution, that a culturally dominant frame of aspirational reference is internalized by members of all social classes. In the case of the U.S.A., this is assumed to place "great emphasis upon certain success goals," success being achieved through accumulation of wealth and possessions which are viewed as conferring status on the individual. As Merton (10) implies, nonadherence to "this syndrome of lofty aspirations" is a deviation from the norm.

Hyman's (4) interesting analysis of some empirical data is influenced by this proposition. Thus he attempts to show "the degree to which individuals in different strata value the *culturally prescribed goal of success,* believe that opportunity is available to them, and hold other values which would aid or hinder them in their attempts to move towards their goal." This conformity of members of all social classes to these "lofty aspirations" might be challenged, certainly for different cultures (e.g., that of Australia, where no *a priori* assumption of conformity can be made). Hence, one purpose of the investigation to be reported was to assess the dominant value systems as well as the possible class differences in and among them.

The approach adopted was to ascertain the *concept of success* of adolescents of different socioeconomic class of origin. If the dominant value system were that defined by Merton as an "Ideology of Success," one would expect to find success defined in terms of achievement of status through possession of wealth. If it can be shown that success does not have this meaning for all, or for members of some classes, it is hypothesized that different value systems are operative. Hence differences in conceptions of, or descriptions of, success and associated paths are viewed as reflecting differences in values systems. The hypotheses to be tested are, *first,* that similarities in the concept of success reflect culturally prescribed value systems; *second,* that adolescents of different social classes will differ significantly in their concept of success; and, *third,* that these differences are sufficient conditions for a rejection of a hypothesis of isolated deviation from a norm (i.e., through membership of social classes different value systems are inculcated).

METHOD

A sample of 819 boys and girls, aged 14–16 years, pupils in secondary schools of New South Wales, Australia, participated in a general study of aspirations.[1] As part of a series of questionnaires and projective tests, the subjects were asked to define their meaning of "success" and to indicate how this was achieved.[2] They were also asked to indicate their relationship to the person used as a model of success.

The assessment of socioeconomic class of origin was made on the basis of father's occupation. Three classes were differentiated for the purpose of this paper: those whose father's occupation was Unskilled manual labor (USK), Skilled manual labor (SK), and White Collar occupations (MC), the latter being a compendium of professional, clerical, and business occupations, and including self-employed farmers.

FINDINGS

Definition of "Success"

It is assumed that answers to the question "what makes you say that he has done well for himself?" provide a measure of a person's concept of success. As Table 1 shows, the criteria of success vary con-

[1] The study was carried out entirely by the author, but for some of the procedures the author is indebted to Prof. C. A. Mace and a research team, Psychology Department, Birbeck College, University of London, one purpose of the present study being a cross-cultural comparison of aspirations. For a preliminary report see Katz (7).

[2] The questions asked were:

Is there anybody that you actually know who has done well for himself?

If yes, who is it (relation, friend, etc.)?

What makes you say that he has done well?

How did he manage to do so well?

When you look around at people who have done well, who have "got on," you may think that in some cases it is because they have been lucky; they just happened to be about at the right time. Sometimes it may be because they knew what they wanted and they worked hard to get it. Or sometimes you might think it was because they knew the right sort of people, who used their influence to help them. How do you think most people who *do well* manage it? By hard work? By being lucky? or By knowing the right people?

It should be noted that responses by *S*s to questions 2 and 3 were entered, where applicable, in more than one category (see Tables 1 and 2).

Table 1 *Percentages of Boys and Girls of Different Socioeconomic Classes of Origin Mentioning Various Criteria of "Success" (Total N: boys = 409; girls = 410)*

	Fathers' Occupation							
	Boys				Girls			
Criteria of "Success"	USK	SK	MC	Total No. of Mentions	USK	SK	MC	Total No. of Mentions
Wealth and possessions	42	55	45	199	34	35	35	144
Occupational or educational status[a]	18	19	44	127	19	29	40	130
Attributes of personality	7	8	6	28	27	23	26	103
Secure job	18	13	10	55	23	22	14	77
Family of procreation	2	5	5	18	3	4	7	21
Not answered	19	9	3	39	12	6	5	38
N	(106)	(164)	(139)	427	(78)	(161)	(171)	475

[a] Differences between classes on number who mention status: boys—for 2 *df*, $x^2 = 20.16$, $p < .001$; girls—for 2 *df*, $x^2 = 12.93$, $.01 > p > .001$.

siderably. Five major categorizations are used. Of these, "wealth and possessions" is most frequently mentioned. It has been suggested that if success is defined in terms of wealth and/or possessions, this would indicate the person's concern with achievement of status (wealth and possessions being viewed as status symbols, conferring prestige on the owner). It is possible, however, to desire possessions not necessarily as a means toward achievement of status. Thus, contrary to the views of Merton (10), it is argued that possessions may have inherent values distinct from their possible significance as status symbols. For instance, a house or a car may have inherent values to the person quite distinct from its possible prestige-endowing qualities. Hence, although the majority of the total sample, and the majority of each class, indicated that they perceived success as a function of wealth or possessions, this is not viewed as necessarily implying concern with status. Rather, it indicates that certain objects have universal appeal: i.e., reflect certain cultural values, but not as status symbols.

Status or prestige, as a criterion of success, is directly referred to in the answers of some subjects. Thus a proportion of the sample attributed success on the basis of the position held by the person in an occupational or educational hierarchy. This is direct evidence of an identification of success with status. Significantly, as Table 1 shows, adolescents of different class of origin differ in their use of status as the criterion of success. Thus adolescents of MC class of origin, by frequently citing status as a criterion of success, indicate that, for this group at least, status achievement is an important component of their value system.

Other criteria of success mentioned by subjects were *attributes of personality*: i.e., possession of certain personality characteristics, viewed as bestowing on the individual personal "worthiness" or even a sense of goal achievement;[3] *a secure job*: i.e., a job description which implied that the successful individual had achieved a secure job (answers were not placed in this category if any indication was given of the characteristic of job satisfaction, derived from status achievement); and, finally, *family of procreation* (a minority of the sample mentioned this criterion, success being defined in terms of the characteristics of social relationships within a family unit).

As Table 1 shows, there are no significant differences between classes on any of these latter criteria which are mentioned by minorities of each class.

Attainment of "Success"

The second element of a culturally prescribed value system defines the procedure towards the achievement of the prescribed goal. As Table 2 shows, there is considerable agreement by subjects on the major procedure used in achieving success. Thus the great majority mentioned, as reason for achieving success, personal effort and personal worthiness. These factors, over which the individual has some control, may be contrasted to conditions independent of and external to the individual: namely, luck or influence. Table 2 shows that, at least in the case of boys, those of MC class of origin more frequently mention personal worthiness and effort as the means towards achievement of success.

This is more clearly demonstrated in Table 3, which shows answers of subjects when asked to indicate which of the three factors, "hard

[3] The significant difference between boys and girls ($p < .001$) in frequency of mentioning this criterion is an interesting phenomenon which correlates significantly with material of projective tests. This will be discussed in a later publication.

Table 2 *Percentage of Boys and Girls of Different Socioeconomic Classes of Origin Who Mention Various Procedures to the Achievement of "Success"*

	Fathers' Occupation							
	Boys				Girls			
Means Used to Achieve "Success"	USK*	SK	MC*	Total No. of Mentions	USK*	SK	MC*	Total No. of Mentions
Personal exertion	57	76	77	290	69	83	82	328
Characteristics of personality	9	16	20	63	18	28	32	104
Luck	11	9	10	41	8	4	7	24
Influence	11	14	8	47	15	10	12	48
Not answered	20	10	3	42	10	5	3	21
N	(106)	(164)	(139)		(78)	(161)	(171)	

* Difference between USK and MC class: Mention "personal exertion"—boys, $p < .001$; girls, $.05 > p > .02$. Mention "characteristics of personality"—boys, $.02 > p > .01$; girls, $.02 > p > .01$.

Table 3 *Selection of Hard Work, Luck, and Influence as General Means for Achieving "Success"*

	Fathers' Occupation					
	Boys			Girls		
Means to "Success"	USK	SK	MC*	USK	SK	MC*
"Hard work," solely	39 (37%)	63 (38%)	79 (57%)	42 (54%)	86 (53%)	95 (56%)
"Luck" and "influence" selected solely or as well as "hard work"	66 (62%)	100 (62%)	57 (41%)	35 (45%)	75 (47%)	74 (43%)
Not answered	1 (1%)	1	3 (2%)	1 (1%)	—	2 (1%)
	106	164	139	78	161	171

* Differences between MC class and others: boys—for 1 *df*, $x^2 = 13.5$, $p < .001$.

work," "luck" and/or "influence" was the most potent factor in ensuring success.[4]

The significant differences between classes as shown in Table 3 indicate that adolescent boys of USK and SK class of origin more frequently perceive the conditions leading to success to be dependent on factors over which the individual has no control. This difference is not apparent in the case of girls.

Model of "Success"

The relationship of the subject to the person identified as successful, or used as a model of success, might be used as an index of the subject's reference group. If the person chosen as a model of success achievement is a member of the subject's immediate family unit, it may be assumed that the family provides a means of identification with success. In turn, this increases the probability of seeking achievement of success, as the model of success is in psychological proximity to the subject. It is of considerable interest to note (see Table 4) that although the majority of the sample (63 per cent) indicate their use of a relative as a model of success, the proportion is much greater for the MC class than for those of USK and SK class of origin. Equally relevant is the total absence of a model for success achievement as indicated by 12 per cent of the USK, suggesting possible absence of "success" in the frame of reference of these individuals.

SUMMARY AND CONCLUSIONS

The basic assumption is that an assessment of a person's concept of "success" provides an index of his frame of aspirational reference. If, for instance, the criterion of success achievement is attainment of status, the procedure toward its achievement—personal exertion and personal worthiness—thus would be taken to indicate a frame of aspirational reference aptly defined by Ichheiser (5) as "The Ideology of Success." Since little information is available on the value systems of the Australian culture pattern, no *a priori* assumption was made about the existence of a culturally prescribed goal of success. However,

[4] Subjects were directed to indicate their choice by choosing one or more of the factors. The same question was used in the investigation carried out in England. It is interesting to note that there approximately 90 per cent chose "hard work" as the procedure to achieve success. The difference in results suggests cross-cultural variation in value systems (7).

Table 4 *Class* Differences in Relationship to Subjects of Person Chosen as a Model of "Success"*

Relationship to Subject	Fathers' Occupation					
	Boys			Girls		
	USK	SK	MC	USK	SK	MC
Model: member of subject's family	53 (50%)	93 (57%)	100 (72%)	45 (58%)	107 (66%)	120 (70%)
Model: friend, acquaintance or known by repute	37 (35%)	63 (38%)	38 (27%)	30 (38%)	48 (30%)	47 (27%)
No "successful" person known to subject	13 (12%)	6 (4%)	1 (1%)	2 (3%)	6 (4%)	2 (1%)
Not answered	3	2	—	1	—	2
	106	164	139	78	161	171

* Differences between classes: boys—for 2 *df*, $x^2 = 14$, $p < .001$; girls—for 2 *df*, $x^2 = 6$, $p < .05$.

the facility with which adolescents in the sample defined the goal and paths toward success suggests that success is at least an important element in the frame of reference of adolescents growing up in Australia.

The criteria used in the definition of success show some basic similarities, but also some significant differences for adolescents of different socioeconomic class of origin. This would suggest the existence of cultural prescriptions, and subcultural or class variations in the frame of aspirational reference which is internalized in the process of socialization. Thus it was seen that the majority of subjects judged success in terms of accumulation of possessions and wealth. Also used by a significant proportion of the sample as criteria of success were attainment of a secure job, and achievement of status, the latter being defined in terms of position in a vocational or educational hierarchy. The use of status in the definition of success varies significantly between adolescents of different social class of origin. We might tentatively conclude that achievement of possessions is part of the culturally prescribed frame of aspirational reference, whereas success measured by the degree of status achievement is confined largely to adolescents of "middle-class" origin.

To assess values embodied in the frame of aspirational reference, it is necessary to consider (as well as the goal) the institutionalized norms toward achieving it. As Merton (10) suggests, these "operate jointly to shape prevailing practices." The explanation of means to success given by subjects in the present investigation again shows evidence of cultural prescriptions. Thus we note that the majority of the sample suggests that the procedure for achieving success is personal exertion and personal worthiness. Adolescents of USK and SK class origin, however, also view achievement of success as dependent on conditions over which the individual has no control: "Luck" and/or "influence" are as important as hard work.

There is evidence, therefore, of considerable variation in the concept of success for adolescents of different socioeconomic class of origin. This is seen as indicative of a major difference in the frame of aspirational reference internalized by members of different social classes. The concept of success in the case of the MC-class adolescent approximates to that previously described as the "Ideology of Success," with the goal emphasizing status achievement and the procedure emphasizing personal effort and personal worthiness.

Those of USK class of origin, on the other hand, appear to have a frame of aspirational reference markedly different from that described above. There is little evidence of concern with status. Achievement of "success" is defined in terms of possessions which are procured by personal exertion, but limited in possibility of attainment by factors over which the individual has no control.

In the sample studied, the adolescent of SK class of origin showed marked within-group variation. This suggests that a proportion of this class may have internalized the value systems of the MC class, while others approximate to those of USK class of origin. This characteristic of marginal status is supported by other evidence.[5]

The finding of class variations in value systems of adolescents indicates that, through the class membership of the family of origin, different values are inculcated. Some direct evidence of the role of the family is provided by the use of family members as models of success. Thus the majority of the sample identify the "successful" person as a member of their immediate family. However, identification with a relative is much more frequent for adolescents of MC-class origin. It is concluded that this again suggests a fundamental class difference in the frame of aspirational reference affecting the adolescent's orientation of his future.

[5] For a description of the concept of marginal status see Lewin (8).

REFERENCES

1. Bendix, R., & Lipset, S. M., Eds. *Class, status and power: A reader in social stratification.* Glencoe, Ill.: Free Press, 1953.
2. Douvan, E. Social status and success striving. *J. Abnorm. Soc. Psychol.*, 1956, **52**, 219–223.
3. Elkin, A. P., Ed. *Marriage and the family in Australia.* Sydney: Angus & Robertson, 1957.
4. Hyman, H. H. The value system of different classes: A social psychological contribution to the analysis of stratification. In Bendix, R., & Lipset, S. M., Eds., *Class, status and power: A reader in social stratification.* Glencoe, Ill.: Free Press, 1953.
5. Ichheiser, G. The ideology of success. *Ethics,* 1943, **53**, 137–141.
6. Kahl, J. A. Educational and occupational aspirations of "common man boys." *Harvard Educ. Rev.*, 1953, **23**, 188.
7. Katz, F. M. A cross-cultural study of adolescent aspirations to the future. *J. Soc. Psychol.*, 1962, **57**, 277–281.
8. Lewin, K. The field theory approach to adolescence. *Am. J. Sociol.*, 1939, **44**, 868–897.
9. Linton, R. *Study of man.* New York: Appleton-Century, 1936.
10. Merton, R. K. *Social theory and social structure.* Glencoe, Ill.: Free Press, 1949.
11. Oeser, O. A., & Hammond, S. M. *Social structure and personality in an urban community.* London: Routledge & Kegan Paul, 1954.
12. Rosen, B. C. The achievement syndrome: A psychocultural dimension of social stratification. *Am. Sociol. Rev.*, 1956, **21**, 206.

6.2 SOCIAL CLASS AND PARENT-CHILD RELATIONSHIPS: AN INTERPRETATION

Melvin L. Kohn

This essay is an attempt to interpret, from a sociological perspective, the effects of social class upon parent-child relationships. Many past discussions of the problem seem somehow to lack this perspective, even though the problem is one of profound importance for sociology. Because most investigators have approached the problem from an interest in psychodynamics, rather than social structure, they have largely limited their attention to a few specific techniques used by

Source: Reprinted with slight abridgment from the *American Journal of Sociology,* 1963, **68,** 471–480, with permission of the author and the University of Chicago Press.

mothers in the rearing of infants and very young children. They have discovered, *inter alia*, that social class has a decided bearing on which techniques parents use. But, since they have come at the problem from this perspective, their interest in social class has not gone beyond its effects for this very limited aspect of parent-child relationships.

The present analysis conceives the problem of social class and parent-child relationship as an instance of the more general problem of the effects of social structure upon behavior. It starts with the assumption that social class has proved to be so useful a concept because it refers to more than simply educational level, or occupation, or any of the large number of correlated variables. It is so useful because it captures the reality that the intricate interplay of all these variables creates different basic conditions of life at different levels of the social order. Members of different social classes, by virtue of enjoying (or suffering) different conditions of life, come to see the world differently—to develop different conceptions of social reality, different aspirations and hopes and fears, different conceptions of the desirable.

The last is particularly important for present purposes, for from people's conceptions of the desirable—and particularly from their conceptions of what characteristics are desirable in children—one can discern their objectives in child-rearing. Thus, conceptions of the desirable—that is, values[1]—become the key concept for this analysis, the bridge between position in the larger social structure and the behavior of the individual. The intent of the analysis is to trace the effects of social class position on parental values and the effects of values on behavior.

Since this approach differs from analyses focused on social class differences in the use of particular child-rearing techniques, it will be necessary to reexamine earlier formulations from the present perspective. Then three questions will be discussed, bringing into consideration the limited available data that are relevant: What differences are there in the values held by parents of different social classes? What is there about the conditions of life distinctive of these classes that might

[1] "A value is a conception, explicit or implicit, distinctive of an individual or characteristic of a group, of the desirable which influences the selection from available modes, means, and ends of action" (Clyde Kluckhohn, "Values and Value Orientations," in Talcott Parsons, & Edward A. Shils, Eds., *Toward A General Theory of Action*, Cambridge, Mass.: Harvard Univ. Press, 1951, p. 395). See also the discussion of values in Robin M. Williams, Jr., *American Society: A Sociological Interpretation*, New York: Knopf, 1951, Chap. XI, and his discussion of social class and culture on p. 101.

explain the differences in their values? What consequences do these differences in values have for parents' relationships with their children?

SOCIAL CLASS

Social classes will be defined as aggregates of individuals who occupy broadly similar positions in the scale of prestige.[2] In dealing with the research literature, we shall treat occupational position (or occupational position as weighted somewhat by education) as a serviceable index of social class for urban American society. And we shall adopt the model of social stratification implicit in most research, that of four relatively discrete classes: a "lower class" of unskilled manual workers, a "working class" of manual workers in semiskilled and skilled occupations, a "middle class" of white-collar workers and professionals, and an "elite," differentiated from the middle class not so much in terms of occupation as of wealth and lineage.

Almost all the empirical evidence, including that from our own research, stems from broad comparisons of the middle and working class. Thus we shall have little to say about the extremes of the class distribution. Furthermore, we shall have to act as if the middle and working classes were each homogeneous. They are not, even in terms of status considerations alone. There is evidence, for example, that within each broad social class, variations in parents' values quite regularly parallel gradations of social status. Moreover, the classes are heterogeneous with respect to other factors that affect parents' values, such as religion and ethnicity. But even when all such considerations are taken into account, the empirical evidence clearly shows that being on one side or the other of the line that divides manual from nonmanual workers has profound consequences for how one rears one's children.[3]

STABILITY AND CHANGE

Any analysis of the effects of social class upon parent-child relationships should start with Urie Bronfenbrenner's analytic review of the

[2] Williams, *op. cit.*, p. 89.

[3] These, and other assertions of fact not referred to published sources, are based on research my colleagues and I have conducted. For the design of this research and the principal substantive findings see my "Social Class and Parental Values," *Am. J. Sociol.*, 1959, **64**, 337–51; my "Social Class and the Exercise of Parental Authority," *Am. Sociol. Rev.*, 1959, **24**, 352–66; and with Eleanor E. Carroll, "Social Class and the Allocation of Parental Responsibilities," *Sociometry*, 1960, **23**, 372–92.

studies that had been conducted in this country during the twenty-five years up to 1958.[4] From the seemingly contradictory findings of a number of studies, Bronfenbrenner discerned not chaos but orderly change: there have been changes in the child-training techniques employed by middle-class parents in the past quarter-century; similar changes have been taking place in the working class, but working-class parents have consistently lagged behind by a few years; thus, while middle-class parents of twenty-five years ago were more "restrictive" than were working-class parents, today the middle-class parents are more "permissive"; and the gap between the classes seems to be narrowing.

It must be noted that these conclusions are limited by the questions Bronfenbrenner's predecessors asked in their research. The studies deal largely with a few particular techniques of child-rearing, especially those involved in caring for infants and very young children, and say very little about parents' overall relationships with their children, particularly as the children grow older. There is clear evidence that the past quarter-century has seen change, even faddism, with respect to the use of breast-feeding or bottle-feeding, scheduling or not scheduling, spanking or isolating. But when we generalize from these specifics to talk of a change from "restrictive" to "permissive" practices—or, worse yet, of a change from "restrictive" to "permissive" parent-child relationships—we impute to them a far greater importance than they probably have, either to parents or to children.[5]

There is no evidence that recent faddism in child-training techniques is symptomatic of profound changes in the relations of parents to children in either social class. In fact, as Bronfenbrenner notes, what little evidence we do have points in the opposite direction: the overall quality of parent-child relationships does not seem to have changed substantially in either class.[6] In all probability, parents have changed techniques in service of much the same values, and the

[4] Urie Bronfenbrenner, "Socialization and Social Class through Time and Space," in Eleanor E. Maccoby, Theodore M. Newcomb, & Eugene L. Hartley, Eds., *Readings in Social Psychology*, New York: Holt, 1958.

[5] Furthermore, these concepts employ a priori judgments about which the various investigators have disagreed radically. See, e.g., Robert R. Sears, Eleanor E. Maccoby, & Harry Levin, *Patterns of Child Rearing*, Evanston, Ill.: Row, Peterson, 1957, pp. 444–447; and Richard A. Littman, Robert C. A. Moore, & John Pierce-Jones, "Social Class Differences in Child Rearing: A Third Community for Comparison with Chicago and Newton," *Am. Sociol. Rev.*, 1957, **22**, 694–704, esp. p. 703.

[6] Bronfenbrenner, *op. cit.*, pp. 420–422 and 425.

changes have been quite specific. These changes must be explained, but the enduring characteristics are probably even more important.

Why the changes? Bronfenbrenner's interpretation is ingenuously simple. He notes that the changes in techniques employed by middle-class parents have closely paralleled those advocated by presumed experts, and he concludes that middle-class parents have changed their practices *because* they are responsive to changes in what the experts tell them is right and proper. Working-class parents, being less educated and thus less directly responsive to the media of communication, followed behind only later.[7]

Bronfenbrenner is almost undoubtedly right in asserting that middle-class parents have followed the drift of presumably expert opinion. But why have they done so? It is not sufficient to assume that the explanation lies in their greater degree of education. This might explain why middle-class parents are substantially more likely than are working-class parents to *read* books and articles on child-rearing, as we know they do.[8] But they need not *follow* the experts' advice. We know from various studies of the mass media that people generally search for confirmation of their existing beliefs and practices and tend to ignore what contradicts them.

From all the evidence at our disposal, it looks as if middle-class parents not only read what the experts have to say but also search out a wide variety of other sources of information and advice: they are far more likely than are working-class parents to discuss child-rearing with friends and neighbors, to consult physicians on these matters, to attend Parent-Teacher Association meetings, to discuss the child's behavior with his teacher. Middle-class parents seem to regard child-rearing as more problematic than do working-class parents. This can hardly be a matter of education alone. It must be rooted more deeply in the conditions of life of the two social classes.

Everything about working-class parents' lives—their comparative lack of education, the nature of their jobs, their greater attachment to the extended family—conduces to their retaining familiar methods. Furthermore, even should they be receptive to change, they are less

[7] Bronfenbrenner gives clearest expression to this interpretation, but it has been adopted by others, too. See, e.g., Martha Sturm White, "Social Class, Child-Rearing Practices, and Child Behavior," *Am. Sociol. Rev.*, 1957, **22**, 704–712.

[8] This was noted by John E. Anderson in the first major study of social class and family relationships ever conducted, and has repeatedly been confirmed (*The Young Child in the Home: A Survey of Three Thousand American Families*, New York: Appleton-Century, 1936).

likely than are middle-class parents to find the experts' writings appropriate to their wants, for the experts predicate their advice on middle-class values. Everything about middle-class parents' lives, on the other hand, conduces to their looking for new methods to achieve their goals. They look to the experts, to other sources of relevant information, and to each other not for new values but for more serviceable techniques.[9] And within the limits of our present scanty knowledge about means-ends relationships in child-rearing, the experts have provided practical and useful advice. It is not that educated parents slavishly follow the experts but that the experts have provided what the parents have sought.

To look at the question this way is to put it in a quite different perspective: the focus becomes not specific techniques nor changes in the use of specific techniques but parental values.

VALUES OF MIDDLE- AND WORKING-CLASS PARENTS

Of the entire range of values one might examine, it seems particularly strategic to focus on parents' conceptions of what characteristics would be most desirable for boys or girls the age of their own children. From this one can hope to discern the parents' goals in rearing their children. It must be assumed, however, that a parent will choose one characteristic as more desirable than another only if he considers it to be both important, in the sense that failure to develop this characteristic would affect the child adversely, and problematic, in the sense that it is neither to be taken for granted that the child will develop that characteristic nor impossible for him to do so. In interpreting parents' value choices, we must keep in mind that their choices reflect not simply their goals but the goals whose achievement they regard as problematic.

Few studies, even in recent years, have directly investigated the rela-

[9] Certainly middle-class parents do not get their values from the experts. In our research, we compared the values of parents who say they read Spock, Gesell, or other books on child-rearing, to those who read only magazine and newspaper articles, and those who say they read nothing at all on the subject. In the middle class, these three groups have substantially the same values. In the working class, the story is different. Few working-class parents claim to read books or even articles on child-rearing. Those few who do have values much more akin to those of the middle class. But these are atypical working-class parents who are very anxious to attain middle-class status. One suspects that for them the experts provide a sort of handbook to the middle class; even for them, it is unlikely that the values come out of Spock and Gesell.

tionship of social class to parental values. Fortunately, however, the results of these few are in essential agreement. The earliest study was Evelyn Millis Duvall's pioneering inquiry of 1946.[10] Duvall characterized working-class (and lower middle-class) parental values as "traditional"—they want their children to be neat and clean, to obey and respect adults, to please adults. In contrast to this emphasis on how the child comports himself, middle-class parental values are more "developmental"—they want their children to be eager to learn, to love and confide in the parents, to be happy, to share and co-operate, to be healthy and well.

Duvall's traditional-developmental dichotomy does not describe the difference between middle- and working-class parental values quite exactly, but it does point to the essence of the difference: working-class parents want the child to conform to externally imposed standards, while middle-class parents are far more attentive to his internal dynamics.

The few relevant findings of subsequent studies are entirely consistent with this basic point, especially in the repeated indications that working-class parents put far greater stress on obedience to parental commands than do middle-class parents.[11] Our own research, conducted in 1956–1957, provides the evidence most directly comparable to Duvall's.[12] We, too, found that working-class parents value obedience, neatness, and cleanliness more highly than do middle-class parents, and that middle-class parents in turn value curiosity, happiness, consideration, and—most importantly—self-control more highly than do working-class parents. We further found that there are characteristic clusters of value choice in the two social classes: working-class parental values center on conformity to external proscriptions, middle-class parental values on *self*-direction. To working-class parents, it is the overt act that matters: the child should not transgress externally imposed rules; to middle-class parents, it is the child's motives and feelings that matter: the child should govern himself.

In fairness, it should be noted that middle- and working-class parents share many core values. Both, for example, value honesty very highly—although, characteristically, "honesty" has rather differ-

[10] "Conceptions of Parenthood," *Am. J. Sociol.*, 1946, **52**, 193–203.

[11] Alex Inkeles has shown that this is true not only for the United States but for a number of other industrialized societies as well ("Industrial Man: The Relation of Status to Experience, Perception, and Value," *Am. J. Sociol.*, 1960, **66**, 20–21 and Table 9).

[12] "Social Class and Parental Values," *op. cit.*

ent connotations in the two social classes, implying "trustworthiness" for the working-class and "truthfulness" for the middle class. The common theme, of course, is that parents of both social classes value a decent respect for the rights of others; middle- and working-class values are but variations on this common theme. The reason for emphasizing the variations rather than the common theme is that they seem to have far-ranging consequences for parents' relationships with their children and thus ought to be taken seriously.

It would be good if there were more evidence about parental values —data from other studies, in other locales, and especially, data derived from more than one mode of inquiry. But, what evidence we do have is consistent, so that there is at least some basis for believing it is reliable. Furthermore, there is evidence that the value choices made by parents in these inquiries are not simply a reflection of their assessments of their own children's deficiencies or excellences. Thus, we may take the findings of these studies as providing a limited, but probably valid, picture of the parents' generalized conceptions of what behavior would be desirable in their preadolescent children.

EXPLAINING CLASS DIFFERENCES IN PARENTAL VALUES

That middle-class parents are more likely to espouse some values, and working-class parents other values, must be a function of differences in their conditions of life. In the present state of our knowledge, it is difficult to disentangle the interacting variables with a sufficient degree of exactness to ascertain which conditions of life are crucial to the differences in values. Nevertheless, it is necessary to examine the principal components of class differences in life conditions to see what each may contribute.

The logical place to begin is with occupational differences, for these are certainly pre-eminently important, not only in defining social classes in urban, industrialized society, but also in determining much else about people's life conditions. There are at least three respects in which middle-class occupations typically differ from working-class occupations, above and beyond their obvious status-linked differences in security, stability of income, and general social prestige. One is that middle-class occupations deal more with the manipulation of interpersonal relations, ideas, and symbols, while working-class occupations deal more with the manipulation of things. The second is that middle-class occupations are more subject to self-direction, while working-class occupations are more subject to standardization and direct supervision. The third is that getting ahead in middle-class occupations is more dependent upon one's own actions, while in working-class occupations it is more dependent upon collective action, particularly in unionized industries. From these differences, one can sketch differences in the characteristics that make for getting along, and getting ahead, in middle- and working-class occupations. Middle-class occupations require a greater degree of self-direction; working-class occupations, in larger measure, require that one follow explicit rules set down by someone in authority.

Obviously, these differences parallel the differences we have found between the two social classes in the characteristics valued by parents for children. At minimum, one can conclude that there is a congruence between occupational requirements and parental values. It is, moreover, a reasonable supposition, although not a necessary conclusion, that middle- and working-class parents value different characteristics in children *because* of these differences in their occupational circumstances. This supposition does not necessarily assume that parents consciously train their children to meet future occupational requirements; it may simply be that their own occupational experiences have significantly affected parents' conceptions of what is desirable behavior, on or off the job, for adults or for children.[13]

These differences in occupational circumstances are probably basic to the differences we have found between middle- and working-class parental values, but taken alone they do not sufficiently explain them. Parents need not accord pre-eminent importance to occupational requirements in their judgments of what is most desirable. For a

[13] Two objections might be raised here. (1) Occupational experiences may not be important for a mother's values, however crucial they are for her husband's, if she has had little or no work experience. But even those mothers who have had little or no occupational experience know something of occupational life from their husbands and others, and live in a culture in which occupation and career permeate all of life. (2) Parental values may be built not so much out of their own experiences as out of their expectations of the child's future experiences. This might seem particularly plausible in explaining working-class values, for their high valuation of such stereotypically *middle-class* characteristics as obedience, neatness, and cleanliness might imply that they are training their children for a middle-class life they expect the children to achieve. Few working-class parents, however, do expect (or even want) their children to go on to college and the middle-class jobs for which a college education is required. (This is shown in Herbert H. Hyman, "The Value Systems of Different Classes: A Social Psychological Contribution to the Analysis of Stratification," in Reinhard Bendix & Seymour Martin Lipset, Eds., *Class, Status and Power: A Reader in Social Stratification*, Glencoe, Ill.: Free Press, 1953, and confirmed in unpublished data from our own research.)

sufficient explanation of class differences in values, it is necessary to recognize that other differences in middle- and working-class conditions of life reinforce the differences in occupational circumstances at every turn.

Educational differences, for example, above and beyond their importance as determinants of occupation, probably contribute independently to the differences in middle- and working-class parental values. At minimum, middle-class parents' greater attention to the child's internal dynamics is facilitated by their learned ability to deal with the subjective and the ideational. Furthermore, differences in levels and stability of income undoubtedly contribute to class differences in parental values. That middle-class parents still have somewhat higher levels of income, and much greater stability of income, makes them able to take for granted the respectability that is still problematic for working-class parents. They can afford to concentrate, instead, on motives and feelings—which, in the circumstances of their lives, are more important.

These considerations suggest that the differences between middle- and working-class parental values are probably a function of the entire complex of differences in life conditions characteristic of the two social classes. Consider, for example, the working-class situation. With the end of mass immigration, there has emerged a stable working class, largely derived from the manpower of rural areas, uninterested in mobility into the middle class, but very much interested in security, respectability, and the enjoyment of a decent standard of living. This working class has come to enjoy a standard of living formerly reserved for the middle class, but has not chosen a middle-class style of life. In effect, the working class has striven for, and partially achieved, an American dream distinctly different from the dream of success and achievement. In an affluent society, it is possible for the worker to be the traditionalist—politically, economically, and, most relevant here, in his values for his children.[14] Working-class parents want their children to conform to external authority because the parents themselves are willing to accord respect to authority, in return for security and respectability. Their conservatism in child-rearing is part of a more general conservatism and traditionalism.

Middle-class parental values are a product of a quite different set of conditions. Much of what the working class values, they can take

[14] Relevant here is Seymour Martin Lipset's somewhat disillusioned "Democracy and Working-Class Authoritarianism," *Am. Sociol. Rev.*, 1959, 24, 482–501.

for granted. Instead, they can—and must—instil in their children a degree of self-direction that would be less appropriate to the conditions of life of the working class.[15] Certainly, there is substantial truth in the characterization of the middle-class way of life as one of great conformity. What must be noted here, however, is that *relative to* the working class, middle-class conditions of life require a more substantial degree of independence of action. Furthermore, the higher levels of education enjoyed by the middle class make possible a degree of internal scrutiny difficult to achieve without the skills in dealing with the abstract that college training sometimes provides. Finally, the economic security of most middle-class occupations, the level of income they provide, the status they confer, allow one to focus his attention on the subjective and the ideational. Middle-class conditions of life both allow and demand a greater degree of self-direction than do those of the working class.

CONSEQUENCES OF CLASS DIFFERENCES IN PARENTS' VALUES

What consequences do the differences between middle- and working-class parents' values have for the ways they raise their children?

Much of the research on techniques of infant- and child-training is of little relevance here. For example, with regard to parents' preferred techniques for disciplining children, a question of major interest to many investigators, Bronfenbrenner summarizes past studies as follows: "In matters of discipline, working-class parents are consistently more

[15] It has been argued that as larger and larger proportions of the middle class have become imbedded in a bureaucratic way of life—in distinction to the entrepreneurial way of life of a bygone day—it has become more appropriate to raise children to be accommodative than to be self-reliant. But this point of view is a misreading of the conditions of life faced by the middle-class inhabitants of the bureaucratic world. Their jobs require at least as great a degree of self-reliance as do entrepreneurial enterprises. We tend to forget, nowadays, just how little the small- or medium-sized entrepreneur controlled the conditions of his own existence and just how much he was subjected to the petty authority of those on whose pleasure depended the survival of his enterprise. And we fail to recognize the degree to which monolithic-seeming bureaucracies allow free play for—in fact, require—individual enterprise of new sorts: in the creation of ideas, the building of empires, the competition for advancement.

At any rate, our data show no substantial differences between the values of parents from bureaucratic and enterpreneurial occupational worlds, in either social class. But see Daniel R. Miller, & Guy E. Swanson, *The Changing American Parent: A Study in the Detroit Area*, New York: Wiley, 1958.

likely to employ physical punishment, while middle-class families rely more on reasoning, isolation, appeals to guilt, and other methods involving the threat of loss of love."[16] This, if still true,[17] is consistent with middle-class parents' greater attentiveness to the child's internal dynamics, working-class parents' greater concern about the overt act. For present purposes, however, the crucial question is not *which* disciplinary method parents prefer, but when and why they use one or another method of discipline.

The most directly relevant available data are on the conditions under which middle- and working-class parents use physical punishment. Working-class parents are apt to resort to physical punishment when the direct and immediate consequences of their children's disobedient acts are most extreme, and to refrain from punishing when this might provoke an even greater disturbance.[18] Thus, they will punish a child for wild play when the furniture is damaged or the noise level becomes intolerable, but ignore the same actions when the direct and immediate consequences are not so extreme. Middle-class parents, on the other hand, seem to punish or refrain from punishing on the basis of their interpretation of the child's intent in acting as he does. Thus, they will punish a furious outburst when the context is such that they interpret it to be a loss of self-control, but will ignore an equally extreme outburst when the context is such that they interpret it to be merely an emotional release.

It is understandable that working-class parents react to the consequences rather than to the intent of their children's actions: the important thing is that the child not transgress externally imposed rules. Correspondingly, if middle-class parents are instead concerned about the child's motives and feelings, they can and must look beyond the overt act to why the child acts as he does. It would seem that middle- and working-class values direct parents to see their children's misbehavior in quite different ways, so that misbehavior which prompts middle-class parents to action does not seem as important to working-class parents, and vice versa.[19] Obviously, parents' values are not the only things that enter into their use of physical punishment. But unless one assumes a complete lack of goal-directedness in parental behavior,

16 Bronfenbrenner, *op. cit.*, p. 424.

17 Later studies, including our own, do not show this difference.

18 "Social Class and the Exercise of Parental Authority," *op. cit.*

19 This is not to say that the methods used by parents of either social class are necessarily the most efficacious for achievement of their goals.

he would have to grant that parents' values direct their attention to some facets of their own and their children's behavior, and divert it from other facets.

The consequences of class differences in parental values extend far beyond differences in disciplinary practices. From a knowledge of their values for their children, one would expect middle-class parents to feel a greater obligation to be *supportive* of the children, if only because of their sensitivity to the children's internal dynamics. Working-class values, with their emphasis upon conformity to external rules, should lead to greater emphasis upon the parents' obligation to impose constraints.[20] And this, according to Bronfenbrenner, is precisely what has been shown in those few studies that have concerned themselves with the over-all relationship of parents to child: "Over the entire twenty-five-year period studied, parent-child relationships in the middle-class are consistently reported as more acceptant and equalitarian, while those in the working class are oriented toward maintaining order and obedience."[21]

This conclusion is based primarily on studies of *mother*-child relationships in middle- and working-class families. Class differences in parental values have further ramifications for the father's role.[22] Mothers in each class would have their husbands play a role facilitative of the child's development of the characteristics valued in that class: Middle-class mothers want their husbands to be supportive of the children (especially of sons), with their responsibility for imposing constraints being of decidedly secondary importance; working-class mothers look to their husbands to be considerably more directive—support is accorded far less importance and constraint far more. Most middle-class fathers agree with their wives and play a role close to what their wives would have them play. Many working-class fathers, on the other hand, do not. It is not that they see the constraining role

[20] The justification for treating support and constraint as the two major dimensions of parent-child relationships lies in the theoretical argument of Talcott Parsons & Robert F. Bales, *Family, Socialization and Interaction Process*, Glencoe, Ill.: Free Press, 1955, esp. p. 45, and the empirical argument of Earl S. Schaefer, "A Circumplex Model for Maternal Behavior," *J. Abnorm. Soc. Psychol.*, 1959, **59**, 226–234.

[21] Bronfenbrenner, *op. cit.*, p. 425.

[22] From the very limited evidence available at the time of his review, Bronfenbrenner tentatively concluded: "though the middle-class father typically has a warmer relationship with the child, he is also likely to have more authority and status in family affairs" (*ibid.*, p. 422). The discussion here is based largely on subsequent research, esp. "Social Class and the Allocation of Parental Responsibilities," *op. cit.*

as less important than do their wives, but that many of them see no reason why they should have to shoulder the responsibility. From their point of view, the important thing is that the child be taught what limits he must not transgress. It does not much matter who does the teaching, and since mother has primary responsibility for child care, the job should be hers.

The net consequence is a quite different division of parental responsibilities in the two social classes. In middle-class families, mother's and father's roles usually are not sharply differentiated. What differentiation exists is largely a matter of each parent taking special responsibility for being supportive of children of the parent's own sex. In working-class families, mother's and father's roles are more sharply differentiated, with mother almost always being the more supportive parent. In some working-class families, mother specializes in support, father in constraint; in others, perhaps in most, mother raises the children, father provides the wherewithal.[23]

Thus, the differences in middle- and working-class parents' values have wide ramifications for their relationships with their children and with each other. Of course, many class differences in parent-child relationships are not directly attributable to differences in values; undoubtedly the very differences in their conditions of life that make for differences in parental values reinforce, at every juncture, parents' characteristic ways of relating to their children. But one could not account for these consistent differences in parent-child relationships in the two social classes without reference to the differences in parents' avowed values.

CONCLUSION

This paper serves to show how complex and demanding are the problems of interpreting the effects of social structure on behavior. Our inquiries habitually stop at the point of demonstrating that social position correlates with something, when we should want to pursue

[23] Fragmentary data suggest sharp class differences in the husband-wife relationship that complement the differences in the division of parental responsibilities discussed above. For example, virtually no working-class wife reports that she and her husband ever go out on an evening or weekend without the children. And few working-class fathers do much to relieve their wives of the burden of caring for the children all the time. By and large, working-class fathers seem to lead a largely separate social life from that of their wives; the wife has full-time responsibility for the children, while the husband is free to go his own way.

the question, "Why?" What are the processes by which position in social structure molds behavior? The present analysis has dealt with this question in one specific form: Why does social class matter for parents' relationships with their children? There is every reason to believe that the problems encountered in trying to deal with that question would recur in any analysis of the effects of social structure on behavior.

In this analysis, the concept of "values" has been used as the principal bridge from social position to behavior. The analysis has endeavored to show that middle-class parental values differ from those of working-class parents; that these differences are rooted in basic differences between middle- and working-class conditions of life; and that the differences between middle- and working-class parental values have important consequences for their relationships with their children. The interpretive model, in essence, is: social class—conditions of life—values—behavior.

The specifics of the present characterization of parental values may prove to be inexact; the discussion of the ways in which social class position affects values is undoubtedly partial; and the tracing of the consequences of differences in values for differences in parent-child relationships is certainly tentative and incomplete. I trust, however, that the perspective will prove to be valid and that this formulation will stimulate other investigators to deal more directly with the processes whereby social structure affects behavior.

SUMMARY

The argument of this analysis is that class differences in parent-child relationships are a product of differences in parental values (with middle-class parents' values centering on self-direction and working-class parents' values on conformity to external proscriptions); these differences in values, in turn, stem from differences in the conditions of life of the various social classes (particularly occupational conditions —middle-class occupations requiring a greater degree of self-direction, working-class occupations, in larger measure, requiring that one follow explicit rules set down by someone in authority). Values, thus, form a bridge between social structure and behavior.

6.3 SOCIAL AND ATTITUDINAL CHARACTERISTICS OF SPANISH-SPEAKING MIGRANT AND EX-MIGRANT WORKERS IN THE SOUTHWEST

Horacio Ulibarri

A study of the educational needs relating to the adult migrant workers was jointly conducted by agencies in Arizona, Colorado, New Mexico, and Texas (Cooperative Research Project #K-005). The study was divided into two parts, namely, demographic and sociopsychological. This report is concerned with the sociopsychological characteristics of the migrant and agrarian culture oriented workers in the four-state area.

In order to analyze the social and attitudinal orientations of the migrant and ex-migrant workers, a series of depth open-end interviews was conducted. The interviews attempted to draw out the individual's attitudinal characteristics by delving in depth into his life history, his level of educational attainment, and his work history. The interviews were conducted in the vernacular, tape recorded, transcribed, and translated. A total of sixty-five persons was interviewed. All subjects were Spanish-speaking. They comprised a comparable number of Spanish-Americans, Mexican-Americans, and Mexican Nationals.

A model for interpretation of the data was developed from the attitudinal patterns that emerged from the interviews. These patterns were present time orientation, submissiveness, passivity, dissatisfaction, a sense of failure, fear, apathy, particularism, familism, ethnocentrism, and a sense of being objects of discrimination. A seven-point scale for each pattern was developed. The scale ranged from an abnormal extreme on one side to the opposite abnormal extreme on the other. For example, the scale for *reward expectation* has the following range:

1. All rewards will come in the future.
2. Long-range, well-planned rewards are expected.
3. Medium to short-range in expectation of future rewards.

Source: Reprinted with slight abridgment from *Sociology and Social Research*, 1966, **30**, 361–370, with permission of the author and *Sociology and Social Research*.

4. Immediate reward expectation.

5. Immediate reward expectations, but wishing to be able to get rewards available in the past.

6. Present rewards less worthy than past ones.

7. Rejection of present rewards; not capable of accepting rewards after they have been earned.

These scales, when applied to the institutional life activities afforded a quantification of the patterns emerging from each interview. Besides this type of quantification, a simple numerical count regarding the number of times an individual referred to a given activity in a specific manner was made to determine salience. For example, the most salient characteristic of the sample group was concern, bordering on fear, for earning a living.

THE FINDINGS AND ANALYSIS OF THE FINDINGS

The analysis of the findings was made by applying the several attitudinal orientations to the institutional areas. A summary was made by applying each attitudinal characteristic across the institutional area. No significant *basic* differences were found among the three Spanish-speaking groups. Whatever differences existed were factors of social mobility rather than cultural differences.

Religion

The area of religion did not emerge as a strong factor in the lives of these people. These people did not seem to have the preoccupation with religion that was characteristic of the traditional Spanish-speaking cultures. One may conclude that the sample generally showed an attitude of detachment and irregularity in their religious practices even though they did not express an a-religious or anti-religious feeling.

Most studies dealing with the cultures of the Spanish-speaking people have generally indicated an almost blind submission toward the clergy on the part of the people. The sample did not indicate this orientation. Rather a complacent contentment toward religion, where involvement in religious affairs was minimal, seemed to prevail among the migrant and ex-migrant workers in the sample.

The Family

The family tended to emerge as one of the strongest areas of life activity in this study. The migrant's nuclear family tended to be a closely knit unit, where all members seemed to enjoy great status and esteem. The indications were that the concept of the extended family has been lost among these people. The only expression of extended familism was a feeble uneasiness for distant relatives and some concern for married brothers and sisters. When asked if they would help their relatives when in distress the usual answer was, "I don't think that we can afford it."

The nuclear family seemed to be rather strongly oriented to the present. They were content with the fact that they were together at the moment. As a family unit they seemed to be rather passive about taking any action to ameliorate their problems. An atmosphere of contentment seemed to prevail within the family's activities. When relating other areas of life to family living, dissatisfaction was expressed as to their living conditions, the fact that they could not provide adequately for their children, that they could not provide such things as clothing for themselves, and that they could not better their lot in life. Their anxiety was often summed up in these words, "I wish I could do more, but what can I do?"

Despite their passivity some expressed a sense of shame at not being able to do better for their children. Yet from a broad perspective, perhaps the most successful involvement of the migrant and ex-migrant worker in all his life's endeavors was with his family. The migrant and ex-migrant's nuclear family exhibited itself as a well-organized unit where all members enjoyed wholesome status and prestige and where there was mutual concern for each other.

Education—Adult

In general, disassociation seemed to be prevalent among the adults in the sample as to education for themselves. They saw no reward resulting from further education and, therefore, did not project themselves into any possibility for improvement through education. For example, when asked "What do you think that you could do to better your lot in life?," the answer never was that they wanted more formal education.

The only ones who expressed any enthusiasm for education were the Mexican Nationals who could not speak English. They desired literacy training in English. With the exception of two young migrants none expressed any traumatic experience in separating themselves from school. Either they had just drifted away or there were no educational opportunities available to them in their youth. It seemed that the vast majority of the people in the sample had experienced so much failure in life they seriously doubted their potential for further learning. Most of them replied to a question of whether they would attend tuition-free adult education classes if they were established, "Yes, but we are too old to learn anymore." Some answered, "I am too stupid to learn." Others replied, "I am so far behind that I don't think that I can learn anymore."

Education—Children

At first glance, the sample seemed to feel a ray of hope that perhaps through education their children might be able to enjoy a better life than they had experienced. When these people were asked what their hopes for their children were, most of them expressed desires such as wanting their children to become lawyers, doctors, or "at least teachers." Further probing into the attitudinal characteristic indicated a blind faith for education summarized thus: "I want my children to get an education, so that they will not have to work as hard as I have." Furthermore, the majority in the sample were doubtful that their children would finish high school. More important still, the children expressed the same attitude, and neither parent nor child was concerned about the problem.

There was minimal participation on the part of the migrant and ex-migrant in school affairs. This lack of articulation with the school rendered this class victims of inequality of educational opportunities for their children. Because of ignorance regarding the nature of education, complacency seemed to prevail regarding the schools. Hostility toward the schools was minimal. When dissatisfaction was expressed, it revolved around some minute particular of the total school situation. For example, one mother condemned the total high school from which her child had dropped the year before because they made the students wear gym suits for physical education classes.

In such a life space, academic achievement can hardly be expected. This was very true of the people in the sample. The average level of educational achievement for the adults was fifth-grade level. The children, who with rare exceptions were not achieving in school at a high level, were dropping out about three to four grades above where their parents had dropped out of school. There seemed total lack of concern for the bleak future that they would undoubtedly face because of lack of educational achievement. Their impoverished condition apparently placed earning a living above getting an education, and, therefore, both parents and children seemed to be totally apathetic regarding progress in education.

Health

The area of health, initially, did not seem to be of particular concern to the sample group. Statements regarding health were only interspersed through the interview, but when these statements were isolated, it became evident that a high degree of importance was relegated to health by these people.

For the most part, these people expressed happiness at enjoying their present good health. They seemed to take their present state of good health for granted. Paradoxically, they were extremely concerned about becoming ill. Yet aside from a few minor activities, there seemed to be no directed efforts at promoting and preserving good health. The only preventive efforts seemed to be the kind imposed on them, e.g., vaccination.

Schulman found that among the Spanish-Americans, unless pain or other dyfunctioning factors of life's activities were present, sickness was not recognized.[1] The same tendency seemed to exist in the sample group. Thus, because they did not seem to understand the true nature of health and illness, whenever illness struck often they failed to see the causal factors. Therefore, unless the cause was readily evident, sickness was thought to be a complete matter of destiny. During protracted illness, some in the group thought that little could be done to help the person recover. What needed to be done by all concerned was to resign themselves to the problem rather than to become anxious over it.

The most important attitude regarding health was a very strong apprehension, bordering on fear, about being sick. When they were asked, "What is the saddest thing in life for you?" invariably the response was, "Being sick." No one was able to explain rationally this fear of illness. Most attempted an explanation with, "When you are sick you have nothing." Some gave a vague indication that sickness prevented them from earning a living. This attitude had family-wide dimensions. Regardless of who was sick, all said that illness caused everybody in the family to be sad. Some said that it was sadder to have small children sick than to have adults ill.

Economics

The most obvious and intense concern of the total group was in the area of earning a living. Usually, the greater part of the inter-

[1] Sam Schulman *et al.*, "The Concept of 'Health' Among Spanish-speaking Villagers of New Mexico and Colorado," *J. Health Hum. Behav.*, 1963, 4, 226–234.

view was related to the problems of earning a living and the difficulties encountered in providing adequately for their families.

Most of the individuals in the sample felt that they were not earning enough money to sustain their families. They believed that the government should develop projects to provide them with job opportunities. Despite their impoverished conditions these migrants and ex-migrants did not seem to have internalized what may loosely be called the "welfare complex." They expressed a necessity to have their earnings supplemented by the free commodity distribution or food stamp programs, but none expressed a desire to become public welfare clients.

Most in the sample group had not attempted in the recent past to qualify themselves for a better type of job. Those, yet in the stream, realized that they were not actually improving themselves. Those no longer migrating seemed to have given up hope of trying to improve themselves. In either case, the idea of getting training for other types of better paying jobs had apparently not entered into their thinking.

The spending patterns also indicated a strong present-time orientation. Of course, most of the income, since it was so low, was spent for basic necessities. There was, however, strong evidence of much impulsive buying. Rather expensive items, such as encyclopedias and television sets, were noted about the house. Useless buying was also noticed. All stated that they spent their money as they earned it. None had any money in the bank; none had any savings.

The whole family was affected seriously by the amount of, and the manner in which, earnings were made available to them through the year. During the working season, the typical seasonal worker in the sample worked as much as sixty hours a week and earned up to seventy dollars a week. During the off-season, however, he worked sporadically, and his earnings seldom amounted to more than twenty-five dollars a week. One of the most evident results of this low income was the impoverished conditions under which these people lived. All the homes visited, with the notable exception of two crew-leaders, were run down or dilapidated, over-crowded, and poorly furnished. Similarly, their poverty was noticed in their dress and in their nutrition.

Because of their low educational attainment level, relatively few jobs were open to the migrant and ex-migrant. Some stated that they had tried looking for other types of jobs, but had been unsuccessful. The factor of not possessing saleable skills in an era of technology, coupled with the factor of discrimination, apparently reinforced their depressed state of mind. Most seemed to have resigned themselves to the problem of poverty instead of trying to fight it any longer. A typical saying among the Mexican-Americans was, "You are Mexican; you have to pick cotton." This fatalistic attitude, however, did not make them aggressive in a socially unacceptable manner. Rather much timidity was noticed both in job-seeking and the toleration of the conditions under which they worked, for example, housing, hours worked, and wages earned.

Dissatisfaction in the area of economics ranged from mild to very strong coupled with bitterness. In most cases the dissatisfaction centered around the working conditions, the housing conditions, and having to exist in a state of fear of want. This fear of want was projected mostly in the form of providing the basic necessities such as food and clothing for their children. The total group considered themselves failures in the area of steady employment. Their typical statement was, "There are no more jobs available; I don't know what we are going to do."

Government

The majority of the sample seemed to have disassociated themselves almost completely from the government. In general, they seemed to be ignorant of the governmental structure. By their manner of referring to the government, they seemed to think of the government as a personality.

In general, most of the people in the sample seemed oblivious to the types of help available from governmental agencies. Neither did they involve themselves in politics or in any other form of activity where conscious responsibility as American citizens was exhibited. Rather, the ignorance about government seemed to be so great and the apathy so enervating that one could almost conclude that these people, even though living in the United States, functionally are not citizens of the United States.

Recreation

Recreation among the sample group was confined almost entirely to the nuclear family. The forms of recreation in which they participated were watching television, playing cards, visiting, going to the movies, and dancing. None belonged to social or fraternal organizations. In general, the total amount of recreational activities was either confined to the nuclear family or to the ethnic group to which they belonged.

Ethnocentrism and Discrimination

Relatively little contact existed between the Spanish-speaking and the Anglo-American in the sample. About the only contact evident existed in the relationship of boss to worker or foreman to farm hand. All said that they had very little social relations with the Anglo. None stated that he had any close Anglo friends. Rather, whatever contact existed seemed to be of the negative type, that is, in the form of discrimination. Very little contact seemed to have existed among the three Spanish-speaking groups, namely, the Spanish-Americans, the Mexican-Americans, and the Mexican Nationals, although no animosity among the three groups was detected.

Regarding discrimination, the Spanish-Americans from northern New Mexico and the Mexican Nationals were not conscious of being objects of discrimination. The Spanish-Americans from Colorado, especially the San Luis Valley, were very conscious of being discriminated against by the Anglo. Similarly, the Mexican-Americans from Texas felt intense, and sometimes vicious, discrimination directed against them.

To interpret these phenomena one must go beyond the data acquired for this study. The Spanish-Americans from northern New Mexico have had minimal contact with the Anglo and are just one step above the social ladder from the agrarian Spanish-American. The Mexican National has been virtually insulated from the Anglo world because of the language barrier. A further mental insulation was provided by the "comparison factor," where the Mexican National is forever comparing the conditions under which he is at present living with those that prevail in Mexico. Thus, when these people move out of their "cultural island" they are almost totally unaware of being discriminated against even when discrimination is very obvious.

The problems of discrimination in Colorado and Texas seemed to be almost identical in nature. One form of discrimination was in the working conditions—long hours of work and low wages prevailing. The other type of discrimination was that brought about by fear, especially in the area of economic competition, by Anglo-Americans who were in the same social class or just one step above the Spanish-speaking. The only important difference between the two situations is that Texas, being the gateway for the Mexicans entering the United States, has a consistent stream of immigrants from Mexico. These newly arrived groups cannot participate widely in the general milieu of American life because of their foreign language and foreign culture.

This consistent group of new arrivals helps to keep alive the stereotypes relegated to the Spanish-speaking even though there is constant horizontal and vertical mobility within the group as they progress in the process of acculturation.

CONCLUSIONS

No basic differences in social and attitudinal characteristics were found among the Spanish-American, Mexican-American, and Mexican Nationals. Whatever dissimiliarities existed tended to be factors of social mobility. The total sample showed the following social and attitudinal characteristics:

1. Strong present-time orientation in reward expectation in all areas and strong present-time orientation in self-projection in all areas.

2. The sample showed timidity in action and a tendency to avoid facing the situation in the area of education by having their children drop out of school. They showed great passivity in the area of health. They tended to be timid in trying to improve themselves in the area of economics. By default, they were escaping the situation in the area of involvement in government. They were passive in the area of recreation, confining their recreational activities to the nuclear family or to their ethnic group.

3. The sample showed strong satisfaction in the area of the family life; complacent satisfaction in the areas of religion and government, and in education as it related to education for the children; and strong dissatisfaction and bitterness at their inability to earn a better living and to provide more adequately for their families.

4. The sample group felt that they were achieving to their utmost capacities in the area of the family; that they had exhausted their own potential for education for themselves, and financially they were futilitarian about the education of their children; that they were exhausting their potential in the area of economics.

5. The sample was not concerned with the dominance-subordinance factor in the area of the family; they were submissive by default in the area of education for their children and thought that their own lack of education was only lack of educational opportunity. They thought that health was mostly a matter of one's destiny. They showed tendencies of resignation to poverty in the area of economics.

6. The sample showed concern about the area of education for their children. They showed some fear of not finding a job and of not being able to provide for their families. They showed fear of ill health, although they were not directing any activities toward preserving or promoting their good health.

7. The sample felt successful involvement with the nuclear family. They were apathetic about most problems concerning education for their children, involving themselves very little in school affairs. They were completely

apathetic about education for themselves. They were apathetic, meeting slight success, in the area of economics. They showed almost complete disassociation with government. They felt complacent about recreation and religion.

8. The sample showed an overall particularistic attitude in all areas except the nuclear family, where they gave equal importance to particulars and universals—namely, they thought that the family existed because of the members, to whom they relegated great status and esteem.

9. The sample indicated that the limits of their familism was the nuclear family, and this orientation extended into education, health, economics, and recreation.

10. The sample showed definite ethnocentric tendencies where few contacts were made with anyone outside their ethnic group. Contact was generally maintained only with primary groups of the same ethnic stock.

11. The group in the sample from northern New Mexico showed little awareness toward discrimination, except in work relations; the Mexicans seemed to be unaware of discrimination; the Spanish-Americans from Colorado indicated strong awareness of discrimination; and the Mexican-Americans were similarly aware.

SUMMARY

A sample of sixty-five migrant and ex-migrant workers was interviewed in depth in order to ascertain their social and attitudinal characteristics. The sample expressed an overwhelming fear of want. Their destitution basically dominated all their orientations toward life, resulting in negative attitudes and disorganization. They indicated little motivation toward helping themselves, and their existence was one of fatalism and anomie.

6.4 SELF-REJECTION AMONG NORTH AFRICAN IMMIGRANTS TO ISRAEL

Judith T. Shuval

Research evidence has accumulated in recent years to demonstrate the prevalence of certain patterns of interethnic strain in Israel. Specifically, a fairly widespread but relatively mild form of prejudice has been shown to focus largely on the Oriental segments of the popula-

Source: Reprinted with slight abridgment from *Israel Annals of Psychiatry and Related Disciplines*, 1966, 4, 101–110, with permission of the author and the *Annals*.

tion but more particularly on immigrants of North African origin. The prejudice referred to functions largely on an attitudinal level or in areas of social interaction; we have observed little overt discrimination in Israeli society. Indeed the official norms of the society are strongly equalitarian and operate against any form of discrimination. It is our impression, however, that such norms have been ineffective in preventing the growth of certain prejudiced *attitudes* which prevail among large segments of the population. While these prejudiced attitudes may be mild compared to the prejudice found in other societies and may carry relatively few behavioral consequences, the phenomenon is nevertheless disquieting, both in terms of its possible growth in the future and in terms of the emerging structure of Israeli society. Some attempt has been made to explain this phenomenon in terms of the increasing differentiation of Israeli society as well as in terms of the high visibility and lower-class status of North African immigrants (1).

If, as has been suggested, this prejudice toward North African immigrants is becoming increasingly normative in the society, it is of some interest to determine the response of that ethnic[1] group to this rather widespread attitude. We shall propose in this paper that there is a wide measure of acceptance on the part of North African immigrants of this norm of prejudice toward themselves. Self-rejection and internalization of a negative stereotype of themselves will be interpreted here as additional evidence for the normative nature of this pattern of prejudice in Israeli society. This interpretation assumes that an intropunitive attitude such as self-rejection in terms of group membership probably represents the group's response to a widespread attitude of hostility in the community toward it. From one point of view self-hatred can be thought of as an indication of the ambivalent status of the group in the social system; group members come to internalize what the prevalent stereotype says about them. This general process is familiar from the work of George H. Mead (2).

From another point of view rejection of self may be thought of as behavior instrumental to conformity with the norms of the society and thus as a means of gaining acceptance by the majority who hold this attitude. If prejudice toward North Africans is a norm of the society, newcomers in order to become socialized into it, will tend to accept this norm along with many others which are perceived as dominant

[1] As used here, "ethnic" refers to the country of origin of the respondent, since all were Jews.

in the culture context. Socially mobile North African immigrants in particular may hasten to internalize this norm in order to gain acceptance.

FREQUENCY OF SELF-REJECTION

We shall present some empirical evidence to demonstrate the prevalence of rejection among North Africans of themselves as a group. The data are drawn from a study carried out in 1959 in four immigrant development centers in Israel. A sample of 1511 men and women were interviewed: of these 719 were immigrants from North Africa, all of whom had arrived in Israel after the establishment of the state in 1948.[2]

Residents in these communities were randomly distributed in terms of ethnic origin, there being no explicit policy at the time concerning desirable ecological patterns of residence. Immigrants were housed on a first-come, first-served basis, and apartments were allocated accordingly. Neighborhoods were therefore ethnically heterogeneous and the ethnic origin of one's neighbors was important in terms of local relationships and friendships (3). Residents were asked, among other things, from which ethnic group they would least and most prefer to have neighbors.

Table 1 indicates that the ethnic group most frequently mentioned as least desired as neighbors is the North African. Although Near Eastern immigrants are also mentioned with relatively high frequency, it appears that rejection is most focused on the North African group. The latter are cited most frequently as least desirable neighbors not only by the European and Near Eastern respondents, but by *themselves* as well. What is perhaps most striking is the fact that the percentage of North Africans rejecting members of their own group as neighbors is approximately equal to the percentage of Europeans and Near Easterners expressing this attitude.

If we assume, as suggested by Table 1, that the Near Easterners represent the second target of neighborly rejection, the self-rejection of the North Africans appears even more marked. For one might

[2] The names of these development centers and the number of residents interviewed in each were as follows:

Kiryat Gat	343
Ashkelon	357
Beersheva	443
Kiryat Shmona	368

Table 1 *Rejection of Various Ethnic Groups as Neighbors by Three Major Ethnic Groups in the Communities*

Ethnic Origin of Respondent	Percentage Indicating That They Would Not Like to Have Members of the Following Ethnic Groups as Neighbors[a]				
	Europeans	North Africans	Near Easterners	No Opinion[b]	No. of Cases
Europeans	10	32	22	36	(542)
North Africans	12	33	24	31	(722)
Near Easterners	7	38	25	30	(238)

[a] In the interview respondents were asked for the specific country from which they preferred not to have neighbors. For purposes of analysis these replies have been grouped into three general ethnic groups.

[b] The large group which did not answer can be explained by refusals in terms of the strong equalitarian norm in Israeli society which presses against overt rejection of any specific ethnic group. Interviewers were instructed to probe as much as possible in order to encourage responses despite this norm.

expect them to indicate the Near Easterners as a legitimate response to this question *more frequently* than they mention themselves. However, the data indicate that, following the dominant pattern of the other ethnic groups in this regard, the North Africans cite themselves most frequently as least desirable neighbors.

Nor does there appear to be any evidence that the North Africans reciprocate the hostility expressed by the European residents toward them. A relatively small per cent (12%) indicate a rejection of Europeans in their responses. There seems to be some anxiety among them about expressing hostility toward the dominant group which in absolute terms undoubtedly reveals more hostility toward them than do the Near Easterners.[3] Such evidence would tend indirectly to confirm our suggestion that self-rejection represents a means of conformity with a norm of the dominant culture. For rejection of the Europeans, who are the major carriers of this norm, would somehow indicate a failure to conform to the norms of the dominant group.

It is of some interest to note that the Near Easterners, who are also a target of some measure of hostility, exhibit relatively less self-

[3] There were almost two and a half times as many Europeans as Near Easterners in these communities, so that despite the equal proportion who express rejection of North Africans as neighbors, in an absolute sense the hostility of Europeans would be much more frequently encountered.

rejection than do the North Africans. Their behavior in this regard might also be interpreted as conformity to the dominant norm; however, it is striking to contrast their lower level of self-rejection with that of the North Africans.

If we glance at the opposite side of the coin, we find a complementary picture. In a situation of ethnically mixed housing, it would seem most reasonable for residents to prefer members of their own or culturally similar groups as neighbors. And indeed among the European respondents fully 60 per cent (542) indicate that they prefer other Europeans. However, among the North Africans only 19 per cent (722) said that they prefer other North Africans as neighbors in the community. Such a relatively low self-preference appears to suggest the kind of attitude we have been suggesting. Furthermore, fully 60 per cent of the North Africans indicate that they would prefer Europeans as neighbors—an attitude which does not seem to be reciprocated as enthusiastically.[4]

STEREOTYPE OF SELF

Following the question discussed above ("Which of the various ethnic groups would you least prefer to have as neighbors in this community?"), respondents were asked to indicate the reasons for their choice of any specific group. These replies were completely free and unstructured. Responses were recorded as completely as possible by the interviewer on the spot. Needless to say, as in all "why" questions, the level of causation selected by respondents varied considerably. However, what did emerge from these answers was an apparent qualitative image of the outstanding traits (negative[5]) of the group mentioned. These replies were categorized in such a way that the negative stereotype of the group became clear. In a sense this represents an incomplete stereotype since positive traits are not included. It may be argued, however, that persons disliking a given group are not too likely to maintain a positive image of it. At the same time the logical possibility undoubtedly exists that Moroccans, for example, may be perceived in generally negative terms but at the same time *certain* positive attributes may be associated with them. In

[4] Only 8 per cent of the Europeans prefer North Africans as neighbors.

[5] A parallel question of "why" followed the question concerning respondents' *positive* choice of ethnic groups as neighbors, and a similar stereotype image analyzed. Here, however, we shall deal only with the negative stereotype.

Table 2 *Negative Stereotype of North Africans as Perceived by Ethnic Groups*

Percentage Indicating Following Traits as Reasons for Rejecting North Africans as Neighbors	Ethnic Group of Respondents		
	Europeans	Near Easterners	North Africans
	(204) [a]	(122) [a]	(268) [a]
Dirty	12	18	10
Too religious	1	1	—
Disloyal to country	—	1	—
Proud, superior	2	—	3
Uncultured	15	5	11
No common language	11	1	3
Bothersome children	9	8	10
Aggressive	31	42	33
Undesirable personal traits	7	14	20
Different customs	5	2	1
"Primitive"	3	2	1
Other	2	5	8
No answer	2	1	—

[a] Some respondents indicated more than one trait and these were all recorded. Likewise a few respondents did not indicate any reasons for their dislike of North Africans. The totals in this table represent the total number of traits mentioned and percentages are calculated on these totals. The latter, therefore, do not always correspond to the number of persons who indicated dislike of North Africans.

the interests of caution we have therefore termed the image analyzed a "negative stereotype" and have not precluded the latter possibility.

Table 2 represents the negative stereotype of North Africans as perceived by each of the three major ethnic groups. The far right-hand column gives the self-image of North Africans. The outstanding trait of the stereotype perceived by all three groups appears to be the "aggressiveness" of North Africans. Other outstanding traits are "dirty," "uncultured," "no common language," and "bothersome children."[6] The Near Easterners and North Africans themselves tend more than the Europeans to perceive "undesirable personal traits." It is of some interest to note that the stereotype held by the Near

[6] This apparently extraneous element appeared in the stereotype because of the specific nature of the interview situation, i.e., in a development center made up of low-cost immigrant housing units. In this sort of situation, "bothersome children" become an extremely salient problem.

Easterners appears to be more clearly defined and somewhat less diffuse than that perceived by the Europeans. This observation is based on the fact that the Near Easterners mention three traits with rather high frequency and virtually no others with any frequency to speak of. These are: "aggressive," "dirty," and "undesirable personal traits."

What is of particular interest to us is the general similarity of the self-stereotype of the North Africans to the image perceived by the Europeans. The only clear exceptions to this are the percentage indicating "no common language" which is, of course, inapplicable to the North Africans in perceiving *themselves,* and the North Africans' greater emphasis on "undesirable personal traits." The outstanding traits perceived by the North Africans themselves *as well as* by the European and Near Eastern respondents are "aggressive," "dirty," "bothersome children," and "uncultured." In other words it would appear that North Africans who reject members of their own group as neighbors do so for essentially the same reasons as other groups. Furthermore, their self-image conforms to a remarkable degree with the negative stereotype others hold of them.

RESIDENTIAL CONTACT AND ATTITUDE TOWARD NEIGHBORS

We shall now look at this problem from a somewhat different angle. As already noted, residents in the communities studied were ecologically distributed in what amounted to a random manner in terms of ethnic background. However, such "randomness" resulted in some residents living in close proximity to members of their own ethnic group and some residents living surrounded, as it were, by members of other ethnic groups. We have attempted to systematize the analysis of residential contact among ethnic groups in such communities by the use of what we have termed an "index of the homogeneity of the microneighborhood (3)." This technique takes as its unit of analysis a complex of three families, i.e., that of the respondent and his two closest neighbors. The microneighborhood can vary from complete ethnic homogeneity when the respondent is flanked by neighbors from his own specific country of origin to complete ethnic heterogeneity in which the respondent is living adjacent to immigrants from radically different countries of origin. For purposes of the present analysis, we shall present four levels of homogeneity which are defined in terms of the cultural closeness of the respondent's two closest neighbors to his own ethnic background.

We shall demonstrate that the North Africans' evaluation of their own immediate neighbors in the community varies with the homogeneity of the microneighborhood in which they live, and that this variation can probably be explained in terms of a pattern of self-rejection among them.

The dependent variable used was defined by an evaluation of neighbors in terms of prior expectations: "How do your present neighbors measure up to your expectations before coming to live here?" Table 3 shows that among North Africans this evaluation

Table 3 *Ethnic Homogeneity of Microneighborhood and Evaluation of Neighbors by North African Respondents*

Level of Homogeneity of Microneighborhood in Which North Africans Live[a]	Percentage of North Africans Indicating a Positive Evaluation of Their Neighbors in Terms of Prior Expectations*	
Completely homogeneous	34	(151)
Partly homogeneous	33	(391)
Partly heterogeneous	44	(203)
Completely heterogeneous	56	(45)

* $\chi^2 = 7.92$; $df = 3$; $.02 < p < .05$.

[a] The levels of homogeniety of the microneighborhood were defined here as follows:

Completely homogeneous — both contiguous neighbors are from the same specific country of origin as the respondent;

Partly homogeneous — both contiguous neighbors are from countries with relatively similar cultural backgrounds to that of the respondent, e.g., Iraq, Yemen, etc., but are *not* European;

Partly heterogeneous — *one* of the contiguous neighbors is European while the other is from a country with a relatively similar cultural background to that of the respondent;

Completely heterogeneous — both neighbors are of European origin.

On the subject of the microneighborhood, see (3).

becomes increasingly positive as the microneighborhood in which the respondent lives becomes more heterogeneous. What this means is that North Africans living in apartments which border on the apartments of *other* North Africans are significantly less pleased with their neighbors than are North Africans who live in heterogeneous micro-neighborhoods, i.e., surrounded by Europeans. The less residential contact a North African has with members of his own group, the more positively he tends to evaluate his immediate neighbors. In a certain sense these data complement the findings presented in Table 1 concerning frequency of rejection of certain groups as neighbors. There too a certain preference for Europeans was shown and a rejection of self. The data in Table 3 present these findings within the context of the actual experience of residential contact with different ethnic groups.

CORRELATES OF SELF-REJECTION

We have been unable with the data at our disposal to carry through any sort of a broad analysis of outside correlates of the self-rejection observed. This question awaits the findings of further research. The limited number of background variables which were examined for a possible correlation with self-rejection among North Africans showed no significant relationship to exist. These were: sex, length of time immigrant had been in Israel, level of education attained, occupation of chief breadwinner in the family, extent of religious orthodoxy.

Table 4 *Self-rejection among North Africans as Related to Age*

Age of Responent	Percentage Rejecting Own Group as Neighbors*	
18–24 years	40	(119)
25–39 years	33	(364)
40–59 years	32	(199)
60 years or over	18	(34)

* $\chi^2 = 6.02$; $df = 3$; $.05 > p > .02$.

The only variable which showed a significant relationship with self-rejection was *age* of the respondent. The younger the immigrant, the more likely he is to reveal feelings of self-rejection in terms of his group membership. This relationship may be seen in Table 4. The study did not include such variables as measures of social mobility, conformity needs, sensitivity to rejection by others, or identification with the overall society. We are therefore unable to pursue these generalizations any further.

CONCLUSIONS

Research over the past several years has demonstrated the growth of a pattern of normative but relatively mild prejudice toward North African immigrants in Israel. This paper has attempted to determine the nature of the response of the North African group itself to this relatively widespread norm.

Evidence has been presented to indicate a response of widespread self-rejection among the North Africans. This attitude is interpreted either as a response to the ambivalent status of the North Africans as the major target of ethnic hostility, or as an attempt on the part of immigrants from North Africa to conform to one of the prevailing normative patterns of the society.

The first finding on which the above generalizations are based is the high frequency with which North Africans indicate a rejection of members of their own group as possible neighbors in housing developments. Data were presented showing that North Africans reject members of their own group as neighbors as frequently as they themselves are rejected by other ethnic groups. Furthermore there is no evidence that they displace a major portion of their hostility to another, ostensibly acceptable target group, i.e., the Near Easterners; instead they choose to focus specifically on themselves. Nor was there any evidence that hostility is reciprocated toward the Europeans who generate the largest absolute amount of hostility toward the North Africans. Rather it would appear that North Africans display a disproportionate desire for Europeans as neighbors. In fact the more residential contact they have with Europeans, the more positive is their attitude toward these neighbors. In addition it was shown that North Africans who in fact live adjacent to other North Africans display the lowest level of satisfaction with their neighbors. Finally, the data indicate that the stereotype image North Africans hold of themselves corresponds remarkably to that held by the Europeans and Near Easterners concerning them. The one background factor that was found to correlate with self-rejection among the North Africans was age: the younger immigrants in this group tend to reject the group more than the older ones. Much of this evidence points, in our opinion, to an attempt on the part of the North Africans to conform to a norm of the dominant groups in the social system in an attempt to gain more complete acceptance into it.

Status and Role

These findings arouse some concern over the apparent direction in which ethnic relations are developing in Israel. The attitudes of the North Africans described here can be taken as additional evidence for the normative nature of the prejudice toward them prevailing in substantial segments of Israeli society. It would seem difficult to interpret their self-rejection in other terms. Furthermore, such self-rejection can hardly be conducive to stability or positive mental health of this group.

Since the phenomenon described here is seen as a response of the group to a situation prevailing in the larger social system, it is clear that solutions to the problem must be sought not so much within the group itself but in the context of the social structure.

SUMMARY

This paper attempts to determine the nature of the response of North African immigrants to a mild but widespread norm of prejudice in Israeli society. Data are presented showing that North Africans reject members of their own groups as neighbors as frequently as they themselves are rejected by other ethnic groups. Nor do they displace their hostility to other potential target groups in the society. The stereotype image North Africans hold of themselves corresponds to that held by the Europeans and the Near Easterners concerning them. In their attempt to gain more complete acceptance, it is suggested that North Africans are conforming to norms of the dominant groups in the social system, even when these include certain forms of prejudice toward them.

REFERENCES

1. Judith T. Shuval, Emerging patterns of ethnic strain in Israel, *Soc. Forces,* Spring 1962; and *ibid.,* Patterns of inter-group tension and affinity, *Unesco, Inter. Soc. Sci. Bull.,* **8** (1), 72–123.
2. George H. Mead, *Mind, self, and society,* Chicago: Univ. of Chicago Press, 1947. Pp. 135–226.
3. Judith T. Shuval, The micro-neighborhood: An approach to ecological patterns of ethnic groups, *Soc. Prob.,* **9,** (3).

6.5 THE EFFECTS OF CHANGES IN ROLES ON THE ATTITUDES OF ROLE OCCUPANTS

Seymour Lieberman

One of the fundamental postulates of role theory, as expounded by Newcomb (2), Parsons (3), and other role theorists, is that a person's attitudes will be influenced by the role that he occupies in a social system. Although this proposition appears to be a plausible one, surprisingly little evidence is available that bears directly on it. One source of evidence is found in common folklore. "Johnny is a changed boy since he was made a monitor in school." "She is a different woman since she got married." "You would never recognize him since he became foreman." As much as these expressions smack of the truth, they offer little in the way of systematic or scientific support for the proposition that a person's attitudes are influenced by his role.

Somewhat more scientific, but still not definitive, is the common finding, in many social-psychological studies, that relationships exist between attitudes and roles. In other words, different attitudes are held by people who occupy different roles. For example, Stouffer et al. (5) found that commissioned officers are more favorable toward the Army than are enlisted men. The problem here is that the mere existence of a relationship between attitudes and roles does not reveal the cause and effect nature of the relationship found. One interpretation of Stouffer's finding might be that being made a commissioned officer tends to result in a person's becoming pro-Army—i.e., the role a person occupies influences his attitudes. But an equally plausible interpretation might be that being pro-Army tends to result in a person's being made a commissioned officer—i.e., a person's attitudes influence the likelihood of his being selected for a given role. In the absence of longitudinal data, the relationship offers no clear evidence that roles were the "cause" and attitudes the "effect."

The present study was designed to examine the effects of roles on attitudes in a particular field situation. The study is based on longi-

Source: Reprinted with slight abridgment from *Human Relations,* 1956, 9, 385–402, with permission of the author and *Human Relations.*

tudinal data obtained in a role-differentiated, hierarchical organization. By taking advantage of natural role changes among personnel in the organization, it was possible to examine people's attitudes both before and after they underwent changes in roles. Therefore, the extent to which changes in roles were followed by changes in attitudes could be determined, and the cause and effect nature of any relationships found would be clear.

METHOD: PHASE 1

The study was part of a larger project carried out in a medium-sized Midwestern company engaged in the production of home appliance equipment. Let us call the company the Rockwell Corporation. At the time that the study was done, Rockwell employed about 4000 people. This total included about 2500 factory workers and about 150 first-level foremen. The company was unionized and most of the factory workers belonged to the union local, which was an affiliate of the U.A.W., C.I.O. About 150 factory workers served as stewards in the union, or roughly one steward for every foreman.

The study consisted of a "natural field experiment." The experimental variable was a change in roles, and the experimental period was the period of exposure to the experimental variable. The experimental groups were those employees who underwent changes in roles during this period; the control groups were those employees who did not change roles during this period. The design may be described in terms of a three-step process: "before measurement," "experimental period," and "after measurement."

Before Measurement

In September and October 1951, attitude questionnaires were filled out by virtually all factory personnel at Rockwell—2354 workers, 145 stewards, and 151 foremen. The questions dealt for the most part with employees' attitudes and perceptions about the company, the union, and various aspects of the job situation. The respondents were told that the questionnaire was part of an overall survey to determine how employees felt about working conditions at Rockwell.

Experimental Period

Between October 1951 and July 1952, twenty-three workers were made foremen and thirty-five workers became stewards. Most of the workers who became stewards during that period were elected during the annual steward elections held in May 1952. They replaced stewards who did not choose to run again or who were not reelected by their constituents. In addition, a few workers replaced stewards who left the steward role for one reason or another throughout the year.

The workers who became foremen were not made foreman at any particular time. Promotions occurred as openings arose in supervisory positions. Some workers replaced foremen who retired or who left the company for other reasons; some replaced foremen who were shifted to other supervisory positions; and some filled newly created supervisory positions.

After Measurement

In December 1952, the same forms that had been filled out by the rank-and-file workers in 1951 were readministered to:

1. The workers who became foremen during the experimental period ($N = 23$).
2. A control group of workers who did not become foremen during the experimental period ($N = 46$).
3. The workers who became stewards during the experimental period ($N = 35$).
4. A control group of workers who did not become stewards during the experimental period ($N = 35$).

Each control group was matched with its parallel experimental group on a number of demographic, attitudinal, and motivational variables. Therefore, any changes in attitudes that occurred in the experimental groups but did not occur in the control groups could not be attributed to initial differences between them.

The employees in these groups were told that the purpose of the follow-up questionnaire was to get up-to-date measures of their attitudes in 1952 and to compare how employees felt that year with the way that they felt the previous year. The groups were told that, instead of studying the entire universe of employees as was the case in 1951, only a sample was being studied this time. They were informed that the sample was chosen in such a way as to represent all kinds of employees at Rockwell—men and women, young and old, etc. The groups gave no indication that they understood the real bases on which they were chosen for the "after" measurement or that the effects of changes in roles were the critical factors being examined.[1]

[1] Some of the top officials of management and all of the top officers of the union at Rockwell knew about the nature of the follow-up study and the bases on which the experimental and control groups were selected.

RESULTS: PHASE 1

The major hypothesis tested in this study was that people who are placed in a role will tend to take on or develop attitudes that are congruent with the expectations associated with that role. Since the foreman role entails being a representative of management, it might be expected that workers who are chosen as foremen will tend to become more favorable toward management. Similarly, since the steward role entails being a representative of the union, it might be expected that workers who are elected as stewards will tend to become more favorable toward the union. Moreover, in so far as the values of management and of the union are in conflict with each other, it might also be expected that workers who are made foremen will become less favorable toward the union and workers who are made stewards will become less favorable toward management.

Four attitudinal areas were examined: (1) attitudes toward management and officials of management; (2) attitudes toward the union and officials of the union; (3) attitudes toward the management-sponsored incentive system; and (4) attitudes toward the union-sponsored seniority system. The incentive system (whereby workers are paid according to the number of pieces they turn out) and the seniority system (whereby workers are promoted according to the seniority principle) are two areas in which conflicts between management and the union at Rockwell have been particularly intense. Furthermore, first-level foremen and stewards both play a part in the administration of these systems, and relevant groups hold expectations about foreman and steward behaviors with respect to these systems. Therefore, we examined the experimental and control groups' attitudes toward these two systems as well as their overall attitudes toward management and the union.

The data tend to support the hypothesis that being placed in the foreman and steward roles will have an impact on the attitudes of the role occupants. As shown in Tables 1 through 4,[2] both experimental groups undergo systematic changes in attitudes, in the predicted directions, from the "before" situation to the "after" situation. In the control groups, either no attitude changes occur, or less marked changes occur, from the "before" situation to the "after" situation.

Although a number of the differences are not statistically significant,

[2] Interested readers are referred to the original article for Tables 1 through 4, which have been omitted for sake of brevity.

those which are significant are all in the expected directions, and most of the nonsignificant differences are also in the expected directions. New foremen, among other things, come to see Rockwell as a better place to work compared with other companies, develop more positive perceptions of top management officers, and become more favorably disposed toward the principle and operation of the incentive system. New stewards come to look upon labor unions in general in a more favorable light, develop more positive perceptions of the top union officers at Rockwell, and come to prefer seniority to ability as a criterion of what should count in moving workers to better jobs. In general, the attitudes of workers who become foremen tend to gravitate in a pro-management direction and the attitudes of workers who become stewards tend to move in a pro-union direction.

A second kind of finding has to do with the relative *amount* of attitude change that takes place among new foremen in contrast to the amount that takes place among new stewards. On the whole, more pronounced and more widespread attitude changes occur among those who are made foremen than among those who are made stewards. Using a p level of .10 as a criterion for statistical significance, the workers who are made foremen undergo significant attitude changes, relative to the workers who are not made foremen, on ten of the sixteen attitudinal items presented in Tables 1 through 4. By contrast, the workers who are made stewards undergo significant attitude changes, relative to the workers who are not made stewards, on only three of the sixteen items. However, for the steward role as well as for the foreman role, most of the differences found between the experimental and control groups still tend to be in the expected directions.

The more pronounced and more widespread attitude changes that occur among new foremen than among new stewards can probably be accounted for in large measure by the kinds of differences that exist between the foreman and steward roles. For one thing, the foreman role represents a relatively permanent position, while many stewards take the steward role as a "one-shot" job and even if they want to run again their constituents may not reelect them. Second, the foreman role is a full-time job, while most stewards spend just a few hours a week in the performance of their steward functions and spend the rest of the time carrying out their regular rank-and-file jobs. Third, a worker who is made a foreman must give up his membership in the union and become a surrogate of management, while a worker who is made a steward retains the union as a reference group and simply takes on new functions and responsibilities as a representative of it.

All of these differences suggest that the change from worker to foreman is a more fundamental change in roles than the change from worker to steward. This, in turn, might account to a large extent for the finding that, although attitude changes accompany both changes in roles, they occur more sharply among new foremen than among new stewards.

A third finding has to do with the *kinds* of attitude changes which occur among workers who change roles. As expected, new foremen become more pro-management and new stewards become more pro-union. Somewhat less expected is the finding that new foremen become more anti-union but new stewards do not become more anti-management. Among workers who are made foremen, statistically significant shifts in an anti-union direction occur on four of the eight items dealing with the union and the union-sponsored seniority system. Among workers who are made stewards, there are no statistically significant shifts in either direction on any of the eight items having to do with management and the management-sponsored incentive system.

The finding that new foremen become anti-union but that new stewards do not become anti-management may be related to the fact that workers who become foremen must relinquish their membership of the union, while workers who become stewards retain their status as employees of management. New foremen, subject to one main set of loyalties and called on to carry out a markedly new set of functions, tend to develop negative attitudes toward the union as well as positive attitudes toward management. New stewards, subject to overlapping group membership and still dependent on management for their livelihoods, tend to become more favorable toward the union but they do not turn against management, at least not within the relatively limited time period covered by the present research project. Over time, stewards might come to develop somewhat hostile attitudes toward management, but, under the conditions prevailing at Rockwell, there is apparently no tendency for such attitudes to be developed as soon as workers enter the steward role.

METHOD: PHASE 2

One of the questions that may be raised about the results that have been presented up to this point concerns the extent to which the changed attitudes displayed by new foremen and new stewards are internalized by the role occupants. Are the changed attitudes expressed by new foremen and new stewards relatively stable, or are they ephemeral phenomena to be held only as long as they occupy the foreman and steward roles? An unusual set of circumstances at Rockwell enabled the researchers to glean some data on this question.

A short time after the 1952 resurvey, the nation suffered an economic recession. In order to meet the lessening demand for its products, Rockwell, like many other firms, had to cut its work force. This resulted in many rank-and-file workers being laid off and a number of the foremen being returned to nonsupervisory jobs. By June 1954, eight of the twenty-three workers who had been promoted to foreman had returned to the worker role and only twelve were still foremen. (The remaining three respondents had voluntarily left Rockwell by this time.)

Over the same period, a number of role changes had also been experienced by the thirty-five workers who had become stewards. Fourteen had returned to the worker role, either because they had not sought reelection by their work groups or because they had failed to win reelection, and only six were still stewards. (The other fifteen respondents, who composed almost half of this group, had either voluntarily left Rockwell or had been laid off as part of the general reduction in force.)

Once again, in June 1954, the researchers returned to Rockwell to readminister the questionnaires that the workers had filled out in 1951 and 1952. The instructions to the respondents were substantially the same as those given in 1952—i.e., a sample of employees had been chosen to get up-to-date measures of employees' attitudes toward working conditions at Rockwell and the same groups were selected this time as had been selected last time in order to lend greater stability to the results.

In this phase of the study, the numbers of cases with which we were dealing in the various groups were so small that the data could only be viewed as suggestive, and systematic statistical analysis of the data did not seem to be too meaningful. However, the unusual opportunity to throw some light on an important question suggests that a reporting of these results may be worthwhile.

RESULTS: PHASE 2

The principal question examined here was: on those items where a change in roles resulted in a change in attitudes between 1951 and

1952, how are these attitudes influenced by a reverse change in roles between 1952 and 1954?

The most consistent and widespread attitude changes noted between 1951 and 1952 were those that resulted when workers moved into the foreman role. What are the effects of moving out of the foreman role between 1952 and 1954? The data indicate that, in general, most of the "gains" that were observed when workers became foremen are "lost" when they become workers again. The results on six of the items, showing the proportions who take pro-management positions at various points in time, are presented in Table 5. On almost all of the items, the foremen who remain foremen either retain their favorable attitudes toward management or become even more favorable

Table 5 *Effects of Entering and Leaving the Foreman Role on Attitudes toward Management and the Union*

	Workers Who Became Foremen and Stayed Foremen ($N = 12$)			Workers Who Became Foremen and Were Later Demoted ($N = 8$)		
	(W) 1951	(F) 1952	(F) 1954	(W) 1951	(F) 1952	(W) 1954
% who feel Rockwell is a good place to work	33	92	100	25	75	50
% who feel management officers really care about the workers at Rockwell	8	33	67	0	25	0
% who feel the union should not have more say in setting labor standards	33	100	100	13	63	13
% who are satisfied with the way the incentive system works out at Rockwell	17	75	75	25	50	13
% who believe a worker's standard will not be changed just because he is a high producer	42	83	100	25	63	75
% who feel ability should count more than seniority in promotions	33	58	75	25	50	38

toward management between 1952 and 1954, while the demoted foremen show fairly consistent drops in the direction of readopting the attitudes they held when they had been in the worker role. On the whole, the attitudes held by demoted foremen in 1954, after they had left the foreman role, fall roughly to the same levels as they had been in 1951, before they had ever moved into the foreman role.

Table 6 *Effects of Entering and Leaving the Steward Role on Attitudes toward Management and the Union*

	Workers Who Were Elected Stewards and Were Later Reelected ($N = 6$)			Workers Who Were Elected Stewards but Were Not Later Reelected ($N = 14$)		
	(W) 1951	(S) 1952	(S) 1954	(W) 1951	(S) 1952	(W) 1954
% who feel Rockwell is a good place to work	50	0	0	29	79	36
% who feel management officers really care about the workers at Rockwell	0	0	0	14	14	0
% who feel the union should not have more say in setting labor standards	0	17	0	14	14	14
% who are satisfied with the way the incentive system works out at Rockwell	17	17	0	43	43	21
% who believe a worker's standard will not be changed just because he is a high producer	50	50	17	21	43	36
% who feel ability should count more than seniority in promotions	67	17	17	36	36	21

The results on the effects of moving out of the steward role are less clear-cut. As shown in Table 6, there is no marked tendency for ex-stewards to revert to earlier-held attitudes when they go from the steward role to the worker role. At the same time, it should be recalled that there had not been particularly marked changes in their attitudes when they initially changed from the worker role to the steward role. These findings, then, are consistent with the interpretation offered earlier that the change in roles between worker and steward is less significant than the change in roles between worker and foreman.

A question might be raised about what is represented in the reversal of attitudes found among ex-foremen. Does it represent a positive taking-on of attitudes appropriate for respondents who are reentering the worker role, or does it constitute a negative, perhaps embittered reaction away from the attitudes they held before being demoted from the foreman role? A definitive answer to this question cannot be arrived at, but it might be suggested that if we were dealing with a situation where a reversion in roles did not constitute such a strong psychological blow to the role occupants (as was probably the case among demoted foremen), then such a marked reversion in attitudes might not have occurred.[3]

One final table is of interest here. Table 7[4] compares the attitudes of two groups of respondents: (1) the twelve employees who were rank-and-file workers in 1951, had been selected as foremen by 1952, and were still foremen in 1954; and (2) the six employees who were rank-and-file workers in 1951, had been elected as stewards by 1952, and were still stewards in 1954. At each time period, for each of the sixteen questions examined earlier in Tables 1 through 4, the table shows (1) the proportion of foremen or future foremen who took a pro-management position on these questions; (2) the proportion of stewards or future stewards who took a pro-management position on these questions; and (3) the difference between these proportions. The following are the mean differences in proportions for the three time periods:

1. In 1951, while both future foremen and future stewards still occupied the rank-and-file worker role, the mean difference was only —.1 per cent,

[3] There were a number of reactions to demotion among the eight ex-foremen, as obtained from informal interviews with these respondents. Some reacted impunitively (i.e., they blamed uncontrollable situational determinants) and did not seem to be bothered by demotion. Others reacted extrapunitively (i.e., they blamed management) or intrapunitively (i.e., they blamed themselves) and appeared to be more disturbed by demotion. One way of testing the hypothesis that attitude reversion is a function of embitterment would be to see if sharper reversion occurs among extrapunitive and intrapunitive respondents. However, the small number of cases does not permit an analysis of this kind to be carried out in the present situation.

[4] Table 7 has been omitted for sake of brevity.

which means that practically no difference in attitudes existed between these two groups at this time. (The minus sign means that a slightly, but far from significantly, larger proportion of future stewards than future foremen expressed a pro-management position on these items.)

2. In 1952, after the groups had been in the foreman and steward roles for about one year, the mean difference had jumped to +47.8 per cent, which means that a sharp wedge had been driven between them. Both groups had tended to become polarized in opposite directions, as foremen took on attitudes consistent with being a representative of management and stewards took on attitudes appropriate for a representative of the union.

3. In 1954, after the groups had been in the foreman and steward roles for two to three years, the mean difference was +62.4 per cent, which means that a still larger gap had opened up between them. Although the gap had widened, it is interesting to note that the changes that occurred during this later and longer 1952 to 1954 period are not as sharp or as dramatic as the changes that occurred during the initial and shorter 1951 to 1952 period.

These findings offer further support for the proposition that roles can influence attitudes. The data indicate that changes in attitudes occurred soon after changes in roles took place. And inside a period of three years those who had remained in their new roles had developed almost diametrically opposed sets of attitudinal positions.

DISCUSSION

A role may be defined as a set of behaviors that are expected of people who occupy a certain position in a social system. These expectations consist of shared attitudes or beliefs, held by relevant populations, about what role occupants should and should not do. The theoretical basis for hypothesizing that a role will have effects on role occupants lies in the nature of these expectations. If a role occupant meets these expectations, the "rights" or "rewards" associated with the role will be accorded to him. If he fails to meet these expectations, the "rights" or "rewards" will be withheld from him and "punishments" may be meted out.

A distinction should be made between the effects of roles on people's attitudes and the effects of roles on their actions. How roles affect actions can probably be explained in a fairly direct fashion. Actions are overt and readily enforceable. If a person fails to behave in ways appropriate to his role, this can immediately be seen, and steps may be taken to bring the deviant or nonconformist into line. Role deviants may be evicted from their roles, placed in less rewarding roles, isolated from other members of the group, or banished entirely from the social system.

But attitudes are not as overt as actions. A person may behave in such a way as to reveal his attitudes, but he can—and often does—do much to cover them up. Why, then, should a change in roles lead to a change in actions? A number of explanatory factors might be suggested here. The present discussion will be confined to two factors that are probably generic to a wide variety of situations. One pertains to the influence of reference groups; the other is based on an assumption about people's need to have attitudes internally consistent with their actions.

A change in roles almost invariably involves a change in reference groups. Old reference groups may continue to influence the role occupant, but new ones also come into play. The change in reference groups may involve moving into a completely new group (as when a person gives up membership in one organization and joins another one) or it may simply involve taking on new functions in the same group (as when a person is promoted to a higher position in a hierarchical organization). In both situations, new reference groups will tend to bring about new frames of reference, new self-percepts, and new vested interests, and these in turn will tend to produce new attitudinal orientations.

In addition to a change in reference groups, a change in roles also involves a change in functions and a change in the kinds of behaviors and actions that the role occupant must display if he is to fulfill these functions. A change in actions, let us assume, comes about because these actions are immediately required, clearly visible, and hence socially enforceable. If we further assume a need for people to have attitudes that are internally consistent with their actions, then at least one aspect of the functional significance of a change in attitudes becomes clear. A change in attitudes enables a new role occupant to justify, to make rational, or perhaps simply to rationalize his change in actions. Having attitudes that are consistent with actions helps the role occupant to be "at one" with himself and facilitates his effective performance of the functions he is expected to carry out.

The reference-group principle and the self-consistency principle postulate somewhat different chains of events in accounting for the effects of roles on attitudes and actions. In abbreviated versions, the different chains may be spelled out in the following ways:

1. Reference-group principle: A change in roles involves a change in reference groups . . . which leads to a change in attitudes . . . which leads to a change in actions.
2. Self-consistency principle: A change in roles involves a change in functions . . . which leads to a change in actions . . . which leads to a change in attitudes.

In the former chain, a person's attitudes influence his actions; in the latter chain, a person's actions influence his attitudes. Both chains might plausibly account for the results obtained, but whether either chain, both chains, or other chains is or are valid cannot be determined from the data available. A more direct investigation of the underlying mechanisms responsible for the impact of roles on attitudes would appear to be a fruitful area for further research.

But apart from the question of underlying mechanisms, the results lend support to the proposition that a person's attitudes will be influenced by his role. Relatively consistent changes in attitudes were found both among workers who were made foremen and among workers who were made stewards, although these changes were more clear-cut for foremen than for stewards. The more interesting set of results—as far as role theory in general is concerned—would seem to be the data on the effects of entering and leaving the foreman role. It was pointed out earlier that the foreman role, unlike the steward role, is a full-time, relatively permanent position, and moving into this position entails taking on a very new and different set of functions. When workers are made foremen, their attitudes change in a more pro-management and anti-union direction. When they are demoted and move back into the worker role, their attitudes change once again, this time in a more pro-union and anti-management direction. In both instances, the respondents' attitudes seem to be molded by the roles which they occupy at a given time.

The readiness with which the respondents in this study shed one set of attitudes and took on another set of attitudes might suggest either that (1) the attitudes studied do not tap very basic or deep-rooted facets of the respondents' psyches, or (2) the character structures of the respondents are such as not to include very deeply ingrained sets of value orientations. Riesman (4) deals with this problem in his discussion of "other-directedness" versus "inner-directedness." How much the rapid shifts in attitudes observed here reflect the particular kinds of respondents who underwent changes in roles in the present situation, and how much these shifts reflect the national character of the American population, can only be speculated on at the present time.

SUMMARY

This study was designed to test the proposition that a person's attitudes will be influenced by the role he occupies in a social system. This is a commonly accepted postulate in role theory but there appears to be little in the way of definitive empirical evidence to support it. Earlier studies have generally made inferences about the effects of roles on attitudes on the basis of correlational data gathered at a single point in time. The present study attempted to measure the effects of roles on attitudes through data gathered at three different points in time.

In September and October 1951, 2354 rank-and-file workers in a factory situation were asked to fill out attitude questionnaires dealing with management and the union. During the next twelve months, twenty-three of these workers were promoted to foreman and thirty-five were elected by their work groups as union stewards. In December 1952, the questionnaires were readministered to the two groups of workers who had changed roles and to two matched control groups of workers who had not changed roles. By comparing the attitude changes that occurred in the experimental groups with the attitude changes that occurred in their respective control groups, the effects of moving into the foreman and steward roles could be determined.

The results on this phase of the study showed that the experimental groups underwent systematic changes in attitudes after they were placed in their new roles, while the control groups underwent no changes or less marked changes from the "before" situation to the "after" situation. The workers who were made foremen tended to become more favorable toward management, and the workers who were made stewards tended to become more favorable toward the union. The changes were more marked among new foremen than among new stewards, which can be probably accounted for by the fact that the change from worker to foreman seems to be a more significant and more meaningful change in roles than the change from worker to steward.

In the months following the second administration of the questionnaire, a number of the workers who had become foremen and stewards reverted to the rank-and-file worker role. Some of the foremen were cut back to nonsupervisory positions during a period of economic recession, and some of the stewards either did not run again or failed to be reelected during the annual steward elections. In June 1954, the questionnaires were once again administered to the same groups of respondents. By comparing the attitude changes that occurred among foremen and stewards who left these roles with the attitude changes that occurred among foremen and stewards who remained in these roles, the effects of moving out of these roles could be assessed.

The results of this phase of the study showed that foremen who were demoted tended to revert to the attitudes they had previously held while they were in the worker role, while foremen who remained in the foreman role either maintained the attitudes they had developed when they first became foremen or moved even further in that direction. The results among stewards who left the steward role were less consistent and less clear-cut, which parallels the smaller and less clear-cut attitude changes that took place when they first became stewards.

The findings support the proposition that a person's role will have an impact on his attitudes, but they still leave unanswered the question of what underlying mechanisms are operating here. A more direct investigation of these underlying mechanisms might comprise a fruitful area for further research.

REFERENCES

1. Jacobson, E., Charters, W. W., Jr., & Lieberman, S. "The use of the role concept in the study of complex organizations." *J. Soc. Issues*, 1951, 7 (3), 18–27.
2. Newcomb, T. M. *Social psychology*. New York: Dryden Press, 1950; London: Tavistock Publications, 1952.
3. Parsons, T. *The social system*. Glencoe, Ill.: Free Press, 1951; London: Tavistock Publications, 1951.
4. Riesman, D. *The lonely crowd*. New Haven: Yale Univ. Press, 1950.
5. Stouffer, S. A., Suchman, E. A., DeVinney, L. C., Star, S. A., & Williams, R. M., Jr. *The American soldier: Adjustment during Army life,* Vol. 1. Princeton: Princeton Univ. Press, 1949.
6. Walker, H. M., & Lev, J. *Statistical inference*. New York: Holt, 1953.

6.6 RISK-TAKING IN CHILDREN: AGE AND SEX DIFFERENCES

Paul Slovic

A prevalent belief in our culture is that men should, and do, take greater risks than women. For the child, a man's role is defined to a considerable extent in terms of courage. For example, Alpenfels and Hayes (1961) note that

> success stories throughout our history [place] a high premium on "taking a chance." The pioneers took a chance; they were courageous "killers of bears." These themes are instilled into the growing child without regard to sex. This is what Davy Crockett did, this is what the space cadet does. . . . Girls emerging from common patterns of babyhood suddenly learn, however, that their adult role is to be a different one [Alpenfels & Hayes, 1961, p. 107].

The foregoing quotation, besides illustrating the value of taking a chance as a masculine goal, implies that sex differences in risk-taking will emerge at some early age. A factor that would seem to result in boys becoming more daring than girls is the process of sex-typing described by Mussen, Conger, and Kagan (1963). One consequence of the cultural pressures exerted at home and school is that children become highly sensitive to male and female personality characteristics, interests, and activities. They develop well-defined conceptions of "boy-traits" and "girl-traits." According to Tuddenham (1952), children as early as in the primary grades picture the typical boy as more daring than the typical girl. Furthermore, boldness has been found to be positively correlated with popularity for boys but negatively correlated with popularity for girls (Tuddenham, 1951). It would be quite surprising if these social pressures did not result in an increased sex difference in risk-taking propensity.

At present, evidence indicating that boys are willing to take greater risks than girls is scarce. In a study by Swineford (1941), ninth-grade *Ss* were asked to indicate the number of points they wanted each

Source: This study was supported by the National Institute of Mental Health. Reprinted with slight abridgment from *Child Development*, 1966, **37**, 169–176, with permission of the author and The Society for Research in Child Development, Inc.

question on an achievement examination to be worth. Possible values ranged from one to four points and, if the item was answered incorrectly, the indicated number of points was subtracted from the *S*'s score. Swineford's index of test risk-taking, the number of errors on four-point questions divided by the total number of errors and omissions, was found to be independent of ability and higher for boys than for girls. Similarly, Crandall and Rabson (1960) reported that boys were less ready to withdraw from threat of failure on an intellectual-achievement task than were girls. Perhaps the most relevant decision-making study has recently been reported by Kass (1964). Subjects aged 6, 8, and 10 years repeatedly played their choice of three slot machines. The machines were programmed to be equal in expected monetary return but differed in probability of payoff. Boys chose the low and intermediate probabilities of payoff significantly more often than did girls. The fact that Kass did not find a significant interaction between sex differences and age may have been due to the small number (seven) of *S*s in each age and sex category.

Adult observers, around the playground and home, rate boys and their activities as adventurous; girls are seen as more sedentary and conservative (Anastasi, 1958). Prior expectations of greater risk-taking in boys, however, may well bias raters' perceptions in the direction of the stereotype. Also, differences in size, strength, and motor coordination rather than in risk-taking propensities may dictate the child's choice of activities.

Risk-taking tendencies have been invoked as possible determiners of accidents (Suchman & Schertzer, 1960) and criminality (Cohen & Hansel, 1956). It is perhaps significant that boys greatly exceed girls in the frequency and severity of childhood accidents (Douglas & Blomfield, 1956; Powers & Lincoln, 1953) and delinquent offenses (Anastasi, 1958). Whether these facts are due to differential risk-taking as opposed to other nonrisk factors is hard to determine. As Suchman and Schertzer aptly point out:

> We need to know much more about the relationship of intellect, including cognition, judgment, and decision-making, to risk-taking among children, and the way in which these mental processes develop in the growing child [Suchman & Schertzer, 1960, p. 15].

The present investigation attempts to provide evidence for the validity of the masculinity-boldness stereotype by studying the influence of age and sex upon children's performance on a decision-making task designed to assess risk-taking.

THE TASK

The criteria used in the selection of an appropriate task were: (*a*) the task should be a decision-making procedure that explicitly focuses the child's attention on risk-taking, that is, one which requires the subject to assess probabilities of winning and losing and their corresponding utilities prior to making a choice; (*b*) the task should be standard for all *S*s; (*c*) the instructions should be easily understood by even the youngest of the *S*s; (*d*) the task should not require motor or physical abilities that are possessed in greater measure by children of a particular age or sex.

In view of the above criteria, the present study employed a variation of the risk-taking tasks described by Edwards and Slovic (1965). The *S* was seated before a panel of ten small knife switches. He was told that nine of these switches were "safe" and the tenth was a "disaster" switch. It was impossible to tell which was the disaster switch. Disaster was assigned randomly and equiprobably to each of the switch positions. This was made clear to *S* in language he could understand. The *S* was asked to pull one of the switches. If he was safe, he was allowed to place one spoonful of M & M candies into a glass bowl. He then had to decide whether to pull another switch and try for another spoonful of candy or stop and keep the candy he had already won. If *S* decided to try for more candy and pulled the disaster switch, a buzzer sounded, and he lost everything he had already earned. The game ended when *S* either stopped and collected his winnings or pulled the disaster switch. In the event that *S* pulled nine safe switches, he was automatically forced to stop and take his nine spoonfuls of candy. Each *S* was allowed to play the game only one time except in the event that the first switch pulled brought disaster. If this occurred, the game was reset, and *S* was given another chance. Therefore, every *S* pulled at least one safe switch.

Each *S* was informed that, since a switch could be pulled only once, the likelihood of pulling the disaster switch on the next try increased with the number of safe switches already pulled. One could try any switch providing it had not previously been pulled, and he could stop and take his winnings any time prior to pulling the disaster switch.

Since both the probability and magnitude of one's potential loss increase with the number of switches pulled, stopping performance on this task can be considered an index of risk-taking tendencies providing that one can assume equal utility of M & M candies for groups of children that one wishes to compare. This assumption seems legitimate for groups of similar age, though one might hesitate to assume equal utilities for groups differing greatly in age. Also, in the event that a child pulled the disaster switch, it was impossible to tell how many switches he would have pulled before stopping voluntarily. This necessitated a second assumption, namely, that chance would be equally favorable (or unfavorable) for all comparison groups. A rather large sample size was obtained to help insure the equality of chance disasters across age and sex classes.

SUBJECTS

The experiment was conducted at a county fair. Subjects were 1047 children and young adults who volunteered to play the game for the chance of winning M & M candies. Admission to the game was free.

The distribution of *S*s by age and sex is shown in Table 1 to the extent that the greater predominance of boys in the sample and the increase with age of the ratio of boys to girls was due to an unwillingness of the less daring girls to participate, the magnitude of sex differences on the experimental task may have been reduced.

Table 1 *Distribution of Subjects by Age and Sex*

	Age						
	6, 7, 8	9, 10	11	12	13	14, 15, 16	Total
Girls	50	85	46	42	40	49	312
Boys	89	137	108	117	111	173	735
Total							1,047

RESULTS AND DISCUSSION

Figure 1 illustrates the percentage of *S*s in each age and sex category who stopped and took their winnings when they could have pulled additional switches. Sex differences in stopping behavior were tested for statistical significance at each age level, using the critical-ratio procedure described by McNemar (1962, pp. 56–61). Girls stopped more often than boys at every age level except the youngest. However, sex differences at the two youngest age levels were small and not statistically significant. The differences at ages 11 and 14–16 were significant at $p < .05$. Although the differences at ages 12 and 13 failed

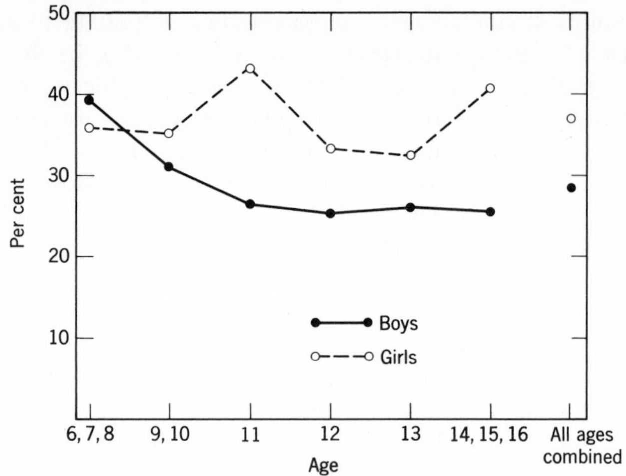

Figure 1. Percentage of *Ss* who stopped voluntarily.

to reach the .05 level of significance, they are consistent with the results shown by *Ss* in the adjacent age categories.

It seems reasonable to conclude that there was an age-by-sex interaction, with both sexes stopping about equally often at the younger age levels and boys becoming more daring than girls by age 11.

Figure 2 provides further insight into the analysis of stopping behavior by illustrating the times during the game at which *Ss* decided to stop. This figure indicates that girls exhibited greater caution than boys after safely pulling the fifth, seventh, and eighth switches.

The caution exhibited by the girls worked to their advantage. They did not stop excessively before switch five when the expectation for continuing was in their favor. Instead, they were more cautious than boys at points where boldness would have been costly. As a result, the girls won an average of 2.20 spoonfuls of candy per person while the boys averaged only 1.84 spoonfuls. It is well known that girls exceed boys in school achievement. One might argue that the superiority of girls on the present task might, like their superiority in school, be due to some sort of greater intellectual maturity or capability, rather than any risk-taking factor. In defense of the risk-taking interpretation, it should be noted that the rank-order correlation between the average number of spoonfuls earned and chronological age was −.04. However,

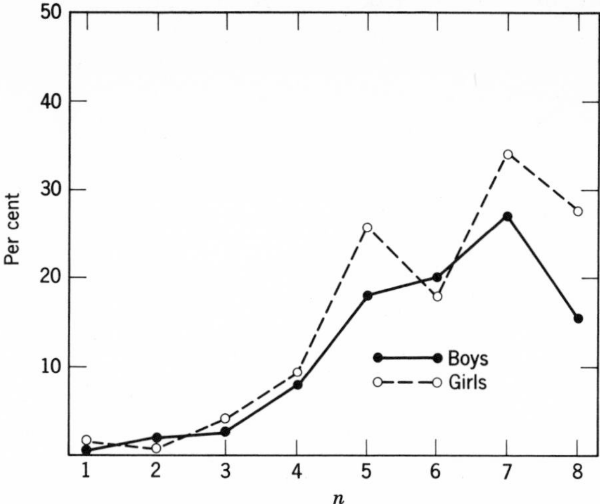

Figure 2. Percentage of *S*s who elected to stop after pulling *n* switches safely. Data are combined over all age groups.

it would not be difficult to vary the payoff structure of the present task in order to create an environment where it would always be to *S*'s advantage to pull another switch. One way to do this would be to make the reward for safely pulling switch *n* greater than the reward for safely pulling switch $n - 1$. Future experimentation should employ a variety of payoff conditions in order to make the interpretation of stopping behavior less ambiguous. For an example of a study where this was done, see Edwards and Slovic (1965).

Any generalizations that one might wish to draw from the present study are limited by the fact that the *S*s included only those children who were curious and daring enough to volunteer to play what was obviously a risk-taking game. This study needs to be replicated with a more representative sample of boys and girls. Furthermore, more efficient use should be made of each *S* by running the game for several trials or by surreptitiously deactivating the disaster switch so that *S* would always be able to stop voluntarily.

SUMMARY

A number of children (735 boys and 312 girls) between the ages of 6 and 16 participated in a decision-making game designed to assess their willingness to take risks. The results indicated a sex difference in risk-taking propensity which emerged between the ninth and eleventh year of age. The difference was in the direction of our cultural stereotype: boys were bolder than girls.

REFERENCES

Alpenfels, Ethel J., & Hayes, A. B. Cultural factors affecting accidents among children. *Behavioral approaches to accident research.* New York: Assn. Aid of Crippled Children, 1961.

Anastasi, Anne. *Differential psychology.* New York: Macmillan, 1958.

Cohen, J., & Hansel, M. *Risk and gambling.* New York: Philosophical Library, 1956.

Crandall, V. J., & Rabson, Alice. Children's repetition choices in an intellectual achievement situation following success and failure. *J. Genet. Psychol.*, 1960, **97**, 161–168.

Douglas, J. W. B., & Blomfield, J. M. *Children under five.* Fair Lawn, N.J.: Essential Books, 1956.

Edwards, W., & Slovic, P. Seeking information to reduce the risk of decisions. *Am. J. Psychol.*, 1965, **78**, 188–197.

Kass, N. Risk in decision-making as a function of age, sex, and probability preference. *Child Develpm.*, 1964, **35**, 577–582.

McNemar, Q., *Psychological statistics.* New York: Wiley, 1962.

Mussen, P. H., Conger, J. J., & Kagan, J. *Child development and personality*, 2nd ed., New York: Harper, 1963.

Powers, J. H., & Lincoln, J. F. Accidents during infancy and childhood. *N.Y. State J. Med.*, 1953.

Suchman, E. A., & Schertzer, A. L. *Current research in childhood accidents.* New York: Assn. Aid of Crippled Children, 1960.

Swineford, F. Analysis of a personality trait. *J. Educ. Psychol.*, 1941, **32**, 438–444.

Tuddenham, R. D. Studies in reputation: III. Correlates of popularity among elementary-school children. *J. Educ. Psychol.*, 1951, **42**, 257–276.

Tuddenham, R. D. Studies in reputation: I. Sex and grade differences in school children's evaluation of their peers. II. The diagnosis of social adjustment. *Psychol. Monogr.*, 1952, **66**, No. 333.

6.7 EFFECTS OF PATERNAL ABSENCE ON SEX-TYPED BEHAVIORS IN NEGRO AND WHITE PREADOLESCENT MALES

E. Mavis Hetherington

This study investigated the effects of father absence on the development of sex-role preferences, dependency, aggression, and recreational activities of Negro and white preadolescent boys. All children had mothers but no father substitute present in the home and no contact with the fathers subsequent to separation.

In previous studies of the effects of father absence on the development of children, total and final absence of the father usually had not occurred. The father was either temporarily away due to war (Bach, 1946; Sears, Pintler, & Sears, 1946) or to occupational demands (Lynn & Sawrey, 1959; Tiller, 1958). An exception to this is the McCord, McCord, and Thurber (1962) study of boys from broken homes. These studies frequently indicated disruption of masculine identification in boys whose fathers were absent. Boys with fathers absent from the home tended to be less aggressive in doll-play situations (Sears et al., 1946), had father fantasies more similar to those of girls (Bach, 1946), and were more dependent (Stolz et al., 1954; Tiller, 1958) than boys whose fathers were living in the home. In contrast to these findings McCord et al. found no differences in dependency between boys from homes in which the father was absent and those in which the father was present and found the former group was more aggressive. The Lynn and Sawrey study also indicated that boys deprived of regular contact with their fathers made stronger strivings toward masculine identification shown by preference for a father versus a mother doll in a Structured Doll Play Test, and manifested an unstable compensatory masculinity. They found no differences between boys whose fathers were absent and those whose fathers were present in ratings of dependency in the doll-play situation and attribute this to a "compensatory masculine reluctance to express dependency [p. 261]."

Source: Reprinted from the *Journal of Personality and Social Psychology*, 1966, 4, 87–91, with permission of the author and the American Psychological Association, Inc.

It might be expected that if boys with absent fathers in contrast to those with a father present manifest compensatory masculinity they would score high on behaviors associated with masculinity such as independence, aggression, masculine sex-role preferences, and participation in activities involving force and competition. Moss and Kagan (1961) suggested that for boys, participation and skill in sports is closely involved with maintenance of sex-role identification. However, if father absence results in a direct expression of a failure to establish masculine identification, boys without fathers would be rated low on the previous variables.

The age at which separation from the father occurs could differentially affect the form of disrupted identification in boys. Early separation may result in greater disruption of sex-typed behaviors than would later separation when identification is well under way or completed. Early separation might result directly in less masculine sex-role behaviors since identification with the father has never developed. In contrast later separation may have little effect on these behaviors or result in exaggerating masculine behavior in an attempt to sustain the already established masculine identification with the major role model, the father, absent.

It might also be expected that the effects of father absence would interact with the race of the family. It has frequently been suggested that the Negro family structure is basically matriarchal (Karon, 1958). Maternal dominance has been demonstrated to have a disruptive effect on sex typing in boys (Hetherington, 1965; Mussen & Distler, 1959). In such mother-dominated families, absence of the father might be expected to have a less disruptive effect on sex-typed behavior of boys than it would in a father-dominant family.

Kardiner and Ovesey (1951) suggest that Negroes have strong inhibited aggressive needs which are displaced and expressed in competitive sports. It would therefore be predicted that Negroes would be rated lower in overt social aggression than would white boys, but would show a marked preference for aggressive, competitive activities.

METHOD

Subjects were 32 Negro and 32 white first-born boys between the ages of 9 and 12, who were attending a recreation center in a lower-class urban area. Sixteen of the boys in each group were from homes in which both parents were present, and 16 from homes in which the father was absent. In half of the father-absent homes for Negro and white families, separation had occurred at age 4 or earlier, and in half, after age 6. Father separation was caused by desertion, divorce, death, and illegitimacy. No father substitutes lived in the home. There were no significant differences in causes of father separation between groups, although illegitimacy was a cause only in the early groups.

Forty-nine of the subjects were only children, seven subjects had a younger male sibling, and eight subjects had a younger female sibling. These subjects were distributed approximately evenly across groups, although there was a slightly larger proportion of only children in the group of children whose fathers left early than in the groups whose fathers were present or had left the home after age 6.

Procedure

Two male recreation directors who had known the subjects for at least six months rated them on seven-point scales measuring dependence on adults, dependence on peers, independence, aggression, and on an activities test. The scales ranged from 1, very rarely and without persistence, to 7, very often and very persistently. Interraters reliabilities ranged from .85 to .94. All subjects were also individually administered the It Scale for Children (ITSC; Brown, 1956).

Measures

Scales for dependence and independence were based upon those used by Beller (1957). The aggression scale was based on that of Sears, Whiting, Nowlis, and Sears (1953). Behaviors involved in each scale were more fully elaborated as in Beller (1957), but used behaviors appropriate to the age group of the present study. A total rating for each of these three scales was obtained.

Rating Scale for Dependence on Adults was comprised of ratings of:

1. How often does the boy seek physical contact with adults?
2. How often does the boy seek to be near adults?
3. How often does the boy seek recognition (any form of praise and punishment) from adults?
4. How often does the boy seek attention from adults?

Rating Scale for Dependence on Peers was composed of the same items as dependence on adults oriented toward children.

Rating Sale for Independence involved the following four of Beller's autonomous achievement-striving scales:

1. How often does the boy derive satisfaction from his work?
2. How often does the boy take the initiative in carrying out his own activity?
3. How often does the boy attempt to overcome obstacles in the environment?
4. How often does the boy complete an activity?

Rating Scale for Aggression involved the following items:

1. How often does the boy act to necessitate correction, scolding, or reminding?
2. How often does the boy ask for special privileges?
3. How often does the boy attack other children or their property to show envy?
4. How often does the boy threaten adults?
5. How often does the boy threaten other children?
6. How often does the boy destroy the property of the Center or of other children?
7. How often does the boy derogate others?
8. How often does the boy quarrel with other children?
9. How often does the boy display undirected aggression?
10. How often does the boy attack other children physically?
11. How often does the child exhibit displaced aggressive attacks?

The Activities Test was comprised of ratings on a seven-point scale ranging from 1, very rarely participates in this activity, to 7, very often and persistently participates in the activity. Five activities in each of four categories were rated. In standardizing the Activities Test three recreation directors were asked to sort a group of 48 activities into the following four categories. Only those in which the three judges agreed were retained.

1. Physical skill involving contact—boxing, wrestling, football, basketball, battle ball.
2. Physical skill not involving contact—foot-racing, bowling, horseshoes, table tennis, darts.
3. Nonphysical competitive games—dominoes, checkers, scrabble, monopoly, cards.
4. Nonphysical noncompetitive games—reading, watching television, building things, working on puzzles, collecting things.

Total ratings for each of the four types of activities were obtained.

The ITSC (Brown, 1956) is a test of sex-role preference which presents the child with an ambiguous figure (It) and asks the child to select from a group of toys and objects those that "It" prefers. A high score indicates masculine preference.

RESULTS

Separate two-way analyses of variance involving race and father status (early absent, late absent, and present) were calculated for each scale. When significant F ratios were obtained, t tests between means were calculated. Table 1 presents the means for all groups on all variables.

The analysis of variance of total dependence on adults yielded no significant differences; however, the analysis of dependence on peers yielded a significant F ratio ($F = 10.18$, $p < .005$) for father status. Subsequent t tests indicated that both early separated and late-separated boys were significantly more dependent on peers than were the boys with fathers living in the home ($t = 2.23$, $p < .05$; $t = 2.90$, $p < .005$).

No significant differences were found between groups on total independence scores.

The analysis of total aggression scores indicated a significant effect of father status ($F = 10.39$, $p < .005$) on aggressive behavior. Both boys who were deprived of their fathers after age 6 and boys whose fathers are present manifested more aggression than boys who were deprived of their fathers at an early age ($t = 3.20$, $p < .005$; $t = 2.21$, $p < .05$, respectively).

The results of the ITSC also yielded a significant effect for father status ($F = 4.966$, $p < .025$). Boys experiencing late separation from the father and boys from unbroken homes have more masculine sex-role preferences than early-separated boys ($t = 2.32$, $p < .05$; $t = 3.14$, $p < .005$).

The Activities Test indicates that early separated boys play fewer physical games involving contact than do either late-separated boys or boys with fathers living in the home ($t = 2.06$, $p < .05$; $t = 2.60$, $p < .025$). Negro boys tend to play more games of this type than do white boys ($t = 2.22$, $p = .05$). It should be noted that this is the only significant racial difference found in the entire study. No significant effects were obtained in the analysis of physical activities involving no contact or in nonphysical competitive activities. However, a significant effect ($F = 8.236$, $p < .005$) for father status was found in nonphysical, noncompetitive activities. Early separated boys spend more time in these activities than do boys living with both parents.

Table 1 *Means for Father Separation Early, Father Separation Late, and Father Present, Negro and White Boys*

	Father Present		Early		Late	
	White	Negro	White	Negro	White	Negro
Dependency on adults	15.69	15.19	14.25	14.00	12.75	13.00
Dependency on peers	15.31	15.50	17.62	18.25	18.25	19.12
Independence	15.75	15.69	18.25	15.37	15.25	18.25
Aggression	39.87	47.06	32.00	30.75	51.00	52.12
ITSC	67.56	70.69	53.50	55.00	65.12	73.25
Physical contact	20.62	23.62	14.87	18.87	21.50	21.87
Physical noncontact	21.06	18.75	15.37	17.50	21.12	17.00
Nonphysical, competitive	21.44	20.81	16.87	18.62	20.12	17.62
Nonphysical, noncompetitive	17.69	16.62	24.25	22.37	21.37	19.12

Table 2 *Correlations among All Variables for All Subjects*

	1	2	3	4	5	6	7	8	9
1. Dependence on adults	1.00	.02	—.25**	.06	.04	.04	.06	.11	—.06
2. Dependence on peers		1.00	—.10	.06	.04	—.02	.03	—.26	.10
3. Independence			1.00	.05	.02	—.01	.11	.17	—.17
4. Aggression				1.00	.21*	.40****	.22*	—.01	—.33***
5. ITSC					1.00	.38***	.02	.09	—.29***
6. Physical contact						1.00	.13	.03	—.59****
7. Physical noncontact							1.00	.17	—.16
8. Nonphysical, competition								1.00	—.23
9. Nonphysical, noncompetition									1.00

Note: Numbered variables in columns correspond to those in rows.

* $p = .10$.

** $p = .05$.

*** $p = .01$.

**** $p = .001$.

It seemed possible that the obtained differences between early and late-separated boys were a result of the total time elapsed since the father left the home, rather than the developmental stage at which separation occurred. The early separated children may have had more time for a loss of cathexsis on masculine behaviors. In order to investigate this possibility, an attempt was made to compare subjects in the early and late-separation groups who had been deprived of their fathers for six years. The resulting *N*s in each group were too small to permit an adequate analysis of the scores ($N = 4$ in early separated, $N = 3$ in late separated); however, the results appeared to parallel those of the total early and late-separated groups.

The small sample size and predominance of only children did not permit a satisfactory analysis of the effect of family size and sex of sibling on the behavior studied.

Table 2 presents the intercorrelations among all variables studied for all subjects.

Dependence on adults but not on peers is negatively related to independence. Masculine sex-role preferences, aggressive behavior, and participation in physical activities cluster together. Conversely, it appears that boys who enjoy nonphysical, noncompetitive activities are low in masculine sex-role preferences, aggression, and in participation in activities involving physical contact or nonphysical competition.

DISCUSSION

The results of the study indicate that absence of the father after age 5 has little effect on the sex-typed behaviors of boys. These boys in most respects do not differ from boys who have their fathers present. They are similar in their independence, dependence on adults, aggression, and sex-role preferences. In preferences for activities involving physical force or competition which might permit socially accepted expression of compensatory masculinity we again find no differences. An increased dependence on the adult all-male staff of the recreation center might have been expected if the boys lacking fathers were seeking attention from other adult males as father substitutes. This did not occur. It appears that any frustrated dependency needs which loss of a father might have produced do not generalize to other adult males. In fact there was a trend for boys with no fathers to be less dependent on adults ($F = 2.56$, $p < .10$). The greater dependence on peers of boys who had lost their fathers early or late is difficult to explain. It may be that loss or lack of a father results in a mistrust of adults with a consequent compensatory increase in dependence on peers. This general pattern of relations was reported by Freud and Burlingham (1944) in their studies of children separated from their parents by World War II. These children showed strong ties to their peers but few emotional ties to adult caretakers in institutions.

Boys who lost their fathers early, before identification can be assumed to have been completed, showed considerable deviation in sex-typed traits. They are less aggressive and show more feminine sex-role preferences than the other boys. They also participate less in physical games involving contact and more in nonphysical, noncompetitive activities. This preference for the latter type of activity could be considered an avoidance of activities involving the appropriate masculine behaviors of competition and aggressive play. An alternative explanation might be that it is a manifestation of social withdrawal since the activities in that category tend to be ones which involve a minimum of social interaction. It is difficult to accept this interpretation in view of the high dependency on peers ratings obtained by these boys. One could speculate that these boys make unsuccessful dependent overtures to peers, are rebuffed, and remain socially isolated.

The results suggest that adequate masculine identification has occurred by age 6 and that this identification can be maintained in the absence of the father. If the father leaves in the first 4 years before identification has been established, long-lasting disruption in sex-typed behaviors may result.

The predictions concerning racial differences were only partially confirmed. Differences between Negro and white boys in overt aggression which would be expected if Negroes inhibit direct expression of aggression were not obtained. However, the predicted high participation of Negroes in competitive activities involving contact was found. On the basis of this study it must be concluded that the behavior of Negro and white boys observed in the setting of a recreation center appears very similar.

SUMMARY

This study investigated the effects of race, father absence, and time of departure of the father on sex-typed behaviors of preadolescent males. If the father left after the age of 5, sex-typed behaviors are similar to those of boys from homes in which the father is present; however, if the father left in the first four years of life, considerable disruption of these behaviors are found. Both groups of boys with fathers absent are significantly more dependent on their peers than father-present boys. The only racial difference obtained indicated that Negro boys participate more in competitive activities involving force than do white boys.

REFERENCES

Bach, G. R. Father-fantasies and father typing in father-separated children. *Child Develpm.*, 1946, **17**, 63–79.

Beller, E. K. Dependency and autonomous achievement-striving related to orality and anality in early childhood. *Child Develpm.*, 1957, **29**, 287–315

Brown, D. G. Sex-role preference in young children. *Psychol. Monogr.*, 1956, **70** (14, Whole No. 421).

Freud, A., & Burlingham, D. T. *Infants without families.* New York: International Univ. Press, 1944.

Hetherington, E. M. A developmental study of the effects of sex of the dominant parent on sex-role preference, identification, and imitation in children. *J. Pers. Soc. Psychol.*, 1965, **2**, 188–194.

Kardiner, A., & Ovesey, L. *The mark of oppression.* New York: Norton, 1951.

Karon, B. P. *The Negro personality.* New York: Springer, 1958.

Lynn, D. B., & Sawrey, W. L. The effects of father-absence on Norwegian boys and girls. *J. Abnorm. Soc. Psychol.*, 1959, **59**, 258–262.

McCord, J., McCord, W., & Thurber, E. Some effects of paternal absence on male children. *J. Abnorm. Soc. Psychol.*, 1962, **64**, 361–369.

Moss, H. A., & Kagan, J. Stability of achievement and recognition seeking behaviors from early childhood through adulthood. *J. Abnorm. Soc. Psychol.*, 1961, **62**, 504–513.

Mussen, P., & Distler, L. Masculinity, identification, and father-son relationships. *J. Abnorm. Soc. Psychol.*, 1959, **59**, 350–356.

Sears, R. R., Pintler, M. H., & Sears, P. S. Effects of father-separation on preschool children's doll play aggression. *Child Develpm.*, 1946, **17**, 219–243.

Sears, R. R., Whiting, J. W. M., Nowlis, H., & Sears, P. S. Some childrearing antecedents of dependency and aggression in young children. *Genet. Psychol. Monogr.*, 1953, **47**, 135–234.

Stolz, L. M., *et al. Father relations of war-born children.* Stanford: Stanford Univ. Press, 1954.

Tiller, P. O. Father-absence and personality development of children in sailor families: A preliminary research report. *Nordisk Psykologi,* 1958, Monogr. No. 9.

§ 7 PERSONALITY AS A SOCIAL AND CULTURAL PHENOMENON

The papers presented so far in this book have included a variety of factors that influence personality: social attraction, social learning, social influence, social status, and roles. The first two studies in this section are concerned with the personality as such, especially with discrepancies between the self and the ideal self. The paper on birth order deals with the relationship between the position and status the individual holds during childhood and the kind of personality and social behavior he displays during adulthood. The two final papers are concerned with the relationship between culture and personality patterns.

The first study, which reports research by Phyllis Katz and Edward Zigler, investigates some of the conditions under which disparities between the individual's "real self" and his "ideal self" normally occur. Their results, whose implications run counter to some personality theories, show that the disparity tends to increase during childhood and adolescence and is greater for more intelligent than for less intelligent children.

The study by Robert I. McDonald and Malcolm D. Gynther explores the relationship between the self-concept and the ideal-self-concept of high-school students of different races, sexes, and social classes. They find that race and sex have a marked effect on these concepts, but that social class does not. They also found differences among the races and sexes with respect to the relative rating students gave themselves on dominance and love, the two dimensions tested in the study.

The paper by Helmreich and Collins in Section 2 of this book reported some interesting differences between individuals who had been firstborn in their families and those who had been later-born. The paper by William D. Altus, the third in this section, presents additional data showing that firstborn children tend to have the edge over later-born children, as far as success in school, intelligence, and occupational success are concerned. However, Altus makes little attempt to explain the reason for the firstborn's preeminence, and the reader is invited to develop some hypothesis of his own to explain this phenomenon.

Robert F. Peck presents a survey of the values held by Mexican and American university students and notes marked differences which not only reflect different patterns in social learning, but also are related to the modal personalities characteristic of individuals from the two cultures.

The study by Gallimore, Howard, and Jordan presents data that are in some ways contrary to common sense. Although a Hawaiian mother discourages dependent behavior on the part of her children and expects them to behave independently, they grow up to be adults who are dependent in a number of different ways. Haole (white) mothers, on the other hand, expect less independence from their children, who in turn grow up to be relatively independent adults. The reason for the difference may be found in the fact that Hawaiian mothers do not reward their children's attempts at independence, whereas Haole mothers do.

7.1 SELF-IMAGE DISPARITY: A DEVELOPMENTAL APPROACH

Phyllis Katz
Edward Zigler

A frequently used measure in many empirical and theoretical contexts (cf. Wylie, 1961) has been the disparity between the individual's real-self image and ideal self. At least three different interpretations of this real- ideal-self disparity have been advanced. The most widely noted position is that of Rogers and his co-workers (Rogers & Dymond,

Source: This research was supported by grants from the National Institute of Mental Health and New York University. Reprinted from the *Journal of Personality and Social Psychology*, 1967, 5, 186–195, with permission of the authors and the American Psychological Association, Inc.

1954) who view such a disparity as a general indicator of maladjustment. Evidence of the popularity of this view can be seen in the practice of employing self-image disparity as an operational measure of mental illness (Scott, 1958).

A second position represents a qualification of the Rogerian thesis. A number of investigators have advanced evidence that while a large self-ideal disparity is invariably ominous, it would be found only among individuals employing particular psychological defenses, for example, sensitizers and psychoneurotics (e.g., Altrocchi, Parsons, & Dickoff, 1960; Hillson & Worchel, 1958). Within this position, maladjusted individuals employing other modes of defense, for example, denial, would be expected to show little self-ideal discrepancy.

A third position was recently advanced by Achenbach and Zigler (1963) who employed developmental theory to generate the prediction that real- ideal-self discrepancy was positively related to the individual's level of maturity. Using the social competence index devised by Phillips and Zigler (1961) as their measure of maturity, these investigators did find a greater disparity in more mature than in less mature individuals. Contrary to Rogerian theory, the magnitude of the disparity was unrelated to the level of the individual's psychological adjustment.

The developmental rationale underlying the predicted positive relationship between self-image disparity and maturity level was based upon two factors. The first of these was that the higher the maturity level, the greater the individual's capacity for incorporating social demands, mores, and values. The high developmental person, then, makes greater self-demands, is more often unable to fulfill them, and consequently experiences more guilt than the low developmental person (Phillips & Rabinovitch, 1958; Phillips & Zigler, 1961). The second factor is based upon the work of Werner and Piaget who have discovered a greater degree of cognitive differentiation at higher levels of development. In any cognition, the more mature individual should employ more categories and make finer distinctions within each category than a less mature individual. This greater differentiating ability should result in a greater disparity when an individual first judges his real self and then his ideal self.

This view that self-ideal discrepancy is a product of both social guilt and cognitive differentiation was tested (Achenbach & Zigler, 1963) by employing a number of measures which differentially tapped these two factors. The disparity between real self and social self, that is, the self as one believes others see it (Brownfain, 1952), was assumed to be less influenced by social guilt and did indeed result in a smaller disparity than obtained with the real- ideal-self instruments. Furthermore, the assessment of these disparities by means of an adjective check list, which allows only a "yes" or "no," and is thus less sensitive to the effects of the cognitive differentiation factor, resulted in smaller disparity scores than obtained with a questionnaire format involving six alternatives to each item. Consistent with their developmental position, Achenbach and Zigler found that the differences between high and low maturity groups in self-image disparity were greatest on instruments involving both the guilt and differentiation factors (i.e., real- ideal-self questionnaire), smaller on instruments involving a single factor (real-ideal check list and real-social questionnaire), and nonexistent on a measure in which both factors were minimized (i.e., real-social check list).

Although the findings of the Achenbach and Zigler study were in keeping with developmental thinking, it should be noted that all of the subjects employed were adults whose developmental level was assessed by a social competence index consisting of the variables of education, intelligence, employment history, occupation, and marital status. Some exception could be taken to the assumption that such an index is a very sensitive indicator of developmental level. A more direct test of the developmental position suggests itself. This position clearly generates the view that there is an ontogenetic sequence in the development of self-image disparity. A major purpose of the present study, then, was to test the specific prediction that younger children exhibit less disparity between perceived and ideal self than do older children.

Although chronological age is perhaps the most frequently used indicator of development, there is little question that chronological age is not the most sensitive reflector of the cognitive structures which are assumed to be changing with various developmental levels or stages (Piaget, 1932; Zigler, 1963). A better indicator of the child's cognitive structure, and thus his developmental level, is his mental age. In terms of the design of the present study, then, we would not only expect more self-image disparity with increasing age, but also more disparity in high- than in low-IQ children within each age level.

As in the earlier study, six measures were collected on every subject —three image measures (real self, ideal self, and social self), each in two formats (questionnaire and adjective check list). The general expectation here was that the disparity would be highest where both guilt and cognitive differentiation were reflected, that is, real- ideal-self disparity on the questionnaire, and lowest where the effects of both these factors were minimized, that is, real- social-self disparity on the adjective check list. Furthermore, the developmental position would generate the prediction that the differences between developmental groups, defined by age and/or IQ, on self-image disparity should be greatest on measures sensitive to both factors, less on measures sensitive to a single factor, and least on measures relatively insensitive to both factors.

An ambiguity in the Achenbach and Zigler study was the failure to delineate the exact nature of the larger self-image disparity found in the more mature subjects. It would be interesting to discover whether a larger self-ideal discrepancy in more mature individuals was due to a lower self-evaluation, a higher self-expectation, or some particular combination of the two. The present study attempted to obtain data on this issue by assessing not only the amount of disparity, but these particular features of the disparity as well.

METHOD

Subjects

One-hundred-twenty children were randomly selected from all fifth-, eighth-, and eleventh-grade classes of the Carl Place, Long Island, public school system. The particular grades were chosen to include elementary school and junior and senior high school children. Since the questionnaires used were self-administering and dependent on the subject's ability to read, it was not deemed feasible to employ subjects younger than 10 years of age (fifth grade).

Within each grade level, subjects were dichotomized on the basis of Otis Quick-Scoring Mental Ability Test scores into high and low groups. The mean IQs of the low groups were 91, 93, and 94 for the fifth, eighth, and eleventh grades, respectively. The mean IQs of the high groups were 124, 127, and 125 for the fifth, eighth, and eleventh grades, respectively. An equal number of male and female subjects was employed within each age and intelligence classification. Thus, a three-way factorial design (Age $\times$ IQ $\times$ Sex) was employed which consisted of 12 groups of 10 subjects each.

Although a number of earlier studies (reviewed by Wylie, 1961) and a more recent one (McDonald & Gynther, 1965) have indicated no clear relationship between self-image disparity and socioeconomic status, use of the IQ variable sensitized the authors to the social class issue. For this reason a middle-class community was chosen that was very homogeneous in respect to socioeconomic status.

Self-Image-Disparity Measures

Two self-image-disparity measures were employed. These were designed to be as similar as possible to those employed in the Achenbach-Zigler study and still be relevant for children. Some of the items used were taken from Coopersmith's (1959) scale of self-esteem. The first instrument was a questionnaire composed of 20 statements. The subject's task was to select one of six alternatives for each statement ranging from "very true" to "very untrue." Half of the statements were negative, for example, "I often wish I were someone else," and half were positive, for example, "I'm popular with the other kids." The same 20 statements were used in different orders when assessing real self, ideal self, and social self. When measuring real self, response alternatives were phrased "This is very true of me," etc.; for ideal self, "I would like this to be very true of me"; finally, for social self, "People think this is very true of me." The most positive alternative was scored with 1 point ("very true" on positive items and "very untrue" on negative items), whereas the most negative received a score of 6. Thus, the possible range for each self-measure was from 20 (most positive) to 120 (most negative).

The second instrument consisted of a list of 20 adjectives, 10 positive, for example, "successful," and 10 negative, for example, "sneaky." For each adjective there were only two response alternatives, "yes" or "no." Analogous to the questionnaire, three different orders of the list were given to assess real self, ideal self, and social self. Positive responses were scored 0 ("no" to negative or "yes" to positive adjectives) and negative responses scored 1. The possible range on this instrument was from 0 (most positive) to 20 (most negative).

Considerable evidence has now been presented that the type of instruments used in this study are reliable in the chronological and mental age groups employed in this study (Engel, 1959; McAfee & Cleland, 1965; Perkins & Shannon, 1965).

Procedure

The instruments were group administered to entire classes in their schoolrooms. The subjects were told that the experimenter wanted to find out what children thought about themselves. They were told that there were no right or wrong answers, that their responses would be kept in strict confidence, and that nobody at the school would be permitted to see the questionnaires. Specific instructions as to how to respond were printed at the top of each section, and a sample item was demonstrated by the experimenter on the blackboard. The questionnaires and adjective lists were always administered in the same order, namely, real self, ideal self, and social self with the three questionnaires first and the three adjective lists next.

RESULTS

The mean group absolute and disparity scores obtained on both the questionnaire and the adjective check list are contained in Table 1.

Disparity between Real and Ideal Self

A Lindquist (1953) repeated-measures analysis of variance (Measure × Age × IQ × Sex) was conducted on the real- and ideal-self questionnaire scores. The findings relevant to the hypotheses of this study are contained in the within-subjects portion of this analysis. These findings revealed a significant measure effect ($F_{1,108} = 267.64$, $p < .001$), a significant Measure × Age interaction ($F_{2,108} = 11.60$, $p < .001$), and a significant Measure × IQ effect ($F_{1,108} = 11.12$, $p < .01$). As can be seen in Table 1, real-self scores are greater (more negative) than ideal-self scores. The two significant interactions indicate that the magnitude of this difference between real and ideal scores is influenced by both age and IQ. The Measure × Age interaction reflects the greater differences between real and ideal scores at Grades 11 and 8 than at Grade 5. The mean differences at these grades were 23.0, 22.1, and 11.1, respectively. The Measure × IQ interaction reflects the finding that the high-IQ subjects exhibit a greater discrepancy between real and ideal scores than do low-IQ subjects (22.3 versus 15.1).

In order to further assess these differential discrepancy scores, real-self and ideal-self questionnaire scores were analyzed separately in Age × IQ × Sex analyses of variance. The analysis of real-self scores revealed a significant difference associated with age ($F_{2,108} = 5.36$, $p < .01$). The real-self ratings were found to be more negative at Grades 11 and 8 than at 5 (59.1, 61.0 versus 54.3). A significant Age × IQ interaction ($F_{2,108} = 3.06$, $p < .05$) was also found. As can be seen in Table 1, this interaction reflected the different relative positions of high- and low-IQ children at the three grade levels. In the fifth

Table 1 *Self-image Scores for Each Group*

Group	*N*	Questionnaire					Adjective-Check List				
		Absolute Scores			Disparity		Absolute Scores			Disparity	
		Real	Ideal	Social	Real-Ideal	Real-Social	Real	Ideal	Social	Real-Ideal	Real-Social
5th grade											
Low IQ	20	57.4	46.4	55.6	11.0	2.2	4.2	1.9	4.8	2.3	—.6
High IQ	20	51.2	40.0	49.0	11.2	2.2	3.2	.9	3.0	2.3	.2
8th grade											
Low IQ	20	61.6	46.2	54.2	15.4	7.4	5.5	1.0	4.3	4.5	1.2
High IQ	20	60.4	31.6	57.1	28.8	3.3	6.6	1.0	5.4	5.6	.8
11th grade											
Low IQ	20	57.4	38.4	51.4	19.0	6.0	4.6	.5	4.4	4.1	.2
High IQ	20	60.8	33.9	54.7	26.9	6.1	6.5	.6	5.4	5.9	1.1

grade, high-IQ subjects express more positive feelings about themselves than the low-IQ subjects; at the eighth grade, high- and low-IQ subjects are similar; and at the eleventh grade, high-IQ subjects express more negative real-self ratings than their less intelligent peers. On the ideal-self analysis, significant age ($F_{2,108} = 4.36$, $p < .05$) and IQ ($F_{1,108} = 18.77$, $p < .001$) main effects were found, indicating that the older or brighter the child, the more positive was his ideal self.

The repeated-measures analysis of variance of the real- and ideal-self scores on the adjective check list resulted in findings similar to those obtained on the questionnaire instrument. A significant measure effect ($F_{1,108} = 253.33$, $p < .001$) and a significant Measure × Age interaction ($F_{2,108} = 12.69$, $p < .001$) were found, reflecting greater negative scores on the real than on the ideal measure, and an increase in real-ideal disparity with age. A Measure × IQ interaction of borderline significance ($p < .10$) was also found. This trend was in the same direction as the significant findings on the questionnaire and reflects the tendency for greater real-ideal disparity in high- than in low-IQ subjects.

Analyses conducted separately on the real- and on the ideal-self adjective scores revealed only significant age effects on both the real ($F_{2,108} = 7.09$, $p < .01$) and ideal ($F_{2,108} = 4.22$, $p < .05$) scores. With increasing age, the real scores became more negative, and the ideal scores more positive.

Disparity between Real and Social Self

The repeated-measures analysis done on the real and ideal scores was also run on the real and social scores. On the real and social questionnaire scores this analysis resulted in a significant measure effect ($F_{1,108} = 45.30$, $p < .001$) and a significant Measure × Age interaction ($F_{2,108} = 3.93$, $p < .05$). As can be seen in Table 1, the social-self scores were smaller (more positive) than the real-self scores. The interaction indicates that the magnitude of difference between real- and social-self scores increases with age. Unlike the real-ideal discrepancy, however, the real-social discrepancy was not significantly influenced by IQ.

An Age × IQ × Sex analysis of variance conducted on the social questionnaire scores alone revealed no significant effects.

The repeated-measures analysis conducted on the real and social adjective check-list scores revealed a significant measure effect ($F_{1,108} =$ 10.59, $p < .01$) and a significant Measure × Age interaction ($F_{2,108} =$ 6.80, $p < .01$), similar to those found on the questionnaire instruments. Social-self scores were smaller (more positive) than real-self scores, and the difference between the two scores was greater at Grades 8 and 11 than at 5. In addition, a significant Measure × Age × Sex interaction ($F_{2,108} = 4.41$, $p < .05$) and a significant Measure × Age × Sex × IQ interaction ($F_{2,108} = 3.24$, $p < .05$) were found. These interactions primarily reflect the finding that fifth-grade male subjects perceived others evaluating them more negatively than they evaluated themselves. This trend was particularly pronounced in the low-IQ subjects at this age level. All other groups exhibited a real-social disparity in the opposite direction.

An Age × IQ × Sex analysis of variance conducted separately on the social adjective check-list scores revealed a significant Age × IQ interaction ($F_{2,108} = 3.18$, $p < .05$) and a significant Age × Sex interaction ($F_{2,108} = 5.59$, $p < .01$). The Age × IQ interaction reflects the fact that the social scores are greater for low- than for high-IQ subjects at Grade 5, whereas an opposite pattern is exhibited at Grades 8 and 11. The Age × Sex interaction can be described as follows: At the fifth grade the boys see themselves being evaluated more negatively than girls; at the eigth grade, girls see themselves being evaluated more negatively than boys; finally, at the eleventh grade, boys and girls see themselves evaluated approximately the same.

Comparisons of Self-image Disparity across the Different Measures

The findings reported to this point are generally in keeping with the major hypothesis that the magnitude of self-image disparity is related to developmental factors. A subsidiary hypothesis was that this positive relationship between development and self-image disparity is due specifically to two factors—an increase in guilt, and an ability to make finer cognitive judgments. A test of this hypothesis requires comparisons of self-image disparity on instruments differing in their susceptibility to the effects of these two factors. The expectation here was that the greatest disparity should be found on the instrument most sensitive to both factors (the real-ideal questionnaire), and the smallest disparity on the instrument least sensitive to both factors (the real-social adjective check list). Furthermore, it is the most sensitive instrument that should maximally reflect the developmental variables of age and IQ.

It is clearly inappropriate to test this hypothesis by comparing the discrepancy scores obtained on the questionnaires (a maximum possible score of 100) with those obtained on the check list (a maximum possible score of 20). In order to make all the discrepancy scores comparable, the following analyses were conducted on the total number of items changed between the two measures, ignoring magnitude of change. It should be noted that a discrepancy score defined by frequency of change was the same as that employed by Achenbach and Zigler (1963). Table 2 presents these discrepancy scores for each group.

Table 2 *Disparity Scores Defined by Number of Changes*

	Real-Ideal-Self Disparity		Real-Social-Self Disparity	
Group	Questionnaire	Check List	Questionnaire	Check List
5th grade				
Low IQ	11.00	5.10	10.80	5.60
High IQ	10.10	3.90	9.25	4.65
8th grade				
Low IQ	13.50	6.35	11.90	7.50
High IQ	15.20	6.90	10.55	6.70
11th grade				
Low IQ	12.55	4.80	11.30	6.80
High IQ	16.50	6.70	11.50	7.05
Total	78.85	33.45	64.80	38.30

These scores were subjected to a Measure (real-ideal versus real-social) × Instrument (questionnaire versus check list) × Age × IQ repeated-measures analysis of variance. With the exception of the higher than expected scores obtained on the real-social check list, the findings of this analysis were consistent with the hypotheses advanced. The main effect of measure was significant ($F_{1,114} = 14.01$, $p < .001$), reflecting the finding that real-ideal disparity was greater than the real-social disparity across the two instruments. This would be predicted from the hypothesis since the real-ideal questionnaire is assumed to be sensitive to two factors, the real-ideal check list to one factor, and the real-social check list to no factors. Similarly, a significant instrument effect ($F_{1,114} = 401.41$, $p < .001$) was obtained reflecting the greater total discrepancy scores on the questionnaires (sensitive to two and one factor) than on the check lists (sensitive to one and no factors). A significant Measure × Instrument interaction ($F_{1,114} = 113.42$, $p < .001$) was found. This is a complex interaction that reflects a number of findings congruent with the predictions and one finding antithetical to the prediction. The discrepancy scores on the self-ideal questionnaire are significantly larger ($t = 5.21$, $p < .001$) than those made on the self-social questionnaire (predicted), whereas the discrepancy scores on the self-ideal check list tend to be smaller ($t = 1.85$, $p < .01$) than those on the self-social check list (opposite to prediction). The discrepancy scores on the self-ideal questionnaire were greater ($t = 17.16$, $p < .001$) than those on the self-ideal check list (predicted). Finally, the self-social questionnaire disparity is greater ($t = 11.11$, $p < .001$) than the self-social check-list disparity (predicted).

As predicted, a number of interactions between the particular disparity scores and the developmental variables were obtained. The effect of measure interacts significantly with both grade ($F_{2,114} = 4.24$, $p < .05$) and IQ ($F_{1,114} = 17.99$, $p < .001$), indicating that the difference between real-ideal and real-social scores is greater with increasing age and higher IQ. A significant Measure × Grade × IQ interaction ($F_{2,114} = 3.63$, $p < .05$) was found. Although a number of differences contribute to this interaction, a sizable portion of it would appear to be due to the finding that the greatest difference between high- and low-IQ groups was obtained with real-ideal disparities at the eleventh grade. A predicted Measure × Instrument × Grade interaction ($F_{2,114} = 11.37$, $p < .001$) was also found. This interaction primarily reflects the greater sensitivity of the self-ideal questionnaire disparity to grade differences. This is especially noticeable between the fifth and eighth grades, where the difference on this instrument is considerably greater than that found with the other three instruments.

The final significant finding revealed by this analysis was an Instrument × Measure × IQ interaction ($F_{1,114} = 7.65$, $p < .01$). As can be seen in Table 2, this interaction reflects the following: on the two real-ideal measures, high-IQ subjects have greater disparity scores than low-IQ subjects with the reverse being true for the two real-social measures, and the magnitude of this crossover effect is more pronounced on the questionnaire instruments than on the check-list instruments.

Further evidence that the instrument (real-ideal questionnaire) sensitive to both factors is most sensitive to the developmental variables of grade and IQ can be obtained directly from Table 2. It is with this measure of disparity that we obtain the greatest differences between grades and IQ levels. The only finding in Table 2 contrary to prediction is the larger discrepancy scores found in the real-social check list as compared to the real-ideal check list. However, the question of the comparability of these two scores must be raised. A phenomenon not encountered in the earlier study with adults (Achenbach & Zigler, 1963) must be noted. Whereas the disparity on the real-ideal check list was typically in the expected direction, with the ideal being more socially desirable than the real, this was less true on the real-social check list. Unlike adults, the children were quite willing to report that they were seen by their peers as being less socially desirable on certain traits than they had reported themselves as being on the real-self check list. The failure to take into consideration the direction of the discrepancy in the scores reported in Table 2 may have led to an erroneous indicator of what we are primarily concerned with, namely, the disparity score predicated upon a change to a more positive social self. In order to investigate this possibility, new disparity scores were calculated for the real-ideal and real-social check-list data which included only the number of items in which the disparity indicated a change from negative to positive. These scores are presented in Table 3.

Table 3 *Frequency of Negative to Positive Changes in Adjective Check List*

	Disparity	
Group	Real-Ideal	Real-Social
5th grade		
Low IQ	3.65	2.50
High IQ	3.10	2.35
8th grade		
Low IQ	5.35	4.35
High IQ	6.20	3.95
11th grade		
Low IQ	4.45	3.55
High IQ	6.15	4.20
Total	28.90	20.90

A comparison of these scores with those reported in Table 2 supports the hypothesis that the larger disparity scores in the real-social check list reported in Table 2 were due to the large number of plus to minus instances. A Grade × IQ × Measure analysis of variance of the data reported in Table 3 revealed a significant measure effect ($F_{1,108} = 20.56$, $p < .001$) reflecting the predicted greater disparity on the real-ideal than on the real-social check-list scores. It thus appears that the one earlier finding that was in a direction opposite to that predicted by the two-factor developmental hypothesis was the result of ignoring directionality in the discrepancy scores. (In respect to the analysis of the data presented in Table 2, ignoring the directionality factor resulted in a more conservative test of the hypotheses under test, which nevertheless received substantial statistical support.)

Other Findings

The assumption that less mature subjects had a less differentiated response tendency than more mature subjects was tested further by running a repeated-measures analysis (Age × IQ × Sex × Measure) on the frequency with which each subject utilized the extreme response categories of "very true" and "very untrue" on each of the three questionnaires. These scores are presented in Table 4. The significant main and interaction effects found generally support the cognitive

Table 4 *Mean Number of Extreme Responses to Questionnaire*

	Measure		
Group	Real Self	Ideal Self	Social Self
5th grade			
Low IQ	8.8	13.3	11.6
High IQ	7.7	12.0	7.0
8th grade			
Low IQ	7.0	12.3	7.4
High IQ	5.4	11.9	5.0
11th grade			
Low IQ	6.6	11.8	7.7
High IQ	4.2	12.2	4.4

differentiation hypothesis. The children were found to make fewer extreme responses as they got older ($F_{2,108} = 3.75$, $p < .05$) with the brighter children giving fewer extreme responses than the less intelligent ones ($F_{1,108} = 6.40$, $p < .05$). As might be expected, ideal-self ratings evoked more extreme responses than either the real-self or social-self ratings ($F_{2,216} = 126.80$, $p < .001$). The significant Measure × Age ($F_{4,216} = 4.30$, $p < .01$) and Measure × IQ ($F_{2,216} = 9.10$, $p < .001$) interactions reflect the relative insensitivity of the ideal-self measure to the effects of age and IQ. It is on the real- and social-self measures that one finds a decrease in extreme responses with age and/or higher intelligence. A significant IQ × Sex × Measure interaction ($F_{2,216} = 3.65, p < .05$) was also found reflecting the one exception to the general findings. On the ideal-self ratings, and only on the ideal-self ratings, high-IQ boys were found to make more extreme responses than low-IQ boys. This may be accounted for by a higher level of aspiration on the part of brighter males, since extreme scores on ideal-self ratings may indicate perfectionistic strivings. It is interesting to note, however, that this exception did not occur in females.

In order to assess the construct validity of the self-image-disparity concept, a correlation was computed between each subject's real-ideal disparity on the questionnaire and that obtained on the check list. The degree of relationship was highly significant ($r = .69$, $p < .01$).

DISCUSSION

The findings of the present study lend considerable credence to the view that self-image disparity increases with increasing maturity. Real-ideal-self disparity was found to be a positive function of both chronological age and IQ. This is a rather surprising finding in light of the conventionally dim view that has been taken of an increasing self-image disparity and the rather negative psychodynamics that are thought to accompany it (McCandless, 1961; Rogers & Dymond, 1954). The findings are in accordance with earlier results obtained with adults of varying maturity levels (Achenbach & Zigler, 1963) and suggest that self-image disparity might be better conceptualized as an index of development rather than a measure of maladjustment.

Although such a view is an unconventional one, further support can be found in certain underemphasized findings in the literature. Coopersmith (1959), in a study of fifth and sixth graders, did find that self-ideal discrepancy was positively related to anxiety. However, he also discovered that children having the largest self-ideal discrepancies received the highest ratings by others, had the highest need-achievement scores, and the highest actual achievement. This is reminiscent of Brownfain's (1952) finding that college students having unstable self-concepts made better grades and were rated more intelligent than students having more stable self-concepts. McAfee and Cleland (1965), employing retardates having mental ages similar to those of the youngest group in the present investigation, found that self-ideal disparity was unrelated to adjustment, but was positively related to IQ. Perkins and Shannon (1965), employing a sample of sixth graders, did not find a significant relationship between real-ideal disparity and IQ. However, as in the present study they did find a positive relationship between ideal scores and IQ. As noted by Achenbach and Zigler (1963), exponents of the stylistic approach to the understanding of self-image disparity, for example, Altrocchi et al. (1960), Hillson and Worchel (1958), may well have obtained their findings (individuals with certain types of defenses have higher disparity scores than individuals employing other types of defenses) by inadvertently comparing individuals differing in maturity levels. As noted in the earlier paper (Achenbach & Zigler, 1963), the developmental position takes as its given the level of maturity attained by the individual and sees both the defenses employed and the amount of self-image disparity as an outgrowth of this level. Within this framework, the degree of self-image disparity would be expected to be low at low levels of maturity and high at high levels of maturity. However, since one finds both adjusted and maladjusted people at all levels of maturity, no simple relationship between degree of self-image disparity and adjustment would be expected.

While there have been studies with children indicating a positive relationship between self-image disparity and both paper-and-pencil tests of adjustment (Hanlon, Hofstaetter, & O'Connor, 1954) and judgments of being "less secure" (Bruce, 1958), the most consistent finding in research on children's self-image disparity is the positive relationship typically found between self-ideal disparity and anxiety (Bruce, 1958; Coopersmith, 1959; Lipsitt, 1958).

It is this consistently found self-image-disparity–anxiety relationship that has probably led workers, for example, McCandless (1961), to emphasize the ominous nature of an increasing self-image disparity. The implicit assumption that anxiety is an essentially negative agent in the individual's total psychic economy would appear to be open to considerable dispute. There are perhaps as many instances in which anxiety is beneficial as those in which it is detrimental to the individual (Ruebush, 1963). The key determinant would appear to be not the presence or absence of anxiety, but rather the individual's response to anxiety in particular situations. This basically positive view of anxiety is consistent with Hebb's (1958) argument that the capacity for anxiety increases as one ascends the phylogenetic scale due to the increasing cognitive capacity of the organism. Provided one can apply Hebb's position to ontogenetic development, the relationship between self-image disparity and anxiety becomes quite understandable within the developmental framework advanced in this paper. Rather than being ominous in nature, increasing self-image disparity would invariably appear to accompany the attainment of higher levels of development, since the greater cognitive differentiation found at such levels must invariably lead to a greater capacity for self-derogation, guilt, and anxiety. As Achenbach and Zigler (1963) noted, the attainment of higher developmental levels does not constitute an unmitigated blessing. While such attainment guarantees the individual a greater ability to deal with whatever problems confront him, his greater cognitive differentiation also gives him the capacity to construct more problems for himself.

Support was found for the subsidiary hypothesis that self-ideal disparity, as usually measured, is a function of two underlying factors related to maturity level, namely, capacity for guilt and cognitive differentiation. On the basis of this hypothesis, it was predicted that various instruments differing in their sensitivity to these two factors should differentially assess the magnitude of the self-ideal disparity. Thus, the real-ideal questionnaire measure (assumed to be reflecting both social guilt and cognitive differentiation) was expected to be maximally sensitive to developmental trends, the real- social-self questionnaire (cognitive differentiation only) and real-ideal adjective (social guilt only) measures to be next most sensitive, and finally the real-social adjective measure (reflecting neither factor) to be least sensitive to age and intelligence effects. For the most part, the results supported these expectations.

An additional indication of the importance of the cognitive differentiation factor was revealed in the finding that the number of extreme responses is negatively related to maturity level, defined by both age and IQ. These findings were perfectly consistent with those reported by Light, Zax, and Gardener (1965). These investigators, employing exactly the same developmental rationale concerning cognitive differentiation as that utilized in this study, found that older and brighter children made fewer extreme responses in rating Rorschach inkblots on semantic differential scales.

Another finding of interest relates to the question of just what aspect of the self-image disparity changes with development. McCandless (1961) has posited that self-ideal-discrepancy scores could be easily replaced by single real-self measures. This argument is based upon the assumption that ideal-self ratings are not ordinarily subject to individual variation. The results of the present investigation contradict this assumption. The increase in real- ideal-self disparity with age was accounted for by both significantly lowered self-evaluations and more positively defined ideal-self ratings. Thus, both aspects of the disparity are related to development. In general, the magnitude of difference was greatest between the fifth- and eighth-grade children and least between the eighth- and eleventh-grade groups, thus suggesting that early adolescence may be a pivotal point in the development of self-image disparity.

The authors have presented their argument in such a way as to highlight the differences between their position and the Rogerian view that a large self-image disparity is ominous in nature. It should be noted, however, that this latter position is a logically appealing one, and considerable evidence has been presented indicating that a large self-image disparity is often accompanied in adults by a state of malaise and maladaptive behavior (Rogers & Dymond, 1954). Perhaps a judicious conclusion of the present study would be that future investigators should be cognizant of developmental factors when interpreting self-image-disparity findings and should expend some energy in determining exactly how the psychodynamic factors emphasized by many workers interact with the developmental phenomena investigated in this paper.

SUMMARY

The present study assessed real-self, ideal-self, and social-self perceptions of fifth-, eighth-, and eleventh-grade children. The major prediction was that self-image disparity is a function of developmental level. This hypothesis was based upon two factors thought to concomitantly increase with maturity: capacity for guilt and ability for cognitive differentiation. A subsidiary prediction was that measuring instruments most sensitive to the assessment of these factors should maximally reflect developmental changes in self-image disparity. Both the major and subsidiary predictions received experimental support. Self-image disparity was found to be positively related to chronological age and intelligence. This larger disparity in older and brighter children was accounted for by both decreased self-evaluations and increased ideal-self images.

REFERENCES

Achenbach, T., & Zigler, E. Social competence and self-image disparity in psychiatric and nonpsychiatric patients. *J. Abnorm. Soc. Psychol.*, 1963, **67**, 197–205.

Altrocchi, J., Parsons, O. A., & Dickoff, H. Changes in self-ideal discrepancy in repressors and sensitizers. *J. Abnorm. Soc. Psychol.*, 1960, **61**, 67–72.

Brownfain, J. J. Stability of the self-concept as a dimension of personality. *J. Abnorm. Soc. Psychol.*, 1952, **47**, 597–606.

Bruce, P. Relationship of self-acceptance to other variables with sixth-grade children oriented in self-understanding. *J. Educ. Psychol.*, 1958, **49**, 229–238.

Coopersmith, S. A method for determining types of self-esteem. *J. Educ. Psychol.*, 1959, **59**, 87–94.

Engel, M. The stability of the self-concept in adolescence. *J. Abnorm. Soc. Psychol.*, 1959, **58**, 211–215.

Hanlon, T. E., Hofstaetter, P. R., & O'Connor, J. P. Congruence of self and ideal self in relation to personality adjustment. *J. Consult. Psychol.*, 1954, **18**, 215–218.

Hebb, D. The mammal and his environment. In C. Ree, J. Alexander, & S. Tomkins (Eds.), *Psychopathology: A source book.* Cambridge: Harvard Univ. Press, 1958. Pp. 127–135.

Hillson, J. S., & Worchel, P. Self-concept and defensive behavior in the maladjusted. *J. Consult. Psychol.*, 1958, **22**, 45–50.

Light, C. S., Zax, M., & Gardener, D. H. Relationship of age, sex, and intelligence level to extreme response style. *J. Pers. Soc. Psychol.*, 1965, **2**, 907–909.

Lindquist, E. *Design and analysis of experiments in psychology and education.* Boston: Houghton Mifflin, 1953.

Lipsitt, L. P. A self-concept scale for children and its relationship to the children's form of the Manifest Anxiety Scale. *Child Develpm.*, 1958, **29**, 463–472.

McAfee, R. O., & Cleland, C. C. The discrepancy between self-concept and ideal-self as a measure of psychological adjustment in educable mentally retarded males. *Am. J. Ment. Defic.*, 1965, **70**, 63–68.

McCandless, B. R. *Children and adolescents.* New York: Holt, Rinehart & Winston, 1961.

McDonald, R. L., & Gynther, M. D. Relationship of self and ideal-self descriptions with sex, race, and class in southern adolescents. *J. Pers. Soc. Psychol.*, 1965, **1**, 85–88.

Perkins, C. W., & Shannon, D. T. Three techniques for obtaining self-perceptions in preadolescent boys. *J. Pers. Soc. Psychol.*, 1965, **2**, 443–446.

Phillips, L., & Rabinovitch, M. S. Social role and patterns of symptomatic behavior. *J. Abnorm. Soc. Psychol.*, 1958, **57**, 181–186.

Phillips, L., & Zigler, E. Social competence: The action-thought parameter and vicariousness in normal and pathological behavior. *J. Abnorm. Soc. Psychol.*, 1961, **63**, 137–146.

Piaget, J. *The moral judgment of the child.* London: Routledge & Kegan Paul, 1932.

Rogers, C., & Dymond, R. *Psychotherapy and personality change.* Chicago: Univ. of Chicago Press, 1954.

Ruebush, B. Anxiety. In H. W. Stevenson (Ed.), *Child psychology: The 62nd Yearbook of the National Society for the Study of Education.* Part 1. Chicago: Univ. of Chicago Press, 1963. Pp. 460–516.

Scott, W. Research definitions of mental health and mental illness. *Psychol. Bull.*, 1958, **55**, 1–45.

Wylie, Ruth. *The self-concept.* Omaha: Univ. of Nebraska Press, 1961.

Zigler, E. Metatheoretical issues in developmental psychology. In M. Marx (Ed.), *Psychological theory*, 2nd ed. New York: Macmillan, 1963. Pp. 341–369.

7.2 RELATIONSHIP OF SELF- AND IDEAL-SELF-DESCRIPTIONS WITH SEX, RACE, AND CLASS IN SOUTHERN ADOLESCENTS

Robert I. McDonald
Malcolm D. Gynther

Psychologists have shown much interest in delineating various parameters of the phenomenal self-concept. Recent studies have investigated the stability of the self-concept through the period of adolescence (Engel, 1959); the relations between self-concept, food aversions, and mother concept in emotionally disturbed children (Davids & Lawton, 1961); as well as the relationship between self-concept, sociometric rankings, and anxiety in elementary school children of various ages (Horowitz, 1962; Lipsitt, 1958).

As yet, little clarification has been obtained concerning the effects of specific demographic variables on phenomenal self or ideal self. Klausner's (1953) early study of white male adolescents focused on the relations between social class and self-concept. His results are quite interesting, but should be considered as only suggestive as N was small (that is, 27). He found that individuals in the higher socioeconomic levels are intropunitive and psychosocially isolated, whereas individuals in the lower socioeconomic stratum react to perceived insecurity and inferiority by aggression and self-assertion. Wylie's (1961) summary of the studies through 1958, including the one just described, is

> The four studies taken together do not permit us to conclude anything about the relationship between socioeconomic class and the self concept [p. 139].

In a more recent experiment, Bieri and Lobeck (1961) assessed the effects of parental identifications, religion, and social class on the self-concepts of male members of an Army reserve unit. This study utilized the Interpersonal Check List (ICL; LaForge & Suczek, 1955), an instrument which analyzes self- and ideal-self-descriptions in terms of dominance (Dom) and love (Lov) scores. The former is a measure of assertive, aggressive, leadership qualities while the latter is a measure of friendly, warm, cooperative characteristics. These investigators

Source: Reprinted with slight abridgment from the *Journal of Personality and Social Psychology*, 1965, **1**, 85–88, with permission of the authors and the American Psychological Association, Inc.

obtained significantly higher Lov scores from Catholics than from Jewish subjects, and also found that upper-class subjects scored higher on Dom than lower-class subjects.

Wylie (1961) has also reviewed the studies which deal with sex differences in self-concepts. She found marked inconsistencies in the findings and concluded that "resolution of possibly contradictory results in this area awaits further research [p. 147]."

Another important demographic variable whose relations with self-concept have not yet been explicated is race. Other data (McDonald & Gynther, 1963) suggest that Negro and white adolescent subjects' reactions to statements about their emotional states, physical well being, and interests are remarkably influenced by these variables. The study referred to, however, found no differences ascribable to social class, a result which is in contrast with Bieri and Lobeck's (1961) and Klausner's (1953) tentative findings. The purpose of this study is to assess the effects of sex, race, and class on the self- and ideal-self-concepts of adolescent Negroes and whites and to determine if there are any interactions between these variables.

METHOD

Subjects

The Negro subjects consisted of 261 (151 female and 110 male) high school seniors who comprised the entire group of graduates for 1961 and 1962 from the only Negro high school in a southern urban area. This school is located on the edge of the city and draws its students equally from the city and outlying areas. The white subjects consisted of 211 (114 female and 97 male) high school seniors who were the 1961 and 1962 graduates from three of the seven white high schools in the community. These three schools were selected as representative of different social classes and cultural settings in the area: an urban school whose children were drawn largely from professional and managerial families, a suburban school whose students came from laboring class and enlisted military personnel families, and a county school which drew adolescents from lower middle class and laboring class families. Ages ranged from 16 to 19 with no mean age differences between sex or race.

Instrument

The ICL (LaForge & Suczek, 1955) was used to obtain self- and ideal-self-ratings. This instrument consists of 128 adjectives and phrases (for example, forceful, usually gives in, considerate, sarcastic) with 16 items for each of eight different kinds of interpersonal behavior. Dom and Lov raw scores are derived for each rating by means of arithmetical formulae given in the manual (Leary, 1956). These scores are then converted to standard scores with a mean of 50 and a standard deviation of 10.

Separate tables are provided for the conversion of self- and ideal-self-raw-scores into *T* scores. However, the present study utilized the self-rating table for both sets of data as this provides a more accurate indication of discrepancies between ideal and self-descriptions in individual cases and as the derivation of *T* scores for the ideal ratings is based on somewhat questionable assumptions and procedures.

Social Class

An occupational classification scheme by Schneider and Lysgaard (1953) was applied to subjects' parents in order to classify subjects with regard to the social class factor. Four occupational classes are derived in terms of the degree of supervisory control over "lower" occupations and independence of supervisory control from "higher" occupations. The four classes are: (*a*) independent occupations, (*b*) dependent occupations involving skill and supervision or manipulation of others, (*c*) dependent occupations involving skill but little supervision or manipulation of others, and (*d*) dependent occupations involving little skill and little supervision or manipulation of others. In addition, the present study employed an "unclassifiable" category for those parents listed as deceased, living in another city with job unspecified, or unemployed. The groupings were made, when possible, on the basis of paternal occupation. In that minority of cases where the father's occupation was unclassifiable, the maternal occupational status was used for classification purpose.

Procedure

ICLs were administered by school counselors during special group testing periods in connection with another study (McDonald & Gynther, 1963). Each student was asked to rate self and ideal. In addition, each student was also instructed to list the occupational status and job title, if known, of both parents on a form provided for this purpose. Two judges, the junior author and a second clinical psychologist, independently rated the maternal and paternal occupations in terms of the various classifications with a resulting 88 per cent agreement. In cases of disagreement between these raters, the final rating was made by the senior author.

To provide sufficient numbers in each cell for statistical analysis, it was necessary to combine Classes *a* and *b* which resulted in the use of only three socioeconomic categories. The number of subjects varied from cell to cell, ranging from 64 Class *d* Negro females to 22 Class *d* white males. Due to the unequal *N*s in each cell, formulae provided by Walker and Lev (1953) were used for the analyses of variance.

RESULTS

The major findings of this study are presented in two tables. Table 1[1] gives the *F* values from the analyses of variance for the four ICL variables. Inspection of this table reveals that race and sex have a marked influence on one's self- and ideal-self-concepts, whereas socioeconomic status does not affect these concepts.

Negro students' self-descriptions yielded higher scores on Dom ($t = 19.10$, $p < .001$) and Lov ($t = 13.53$, $p < .001$) than did those of white students. The white subjects' ideal-self-descriptions, on the other hand, yielded higher scores on Dom ($t = 11.90$, $p < .001$) and Lov ($t = 2.53$, $p < .01$) than those of the Negro subjects.

Male adolescents described themselves as higher on Dom than their female counterparts ($t = 4.10$, $p < .01$) while female subjects rated themselves higher on the Lov variable than the male subjects did ($t = 5.52$, $p < .01$). The same pattern was found for the ideal descriptions ($t = 1.92$, $.05 < p < .10$ for Dom; $t = 4.00$, $p < .01$ for Lov).

The only significant interaction pertains to the finding that Negro males obtained much higher Dom scores than white males ($t = 8.06$, $p < .001$) while Negro females' Dom scores, although higher than those of white females ($t = 3.22$, $p < .01$), showed considerably less difference between the means.

Table 2 presents the means and standard deviations of the ICL variables by sex and race. Inspection of these data shows that there is much less discrepancy between self- and ideal-self-descriptions of the Negro students than the white students ($t = 32.90$, $p < .001$ for Dom; $t = 21.61$, $p < .001$ for Lov). Comparisons of self-ideal-self discrepancies by sex reveal less discrepancy for the males on Dom ($t = 7.82$, $p < .01$) while the reverse was found for Lov ($t = 9.08$, $p < .01$).

[1] Interested readers are referred to the original paper for Tables 1 and 2, which are omitted here in the interest of brevity.

DISCUSSION

Our negative findings for class are not consistent with those of previous investigators who have demonstrated that social status affects self-descriptions. This is not to say that previous results have themselves been consistent; for example, Klausner's (1953) and Bieri and Lobeck's (1961) results regarding the relationship between dominance and class membership are quite contradictory. A possible explanation of these discrepancies is that each study used a different measure of social class. Two suggestions for future work are: for relationships between different classification methods to be clarified by, for example, using several different indices on one sample; and for consensus to be reached in the use of the procedure with the most satisfactory reliability and validity coefficients so that later findings might be more comparable.

The results concerning the sex variable (i.e., boys higher on Dom, girls higher on Lov) conform with the role expectations traditionally associated with being a boy or a girl, at least in the white culture, although the studies cited by Wylie (1961) gave no clear-cut evidence related to this point. The similar findings for Negro adolescents might not have been as confidently predicted, considering the characteristic description of Negro culture as matriarchal. Of course, such conclusions have been principally based on observations of adult, not teen-age, interactions.

If the present results concerning the sex variable seem fairly obvious, the results involving race would seem contrary to lay expectations, as well as to Grossack's (1957) findings that Negro males and females obtain significantly lower Edwards Personal Preference Schedule Dominance scores than white normative samples. That is, it would probably be anticipated that whites would describe themselves as more dominant than Negroes, whereas in fact the exact opposite was found. Although one could give sociological, psychodynamic, or cultural "explanations" of this finding, the most important next step would appear to be replication to confirm or disconfirm the results.

SUMMARY

This study evaluated the effects of sex, race, and social class on the self- and ideal-self-concepts of adolescent *S*s. Interpersonal Check

Self-, Ideal-Self-descriptions Related to Sex, Race, and Class

List data were obtained from 261 Negro and 211 white high school seniors from urban segregated schools whose social class was determined on the basis of parental occupations as reported by the students. Sex and race markedly influenced the results, but class was not found to have any effect. Negro students obtained higher dominance and love scores than the white students for self-ratings, but lower scores on ideal descriptions. Males' self- and ideal-self-ratings yielded higher scores on dominance while females' ratings yielded higher scores on the love variable. There was less discrepancy between ideal and self-ratings of: (a) Negroes compared with whites, (b) males compared with females on dominance, and (c) females compared with males on love.

REFERENCES

Bieri, J., & Lobeck, R. Self-concept differences in relation to identification, religion, and social class. *J. Abnorm. Soc. Psychol.*, 1961, **62,** 94–98.

Davids, A., & Lawton, Marcia J. Self-concept, mother concept, and food aversions in emotionally disturbed and normal children. *J. Abnorm. Soc. Psychol.*, 1961, **62,** 309–314.

Engel, Mary. The stability of the self-concept in adolescence. *J. Abnorm. Soc. Psychol.*, 1959, **58,** 211–215.

Grossack, M. M. Some personality characteristics of southern Negro students. *J. Soc. Psychol.*, 1957, **46,** 125–131.

Horowitz, Frances D. The relationship of anxiety, self-concept, and sociometric status among fourth, fifth, and sixth grade children. *J. Abnorm. Soc. Psychol.*, 1962, **65,** 212–214.

Klausner, S. J. Social class and self-concept. *J. Soc. Psychol.*, 1953, **38,** 201–205.

LaForge, R., & Suczek, R. F. The interpersonal dimension of personality: III. An Interpersonal Check List. *J. Pers.*, 1955, **24,** 94–112.

Leary, T. *Multilevel measurement of interpersonal behavior.* Berkeley, Calif.: Psychological Consultation Service, 1956.

Lipsitt, L. P. A self-concept scale for children and its relationship to the children's form of the manifest anxiety scale. *Child Develpm.*, 1958, **29,** 463–472.

McDonald, R. L., & Gynther, M. D. MMPI differences associated with sex, race, and social class in two adolescent samples. *J. Consult. Psychol.*, 1963, **27,** 112–116.

Schneider, L., & Lysgaard, S. The deferred gratification pattern. *Am. Sociol. Rev.*, 1953, **18,** 142–149.

Walker, Helen, & Lev, J. *Statistical inference.* New York: Holt, 1953.

Wylie, Ruth. *The self concept.* Lincoln: Univ. of Nebraska Press, 1961.

7.3 BIRTH ORDER AND ACADEMIC PRIMOGENITURE

William D. Altus

In *The Psychology of Affiliation,* Schachter (1959) emphasized the group orientation of the firstborn under anxiety-producing situations. One fact which he did not comment on in this earlier publication is implicit in Tables 22a and 22b of that book: It is the marked preponderance of the firstborn among his sample of 298 students from the undergraduate psychology classes at the University of Minnesota. If the only child is considered a firstborn (as he usually is in studies of ordinal position), some 164 (55.03%) were firstborn while 134 (44.97%) were laterborns. Even with the only child excluded from consideration, some 48.46 per cent, or nearly one-half the total, were firstborn. Such a statistic would not be surprising if all students came from two-child families where equality of number might be postulated; but since representatives of families of diverse sizes are to be expected, such a statistic *is* surprising.

Bender (1928) reported a study involving sophomore Dartmouth students, from which it is possible to calculate that 42.31 per cent were firstborn, when the only child is excluded from consideration, and 53.13 per cent when the only child is included among the firstborn. Hayes (1938) published a study of 76 females at Mt. Holyoke College. Of these, 50.84 per cent were firstborn when the only child is excluded, and 61.84 per cent are firstborn when the only child is included. Abernethy (1940) reported on 300 women from Queens College, North Carolina; among this group 39.85 per cent or 46.66 per cent were firstborn, depending upon how the only child is treated in the calculations. It is clear that all these studies point to an overrepresentation of the firstborn at the college level, if one may assume some modicum of representativeness among the various samples of the total college populations involved.

It should also be noted that Terman et al. (1925) found a bias

Source: Reprinted from the *Journal of Personality and Social Psychology,* 1965, **2,** 872–876, with permission of the author and the American Psychological Association, Inc.

favoring the firstborn in their study of the gifted, particularly among those coming from families of two, three, and four children. He noted the similarity of the ratios he found to those of Cattell (1947), in his survey of the eminent American scientist. To illustrate with the two-child family, Terman reported that 56.1 per cent of his gifted sample were among the first born; in Cattell's study of eminence among American men of science, the corresponding percentage is 57.4. The figures for all birth-order positions among representatives of the three- and four-child family were likewise quite similar in both studies. Ellis (1926) in his study of eminence among the British found that 56 per cent were firstborns among those who came from two-child families. The congruence of these data is rather unexpected since the criterion for Terman was simply psychometric brightness among children, while for Cattell and Ellis the criterion was achieved eminence in science for one and eminence in general in the other.

The tabular data from Schachter (1959) show that 62.22 per cent of his representatives from the two-child family were among the firstborn. The comparable data from Hayes (1938) yields a percentage of 57.69 favoring the firstborn in the two-child family; for Abernethy (1940), it is 63.16. Bender (1928) did not report his data so that the statistic for the two-child family could be computed.

The uniformity and consistency of these data led the writer to embark on a program of birth-order studies, one facet of which concerned the ratios of the birth order of all students entering the University of California, Santa Barbara, for the years of 1960, 1961, 1962, and 1963. It was predicted that the firstborn would be overrepresented, regardless of the sex of the student.

RESULTS

The record for about one student in twenty had to be discarded since half siblings, step siblings, and foster siblings were judged to render a birth order invalid for research purposes. The data on all the valid records for students coming from families of one, two, three, or four children are given in Table 1. Only 6.96 per cent of the male and 6.25 per cent of the female students come from families of five or more children. Such small numbers were entailed among the larger families that data beyond the four-child family are not shown.

The consistency of percentages for the various birth orders stands out clearly in the tabular data. The only child shows a percentage variation of less than five points, 12.06 to 16.99. The firstborn from

Table 1 *Sibling Order for Students Entering in 1960, 1961, 1962, and 1963, from Families of One, Two, Three, or Four Children*

	Birth Order[a]										
Group	1/1	1/2	2/2	1/3	2/3	3/3	1/4	2/4	3/4	4/4	Total
1960											
Men	16.99	29.81	12.50	17.31	10.90	3.85	4.49	2.24	1.28	0.64	100.01
Women	14.29	29.96	16.64	16.37	7.07	4.02	6.66	2.91	1.25	0.83	100.00
1961											
Men	13.92	25.63	12.03	18.04	10.13	5.70	5.70	5.38	2.22	1.27	100.02
Women	16.59	26.54	14.22	15.40	11.37	6.40	5.21	2.13	1.18	0.95	99.99
1962											
Men	13.33	26.92	16.41	13.59	8.21	5.90	6.66	4.36	2.82	1.79	99.99
Women	16.33	27.10	16.16	12.79	9.60	6.06	5.39	3.03	2.36	1.18	100.00
1963											
Men	12.64	24.02	17.94	14.66	11.70	5.30	6.55	3.28	2.03	1.87	99.99
Women	12.06	25.75	16.36	16.13	8.24	7.42	8.12	3.36	1.39	1.16	99.99
Total											
Men											
(*N*)	230	433	256	258	173	87	100	62	35	25	1,659
Men	13.86	26.10	15.43	15.55	10.43	5.24	6.03	3.74	2.11	1.51	100.00
Women											
(*N*)	374	711	417	398	227	156	172	77	40	27	2,599
Women	14.39	27.36	16.04	15.31	8.73	6.00	6.62	2.96	1.54	1.04	99.99

Note: In percentages.

[a] Read thus: 1/1 means an only child; 1/2 is the firstborn of two; 2/2 is the younger in a family of two; 1/3 is the firstborn in a three-child family; and so on.

the two-child family shows relatively even less variation than does the only child since the older of two ranges from a low of 24.02 per cent to a high of 29.96 per cent. The later-born in the two-child family shows the same relative incidence as does the only child, ranging as he does from 12.03 per cent to a high of 17.94 per cent. The first-born in the three-child family shows a comparable constancy, ranging from 12.79 per cent to a high of 18.04 per cent. The variation is somewhat greater in the later birth orders, where smaller numbers reduce the reliability and increase the discrepancy somewhat. Still, the predictability from sex to sex and from year to year is good: The youngest in the four-child family hovers about a mode of 1 per cent, dipping from a low of .64 per cent to a high of 1.87 per cent.

Men and women show strikingly similar birth-order ratios. What variability there is could easily be explained by chance fluctuation. Sex factors enter negligibly, if at all, in the ratios noted in Table 1. The size of the family is shown to be of marked significance, however, in terms of the student population. The representatives of two-child families comprise 42.68 per cent of all the students who come from families of one through four children; and the families of one through four children, it will be remembered, contribute 93 per cent of all the entering students to whom a birth order could validly be assigned. The three-child family contributes 30.51 per cent; the four-child family, 12.63; the one-child family, 14.19 per cent. The percentages for the total population of students, without restriction as to family size, are not much different: one-child family, 11.43 per cent; two-child, 39.17 per cent; three-child, 29.51 per cent; four-child, 13.02 per cent; five-child, 3.95 per cent; all other orders, 2.92 per cent. This linkage with size of family is in part explicable by the observed linkage of intelligence and number of children (Maxwell & Pilliner, 1960). It seems likely that differential academic motivations as social class is varied must account for part of the variance. Economic factors also probably enter since family income tends to drop among families of larger size.

The most significant aspect of Table 1 is, for the writer, the observed effect of birth order on the four entering college classes. The total number of firstborn males from families of two children is seen to be 433 or 62.84 per cent, while 256 or 37.16 per cent are the second-born or younger. For women from two-child families, the first-born accounts for 63.03 per cent, while the second-born yields 36.97 per cent. It is thus clear that for each eight entering students who come from two-child families, five will be the firstborn or older while only three will be the second-born or younger. For the three-child family, 49.81 per cent of the males are firstborn; 33.40 per cent are second-born; 16.80 per cent are third out of three. The ratios are roughly ½ for the firstborn, ⅓ for the second-born, and ⅙ for the third-born. For women from three-child families, the percentages are 50.96 for the firstborn, 29.07 for the second-born, and 19.97 for the third-born or youngest. Again, there is a marked aberration from the theoretical expectancy, which would be ⅓ or 33.33 per cent for each of three birth orders. The four-child family continues the same trend: When men and women are considered as a total, about ½ of all representatives of the four-child family are firstborn; about ¼ are second-born; the remaining ¼ are divided between the last two birth orders, with the younger of the two getting a slightly smaller percentage.

The percentage of firstborns for *all* entering students regardless of sex and family size is 61.34 when the only child is considered a firstborn and 55.05 when the firstborn is disregarded in the computation. For women, the figures are 62.29 and 55.80; for men, 59.87 and 53.49—the percentages varying with the inclusion or exclusion of the only child.

DISCUSSION

It would appear that to the extent the data reported in this paper are representative, the probability of attending college is closely associated with size of family and that within families of the same size the firstborn has the cards stacked in his favor. Over 90 per cent of the local student population comes from families of one, two, three, or four children. Of the entering students, over 60 per cent are firstborn if the only child is considered as a firstborn without any siblings; if the only child is left out of the computations, then about 55 per cent are still among the firstborn group.

Some evidence which has come to light since this program of studies was begun tends to corroborate the findings here noted. Capra and Dittes (1962) reported that 61 per cent of two samples of Yale undergraduates were either only children or firstborns. This figure corresponds almost exactly to the 61.34 per cent found locally. The figure for a sample of 133 students at Reed College[1] in 1962 showed 73 per cent to be either only children or firstborns; when the only child was left out of the equation, the percentage was 66. Stewart

[1] Personal communication, 1964.

(1962) in a study of 7000 boys and girls in grammar and modern secondary schools in a London borough found that the firstborn tended to be significantly overrepresented, a tendency which became more marked in the upper grades since the firstborn tended to persist in school longer than did the later-born. The phenomenon of academic primogeniture, which has been noted among American colleges for the past 40 years, appears therefore to have its analog when the geographical locus is shifted to England and the educational level to the state-supported secondary school.

Schachter's (1963) publication belatedly came to the writer's attention as he was in process of final revision of the present paper subsequent to its acceptance for publication. Schachter stresses, in this significant recent paper of his, the linkage of eminence to order of birth, citing many previous reports beginning with Galton. He then proceeds to show that at the University of Minnesota some 4013 students taking introductory psychology in 1959 and 1961 give similar evidence for a preponderance of the firstborn. To make his findings comparable to those reported in the present study, the percentages of firstborn students from families of two, three, and four children were calculated from his data. Some 55.43 per cent of the representatives of the two-child family at the University of Minnesota are firstborn; the comparable figure at Santa Barbara is 62.96 per cent. For representatives of the three-child family, the firstborn at Minnesota comprise 45.97 per cent; at Santa Barbara the figure is 50.50 per cent. For the four-child family, the figures for the firstborn are 41.07 per cent at Minnesota and 50.56 per cent at Santa Barbara. Some 48.94 per cent of the two-, three-, and four-child family representatives among University of Minnesota students are firstborn; at Santa Barbara, the figure is 56.70 per cent, higher by some 7.76 points. This somewhat larger percentage of firstborn students at Santa Barbara may be due to the relatively high entrance standards at the University of California, where only the top 10–15 per cent of graduating high-school seniors are found admissible on the basis of secondary grade averages. The data on firstborns at Yale and at Reed previously noted would lend some credence to the linkage of higher entrance standards to a greater ratio of firstborn students. If this inference is a correct one—the writer has no data to corroborate it—then public junior colleges which must accept any high-school graduate should show a greater proportion of later-born students than obtains in collegiate institutions with comparatively stringent entrance standards.

Schachter also furnished data on two-child family representatives matriculating at Columbia University between 1943 and 1962; here, likewise, the firstborn is overrepresented in every comparison. Among graduate students in the Department of Psychology and the Institute of Child Welfare at the University of Minnesota, Schachter again found the firstborn overrepresented. He calculates that 57.79 per cent of this latter group is firstborn but this is done by including the only child in the firstborn category. If the only child is removed from the computations, the figure drops to 46.84 per cent, which is slightly under the 48.94 per cent found for the firstborn representatives from families of two, three, and four children matriculated at Minnesota as undergraduates. One reason for this drop is that the proportion of only children who are graduate students in Schachter's study is approximately double that for the local undergraduate population, who take introductory psychology courses.

In the same article, Schachter reports the relation of birth order to grade averages for 628 students from a Minneapolis high school. The firstborn is shown to have a higher grade average which is consistent though small. In discussing this finding, Schachter disclaims any belief that it may be caused by differences in tested aptitude between first- and later-borns, saying that "Sanity certainly would suggest a conclusion of no association." The explanation for the grade differentials he believes to reside in motivational factors. He goes on to suggest that since he has found (Schachter, 1964) the firstborn to be less popular than the later-born, "Perhaps with little else to do, firstborns simply spend more time at their books."

Despite Schachter's belief that aptitude is not a parameter relating to order of birth, there is some evidence that for high levels of aptitude there may well be linkages between birth order and measures of aptitude. It will be remembered that Terman et al. (1925) found the firstborn overrepresented among his gifted. Altus (1965) reports the firstborn students at the Santa Barbara campus of the University of California earn higher scores than do later-born students on the Verbal Aptitude section of the Scholastic Aptitude Test. In a later study (unpublished) he found it possible to demonstrate significant mean differences, for both men and women, between firstborn (older) and second-born (younger) students from two-child families at the Santa Barbara campus while employing an aptitude test of only ten items, eight verbal and two quantitative. The mean differences on the short aptitude test favored the firstborn, of course. Nichols (1964) has found in an 84 per cent sample of 1618 finalists in the National Merit Scholarship Qualifying Test that the firstborn is markedly overrepresented: 66 per cent of the two-child family representatives were firstborn; 52 per cent is the corresponding figure for the three-child family; 59 per cent for the four-child family; and 52 per cent for the five-child family. In all, he found slightly over 59 per cent of the representatives of two-, three-, four-, and five-child families were first born. Since the merit finalists represent a sample some three standard deviations above the average of the high-school population from which they come, they are probably superior in aptitude to the mean of any college student body in the United States. The fact that primogeniture effects stand out so strikingly when the criterion of evaluation is aptitude test scores rather than performance in the classroom lends significant corroboration to the general implied thesis of this paper that order of birth is a parameter which future studies—at least of the very able—must reckon with.

The data in the present paper relating order of birth to college attendance are in accord with what Schachter (1963) has found and what many others have occasionally reported since the 1920s about college attendance in the United States. The documentation of the case for academic primogeniture seems fairly adequate and complete. The parts which motivation and aptitude—if they can be separately dealt with—play in determining the composition of college student bodies are, of course, beyond the scope of this paper. The mere fact of the overrepresentation of the firstborn does have a peculiar social relevance which deserves comment, however.

The most significant aspects of birth-order linkage to college attendance are the loss to society from the untrained, though presumptively educable, later-borns; the effect upon our rapidly changing society, with its increasing emphasis upon technology, if the society and its technology come more and more under the control of the firstborn, assuming that he is, as Adler (1928) once wrote, a "power-hungry conservative." No one has corroborated Adler's dictum and it may be that he was wrong. It can be safely asserted, however, that to the extent the firstborn differs as a person from the later-born, our society will increasingly feel that difference as college and professional training become more and more a *sine qua non* for achieving a managerial position in our power structure.

SUMMARY

Data were obtained on the birth order of students entering in 1960, 1961, 1962, and 1963, at the University of California, Santa

Barbara. Previous studies had shown the firstborn to be overrepresented among college students. The present study confirms this trend: Over 60 per cent of all entering students are firstborn if the only child is included as a firstborn; if the only child is excluded, the figure is about 55 per cent. Among representatives of the two-child family, 62.96 per cent were firstborn; 50.50 per cent were firstborn among three-child family representatives; and 49.72 per cent were firstborn among those coming from families of four. The sex of the student appeared unrelated to these birth-order trends. It is suggested that the overrepresentation of the firstborn at the college level must have marked social effects in the competition for power and place in our increasingly technological society.

REFERENCES

Abernethy, E. M. Further data on personality and family position. *J. Psychol.*, 1940, **10**, 303–307.

Adler, A. Characteristics of the first, second, and third child. *Children*, 1928, **3**, 14–52.

Altus, W. D. Birth order and scholastic aptitude. *J. Consult. Psychol.*, 1965, **29**, 202–205.

Bender, I. E. Ascendance-submission in relation to certain other factors in personality. *J. Abnorm. Soc. Psychol.*, 1928, **23**, 137–143.

Capra, P. C., & Dittes, J. E. Birth order as a selective factor among volunteer subjects. *J. Abnorm. Soc. Psychol.*, 1962, **64**, 302.

Cattell, J. M. *Man of science*. Vol. 1. Lancaster, Pa.: Science Press, 1947.

Ellis, H. *A study of British genius*, rev. ed. Boston: Houghton Mifflin, 1926.

Hayes, S. P. A note on personality and family position. *J. Appl. Psychol.*, 1938, **22**, 347–349.

Maxwell, J., & Pilliner, A. E. The intellectual resemblance between sibs. *Ann. Hum. Genet.*, 1960, **24**, 23–32.

Nichols, R. C. Birth order and intelligence. Unpublished research, National Merit Scholarship Corporation, Evanston, Ill., 1964. (Mimeo)

Schachter, S. *The psychology of affiliation*. Stanford: Stanford Univ. Press, 1959.

Schachter, S. Birth order, eminence, and higher education. *Am. Sociol. Rev.*, 1963, **28**, 757–768.

Schachter, S. Birth order and sociometric choice. *J. Abnorm. Soc. Psychol.*, 1964, **68**, 453–456.

Stewart, Mary. *The success of the first born child*. London: Workers Educational Assn., 1962.

Terman, L. M., et al. *Genetic studies of genius:* Vol. 1, *The mental and physical traits of a thousand gifted children*. Stanford: Stanford Univ. Press, 1925.

7.4 A COMPARISON OF THE VALUE SYSTEMS OF MEXICAN AND AMERICAN YOUTH

Robert F. Peck

For the past six years, in collaboration with Dr. Rogelio Diaz-Guerrero of the National University of Mexico, work has been progressing on a multifaceted research known as the Cross-Cultural Study of Values. Nine instruments have been devised, with parallel forms in English and in Spanish, to investigate similarities and differences in the conceptions held by Mexican and American youth about several major aspects of human relationships. The instruments include three questionnaires designed to discover the meaning of the "respect" relationship in the two cultures. Another set of three different questionnaires concerns the concept of "love." Another instrument is designed to elicit conceptions of masculinity and femininity in the two cultures. A One-Word Sentence Completion instrument, especially designed for computer analysis, is part of the battery. Finally, a "value-hierarchy" instrument is included.

The present report concerns the results of the "value-hierarchy" instrument, and one of the "respect" questionnaires. "Respect" was chosen for study because, along with love, authority, friendship, and duty, it is one of the central motives that bind human society together. Moreover, there was some reason to believe that the relationship of respect takes a somewhat different form—different ways of feeling and acting—in the U.S. and in Latin America. Although the Spanish word "respetar" and the English word "respect" are identical in origin, very similar in form, and similar in dictionary definition, the actual behavior patterns and the conceptual associations surrounding these terms might, we thought, differ significantly in the two cultures.

In order to get a first estimate of the relative importance of various major values in the two cultures, a simple, straightforward questionnaire was devised which asked the people to rank-order fifteen de-

Source: This study was supported in part by a grant from the Hogg Foundation for Mental Health of the University of Texas. Reprinted from the *Interamerican Journal of Psychology*, 1967, 1, 41–50, with permission of the author and the Revista Interamericana de Psicologia, Inc.

sirable conditions or goals of life. This is the "value hierarchy" instrument.

METHOD

A check list was constructed, made up of twenty different possible meanings that might be associated with the term "respect." This questionnaire was composed first in English, then an exact counterpart was prepared in Spanish. We strove for *semantically* identical meaning, which was not always the same as a linguistically literal translation.

The English version was administered to the University of Texas sample. The Spanish version was used at the University of Mexico. The respondent was simply asked to check any of the twenty possible meanings that he or she would attribute to "respect." After all samples were completed, an F test was applied to determine whether any one sample consistently tended to check a larger or smaller total number of items. There was no significant response bias in any sample, so a direct comparison of percentage response to each item of the questionnaire was possible.

The "value-hierarchy" instrument consisted simply of a list of the fifteen desiderata shown in Table 1, with instructions to number them from one to fifteen, in order of their relative importance to the individual. Again, the English form was used with the U.S. sample and the Spanish language form was used with the Mexican sample.

For each item in the "respect" questionnaire, an analysis of variance was performed on the CDC 1604 computer at the University of Texas, using a program written especially for this study by Dr. Donald Veldman. An analogous procedure was used with the value hierarchy. Analysis of variance was applied to the average rank assigned to each term in the instrument by four subgroups: U. S. males, U. S. females, Mexican males, and Mexican females. Following this, the values could be arrayed in descending order of importance as assigned by the members of each of the four subgroups, and points of significant difference between the two cultures could be identified.

THE SAMPLE POPULATIONS

Partly because they were accessible and cooperative, but also because they represent the future leaders and opinion-makers of their societies, college students were selected for initial study. If anything,

Table 1 *The Value Hierarchy of Mexican and American Youth*

		U. of Mexico		U. of Texas	
Rank	Mexican Value[a]	Men	Women	Men	Women
1	+	Career success	Health	Love	Love
			Career success		Religious faith
2	+	Health		Freedom	
					Freedom
3	+	Knowledge	Honor	Health	Health
4	+	Honor	Knowledge	Career success	
5	+	Economic security	Economic security		Character
				Knowledge	Friendship
6	—	Freedom	Character	Friendship	Knowledge
7	—	Friendship	Freedom	Character	
8	+	Respect	Religious faith	Honor	Honor
				Religious faith	Good disposition
9	—	Character	Friendship		
				Economic security	
10	—	Love	Respect		Respect
11	—	Religious faith			Economic security
			Love	Respect	
12		Good disposition	Good disposition	Good disposition	Career success
13		Humor	Humor	Wealth	Humor
14		Wealth	Power	Humor	Wealth
15		Power	Wealth	Power	Power

[a] Values rated more highly by Mexicans than Texans are indicated by +, whereas values rated lower by Mexicans are indicated by —.

similarities in their intellectual orientation and in their social background might be expected, that transcend national differences. Thus, any value differences found are likely to be genuine. Greater differences might be expected if noncollege populations were compared. The U. S. sample consisted of 310 arts and science students at the University of Texas and 242 arts and science undergraduates at the National University of Mexico. There were somewhat more men than women in the Mexican sample and somewhat more women than men in the University of Texas sample. These figures pertain to the samples drawn for the value-hierarchy study.

Two different samples were used in the "respect" study, consisting of 340 arts and science majors at the University of Texas and 298 arts and science majors at the University of Mexico.

Since the results from the two instruments are derived from two different samples from the general populations of Mexico and the U. S., it cannot be said that the same people showed identical response patterns in the two different instruments. On the other hand, where results from the two different inquiries show similar or psychologically compatible patterns between the two samples from a culture, it might reinforce the idea of generalized traits of "national character."

RESULTS

The Value Hierarchy

The Texas youth, both male and female put *love* at the top of their list of values. This was closely followed by *freedom* and *health,* in both sexes. Thereafter, the next most important thing to men was *career success,* although for the women it was very far down on the list. The Texas coeds, on the other hand, gave second highest place to *religious faith,* whereas the male students put it below the middle of the hierarchy. The next three values in order of importance to the American students were *good character, knowledge,* and *friendship,* with *character* being significantly more important to the women than to the men. Personal *honor* was given a middle place in the hierarchy, with *economic security* of less than average concern to either sex. The girls favored a *good disposition* significantly more than the men, to whom it was a relatively unimportant value, compared with the other alternatives. Both sexes agreed that a *sense of humor, wealth,* and the *power to shape events* were least important to them.

In considerable contrast to the U. S. picture, the Mexican students put *success* and *health* at the head of their lists. *Success in a career* was almost as important for the Mexican coeds as for the Mexican male students. In both these values, the Mexican students gave much greater importance to these considerations than did the American students, even though *health* stood high for the Americans. Next, and very important to the Mexicans, were *knowledge, honor,* and *economic security.* These considerations were much more important to them than to the American students. *The respect of society* was the final value on which the Mexicans placed significantly more importance than did the Americans. Although *freedom* was listed sixth or seventh out of the fifteen by the Mexicans, their concern for this was a great deal less than the Americans demonstrated. Perhaps the most dramatic difference is the low value placed on *love* by the Mexican students, in contrast with the Texans. They also gave somewhat less weight to *friendship, good character,* and *religious faith* than did the American sample.

The one area of substantial agreement between the two cultures was the low value given to *humor, wealth,* and *power,* by comparison with the other values in life.

In interpreting results such as this, it is extremely important to be aware of the differences in the practical circumstances in which these two groups of students find themselves. While the value pattern of the U. S. students emphasize love, freedom, and other nonmaterial considerations, far above such things as economic security, wealth or power, it must be remembered that the majority of the American students can take for granted a reasonable degree of economic security, certainly by contrast with a great many of the Mexican students. Insofar as an instrument such as this reflects their true value system, the American students certainly dispel the picture of rank materialism that is so often leveled at them by people in other countries. They see themselves as much more concerned to achieve personal warmth in their human relationships than to defend personal "honor," or worry about social recognition and respect. If these are attractive qualities, as they well may be, it must be said that most of the American students can rather easily afford to be unmaterialistic in this way.

The young Mexicans greatly stress career success. It must be remembered that in Mexico, university education is almost the only route for social mobility and self-betterment. There may well be a good deal of selection operating to make career-oriented young people the most likely to attend and survive at the National University. In the case of the young women, practical circumstances in Mexico seem likely to cause them a good deal of frustration in the not too distant future, in most cases. There are actually few opportunities, as yet, for professional careers for women in Mexico. If, as may conceivably be the case, their interest in a career is symptomatic of a desire for greater independence and self-realization, this too may be frustrated for many of these female students, before social conditions change enough to permit such realization to occur.

The emphasis on health is understandable in a society where there is still a high mortality rate. It should be noted, of course, that this emphasis was not a great deal more than that given to health by the American students, which must be emphasized by the Americans for quite different psychological reasons, in view of the superior health conditions in the United States.

The Mexican students put great emphasis, also, on knowledge and economic security, again quite probably because both are difficult to come by in their society, at least until recently. Their emphasis on personal honor reflects the Latin pride which is well known in history and literature. The relatively low emphasis given to religious faith undoubtedly reflects the secularization of Mexican society, but it also may reflect even more the self-selection of secular-minded students to attend the University.

The quite low value given to love by both male and female Mexicans is in marked contrast with the Americans. While the results of the other questionnaires on the meaning of "love" remain to be analyzed, it can be said already that the relationship of love between the sexes in Mexico seems to be a somewhat more ambivalent one than is commonly the case in America. Speculation on this, however, is best left to more concrete evidence in later parts of the research.

The Concept of Respect

With the exception of one item, one or another person in every group checked each item in the "respect" instrument. Thus, differences between the groups is a matter of degree, not of total dissimilarity. Nonetheless, the analysis of variance showed that there were significant differences between the two groups on nineteen of the twenty items.

In order to establish a picture of the "core-value pattern" in the samples from the two cultures, Table 2 was constructed. It shows that the University of Texas students picked six items significantly more often than did the students from the University of Mexico. Conversely, the Mexican students checked eleven other items significantly more than the Texas students.

Reading the items in the two halves of Table 2, an interesting contrast is visible in relationship patterns. The American pattern ("Texan" would be a more safely limited term) depicts the respect relationship as one between equals. One can admire and look up to another person, perhaps for some specific attribute, without feeling generally inferior or subordinate. Indeed, there is a suggestion of calmly confident self-assurance in the emphasis on giving the other person "a chance," and being considerate of his feelings and his

Table 2 *"Respect": The "Core-Culture" Pattern in Mexico and in Texas*

U.S. (U. of Texas)	Mexico
1. Look up to with admiration	
	2. Awe
	3. Fear
	4. Love
5. Treat as an equal	
6. Give the other a chance	
	7. Affection
8. Admire	9. Expect protection from
	11. Feel protective toward
	12. Dislike
	13. Don't trespass on rights
	15. Have to obey, like it or not
	16. Duty to obey
17. Consider other's feelings	
18. Consider other's ideas	20. Don't interfere in other's life

ideas. Much less often than the Mexicans do Texas students associate "respect" with the idea of obedience or protection; and they rarely connect it with fear or dislike. In fact, in general, the respect relationship is less laden with intense, personal emotion for the Texas students. While the difference is only one of degree, there seems to be a consistent overall pattern of relatively detached, democratic give-and-take among equals, when the Texans picture the respect relationship.

The Mexican pattern looks equally self-consistent, and quite different. It pictures "respect" as an extremely intimate relationship, involving a good deal of strong personal feeling. For some, part of this feeling is negative, in opposition to the very positive emotions of love and affection that are also expressed. Reciprocal protectiveness is another major theme. Finally, there is considerable concern about not interfering in the other person's life, or trespassing on his rights—perhaps a more immediate danger when life is so close, so emotion-laden, and so intimately bound up, as the Mexican students portray it. The overall pattern tends to be on the authoritarian model. Most of the Mexicans think that respect involves a positive duty to obey; and a third to a half of them, unlike most American students, feel that respect means you *have* to obey the respected person, whether you like it or not. Thus, in contrast to the American pattern, most of the Mexicans portray the respect relationship as an intricate web of reciprocal duties and dependencies, cast in a hierarchical mold, with strong feelings of emotional involvement to support it—and, sometimes, to strain it.

CONCLUSIONS

Results from the two different instruments show highly significant differences in the value patterns of Mexican college students and American college students. There is substantial agreement within each culture on a common array of values. This might well be termed a "core-culture pattern." The patterns for the two different cultures are very significantly different. The American pattern portrays life as a relatively secure place, economically, with emphasis on equalitarian friendliness and rather comfortable self-assurance.

The Mexican pattern shows characteristics of a close-knit, highly emotionalized, reciprocal dependence and dutifulness, within a firmly authoritarian framework. In addition, the Mexican students seem to be powerfully motivated to strive for career success, knowledge, and economic security, undoubtedly because they are by no means sure of possessing or achieving these without great effort, in many cases.

It seems important to note that the college students in both countries gave least value to achieving power to influence events, and to achieving really substantial wealth. Since the future possessors of both wealth and power in both cultures are almost certain to come from these college populations, in large degree, either these students do not accurately report the true value systems that will guide their future behavior, or these values may be ones which achieve top priority only later in life for most people. For many of the students, of course, perhaps the majority, this may be a simple statement of the truth about their values, that they neither avidly seek power or wealth, nor will they be likely to achieve it to an outstanding degree.

These are just pieces in a larger mosaic of research which we expect to extend to other values, and to a number of other countries. The general method developed for this research does look readily usable both in other regions and in other areas of values. It can be used where more complex forms of data gathering are unmanageable; and it is adapted for analysis of large numbers of cases by high-speed computer. As a large-scale survey method, therefore, to be supplemented by depth techniques with selected small samples, it offers useful promise for cross-cultural studies of several kinds. Within its limitations, it provides a totally objective way in comparing the values of people from two or more cultures, and thus of measuring the similarity or difference of the cultures. In the present instance, it furnished an illuminating initial probe into certain culturally differentiated values, and into certain facets of national character in Mexico and the United States.

SUMMARY

The present paper reports findings with two different instruments which are part of the nine-instrument battery used in a multifaceted research known as the Cross-Cultural Study of Values. One is the Values Hierarchy and the other, one of the three Respect Questionnaires.

Parallel forms of the tests in English and in Spanish were administered to two samples of college students; the English version was administered at the University of Texas and the Spanish version at the Universidad Nacional Autónoma de México.

Results from these instruments show highly significant differences in the value patterns of Mexican college students and American college students. The American pattern portrays life as a relatively secure place, economically, with emphasis on equalitarian friendliness and rather comfortable self-assurance. The Mexican pattern shows characteristics of a close-knit, highly emotionalized, reciprocal dependence and dutifulness, within a firmly authoritarian framework.

There is substantial agreement within each culture on a common array of values. This might well be termed a "core-culture" pattern.

REFERENCES

Anderson, H. H. Children's values in western Europe and the Americas. Presented at Symposium: Recent Advances in Cross-Cultural Research, Divisions 8 and 9, American Psychological Association, Chicago, September 5, 1960.

Coelho, George V., & Steinberg, Alma G. B. Cross-cultural assessment of coping behavior: Student-TAT responses of competent adolescents in Maryland and Puerto Rico. A Cross-National Conference on Childhood and Adolescence.

Diaz-Guerrero, R., & Peck, R. F. Respecto y posición social en dos culturas. *Proceed-* Invited paper for Section XVII, XVII International Congress of Psychology, held in Washington, August 20–26, 1963.

Diaz-Guerrero, R., & Peck, R. F. Respecto y posición social en dos culturas. *Proceed-*

ings of the Seventh Interamerican Congress of Psychology. Mexico, D.F., 1963 (July), 116–137.

Havighurst, R. J., Dubois, Maria Eugenia, Csikszentmihalyi, M., & Doll, R. University of Chicago. *Vita Humana,* Fasc. 3, A cross-national study of Buenos Aires and Chicago adolescents.

Peck, R. F., & Diaz Guerrero, R. The meaning of love in Mexico and the United States. *Am. Psychol.,* 1962, 17 (6), 329.

Peck, R. F., & Galliani, C. Intelligence, ethnicity and social roles in adolescent society. *Sociometry,* 1962 (March), 25 (1), 64–72.

Peck, R. F., & Havighurst, R., et al. *The psychology of character development.* New York: Wiley, 1960.

7.5 INDEPENDENCE TRAINING AMONG HAWAIIANS: A CROSS-CULTURAL STUDY

Ronald Gallimore
Alan Howard
Cathie Jordan

This report is based on a portion of the data collected during an investigation of Hawaiians of Polynesian ancestry on the Island of Oahu during 1965–1966. From these initial efforts a set of hypotheses was constructed to account for the social and psychological characteristics of the Hawaiian subculture. The second phase of the project, currently in progress, involves systematic testing of these hypotheses. This report presents some of the preliminary findings on child rearing and socialization obtained during the testing period.

Racially and ethnically, Americans of Hawaiian descent are best considered part Hawaiian. Virtually all have some Hawaiian ancestry but few, if any, can be considered "pure" Hawaiians. Most identify themselves as Hawaiian-other combinations, the other usually being Chinese, Filipino, Japanese, Portuguese, Korean, Puerto Rican, or Haole (i.e., Caucasian). They speak a colloquial dialect of English, often described as "pidgin," which includes some words from Hawaiian as well as a few from other languages. Hawaiian is spoken by a minority, most of whom are elderly: in general, familiarity with the old culture has been substantially eroded. There is, however, a distinct Hawaiian subculture, particularly in those areas set aside as the

Source: This paper was delivered at the Western Psychological Association convention, San Francisco, May 1967. It is reprinted here, in slightly abridged form, with the permission of the authors.

Hawaiians' homelands. One of these areas, Aina Pumehana,[1] is the focus of our research.

The ethnographic study strongly suggests that Hawaiian mothers are indulgent of infants and toddlers to the point of fostering extreme dependency. After a child has become mobile and verbal, or the next child is born, mothers grow weary of the burdensome dependency which previously was encouraged and in which they had taken pleasure. The child's overtures are increasingly punished and he is forced to rely more often on his own efforts or the capricious aid of older children. The child initially responds with redoubled efforts to secure the once plentiful nurturance—predictably, the response of the mother is punitive and rejecting.

Although the Hawaiian mother discourages and punishes dependency, she does not, so it appears, reward independence. With time, independent behavior is acquired but is limited to those responses which the child finds gratifying but do not provoke the mother. The Hawaiian child becomes independent, therefore, not because his mother rewards self-sufficiency but because she punishes him when he fails to meet her expectations or because he has no alternative means of securing gratification except through independent action. Therefore, the most salient feature of Hawaiian independence training is the withdrawal of nurturance coupled with the active punishment of dependency demands.

On the basis of the ethnographic data it was predicted that Hawaiian mothers would except independence earlier than Haole mothers. The anticipation of a Haole-Hawaiian difference was based on two pieces of information: (1) Hawaiian children, in contrast to Haole children, are notoriously indifferent scholars at all grade levels and seem genuinely independent of the performance-reward contingencies typically employed by teachers, and (2) Chance (1961) has shown that poor first-grade achievement is related to early pressure for independence.

STUDY 1

In the first study, 32 Hawaiian mothers responded to the pressure-for-independence questionnaire originally developed by Winterbottom (1958) and expanded by Chance (1961). The mother is asked to give the age at which she expects children to perform competently

[1] Aina Pumehana is a pseudonym.

each of 28 tasks. Tasks include, for example, eating alone, playing outdoors, staying home alone, trying hard tasks without asking for help, and so forth.

Table 1 *Distribution of Hawaiian-Haole Differences in Expected Age of Task Competence* (Original 20-Item Winterbottom Scale)*

Number of items Hawaiian mothers expecting earlier independence	16	(80%)
Number of items no difference between Hawaiian and Haole mothers	2	(10%)
Number of items Haole mothers expecting earlier independence	2	(10%)

* $\chi^2 = 19.59$; $p < .001$.

The overall median age obtained for each item from the Hawaiian group was contrasted with comparable data for 52 middle-income Haole mothers reported by Chance (1961). The results are entirely consistent with expectation. On 80 per cent of items from the original Winterbottom scale, the median age for the Hawaiian mothers was at least one year under the age reported for Haole mothers. Comparisons made with the Chance revision and a Hawaii revision[2] also yielded differences of significant magnitude. The obtained chi squares were significant at the .001, .01, and .02 levels of significance for the three scales respectively.

These findings reinforce the field observations of the ethnographic study and are consistent with preliminary analysis of a recently completed set of Sears-type (Sears, Rau, & Alpert, 1966) mother interviews. Whether this Hawaiian-Haole difference can be attributed to ethnic variables is problematic at this stage of the research—here, as in other studies of the ethnic poor (Gallimore & Howard, 1967), the inevitable confounding of social and cultural variables is present.

In this instance, it is plausible that early independence pressure among the mothers in our Hawaiian sample had a cultural origin but is presently maintained by socioeconomic factors. Studies of child-rearing practices among low-income mainland U. S. groups (Sears, Maccoby, & Levin, 1957) support a socioeconomic explanation of the Hawaiian-Haole difference. Poverty may press mothers to expect early independence both on the mainland and in Hawaii.

[2] The Hawaii Scale excluded items which Hawaiian mothers found unusual.

STUDY 2

The combination of independence pressure, nurturance withdrawal, and punitiveness for dependency ought to produce dependency inhibited children. That is, Hawaiian children ought to be more reluctant to seek adult assistance than Haole children.

In the second study, measures of dependency inhibition were obtained from 27 Hawaiian children and 14 Haole children. The Hawaiian children were from low-income families and were members of the prekindergarten Headstart program. The Haole children were attending a private preschool in a middle-income community in Hawaii and were from middle-class families. Ages ranged from 3–0 to 5–2 with the Haole median at 4–7 and the Hawaiian median at 4–5.[3]

***Table* 2** *Distribution of Hawaiian and Haole Children Asking and Not Asking for Help**

	Asking for Help	Not Asking for Help	Persisting
Hawaiian	7 (25.9%)	17 (62.9%)	3 (11.2%)
Haole	13 (92.8%)	0	1 (7.2%)

* $\chi^2 = 14.23$; $p < .001$.

Each child was asked to solve a puzzle which pretesting had shown to be too difficult for children under 7. The child was first shown the assembled puzzle (consisting of nine pieces of wood, forming a three-dimensional rectangle) and given a demonstration on how to proceed. The child was told "go ahead and play with the puzzle and if you want me to help you, just ask and we will play with it together. This is a very hard puzzle." The injunction to ask for help was repeated immediately after the child began to work. Time spent working was recorded as well as notes on the child's behavior. If the child stopped working and did not ask for help, *E* waited one minute and offered help. A ten-minute time limit was imposed.

The data are unambiguous. Ninety-three per cent of the Haole group spontaneously asked for assistance. In contrast, only 26 per cent of the Hawaiian children requested aid while 63 per cent stopped working, but did not ask for help. The Hawaiian nonasker typically

[3] The Haole group was significantly older which weighs in favor of the findings since dependency has generally been found to decrease with age.

worked with interest and attention for three to four minutes, followed by a gradual decrease in activity. After ceasing to work, the nonasker often appeared apprehensive and uncomfortable. The askers, in both groups, tended to stop work abruptly after three to four minutes and ask for help in a clearly and openly dependent fashion.

There were no significant age or sex differences between askers and nonaskers for the Hawaiian group. Eleven per cent and 7 per cent of the Hawaiian and Haole children, respectively, worked steadily for the ten-minute period without stopping and without asking for help: the difference is not significant.

The difference in time spent working for Hawaiian and Haole askers also was not significant.

Unfortunately there was insufficient overlap between the mother sample and the preschool sample, making impossible a test of the relationship between pressure for independence and dependency inhibition.

DISCUSSION

The results of these two studies lend a satisfactory degree of support for the hypotheses derived from the ethnographic study. Presuming dependency inhibition to be a high-probability response among Hawaiians accounts for a significant range of the behavior. Already noted is the generally inadequate academic performance of Hawaiian children, attributable, in our view, to their indifference to performance-reward contingencies. Hawaiian children are trained by their parents to avoid the vulnerability of evaluative dependence.

The general inhibition of dependency should, and apparently does, reduce the effectiveness of social reinforcers employed by adult agents assigned the task of controlling Hawaiian adolescents. Exceptions are distinguished by a high degree of reward for approach-dependency behavior.

NOTES

Despite the inhibition of dependency so clearly characteristic of children and adolescents, other ethnographic data strongly suggest that adults persist in the establishment of dependent relations among peers and less often with marital partners. Adults often describe dependent relations as painful and anxiety-producing, but inescapable.

Also characteristic of the adult population is a cultural distaste for individual achievement, in terms of status, material wealth, and signification. More important is the pursuit of social approval, and it is this motive which appears to be central for an explanation of Hawaiian behavior. It is therefore hardly speculation to propose that dependency inhibition or its antecedent, dependency anxiety, may account for the importance of the approval motive and the relative unimportance of the achievement motive.

Hawaiians highly value amiable, noncompetitive peer relations. It is regarded as socially impolite to pursue acceptance and approval by a recounting of personal accomplishment, irrespective of subtlety. When confrontations do occur, they are likely to be highly destructive—it is not uncommon for example, for close friends to be offended by a wholly inconsequential act or word to the extent that a relationship is permanently severed. Hostile and direct confrontations are rare, however; avoidance is the much preferred solution to interpersonal conflict.

REFERENCES

Chance, June E. Independence training and first graders achievement. *J. Consult. Psychol.*, 1961, 25, 149–154.

Sears, R. R., Eleanor Maccoby, & H. Levin. *Patterns of child rearing*. Evanston, Ill.: Row, Peterson, 1957.

Sears, R. R., Lucy Rau, and R. Alpert *Identification and child rearing*. Stanford: Stanford University Press, 1966.

Winterbottom, Marian R. The relation of need for achievement to learning experience in independence and mastery. In J. W. Atkinson (Ed.), *Motives in fantasy, action, and society*. Princeton: Van Nostrand, 1958.

§ 8 COMMUNICATION

An essay by Raymond A. Bauer begins this section by challenging the commonly held stereotype of the audience as helpless, or at least passive, where influence is attempted via the mass media of communication. Research results, however, which find their expression in the model of communication as a transactional process, show that the audience can be influenced only when it is an active participant.

The second paper, an experiment reported by Triandis, Loh, and Levin, presents evidence to show that the kind of spoken language used by an individual may be a more significant factor than race in determining the extent to which he will be accepted as a friend. Spoken language also tends to be a major factor in the amount of social distance subjects perceive between themselves and target individuals.

The semantic differential, a device used to measure the connotative meanings of words, objects, and other events, is employed in the third paper as a means of analyzing the attitudes of American Indian adolescents. Malcolm M. Helper and Sol L. Garfield, the researchers, found significant differences between the values held by Indians and whites. The attitudes expressed by Indians who were doing well in school also were found to be different from those of low-achieving Indians, and in some respects were similar to those of white students.

8.1 THE OBSTINATE AUDIENCE: THE INFLUENCE PROCESS FROM THE POINT OF VIEW OF SOCIAL COMMUNICATION

Raymond A. Bauer

I shall here discuss the relationship of two models in the area of social communication. First, the social model of communication: the model held by the general public, and by social scientists when they talk about advertising, and somebody else's propaganda, is one of the exploitation of man by man. It is a model of one-way influence: the communicator *does* something to the audience, while to the communicator is generally attributed considerable latitude and power to do what he pleases to the audience. This model is reflected—at its worst—in such popular phrases as "brainwashing," "hidden persuasion," and "subliminal advertising."

A second model—the model which *ought* to be inferred from the data of research—is of communication as a transactional process in which two parties each expect to give and take from the deal approximately equitable values. This, although it *ought* to be the scientific model, is far from generally accepted as such, a state of affairs on which W. Philips Davison (1959) makes the comment:

> the communicator's audience is not a passive recipient—it cannot be regarded as a lump of clay to be molded by the master propagandist. Rather, the audience is made up of individuals who demand something from the communications to which they are exposed, and who select those that are likely to be useful to them. In other words, they must get something from the manipulator if he is to get something from them. A bargain is involved. Sometimes, it is true, the manipulator is able to lead his audience into a bad bargain by emphasizing one need at the expense of another or by representing a change in the significant environment as greater than it actually has been. But audiences, too, can drive a hard bargain. Many communicators who have been widely disregarded or misunderstood know that to their cost [p. 360].

Davison does not contend that all the exchanges are equitable, but that the inequities may be on either side. He only implies that neither

Source: Reprinted in abridged form from the *American Psychologist,* 1964, **19,** 319–328, with permission of the author and the American Psychological Association, Inc.

the audience nor the communicator would enter into this exchange unless each party expected to "get his money's worth," at least most of the time. After all, Davison is not speaking as a social philosopher nor as an apologist for the industry, but as an experienced researcher trying to make sense out of the accumulated evidence.

Whether fortunately or unfortunately, social criticism has long been associated with the study of communication. The latter was largely stimulated by the succession of exposés of propaganda following World War I, particularly of the munitions-makers' lobby and of the extensive propaganda of the public utilities. There was also social concern over the news media, the movies and radio, and the increasingly monopolistic control of newspapers. Propaganda analysis, which is what research communication was called in those days, was occupied with three inquiries: the structure of the media (who owns and controls them, and what affects what gets into them); content analysis (what was said and printed); and propaganda techniques (which are the devil's devices to influence people). In this period, *effects* for the most part were not studied: they were taken for granted. Out of this tradition evolved Laswell's (Smith, Laswell, & Casey, 1946) formulation of the process of communication that is the most familiar one to this day: "Who says what, through what channels [media] of communication, to whom [with] what . . . results [p. 121]." This apparently self-evident formulation has one monumental built-in assumption: that the initiative is exclusively with the communicator, the effects being exclusively on the audience.

While the stimulus and the model of research on communication were developing out of the analysis of propaganda, survey research, relatively independently, was evolving its technology in the commercial world of market research and audience and leadership measurement. As is well known, Crossley, Gallup, and Roper each tried their hands at predicting the 1936 presidential election and whipped the defending champion, the *Literary Digest*. By 1940, Lazarsfeld was ready to try out the new technology on the old model with a full-scale panel study of the effects of the mass media on voting in a national election, having tested his strategy in the New Jersey gubernatorial race in 1938.

The results of this study, again, are well known. Virtually nobody in the panel changed his intention, and most of the few who did so attributed it to personal influence (Lazarsfeld, Berelson, & Gaudet, 1948). The mass media had had their big chance—and struck out. Negative results had been reached before but none which had been demonstrated by such solid research. A number of equally dramatic failures to detect effects of campaigns carried on in the mass media followed, and by the end of the decade Hyman and Sheatsley (1947) were attempting to explain why. No one could take the effects of communication for granted.

In the meantime, at just about the time that the students of the effect of communication in a natural setting were beginning to wonder if communication ever had effects, experimental studies were burgeoning under essentially laboratory conditions. Experiments had been conducted before, but the tradition of experimenting on the effects of communication was vastly enhanced by the War Department's Information and Education Division, and after the war by Hovland and his associates at Yale (Hovland, Lumsdaine, & Sheffield, 1949). The Yale group's output, and that of colleagues and students of Kurt Lewin, account for a very high proportion of the experimental work on the subject in the past two decades.

The experimenters generally had no trouble conveying information or changing attitudes. Of course nobody stopped to record very explicitly the main finding of all the experiments: that communication, given a reasonably large audience, varies in its impact. It affects some one way, some in the opposite way, and some not at all. But nevertheless the experimenters got results.

By the end of the 'fifties it was quite clear that the two streams of investigation needed reconciling, and Carl Hovland (1959) did so. More recently, pursuing the same theme, I stated Hovland's major point as being that the audience exercises much more initiative outside the laboratory than it does in the experimental situation (Bauer, 1962). The audience selects what it will attend to. Since people generally listen to and read things they are interested in, these usually are topics on which they have a good deal of information and fixed opinions. Hence the very people most likely to attend to a message are those most difficult to change; those who can be converted do not look or listen. A variety of studies attribute to this circumstance alone: the fact that actual campaigns have often produced no measurable results, while quite marked effects could be produced in a laboratory.

Two favorite problems of the laboratory experimenters take on quite a different aspect when considered in a natural setting. One is the question of the order of presentation of arguments. Is it an advantage to have your argument stated first (the so-called law of primacy) or stated last (the so-called law of recency)? In a laboratory the answer is complex but it may be quite simple in a natural situation: he who presents his argument first may convert the audience and they in turn may exercise their oft-exercised prerogative of not listening to the opposing case. Hence to have the first word rather than the last could be decisive in the real world, but for a reason which may seem irrelevant to the relative merits of primacy versus recency.

Of course, another important variable is the credibility of the source. By creating an impression of the credibility of the stooge or experimenter in the laboratory, it is often possible to convert a person to a position far removed from his original one. But in real life, the audience usually does its own evaluation of sources, and at a certain point sometimes arrives at a result quite the opposite of that reached experimentally. If the audience is confronted with a communicator trying to convert it to a position opposed to its own, it is likely to see him as "biased," and the like, and come away further strengthened in its own convictions.

In a sense, Joseph Klapper's 1960 book, *The Effects of Mass Communication,* marks the end of an era. Twenty years earlier, a social scientist would have taken effects for granted and specified the devices the propagandist employed to achieve them. But Klapper (1960) makes statements like these: "[my position] is in essence a shift *away* from the tendency to regard mass communication as a necessary and sufficient cause of audience effects, toward a view of the media as influences, working amid other influences, in a total situation [p. 5]." He sees communications as operating through mediating factors—group membership, selective exposure, defense mechanisms—"such that they typically render mass communication a contributory agent, but not the sole cause in a process of reinforcing the existing conditions. (Regardless of the condition in question . . . the media are more likely to reinforce [it] than to change) [p. 8]." Change takes place, according to Klapper, in those rare circumstances when mediating forces are inoperative, when they are occasionally mobilized to facilitate change, or in certain residual situations. He reviews the literature on the effect of variation in content, mode of presentation, media, and so on, but rather than taking effects for granted, he searches for the exceptional case in which the mass media change rather than fortify and entrench.

Klapper recommends what he calls the "phenomenalistic" and others have called the functional approach. The study of communication has traditionally (although not exclusively) been conducted from the point of view of the *effects intended by the communicator*. From this perspective, the disparity between actual and intended results has often been puzzling. The answer has come increasingly to be seen in entering the phenomenal world of the audience and studying the functions which communication serves. The failure in research to this point has been that the audience has not been given full status in the exchange: the intentions of its members have not been given the same attention as those of the communicator.

Some will argue that these generalizations do not hold true of advertising. They do. But until now no one has undertaken to match the effects of communication in various areas according to comparable criteria and against realistic expectation.

Actually much more is expected of the campaigns with which academic psychologists are associated than is expected of commercial promotion. For example, a paper on governmental informational campaigns concluded with these words (Seidenfeld, 1961): "while people are willing to walk into a drugstore and buy low calorie preparations and contraceptives, they are not very anxious to take shots for protection against polio or attend a clinic dealing with sexual hygiene." By the author's own figures, 60 per cent of the public had had one or more polio shots and 25 per cent had had the full course of four. According to his expectations, and probably ours, these were hardly satisfactory accomplishments.

Yet, what about the highly advertised product, low in calories, with which he was comparing polio inoculations? Presumably he had heard that it was a smashing commercial success, or had seen some dollar volume figure on gross sales. Actually, it was being bought by 4 per cent of the market—60 per cent and even 25 per cent are larger figures than 4 per cent. Our unacknowledged expectations must be reckoned with.

These differences in expectation and criteria produce much confusion, usually on the side of convincing people that commercial campaigns are more successful than others. Yet, consistently successful commercial promotions convert only a very small percentage of people to action. No one cigarette now commands more than 14 per cent of the cigarette market, but an increase of one per cent is worth $60,000,000 in sales. This means influencing possibly .5 per cent of all adults, and 1 per cent of cigarette smokers. This also means that a successful commercial campaign can alienate many more than it wins, and still be highly profitable.

But commercial promotions often do not pay their way. The word is currently being circulated that a mammoth corporation and a mammoth advertising agency have completed a well-designed experiment that proves the corporation has apparently wasted millions of dollars on promoting its corporate image. Some studies have shown that an increase in expenditures for advertising has, under controlled experimental conditions, produced a decrease in sales.

The truth is now out: that our social model of the process of communication is morally asymmetrical; it is concerned almost exclusively with inequities to the advantage of the initiators, the manipulators. From the social point of view this may be all to the good. The answer to the question whether our social and scientific models should be identical is that there is no reason why we should be equally concerned with inequities in either direction; most of us consider it more important to protect the weak from the powerful, than vice versa. However, no matter how firmly committed to a morally asymmetrical social model, investigators should note that inequities fall in either direction and in unknown proportions.

The combination of this asymmetry and the varying expectations and criteria mentioned earlier fortifies the model of a one-way exploitative process of communication. And it is probably further reinforced by the experimental design in which the subject is seen as *re*acting to conditions established by the experimenter. We forget the cartoon in which one rat says to another: "Boy, have I got this guy trained! Every time I push this bar he gives me a pellet of food." We all, it seems, believe that *we* train the *rats*. And while the meaning of "initiative" in an experimental situation may be semantically complicated, the experimenter is usually seen there as *acting* and the subjects as *reacting*. At the very least and to all appearances, the experimental design tends to entrench the model of influence flowing in one direction.

The tide is, in fact, turning, although it is difficult to say whether the final granting of initiative to the audience, which seems to be imminent, is a "turn" or a logical extension of the research work of the past 25 or 30 years. Obviously Davison and Klapper and others, such as the Rileys, Dexter and White, Charles Wright, and Talcott Parsons, regard their position as the logical conclusion of what has gone before rather than a drastic inversion. So-called "functional" studies are increasing in volume, and appear now to be a matter of principle. In any event, Dexter and White (in press), the editors of the forthcoming reader whose tentative title is *People, Society, and Mass Communication*, are firmly committed to this point of view and have organized the book upon it.

Traditionally, the name "functional studies" has been applied to any work concerned with a range of consequences wider than or different from those intended by the communicator. Two early classics, both done in the 'forties, are studies of listening to daytime radio serials: one by Herta Herzog (1944), and the other by Warner and Henry (1948). They established that women used the radio serials as models for their behavior in real life. In the late 'forties, Berelson (1949) studied how people reacted to not having newspapers during a strike, work which Kimball (1959) replicated in the newspaper strike of 1948. The variety of functions the newspapers proved to serve is amazing, including the furnishing of raw material for conversation. "The radio is no substitute for the newspaper. I like to make intelligent conversation [Kimball, 1959, p. 395]." There was also research on the adult following of comics (Bogart, 1955), children's use of television (Maccoby, 1954), and the reading of *Mad* magazine (Winick, 1962).

From a cursory glimpse, one concludes that early functional studies suffered from a tendency to focus on the deviant. Or, put another way, functional or motivational analysis (motivation research can be regarded as a subdivision of functional analysis) was ordinarily evoked only when the stereotyped model of economic rational man broke down. The findings advanced scientific knowledge but did little to improve the image of man in the eyes of those committed to a narrow concept of economic rationality. We may well argue that the social scientists' model of man is in reality broader, more scientifically based, and even more compassionate; but the public may not think so.

Thus, the early functional studies added to knowledge of the process of communication by including effects intended by the audience. There is a question, however, as to what they did to the social model of the process. Certainly the work of motivation research was written up in such a way as to confirm the exploitative model. But more recent functional studies focus on ordinary aspects of communication, and present the audience in a more common, prosaic, and, therefore, more sensible light.

Meanwhile, new trends have been developing in psychological research on communication. Until about a decade ago, the failure of experimental subjects to change their opinions was regarded as a residual phenomenon. Little systematic or sympathetic attention was paid to the persistence of opinion. The considerable volume of recent research using what the Maccobys (Maccoby & Maccoby, 1961) call a homeostatic model is dominated by theories based on the psychology of cognition, Heider's balance theory, Festinger's dissonance theory, Osgood and Tannenbaum's congruity theory, and Newcomb's strain for symmetry. While the proponents of each theory insist on adequate grounds on their distinctiveness, all agree that man acts so as to restore equilibrium in his system of belief. In any event, homeostatic studies do finally accord some initiative to the audience. Specifically, they reveal individuals as deliberately seeking out information on persons either to reinforce shaken convictions or consolidate those recently acquired. Festinger, for example, is interested in the reduction of dissonance following upon decisions—which means he views people as reacting to their own actions as well as to the actions of others. This influx of new ideas and new research is a valuable and welcome addition to both the theory and practice of social communication.

Restoring cognitive equilibrium is, however, only one of the tasks for which man seeks and uses information. Furthermore, the homeostatic theories, while according initiative to the audience, make it peculiarly defensive. They do little to counteract the notion of a one-way flow of influence—although it must be conceded that a scientific model is under no moral obligation to correct the defects, if any, of the social model.

Much is gained by looking upon the behavior of the audience as full-blown problem solving. Such a viewpoint requires the assumption that people have more problems to solve than simply relating to other people and reducing their psychic tension, among them being the allocation and conservation of resources.

The necessity for taking explicit cognizance of the audience's intention was forced on us when we were studying Soviet refugees. We knew that virtually every Soviet citizen was regularly exposed to meetings at which were conveyed a certain amount of news, the party line on various issues, and general political agitation and indoctrination. In free discussion our respondents complained endlessly of the meetings so we knew they were there. But when we asked them, "From what sources did you draw most of your information about what was happening?" only 19 per cent specified them, in contrast to 87 per cent citing newspapers, 50 per cent citing radio, and another 50 per cent word of mouth (Inkeles & Bauer, 1959, p. 163). Gradually the obvious dawned on us; our respondents were telling us where they learned what *they* wanted to know, not where they learned what the regime wanted them to know.

A similar perplexity arose with respect to the use of word-of-mouth sources of information. It was the least anti-Soviet of our respondents who claimed to make most use of this unofficial fountain of information. Rereading the interviews, and further analysis, unraveled the puzzle. It was the people most involved in the regime, at least in the upper social groups, who were using word-of-mouth sources the better to understand the official media, and the better to do their jobs (Inkeles and Bauer, 1959, p. 161)! As a result we had to conduct analysis on two levels, one where we took into account the intentions of the regime, the other, the intentions of the citizen. Thus, viewed from the vantage point of the regime's intention, the widespread dependence upon word of mouth was a failure in communication. From the point of view of the citizen and what he wanted, his own behavior made eminent sense.

At the next stage, we benefited from the looseness of our methods, the importance of the people we were studying, and from highly imaginative colleagues from other disciplines. We were studying the processes of decision, communication, and the like, in the business and political community. As we studied "influence" by wandering around and getting acquainted with the parties of both camps, and kept track of what was going on, the notion of a one-way flow became preposterous. It also became clear that men in influential positions did a great deal to determine what sort of communication was directed toward them (Bauer, Pool, & Dexter, 1963). At this juncture, Ithiel de Sola Pool crystallized the proposition that the audience in effect influences the communicator by the role it forces on him. This idea became the organizing hypothesis behind the Zimmerman and Bauer (1956—this experiment was replicated by Schramm & Danielson) demonstration that individuals process new information as a function of their perceived relationship to future audiences. Specifically, they are less likely to remember information that would conflict with the audience's views than they are to remember information to which the audience would be hospitable.

The final crystallization of my present views began several years ago when a decision theorist and I together reviewed the studies by motivation researchers of the marketing of ethical drugs to doctors. Surprisingly, I found the level of motivation discussed in these reports quite trivial, but the reports provided perceptive cognitive maps of the physician's world and the way he went about handling risk. The now well-known studies of the adoption of drugs by Coleman, Menzel, and Katz (1959) contributed data consistent with the following point: physicians become increasingly selective in their choice of information as risk increases either because of the newness of the drug or difficulty in assessing its effects. Thereupon, a group of Harvard Business School students (in an unpublished manuscript) established by a questionnaire survey that as the seriousness of the disease increased, physicians were increasingly likely to prefer professional to commercial sources of information.

Why doesn't the physician always prefer professional to commercial sources of information? The physician is a busy man whose scarcest resources are time and energy, two things which commercial sources of information, on the whole, seem to help him conserve. Even so, he is selective. Let us assume two components in the choice of source of information: social compliance and the reduction of risk. Consider, then, that the doctor may be influenced by his liking either for the drug company's salesman who visits his office, or for the company itself. We may assume that, of these two components of influence, social compliance will be more associated with his sentiments toward the salesman and risk reduction with the company's reputation.

In a study conducted with the Schering Corporation (Bauer, 1961), I found that in the case of relatively riskless drugs, the correlation of preference for drugs with preference for salesman and for company was about equal. However, with more hazardous drugs—and with large numbers of subjects—preference for the company carried twice the weight of preference for the salesmen: the physicians selected the source closest associated with reduction of risk.

In the latest and fullest development of this point of view, Cox (1962) asked approximately 300 middle-class housewives to evaluate the relative merits of "two brands" of nylon stockings (Brand N & Brand R) as to overall merits and as to each of 18 attributes. After each rating the subject was asked to indicate how confident she was in making it. The subjects then listened to a tape-recorded interview with a supposed salesgirl who stated that Brand R was better as to six attributes, whereupon they were asked to judge the stockings again and to evaluate the salesgirl and their confidence in rating her. Finally, they completed a questionnaire which included three batteries of questions on personality, one of which was a measure of self-confidence.

The findings of interest here bear upon personality and persuasibility. Male subjects low in generalized self-confidence are generally the more persuasible. Females are more persuasible in general but on the whole this is not correlated with self-confidence or self-esteem.

The reigning hypotheses on the relationship of self-confidence to persuasibility have been based either on the concept of ego defense (Cohen, 1959) or social approval (Janis, 1954), and Cox chose to add *perceived self-confidence in accomplishing a task.* He was dealing, then, with two measures of self-confidence: generalized self-confidence, presumably an attribute of "personality"; and specific self-confidence, that is, perceived confidence in judging stockings.

It has been suggested that the reason that in women personality has not been found correlated with persuasibility is that the issues used in experiments have not been important to them. And importance may account for the strong relationship Cox found when he gave them the task of rating stockings. That he was testing middle-class housewives may be why the relationship was curvilinear. (That is to say, his subjects may have covered a wider range of self-confidence than might be found in the usual experimental groups.) Women with *medium* scores on the test of self-confidence were the most likely to alter their rating of the stockings in the direction recommended by the salesgirl; those scoring *either* high or low were less likely to accept her suggestion. As a matter of fact, countersuggestibility apparently crept in among the women low in self-confidence; those who rated lowest were almost three times as likely as the others to change in the *opposite* direction. Since these findings were replicated in three independent samples, ranging from 62 to 144 subjects, there is little reason to question them for this type of person and situation. The differences were both significant and big.

The curvilinear relationship was not anticipated and any explanation must, of course, be ad hoc. One might be that, faced with the difficult task of judging between two identical stockings and the salesgirl's flat assertion that one was better than the other, the women tacitly had to ask themselves two questions: Do I need help? Am I secure enough to accept help? Accordingly, the subjects most likely to accept the salesgirl's suggestion would be those with little enough self-confidence to want help, but still with enough to accept it. As an explanation, this is at least consistent with the curvilinear data and with the apparent countersuggestibility of the subjects with little self-confidence.

This explanation, however, should not apply to individuals confident of their ability to perform the task. And this turned out to be the case. Among the subjects confident they could perform the *specific* task, generalized self-confidence played little or no role. The usual notions of social compliance and ego defense were virtually entirely overriden by the subject's confidence in her handling of the task—a conclusion which is supported, no matter how the data are combined.

The virtue of Cox's data is that they enable us to relate the problem-solving dimensions of behavior to social relationships and ego defensive. It is interesting that—in this study—the more "psychological" processes come into play only at the point at which felt self-confidence in accomplishing the task falls below a critical point. Thus, tendency to accept the suggestions of the alleged salesgirl in Cox's experiment must be seen as a function of both ability to deal with the task and personality.

The difficulty of the task may either fortify or suppress the more "social-psychological" processes, depending on the specific circumstances. Thus, study of drug preference shows that as the task gets easier, the individual can indulge in the luxury of concurring with someone whom he likes, whereas when risk is great he has to concentrate on the risk-reducing potentialities of the source of information.

Thus the full-blown, problem-solving interpretation of the behavior of an audience in no sense rules out the problems with which students of communication have recently concerned themselves: ego defense and social adjustment. As a matter of fact, such problems seem explorable in a more profitable fashion if, simultaneously, attention is paid to the more overt tasks for which people use information. Yet, while there has been a consistent drift toward granting the audience more initiative, it cannot be said that the general literature on communication yet accords it a full range of intentions.

Of course, the audience is not wholly a free agent: it must select from what is offered. But even here, the audience has influence, since it is generally offered an array of communications to which it is believed it will be receptive. The process of social communication and of the flow of influence in general must be regarded as a transaction. "Transactionism," which has had a variety of meanings in psychology, is used here in the sense of an exchange of values between two or more parties; each gives in order to get.

The argument for using the transactional model for *scientific* purposes is that it opens the door more fully to exploring the intention and behavior of members of the audience and encourages inquiry into the influence of the audience on the communicator by specifically treating the process as a two-way passage. In addition to the influence of the audience on the communicator, there seems little doubt that influence also operates in the "reverse" direction. But the persistence of the one-way model of influence discourages the investigation of both directions of relationship. With amusing adroitness some writers have assimilated the original experiment of Zimmerman and Bauer to established concepts such as reference groups, thereby ignoring what we thought was the clear implication of a two-way flow of influence.

At our present state of knowledge there is much to be said for the transactional model's pragmatic effect on research, but at the same time it is the most plausible description of the process of communication as we know it. Yet there seems to be a tendency to assume that words such as "transaction," "reciprocity," and the like imply exact equality in each exchange, measured out precisely according to the value system and judgment of the observer. This is nonsense. Obviously there are inequities, and they will persist, whether we use our own value systems as observers or if we have perfect knowledge of the people we observe.

The rough balance of exchange is sufficiently equitable in the long run to keep *most* individuals in our society engaged in the transactional relations of communication and influence. But some "alienated" people absent themselves from the network of communication as do, also, many businessmen who have doubts about the money they spend on advertising. The alienation is by no means peculiar to one end of the chain of communication or influence.

This point of view may be taken as a defense of certain social institutions such as advertising and the mass media. There is a limited range of charges against which *impotence* may indeed be considered a defense. Once more, ironically, both the communicator and the critic have a vested interest in the exploitative model. From the point of view of the communicator, it is reassuring that he will receive *at least* a fair return for his efforts; to the critic, the exploitative model gratifies the sense of moral indignation.

REFERENCES

Bauer, R. A. *The new man in Soviet psychology*. Cambridge: Harvard Univ. Press, 1952.

Bauer, R. A. Risk handling in drug adoption: The role of company preference. *Publ. Opin. Quart.*, 1961, **25**, 546–559.

Bauer, R. A. The initiative of the audience. Paper read at New England Psychological Association, Boston, November 1962.

Bauer, R. A., Pool, I. de Sola, & Dexter, L. A. *American business and public policy*. New York: Atherton Press, 1963.

Berelson, B., What missing the newspaper means. In P. F. Lazarsfeld & F. N. Stanton (Eds.), *Communications research, 1948–1949*. New York: Harper, 1949. Pp. 111–129.

Bogart, L. Adult talk about newspaper comics. *Am. J. Sociol.*, 1955, **61**, 26–30.

Cohen, A. R. Some implications of self-esteem for social influence. In C. I. Hovland & I. L. Janis (Eds.), *Personality and persuasibility*. New Haven: Yale Univ. Press, 1959. Pp. 102–120.

Coleman, J., Menzel, H., & Katz, E. Social processes in physicians' adoption of a new drug. *J. Chron. Dis.*, 1959, **9**, 1–19.

Cox, D. F. Information and uncertainty: Their effects on consumers' product evaluations. Unpublished doctoral dissertation, Harvard University, Graduate School of Business Administration, 1962.

Davison, W. P. On the effects of communication. *Publ. Opin. Quart.*, 1959, **23**, 343–360.

Dexter, L. A., & White, D. M. (Eds.). *People, society and mass communication.* (Tentative title) Glencoe, Ill.: Free Press, in press.

Herzog, Herta. What do we really know about daytime serial listeners? In P. F. Lazarsfeld & F. N. Stanton (Eds.), *Radio research, 1942–1943.* New York: Duell, Sloan & Pearce, 1944. Pp. 3–33.

Hovland, C. I. Reconciling conflicting results derived from experimental survey studies of attitude change. *Am. Psychol.*, 1959, **14**, 8–17.

Hovland, C. I., Lumsdaine, A. A., & Sheffield, F. D. *Experiments in mass communication.* Princeton: Princeton Univ. Press, 1949.

Hyman, H. H., & Sheatsley, P. B. Some reasons why information campaigns fail. *Publ. Opin. Quart.*, 1947, **11**, 412–423.

Inkeles, A., & Bauer, R. A. *The Soviet citizen.* Cambridge: Harvard Univ. Press, 1959.

Janis, I. L. Personality correlates of susceptibility to persuasion. *J. Pers.*, 1954, **22**, 504–518.

Kimball, P. People without papers. *Publ. Opin. Quart.*, 1959, **23**, 389–398.

Klapper, J. *The effects of mass communication.* Glencoe, Ill.: Free Press, 1960.

Lazarsfeld, P. F., Berelson, B., & Gaudet, Hazel. *The people's choice.* New York: Columbia Univ. Press, 1948.

Maccoby, Eleanor E. Why do children watch T.V.? *Publ. Opin. Quart.*, 1954, **18**, 239–244.

Maccoby, N., & Maccoby, Eleanor E. Homostatic theory in attitude change. *Publ. Opin. Quart.*, 1961, **25**, 535–545.

Seidenfeld, M. A. Consumer psychology in public service and government. In R. W. Seaton (Chm.), Consumer psychology: The growth of a movement. Symposium presented at American Psychological Association, New York, September 1961.

Smith, B. L., Laswell, H. D., & Casey, R. D. *Propaganda, communication and public opinion.* Princeton: Princeton Univ. Press, 1946.

Warner, W. L., & Henry, W. E. The radio daytime serial: A symbolic analysis. *Genet. Psychol. Monogr.*, 1948, **37**, 3–71.

Winick, C. Teenagers, satire and *Mad. Merrill-Palmer Quart.,* 1962, **8**, 183–203.

Zimmerman, Claire, & Bauer, R. A. The effects of an audience on what is remembered. *Publ. Opin. Quart.*, 1956, **20**, 238–248.

8.2 RACE, STATUS, QUALITY OF SPOKEN ENGLISH, AND OPINIONS ABOUT CIVIL RIGHTS AS DETERMINANTS OF INTERPERSONAL ATTITUDES

Harry C. Triandis
Wallace D. Loh
Leslie Ann Levin

Recent studies of social distance have demonstrated that it is possible to obtain a number of lawful relationships between the characteristics of a person and the behavioral intentions and evaluations of this person by subjects. These judgments are largely determined by cultural factors (Triandis, 1964a; Triandis, Davis, & Takezawa, 1965; Triandis & Triandis, 1960, 1962). A multidimensional instrument which measures the behavioral component of attitudes, called the behavioral differential (Triandis, 1964b) may be used to measure the behavioral intentions toward the stimuli, while the semantic differential (Osgood, Suci, & Tannenbaum, 1957) may be used to measure the evaluation, potency, and perceived activity of the stimulus persons. With American subjects, race was found to be a powerful determinant of variance in social distance judgments; with Greek subjects religion was very important; with German and Japanese subjects occupation was the important determinant of variance.

The above-mentioned work has relied on questionnaires in which complex stimulus persons, such as a "Negro, Portuguese, Roman Catholic, Physician," were judged in connection with social distance items forming an equal-interval scale, standardized in the culture in which the study took place. More recently, similar stimuli were used with semantic differential and behavioral differential scales. Since stimuli presented as verbal descriptions may have limitations, it was decided that an approximation of real persons, having the abstract characteristics described in our questionnaires, would provide a test of the generality of previous findings.

Source: This research was supported by the National Science Foundation, in support of a program of Undergraduate Research Participation. Reprinted with slight abridgment from the *Journal of Personality and Social Psychology*, 1966, 3, 468–472, with permission of the senior author and the American Psychological Association, Inc., copyright holder.

METHOD

Subjects

All subjects were Caucasian, native-born Americans attending the 1964 summer school session at the University of Illinois. Fifty-six males and 38 females were tested. Eighty per cent of the subjects perceived themselves as belonging to the middle-class, 73 per cent came from urban environments, mostly from Illinois. Seventy-seven per cent were Christian, 6 per cent Jewish, and 17 per cent considered themselves nonreligious. When asked to describe their coloring, 42 per cent checked "light," 52 per cent "medium," and 6 per cent "dark."

Procedure

The stimuli employed in the experiment consisted of color slides of two young men with simultaneous presentation of a tape-recorded voice making a statement about civil rights. Sixteen combinations of stimulus characteristics, generated by a $2 \times 2 \times 2 \times 2$ factorial design, were employed in a fixed order after presentation of a warm-up and two anchoring pictures. The slides showed (*a*) a Negro or white man, who was (*b*) wearing a suit and carrying an attaché case or in overalls and carrying a lunch pail. The tape-recorded voices presented a message that was (*c*) either in favor or against integrated housing and (*d*) either in excellent English or in poor English. The verbal statements had been previously scaled by Davis and Triandis (1965) to represent extreme positions on the particular civil rights issue. Examples of the statements representing the two extremes in opinion and the two extremes in grammar are shown below. The actor who read the statements into the tape recorder attempted to employ an appropriate Negro or white accent, and a polished or a "poor" accent, depending on the combination of treatments involved in the particular condition.

1. The City Council should pass a law prohibiting discrimination on the basis of race, religion, or ethnic background in any and all housing.
2. Discrimination in housing is strictly a private affair and no action should be taken by the City Council or any other government body which would interfere with private property rights in any way.
3. Them guys in City Hall better pass a law that ain't gonna let nobody keep anybody out of a house they wanna live in.
4. Them guys in City Hall better not put their noses in with no law when a private homeowner wants to sell his house only to people like him.

For each of the stimulus conditions, after the slide and tape-recorded voice had been presented, the subjects responded to fifteen behavioral differential scales taken from the factor analysis of Triandis (1964b). In the analysis that follows only three of the factors will be employed: the admiration factor, determined by the subject judgments on the "would admire the character of this person" and "would admire the ideas of this person" scales; the social distance factor, determined by the judgments on "would exclude from the neighborhood" and "would not accept as a close kin by marriage"; and the friendship factor, determined from the subject judgments on the scales "would accept as an intimate friend" and "would eat with this person." The analysis of the responses to two semantic differential scales (good-bad, wise-foolish) will also be reported.

Two of the stimulus conditions were repeated to obtain an estimate of the reliability of these judgments. After the subjects completed responding to the stimulus slides and tape recordings, they completed a questionnaire in which a number of civil rights issues were judged against a set of evaluative semantic differential scales.

Analysis

A scalogram analysis of the responses of the subjects to the civil rights issues established five types of subjects. Type I is in favor of interracial marriages, sit-ins, and freedom marches, integrated housing, integrated schools, and is opposed to segregated schools. Type II is opposed to interracial marriages, but is otherwise like Type I. Type III is opposed to both interracial marriages and sit-ins, freedom marches, etc., but, is in favor of integrated housing and integrated schools and against segregated schools. Type IV is opposed to interracial marriages, sit-ins and freedom marches, and integrated housing, but is in favor of integrated schools. Finally, Type V is opposed to interracial marriages, sit-ins, freedom marches, and integrated housing or schools, and is in favor of segregated schools. Thus, the affective responses of the subjects form a Guttman scale, with interracial marriages as the most extremely favorable item, followed by sit-ins and freedom marches, followed by integrated housing, then by integrated schools, and finally by opposition to segregated schools. The data from these types of subjects were analyzed separately and a combined analysis was also performed.

Analyses were carried out separately for each of the four response continua employed in the present experiment (the admiration, social distance, friendship, and evaluation factors of the behavioral and semantic differentials). Analyses of variance were performed on the means of the responses of the subjects of a particular type, to the particular stimulus.

RESULTS

Reliability

The reliability of the judgments was obtained by repetition of two stimuli. The obtained reliabilities for the various factors ranged between Pearson *r*'s of .59 and .85.

Relative Importance of the Characteristics

Table 1 presents the summaries of the analyses of variance based on the sums of the responses of the 94 subjects. The data were also broken down by experimenter, by sex of the subject, by social class, and by religion of the subject. No systematic deviations from the results of Table 1 were obtained. An analysis of the responses of the six subjects who considered themselves to be dark showed a dramatic difference in social distance towards Negroes, as compared to the subjects who consider themselves to be of light or medium color. The dark subjects emphasized race about eight times less than did the others, while they emphasized the level of English about twice as much as the others. Because of the small number of dark subjects, these results must be considered as purely exploratory.

Table 2 shows the results of analyses of the subjects classified into each of the five attitude types, as per the Guttman scalogram analysis.

DISCUSSION

The results of the present study are consistent with previous research. Triandis, Fishbein, and Hall (1964) found high correlations between the admiration (social acceptance) factor of the behavioral differential and the evaluative factor of the semantic differential in person perception. The present results confirm this finding by showing that in the case of both of these factors the level of spoken English is by far the most important determinant and the belief is the next most important. The importance of English as a factor in person perception was also established in that previous study. Previous work (Triandis & Triandis, 1960, 1962) had shown that race is a most important determinant of the social distance factor among American subjects. Again, race and level of English are important in the present study. Friend-

Table 1 *Analysis of Variance of Complex Stimulus Persons Based on Composite Scores for Three Behavioral Differential and One Semantic Differential Factors* (N = *94*)

		Friendship			Evaluation			Admiration			Social Distance		
Source	*df*	*SS*	*F*	% Variance	*SS*	*F*	% Variance	*SS*	*F*	% Variance	*SS*	*F*	% Variance
Race (A)	1	32,761	29.7**	9.3	576	0.3	0.2	2,352	0.6	0.3	344,951	104.9**	57.0
Belief (B)	1	4,692	4.3	1.3	45,796	21.3**	12.8	106,276	26.6**	14.0	298	0.1	0.1
Dress (C)	1	8,464	7.7*	2.4	1,849	0.9	0.5	56	0.01	0.01	6,202	1.9	1.1
English (D)	1	277,202	251.5**	78.3	269,980	125.6**	75.4	566,256	141.7**	74.7	189,442	59.3**	31.2
B × C				0.2			0.4			1.9			0.4
B × A				0.2			1.9			1.0			0.8
B × D				1.7			3.3			2.1			0.01
C × D				0.1			0.2			0.03			0.01
C × A				0.01			0.3			0.8			4.8
A × D				1.2			0.6			0.01			
Σ interactions	11	12,124			23,703			43,955			35,137		

* $p < .05$.
** $p < .01$.

Table 2 *Percentage of Variance of Subject Types Classified by Position on the Civil Rights Issues as Determined by Scalogram Analysis*

Determinant	Social Distance			Admiration			Friendship			Evaluation		
	Liberal I and II	Moder-ate III	Preju-diced IV and V	Liberal I and II	Moder-ate III	Preju-diced IV and V	Liberal I and II	Moder-ate III	Preju-diced IV and V	Liberal I and II	Moder-ate III	Preju-diced IV and V
Race	21	54	80	0	0	7	0	13	55	0	0	3
English	59	31	15	43	81	22	78	80	33	58	76	57
Belief (opinion)	0	0	1	37	10	15	3	0	6	24	14	26
Dress	2	1	0	0	0	1	3	2	1	3	0	1

Note: Type I = 18, Type II = 31, Type III = 34, Type IV = 5, Type V = 6; total N = 94.

ship is mainly determined by the quality of English, then by race, and least by the dress of the stimulus person.

It is notable that each of the four stimulus characteristics employed in the present study had some influence in the determination of significant amounts of variance in one or another of the behavioral differential factors. Thus, the present findings confirm previous research which demonstrated that different aspects of the behavioral intentions of subjects towards stimulus persons are determined by different combinations of the characteristics of these stimulus persons.

The results of Table 2 are consistent with common-sense expectations. Race was a more important factor in the determination of the social distance of prejudiced than in the determination of the social distance judgments of unprejudiced subjects. In the case of admiration, English was the primary determinant for all subjects, but the weight given to it differed between the subgroups. Prejudiced subjects gave some weight to race and belief (opinion). In the case of friendship we find again the tolerant subjects giving no weight to race and the prejudiced giving a substantial weight to that characteristic as a determinant of their judgments.

These and similar previous findings suggest that studies of "prejudice" should examine the problem in greater detail. While race is an extremely important determinant of social distance, it is quite unimportant as a determinant of admiration, at least for our subjects. Thus, while most of our subjects are willing to admire the ideas of a qualified Negro, many of the same subjects are not willing to accept him in their neighborhood.

To understand prejudice in its full complexity, it is necessary to think of a matrix the rows of which are defined by various "undesirable" characteristics. In addition to those examined in the present study, we have asked subjects to respond to stimulus persons who differed from them in religion, age, sex, nationality, competence in doing a job, degree of sociability, etc. We presented stimulus persons with physical disabilities (e.g., deaf), with "a prison record," with different shades of skin color, etc. On the column side of this analysis, we examined behaviors such as "would not admire the ideas of," "would not marry," "would not accept as an intimate friend," "would treat as a subordinate," "would exclude from the neighborhood," and "would not hire" (Rickard, Triandis, & Patterson, 1963; Triandis, 1963). When all of the information collected in these studies is placed together, it becomes clear that the classes of behavioral intentions mentioned above are distinct, and influenced by different combinations of "undesirable" characteristics. "Admire the ideas of" is most sensitive to characteristics indicative of status—for example, kind of English spoken, occupation—and also to the opinions of the stimulus persons; marital acceptance is sensitive to English, but also to race and age; friendship acceptance is sensitive to age, sex, religion, English, race, dress, and skin color; subordination is likely when the stimulus person is of a high status occupation; exclusion from the neighborhood is primarily sensitive to race and English, and slightly to religion; acceptance as an employee is primarily sensitive to competence and disability, and secondarily to race and sociability.

In dealing with this problem it is necessary to face the enormously difficult task of separating valid from invalid cues. It might be argued that when a person speaks ungrammatical English this is a valid cue that the college student subject would not be likely to experience much satisfaction if he were to establish a friendship with such a person. (Or is this snobbery?) On the other hand, when he sees a Negro and he comes to the same conclusion, it might be argued that he is making an incorrect inference, hence, the designation prejudiced. However, to argue that the subject is making an incorrect inference implies that the social scientist knows the ecological validity (Brunswik, 1947) of the cue, in connection with each of the behaviors in question. In fact, the scientist usually does not know these validities. A new approach to the study of prejudice would require the prior study of the ecological validities of each of the supposedly undesirable personal characteristics, for each of the classes of behavior under investigation. Subsequently, an examination of the weights given by a subject to these characteristics of stimulus persons may lead to a comparison with the ecological validities of the cues. Large discrepancies between the value of the validity coefficients for each cue, and the weights given by the subject would lead to the conclusion that the subject is prejudiced about a particular characteristic in connection with the particular class of behaviors. Thus, each cell in the matrix described above, would potentially define one kind of prejudice. A highly prejudiced person would most likely be found to be prejudiced in a large number of these cells, while other individuals might have only certain "blind spots." To begin such a research effort it would be necessary to develop criteria of "effective behavior" and "satisfaction with own behavior," which would permit the determination of the ecological validities required by the research program. This approach would involve a reorientation of present research on prejudice, but it would place such research in the center of the fundamental problems of social psychology.

SUMMARY

Ninety-four *S*s were shown slides of either a Negro or a white young man, who was either well dressed or poorly dressed and simultaneously heard a tape-recorded statement which was either in favor or opposed to integrated housing and which was spoken either in excellent or in ungrammatical English. The stimuli formed a $2 \times 2 \times 2 \times 2$ factorial design. The evaluation of the stimulus person was measured by the evaluative factor of the semantic differential; the behavioral intentions of *S*s toward the stimulus persons were measured by three factors of the behavioral differential. It was shown that liberal *S*s differed from nonliberal *S*s in the relative weights they employed for the characteristics race, dress, English, and opinion. Furthermore, English and opinion were the determinants of the evaluation judgments, as well as the social acceptance judgments on the behavioral differential. Race and English were the important determinants of the judgments on the social distance factor. English, race, and dress, in that order, were important in the determination of the judgments on the friendship factor.

REFERENCES

Brunswik, E. *Systematic and representational design of psychological experiments.* Berkeley: Univ. California Press, 1947.

Davis, E. E., & Triandis, H. C. An exploratory study of intercultural negotiations. Technical Report No. 26, 1965, University of Illinois, ONR Contract Nr 177–472, Nonr-1834 (36), Office of Naval Research.

Osgood, C. E., Suci, G. J., & Tannenbaum, P. H. *The measurement of meaning.* Urbana: Univ. of Illinois Press, 1957.

Rickard, T. E., Triandis, H. C., & Patterson, C. H. Indices of employer prejudice toward disabled applicants. *J. Appl. Psychol.*, 1963, **47**, 52–55.

Triandis, H. C. Factors affecting employee selection in two cultures. *J. Appl. Psychol.*, 1963, **47**, 89–96.

Triandis, H. C. Cultural influences upon cognitive processess. In L. Berkowitz (Ed.), *Advances in experimental social psychology.* New York: Academic Press, 1964. Pp. 1–48. (a)

Triandis, H. C. Exploratory factor analyses of the behavioral component of social attitudes. *J. Abnorm. Soc. Psychol.*, 1964, **68**, 420–430. (b)

Triandis, H. C., Davis, E. E., & Takezawa, S.-I. Some determinants of social distance among American, German, and Japanese students. *J. Pers. Soc. Psychol.*, 1965, **2**, 540–551.

Triandis, H. C., Fishbein, M., & Hall, Eleanor R. Person perception among American and Indian students. Technical Report No. 15, 1964, University of Illinois, Contract Nr 177-472, Nonr-1834 (36), Office of Naval Research.

Triandis, H. C., & Triandis, Leigh M. Race, social class, religion, and nationality as determinants of social distance. *J. Abnorm. Soc. Psychol.*, 1960, **61**, 110–118.

Triandis, H. C., & Triandis, Leigh M. A cross-cultural study of social distance. *Psychol. Monogr.*, 1962, **76**(21, Whole No. 540).

8.3 USE OF THE SEMANTIC DIFFERENTIAL TO STUDY ACCULTURATION IN AMERICAN INDIAN ADOLESCENTS

Malcolm M. Helper
Sol L. Garfield

Past research on values and value conflicts in the American Indian has relied largely on projective methods and open-ended questionnaires (Macgregor, 1946). While these methods have yielded important results, they often involve subjective judgments, which can be unreliable, and difficult to replicate. The present study represents an attempt to apply the technique of the semantic differential to the question of the assimilation of values by adolescent Indians. This technique is objective and has the advantage of relating research in this area to a broader body of psychological theory and research.

While the semantic differential has been used to compare the values of one cultural group with those of another (Maclay & Ware, 1961; Osgood, 1960; Rosen, 1959; Triandis & Osgood, 1958), it apparently has not been applied in the situation in which the value systems of two cultures impinge upon the same individual. In the present study, the semantic differential technique was used to compare values of American Indian and white adolescents, and within the Indian group, to determine whether semantic differences can be detected between those showing high and low acculturation by another criterion (academic achievement).

Source: This study was supported by a mental-health research grant from the U.S. Public Health Service. Reprinted with slight abridgment from the *Journal of Personality and Social Psychology*, 1965, **2**, 817–822, with permission of the authors and the American Psychological Association, Inc.

METHOD

The method used consisted of three steps: (*a*) Determining the number and nature of differences between Indian and white groups on a semantic differential designed to tap the connotative meaning of concepts related to distinctive values of both groups. (*b*) Within the Indian group, determining the differences on the instrument between subgroups showing high and low acculturation by the achieving criterion. (*c*) Assessing the direction of these semantic differences to determine if the groups with high academic acculturation tend to be more like the whites semantically than the low academic acculturation groups.

Subjects

American Indian: The freshman and senior classes of the Flandreau Indian School (FIS) located in Flandreau, South Dakota, provided data for the study. FIS is a boarding school serving eighteen reservations in North and South Dakota, Nebraska, Wyoming, and Montana, and includes individuals from various Plains Indian groups. Students are sent to FIS for a variety of reasons, including educational needs which cannot be met in the local reservation schools, family instability, and adjustment problems of the individual. More than one factor may be operative in a given case. The aim of the school is to provide a basic high-school education, plus opportunities for acquiring vocational skills. In this study, the entire freshman and senior classes were tested, resulting in a sample of 101 boys and 131 girls.

Whites: The public high school in the town near which FIS is located provided the white subjects. Freshman and senior classes were again involved in their entirety, resulting in 62 boys and 61 girls. Students of Indian extraction in these classes filled out the questionnaires, but these were not included in the analyses.

Semantic Differential

Ten scales were used, three for each of the three major factors found in previous studies (Osgood, Suci, & Tannenbaum, 1957) plus an additional scale included on a trial basis. The scales, listed according to the factor represented, were as follows: Evaluation—happy-sad, fair-unfair, bad-good; Potency—weak-strong, hard-soft, manly-womanly; and Activity—fast-slow, cold-hot, dull-sharp. The experimental scale was like me-not like me. It will not be reported in this paper since it was not used in deriving any of the factor scores.

The fifteen concepts included are listed below, together with comments regarding the rationale for their selection.

Race labels: INDIAN and WHITE PERSON were included to determine whether the technique would show differences in attitudes toward ethnic group membership.

Time concepts: THE FUTURE, BEING ON TIME, and PLANNING AHEAD were included because it was felt that concern about scheduling and about the future were hallmarks of the dominant culture, and much less important in the Indian culture (Macgregor, 1946).

Self-concepts: ME and ME AS I WANT TO BE were used to determine if the technique might be useful in detecting self-depreciation or other features of attitudes toward the self that have been hypothesized to accompany acculturation (Hartley & Hartley, 1952).

Parent concepts: MY MOTHER and MY FATHER were included because attitudes toward parents are thought to be influenced by the acceptance of a different value system. GOING HOME was intended to represent a somewhat indirect check on attitudes toward parents and the reservation culture among the Indians.

School-related concepts: FLANDREAU SCHOOL and QUITTING SCHOOL were included as a possible means of tapping attitudes toward the school, considered to be a major agent of acculturation.

Specific behaviors: DRINKING, SPEAKING ENGLISH, and GETTING MAD were included because it was thought, on the basis of initial contacts with personnel of the Indian school, that they would have different connotations in the two groups.

The concepts were presented two to a page in eight-page, multilithed, booklets, each concept being followed by the ten scales in the following format:

THE FUTURE

fast____:____:____:____:____:____:____slow
weak____:____:____:____:____:____:____strong
etc.

The concepts were presented in the same order for all subjects. The scales were presented in the same order for each concept, in the following order and left-right orientations: fast-slow, weak-strong, happy-sad, hard-soft, fair-unfair, cold-hot, like me-not like me, bad-good, manly-womanly, dull-sharp.

Testing was done in a regular classroom with no more than 35 subjects in each group. Oral instructions and blackboard demonstrations were given to supplement printed directions. The experimenter introduced the study as part of a larger project aimed at uncovering how high-school students viewed various ideas, with special consideration of differences between freshmen and seniors. At no time were Indian-white comparisons mentioned to either set of subjects.

Independent Measure of Acculturation

Study of acculturation within the Indian group requires an independent measure of acceptance of white culture by the Indian subjects. It was concluded that the academic achievement test scores already available on these subjects would be appropriate. Acquisition of formal academic skills and knowledge, which are almost totally foreign to historic Indian culture, would seem to represent one crucial aspect of acculturation. As noted below, the scores of the Indian subjects on the test used were well below white norms, suggesting that factors other than basic learning ability are important in the Indian scores. These other factors would presumably include amount of formal or informal exposure to white culture, and attitudes toward accepting it.

The scores available were on the Iowa Test of Educational Development, Form X3-CP. The percentile value of the Composite score on this test was used. The median percentile for the freshmen students was 32, and for the senior students, 22. Only five subjects in the entire Indian group scored above the seventieth percentile. This underachievement relative to white standards is similar to that found in other culturally deprived minority groups (Kennedy, Van DeRiet, & White, 1963).

RESULTS

Invalid Responses

For each subject, the ten ratings on each concept were scanned (via a computer program) for omissions and for stereotyped response patterns. A subject's ratings on a given concept were considered invalid and were discarded from further analysis if they had any of the following characteristics: one or more blank scales; eight or more identical responses; a pattern of strict alternation of extremes for all ten responses. By these criteria, 9.2 per cent of all concepts rated by Indian subjects were invalid, as compared to 4.1 per cent of those rated by white subjects. WHITE PERSON had the greatest proportion of invalid responses in both groups, 19 per cent among Indians, 13 per cent among whites. DRINKING was second for Indians (16%), while INDIAN was second for whites (11%), ME AS I WANT TO BE had a minimal number of invalid response patterns in both groups, 5 per cent for Indians, 1 per cent for whites.

Independence of Factors

For each race, mean scores on the three factors were computed for each concept for each sex separately. Within each group, rank-order correlations were computed among the three factors over the concept means in order to determine the extent of similarity between the factor scores. In each group, the correlations between concept rankings on the Evaluation and Activity factors proved to be higher than the other two correlations. In three of the four groups, this correlation was over .90 (the value in the fourth group, white boys, was .76). Potency was largely independent of the other two factors in girls of both races (rho's ranging from .12 to .30), but was significantly related to them in boys of both races (rho's ranging from .45 to .79). It thus appears that the three factors tap very similar dimensions in this sample of subjects and concepts, except for the differentiation of the Potency factor from the other two by girls.

Comparison of Indians and Whites

Examination of the grand means for the three factors (over the 15 concepts) indicated differences between the racial groups in the use of the rating scales. Indian boys had higher overall means on all three factors than white boys, the discrepancy ranging from .24 scale unit for Evaluation to .10 for Activity. Furthermore, comparison of the means occupying each rank for Indian and white boys indicated that the tendency toward higher means for Indians occurred at all levels, and did not arise from higher ratings by them on just a few concepts. Constant differences of the magnitude observed would have a significant impact on the results of t tests, since the standard error of most of the means involved falls between .10 and .20 scale unit. For girls, the greatest difference on overall means (.13 scale unit) was found for Activity and was in the opposite direction from that for boys.

Because of the apparent differences in response habits, Indians and whites were not compared on concept means directly, but rather with respect to the relative ranks occupied by the concepts. Table 1 presents the rankings of the concepts on the three factors by Indian and white groups of each sex. A rank of 1 indicates the highest mean; a rank of 15, the lowest.

The general level of agreement between Indians and whites, as indicated by the rho's in Table 1, is high. Except for boys on the Activity score, all of the correlations reach the .01 level. The significance of between-group differences in the ranks of individual concepts was not evaluated statistically because of the apparent lack of appropriate tests for this kind of data. However, the consistency of these discrepancies in the two sex groups give some assurance as to their reality. Eighteen instances were found in which an Indian-white difference of two ranks or more occurred on the same concept and factor for both sexes. In fifteen of these, the direction of differences was the same for the two sexes, significantly in excess of the nine expected by chance ($\chi^2 = 6.72$, $p < .01$).

Comparison of High- and Low-Achieving Indians

The median achievement score was determined for each sex in each school class. Those above the median in each group were considered to be high achievers (highs), and those below were considered to be low achievers (lows). Freshman and senior highs were pooled within each sex, as were freshmen and senior lows. Highs and lows showed differences in response pattern which paralleled those between the Indian group as a whole and the white group. Low boys had overall means which exceeded those of high boys by .38, .10, and .21 scale unit on the three factors. On each factor, the high boys have the response pattern more similar to that of white boys. The low girls among the Indians showed a positive bias of .12 scale unit (as compared to the highs) on Evaluation, but a negative bias on Potency and Activity. The high girls were thus the more like white girls on the Evaluation and Activity factors, while the lows had the greater similarity to whites on Potency.

Concepts were ranked for the highs and lows just as they were for the white versus Indian comparisons in Table 1. Table 2 lists these rankings.

As one approach to the hypothesis that highs are more similar to whites than lows, the concept rankings of highs and lows were each correlated with the rankings from the appropriate white criterion group. These correlations, shown in Table 2, indicate, as expected, closer agreement in each case between the highs and the white norms than between the lows and the white norms. The differences are not large, but it should be noted that they are markedly restricted by the high similarity of the high and low Indian groups to each other, as indicated by the low versus high rho's in Table 2. In other words,

Table 1 *Rankings of Concepts on Three Factors by Whites and Indians*

	Boys						Girls					
	Evaluation		Potency		Activity		Evaluation		Potency		Activity	
Concept	White	Indian	White	Indian	White	Indian	White	Indian	White	Indian	White	Indian
1. The future	9	11	3.5	6	6	10	7	7	5	4	7	6
2. My father	7	9	2	3	8	8	6	10	1	1	4	7
3. Flandreau school	12	8	13	10	14	11	12	8	9	3	13	10
4. Going home	5	2	11	7	10	3	8	2	11	6	11	4.5
5. Drinking	13	13	12	13	13	14	13	13	10	12	14	14
6. White person	10	12	7	12	5	12	10	12	3	11	8	13
7. Quitting school	15	15	15	15	15	15	15	15	14	13	15	15
8. Me	6	7	3.5	4	3	6	9	9	15	15	9	9
9. Being on time	4	10	8	9	2	9	5	11	4	8.5	6	11
10. My mother	3	3	14	14	4	7	4	3	13	14	2	3
11. Indian	11	6	6	2	7	2	11	5	2	2	10	2
12. Speaking English	8	5	10	8	11	4	2	4	7	10	3	4.5
13. Me as I want to be	1	1	1	1	1	1	1	1	12	8.5	1	1
14. Getting mad	14	14	9	11	12	13	14	14	8	7	12	12
15. Planning ahead	2	4	5	5	9	5	3	6	6	5	5	8
Rho (White versus Indian)	.80		.85		.50		.72		.69		.66	

Table 2 *Rankings of Concepts on Three Factors by Low- and High-Achieving Indians*

	Boys[a]						Girls[a]					
	Evaluation		Potency		Activity		Evaluation		Potency		Activity	
Concept	Low	High	Low	High	Low	High	Low	High	Low	High	Low	High
1. Future	11	10	3	6	11	10	8	7	7	4	5	8
2. My father	5	11	4	3	4	8	10	10	1	1	7	7
3. Flandreau school	7	9	7	10	7	11	7	9	3	5	9	11
4. Going home	1	4	8	8	3	4	6	2	5	8	4	4
5. Drinking	13	13	13	13	14	14	13	14	14	11	14	14
6. White person	12	12	12	12	12	12	12	12	11	13	12.5	13
7. Quitting school	15	15	15	15	15	15	15	15	13	14	15	15
8. Me	9	7	5	4	10	7	5	8	15	12	8	10
9. Being on time	10	6	9	9	9	9	11	11	12	6	11	9
10. My mother	3	5	14	14	6	6	2	3	8.5	15	3	3
11. Indian	4	8	2	2	2	5	4	5	2	2	2	5
12. Speaking English	8	2	11	7	8	2	3	4	10	7	6	2
13. Me as I want to be	2	1	1	1	1	1	1	1	4	9	1	1
14. Getting mad	14	14	10	11	13	13	14	13	6	10	12.5	12
15. Planning ahead	6	3	6	5	5	3	9	6	8.5	3	10	6
Rho (Low versus High)	.76		.93		.84		.92		.64		.89	
Rho (Low and High versus White criterion)	.71	.85	.83	.86	.39	.46	.64	.73	.43	.71	.60	.78

[a] *N*s were variable from concept to concept because of the screening for invalid response patterns. Ranges of *N* were as follows: low boys, 34–39; high boys, 39–47; low girls, 33–43; high girls, 44–58.

the relatively few differences which do occur between the high and low Indian groups tend rather consistently to put the high group closer to the white norms. This can be studied more directly by noting, for each difference between highs and lows, which of the two groups stands in the same relation to the total Indian group as does the white group. In the 27 instances in which whites differ from Indians by two or more ranks and the high Indians also differ from low Indians by this amount, the high group is found to parallel the whites in 21 instances, while the lows do so in only 6. On the assumption that each of these differences could have gone either way by chance alone, the chi-square value for the observed distribution is 7.26, significant at the .01 level.

High-achieving Indians thus appear to be more like whites than do low-achieving Indians, both with respect to response bias and with respect to the ranking of value-related concepts on semantic factors.

DISCUSSION

Perhaps the first lesson to be learned from the present study is that response sets can differ in different cultural groups, and can seriously affect the interpretation of questionnaire data. The data also suggest that the response biases themselves may be susceptible to the influences of acculturation.

A second methodological point is that semantic ratings of these value-oriented concepts are highly saturated with the evaluative factor. Concept rankings on Evaluation and Activity are highly correlated in all groups, and these two rankings are each significantly correlated with Potency rankings in boys. Girls apparently differentiate Potency from the other two factors most markedly in rating self, ideal, and mother concepts, all of which are seen as weak but good.

The present study indicates, thirdly, that semantic ratings can provide evidence of both similarities and differences between a dominant culture and different subgroups of a minority population. In the present study, the similarity is evidenced by the high correlations between rankings of concepts by whites and by Indians. The concepts which produce the most agreement between the groups, and also between high- and low-achieving Indian subgroups, are concepts which are seen very negatively (DRINKING, QUITTING SCHOOL) or very positively (ME AS I WANT TO BE). To what extent acculturation is a factor in this similarity is not, however, revealed by the present methodology.

The evidence for differences between groups appears in their consistent difference in ranking of certain of the concepts. A major problem introduced by the discovery of response biases, is, of course, the lack of significance tests for differences between ratings of individual concepts by different groups. Nonetheless, the Indian-white differences tend to be replicated in the two sex groups. More importantly, differences between Indians high and low on a measure of acculturation tend to parallel in direction those between whites and Indians. This finding indicates that both kinds of differences are meaningful rather than accidental.

This apparent displacement of high achievers, as compared with low achievers, toward white norms also is in line with the initial hypothesis of the study, and suggests that semantic ratings offer a useful means of assessing the relative acculturation of subgroups of minority populations.

In addition to providing a general picture of similarity and difference between groups, semantic data may help elucidate attitude patterns around topics of specific relevance to the process of acculturation. In the present study, the results for INDIAN and WHITE PERSON suggest potentially important differences in attitudes toward group membership. The data in Table 1 indicate that each race rates its own label more positively than the other group does. It can also be noted that Indians rank INDIAN higher than whites rank WHITE PERSON in every instance. Comparisons within each racial group shows that Indians differentiate the two concepts on each factor to a much greater extent than whites do. Furthermore, the race labels stand in a different relationship to self and ideal concepts in the two racial groups. For Indians, INDIAN is closer than ME to ME AS I WANT TO BE in five of six comparisons; for whites, the reverse is true—ME is closer to the ideal than is WHITE PERSON in five of six comparisons. Indians thus appear to see their racial group as more valuable than themselves as individuals, while whites tend to see their racial group as less valuable than themselves as individuals. This tendency to elevate race over self appears slightly reduced in high boys, who rate ME somewhat higher and INDIAN somewhat lower on the evaluative factors than do low boys, but appears to be about equal in high and low girls. These results suggest that the concept INDIAN is more highly salient and more highly valued in Indian youth than WHITE PERSON is in whites. This conclusion stands in contrast to certain previous research which has indicated very substantial devaluations of their own group by members of disadvantaged minorities (Clark, 1963; Macgregor, 1946). This difference may indicate only that semantic ratings tap more superficial, defensive attitudes and fail to reveal more deep-seated negative feelings; or it may be a function of the specific groups studied. In any event, the method appears to generate rather clear-cut contrasts in attitudes toward racial group membership.

SUMMARY

Two hundred and thirty-two Indian adolescents in an Indian boarding school and 123 white adolescents in a community high school rated concepts referred to values thought to be distinctive in the two groups. Academic achievement test scores were used as an independent measure of acculturation within the Indian group. Indians and whites, and high- and low-achieving Indians, differed in response biases. Indians and whites were found to be highly similar on overall rank ordering of the concepts, as were high- and low-achieving Indians. Nonetheless, apparently consistent differences were noted between the races for certain concepts. Such differences were also noted between high- and low-achieving Indians. Most of these latter differences put the high achievers closer to white norms than the low achievers. With appropriate precautions against response bias, the semantic differential appears potentially useful in studying acculturation and attitudes toward ethnic group membership.

REFERENCES

Clark, K. B. *Prejudice and your child,* 2nd ed. Boston: Beacon Press, 1963.

Hartley, E. L., & Hartley, R. E. *Fundamentals of social psychology.* New York: Knopf, 1952.

Kennedy, W. A., Van DeRiet, V., & White, J. C., Jr. A normative sample of intelligence and achievement of Negro elementary school children in the southeastern United States. *Monogr. Soc. Res. Child Develpm.,* 1963, 28(6, Ser. No. 90).

Macgregor, G. *Warriors without weapons.* Chicago: Univ. of Chicago Press, 1946.

Maclay, H., & Ware, E. E. Cross-cultural use of the semantic differential. *Behav. Sci.,* 1961, **6,** 185–190.

Osgood, C. E. The cross-cultural generality of visual-verbal synesthetic tendencies. *Behav. Sci.,* 1960, **5,** 146–169.

Osgood, C. E., Suci, G. J., & Tannenbaum, P. H. *The measurement of meaning.* Urbana: Univ. of Illinois Press, 1957.

Rosen, E. A cross-cultural study of semantic profiles and attitude differences: Italy. *J. Soc. Psychol.,* 1959, **48,** 137–144.

Triandis, H. C., & Osgood, C. E. A comparative factor analysis of semantic structures in monolingual Greek and American college students. *J. Abnorm. Soc. Psychol.,* 1958, **57,** 187–196.

§ 9 GROUP PROCESSES

The seven papers in this section show what happens to the behavior of groups and their members when the following variables are manipulated: stability of membership, clarity of member roles, competition, and the extent to which responsibility is shared by members. Although these are only a sampling of the kinds of variables that may affect group behavior, they do relate to conditions that are likely to occur at some time or other in the history of almost any group.

The experiment by Moses H. Goldberg and Eleanor E. Maccoby shows that children have difficulty with tasks requiring cooperation when the composition of groups is changed at frequent intervals. In such groups, the more able children tend to dominate the less able.

The study conducted by Ewart E. Smith shows that the presence of nonparticipating members interferes with the productivity and satisfaction of other group members. This effect was particularly pronounced when members had not been notified that the nonparticipants would remain silent.

The research by Robert E. Dunn and Morton Goldman is concerned with the effect that competition and assigning rewards on individual or group merit have on members' attitudes. They report a tendency for the highest degree of satisfaction to be achieved when members share equally in rewards and are not required to compete with other groups. Competition appears to lower the members' acceptance of one another, as well as of members of competing groups.

Research by Julian, Bishop, and Fiedler with Army combat engineers, however, puts intergroup competition in a more favorable light. They report that such competition improved the morale and personal adjustment of members of companies of Army combat engineers. After reading these two studies, the reader is encouraged to develop hypotheses that may explain the contradictions between the results of this study and that of Dunn and Goldman.

Cooperation and competition are also the theme of the experiment conducted by McClintock, Gallo, and Harrison. This study took place within the context of a two-person, nonzero-sum game, of a type known as the Prisoner's Dilemma. The antagonists in this experiment were subjects whose test scores had revealed them as being markedly internationalist or isolationist. Although common sense might lead one to expect that internationalists generally would use cooperative strategies in such a game, results indicated the contrary. Differences did appear, however, in the behavior of the two types of subjects.

The paper by Roby, Nicol, and Farrell reports the results of research conducted with two types of group organization in which the power to make decisions was either centralized in one member or shared by all members (decentralized). Results showed that each type of organization had its advantages, with coordination of members' actions being accomplished more efficiently under centralized conditions, accommodation to environmental changes being done more efficiently under centralized conditions, and accommodation to environmental changes being carried out more effectively with decentralized structures.

Salomon Rettig contributes the final paper in this section. His research deals with the commonly observed tendency of people to try things in groups which they are unlikely to undertake on their own. His findings show that group discussion does facilitate risk taking, but just why this occurs is not clear. Rettig believes that group discussion reduces anticipated censure (or anxiety) by giving members a chance to test the approval or disapproval of the rest of the group with respect to proposed actions.

9.1 CHILDREN'S ACQUISITION OF SKILL IN PERFORMING A GROUP TASK UNDER TWO CONDITIONS OF GROUP FORMATION

Moses H. Goldberg
Eleanor E. Maccoby

The present study deals with the individual's ability to maximize his own gains in a situation requiring cooperation with others for the achievement of individual goals. Our experiment grows out of the classic earlier work of Mintz (1951), who used a situation in which several individuals had to pull cones out of a single narrow-necked jar. "Traffic jams" usually developed at the neck of the jar, so that none of the participants could get their cones out, when rewards and punishments were administered to each individual on the basis of his own time score. When *groups* of participants received a single score based on the total time for all the cones to be withdrawn from the jar, however, there was efficient cooperative performance. The group worked out a strategy of taking turns and cones were withdrawn smoothly in a relatively short time.

We are interested in the situation of individual rewards and punishments—the situation which resulted in failure for most participants in Mintz' experiment. We assume that even in situations where individuals are motivated to maximize their own gains, they do ultimately acquire the ability to work out cooperative strategies if their individual success depends upon their doing so. We expect that if a game similar to that employed by Mintz is continued over a series of trials, it will be possible to chart the development of these cooperative strategies. We wished to discover how efficiently a group would perform on such a task if, although the group had not previously worked together, they had all previously worked with other groups on the task and thus had an opportunity to acquire certain skills in getting and maintaining group cooperation.

Specifically, we wished to discover whether the acquisition of such skill would be facilitated or hindered by constantly changing group membership during the initial phases of experience with the task. It

Source: Reprinted from the *Journal of Personality and Social Psychology*, 1965, 2, 898–902, with permission of Dr. Maccoby and the American Psychological Association, Inc., copyright holder.

could be argued that if an individual is to be brought together with a group of strangers to work with them on an individual-reward task with which all are familiar, successful group performance will be most likely if the individuals involved have all had fairly extensive previous experience in adapting themselves to a variety of partners. Individuals who had previously worked on the task in the company of only one fixed set of partners would presumably be at a disadvantage in interacting with a group of strangers, having had exposure to a lesser range of other individuals to whom they would have had to learn to adapt their own behavior. Putting the issue in terms of acquisition of roles, the individual who has worked in several different groups, composed of a variety of other personalities, will have had experience in taking a variety of roles; a stable group, by contrast, which does not change personnel during the series of training trials, should develop a set of stable role relationships and the members of such groups may find that the role they have acquired does not transfer easily to a new group setting.

Our hypothesis is: when tested with a group of strangers on a task requiring group cooperation for achievement of individual goals, the individuals who will be most successful will be the ones who have had previous experience in groups of changing composition; those least successful will be those whose previous experience had been with a single unchanging group.

METHOD

Design

Changing Groups: Groups of children performed a cooperative task for eight consecutive trials—the "training period." After each pair of trials, the composition of the groups was changed, so that each of the subjects in these groups worked with four different sets of co-workers during the training trials. The subjects were reassorted once more, after which they performed the task eight more times (test trials) without further shuffling of group membership.

Stable Groups: Subjects assigned to this condition had their eight training trials with the same group of co-workers. They were then shifted to new groups, and performed eight test trials. (See Figure 1.)

Subjects

The subjects were 64 second-grade children, 32 boys and 32 girls, from two schools in Palo Alto, California. Four groups of 16 were

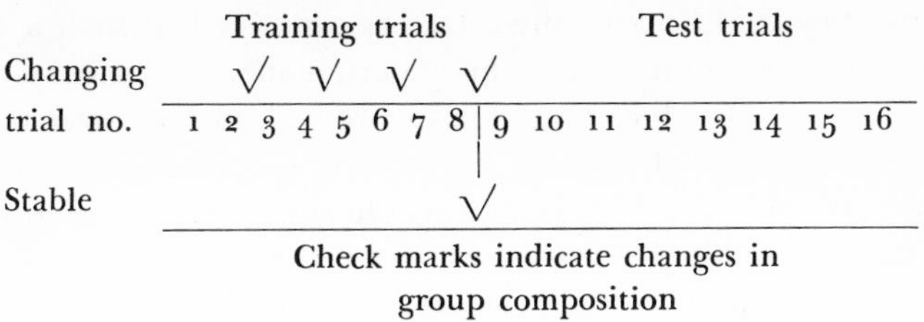

Figure 1. Points at which membership changes were made in the two types of groups.

used, and from these pools of 16, four subgroups of four children each were formed. The groups were then designated as follows: 16 boys, stable-membership condition (SB); 16 girls, stable-membership condition (SG); 16 boys, changing-membership condition (CB); 16 girls, changing-membership condition (CG). Groups CG and SB were from one school, SG and CB from the other. An attempt was made to form groups from children who knew each other as little as possible. Cases were randomly assigned to the two conditions.

Procedure

We wished to devise a task which would meet the following criteria:

1. It must require close group cooperation for successful performance, with an uncooperative member able to jeopardize the group's success.

2. It must permit individual differences in performance, and permit reward to be given to the individual on the basis of his own performance, independent of the total group achievement.

3. It should provide a range of scores, rather than simply a "pass" or "fail" score.

We chose a tower-building task, in which the group of four children working together had to build a single tower of blocks, and build it as high as they could within the 15-second time period allowed for each trial. Each child was given a pile of eight 3-inch blocks of a distinctive color, and his score at the end of the trial was the number of his own blocks that were on the jointly built tower when time was called. No two children could place blocks at the same moment. Even with perfect cooperation (e.g., regularly taking turns placing a block) it was not possible for all the children to place all their blocks. The time allotted was too short, and there was an upper limit to the height of the tower due to the height of the children and the stability of the structure they could build; these factors combined in such a way that the highest tower built during the experiment was 19 blocks. An individual child could reduce everyone's score by knocking over the tower, through carelessness, deliberate negativism, or overzealous addition of blocks to an already wobbly structure. On this task, the potential range of scores for individual children was 0–8 on each trial.

The experimental setting consisted of a large multipurpose room located at the respective schools. Four "stations" were established in the four corners of the room, and a judge was assigned to each station, the senior author serving as coordinator and timer. Also placed at each station was a set of 32 3-inch cubes, 8 each of green, yellow, blue, and red. The 16 children who were to participate in the session were then assembled in the center of the room and the following instructions were read:

> This morning we are going to play a little game—and if you listen carefully and follow the rules, you can win some prizes. Does everybody like M & Ms? . . . OK. . . . Here's what you have to do. Do you see the numbers 1, 2, 3, and 4 in the corners? In a minute I'm going to call all of your names and tell you each one of the numbers. Then you will all go to the number I tell you. But first I'll tell you what you are going to do. When I say "Go" I want everybody at each number to build one tower with blocks. There will be four boys [girls] at each number and all four of you have to build the same tower. I want you to build it as high as you can. There's one thing, though, I want you each to use different color blocks. That way we can see how many blocks each one of you put on the tower. We are going to give you one M & M for each block of your own color that's on the tower. So the more blocks of your color you put on, the more M & Ms you'll get. Be careful, though, if the tower gets knocked down, it doesn't count and you have to start over. No fair holding the tower, either; it has to stand up by itself. You will have to work quickly because I'm only going to give you a short time. Watch, and I'll show you what I mean. Suppose you build a tower and when I say stop, it looks like this: [blue, red, green; red, blue]. The boy [girl] with the red blocks would get two M & Ms, because there are two red blocks on the tower, the one with blue would get two, the one with green would get one, and the one with yellow wouldn't get anything, because there aren't any yellow blocks on the tower. . . . Does everybody understand? . . .

After this instruction the groups were divided into four subgroups of four children each and these were sent to the four stations. Each group had 16 trials of tower building. The judges distributed rewards (as per instructions to the children) after each trial, and enforced the rules. Each trial was 15 seconds in duration, and there were no rewards for blocks placed after the signal to stop. Towers which collapsed between the signal to stop and the time necessary for the judge to count the blocks were treated as if they had fallen during the trial, and only those blocks still standing erect in the original spot were rewarded.

After the second, fourth, sixth, and eighth trial, the following instructions were given:

> Now before we try it again, I'm going to give you all another number, and I want you to move to the new place. Some of you will stay at the same number, but most of you will have to move.

The subgroups were then reconstituted.

In the changing-membership condition, complete reconstitution took place. No child ever worked with the same other child again when he moved to a new "station." In the stable-membership condition, all of the children moved, but the subgroups were identical, that is, they moved as a unit of four, except for the last move, the one after Trial 8. At this time they, too, were reconstituted with different partners. The last eight trials (9–16) are regarded as a testing period, and no movements or reconstitutions took place.

RESULTS AND DISCUSSION

We predicted that children who had been trained in subgroups of changing composition would be more successful when placed with still another group in the test trials than would subjects whose training had occurred in groups of constant composition. The reverse proved to be the case. The mean total number of blocks placed per trial by the 32 subjects in the changing composition groups during their eight test trials was 45.4. That of the constant composition groups was 72. This means that each of the eight four-person changing subgroups built towers averaging 5.7 blocks in height during the eight test trials, while the stable subgroups built towers which averaged 9 blocks in height. This difference is significant, $p < .01$ ($t = 3.02$, $df = 14$). During the eight training trials, the performance of the groups under the two training conditions was not significantly different. The average number of blocks placed per trial by four-man subgroups during training was 7.4 for the stable groups, 6.9 for the changing groups. Figure 2 shows the trial-by-trial totals for all of the 32 subjects in each condition combined. Dividing the totals in this graph by 8 will yield the mean performance of four-man subgroups, and dividing by 32 will give the individual mean performance for each trial.

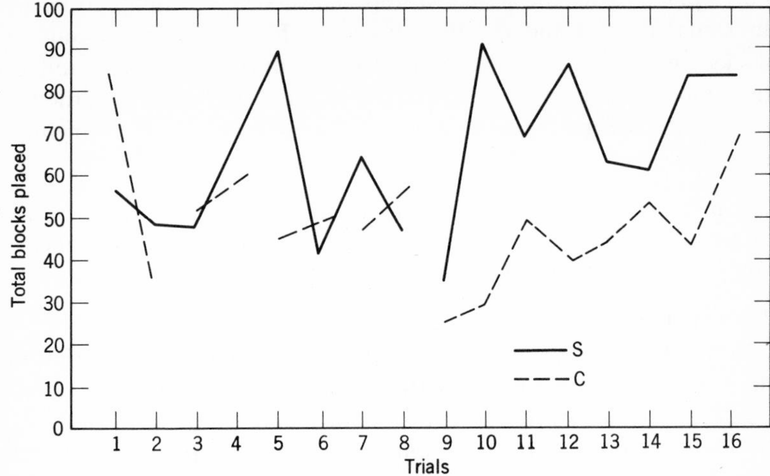

Figure 2. Changing (C) versus stable (S) groupings. (Total number of blocks placed in each condition trial by trial by 32 subjects in eight subgroups. Break in line indicates reconstitution of membership of four-person subgroups.)

How can we account for the superiority of the constant-composition groups during the test trials? We first entertained the hypothesis that in the constant-membership condition, there was time for the formation of stable role relationships—that some subjects emerged as leaders, others as followers, and that this role acquisition somehow permitted subjects to function more effectively in a new group. It is true that the task permitted the establishment of leadership and followership roles. The situation frequently occurred in which more than one child would place a first block and insist that the tower should be built upon his starting point. The child who succeeded in persuading the group to build on his first-placed block had at least a one-block advantage, of course, but his dominance gave him a greater advantage than this. The number of first blocks placed was significantly correlated with total additional blocks placed. That is, the child who succeeded in establishing the starting point for the tower was able to get more of his blocks on the tower, not counting the first block. It is meaningful, then, to speak of dominance of some individuals in the performance of this task, and we may ask whether leadership or dominance became more polarized, more stably characteristic of specific individuals, in the constant than in the changing condition.

We can obtain information relevant to this question by examining the variability of scores in each group. If stable dominance patterns were emerging in one of the experimental conditions, this should mean that some individuals would earn consistently high scores and others consistently low scores over a series of trials. If groups were functioning with little polarization, the variance among individual scores should be less.

During the training trials, the scores of individuals were more variable under the changing-composition condition than under the constant-composition condition ($F = 1.97$, $p < .05$). The difference in variability was even more marked during the test trials. For each child, we computed a ratio score—the ratio of the number of blocks he placed during the eight test trials to the total number placed by his group. The average of these ratios was, of course, .25. But in the groups which had been trained under changing-membership conditions, the variability was considerably greater ($F = 2.42$, $p < .01$). There were two children in these groups who clearly exercised coercive dominance over the other children in their groups—one placed 59 per cent of all the blocks placed by his group, the other 50 per cent; there was one child in a group dominated by a high-scoring child who placed no blocks during the test trials, and two others who placed only 7 per cent each of the total being placed by their group. No such extremes were found among the children trained under constant-group condition. Observers' reports on the changing groups indicated that in some instances the dominant child was shouldering others away from the tower. Sometimes he would have a confederate who helped exclude the other two children and in return be allowed to place some of his own blocks.

Several of the groups trained under constant-composition conditions, by contrast, developed smooth cooperative techniques including all group members during the test trials. For example, the four members of a group would each pick up four blocks and stand poised for the starting signal—one child on his knees to place the bottom four blocks, the next child stooped to place the next four just above, etc. At the starting signal, the four sets of blocks would be quickly superimposed; out-of-line blocks would be straightened to stabilize the structure, and then the group would stand back and restrain one another from placing additional blocks so as not to topple the tower. Such a procedure resulted in equal scores for all participants and a high group score. The more equal distribution of scores among the constant-composition group suggests that cooperative techniques of this kind may have been responsible for their high scores during the test trials.

If equalitarian rather than dominance techniques are more effective in maximizing group scores, and constant-composition groups more often employ equalitarian techniques, how does it happen that these groups did not excel during the training trials? We have already seen that in the constant-group condition, different group members obtained more similar scores during this period as well as during the test trials, yet they did not consistently build higher towers at this time than the changing-membership group. Our observations suggest that it takes time to develop genuinely cooperative processes, because the group must first devise means of controlling would-be coercive individuals. It frequently happened in our control groups that an individual would obtain a high score on early trials by using coercive techniques. But on subsequent trials, he would obtain a score of 0, when other members of the group took measures against him, sometimes by deliberately knocking down the tower. In the groups with constantly changing membership, this mobilization of the group against the bully does not appear to have taken place so readily. We suspect it may have begun to occur during the test trials when the experimental group children continued with the same group of co-workers for a longer period of time than they had done during their training trials, and that the countermeasures which the low-scoring children began to take may be in part responsible for the changing groups' failure to improve their performance during the test trials as much as the stable groups did. It is likely that the course of development of cooperative techniques would be greatly influenced by the characteristic behavior dispositions of group members, for example, whether one was habitually dominant and the others submissive. We suggest that experimental variation of group composition would be a fruitful line of further research, as well as more systematic observation of group process during training and test trials.

SUMMARY

This study, related to earlier work by Mintz, deals with the behavior which occurs when individuals must interact effectively with others in order to maximize their own goals. The major question investigated was whether effective interaction is facilitated more by experience with a variety of partners or by continued interaction with a stable group of partners. Four-child groups of second-grade children were set the task of building a single tower of blocks, each child being rewarded for the number of his own blocks he placed on the tower within a short time interval. Eight groups had their initial experience with this task under conditions of periodic changes in the membership of the groups; another set of eight groups were trained under constant-membership conditions. Then all groups were reconstituted, and a series of test trials conducted. The children who had been trained under conditions of stable group membership performed more effectively. The groups with constantly changing membership tended, more often than contant-membership groups, to have high-scoring children who exercised coercive dominance over low-scoring children.

REFERENCE

Mintz, A. Non-adaptive group behavior. *J. Abnorm. Soc. Psychol.*, 1951, **46**, 150–159.

9.2 THE EFFECTS OF CLEAR AND UNCLEAR ROLE EXPECTATIONS ON GROUP PRODUCTIVITY AND DEFENSIVENESS

Ewart E. Smith

In all groups, people invest considerable time and energy trying to develop sufficient understanding of other members in order to feel they can predict how these other members will behave. In role theory concepts (5), this is attempting to locate the position of the other so that one may have valid role expectations of the other's role enactments. The same phenomena have been discussed in other theoretical terms. Bales (1) states that the social structure of groups develops in order to ". . . reduce the tensions growing out of uncertainty and unpredictability in the actions of others."

Source: This work was supported by a research grant from the Group Psychology Branch of the Office of Naval Research. Reprinted with slight abridgment from the *Journal of Abnormal and Social Psychology*, 1957, **55**, 213–217, with permission of the author and the American Psychological Association, Inc.

The general hypothesis of the present study is that the time and energy used by group members in attempting to predict the behavior of others reduces the amount of group energy available for any given group goal or task. This hypothesis is consistent with the conception of group energy formulated by Cattell (2), who states that group members have a finite amount of energy available in a group situation, and that the amount of energy absorbed by the internal group structure is subtracted from the amount available for group productivity.

The present investigation is primarily concerned with the relationship between the degree to which members of a small group feel they can predict each other's behavior, and the group's task efficiency. In addition to the positive relationship anticipated between these variables, it was expected that uncertainty regarding the roles of the other group members would be reflected in increased defensiveness and dissatisfaction with the group experience.

While these problems have not previously been studied experimentally, as far as the author can ascertain, Torrance (8) developed similar views from his study of 1000 critical incidents of Air Force crews downed in enemy territory. He concluded that the two major detrimental factors in group survival were an unclear situation and an unclear group structure. Regarding the latter factor, he states, in part:

> Under stress, these linkages between members may become confused and thus people do not have a clear perception of what they can expect from one another, with whom they can relate, how they can relate to one another, and so on. The fact that this happens apparently influences the ability of the group to survive.

In order to induce ambiguous role expectations, paid accomplices were assigned roles as silent members in small groups of persons who were, initially, strangers to each other. In the initial meeting of such a group, each member should find the behavior of all of the others equally unpredictable. But in the course of group interaction the behavior of those who spoke should become more predictable, while the behavior of those who remained silent should remain unpredictable. Eventually the group members would undoubtedly come to predict with confidence the simple fact that the silent members would remain silent. Since only short-term groups were studied, however, the latter effect is not relevant to the present experiment.

This reasoning was substantiated in several preliminary investigations. The presence of silent group members in short-term groups had little, if any, effect on productivity during the first few minutes, but productivity decreased to a low point at about thirty minutes, followed by a gain until the presence of silent members resulted in no decrement in productivity.

The hypotheses tested in the present study are:

1. The presence of silent members in a group produces (*a*) decreased productivity, (*b*) increased defensiveness, and (*c*) increased dissatisfaction with the group experience.
2. Decreasing the ambiguity of role expectations in a group that contains silent members counteracts the effects predicted in Hypothesis 1.

METHOD

Subjects and Task

The subjects (*S*s) were 50 males and 90 females from the introductory psychology classes at the University of Colorado. The task, taken from an experiment by Taylor and Faust (7), is an adaptation of the parlor game, "Twenty Questions," in which the *S*s had to identify items designated by the experimenter (*E*) as either animal, vegetable, or mineral. Each problem had to be solved with less than forty questions for the group to receive credit. There was no time limit on individual problems. To each question asked by a group member, *E* replied in one of the following ways: (*a*) Yes; (*b*) No; (*c*) Partly; (*d*) Sometimes; (*e*) Not in the usual sense of the word; (*f*) I don't know (no charge for the question); (*g*) Please restate the question (if the question was unclear or could not be answered in one of the above ways). Difficult items like wrench, ruby, and bread were used.

Experimental Design

In the experimental Conditions A and B, each group was composed of three participating *S*s, two females and one male, and two silent members, one female and one male. Condition A was designed to induce ambiguous role expectations. Condition B differed from Condition A in that the roles of the silent members were clarified prior to experimentation; all group members checked their "usual role" in a group on a check list. Everyone then announced the role he had checked, which was then checked by *E* on a large replica of the "Usual Roles" check list. The silent members always checked the "Listener" role.

Group Processes

In the control Conditions C and D, there were no paid silent members. In Condition C each group was composed of three participating *S*s, two females and one male. In Condition D, each group was composed of five participating members, three females and two males.

In all conditions, *S*s worked on the task for two periods. The first work period, which lasted fifteen minutes, was intended to allow ambiguous role expectations of the silent members to develop. In the second work period, which was ten minutes long, group productivity was measured. The problems, and their order, were the same for all groups. Regardless of how many problems the group had solved in the first work period, each group started with a new, and identical, set of problems in the second work period.

The thirteen silent paid participants were not known to the *S*s in their groups. Each silent member was assigned to Condition A and B groups an equal number of times.

Dependent Variable Measurements

Group productivity was measured by the number of problems solved. *Defensiveness* was measured by a 25-item Likert scale, with a corrected, split-half reliability of .79, which had been validated by the known group method (4). A typical item is "I felt free to express all my ideas in this group." *Group satisfaction* was measured by a 15-item Likert scale, with a corrected split-half reliability of .93, which had been validated by the known group method. A typical item is "This is the most stimulating experience I've had in a long time." A single item was used as an index of *role ambiguity:* "I can predict how this person would act in other situations." The *S*s rated each group member on a scale from -3 to $+3$. A numbering system was used so that *S*s did not give their names. This measure was used as a check on the effectiveness of the experimental manipulation.

RESULTS AND DISCUSSION[1]

Table 1 contains the findings on the ambiguity item, "I can predict how this person would act in other situations." Plotting the scores on this item revealed that normal distributions could not be assumed. Consequently, nonparametric rank tests have been used (3, 6). An *H* test, which is functionally equivalent to a one-way analy-

[1] Statistical significance at the .05 level has been indicated by a single asterisk; at the .01 level or better by a double asterisk.

Table 1 *Median Rating of Ss and Silent Paid Participants on Role Ambiguity*

Statistics on Role Ambiguity Rating	Data under Each Condition					
	A Ambiguity (Silent Members)		B Clarity (Silent Members)		C Control ($N = 3$)	D Control ($N = 5$)
	Rating of *Ss*	Rating of Silent Members	Rating of *Ss*	Rating of Silent Members	Rating of *Ss*	Rating of *Ss*
Median	11.00	6.00	11.00	8.00	8.50	8.00
N	29	29	30	30	30	50

Note: Low scores indicate role ambiguity.
H for these data is 34.89, $p < .01$.
N is 29 in Condition A as one S failed to fill out the rating form.

sis of variance, has been computed on the data in Table 1. As this H is statistically significant. additional rank tests have been computed. Using this method, z's are obtained which are normal deviates evaluated by the use of the normal probability table. The z (for related measures) on the ratings of silent members compared to the ratings of *Ss* in the Condition A groups is 4.46**, indicating that the independent variable manipulation in Condition A was successful; i.e., that the silent paid participants were seen as less predictable than the *Ss*.

Additional support for the hypothesis that silent members were seen as less predictable is given by the significant z, 4.37**, between the ratings of silent members and *Ss* in the Condition B groups. However, comparison of the ratings of the silent members in Condition A with the ratings of the silent members in Condition B indicates that the difference, although in the predicted direction, is not significant. Therefore, the hypothesis that role clarification reduces the ambiguity of the roles of silent members is not supported.

This failure may be due to a temporal factor. At the time that the *Ss* rated the silent members on predictability, they had a period of 30 minutes of observations upon which to base their ratings. This 30-minute time sample was the same in Conditions A and B, and was apparently more powerful than the earlier one-minute role clarification in Condition B, perhaps resulting in a leveling effect on the comparison of Conditions A and B with respect to the ratings of the silent members. Results more in line with the hypothesis might have been obtained if the rating item had been given earlier.

An interesting, and unpredicted, finding is that the mean rating of the *S*s in both Conditions A and B is significantly higher than the ratings of *S*s in Condition C, with z's of 3.24** and 3.64**, using a rank test for independent samples (3). This finding cannot be explained from the data, but, as a possible explanation, it may be suggested that in the groups containing silent members, the other *S*s were seen by contrast as much more predictable than they otherwise would have been.

Table 2 contains the findings on group productivity. Plotting the group task scores for the second work period (as anticipated, there were no significant differences in the first work period) revealed that normal distributions could not be assumed. Consequently, nonparametric rank tests (for independent measures) were used. The obtained z between Conditions A and B is 2.18*; between A and C, 2.35*; and between A and D, 2.63**.

Table 2 *Number of Problems Solved, under Each of Four Conditions, in First and Second Work Periods*

	Data under Each Condition			
Statistic on Number of Problems Solved	A Ambiguity (Silent Members)	B Clarity (Silent Members)	C Control ($N = 3$)	D Control ($N = 5$)
Median: First work period (15 minutes)	5.50	6.50	6.00	6.00
Median: Second work period (10 minutes)	0.	3.00	2.00	2.50
Number of groups	10	10	10	10

Note: H for these data (second work period) is 9.29, $p < .05$.

Table 2 shows that the silent members reduced group productivity significantly in Condition A. These results support the hypothesis that ambiguous role expectations reduce group productivity. At first glance, some more parsimonious explanations might be suggested. Thus, one might suppose that the decrement in productivity in Condition A was produced by silent members per se, rather than by ambiguous role expectations. However, silent members were also present in the Condition B groups, where they were as silent, "uncooperative," "unproductive," etc., as they were in the Condition A groups. The difference was that in the Condition B groups, the *Ss* expected the silent members to be silent. Therefore, the variable to which the decrement in productivity must be attributed was the unpredictability of the silent members.

The data in Table 3 support the first hypothesis, that the presence of silent members produces increased defensiveness. The t ratios between Conditions A and C, and A and D, are 4.48** and 4.04**, respectively. The second hypothesis, that the presence of silent members does not produce increased defensiveness if the roles of the group members are explicit, is not supported. The differences between Condition B and Conditions C and D on defensiveness are significant, with t's of 3.45** and 2.79**, respectively. The difference between Conditions A and B is not significant.

Table 3 *Average Defensiveness Scale Scores under Each of Four Conditions*

	Data under Each Condition			
Statistic on D-Scale Scores	A Ambiguity (Silent Members)	B Clarity (Silent Members)	C Control ($N = 3$)	D Control ($N = 5$)
Mean	66.00	61.53	49.17	52.74
SD	13.92	12.41	14.14	14.10
N	30	30	30	50

Note: High scores indicate defensiveness.

The analysis of variance is not summarized, to conserve space, as only predicted differences have been tested. However, the overall F on the means is 9.72, $p < .01$.

The data in Table 4 clearly support the first hypothesis, that the presence of silent members reduces group satisfaction. The t between Conditions A and D is 9.26**, and that between Conditions A and C is 6.05**. As the F ratio on the variances of Conditions A and C is 2.31*, a correction for t's computed when variances are heterogeneous has been used (3). The second hypothesis, that the presence of silent members does not reduce group satisfaction if the roles of the group members are explicit, is partially supported by the data. Group satisfaction is higher in Condition B than in Condition A, with a t of 2.48*. However, the decrement in satisfaction produced by the silent members was not completely offset by the role clarification in Condition B groups, as the t ratios between Condition B, and Conditions C and D, on group satisfaction, are 3.23** and 3.81**, respectively.

Table 4 *Average Group Satisfaction Scale Scores under Each of Four Conditions*

	Data under Each Condition			
Statistic on GS-Scale Scores	A Ambiguity (Silent Members)	B Clarity (Silent Members)	C Control ($N = 3$)	D Control ($N = 5$)
Mean	54.80	62.60	74.77	74.50
SD	9.74	13.82	14.81	13.06
N	30	30	30	50

Note: High scores indicate satisfaction.

The F ratio between the variances of Conditions A and C is 2.31; the overall F on the means is 18.34, $p < .01$ in both instances.

At this point, it should be noted that although the primary independent variable, the presence of silent members, produced the expected results in all cases, the lack of significant differences between Conditions A and B on the role ambiguity item and on the Defensiveness scale throws some doubt on the interpretation of the results given here. One must decide whether Conditions A and B were really different, as indicated by the significant differences between them on productivity and the Group Satisfaction scale; or whether they are really similar, as indicated by the lack of significant differences on the ambiguity item and Defensiveness scale.

The argument here is that Conditions A and B were different, and that role ambiguity and role clarification were the variables which lowered and raised group productivity. The lack of significant differences between Conditions A and B on the role ambiguity item and the Defensiveness scale are interpreted as a product of their relatively low reliability and of the decay of the role clarification set-variable by the time the questionnaires were given. However, the data are open to alternate interpretation.

SUMMARY

In a laboratory investigation, paid participants, who were instructed to remain silent, were included in small groups to induce ambiguous role expectations. Five-member problem-solving groups, each including three naive *S*s and two silent members, were used in each experimental condition. Three- and five-member groups were used in control conditions. It was hypothesized that ambiguous role expectations would reduce group productivity and satisfaction, and increase defensiveness.

All these predictions were well supported by the data.

Silent paid participants were included in another condition, where group members revealed their intended role behaviors. Group members thus had accurate expectations that the paid participants would remain silent. It was hypothesized that, as a result of this role clarification, the effects predicted above would be reduced or negated. Thus, the presence of silent participants would not reduce group productivity and satisfaction, or increase defensiveness.

Role clarification, with silent paid participants present in the groups, did, as predicted, result in normal (i.e., control group level) group productivity. Group satisfaction was significantly increased, but not to the normal level. The prediction that role clarification would restore the decrement in defensiveness was not supported.

REFERENCES

1. Bales, R. F. A theoretical framework for interaction process analysis. In D. Cartwright & A. F. Zander (Eds.), *Group dynamics: Research and theory*. Evanston, Ill.: Row, Peterson, 1953.
2. Cattell, R. B. New concepts for measuring leadership, in terms of group syntality. *Hum. Relat.*, 1951, 4, 161–184.
3. Edwards, A. L. *Statistical methods for the behavioral sciences.* New York: Rinehart, 1954.
4. Gibb, J. R. *Factors producing defensive behavior within groups.* Quarterly Status Report, Office of Naval Res., Contract Nonr-1147(03), NR 170–226, Feb. 15, 1956, 5 pp.

5. Sarbin, T. R. Role theory. In G. Lindzey (Ed.), *Handbook of social psychology.* Cambridge, Mass.: Addison-Wesley, 1954.
6. Siegel, S. *Non-parametric statistics for the behavioral sciences.* New York: McGraw-Hill, 1956.
7. Taylor, D. W., & Faust, W. L. Twenty questions: Efficiency in problem solving as a function of size of group. *J. Exptl. Psychol.*, 1952, **44**, 360–368.
8. Torrance, E. P. The behavior of small groups under the stress of conditions of "survival." *Am. Sociol. Rev.*, 1954, **19**, 751–755.

9.3 COMPETITION AND NONCOMPETITION IN RELATION TO SATISFACTION AND FEELINGS TOWARD OWN-GROUP AND NONGROUP MEMBERS

Robert E. Dunn
Morton Goldman

The purpose of this study is to examine groups working in competition and noncompetition situations and to observe the effects of these conditions on the satisfaction of the group members and their feelings toward own-group and nongroup members.

An often-quoted study dealing with cooperation and competition is that by Deutsch (1). In his study, Deutsch was interested in (*a*) the productivity of the groups and (*b*) the type of interpersonal relations and morale that developed among the group members. In a study by Hammond and Goldman (2), which dealt mainly with the productivity factor, it was found that the competition-cooperation variable, as reported by Deutsch, is not the essential component affecting group performance; but that working in concert with others on a goal rather than as an individual is the more important element. The current study will examine again the cooperation-competition variable, attempting to clarify and extend Deutsch's findings, but, in this case, working with variables dealing with satisfaction and with the acceptance of others within and outside of one's own group.

Deutsch established two types of group situations: a "competitive" one and a "cooperative" one. In the "competitive" situation, a subject (*S*) was told that his performance would be evaluated against the

Source: Reprinted with slight abridgment from the *Journal of Social Psychology*, 1966, **68**, 299–311, with permission of the authors and The Journal Press.

performance of other *S*s within his group. *S* was induced to view the other members within his group as competitors for mutually exclusive rewards. These *S*s were generally less satisfied and, as a group, more poorly performing than were the *S*s working in the "cooperative" situation and were believed by Deutsch to have been adversely influenced by the competitive aspect of their group situation. In Deutsch's "cooperative" treatment, all *S*s within a given group worked for a similar and a shared reward. Not only would *S* receive a reward, but he would be working with others for a common goal and would have the added incentive of seeing other members with whom he has worked or helped also receive rewards. Thus, the question raised is whether the difference between behavior in the "competitive" and "cooperative" treatments is due to the "competitive" factor or to the working-for-shared-rewards aspect.

In the "cooperative" situation, in addition to all members in a given group working for a common goal, all the members of the group would also share similarly in receiving or in not receiving the reward, according to the level of the performance of the group. However, Deutsch had a further stipulation that groups would compete with one another. If a given group reached its goal, it could have done so by performing better than the other groups; and the remaining groups thereby were prevented from reaching their goals. This "cooperative" treatment in this respect is similar to the "competitive" treatment in that the "cooperative" treatment involves *intergroup* competition. Deutsch attributed the greater friendliness and better acceptance of other group members in this treatment to its cooperative aspects, deemphasizing the fact that the groups were competing with each other. If the sharing of common goals and rewards is the important and sole consideration, then why include the competitive factor? One should note that Deutsch employed no instrument measuring the feelings toward nongroup members. What would occur if the competitive variable were eliminated? The answer to this question has important implications for intergroup rivalry and tension.

To clarify the issues raised, four treatments will be employed. The first treatment will be similar to Deutsch's "cooperation" situation, but will be called group competition because, as explained, these groups compete against other groups. The second treatment will duplicate Deutsch's "competitive" situation. It will be called individual competition. In this treatment, *S*s within the same group compete for mutually exclusive goals. If a given *S* in the group attains his goal, this accomplishment prevents other members of the group from reaching their goals. The third treatment is designed to promote intragroup cooperation without requiring intergroup competition. All members of the group are similarly rewarded, but rewards are based on the performance of each group independently of the performance of the other groups. One group doing well does not affect the ability of other groups to reach their goals, as was the case in Deutsch's study. This treatment will be called the group-merit treatment. By comparing the group-merit treatment and the group-competition treatments with each other, it will be possible to see the results, positive or negative, that occur from having or not having intergroup competition. The fourth treatment has *S*s in the same group working for individual rewards (as was the case in Deutsch's "competitive" treatment), but with the important change that the group members do not vie for mutually exclusive goals. Instead, each *S* is individually evaluated independently of the performance of the other group members—each *S* being rewarded on the basis of his individual contribution. This treatment is called the individual-merit treatment. By comparing the individual-merit treatment and the individual-competition treatment with each other, it will be possible to examine the effect, if any, that occurs because of competition when *S*s work for individual goals.

By adding these two treatments and retaining the two treatments that Deutsch used, we shall find it possible to see if it is indeed the competition factor that is responsible for the results Deutsch reported. By comparing the two treatments in which *S*s work for individual independent rewards with the two treatments in which all *S*s in the same group are similarly rewarded, we shall find it possible to determine whether or not working alone for independent rewards is the essential factor responsible for the results.

Comparisons can also be made between the group-competition and the group-merit treatments to examine the effects of intergroup competition. Does one need to pit one group against another group to produce strong satisfaction and high morale within a given group? If one does have groups competing against each other, how will this fact affect the feeling toward *S*s who are not members of the same group?

The current study was designed to examine and extend the understanding of competition and cooperation and the sharing or the nonsharing of the same rewards within a group.

METHOD

Subjects

*S*s were recruited from three general-psychology classes by being told they would have opportunity to receive credit toward their final course grade for participation. From each class, four groups of five *S*s each were formed. The four groups from a given class were randomly assigned to one of the four treatments, every class having a group in each one of the four treatments. Because three classes were used, each of the four treatments had three groups, making a total of 12 groups. In all, 60 students participated. Each group met for one hour a week for four weeks to discuss human-relations problems.

Insofar as the limitations of the students' schedules would allow, *S*s in the groups were balanced on a sociometric scale and on the *F* scale. The sociometric balancing was accomplished by asking *S*s to list in order of preference those other members of the class whom they would want to be in their group. Scores were assigned to each choice on the basis of five points for a first choice, four points for a second choice, etc., to one point for a fifth choice and every choice thereafter. Then every *S* was given a score based on the rank and the number of times he was chosen. Groups were then balanced on this basis and on the basis of the number of points of choices within the group. The four groups that met the first semester were further balanced on grades on their first examination, while the eight groups that met the second semester were balanced on the Wonderlic Personnel Test, Form A (timed).

Inducing the Independent Variables

The following set of instructions was read to all groups:

We are interested in finding out to what extent group discussions of psychological problems foster greater insight into these problems. We want to find out if the increased understanding obtained by individuals in these sessions would be sufficient to make these sessions an integral part of the general-psychology course. We will be comparing the final grades that you make with the grades made by students who are not participating in these groups to see the extent to which your grades improve, if any.

Since absences will detract from the adequate performance, regular attendance will be expected. We will meet at this hour for an additional three weeks, or four sessions in all.

You will be presented with a problem that is relevant to your study of psychology and will be asked to discuss it with a view of how to resolve it. You will be allowed 30 minutes to discuss the problems. Then you will be allowed 15 minutes to write up your recommendations in the form of a single written report. You are to decide upon a different person to do the writing each week. This report will represent the contributions of the group as a whole.[1]

Please do not discuss what you do here with other students, as this could affect the performance of the other groups.

To the best of the experimenter's knowledge, this request was honored. No information appeared to leak out to the groups in the different treatments or to the groups taking part the following semester.

In addition to the instructions just quoted there were special instructions for each condition describing the way in which credit was to be allotted.

The instructions read to the groups in the group-competition treatment were as follows:

You are going to receive some credit for the level of work that you are doing here. The credit will depend on the total participation of all group members in the discussion of the problems which will be given and the solutions of these problems in your written reports. All members of this group will receive the same amount of credit. This will be determined by comparing the performance of this group with the performance of three other groups participating in the program. Of the four groups, each member of the group judged best will receive 15 points; each member of the group judged second best will receive 10 points; each member of the group judged third best will receive five points; and the poorest of the groups will receive no points. These points will be added to your total score before your final general-psychology grade is determined. Thus, if this group's performance is judged best in comparison to the performance of the other three groups participating, each of you would receive 15 points which would be added on to your total score in general psychology.[2]

[1] The person writing the report was arbitrarily selected by the experimenter in alphabetical order according to the student's last name. At the end of the group discussion the experimenter asked, "Well, whom would you like to write up your recommendations?" At that point, there was a slight pause; so the experimenter pointed to a student and said, "Why don't *you* do it this week?" Because the groups met for four sessions, four different students were assigned to write a report for each group.

[2] A student's final grade in the general-psychology course is determined by adding the points made on three hour-long examinations to the points made on the final examination. Fifteen additional points made a difference of three letter grades on a

Competition, Noncompetition: Feelings toward Group Members

The instructions read to the groups in the group-merit treatment were as follows:

You are going to receive some credit for the level of work that you are doing here. The credit will depend on the total participation of all group members in the discussion of the problems which will be given and the solutions of these problems in your written reports. All members of this group will receive the same amount of credit. The amount of points which you will receive varies from 15 points to zero points. If this group does a very superior job, each group member will receive 15 points; if this group does a superior job, each group member will receive 10 points; if this group does a fair job, each group member will receive five points; if this group does poorly, members will receive no points. These points will be added to your total score before your final general-psychology grade is determined. Thus, if this group's performance is very superior, each of you would receve 15 points which would be added to your total score in general psychology.

The instructions read to the groups in the individual-competition treatment were as follows:

You are going to receive some credit for the level of work which you are doing here. The credit will depend on your individual contribution in the discussions of the problems which will be given and the individual contributions to the solution of these problems in the written reports. Each member of this group will receive different amounts of credit. This will be determined by comparing the performance of each member with the performance of the other members in this group. Of the five members here, the member of this group whose performance is judged best will receive 15 points; the member of this group whose performance is judged second best will receive 10 points; the member of this group whose performance is third best will receive five points; and the member of this group whose performance is judged poorest in comparison to (that of) other group members will receive no points. The number of points that each individual earns here will be added to his total score before his final general-psychology grade is determined. Thus, the individual whose performance is judged the best in comparison to the performance of the other members would receive 15 points which would be added to his total score in general psychology.

The instructions read to the groups in the individual-merit treatment were as follows:

---

one-hour examination; thus, a student who had obtained a "D" on a one-hour examination could obtain an "A" if 15 points were added to his examination score. Fifteen points added to the score on the final examination would raise the student's mark one letter grade at least.

You are going to receive some credit for the level of work which you are doing here. The credit will depend on your individual contribution in the discussion of the problems which will be given and the individual contributions to the solutions of these problems in the written reports. Each member of this group will receive either the same or different amounts of credit as the other members depending on his individual contribution. The number of points which each of you can receive varies from 15 points to zero points. Those individuals here who do a very superior job will each receive 15 points; those individuals who do a superior job will each receive 10 points; those who do a fair job will each receive five points; and those individuals who perform poorly will each receive no points. The number of points that each individual earns here will be added on to his total score before his final general-psychology grade is determined. Thus, it would be possible for all of you here to receive 15 points if each of you performed in a very superior manner, and this would be added to each of your total scores in general psychology.

Problems

Four problem situations were devised, one for each of the four meetings of the groups. All groups received the problems in the same order. Problem 1 dealt with a new college teacher who was having difficulty in getting students to attend classes. Problem 2 involved a Jewish mother who could not get her 9-year-old son to attend Sunday School. Problem 3 concerned a bright student who was failing a course that to him seemed very dull. Problem 4 consisted of what a fraternity could do if its members discovered that a new member who is well liked belongs to a religious group that is excluded by the national rules of the fraternity.

Evaluating the Dependent Variable

The effects induced by the four treatments were examined with the use of three instruments: (*a*) a subliminal questionnaire, (*b*) a sociometric test, and (*c*) written reports obtained from the experimental *S*s.

The Subliminal Questionnaire: At the end of each session, *S*s were asked to give an additional few minutes of time to help the experimenter with his master's thesis project, a study in subliminal perception. A questionnaire was distributed, and a stick-figure slide composed of four or more "persons" in ambiguous poses was flashed upon the wall at a .01-second exposure rate. The room was normally lighted, so that *S*s could see little more than a flash of light; thus they received only vague impressions of the pictures. The pictures consisted of stick figures in various positions (standing, seated, and holding hands) appearing to be engaged in various tasks. The authors felt that because of the rapid exposure of the picture and the general vagueness of the material *Ss* would resort to their own emotional states in checking a questionnaire distributed to them. The questionnaire required *S* to check positive, neutral, or negative statements dealing with the behavior of the stick figures. The positive statements contained material such as "all the group members are productively engaged in a satisfying task," "they are all smiling," "they are all facing each other and working under happy circumstances." The negative statements contained material such as "the people are frowning," "they are not engaged in the same task," "they are facing in opposite directions." The neutral statements contained material such as "undecided" or "can't tell."

For each of the four group sessions, a different picture and a different questionnaire were used. *Ss* were told that, while it was expected that they would not be able to "see" the projected picture, there was one that they would be allowed to view after the experiment was over. Further, they were assured that a possibility existed that they were "unconsciously" aware of what was in the picture, and that it was the experimenter's belief that this would influence the way they answered the questionnaire. All they had to do was to answer the items on "hunch" or "impulse." They were not requested to sign their names.

Question might arise as to whether or not the stick-figure slides influenced the answers. This problem was not investigated; but, assuming such an influence, any differences between groups would have to be attributed to some other factor. These latter differences are of main interest in the present experiment.

Sociometric Choices and the Written Report: When the four scheduled meetings for all groups were concluded, *E* went to two of the three classrooms (due to an error in scheduling, the third classroom did not participate in this part of the experiment)[3] and distributed additional sociometric questionnaires. *E* told the students that they had participated in an attempt to evaluate different methods of treating discussion groups, and that the psychology department intended to use these results as an aid in forming future discussion groups. Sincerity was requested in *Ss* writing comments relevant to the experiences in the meetings—experiences *Ss* thought might be helpful to the department, including statements of attitudes.

[3] Since each class had one group in each of the four treatments, the loss was equally shared by students in each of the four treatments.

RESULTS

The data available from the three instruments will be analyzed to see if the treatments induced created differences and (if differences exist) to examine the variables responsible for the differences.

The Subliminal Questionnaire

S received a score on the subliminal projective instrument by subtracting the number of negative items checked on the questionnaire from the positive items checked—each of the four group sessions being considered separately. The neutral items checked were counted neither positively nor negatively. For each of the four sessions, the median score for all *S*s was found, and the median chi square test was used to determine significance.

Table 1 *Per Cent of* Ss *Viewing the Subliminal Pictures Positively*

	Session			
Treatment	1	2	3	4
Group-merit	43	50	79	71
Group-competition	57	67	54	54
Individual-merit	46	50	33	45
Individual-competition	53	35	33	53

Table 1 presents the percentage of *S*s for each group session in each of the four treatments that fall above the median. The treatment having the highest percentage of *S*s above the median is the treatment under which *S*s viewed the picture most positively. At only one of the four sessions—the third—is the difference between treatments significant at the .05 level. *S*s in the group-merit treatment gave the greatest number of positive responses, followed by *S*s in the group-competition treatment, while *S*s in the individual-merit and the individual-competition treatments were tied for the least number of positive responses.

Significance at the .05 level was obtained using the median test when comparing the positive responses for the *S*s in the two group-reward treatments with the positive responses for the *S*s in the two individual-reward treatments. No significant differences appeared when the two cooperation treatments were compared with the two competition treatments.

Self-report Statements

At the end of the group sessions, all *S*s were asked to write a brief report expressing their feelings about the meetings. These statements were given to three judges, who were instructed to score each statement "positive" or "negative" according to whether more positive feeling or more negative feeling was expressed. The following is an example of a statement judged negatively:

> I don't want to be overcritical, but I do not feel the outside groups were too beneficial. After coming to the first two, I dreaded coming to the third and fourth. Many times, the problems were so incomplete that we had trouble discussing them. If the groups had been formed for the purpose of helping us learn the information required of the course, I feel they would have been of some help, but as they were, I don't think they help me.

The following is an example of a statement judged positively:

> I enjoyed working with the group, and, although I'm not certain how much psychology I learned by being in the group, I'm sure it helped me some in my learning. I know I learned other things as well, getting to compare some of my opinions with other students' opinions.

No judge was aware of the conditions of the experiment, and they worked independently. Whenever there was a disagreement among the judges, the evaluation of the two judges who agreed was used. The average correlation between judges (using the phi coefficient) is .72.

Table 2 presents the number of *S*s in each of the four treatments whose statements were judged positively and negatively. Using a chi-square test, the differences among treatments are significant at the

Table 2 *Number of Ss in Each Treatment Whose Statements Were Judged Positive and Negative*

	Judgment	
Treatment	Positive	Negative
Group-merit	4	4
Group-competition	8	4
Individual-merit	0	4
Individual-competition	1	9

.01 level. The group-competition treatment received the highest per cent of positively rated statements (66 per cent), followed by the group-merit treatment (50 per cent), the individual-competition treatment (10 per cent), and the individual-merit treatment (zero per cent) respectively.

Significance at the .01 level was obtained using the chi-square test when comparing the positive and negative statements in the two group-reward treatments with the statements in the two individual-reward treatments. No significant differences appeared when the two cooperation treatments were compared with the two competition treatments.

Sociometric Instrument

At the conclusion of the fourth experimental session, *E* again went to the classrooms from which *S*s had been recruited and asked the students to complete a second sociometric instrument by listing the names of individuals in their classes with whom they would want to work for possible future discussion groups. As was the case when the first sociometric instrument was scored to equate for choices across the four treatments, scores were given by assigning five points for the first choice, four points for the second choice, three points for the third, two for the fourth, and one point for all succeeding choices. Each *S* participating in the study received two scores: (*a*) the sum of the choices of individuals who were members of *S*'s experimental group and (*b*) the sum of choices of individuals who were not of *S*'s experimental group. Because the same two scores were computed for each *S* on the first sociometric instrument (i.e., the one completed before the experiment started), the differences between preexperimental choices and postexperimental choices could be obtained for both own-group and nongroup members. Table 3 presents the results comparing the group-merit and the group-competition treatments on the increase in both own-group and nongroup members. With the Mann-Whitney *U* test, results significant at the .05 level were obtained

Table 3 *Average Rank Differences Between Postsociometric and Presociometric Choices for Own-Group and Nongroup Members*

Treatment	Nongroup Members	Own-Group Members
Group-merit	21.31	19.37
Group-competitive	19.03	17.10

for the nongroup choices, and nonsignificant results were obtained for the own-group choices. On both the own-group and non-group choices, the group-merit treatment is above the group-competition treatment in selecting individuals with whom to participate in group sessions.

DISCUSSION

One of the major questions examined in this study is whether or not the satisfaction of individuals working in groups is affected by the competition-cooperation variable or whether or not the more important variable is the sharing or the not sharing of similar rewards with members within the same work group. Because "satisfaction" is an elusive term, the authors decided to measure this factor in two ways, using a self-report and a projective technique.

The projective technique involved flashing a stick-figure picture on the wall at a fast speed and asking *S*s (at the end of each of the four group sessions) to report on whether they saw positive, neutral, or negative material. The authors believed that viewing the pictures positively or negatively would be affected by the satisfaction or dissatisfaction experienced in the group sessions. Significant differences among the treatments at the .05 level were found in the third session. If the relationship between experiencing satisfaction and viewing the stick-figure picture is correct, then evidence was obtained to support the assertion that working in a group and sharing similar common rewards with others is the essential factor—*not* the competition-cooperation variable. In the case of the two individual-reward treatments, the competition factor was of no import. In both of these treatments, the data show that the least amount of positive content for the stick figures was reported, both of these treatments having identical percentage scores.

The second measure used to examine satisfaction was a self-report obtained from all *S*s at the conclusion of the study. On this instrument, students were asked to write a short statement expressing their feelings about the group sessions. Differences among treatments were significant at the .01 level again supporting the assertion that greater satisfaction was experienced by *S*s in the two treatments involving shared rewards as opposed to working for an individual reward. No evidence was found that the satisfaction variable was adversely affected by the competition-cooperation factor.

The results obtained in this study support the research reported by

Deutsch (1) in that *S*s involved in the "cooperation" treatment (our group-competition treatment) experience greater satisfaction than those in the "competition" treatment (our individual-competition treatment). But the results obtained in this study are in opposition to the work of Deutsch in that it was not the competition factor that induced the negative findings, but the working for individual, independent rewards. Deutsch, in setting up his two treatments, introduced both the competition and the working-alone factors. In the present study, there is evidence that the working-alone factor is responsible for the differences obtained in producing less satisfaction.

The second major area of this study concerned feelings toward ingroup and outgroup members. Deutsch found an increased acceptance of members within the same group in the "cooperation" treatment. But in his "cooperation" treatment, one group was pitted against other groups. One group receiving the highest reward automatically prevented other groups from doing so. Is it necessary to introduce this group-competition aspect to obtain greater acceptance among members in the same group? Deutsch deemphasized this group-competition aspect of his study; he used no measure to obtain feelings toward nongroup members. In the present study, there is evidence of differences between preexperiment choices and postexperiment choices for own-group as well as for nongroup members. The results show significantly greater acceptance, in terms of choosing individuals with whom to participate again in group sessions, for nongroup members by the group-merit-treatment *S*s as compared to the choices of nongroup members by *S*s in the group-competitive treatment. For choosing own-group members, the group-merit treatment is also higher than the group-competitive treatment, the differences not being significant, however. Thus, the data show that for *S*s in the group-competition treatment there is a tendency to view other class members as possible rivals and to be less prone to accept them as group members. The results also show the needlessness of including intergroup competition in developing both mutual satisfaction or greater acceptance among members of a group.

There exists the tendency to include intergroup competition as part of a "cooperation" treatment, perhaps under the assumption that this induces cohesiveness or "good in-group feeling." Educators and other professional group workers sometimes include intergroup rivalry in their applied "cooperation systems." The present study points to the possibility that this rivalry may not only be unnecessary, but may do social harm through the intergroup tensions that it arouses.

SUMMARY

One purpose of this study was to evaluate the relative satisfaction of small-discussion-group members under four conditions of reward: (*a*) rewards given individually on a noncompetitive basis (individual merit), (*b*) rewards given equally among a group on a noncompetitive basis (group merit), (*c*) rewards given individually on a competitive basis (individual competition), and (*d*) rewards given equally among a group on a competitive basis (group competition). A second purpose of the study was to compare the group-merit and group-competition treatments with respect to the acceptance or the rejection of own-group and nongroup members.

Significant differences were found on the two measures used to examine satisfaction, showing that greater satisfaction is experienced when individuals share similarly in the rewards for mutual contributions than when given rewards independently for individual contributions. The competition variable does *not* appear to affect the results. With respect to acceptance or rejection, the group-merit treatment as compared with the group-competition treatment produced greater acceptance of own-group as well as of nongroup members.

Our results, based on the study of college students working in small face-to-face discussion groups, emphasize the advantage of having group members share rewards while making mutual contributions on a noncompetitive basis, competing neither against each other nor against other groups. It was suggested that intergroup rivalry might not only be unnecessary in producing "good in-group feelings" but that it might do social harm.

REFERENCES

1. Deutsch, M. An experimental study of the effects of cooperation and competition upon group processes. *Hum. Relat.*, 1949, **2**, 199–232.
2. Hammond, L. K., & Goldman, M. Competition and non-competition and its relationship to individual and group productivity. *Sociometry*, 1961, **24**, 46–60.

9.4 QUASI-THERAPEUTIC EFFECTS OF INTERGROUP COMPETITION

James W. Julian
Doyle W. Bishop
Fred E. Fiedler

The work of Paterson (1955), Harvey (1956), Haefner, Langham, Axelrod, and Lanzetta (1954), and Sherif and Sherif (1953) indicates that members of a group become more cooperative and cohesive when their group is confronted by a common threat. Such a common threat, posed by a common enemy or opponent, should lead to closer interpersonal relations and hence to increased adjustment. Myers (1962a, 1962b) in two earlier studies under this program, has utilized this principle in testing the hypothesis that groups in competition with one another constitute a more quasi-therapeutic environment than comparable groups which do not compete with one another. His study of rifle teams showed that competitive group conditions had adjustive effects even for men in losing teams. A second study (1962a) investigated the effect of competitive and noncompetitive team golf on hospitalized schizophrenics. This investigation again showed that patients in relatively good reality contact improved in their adjustment and social interactions as compared with a comparable control group in which members of the twosomes were rewarded irrespective of their performance. The investigation reported here is the third in the series specifically concerned with quasi-therapeutic effects of intergroup competition.

Previous studies were conducted with ad hoc groups under controlled conditions. The present investigation extends the study of quasi-therapeutic competitive conditions to a field setting in which the group is of considerable salience to the member. Specifically, this study tested the hypothesis that small military groups, which compete in their normal training and garrison activities, will improve to a significantly greater extent in their interpersonal relations and in the

Source: This study was supported by a grant from the Office of the Surgeon General, Department of the Army. Reprinted with slight abridgment from the *Journal of Personality and Social Psychology*, 1966, 3, 321–327, with permission of Drs. Julian and Fiedler and the American Psychological Association, Inc., copyright holder.

psychological adjustment of their members than will controls receiving routine training.

However, as Deutsch (1962) has recently noted, the prototypic condition of completely cooperative relations among group members does not exist in the natural setting. "The members of a basketball team may be cooperatively interrelated with respect to winning the game but competitive with respect to being the 'star' of the team [pp. 277–278]." Men in military groups must also cooperate in the attainment of some common goals but may compete in order to achieve some personal goals such as special consideration from superiors, recommendation for promotion, or simply avoidance of undesirable details. The present investigation attempted to make the group situation more adjustive by shifting the relative emphasis to competitive relations *between groups* rather than among the individual members of the same group.

METHOD

Subjects

Men from 27 squads of a combat engineer battalion participated in the experiment as part of their normal training. This battalion was a combat-ready unit. The 178 men for whom complete data were available had served in the Army at least 6 months and had undergone a minimum of 16 weeks of individual basic training as well as additional training in their combat engineer specialties. The men ranged in age from 18 to 46, with a median age of 22 years; their educational level ranged from 8 to 16 years of school with a median of 12 years.

Design

The combat engineer battalion consisted of three field companies as well as headquarters and supporting troops. One of the field companies was randomly chosen to receive the competitive training condition (EC). The two control companies (CC) proceeded with training and duties on the post as before, without special instructions as far as the experiment was concerned.

Training, routine tasks and recreational activities in the experimental company were designed to emphasize competition among the 9 squads in the company while the 18 squads in the two control companies were not subjected to any experimental changes in training. Criteria of personal adjustment were obtained from questionnaires which were administered before and after a three-month period during which the competitive treatment was applied. Squad averages were computed from the individual adjustment measures. The general design of the investigation was thus a standard before and after comparison of groups which had been assigned to the experimental and control conditions.

Only the battalion commander, the battalion executive officer, and the commander of the experimental company were informed about the study. These officers worked closely with the project staff in devising and administering the experimental treatment. None of the other officers or enlisted men in the battalion knew about the experiment or were aware of any experimental changes in training, as indicated by interviews held after the conclusion of the study. These interviews also showed that the men assigned no particular significance to the questionnaires which were administered as "part of a survey for a medical research project."

Competition among Squads

Life in the military is characterized by continual surveillance and evaluation. A day may begin with a personal clothing inspection at reveille. Before breakfast has settled, a man finds he must clean and arrange his barracks area and then "police" the surrounding landscape to meet the requirements of still another inspection. Training activities also include this regular evaluation of performance. Such a routine offers innumerable opportunities for comparisons among individuals and among military units, together with the possibility of differential recognition and reward.

In essence, the present experimental treatment consisted in making these training and garrison activities into contests among the squads. Demerits, commendations, three-day passes, and other organizational rewards were earned by squads as a whole, in contrast with the control procedure of rewarding or punishing the individual. The investigators intermittently reviewed the procedures that were followed in both the experimental and control companies. These observations indicated that the two groups received approximately the same amount of rewards throughout the experimental period. Emphasis on intersquad competition was introduced into the experimental company (EC) very gradually, and eventually encompassed the various inspections of barracks areas, personal equipment, squad weapons, personal weapons, vehicles, etc. Training exercises were also conducted competitively by comparing squad performances, for example, in obstacle course maneuvers, bivouac, and in recreational games. The commander of the experimental company provided rewards for squad contests and judged the quality of squad performance. It should be stressed that the study involved no activities which were especially devised for the sake of the experiment. The military situation provided more than ample opportunity for intersquad competition, and none of the experimental procedures departed from accepted training procedures and military doctrine. The study merely called for a change in emphasis, designed to enhance the integrity and importance of squad membership and thus to heighten the sense of promotive relations among squad members.

Data analysis was limited to men who were present for both questionnaire testing sessions. The number of men present per squad varied from 2 to 9. The average number of men per squad included in the analysis was 4.4 for both the control and the experimental companies. Subjects attrition from pre- to posttest sessions was primarily due to regular military procedures (e.g., transfers, emergency furloughs, temporary duty assignments, etc.). There was some loss of data due to incomplete questionnaires. Both experimental and control groups, however, showed approximately equal attrition of subjects due to these sources. There was no evidence of differential selectivity or loss of subjects. Care was also taken to avoid involving company and battalion personnel in the administration of questionnaires. Attendance at testing sessions was compulsory for all personnel and men were excused from details to permit them to attend the testing sessions.

Adjustment and Interpersonal Relations Criteria

Self-report Adjustment Measures: The questionnaire battery contained three major indices of squad member adjustment: the Taylor Manifest Anxiety (*MA*) scale, a twelve-item evaluative self-description using a semantic differential format, and a Personal Reaction Form (PRF) composed of a set of graphic rating items which ask about reactions to military life and squad training.

The *MA* scale has been described elsewhere in detail (see Taylor, 1953). Choice of this measure as an index of adjustment is justified by Hoyt and Magoon (1954) and Buss (1955) who reported that *MA* scores are clearly related to such signs of tension and anxiety as hesitant speech, perspiration, and nervousness. Fiedler et al. (1959) also used *MA* scores successfully as one criterion of adjustment of men in small college and military groups.

The semantic differential self-descriptions were composed of twelve eight-point scales bounded by bipolar adjectives. The particular bipolar adjectives used here were chosen to reflect the evaluative dimension of connotative meaning, for example, "good-bad" and "friendly-unfriendly" (see Osgood, Suci, & Tannenbaum, 1957).

To determine whether the various "self-esteem" items could be combined into a single score these twelve scales were intercorrelated for the entire presession sample and factor analyzed separately for the descriptions of self, least-preferred co-worker, squad leader, and fellow squad member. Nine scales loaded sufficiently on the first factor in the four analyses to indicate consistency in the favorability of subject self-ratings. These were: pleasant-unpleasant, friendly-unfriendly, good-bad, lazy-hard-working, distant-close, cold-warm, self-assured-hesitant, efficient-inefficient, and fair-unfair. In addition, three scales appeared to define a second factor. These scales were: patient-impatient, sad-happy, and tense-relaxed; they again clustered in all four analyses. This factor was labeled "emotional adjustment" and was scored separately. Both the "self-esteem" and "emotional adjustment" ratings were obtained by summing the responses across the appropriate scales. The most favorable rating was scored 8, and least favorable, 1. Self-esteem scores thus could range from 72 to 9, and the emotional adjustment rating from 24 to 3.

Eleven graphic rating items were included in both the pre- and postsession Personal Reaction Forms. These PRF items were similarly intercorrelated and factor analyzed for the presession sample to identify those items which clustered. The items had been designed to obtain squad member reactions to, and perceptions of, various phases of Army life. Four clusters were identified and given the following labels: general adjustment to Army life, perceived integration of the squad, identification with own squad, and perceived harmony of the squad. Cluster scores were obtained for each man simply by summing his component item ratings.

Objective Indices of Adjustment: Additional information relevant to military adjustment was obtained at the termination of the experimental training period from disciplinary and medical records of the battalion.

The incidence of recorded disciplinary problems for the men of these units was quite low, and scores are, therefore, highly unreliable. It was possible, however, to compile a rough score for each squad. These scores indicated the history of any disciplinary problems for the men in each squad during the three-month experimental period. Each score was the cumulative incidence of any of the following: courts martial, disciplinary citations submitted to the company commanders by the military police, and disciplinary actions initiated by the respective company commanders.

To assess the probable psychogenic component of medical problems, a record was maintained of those men who reported for sick call during the three months of the investigation. As part of this record, the medical officer in charge of the dispensary rated each man who reported for sick call on the degree to which his complaint seemed to have a psychogenic origin. Those records were used to calculate a cumulative score for each squad in the battalion. The score was a function of the relative frequency of sick call visits multiplied by the psychogenic rating given each complaint by the attending medical officer. Although these scores did not permit the more sensitive before-after comparisons, postexperimental averages could be compared for the experimental and control squads.

Interpersonal Relations among Squad Members: The questionnaire battery also contained three types of measures indicative of the quality of the interpersonal relations among squad members. First, semantic differential descriptions of fellow squad members generated "interpersonal esteem" scores. These scores, calculated in the same manner as the self-esteem score described above, indicated the favorableness with which squad members perceive or judge one another. Such scores have previously been found related to expressions of positive feeling by group members (Julian & McGrath, 1963) and successful task performance (McGrath & Julian, 1962; Myers, 1962b).

Four sociometric nomination items comprised the second index of squad interpersonal relations. These four items asked for nominations of these: with whom you could talk over personal problems, with whom you would like to go on pass, who would make the best leaders for a combat mission, and with whom you work best. Three nominations were obtained for each question. A score was obtained by calculating the number of fellow squad members who were chosen by the men in a squad, as a proportion of the total choices they made. Thus, the higher the score, the greater the proportion of within-squad choices of confidants, friends, leaders, and work partners.

A third assessment indicative of the interpersonal relations among squad members was a measure of interpersonal knowledge or familiarity suggested by the battalion commander. We adopted an inventory of interpersonal knowledge developed by Havron and McGrath (1961) which requires each man to provide biographic information about his fellow squad members, for example, his home state, number of years of schooling received, and his middle name. Each man's familiarity score was computed as a ratio of the amount of correct information he gave to the total of possible correct answers. A high score showed that a man had proportionately close familiarity with his fellow squad members. This score is presumably related to the degree of interpersonal contact and communication among squad members.

RESULTS

Improvement in Adjustment

According to the major hypothesis of this study, intersquad competition should lead to improved interpersonal relations and squad member adjustment. Table 1 presents the statistical comparison of adjustment for the competitive and control squads.

Table 1 *Average Change in Adjustment for Members of Competitive and Control Squads*

	Squads	
Variable	Competitive	Control
Self-esteem	+1.9	−1.5**
Emotional adjustment	+1.3	− .6***
Anxiety (*MA* scale)	−1.4	+ .67***
Adjustment to Army life	+ .94	− .84**
Perceived squad integration	+ .92	− .38*
Identification with squad	+1.77	+ .60
Perceived squad harmony	− .71	−1.19
Perceived competition among squads	+1.22	+ .06***

Note: Statistical evaluation of differences between the competitive and control squads was calculated using the procedure for orthogonal comparisons among treatment means discussed in Edwards (1960, p. 140).

* $p < .10$, $df = 1/24$.
** $p < .05$, $df = 1/24$.
*** $p < .025$, $df = 1/24$.

Changes in self-esteem and emotional adjustment ratings indicated clearly the relative improvement in the self-perceptions of the squad members in competitive groups as compared with members of other squads. Squads trained under competitive conditions also had a lowered level of manifest anxiety on the Taylor scale. This improvement in personal adjustment was also observed in the men's reactions to military life. Improvement in general adjustment to the Army was indicated in responses to the items: "How strongly do you want to make a career of the Army?" and "How satisfied and contented have you been with military life?" (Cluster 1, PRF). Perceived Squad Integration (Cluster 2) included responses to the items: "How well do you feel you have gotten to know the other men in your squad?" "How similar do you feel that the men in your squad are to one another?" and "How well do the members of your squad work together?" A similar pattern of improvement was shown by the clusters designated "Identification with the Squad" and "Perceived Squad Harmony." In total, these changes point to a marked improvement in squad member morale, satisfaction, and personal adjustment under the competitive training conditions.

Table 1 also presents a comparison of the "perceived competition" among squads under the experimental and control training conditions. This item was included in the PRF and provided a check on the impact of the experimental competitive squad training.

Improvement of Squad Interpersonal Relations

Myers' study had shown that the competitive condition led to better interpersonal relations. This result was also expected in the present investigation. As shown in Table 2, changes in the hypothesized direction occurred in six of the seven measures, with two of these statistically significant. Interestingly enough, "esteem received" scores which reflected the favorableness with which squad members judged one another did not change significantly in competitive squads. Indeed, the scores showed a slightly greater improvement under control conditions than experimental conditions. Friendship choices for the sociometric nomination items paralleled the findings obtained for interpersonal esteem. These changes were shown in nominations of: "someone with whom you would talk over a personal problem" and "someone with whom you would like to go on a pass." Changes in intrasquad familiarity similarly paralleled the shifts in interpersonal esteem. Experimental, competitive squad members did not increase in their personal knowledge of one another.

The remaining two sociometric questions which are related to work and task relations among squad members did indicate a significantly greater change in intrasquad relations for competitive squads. Under the competitive training condition choices of "combat leaders" and "work partners" were more frequently made from among fellow squad members. Hence, at least for these small military groups, group com-

Table 2 *Average Change in Interpersonal Relations of Squad Members*

Variable	Squads: Competitive	Squads: Control
Esteem received from fellow squad members	+2.6	+4.5
Perceived emotional adjustment	+ .91	+ .80
Sociometric nominations		
Person with whom you would talk over personal problems	+ .25	+ .17
Person with whom you would like to go on pass	+ .16	+ .09
Person who would make best combat leader	+ .25	− .03**
Person with whom you work best	+ .24	+ .05*
Intrasquad familiarity	+ .32	+ .10

Note: Statistical evaluation of differences between the competitive and control squads was calculated using the procedure for orthogonal comparisons among treatment means discussed in Edwards (1960, p. 140).

* $p < .05$, $df = 1/24$.

** $p < .01$, $df = 1/24$.

petition led to an improvement in both the "work relations" and personal adjustment of the men. These effects, however, did not generalize to other relationships among squad members.

Objective Indices of Adjustment

Only terminal, postsession scores were available to measure medical and disciplinary problems in the squads. The average postsession levels for the experimental and control squads were compared using the Mann-Whitney U test on the ranked scores. No differences were found between conditions either for frequency of sick call visits adjusted for apparent psychogenic origin ($p > .05$, $U \leq 71$), or history of disciplinary problems during the three-month experimental period ($p > .05$, $U \leq 61$).

DISCUSSION

A possible limitation of the study lies in the fact that only one experimental and two control companies were used. In such a field study as this it is desirable to have several experimental units and several control units in order to take account of the variance due to sampling intact groups rather than individuals. For a number of reasons, this was not possible in the present study. Our experimental and control companies might have differed on certain critical variables, and these differences could account for our results. However, our data reveal no large pretest differences between experimental and control groups. Thus, it seems reasonable to conclude that the experimental results are valid.

The major significance of this study lies in the fact that we have been able to validate, under field conditions, the hypothesis that intergroup competition has quasi-therapeutic, adjustive effects on team members. The study supports the assumption that intergroup competition leads to improved work relations in the group, and to higher self-esteem, lower anxiety, and greater satisfaction with the conditions of group life. The quality of the interpersonal relations improves in task-related aspects but not necessarily in such aspects as wanting to go on pass with fellow squad members, or wishing to talk over personal problems with them. The improvement appears to be primarily in the trust and confidence the individual feels for his fellow group members, as shown by the significant increase of sociometric nominations of persons who would make a good combat leader and those with whom the individual can work best. Our data obviously cannot tell us whether the interpersonal relationship improved because the squad members became better adjusted, or whether the squad members adjusted because the interpersonal relationships improved. It seems reasonable to assume, however, that the latter is the case, or else, that improvement in adjustment and interpersonal relations occurred hand in hand. On the basis of our previous work (Fiedler et al., 1959), we are inclined to feel at this point that the improvement of the interpersonal relationship was causal to the improvement in adjustment. This interpretation is also clearly suggested by the findings of Alexander and Drucker (1960) who found that the experimental modification of group members' interpersonal perceptions, and hence, interpersonal relations, affected self-ratings of adjustment on the part of the individual who was the object of the perceptions.

While the results of this study, especially those relating to self-ratings and anxiety scores, are quite clear in support of our original hypothesis, the importance of this experiment is probably in the demonstration that task groups under field conditions can be engineered by appropriate environmental manipulation to contribute to the individual group member's adjustment. It further shows that such effects can be accomplished through administrative channels within the context of routine operational conditions rather than through the intervention of mental health specialists. This quasi-therapeutic effect is all the more striking inasmuch as combat engineer squads are not especially noted for the therapeutic environment which they provide for their members. In fact, it was most unfortunate for our study that the control companies began to imitate the experimental company's emphasis on intersquad competition even before the experiment was concluded. This, no doubt, materially lessened the effects of the manipulation which the study introduced.

In light of the critical shortage of professional personnel in the mental health field, the possibility of promoting better adjustment through relatively minor changes in the administrative structure opens an exciting vista of future possibilities.

The question must be asked whether the experimental manipulation had a favorable or adverse effect upon the groups' effectiveness. The data, based on military performance tests administered at the termination of the experiment, did not show significant differences between control and experimental companies. It is nevertheless noteworthy that the experimental company was later considered by post headquarters to have been the best project company on the post. It is also of interest that the entire battalion changed to the system of training introduced by the experimental company. There is thus ample evidence in this study that the intersquad competition not only aided in the adjustment of the individual, but that it also did not interfere with effective performance, if it did not, indeed, contribute to it.

SUMMARY

Nine combat engineering squads competed in their training and garrison duties to test the hypothesis that intergroup competition promotes close interpersonal relations among group members and improves morale and adjustment. Eighteen squads for whom no changes in training were introduced served as controls. Questionnaire measures of interpersonal relations and adjustment were obtained before and after a three-month experimental period. Changes in self-perceptions and reactions to military life showed a relative improvement in adjustment of the members of competitive squads as compared with members of control squads. Men trained under competitive conditions also had a lowered level of manifest anxiety on the Taylor scale. Improvement in the quality of interpersonal relations was indicated by a significantly greater change in within-squad sociometric choices of combat leaders and work partners for the members of competitive squads. However, these improvements did not generalize to nontask aspects of relations among squad members.

REFERENCES

Alexander, S., & Drucker, E. H. The effects of experimentally modified interpersonal perceptions on social behavior and adjustment. Tech. Rep. No. 9, 1960, U. of Illinois, Group Effectiveness Res. Lab., Contract DA-49-193-MD-2060, Office of the Surgeon General, U. S. Army.

Buss, A. H. A follow-up item analysis of the Taylor anxiety scale. *J. Clin. Psychol.*, 1955, **11**, 409–410.

Deutsch, M. Cooperation and trust: Some theoretical notes. In M. R. Jones (Ed.), *Nebraska symposium on motivation: 1962*. Lincoln: Univ. of Nebraska Press, 1962. Pp. 275–319.

Edwards, A. L. *Experimental design in psychological research*. New York: Rinehart, 1960.

Fiedler, F. E. The nature of teamwork. *Discovery*, 1962, **23**, 36–41.

Fiedler, F. E., Hutchins, E. C., & Dodge Joan S. Quasi-therapeutic relations in small college and military groups. *Psychological Monographs*, 1959, 73 (3, Whole No. 473).

Haefner, D., Langham, P., Axelrod, H., & Lanzetta, J. T. Some effects of situational threat on group behavior. *J. Abnorm. Soc. Psychol.*, 1954, **49**, 445–453.

Harvey, O. J. An experimental investigation of negative and positive relations between small groups through judgmental indices. *Sociometry*, 1956, **19**, 201–209.

Havron, M. D., McGrath, J. E., & Fay, R. J. The effectiveness of small military units: Parts I–III. PRS Report No. 980, 1961, Department of the Army, The Adjutant General's Office, Personnel Research Section, Institute for Research in Human Relations.

Hoyt, D. P., & Magoon, T. M. A validation study of the Taylor manifest anxiety scale. *J. Clin. Psychol.*, 1954, **10**, 357–371.

Julian, J. W., & McGrath, J. E. The influence of leader and member behavior on the adjustment and task effectiveness of negotiation groups. Technical Report No. 17, 1963, University of Illinois, Group Effectiveness Research Laboratory, Contract DA-49-193-MD-2060, Office of the Surgeon General, United States Army.

McGrath, J. E., & Julian, J. W. Negotiation and conflict: An experimental study. Technical Report No. 16, 1962, University of Illinois, Group Effectiveness Research Laboratory, Contract DA-49-193-MD-2060, Office of the Surgeon General, United States Army.

Myers, A. E. Competitive team golf with schizophrenics. Technical Report No. 14, 1962, University of Illinois, Group Effectiveness Research Laboratory, Contract DA-49-193-MD-2060, Office of the Surgeon General, United States Army. (a)

Myers, A. E. Team competition, success, and adjustment of group members. *J. Abnorm. Soc. Psychol.*, 1962, **65**, 325–332. (b)

Osgood, C. E., Suci, G. J., & Tannenbaum, P. H. *The measurement of meaning*. Urbana: Univ. of Illinois Press, 1957.

Paterson, T. T. *Morale in war and work*. London: Parrish, 1955.

Sherif, M., & Sherif, Carolyn W. *Groups in harmony and tension*. New York: Harper, 1953.

Taylor, Janet A. A personality scale of manifest anxiety. *J. Abnorm. Soc. Psychol.*, 1953, **48**, 285–290

9.5 SOME EFFECTS OF VARIATIONS IN OTHER STRATEGY UPON GAME BEHAVIOR

Charles G. McClintock
Philip Gallo
Albert A. Harrison

Several experiments have been conducted recently to investigate the relationship between internationalism-isolationism and game-playing behavior. Lutzker (1960) developed an internationalism scale and found that internationalists made more cooperative responses in a Prisoner's Dilemma game than isolationists. In a subsequent study, McClintock, Harrison, Strand, and Gallo (1963) varied the strategy that the internationalist and isolationist players encountered in a modified Prisoner's Dilemma game. Unbeknownst to the subjects in this experiment, a preprogramed sequence of "other-player" responses was provided by the experimenter. The subjects received either 85 per cent cooperative, 50 per cent cooperative, or 15 per cent cooperative responses. These experimenters found that the internationalist group made more cooperative choices than the isolationist group, but also observed that the three strategies followed by the simulated other player had no differential effect upon the number of cooperative responses within either group. Bixenstine, Potash, and Wilson (1963) also report that no fixed proportion of cooperative behavior on the part of a presumed partner affected differential cooperative behavior on the part of the subject.

The fact that the simulated other player's responses did not have an effect upon the subject's choices poses a difficult problem of interpretation. One cannot determine whether the subjects failed to respond to variations in the other player's strategy, or whether differences in the other player's strategy evoked different subject goals.

Depending upon the strategy of the other, different goals in different subjects, such as maximizing one's own gains regardless of the other player's gains or losses, or maximizing the difference between one's

Source: This research was supported by the Air Force Office of Scientific Research of the Air Research and Development Command. Reprinted with slight abridgment from the *Journal of Personality and Social Psychology*, 1965, 1, 319–325, with permission of the authors and the American Psychological Association, Inc.

own and the other player's gains, could produce the same proportion of cooperative responses across subjects.

The task of determining what predispositions are operative is difficult given the structure of the Prisoner's Dilemma game. The players are in a relationship which is more or less symmetrical and interdependent, and in which the subject may spend a considerable portion of his time attempting to modify the response pattern of the other player. In fact, this latter factor introduces another source of variance in interpreting the subject's responses. That is, one cannot determine whether a given response or response sequence by the subject represents: an attempt to modify the other player's response(s); a characteristic response to the game independent of the other player's response(s); and/or an attempt, given the subject's perception of the other player's strategy, to achieve a given goal such as maximizing his own gains, or the difference between his own and the other player's score.

The present study was designed to obtain additional information regarding some of the factors which contribute to the response patterns of individuals in the Prisoner's Dilemma game. The usual symmetry and interdependence of the Prisoner's Dilemma game were modified so that subjects could be observed under two conditions: a situation in which they could not markedly affect the outcome of the game, and subsequently, a situation in which they had almost complete control over their own and the other player's outcomes.

Thus, during the first situation (Session 1), it was possible for the experimenter, in the guise of the "other player," to vary systematically the experiences of subjects who had little control over their own and no control over the other player's outcome. And during the second situation (Session 2), in which the distribution of power was reversed, it was possible to observe whether the subjects' strategy varied as a function of this initial experience.

More specifically, the matrix employed in Session 1 (Figure 1) is structured to allow the "simulated" other player to select one of two strategies, I—the "X" response, which maximizes his own and the subject's payoffs, but may result in the subject winning more than himself, or II—the "Y" response, which enables the simulated other player to win more than the subject (in fact forces the subject to lose on each trial), but which results in a much lower absolute level of winning for the simulated other.

The subject also has a choice between two alternatives in Session 1. If the simulated other chooses the Y response, the subject's choice has no effect upon the payoffs. However, if the simulated other chooses the

MATRIX FOR SESSION 1

	A	B
X	YOU WIN 5¢ OPPONENT WINS 5¢	YOU WIN 10¢ OPPONENT WINS 5¢
Y	YOU LOSE 1¢ OPPONENT WINS 1¢	YOU LOSE 1¢ OPPONENT WINS 1¢

MATRIX FOR SESSION 2

	X	Y
A	YOU WIN 5¢ OPPONENT WINS 5¢	YOU WIN 1¢ OPPONENT LOSES 1¢
B	YOU WIN 5¢ OPPONENT WINS 10¢	YOU WIN 1¢ OPPONENT LOSES 1¢

Figure 1. Session 1 and Session 2 payoff matrices. (Subject chooses A or B in Session 1, X or Y in Session 2.)

X response, the subject's choice will influence his own payoff but not the payoff to his opponent. The subject may select either the "A" response, which gives each player an equal payoff, or the "B" response, which doubles the subject's payoff but leaves his opponent's unchanged. The choices and the power relationships are reversed in Session 2, with the subject controlling the X and Y choices.

The response alternatives available to the subjects in a conventional Prisoner's Dilemma game (Figure 2) are usually referred to in the literature as cooperative and competitive. An analysis of the structure of the conventional game indicates that a cooperative choice, if reciprocated, has two effects: (*a*) it gives an equal and satisfactory payoff and, (*b*) it is the point of maximum joint payoff. The competitive response, if unreciprocated, has three effects: (*c*) it maximizes the subject's payoff, (*d*) it minimizes his opponent's payoff, and, (*e*) it maximizes the difference between the two payoffs in favor of the competitor.

The consequences of the choices in the present game only partly parallel those of the conventional Prisoner's Dilemma game. The A response fulfills Criterion *a* above, whereas the B response fulfills Criteria *b*, *c*, and *e*. The X response fulfills *a* and can fulfill *b* and the Y response fulfills *d* and *e*. However, since the B and Y responses each fulfill two of the three criteria for competitive responses and the A and X each fulfill at least one criterion for cooperative responses, it would appear that the choice of B or Y is a more competitive response than the choice of A or X. For these reasons, the A and X responses

	PLAYER I	
	A	B
P	YOU WIN 5¢	YOU WIN 7¢
L		
A	OPPONENT	OPPONENT
Y	WINS 5¢	LOSES 4¢
E		
R	YOU LOSE 4¢	YOU LOSE 1¢
II		
	OPPONENT WINS 7¢	OPPONENT LOSES 1¢

Figure 2. An example of a conventional prisoner's dilemma payoff matrix.

will be referred to as the "cooperative" responses and the B and Y responses will be referred to as the "competitive" responses. It is, however, important to maintain the distinction between our definition of these terms and the usual definition encountered in the Prisoner's Dilemma literature.

Thus, in the present study the structure of the Prisoner's Dilemma game is modified so that the subject will be aware that he cannot directly affect the other player's responses and that he cannot be affected by them. Furthermore, the payoff matrices contain more extreme values than those normally employed in Prisoner's Dilemma games. These particular values were selected to determine whether subjects make responses which maximize their own outcomes even though such responses enable the other player to win as much or more than the subject, or responses which markedly reduce their own absolute winnings, but assure the subjects that they are winning more than the other player. Under these conditions, an attempt is made to determine whether either or both the more internationalistic and/or the more isolationistic subjects modify their behavior in Session 2 as a function of differences in the strategy of a simulated other in Session 1.

METHOD

Subjects

Eighteen male and 18 female students in a summer session psychology course at the University of Washington served as subjects. Within each sex, the subjects were randomly assigned to each of two experimental conditions, that is, a "cooperative other" or a "competitive other." Thus, each experimental group was composed of 9 females and 9 males. All subjects were run in like-sexed pairs. Whenever two subjects of the same sex were not available, a paid participant of the same sex was used to maintain the illusion that the subjects were playing against each other. The Internationalism-Isolationism Scale (Lutzker, 1960) was administered at the end of Session 2. For purposes of analysis, each experimental group was split at the median of its respective distribution of scores. There was no median overlap between the two groups, that is, all subjects called "internationalists," regardless of the experimental group, scored higher than all subjects called "isolationists." Thus, four orthogonal groups were employed in the analysis: internationalist-cooperative other, internationalist-competitive other, isolationist-cooperative other, and isolationist-competitive other. Although the distribution of sexes was unequal in the four groups, a separate analysis of variance, using sex as one independent variable, demonstrated that the results of the experiment could not be attributed to sex differences in style of play.

Experimental Procedure

Two game matrices were employed (Figure 1). In the Session 1 matrix the subjects controlled the A and B choices; in the Session 2 matrix, the X and Y. Since the other player was simulated, each subject had the same matrix at any given time, although each was led to believe that the other player controlled the X and Y choices in the Session 1 matrix, and A and B in the Session 2 matrix.

Each subject had a game board in front of him with the appropriate matrix displayed on it. Each of the game boards was connected to a master control panel operated by the experimenter, so that the experimenter had the option of sending the subject either a "cooperative" or a "competitive" response on any given trial. In the cooperative-other condition, in Session 1, the experimenter sent the subject 26 cooperative responses, X, and 4 competitive responses, Y. In the competitive-other condition, in Session 1, the experimenter sent the subject 4 cooperative responses and 26 competitive responses. In Session 2, the subjects in both conditions were sent 27 A and 3 B responses. In this instance an A response by the simulated other indicated to the subject that the other was playing a strategy which would enable both players to win the same amount and that he was not attempting to win more than the subject.

When the subjects entered the experimental room, a coin was flipped by the experimenter to determine the booth assignment. The subjects were informed that one subject had an initial advantage over the other, and the purpose of the coin was to determine the advantage by chance. They were told further that the experiment would be halted halfway through, and that they would then trade booths and reverse the advantage. In actuality, both subjects received the same treatment in both sessions.

The subjects were then seated in partitioned booths. They could not see each other or the experimenter. Each subject's game board was equipped with two response buttons and four lights to indicate mutual choices. The game was then explained and the equipment demonstrated. The instructions were designed to be as neutral as possible. Each subject was given $1.40, and told that they could keep whatever they had at the end of the experiment, they were then handed the matrices, which slipped over the game board, in such a way that they were not aware that they both had identical matrices. Payoffs were made after each trial by slipping coins through slits in the partitions.

At the end of 30 trials the subjects were told to hand the Session 1 matrices to the experimenter, to gather up their money, and to trade booths. When they were settled, Session 2 matrices were handed to them. After 30 more trials, the experiment was concluded. The subjects then completed the Internationalism-Isolationism Scale. When they had completed this task, the experiment was explained to them, and they were awarded $2.50 for having participated.

RESULTS

The choice behavior of internationalistic and isolationistic subjects by condition and by trial are presented in Table 1 in terms of the mean number of cooperative responses. Table 2[1] includes the results of a mixed design analysis of variance which takes into consideration the main effects of internationalism versus isolationism, cooperative versus competitive simulated other, and Session 1 versus Session 2, as well as relevant interaction effects.

In addition to the main analysis of variance, a supplementary analysis of variance was performed on the choice behavior of the ten

[1] Readers are referred to the original article for Table 2, which has been omitted for purposes of brevity.

subjects in each experimental group scoring highest and lowest on the Internationalism-Isolationism Scale. The results of the supplementary analysis are quite similar to the results of the main analysis. The relative position of the means that enter into the three-way interaction is preserved.

Table 1 *Mean Number of Cooperative Choices for Internationalists and Isolationists by Condition and by Session*

Strategy of Simulated "Other Player"	Internationalists		Isolationists	
	Session 1	Session 2	Session 1	Session 2
Cooperative	7.11	23.77	9.44	18.56
Competitive	11.22	16.33	8.56	21.00

It can be seen from these tables that in this particular game situation, internationalists did not demonstrate an overall tendency to be more cooperative than isolationists. In line with previous findings, the cooperative-other and competitive-other strategies did not have an effect on the overall number of cooperative choices made by the subjects. However, the interaction between personality, strategy of the other, and parts of the game is significant. This interaction, using the data from all subjects, is presented visually in Figure 3. Inspection of this interaction indicates that the two-way interaction between parts of the experiment and strategy of the other player was significantly different for internationalists as compared to isolationists. Both groups made significantly more cooperative responses in Session 2, which is not surprising since a cooperative response in this session also maximizes the subjects' absolute gains.

It appears that the strategy of the player had little differential effect upon the isolationists in Session 1 and Session 2. However, the internationalists made more cooperative responses in Session 1 when faced with a competitive opponent than when playing against a cooperative opponent. This pattern was reversed in Session 2 with the internationalists being more likely to allow a previously cooperative opponent to win as much or more than their previously competitive opponent.

Finally, it is apparent that even though a greater proportion of cooperative responses were made in Session 2 than in Session 1, there was still a substantial number of competitive responses made across

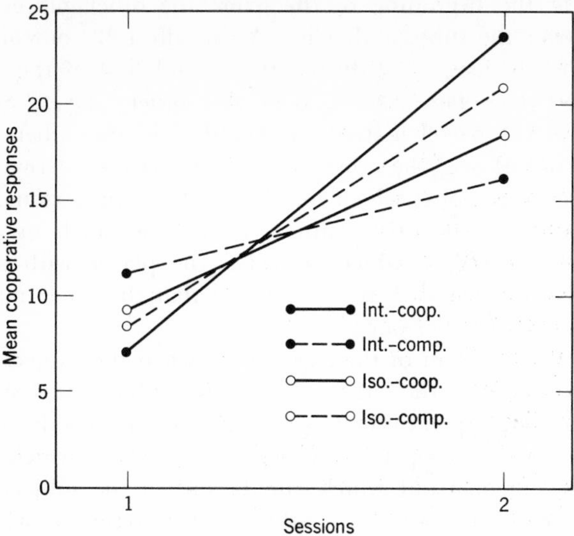

Figure 3. Mean number of "cooperative" responses made by internationalists and isolationists in Session 1 and Session 2 under conditions of "cooperative other" and "competitive other."

subjects in Session 2. These responses occurred even though the subjects knew they would receive $.05 if they made a cooperative response, and only $.01 if they made a competitive response. Thus, it appears that even when it is substantially more profitable in terms of absolute winnings to make a cooperative response, subjects continue to make a surprising proportion of competitive responses to ensure that they win more than the other player.

DISCUSSION

In the present experiment two major modifications of the Prisoner's Dilemma game were made to determine whether differences in the strategy of the other player differentially affected the responses made by internationalistic and isolationistic subjects. First, the nature of the interdependent relationship between players was modified so that the subjects were first in a position where they had a minimal effect upon the outcome of the game (Session 1), and then they assumed a position where they could control the outcome (Session 2). In terms of the theoretical paradigm of Thibaut and Kelley (1959), one could say that at the beginning of the game the other player had "fate control" over the subject, that is, "A can affect B's outcomes regardless of what B does," and during the second half of the experiment the subject had fate control over the other player. Second, the structure of the payoff matrix was modified so that when one player had fate control over the other, he could select one of two behavioral alternatives, a response which maximized his own personal gain, but which permitted the other subject to win as much or more than himself, or a response which provided the player with a markedly smaller absolute payoff, but assured him that the other player would receive an even smaller one.

During the first half of the experiment when the subject was under the fate control of the other player, the subject was still able to exercise an effect upon his own outcome under one condition. Namely, if the other made a cooperative response, that is, one which maximized the other's outcome but which also permitted the subject to win as much or more, the subject could select a response which would enable him to gain equivalent winnings, or a response which would enable him to win twice as much as the other player. If, however, the other player selected a competitive response, that is, one which maximized the difference between his own and the other player's score, the subject's response did not affect the outcome. During this phase of the experiment, a determination was made as to whether the subjects given a simulated competitive or cooperative strategy by the other player would opt for equivalent or higher payoffs should the simulated other select a cooperative response. That is, would the subject attempt to inform the other player who had fate control over him that he was attempting to achieve equivalent rewards (cooperation), or that he was attempting to achieve the highest rewards, and to maximize the difference between his own and the player's winnings (competition).

The data from Session 1 indicate that a substantial proportion of the responses (70%) made by the subject when under the fate control of a simulated other player were ones which reflected an attempt by the subject to achieve the highest reward possible for themselves—one substantially higher than the other player. There were no significant differences in the proportion of such responses selected between subjects who were "cooperated" with or "competed" against by the other player, nor were there significant differences between internationalists and isolationists. In comparing groups (internationalists versus isolationists) by treatments (cooperative versus competitive other), we also find no significant difference in Session 1. We can note that the internationalists who play with a cooperative other tend to select the highest proportion (76%) of competitive responses, whereas the internationalists who play with a competitive other select the lowest proportion (63%) of competitive responses. The two isolationistic groups fall between these two proportions. Thus, the internationalists in the cooperative conditions seem to be more likely to play to maximize their own gain and the difference between their own and the other player's score—perhaps under the assumption that when the positions of fate control are reversed they will support similar behavior on the part of the other player. The internationalists under the competitive condition made the largest proportion of cooperative responses—perhaps to indicate to the other player that they would settle for equivalent rewards if he would shift from a competitive to a cooperative strategy.

When the positions of power of the players were reversed in the second part of the experiment, we observe that indeed the internationalists who were cooperated with during Session 1, and who most frequently selected responses which would enable them to maximize their own gains, show a greater increment in cooperative responses in Session 2. That is, they most frequently select responses which permit themselves the highest absolute reward while permitting the other player to win as much or more than themselves. Conversely, the internationalists who were competed against in Session 1 show the smallest increment in cooperative responses in Session 2. It would appear that when the other player has fate control over the internationalistic subjects, and selects competitive responses, the internationalists attempt to modify the other's behavior by making a greater proportion of responses that indicate they are willing to settle for equivalent rewards. When this fails, and when they assume fate control in Session 2, the internationalists retaliate by selecting the highest proportion of competitive responses, even when such responses markedly reduce their own absolute payoffs. In contrast to the internationalists, the isolationists appear to be less sensitive to differences in the strategy of the other player, both in Session 1 and Session 2.

In general it appears that variations in the strategy of a simulated other player do produce differences in subjects' responses when, those subjects are internationalistic in orientation, and when the Prisoner's Dilemma game is modified in the ways described above. It seems that for internationalistic subjects "cooperation" fosters "cooperation," and "competition" fosters "competition." At this point in research on game-playing behavior, it seems necessary to investigate more intensively the differences between two predispositions or player goals, namely, the selection of a strategy which maximizes personal gains regardless of the outcomes afforded to the other player, and a strategy which maximizes the differences between own and the other player's payoffs. In real life it is likely that there are marked differences between the motives which are expressed in terms of these two strategies.

SUMMARY

Internationalist and isolationist *S*s played a two-part modification of the Prisoner's-Dilemma-type game. Though they did not know it, they were actually playing against *E*, rather than each other. In the first part of the experiment, *S*s had little control over the payoff matrix. In the second part, *S*s had virtually total control over the payoffs. During the first part of the experiment, *E* played a "cooperative" strategy against half of the *S*s and a "competitive" strategy against the other half. The results indicated that neither the strategy played against *S*s nor the personality of *S*s influenced the number of cooperative choices. However, a significant three-way interaction indicated that internationalists are more sensitive to changes in their opponents' strategies.

REFERENCES

Bixenstine, V. E., Potash, H. M., & Wilson, K. V. Effects of level of cooperative choice by the other player on choices in a Prisoner's Dilemma game. Part I. *J. Abnorm. Soc. Psychol.*, 1963, **66,** 308–313.

Lutzker, D. Internationalism as a predictor of cooperative behavior. *J. Conflict Resol.*, 1960, 4, 426–435.

McClintock, C. G., Harrison, A. A., Strand, Susan, & Gallo, P. Internationalism-isolationism, strategy of the other player, and two-person game behavior. *J. Abnorm. Soc. Psychol.*, 1963, **67,** 631–636

Thibaut, J. W., & Kelley, H. H. *The social psychology of groups.* New York: Wiley, 1959.

9.6 GROUP PROBLEM SOLVING UNDER TWO TYPES OF EXECUTIVE STRUCTURE

Thornton B. Roby
Elizabeth H. Nicol
Francis M. Farrell

One of the central problems of organization theory is that of determining the most efficient locus of decision making authority and responsibility. As Simon (1957, pp. 26–28) notes, the usual pronouncements on this problem, couched in terms of "span of control," "unity of command," "specialization," and "minimization of organizational levels" are likely to lead to inconsistencies in any particular case. It appears that a fruitful study of the organizational decision making problem will require a schema that permits the precise specification of all the factors that may be operative.

In a recent article (Roby, 1961), a schema for describing "executive structures" has been proposed that appears to lend itself to this problem. Essentially, this schema reduces the description of such structures to a specification of the particular environmental and response information that is brought to bear on each component decision. It assumes that there are measurable degrees of relevancy of various items of information for any such component decision, and an effective structure is simply one that provides the most relevant information for each decision that must be made. In principle, even such diverse classes of "information" as task *expertise* and human relations skills may be subsumed in this paradigm.

This formulation of the group decision-making problem implies that the optimum locus of authority may depend very critically on the nature of the decisions to be made. Specifically, if the correct response by each group member to a task situation depends on prior or subsequent responses by other group members, then a centralized

Source: The research reported in this paper was conducted by the authors under a joint research arrangement between Tufts University and Decision Sciences Laboratory (L. G. Hanscom Field, Bedford, Mass.) under Contract No. AF 19(604)-5727. Further reproduction is authorized to satisfy needs of the United States Government. This is ESD-TDR-63-139. Reprinted with slight abridgment from the *Journal of Abnormal and Social Psychology*, 1963, 67, 550–556, with permission of the authors and the American Psychological Association, Inc., copyright holder.

structure will result in more rapid attainment of the correct problem solution than a decentralized structure. On the other hand, if the correct response by each group member is independent of the responses performed by other group members, then a decentralized structure will result in a more rapid attainment of the correct problem solution than a centralized structure.

In the former case, a central authority, who decides what responses each person will make, knows directly what those responses will be. This information would not be immediately accessible to other group members.[1] If the principal determinant of correct responses is the state of the external environment, on the other hand, individual group members will typically be in a position to follow very closely the environmental conditions of greatest relevance to their own response decisions.

An extreme example of the former situation is represented by highly ambiguous environmental conditions under which any concerted action by the group may be better than uncoordinated, and perhaps conflicting, efforts by individual group members—however well conceived the latter may be in isolation.[2] Whether or not such conditions ever obtained in fact, they are probably approached in real-life situations. In any case, it seems reasonable to assume that centralization becomes relatively more effective as the various component decisions become more closely interactive.

The present study was intended as a preliminary test of this proposition in a simple laboratory task with well-defined functional relationships between environmental inputs and group actions.

PROCEDURE

Task Description

The task consisted of simple problems whose solution required subjects to acquire environmental state information from display lights and to adjust the settings of certain response switches.

[1] An exception to this assumption should be made in the case of more intimate, face-to-face groups, such as athletic teams or small instrumental ensembles. In such groups, direct observations can be made of other group members' actions and the special advantage of the centralized structure would not obtain.

[2] Simon (1957) gives the example of ten persons who cooperate in building a boat. If each has his own plan, and they do not communicate their plans, the chances are that the resulting craft will not be very seaworthy; they would probably meet with better success if they adopted even a very mediocre design, and if then all followed this same design [pp. 9–10].

Each of four operator booths was provided with a control box on which were mounted two display lights and two double-throw response switches (see Figure 1). Response switches were designated by the letter "R" followed by a number; for example, R1 and R2 were the labels on the response switches in the first booth, R3 and R4 were in the second booth, and so on. The display lights were distinguished by labels with the letter "L" and a number, L1 and L2 being in the first booth, L3 and L4 in the second booth, and so on.

The display lights were controlled by the experimenter from a central console. In connection with the experimental problems, the "on" and "off" states of the lights were assigned values of $+1$ and -1, respectively. The two positions of the switches, "up" and "down," were also assigned $+1$ and -1 values, respectively.

With this equipment, four-man teams of subjects were asked to solve problems consisting of sets of simple equations requiring only multiplication of $+1$ and -1 elements.

To illustrate, subjects may be given the task of setting their switches to $+$ or $-$ values in order to satisfy the following three equations:

$$\text{L1 L4 R2} = +1 \quad (1)$$
$$\text{L2 L5 R4 R6} = -1 \quad (2)$$
$$\text{L3 R1 R6} = +1. \quad (3)$$

On a typical trial, the experimenter might set in the values: L1 = $+1$, L2 = $+1$, L3 = -1, L4 = $+1$, L5 = -1 (L6, L7, L8 are irrelevant in this problem). Then, since the product of L1 and L4 is $+1 \times +1 = +1$, the subject responsible for R2 should set his switch at $+1$ also in order to satisfy Equation 1. From Equation 2 it is noted that the product of L2 and L5 is -1 which is also the value that the entire product on the left must have to satisfy the equation. Thus, the product of R4 and R6 must be $+1$. Both switches must be set alike: either both positive or both negative. Finally, since L3 in Equation 3 is negative, it is necessary for the product of R1 and R6 to be negative in order to obtain the value $+1$ on the right. Thus, R1 and R6 must be set at opposite signs. It should be noted that R6 enters into both Equations 2 and 3; it must be adjusted so as to satisfy both of these equations at the same time. Thus, the subject controlling that switch must coordinate his switch action with the subjects controlling response switches R4 and R1.

The minimum degree of coordination required among switch actions and therefore among subjects can be determined by the design

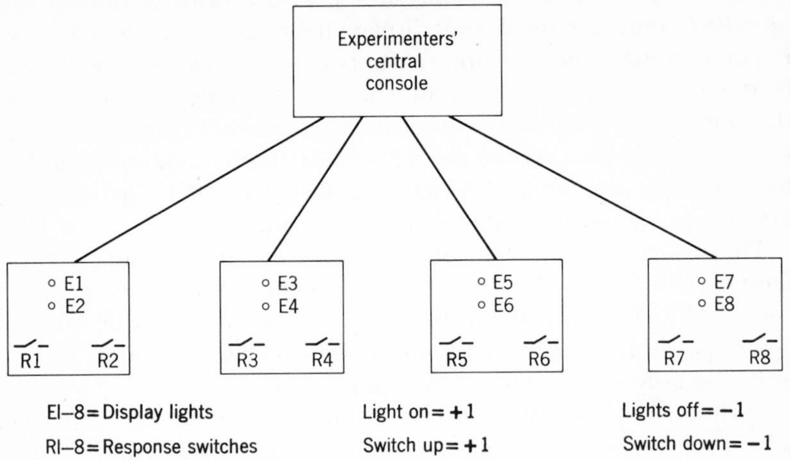

Figure 1. Diagram indicating essential features of problem-solving equipment. (The subjects' display-and-response boxes were located in separate booths.)

of the problems. Since the switches and display lights were numbered consecutively for the four operator booths, an equation containing, for example, the elements L1, L4, L5, and R7 would require the participation of all four subjects: the first three subjects would have to provide information concerning the state of the lights, while the fourth subject would have to adjust Response Switch Number 7. In this experiment all of the problems required the participation of all four subjects.

Two classes of problems were formulated:

1. Problems whose solutions required reaction only to environmental state information. These are called "E contingent problems." Equation 1 illustrates the E contingent function since the correct setting for R2 depends only on the "state of the world" as reflected in L1 and L4.

2. Problems whose solutions require subjects to coordinate response actions. These are called "R contingent." Equation 2 is one example and the *pair* of equations 2 and 3 is another.

A *problem* consisted of a set of four equations all of which had to be satisfied contemporaneously. When this was accomplished, the subjects received a confirming signal after an automatic 15-second delay. The purpose of this delay was to avoid reinforcement for solutions that occurred through random behavior.

The basic equations were set into the central control console by a banana-plug switchboard which permitted up to four elements (L's or R's or combinations thereof) to be used in each equation, but new problems could be introduced by changing the L values. The switchboard has the capacity for stipulating eight equations at one time, but the present experiment required only four.

Experimental Design

The experiment was set up to test the effects of "executive structures" on the speed with which problems are solved by small groups. Two types of executive structure were studied: one in which problem solving responsibility rested in only one team member, and one in which every man in the group had responsibility for solving one part of the problem. These contrasting structures will be referred to as "centralized" and "distributed" conditions.

Groups organized in one or the other of these ways worked the two kinds of problems mentioned earlier: problems requiring reaction primarily to environmental state information (E contingent) and problems requiring coordination of subjects' responses (R contingent). Each E-contingent equation required subjects to take three lights into account in setting one response switch. The R-contingent equations, on the other hand, required them to take one light into account while adjusting three response switches.

The degree of interdependence between the various elements in the separate equations was equated between E-contingent and R-contingent conditions. This could be done very simply with these equations since the problem sets are identical to each other with L and R interchanged, as may be seen in the illustrative problems of Table 1.

Each equation involves either a light or a switch for every subject.

Under the so-called "distributed" executive structure, each of the four team members was given a card bearing only one of the four equations constituting a problem. It was the individual's responsibility to obtain the necessary information from the other group members and to direct the setting of the switches involved in his part of the problem. The equations assigned to individual subjects did not involve the single R for which they were responsible in the E-contingent condition or the single L to which they had direct access in the R-contingent condition.

In the "centralized" type of executive structure, one subject was

Table 1 *Illustrations of the Two Types of Problems*

Equation	E-Contingent Problems	Equation	R-Contingent Problems
1	L1 L3 L8 R5 = +1	1	R1 R3 R8 L5 = +1
2	L2 L3 L5 R7 = +1	2	R2 R3 R5 L7 = +1
3	L4 L5 L7 R1 = −1	3	R4 R5 R7 L1 = −1
4	L1 L6 L7 R3 = −1	4	R1 R6 R7 L3 = −1

Note: L elements refer to specific display lights; R elements indicate response switches.

appointed "leader"; he had the entire set of four equations which were not made available to others in the group. It was his task to obtain the L state information from the others and to direct them in setting their response switches.

The "centralized" condition was further subdivided to afford an additional comparison, "best" leaders versus "worst" leaders: the leader for some trials was the team member with the highest apparent aptitude; for other trials the leader was the person with the lowest apparent aptitude. These two subconditions shall be called "C1" and "C4"; the letter "C" indicates centralization, while the digits 1 and 4 refer to the leader's relative standing in a four-man group. The team members who were rated second or third in apparent aptitude did not serve as leaders in this experiment.

The next section on Administrative Procedure will explain how these ratings of best and worst leader were made by the two experimenters.

Eight groups of subjects took part in the experiment, each group being tested in two separate sessions conducted on consecutive days. On each day the group worked through a problem under each of four combinations of the main experimental variables.

The subjects were airmen from the 3245th AC & W Squadron (Exptl) who were experienced in air surveillance tasks.

Administrative Procedure

Groups were first given a brief orientation talk in which it was explained that the experiments were concerned with problems of group performance in tasks similar to those involved in air defense. It was further explained that in order to obtain adequate control over the relevant conditions it was necessary to study these problems in a highly simplified task requiring information exchange and coordination of response actions.

After the orientation, the group members were assigned to booths and were provided with booklets reviewing the algebra of multiplication; these booklets contained sets of practice problems which the members worked at their own pace. As each set was completed, subjects called on the experimenter to check their answers. This gave the two experimenters an opportunity to assess each subject's aptitude in dealing with problems of this type. Individual instruction was given as needed to subjects experiencing difficulty with the written practice problems.

Following completion of the written practice problems, the use of the equipment in solving equations was then explained and demonstrated. Several sample problems of increasing difficulty were worked by the subjects using the response switches. This equipment-oriented practice period afforded the experimenters another opportunity for rating the subjects according to their apparent ability and grasp of the problem situation. The two experimenters, conferring together, chose the best leader and worst leader on the basis of their observation during the orientation and practice sessions.

Just prior to a test trial, the subjects were given the appropriate problem. If the trial was to be under the "centralized" condition, a card bearing *four* equations was given to the leader. If the trial was to be under the "distributed" condition, a card bearing *one* equation was given to each subject.

Before each trial, subjects were instructed to set their switches in the positive (up) position. Their compliance could be verified from the experimenters' console display. At a "go" signal, the subjects began to solve the problem. Intersubject conversations were tape recorded and an Esterline-Angus 20-pen recorder preserved a record of all switch actions. The time taken to solve each problem was automatically clocked. If a problem was not solved within 15 minutes, the trial was halted and a time score of 15 minutes was entered on the experimental record. This limit was reached only three times in the course of the experiment.

As was mentioned earlier, four problems were run under different conditions in each session. For each problem, two trials were run; these trials differed only in the "L values" (display lights) controlled by the experimenter. After the first trial, some of the display lights were changed and the subjects reworked the problem incorporating the new values.

RESULTS

The chief dependent variable was time to obtain the correct solution to the equations. The 16 time scores for each group were converted into speed scores (reciprocal of time in minutes) and were multiplied by 100 for convenience in computation. The latter scores appear to have an approximately normal distribution with some positive skewness.

The mean speed scores for the principal experimental conditions are shown in Table 2.

Table 2 *Mean Speed Scores under Various Experimental Conditions*

Executive Condition	E-Type Problems	R-Type Problems	Total
Session 1			
C1	44.63	48.25	46.44
C4	45.88	14.25	30.06
D	94.81	35.19	65.00
Total	70.03	33.22	51.63
Session 2			
C1	74.88	59.75	67.31
C4	61.63	22.50	42.06
D	95.56	45.31	70.44
Total	81.91	43.22	62.56
Both sessions pooled			
C1	59.75	54.00	56.88
C4	53.75	18.38	36.06
D	95.19	40.25	67.72
Total	75.97	38.22	57.09

Notes: C1 = best leader, C4 = worst leader, D = distributed responsibility, E-type = environment-contingent problem, R-type = response-contingent problem.

The experimental findings may be summarized as follows:

Problem-Type Differences: Problems requiring reaction to environmental changes were solved more quickly than problems involving coordination of response actions among the subjects. The time taken to solve E-type problems averaged 2.59 minutes, while that for R-type problems averaged 4.35 minutes. The difference is significant at the .001 level.

It will be recalled that these two problem types were entirely equated for the minimum amounts of interaction required among subjects. Thus, it is reasonable to attribute the obtained differences between them entirely to the greater ambiguity of the R-contingent condition. Put rather strongly, the freedom of action offered by the R-contingent task actually makes it more difficult.

Executive Structure Differences: Comparison of the time scores for the three executive structure conditions—best leader, worst leader, and group shared solutions—showed significant differences ($p < .01$). Fastest times were clocked for the best leaders, group shared solutions were next, and the worst leaders were the slowest. Our main interest, however, is not so much in executive structures per se as in the relation of executive structures to the two problem types.

Executive Structures in Relation to Problem Types: The interaction between problem types and executive structures was statistically significant. With problems requiring reaction to environmental states, fastest solutions were reached when crew members shared responsibility equally. For the R-contingent problems (requiring coordination of subjects' responses), the centralized structure with the high aptitude subject as leader was clearly superior. For both types of problems the centralized structure with the low aptitude leader was least effective. The difference between best and worst leaders is most pronounced with R-contingent problems. These results are shown graphically in Figure 2.

As an additional check on the significance of this interaction, the mean square was tested against its own "residual" consisting of those second-order interactions which include the structure and problem-type factors. The resulting F ratio of 6.64 ($df = 2/10$) has a probability of approximately .02. Hence, the interaction between executive structures and problem types is a reliable effect over the conditions of this experiment.

Sequential Effects: It will be recalled that, in each of two sessions, subjects were given two trials on each of four problems (the E values being varied for each trial). The analysis of variance showed no significant variations over the two trials, over the four problems, or over the two sessions. In other words there are no significant variations in speed attributable to sequential effects.

One interaction, however, was marginally significant (slightly above the .05 level). This was the interaction between trials and sessions. In order to check on the reliability of this result, the mean square for the interaction was tested against the mean square of the second-order interactions in which the trial and session factors were involved. The

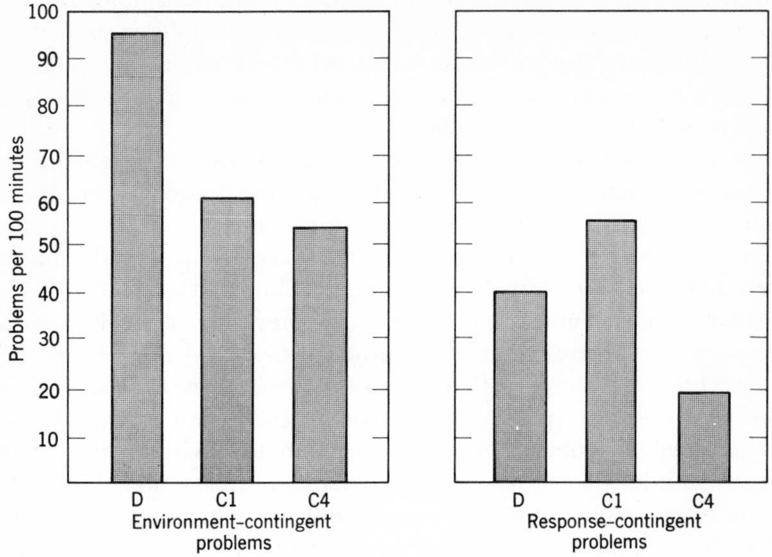

Figure 2. Bar graphs show average speed of solving two types of problems under different conditions of executive structure. ("C1" refers to the scores made under the leadership of the "best" team member, "C4" indicates leadership by the "poorest" team member, and "D" indicates the condition in which all team members shared responsibility equally.)

resulting *F* ratio is insignificant. Inspection of the data also revealed that the apparent effect was entirely attributable to the fact that the two highest speed scores occurred, respectively, on a first trial in one group's first session and on a second trial in another group's second session. Thus, the apparent interaction of trials and sessions is considered a random sampling effect.

DISCUSSION

The hypothesis on which the study was based is that centralized executive structures are *relatively* more effective for decisions or tasks of which the principal determiner of response effectiveness is the identity of other ongoing responses. Distributed executive structures, on the other hand, are *relatively* more effective for decisions or tasks in which response effectiveness is primarily determined by the state of the external environment. These differences in relative effectiveness presumably arise from differential access to the important classes of information. Subject to several qualifications discussed below, the data strongly support this hypothesis.

Perhaps the most important restriction that must be placed on the generality of our hypothesis arises from the results for the C4 condition, indicating that there is a lower bound for leader ability below which the centralized condition may not be effective for any type of problem.

In addition, however, several quite special conditions of this study should be pointed out. The subjects were Air Force personnel and hence may have adapted unusually well to the centralized structure. Further, the distributed structure used in this study, in which each group member was responsible for one equation, is different from an undifferentiated, completely "open" authority structure, in which group members share all decisions uniformly. Finally, the performance criterion here used was speed of problem solution. It is possible that other criteria of effectiveness would not yield the same pattern with respect to experimental conditions.

Granting that the substantive findings of this study require confirmation under a wider range of conditions, the methodological gain seems more secure. Both the conceptual apparatus and the laboratory apparatus here employed appear to lend themselves well to a definite, if rarified, treatment of one aspect of a complex problem. It remains to be demonstrated that these tools can be applied to a systematic, cumulative investigation of other facets of the relation between authority structures and performance.

SUMMARY

Speed of problem solving by four-man teams of airmen was measured for two conditions of group organization: (a) with responsibility centered in one team member, and (b) with responsibility shared equally by all members. Problems in algebraic form required *S*s to acquire environmental state information and to adjust the settings of certain response switches. The two conditions of group structure and two types of problems were varied factorially. Analysis of variance indicates (a) that problems requiring reaction to environmental changes are more quickly solved under the shared responsibility condition, and

(b) that problems involving coordination of action among operators are more efficiently solved with a competent centralized authority. Designation of a low-aptitude group member as leader produced inferior performance on both problem types.

REFERENCES

Roby, T. B. The executive function in small groups. In L. Petrullo & B. M. Bass (Eds.), *Leadership and interpersonal behavior.* New York: Holt, Rinehart, & Winston, 1961. Pp. 118–136.

Simon, H. A. *Administrative behavior: A study of decision-making processes in administrative organization,* 2nd ed. New York: Macmillan, 1957.

9.7 GROUP DISCUSSION AND PREDICTED ETHICAL RISK TAKING

Salomon Rettig

Mob action and the behavior of gangs and crowds seem to suggest a qualitative transformation of individual standards of conduct when acting in groups. Socially undesirable behaviors unlikely to take place in isolation can be observed in crowds. These observations have given rise to much speculation and to some recent experimentation with group-induced assertiveness in behavior. One particularly cogent view maintains that the group situation facilitates risk-taking behavior, and recent experiments with group risk taking have tended to support this view. Wallach, Kogan, and Bem (1962, 1964) have consistently found that group decisions produce shifts toward greater risk taking, whether the payoff is hypothetical or real. The same results were obtained when monetary gains were paired with an aversive stimulation (Bem, Wallach, & Kogan, 1965). Lonergan and McClintock (1961), who had hypothesized a shift toward increased conservatism, also found a consistent increase in risk taking in interdependent groups, although this trend apparently did not reach acceptable

Source: This study was supported by a grant from the National Institutes of Health. Reprinted from the *Journal of Personality and Social Psychology,* 1966, 3, 629–633, with permission of the author and the American Psychological Association, Inc.

levels of statistical significance ($p < .10$). In a very recent experiment Wallach and Kogan (1965) attempted to separate the effects of group discussion and group consensus on risk taking. They found that the shift toward increased risk taking which resulted from group discussion alone was as large as that produced by discussion and consensus. Consensus alone produced no effect. The authors concluded that "group discussion provides the necessary and sufficient condition for generating the risky shift effect [p. 17]."

In their explanation of the above results Wallach et al. (1964) repeatedly conjecture that the group situation produces increased risk taking because it permits the diffusion of responsibility. Since the entire group participates in the decision-making process, each member shares his responsibility with the group. Such spreading of responsibility allows for the choice of higher risk levels and the increased probability of failure associated with it (p. 273). It would seem that the principle of "responsibility diffusion" would have been more plausible had group consensus rather than group discussion been the critical determinant of increased risk taking, since a group can be held collectively responsible only for a decision reached but not for the process of discussion preceding the decision. In their defense of the concept of responsibility diffusion in relation to group discussion Wallach and Kogan (1965) find it necessary to resort to an additional, noncognitive explanation of the results by stating that the group discussion produces affective ties among its members which enable each to feel less blameworthy in case of failure, following a risky decision (p. 19).

In evaluating the noncognitive solution to the problem of group-induced risk taking, one must take into account the fact that the subjects were randomly assigned to the groups (Wallach & Kogan, 1965, p. 5) and that the somewhat artificial atmosphere of an experiment, coupled with the temporary formation of a group, leaves little possibility for the establishment of strong affective ties among the subjects. Instead, the present study wishes to suggest a somewhat different possibility which may account, at least in part, for the observed increased risk taking which follows group discussion; the possibility that group discussion may produce a shift in orientation away from failure avoidance and toward the maximization of gain. This shift in orientation may be accompanied by a tendency to take greater risks. The above explanation has the advantage of simplicity, making it unnecessary to refer to the theorem of responsibility diffusion. The latter, while intuitively appealing, is a very complex explanation of risk taking since it implies that the taking of responsibility in a group is a sharable process which reduces the responsibility of each member.

The present study is designed to relate predictive judgments of unethical behavior to different external conditions of judgment, predominantly that of group discussion. The specific hypothesis tested is that group discussion will produce a shift in predictive judgments of unethical behavior which is similar to that produced by varying other sources of risk, namely, privacy and impersonality of judgment. That is, the occurrence of unethical behavior would (be predicted to) be more frequent if such judgments predict the behavior of a hypothetical person rather than the behavior of the subject himself, and when the judgments are expected to remain private rather than become public, since self-disclosure and publicity about unethical behavior carry a greater likelihood of censure. Conversely, impersonality and privacy about such predictions represent judgment conditions of low risk. If group discussion produces greater risk taking, it should show an effect similar to that obtained by making the predictive judgments impersonal and private.

While predictive judgments about the occurrence of unethical behavior are not the equivalent of actual risk-taking behavior, the multidimensional scale designed to measure such judgments has been shown to predict the actual unethical behavior of the judges (Rettig & Pasamanick, 1964; Rettig & Sinha, 1965). In these experiments it became evident that the intervening variable between predictive judgment and behavior was sensitivity to social censure. Subjects who took behavioral risks (e.g., of cheating in order to increase monetary gains) were found to make greater discrimination in judgment between matched items portraying unethical behavior differing only in the negative reinforcement value of censure (RV_{cens}) than subjects who did not take such risks. Matching the same stimulus items in accordance with other built-in determinants of unethical behavior, such as the expectancy (E_{gn}) and the reinforcement value of gain (RV_{gn}) or the expectancy of censure (E_{cens}), produced no results. The above relationship between unethical (risk-taking) behavior and impersonal predictive judgments was obtained despite the interval of one year between behavior and judgment. The results were explained in terms of differential learning, in that subjects motivated to take unethical risks apparently have learned to be generally more sensitive about censure since it had served as a (negative) reinforcer during previous behavior. Subjects not motivated to take such risks are less sensitive to censure since they have not undergone a similar learning process.

In these and other studies it was also consistently shown that the RV_{cens} component of the stimulus items explained more variance in predictive judgments than the remaining built-in determinants (Rettig, 1964; Rettig & Pasamanick, 1964; Rettig & Rawson, 1963). However, all of these studies were conducted under individual judgment conditions. As will be shown later, group judgment conditions apparently create a difference in orientation, emphasizing the reinforcement value of gain (RV_{gn}) more than the reinforcement value of censure (RV_{cens}).

METHOD

Behavior Prediction Scale

The basic structure of the multidimensional scale was described in a previous report (Rettig & Rawson, 1963). Briefly, the scale consists of a series of stimulus items, each portraying a person (either hypothetical or the subject himself) in conflict about stealing money from a bank. Each item presents four determinants (the expectancy and reinforcement value of gain, and the expectancy and reinforcement of censure) in the same sequence, randomly varying the levels of any one determinant (high or low) from item to item. This combination of determinants and levels required 16 (2^4) stimulus items. Subjects were requested to predict on a scale ranging from 0 (definitely not) to 6 (definitely yes) whether or not the money would be taken. The high and low levels of the determinants were presented as follows:

1. Reinforcement value of gain (RV_{gn}): high—the money is needed for a crucial medical operation; low—the money is needed by other people.
2. Expectancy of gain (E_{gn}): high—the medical operation was guaranteed to cure the illness, the money obtainable would help many people; low—the success of the operation was not guaranteed, the money obtainable would help only very few people.
3. Negative reinforcement value of censure (RV_{cens}): high—the theft would result in expulsion from the bank and charge of criminal conduct; low—the theft would be settled in private with the bank president.
4. Expectancy of censure (E_{cens}): high—the theft would be detected; low—the theft would go unnoticed.

Two forms of the scale were constructed, a personal form on which the subjects predict their own behavior, and an impersonal form on which the subjects predict the behavior of a hypothetical person.

The following are two matched sample items, one from the personal and the other from the impersonal form of the scale.

[Personal] Assuming you are a bank employee in urgent need of a large sum of money for a crucial *medical operation* you need. You are thinking of stealing the money from the bank. The operating surgeon could *not give you any guarantee* that the operation would cure your illness. You are certain that your theft *would be detected* sooner or later. However you are convinced that if you are caught you would settle the matter *privately* with the bank president.

[Impersonal] A bank employee was in urgent need of a large sum of money for a crucial *medical operation* he needed. The employee is thinking of stealing the money from the bank. The operating surgeon could not give the employee any guarantee that the operation would cure his illness. The employee was certain that his theft *would be detected* sooner or later. However, the employee was convinced that if he was caught he would settle the matter *privately* with the bank president.

The instructions accompanying the scale emphasized that subjects were to predict only whether or not the money would be taken, not to judge how wrong it would be to take it. Separate Kuder-Richardson reliability estimates were found to be .94 for the individual condition of judgment, and .90 for the group condition.

Subjects

The subjects were 160 undergraduate students equally distributed by sex and within the various judgment conditions. All subjects were seen in their original classrooms, with entire class sections participating in the study. Fourteen different sections were tested. The equal distribution of subjects within the various cells was accomplished after the experiment, with the aid of a table of random numbers.

Individual versus Group Condition

In the individual condition of judgment, subjects were administered the scale under ordinary classroom procedure. Both forms of the questionnaire were administered at the same time in such a fashion that adjacent students received different forms. In the group condition subjects were asked to cluster themselves into three or four member groups, facing each other. Subjects were then instructed to read each question and to discuss it aloud with the other members in their group. Following discussion each subject made his own judgment; group consensus was not required. Adjacent groups received different forms of the scale.

Public versus Private Condition

In the public judgment condition subjects were informed in the beginning that upon completion of the questionnaire they would exchange their copy with that of another student. The other student would be one of the group members in the group condition of judgment, or another classmate in the individual condition of judgment. In the private judgment condition no instructions for the exchange of questionnaires were given.

Table 1 *Scale Means and Standard Deviations of Predictive Judgments for Low- and High-Rise Conditions*

Condition	*M*	*SD*
Low risk		
Group	35.36	16.40
Impersonal	41.05	15.39
Private	32.10	15.96
High risk		
Individual	30.09	18.10
Personal	24.40	15.28
Public	33.35	18.85

RESULTS

As seen in Table 1 the group condition and the impersonal condition of judgment produce the expected effect of increased prediction of the occurrence of the unethical behavior. While the effect produced by group discussion alone reaches an acceptable level of significance ($F = 5.06$, $df = 1/144$, $p < .05$), and the effect due to the impersonal condition of judgment is similar ($F = 50.40$, $df = 1/144$, $p < .001$), both sources of risk combine to produce a significant interaction ($F = 6.82$, $df = 1/144$, $p < .01$). That is, the group effect is significantly more pronounced when the judgments are personal than when they are impersonal. The effect produced by publicity does not reach statistical significance. However, its interaction with personal conditions of judgment does reach statistical significance ($F = 5.40$, $df = 1/144$, $p < .05$), showing the expected effect of publicity only for personal judgments. For impersonal judgments the effect of publicity is reversed, increasing rather than decreasing the prediction. There were not significant differences in relation to sex. These findings support the hypothesis that group discussion produces a shift toward increased risk taking in judgments.

An inspection of the internal determinants of the predictive judgments, especially in their relationship to the two more critical sources of variation in risk (group discussion and personal judgments), provides further clues about the decision-making process underlying the judgments (Table 2). While personal judgment conditions significantly affect all internal determinants ($p < .001$) except for RV_{gn}, the group condition of judgment affects only RV_{gn} ($F = 16.82$, $df = 1/144$, $p < .001$). These findings indicate that while the overall effects are similar for both conditions of risk, the judgmental process itself apparently differs.

Table 2 *Mean Difference Score of Predictive Judgments by Risk Condition and Item Component*

Condition	E_{gn}	RV_{gn}	E_{cens}	RV_{cens}
Group	6.79	12.94	6.74	9.69
Individual	6.86	7.36	6.69	9.99
Impersonal	8.35	10.60	8.93	11.73
Personal	5.30	9.70	4.50	7.95

DISCUSSION

Group discussion and impersonal conditions of judgment produce increased risk taking, as evidenced by a greater anticipation of the occurrence of unethical behavior. Privacy in judgment shows a similar effect only if the judgments are personal ones, referring to the subject's own behavior. These results were predicted from the general notion that low conditions of risk make for increased risk taking. That is, judgments of unethical behavior made in private rather than in public, and referring to a hypothetical person rather than to the subject himself are less likely to be censured and thus represent low-risk conditions of judgment. More important, previous studies have shown that group discussion also lowers the conditions of risk. The latter is supported by the present study, since the effect produced by group discussion was found to be similar to the effects produced by varying the other conditions of risk.

However, certain important differences must be noted in comparing the present study to previous studies of group effects on risk taking. In the previous studies the higher risk choices were also choices carrying higher reinforcement values of gain, monetary and social ones. Since choice of the higher reinforcement values of gain was not experimentally separated from the selection of the higher levels of risk, it was not possible to observe the effect of one upon the other. In the present study the higher risk judgments are socially undesirable (unethical) ones, and carry no higher monetary incentives for the subjects. Furthermore, the reinforcement value of gain is only one of four different considerations affecting the judgments. This design permits not only the isolation of the reinforcement value of gain and the measurement of its effect on the selection of higher levels of risk, but also the evaluation of the effect of the remaining internal determinants on risk preference in judgment, especially in their interaction with the external sources of variation in risk. It is here that the present study clearly points to the reinforcement values of gain as being largely responsible for the observed differences of risk taking in judgments between individual and group conditions.

Precisely why group discussion should produce an increased emphasis on the reinforcement value of gain is not entirely clear. Perhaps group discussion brings about a reduction in anticipated censure (or anxiety) for the participating group members since the discussion provides each member with the opportunity of testing the approval or disapproval of the other group members and adjust his responses accordingly. In other words, the process of communication set in motion by the group discussion may result in a lowered expectancy of being censured and a concomitantly greater feeling of security. The resulting reduction in anticipated censure would, in turn, permit preference of a more "offensive" strategy (maximization of gain) over a "defensive" one (avoidance of censure). Here one might also expect a reduced emphasis on RV_{cens} in the groups condition of judgment. While RV_{cens} did show a greater drop than the other components, the shift does not attain statistical significance probably because of the greater "end effect" in the individual judgment condition. Such an effect tends to artificially restrict variability in judgments. (Probably for the same reason RV_{cens} is also restricted in personal judgment conditions.)

While the above conjecture is highly speculative at this time, it might offer an explanation as to why group discussion rather than group consensus is the critical antecedent of increased risk taking observed in groups. Consensus alone, in skipping the process of censure testing and subsequent adjustment of one's own position, may tend to increase rather than decrease the anxiety of the participating subjects.

Since riskiness in judgment is not the equivalent of risk taking in other forms of behavior, even if these judgments are predictions by a subject about himself, the present findings must be considered exploratory. Here it is also important to realize that the levels which are selected to represent the various components of the stimulus items are chosen arbitrarily. Although the present findings in the individual condition of judgment are in agreement with the results of previous studies in which somewhat different scales were used, the consistency in the results may partially reflect a common experimenter bias in the selection of the component levels. However, despite the possibility for such common experimenter bias, the group condition of judgment produced results which were clearly different from those consistently shown in individual judgment conditions. In individual judgment conditions the negative reinforcement value of censure was found to be the most important determinant of predictive judgments of unethical behavior as well as of actual unethical behavior. In the group judgment condition the reinforcement value of gain is found to be the most important determinant of predictive judgment. Whether under group conditions the reinforcement value of gain will also prove to be the most important determinant of actual unethical behavior still remains to be tested.

SUMMARY

Recent studies demonstrated that group discussion increases risk taking. These results were explained in terms of responsibility diffusion. The hypothesis tested here is that group discussion affects predictive judgments of unethical behavior in the same way as two other risk conditions: privacy and impersonality. One hundred and sixty *S*s, equally distributed by sex and judgment conditions, predicted the behavior of persons (*S* himself or hypothetical) in conflict about stealing. Sixteen items, each varying the expectancy and reinforcement value of gain or censure, were judged. The findings support the hypothesis. However, the results support an interpretation of censure testing rather than responsibility diffusion during group discussion.

REFERENCES

Bem, D. J., Wallach, M. A., & Kogan, N. Group decision making under risk of aversive consequences. *J. Pers. Soc. Psychol.*, 1965, **1**, 453–460.

Lonergan, B. G., & McClintock, C. G. Effects of group membership on risk-taking behavior. *Psychol. Rep.*, 1961, **8**, 447–455.

Rettig, S Ethical risk sensitivity in male prisoners. *Brit. J. Criminol.*, 1964, **4**, 582–590.

Rettig, S., & Pasamanick, B. Differential judgment of ethical risk by cheaters and noncheaters. *J. Abnorm. Soc. Psychol.*, 1964, **69**, 109–113.

Rettig, S., & Rawson, H. E. The risk hypothesis in predictive judgments of unethical behavior. *J. Abnorm. Soc. Psychol.*, 1963, **66**, 243–248.

Rettig, S., & Sinha, J. B. P. Bad faith and ethical risk sensitivity. *Am. Psychol.*, 1965, **20**, 515. (Abstract)

Wallach, M. A., & Kogan, N. The roles of information, discussion, and consensus in group risk taking. *J. Exptl. Soc. Psychol.*, 1965, **1**, 1–19.

Wallach, M. A., Kogan, N., & Bem, D. J. Group influence on individual risk taking. *J. Abnorm. Soc. Psychol.*, 1962, **65**, 75–86.

Wallach, M. A., Kogan, N., & Bem, D. J. Diffusion of responsibility and level of risk taking in groups. *J. Abnorm. Soc. Psychol.*, 1964, **68**, 263–274.

§ 10 LEADERSHIP AND ORGANIZATIONAL BEHAVIOR

Both leadership and organization are necessary in any group that sets out to accomplish anything. Leadership, broadly defined, refers to the influence that a group member has over the motives and behavior of other members, and organization refers to the structure of the relationships that develop among group members as they undertake their tasks.

The first paper in this group consists of a study by Lana, Vaughan, and McGinnies, who show that leadership and interaction status in group discussions are positively correlated, but that friendship and interaction status are not. Once within the context of a discussion group, friends tend to direct their discussion toward those who have status within the group rather than to one another.

The research conducted by John A. Sample and Thurlow R. Wilson is concerned with comparing two styles of leadership: that of the task-oriented supervisor who is primarily interested in seeing that the group completes the task it has been assigned, and who is only secondarily interested in the affective or "feeling" aspects of group life, and that of the interaction-oriented supervisor, who is more interested in seeing that members have personally satisfying experiences while working in the group. Sample and Wilson's research shows that the first type of leader does a better job of planning and hence is more effective in stress situations, but that affective needs of members need not be thwarted in the course of achieving the group's assigned tasks.

The studies reported in the paper by Bernard M. Bass and George Dunteman are concerned with three styles of group participation: task-, interaction-, and self-orientation. Task-oriented individuals generally are perceived by group members as most valuable, probably because of their leadership skills. Interaction-oriented members enjoy group life for its own sake and not because of the tasks the group is able to accomplish, whereas self-oriented members find little satisfaction within the context of groups, irrespective of whether they are working or socializing.

The factors related to effective performance in branch offices of a nationwide firm are studied in the paper by Bachman, Smith, and Slesinger. They found that the efficiency of offices and the satisfaction of managers and salesmen was related to the amount of control both had over the office and the extent to which they were able to influence one another.

The final paper in this section consists of a field experiment conducted by Nancy C. Morse and Everett Reimer, who restructured departments doing clerical work in a large organization in such a way that higher-level management played a more active part in the decision-making processes in two divisions and that rank-and-file employees played a greater part in decision making in two other divisions. Employee satisfactions were significantly higher in divisions where employees participated in decisions. However, there was no difference in productivity (as measured by clerical costs) between the two treatments.

10.1 LEADERSHIP AND FRIENDSHIP STATUS AS FACTORS IN DISCUSSION GROUP INTERACTION

Robert E. Lana
Willard Vaughan
Elliott McGinnies

The purpose of this study is to examine the relationships between a quantitative index of verbal interaction among the members of a discussion group and indices of sociometric choice on friendship and leadership criteria.

In a recent series of investigations, the authors and their colleagues have been concerned with problems of communicating information

Source: This research was supported by a grant from the National Institute of Mental Health. Reprinted with slight abridgment from the *Journal of Social Psychology*, 1960, 52, 127–134, with permission of the authors and The Journal Press.

concerning mental health to various types of community groups. Several factors that play a role in the persuasion process have been reported, among them certain biographical characteristics of the group members (5), attitudinal composition of the target groups (7), and the use of group discussion following single and multiple communications (6). McGinnies and Vaughan (5), for example, found that participants in group discussion are generally distinguished by superior educational attainment as well as by leadership status in their respective groups. While yielding information concerning the types of individuals who might be expected to dominate discussion, this type of analysis did not reveal the patterns of interaction that occur among these individuals. It seemed probable that the sociometric structure of discussion groups would be a factor determining the direction of participation once the active participants had been recruited. Choices based upon leadership within the group as well as personal contact among the group members seemed to be the most relevant for this purpose.

The leadership variable in discussion behavior has received some attention by other investigators. Bell and French (1) report that the leadership standing of most of the members of informal discussion groups was unaffected by changes in either the composition of the group or the topic of discussion. Studying the effects of status upon interpersonal choice and communications within small discussion groups, Hurwitz, Zander, and Hymovitch (3) found that high-status individuals communicated more than those low in status. Both low- and high-status persons directed more of their remarks to members high in status, so that high-status individuals both initiated and received more communications than did lows. Friendship as a confounding variable was eliminated by selecting individuals having no previous acquaintance with one another.

In actual practice, however, stable patterns of both leadership and friendship are likely to exist within a formed group prior to any experience that the group may have with a persuasive communication. Several interesting questions then arise. Are friendship and leadership standings of the members correlated? If so, do those individuals enjoying high status with respect to these variables also initiate and receive most of the verbal exchanges in group discussion? The findings of Hurwitz and his associates suggest that this would be the case, although their study did not utilize preexisting friendship relations or actual choices within the group as measures of leadership. If friendship and leadership are not related to a significant extent, which of these factors is a more reliable determinant of initiative in discussion? A review of the literature on small group discussion discloses no answer to these questions and confirms what Lindzey and Borgatta (2) have referred to as the relative paucity of ". . . . research aimed at exploring in a regular fashion the kinds of conditions and variables that are related to sociometric response."

PROCEDURE

Two community groups from suburban Washington participated in the investigation. Both discussion groups were drawn from larger PTA organizations, and the members were generally acquainted with one another. Friendship and leadership status in all probability, were substantially determined at the outset of the experiment. One group (*A*) was composed of 18 women organized as a child study group, while the other (*B*) consisted of two male and 16 female members. All of the women in both groups gave their occupation as housewife, and the averages for the two groups were 38.6 and 33.4 years. The mean numbers of years in college were 3.3 and 2.0 for the two groups, while the average yearly income was $9,100 for the first group and $5,700 for the second. One group, therefore, was somewhat older, enjoyed slightly more education, and was higher salaried than the other. These differences, however, were not marked. Each group met at their usual location for three experimental sessions spaced at weekly intervals. During each meeting groups viewed a film portraying a mental health problem, discussed the film for a period limited to 30 minutes, then responded to a questionnaire. Three films, *The Feeling of Rejection, The Feeling of Hostility,* and *Breakdown,* were shown to each group in that order.

With the knowledge and consent of the participating groups, each discussion was tape-recorded so as to provide a verbatim account of the groups' verbal activity. Furthermore, to identify the discussion contribution of each individual member of the group, two experimenters maintained a record of the direction of verbal activity throughout the discussion identifying the initiator and recipient of each comment according to their location in the room, i.e., by row and letter seat number, as described in detail elsewhere (4).

A verbatim transcript was prepared from the tape recording of each discussion, and the sequence of comments was matched with the sequence of commentators. Through this technique every comment in the discussion was identified by source and destination. Although comments were always initiated by an individual, the recipient might have been the leader, the group as a whole, or another member.

Biographical information was obtained from the groups on the occasion of their first meeting, and sociometric data were collected at the second and third meetings. Each questionnaire was coded according to the row letter and seat number of the respondent. Questionnaire responses were thus easily matched with the individual's verbal activity during the discussion.

Following the discussion period of the second meeting, each person was asked to indicate the two members of the group with whom she considered herself to be most friendly. The subjects made their choices by means of a diagram representing the group's seating arrangement. As a row letter and seat number combination identified the location of each individual in the group, the subjects needed only to circle that combination which spatially located each friend. This procedure was necessitated by our original assurance of anonymity in connection with the tape recordings.

At the third and final meeting, each person was asked to identify those members of the group whom she would choose for president and vice-president if the group were to continue and to require officers. These data were gathered by the same technique used to obtain friendship preferences within the group; the subjects made their choices by indicating the row and seat combination corresponding to the location of their nominations.

Indices Developed

Three values were calculated for each member of the two groups.

a. Friendship Status: Total choices received from all other members of the group constituted the friendship score of each member. The individuals were then ranked in order of frequency of choices received on this criterion, and the ranks served as measures of friendship status.

b. Leadership Status: The total of the nominations received for either president or vice-president from all other members of the group yielded a leadership score for each person. The members of each group were then ranked according to these scores, with a high rank indicating greater leadership status.

c. Interaction Status: An index was sought to describe the degree to which each member of the two discussion groups verbally interacted with her fellow members during the discussions. Comments initiated by any individual member of a discussion group can logically take only three directions. They may be directed to the discussion leader, to another member of the group, or to the group as a whole. We recorded and examined each of these contingencies by determining the intercorrelations between them across meetings. In general, these three types of discussion interaction were highly correlated, so that any one of them could have been used independently as a representative index of extent of interaction between an individual and other members of the group. Since most of the comments by the subjects were directed toward other specific individuals, this single measure was taken as an indication of interaction status.

RESULTS AND DISCUSSION

In order to obtain information bearing upon the questions posed by the investigation it was necessary to estimate the degree of relationship between the following sets of variables for each of the two groups: (*a*) interaction status and friendship status, (*b*) interaction status and leadership status, (*c*) friendship status and leadership status.

Since the three indices were obtained by ranking, it was necessary to analyze the results by a statistical technique applicable to ordinal scores, thereby imposing no restrictive assumptions regarding their distribution. Furthermore, since the focus of the study was upon examining relationships between interaction and uncontaminated indices of friendship and leadership, a rank correlation technique was required whose partial had been derived. The single statistical tool meeting these requirements is Kendall's *tau* (8). The partial correlations thus examined were as follows: (*a*) interaction status and friendship status independent of leadership status, (*b*) interaction status and leadership status independent of friendship status, (*c*) friendship status and leadership status independent of interaction status.

Each of the above relationships was tested for significance, with .05 as the level of acceptability. The results are shown in Tables 1 and 2.

It is apparent from Table 1 that a positive correlation exists between interaction status and both friendship and leadership in Group *A* and between interaction status and leadership in Group *B*. From this table, however, it is not clear whether either friendship or leadership considered independent of the other would relate significantly to interaction status. Friendship status and leadership status in both

Table 1 *Summary of Tau Values with Significance Levels**

	Group *A*				Group *B*		
	IS	FS	LS		IS	FS	LS
IS	—	—	—	IS	—	—	—
FS	.287	—	—	FS	.150	—	—
	<.05				>.10		
LS	.490	.654	—	LS	.288	.438	—
	<.01	<.001			<.05	<.01	

* With $N = 18$, *tau* must have a value $\geqq$ .282 to reach significance at the .05 level with a one-tailed test. With this *N*, *tau* is equal to a *Z* of 1.65.

Table 2 *Summary of Partial Tau Values*

Group *A*			Group *B*		
(IS) (F) · (L)	=	−.045	(IS) (F) · (L)	=	.026
(IS) (L) · (F)	=	.411	(IS) (L) · (F)	=	.247
(F) (L) · (IS)	=	.610	(F) (L) · (IS)	=	.421

discussion groups were highly correlated, indicating that those individuals who received the most votes for group officers were also frequently chosen as friends.

The next step in the analysis, therefore, was to partial out the respective contributions of friendship and leadership to the correlation with discussion interaction. Partial *taus* calculated from the *taus* reported above are shown in Table 2.

Conclusions to be drawn from the data are based on the partial *taus* presented above. It must be pointed out, however, that no distribution has been derived for partial *taus* as yet, and any conclusions relating to the statistical significance of a particular partial *tau* must be argued by inference from the significance levels associated with each *tau* used in the calculation of the various partials. It can be argued that because the *tau* values ($\tau_{(IS)\,(L)}$ for Groups *A* and *B*) are significant the partial *taus* reflecting these same relationships, being of approximately the same magnitude, are also significant, since the relationship is not confounded with the effect of a third variable. We have in effect a "purer" measure of the various relationships under investigation. Only if the partial *taus* were of considerably different magnitudes from their respective *taus* would this type of inference be difficult to make. The distribution of the *tau* statistic has been tabled, and significance levels can be associated with any given value.

All *tau* values in Table 1 are significant beyond the .05 level with the exception of $\tau_{(IS)(F)}$ for Group *B*. This is consistent with the fact that $\tau_{(IS)(F)\cdot(L)}$ is not significant for either Group *A* or *B*. The partial *taus* between interaction status and friendship status in the independence of leadership are $-.045$ in Group *A* and .026 in Group *B*, indicating that the significant $\tau_{(IS)(F)}$ for Group *A* is probably an artifact resulting from a contamination of friendship status with leadership status. Since $\tau_{(IS)(F)}$ for both groups is considerably larger than the respective partial *tau* values, the results demonstrate that friendship status in the absence of leadership status of the same magnitude is not related to interaction status in the discussion situation. Also, since the partial *taus* between interaction status and leadership status for both groups are of similar magnitude to their respective *taus*, a positive relationship exists between interaction status and leadership status regardless of friendship status. Following the same line of reasoning, it is also evident that friendship status and leadership status are highly related regardless of discussion contribution (IS), since $\tau_{(F)(L)} = .654$ and .438, while $\tau_{(F)(L)\cdot(IS)} = .610$ and .421.

Inasmuch as it is somewhat difficult to conceive of interaction status being related only to leadership, when leadership is highly correlated with friendship, Figure 1, which consists of a diagram of the logic involved, may be useful.

The results confirm our earlier findings that discussion of a communication in the small group situation is largely confined to that segment of the group that enjoys superior status in a number of respects and chiefly with regard to education and leadership. From the present results, it is apparent that not only are the leaders of such groups the most vocal participants in discussion, they also address most of their comments to each other. Those participants who do not enjoy a high degree of leadership status tend to direct their remarks toward those whom they perceive as the leaders. Although group leaders also rank high with respect to friendship choices, it is leadership rather than friendship which determines the individual's position in the hierarchy of discussion interaction.

SUMMARY

Sociometric choices on friendship and leadership criteria were made by members of two community groups who engaged in three discussion

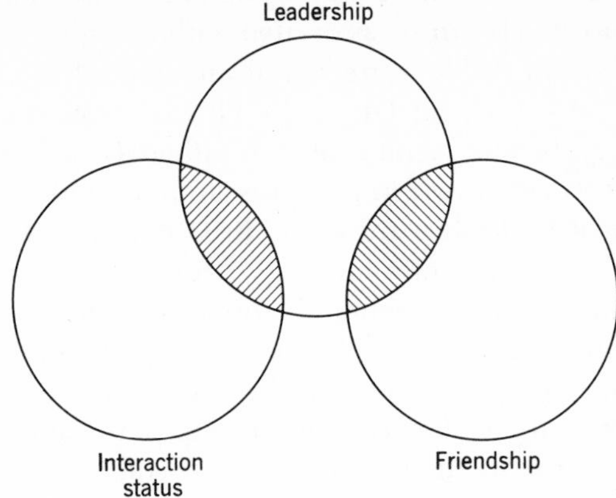

Figure 1. Each circle schematically represents the total variance of each of the three variables. Shaded areas represent approximations of the appropriate common variance between each of two factors.

sessions concerning mental health films. Indices of friendship and leadership status were obtained from these groups and related by nonparametric correlational methods to an index of verbal activity, labeled interaction status. It was found that leadership status and interaction status were highly correlated, as were leadership status and friendship status. Friendship status and interaction status, however, were not correlated. Those discussion participants who were relatively low in leadership status directed their comments to those members whom they identified as leaders. Friendship status apparently does not itself influence an individual's interaction status within the small discussion group. These results suggest that discussion of a communication in the small group situation is largely confined to the perceived leaders of the group.

REFERENCES

1. Bell, C. B., & French, R. L. Consistency of individual leadership position in small groups of varying membership. *J. Abnorm. Soc. Psychol.*, 1950, 45, 764–767.
2. Lindzey, G., & Borgatta, E. F. Sociometric measurement. In Lindzey, G. (Ed.), *Handbook of social psychology*. Cambridge: Addison-Wesley, 1954.
3. Hurwitz, J. I., Zander, A. F., & Hymovitch, B. Some effects of power on the rela-

tions among group members. In Cartwright, D., & Zander, A. F. (Eds.), *Group dynamics*. Evanston, Ill.: Row, Peterson, 1953.

4. McGinnies, E. A method for matching anonymous questionnaire data with group discussion material. *J. Abnorm. Soc. Psychol.*, 1956, **52,** 139–140.
5. McGinnies, E., & Vaughan, W. Some biographical determiners of participation in group discussion. *J. Appl. Psychol.*, 1957, **41,** 179–185.
6. McGinnies, E., Lana, R., & Smith, C. The effects of sound films on opinions about mental illness in community discussion groups. *J. Appl. Psychol.*, 1958, **42,** 40–46.
7. Mitnick, L. L., & McGinnies, E. Influencing ethnocentrism in small discussion groups through a film communication. *J. Abnorm. Soc. Psychol.*, 1958, **56,** 82–90.
8. Siegel, S. *Nonparametric statistics*. New York: McGraw-Hill, 1956.

10.2 LEADER BEHAVIOR, GROUP PRODUCTIVITY, AND RATING OF LEAST PREFERRED CO-WORKER

John A. Sample
Thurlow R. Wilson

Group productivity can be predicted from the way the group leader describes the personality of his least preferred co-worker (LPC), according to a number of investigations by Fiedler (1958, 1962). In several natural groups, the leader who described the LPC in unfavorable or socially undesirable terms tended to have a more productive group. The greater production secured by the leader giving unfavorable ratings to the LPC has been explained by this leader's ability to maintain the necessary social distance between himself and his workers (Fiedler, 1958). (For the remainder of this report an individual who gives generally favorable ratings to the least preferred co-worker will be called "favorable LPC" while the term "unfavorable LPC" will denote someone who rates LPC in a generally unfavorable direction.) The support for the social distance interpretation is based for the most part on the co-worker ratings.

In the present research, natural groups were studied while performing their regular task under stress. The team composition was controlled: some groups had a favorable LPC leader while others had an unfavorable LPC leader. A major objective was to provide a description of the behavior within the two kinds of groups, and in

Source: Reprinted from the *Journal of Personality and Social Psychology*, 1965, **1,** 266–270, with permission of the authors and the American Psychological Association, Inc.

particular, to see if the favorable LPC leader would respond to his group in a more positive socioemotional manner than would the unfavorable LPC leader.

Productivity of the natural groups was determined under stress and also under routine conditions. On the basis of Fiedler's findings, one would expect superior performance of the unfavorable LPC groups under stress. An additional aim of the present investigation was to examine interpersonal attraction expressed between group members in order to determine whether the unfavorable LPC leader generates more social distance between himself and his followers.

METHOD

The independent variable was the LPC score of the appointed leader. Subjects rated their most preferred co-worker and their least preferred co-worker on 24 adjective pairs, such as friendly-unfriendly, quitting-persistent, on eight-point scales (Fiedler, 1958). The results of the experiment are based on the data from fourteen groups—eight with favorable LPC leaders and six with unfavorable LPC leaders. The results are based on teams with endorsed leaders only. Endorsement was determined by the questionnaire given at the end of the investigation period, and a leader was classified as endorsed if all members agreed that they would select him to take charge of the team on a future problem. Two groups with favorable LPC leaders and four with unfavorable LPC leaders did not meet the criterion of endorsement.

Nature of Task and Group

The natural groups under study were four-man sets of students from the undergraduate experimental psychology laboratory course. As part of the course work, each team of students was assigned a Skinner box and a rat and required to perform several operant conditioning exercises according to the Homme and Klaus (1961) manual. Such laboratory teams have been a regular part of the experimental psychology instruction in recent years.

Each group had an appointed male leader who met the criteria of having a good academic record and a score at least one standard deviation from the mean on LPC. Between groups, the followers were equated on LPC, grades, and prior acquaintance.

The role of the appointed leader was to assign tasks, supervise the work of the other students, lead the discussion of questions based on the operant conditioning problem, and write a general report after the problem had been completed. The leader acted as the channel of information between the laboratory instructor and the group. For each operant conditioning exercise, the followers performed the jobs of experimenter, recorder, and timer. The tasks were rotated each week.

Each laboratory team carried out ten operant conditioning problems over a two-month period. The eighth assignment in the series was a laboratory test, and this exercise was completed under somewhat stressful conditions in the small-groups laboratory. The test was assumed to be stressful because the students did not have the help of their laboratory manual, the 90 minutes allowed for the test was 15 minutes less than the time allowed for routine assignments, and furthermore this assignment had more weight than others in determining final grade. No group left before the end of the allotted time.

The academic grades earned by each individual in the laboratory were determined from the grades given his team and not from scores of assignments prepared by that individual.

Measures

Data collected included observer scoring of behavior during the stress problem, the scoring of the laboratory reports, and a questionnaire completed by the students at the end of the academic term. Observers, who did not know the composition of the groups or the rationale of the experiment, scored behavior using the twelve categories of the Bales interaction process analysis (Bales, 1950). Scoring was performed for a ten-minute period followed by a five-minute rest period. For each ten-minute period the observer noted the nature of the group's activity in one of three divisions: planning, running (rat in Skinner box), or paper work. An act was scored as leader-to-member, member-to-member, or member-to-leader.

For each exercise, the graph, the animal behavior notes, and the recording sheet were scored by a key. The key was a check list comparing these products to a model; judgments of presence or absence were required and some judgments of neatness.

One week following the completion of the ten conditioning problems, the team members were given questionnaires to determine endorsement of the leader, judgment of the roles various individuals had performed in the group, social distance between individuals in the group, and perceived group atmosphere.

Rationale Given to Subjects for Manipulations and Measures

All rationales and instructions given to students concerning the laboratory teams, the observation, and the questionnaires followed outlines prepared in advance. The observation of the laboratory teams was explained as a means of providing practice for observers of group behavior. It was made to seem that the laboratory instructor (JS) was merely acquiescing to a professor's demand, and the instructor dissociated himself completely from the observation. All evidence indicates that students accepted the rationales.

RESULTS

Group Productivity

The scores for each of the nine laboratory exercises are summarized in Table 1. Note that each score is based on the work of the followers and does not include the score given to the leader's report. No objective scoring key was developed for the leader's report; the reports were

Table 1 *Mean Scores of Laboratory Assignments for Fall and Winter Terms According to Leader Type*

Assignment	Fall Term Unfavorable[a]	Fall Term Favorable[b]	Winter Term Unfavorable[a]	Winter Term Favorable[b]
2	80	84	84	90
3	87	84	85	86
4	88	87	92	88
5	86	86	79	74
6	84	84	79	73
7	87	88	91	85
8 (stress)	90	80	81	66*
9	86	84	84	87
10	92	90	87	88
Number of groups	2	3	4	5

Note: Score is based on the percentage of possible points earned by followers on the graph, recording sheet, and animal behavior notes and does not include the percentage score given to the leader's report.

[a] Team with unfavorable LPC leader.

[b] Team with favorable LPC leader.

* Difference between unfavorable and favorable for winter term, $p < .05$.

randomly assigned high grades. The teams are separated into fall and winter terms to examine a possible scoring bias for the fall teams; the scoring of the fall groups was performed by one of the authors (JS) while the winter groups were scored by someone who had no knowledge of the experiment. A close correspondence is noted between fall and winter scorings. Favorable and unfavorable LPC teams perform equally well on the routine assignments, but on the stress problem, the favorable-LPC-led team scores below the unfavorable; the difference is significant for the nine winter groups ($p < .05$).[1]

Behavior during Stress Problem

The two kinds of leaders showed little difference in their observed behavior for the stress problem as a whole. For example, mean percentage of leader-to-member acts classified as positive socioemotional was 24 per cent for favorable LPC and 21 per cent for unfavorable LPC teams.

Significantly different patterns do appear for the two types of leaders when their behavior is analyzed for planning, running, and paper work. In Table 2 behavior of the two types of leaders and their followers is described for each of the three problem phases. Phase-by-phase comparison of the behavior of the favorable and unfavorable LPC leaders discloses clear differences in positive acts and attempted answers. During planning, positive reactions account for an average of 30 per cent of the favorable LPC leader's behavior as compared to 11 per cent for the unfavorable LPC leader ($p < .01$). During the running phase the favorable LPC leader drops to 14 per cent and the unfavorable LPC leader increases to 31 per cent positive acts ($p < .01$ for the difference between types of leaders). During the paper-work phase the favorable leader again has a higher proportion of positive acts than the unfavorable supervisor, but the t is only 1.3. The phase-by-phase changes in attempted answers are inverse to the changes in positive reactions; the percentage of attempted answers from planning to running increases for the favorable LPC leader and decreases for the unfavorable LPC supervisor. Analysis of mean number of positive acts and attempted answers for each phase yielded essentially the same picture of leader difference as did the analysis of mean percentages.

When leaders are compared to their followers in Table 2 the follower profile compared to the corresponding leader profile is found to have a smaller percentage of acts in attempted answers and a larger

[1] All reported probabilities for t are based on two-tailed tests.

Table 2 *Mean Percentage of Acts in Categories during Each Problem Phase for Leaders and Their Followers*

Observer Behavior Category	Problem Phase: Planning L[a]	F[b]	Running L[a]	F[b]	Paper Work L[a]	F[b]
Favorable LPC groups						
Positive Socioemotional	30	28	14	30	29	34
Attempted answers	48	39	62	49	50	33
Questions	15	24	11	19	13	24
Negative Socioemotional	6	7	12	4	8	6
Unfavorable LPC groups						
Positive Socioemotional	11	12	31	32	19	19
Attempted answers	71	52	52	40	61	44
Questions	15	25	6	20	15	33
Negative Socioemotional	3	8	10	10	5	4

Note: Percentages are based on six unfavorable LPC groups and eight favorable LPC groups except during the planning phase when one of the favorable LPC groups could not be scored due to equipment failure.

[a] L = Leader to follower.

[b] F = Follower to leader.

percentage in questions. These leader-follower profile differences in the task area are not related to leader type. The emotional behavior of the members is matched to that of the leader except during the running period of the favorable-LPC-led groups; the followers show a higher proportion of positive acts than their leader ($p < .01$) and a lower proportion of negative units ($p < .05$).

The proportions of suggestions given by leaders during the problem phases are given in Table 3. From planning to paper work the favora-

Table 3 *Proportion of Suggestions Given by Leader by Problem Phase*

Team Leader	Problem Phase: Planning	Running	Paper Work
Favorable LPC	.56	.77	.69
Unfavorable LPC	.79	.67	.41

Note: Suggestions are acts recorded by observers in "gives suggestion." For number of groups, see Table 2.

ble LPC supervisor increases his proportion of suggestions while the unfavorable LPC individual gives fewer suggestions relative to his team ($p < .01$).

Subjects' Descriptions of Their Team

The measures of interpersonal attraction failed to yield differences associated with LPC. On the Guttman scale measuring desire for social contact with team members, the two types of leaders were equal. No difference was discovered when members of favorable and unfavorable LPC teams were compared with regard to attraction to their leader.

On a "guess-who" test, the favorable LPC leader received an average of 2.2 votes (of 3 possible votes) for "stimulates ideas" compared to .8 votes for the unfavorable LPC leader ($p < .05$). No differences were found for the other items: was constructive critic, attempted to increase cooperation, attempted to keep the group from getting off the subject, contributed new ideas.

DISCUSSION

Distinctly different behavior patterns emerge for the two types of leaders when the stress problem is broken into phases. The unfavorable LPC leader, who is initially task oriented with a minimum of emotional response, gives a high proportion of positive acts during the time when the team is conditioning its rat. The favorable LPC individual, however, plays these roles in reverse order. He is task oriented during the running period, when his followers are giving a high proportion of positive socioemotional acts. The different patterns of behavior on the stress problem are associated with differences in group production; the unfavorable LPC teams are found to be superior.

One interpretation of the above trends is that the unfavorable LPC leader firmly and quickly structures the groups' procedures during the planning phase and then is able to play a less dominating, and even jovial, role. On the other hand, the favorable LPC leader holds a group discussion during the planning period and the work is not clearly organized at that time. This leader then attempts to organize the work during the later phases, with only partial success.

The failure of the favorable LPC groups is conjectured to come from two sources: from the use of a group discussion procedure which is workable for the routine problem solving but unadaptable to the demands of the test problem and from the inability of the favorable LPC leader to control the positive socioemotional behavior of his followers. Perhaps the problem of socioemotional control was made more difficult by the fact that during the paper work the group was obliged to remain together in the small room. It was observed that in the classroom, team members often moved apart to perform their individual paper-work chores. Spatial separation is a technique for gaining control of positive social-emotional behavior (as any grade school teacher knows).

The investigation supports findings from Fiedler's research on LPC. The production differences under stress occurred as expected from Fiedler's (1958) studies on task groups. The finding that the favorable LPC leader was described by his followers as "stimulating ideas" is congruent with the results (Fiedler, 1962) that groups with favorable LPC leaders are better able to produce at creative tasks than are groups with unfavorable LPC leaders, provided interpersonal stress is minimal.

The present investigation, however, does not support the notion that the unfavorable LPC individual is generally socially distant and unfriendly. The study reveals no difference in the total amount of positive socioemotional behavior between favorable and unfavorable LPC leaders are better able to produce at creative tasks than are groups attraction in the groups with different types of leaders. The investigation demonstrates that both favorable and unfavorable LPC leaders are friendly to group members but at different times during the task. It is not the occurrence of positive behavior which distinguishes the two kinds of leaders, but the timing of this behavior.

SUMMARY

Experimental psychology students formed into teams of controlled composition worked on ten operant conditioning problems—nine problems under routine conditions and one problem under stress. Prior to formation of the teams, eight of the appointed leaders gave favorable ratings to their least preferred co-worker (LPC) and six gave unfavorable ratings. Teams with leaders giving unfavorable ratings to LPC were superior to other teams on performance on the stress problem but equal on the routine problems. The two kinds of leaders showed little difference in observed behavior for the stress problem as a whole, but when the problem was analyzed according to phases, significantly different patterns appeared. Interpersonal attraction did not differ in the two kinds of teams.

REFERENCES

Bales, R. F. *Interaction process analysis: A method for the study of small groups.* Cambridge, Mass.: Addison-Wesley, 1950.

Fiedler, F. E. *Leader attitudes and group effectiveness.* Urbana: Univ. of Illinois Press, 1958.

Fiedler, F. E. Leader attitudes, group climate, and group creativity. *J. Abnorm. Soc. Psychol.*, 1962, **65**, 308–318.

Homme, L. E., & Klaus, D. J. *Laboratory studies in the analysis of behavior.* Albuquerque, N. M.: Teaching Machines, Inc., 1961.

10.3 BEHAVIOR IN GROUPS AS A FUNCTION OF SELF-, INTERACTION, AND TASK ORIENTATION

Bernard M. Bass
George Dunteman

In *Leadership, Psychology and Organizational Behavior* (Bass, 1960), three types of group members, self-, interaction, and task oriented, were conceived. It was argued that attempts to lead under specified circumstances would be different among these three types of individuals. The Orientation Inventory (Bass, 1962), 27 triads of questions about personal preferences, values, and projections, was constructed to screen populations for samples of these idealized types. For each triad, subjects indicate which alternative they prefer most, and which they prefer least.

The Orientation Inventory (Ori), in its final form, had the following test-retest reliabilities: self-orientation, .73; interaction orientation, .76; and task orientation, .75. The built-in negative correlations[1]

[1] Like forced-choice and Kuder inventories, these scales yield ipsative scores. Since the grand mean score is a constant, if an individual is high on one scale, he must be low on another. This accentuates the differentiation in responses of a given individual on the three orientations, making it easier to type him at one extreme or another. Equally important, the forcing fits the conceptualization. We argue that

Source: This research was supported by the Group Psychology Branch of the Office of Naval Research. Reprinted from the *Journal of Abnormal and Social Psychology*, 1963, **66**, 419–428, with permission of the senior author and the American Psychological Association, Inc., copyright holder.

among the three scales and the obtained reliabilities made possible a classification system labeling individuals as of one type or another if they were in the top quartile of a particular distribution. In a classification-reclassification analysis, it was seen that only 6.5 per cent of 84 subjects shifted from one idealized category to another. Most shifts were into and out of the residual category from one of the idealized types (Bass, Frye, Dunteman, Vidulich, & Wambach, 1963).

In addition to sex differences, occupational and educational differences were also found in expected directions. For example, engineers earned significantly higher task scores than nonengineers (Dunteman & Bass, 1963). At all age levels—early adolescent, late adolescent, and middle age—women were more interaction oriented than men (Bass et al., 1963).

Overt choice behavior was found associated in expected directions with Ori scale scores. Subjects with high task orientation scores completed tasks voluntarily more frequently following interruption than subjects with low task scores. Subjects with high task scores volunteered in greater frequency for psychological experiments. Subjects with high interaction scores were more likely to choose to work in a group or to volunteer for discussions rather than working on problems alone. Subjects with high self-orientation scores were more likely to choose to work alone and, of all students, were most likely to shift from nonvolunteering to volunteering for service as a subject of a psychological experiment when an extrinsic monetary reward was added for volunteering (Bass et al., 1963).

On a battery of personality inventories and attitude questionnaires, the highly self-oriented subject described himself, to a statistically significant degree, as disagreeable, dogmatic, aggressive-competitive, sensitive-effeminate, introvertive, suspicious, jealous, tense-excitable, manifestly anxious, lacking in control, immature-unstable, needing

---

in groups, members are concerned with the task, the interaction, or themselves. If they pay more attention to one, then they must devote less to another. Thus, we suggest that if a person is generally task oriented, then he is unlikely to be interaction oriented. Our measurements follow these restraints. The most uniform negative correlation seems to be between task and interaction orientation. This correlation varies between —.3 and —.5. On the other hand, self-orientation sometimes shows less of a negative correlation with the other scales. Thus, "mixed types" of individuals emerge. A recent suicide was extremely high in task *and* self-orientation and extremely low in interaction orientation. Juvenile delinquents in general tend to be low in task orientation and high in self- and/or interaction orientation. (The interaction oriented get along better in the institution and are paroled more readily.)

aggression, needing heterosexuality, lacking in need for change, fearing failure, and feeling insecure. The interaction-oriented subject described himself as significantly in need of affiliation, socially group dependent, lacking in need for achievement, lacking in need for autonomy, needing to be helped by others, tending to warmth and sociability, and lacking in need for aggression.

The task-oriented subject described himself on the other inventories as self-sufficient and resourceful, controlled in will power, needing endurance, aloof and not sociable, sober and excitable, introvertive, radical, not dogmatic, lacking in need for heterosexuality, needing abasement, aggressive and competitive, lacking in need for succorance, low in fear of failure, mature and calm. He also scored higher in intelligence. He was a scholastic overachiever, if above average in ability, compared to equally intelligent subjects lower in task orientation (Bass et al., 1963).

PART I

Orientation and Peer Evaluations of Discussion Performance

The present report deals with several independent studies of differential behavior in groups of members assessed by Ori as self-, interaction, or task oriented. Behavior, as rated by peers, of 32 supervisors and 25 secretaries in sensitivity training groups provided two sets of correlated observations. Another study related orientation to observer's appraisals of the leadership potential of 48 candidates for supervisory positions under intensive observation for three days using "country house" techniques. Finally, contrived groups, homogeneous with respect to orientation, or containing specific proportions of members of each type, yielded further evidence on the overall differences in contribution to group life of the task oriented, the interaction oriented, and the self-oriented.

Procedure

Thirty-two members of a management training laboratory were administered Ori at the beginning of the laboratory. They were assembled in "balanced" discussion groups of eight each, matched in educational and occupational level (but without reference to Ori score). Each group met ten times during two weeks for a total of twenty hours of discussion about miscellaneous matters of their own choosing.

Each of the discussions was of the leaderless type. The groups were sensitivity training groups without any formal leader, without any appointed chairman, and without any previously decided agenda of a formal character. Each discussion lasted about two hours, and different from most training programs, *no laboratory staff members were present during the discussion,* although tape recordings were run of the discussions. The discussants were free to talk about anything and everything they wished, constrained only by the other seven members of the group in the room. Prior to these discussions, staff members encouraged participants to experiment in new ways of behaving, to give each other feedback, and to take time during the discussion to analyze its process.

A similar procedure was carried out for 25 professional women secretaries who met in two groups for sensitivity training for one weekend and nine successive evenings once a week. Trainers were present at the regular meetings. The mean age of both secretaries and supervisors was approximately 35 with a range from the early 20s to the late 50s. After the tenth meeting, each member of a group rated every other subject in that group on 27 items of behavior. A nine-point scale was used to indicate how much the person the subject was rating exhibited each of the behaviors during the 20 hours of discussion (9 = Completely, 8 = Almost completely, . . . , 1 = Not at all). In addition each subject ranked every other subject in his group according to the extent the subject ranked had successfully led or influenced the group.

The seven ratings received by each subject on each item from fellow members in a group yielded a mean rating on each item which in turn was correlated with the Ori scores of that participant (product moment).

Results

Both among supervisors and secretaries, task orientation and interaction orientation scales tended to correlate much more highly with peer ratings than did the self-orientation scale, and to a much greater degree.

Task orientation was correlated significantly (joint probability at the 1 to .1% level) for both supervisors and secretaries with the following peer ratings: helps members express their ideas (.60, .43),[2]

[2] The first value in parenthesis is the product-moment correlation for 32 supervisors between task orientation score and peer rating; the second value is the corresponding correlation for 25 secretaries.

helps group stay on target (.58, .44), helps get to the meat of issues (.57, .38), gives good suggestions on how to proceed (.56, .39), provides good summaries when needed (.52, .44), encourages group to a high level of productivity (.52, .45), takes the lead in selecting topics (.49, 54), works hard (.49, .40), offers original ideas (.46, .37), effectively senses when to talk and when to listen (.45, .38), successfully influences (.44, .43), concerned about successfully completing the group's jobs (.33, .47), and does not run away when faced with a problem (.48, .39).

Task-orientation scores of supervisors but not of secretaries correlated significantly at the 1 per cent level with: provides helpful, objective feedback to members (.55) and easy to understand what he is trying to say (.54). Task-orientation scores of secretaries but not of supervisors correlated significantly at or near the 5 per cent level with: removal from the group would be a loss (.39), continues to push point even after being blocked repeatedly (.51), annoys others (.37), dominates and imposes her will on the group (.46), makes unjustified assumptions (.40), and blocks the group (.38).

Thus, while task-oriented subjects are seen as exhibiting initiative and aiding the group to achieve its ends, among women secretaries, domineering inflexibility is perceived as going along with helpfulness, initiative, and successful influence.

Interaction-orientation scores generally revealed a reversed pattern of rated behavior.[3] Among both supervisors and secretaries, interaction-orientation scores were negatively correlated (at a joint probability at the 1 or 5 per cent level) with: concerned about successfully completing group jobs (−.36, −.30), dominates and imposes will on the group (−.39, −.49), offers original ideas (−.40, −.31), encourages group to a high level of productivity (−.42, −.32), provides good summaries when needed (−.43, −.32), takes the lead in selecting topics (−.46, −.48), and helps group stay on target (−.51, −.38).

Supervisors only who were high in interaction scores were seen as: running away when faced with a problem (.38) and yielding to group pressures (.26) while highly interaction-oriented secretaries were rated highly in making others feel at ease (.30).

Other ratings which correlated negatively in one sample at the 1 or 5 per cent level, but not the other included (for supervisors only): easy to understand what he is trying to say (−.43); gives good suggestions on how to proceed (−.44); provides helpful, objective feedback to

[3] This result is inseparable statistically or conceptually from the negative relation between task and interaction orientation.

members (−.45); works hard (−.45); helps get to the meat of issues (−.46); helps members express their ideas (−.55). For secretaries only, significant negative correlations at the 5 per cent level were obtained between interaction-orientation scores and: annoys others (−.45) and makes unjustified assumptions (−.48).

Interaction-oriented supervisors and secretaries are seen as of little positive help to group work; among supervisors only, as avoiding problems and conflicts; among secretaries, as avoiding being unpleasant and unreasonable.

Self-orientation scores for both supervisors and secretaries were significantly (joint probability at the 5 per cent level) but negatively related with making others feel at ease (−.21, −.20).

PART II

Orientation and Assessed Leadership Potential

A major utility regularly selects journeymen and maintenance workers with promise, according to their performance records and boss' opinions, and sends them to a center for three days of intensive observation in various quasi-real group situational tests following OSS procedures and methods usually described as the "country house" technique (see Vernon, 1950). Observers use a five-point scale to pool their ratings into a single overall evaluation of the promotability to supervisory positions of the candidates screened by the situational tests.

Forty-eight of these candidates were given the Ori. The orientation scores, unknown to the assessors, were then compared for the thirteen candidates earning the highest "promotability" ratings with the thirteen candidates earning the lowest appraisals by the assessment staff. Table 1 shows the mean Ori scores of the thirteen high and low candidates. Downgraded candidates were significantly higher (at the 1%

Table 1 *Mean Orientation Scores of 13 Candidates Appraised Highly Promotable to Supervisory Positions with 13 Appraised as Low in Promotability*

	Mean Orientation		
Promotability	Self	Interaction	Task
High	21.8	23.8	35.5
Low	18.2	29.4	33.4
		$p < .01$	

level) in interaction orientation and comparably lower in self- and task orientation. Evidently, the lack of initiative of the interaction oriented strongly affected their appraisals, consistent with preceding results obtained for secretaries and supervisors. On the other hand, task orientation failed to significantly raise evaluations any more than did self-orientation.

PART III

Recomposed Groups Homogeneous in Orientation

To gain further insight into the behavior of discussants as a function of their orientation, discussion groups were set up of participants, all of a single type. Consistent differences between self-oriented, interaction-oriented, and task-oriented groups, in meaningful ways, were observed for both the supervisors and the secretaries who met once in these recomposed groups.

Procedure

Following the fourth meeting of the regular training groups of supervisors, the groups were recomposed for the next discussion according to members' Ori scores. The members did not know the basis of recomposition. The eight members of the supervisor's laboratory scoring highest on the self-orientation scale were placed in a "Blue" group; the eight scoring highest on the interaction scale were placed in a "Brown" group; and the eight highest on the task-orientation scale were placed in a "Purple" group. The remaining eight were not as high as any of the other individuals on any of the three scales and were placed in an "Orange" or "residual" group of individuals none of whom were high on any of the scales, nor low therefore on any of the scales. Each of these temporarily recomposed groups held a two-hour meeting after which they were dissolved and members returned to their original groups.

A somewhat modified plan was followed for the secretaries. After the tenth regular meeting, 22 of the 25 secretaries present from the two regular training groups were recomposed into three groups—Blue, Brown, and Purple—of seven or eight subjects each of the same orientation. No residual Orange group was composed because of the fewer number of subjects available.

Supervisor Analyses

At the end of each of the four preceding two-hour discussions in his regular training group during the first three days of the laboratory, each supervisor had filled out a postmeeting questionnaire. He did the same at the end of the two-hour discussion in the recomposed group.

The questionnaire contained twelve items. Each item was accompanied by a nine-point scale varying from a generally favorable to a generally unfavorable reaction. For example, the first question was "How do I feel about this group now?" The respondent could indicate a reaction ranging from 1, "worst possible group," to 9, "best possible group."

Results

The recomposed groups behaved as anticipated, although to a degree exceeding expectations.

Table 2 shows the mean extent on each nine-point scale that a recomposed group's discussion was higher in rating by its members than the same members had assigned to the last meeting of the balanced group from which they had come. For example, members of the Blue group, on the average, rated their Blue group .5 lower in quality (Item 1) than the various immediately preceding, regular groups. On the other hand, the interaction-oriented members gave an average of 1 point more to their newly formed Brown group than to the various home groups from which they had come. In evaluating these responses, it should be kept in mind that in a management training laboratory of this sort, a great deal of loyalty is developed for one's regular home training group. Most experienced staff personnel will agree that it is difficult to destroy this loyalty by rearranging memberships temporarily. Thus, in general, members were more favorably inclined to their original "home" group with which they had been meeting for the first three days than to their newly recomposed temporary group. But there was a striking exception—those who met as the Brown group of highly interaction-oriented subjects.

Interaction-oriented members (the Brown group) felt quite differently about their recomposed group than did any of the other members. They seemed much more favorably disposed towards their recomposed group; and in the informal critique that followed they were rather extreme in this feeling. As noted in Table 2, they reported their recomposed group had clearer goals, worked harder, had a more practical and realistic discussion centered in what was going on in the group. Most significantly in view of the question of loyalties, the interaction-oriented members felt more "joined up" with their new

Table 2 *Differences in Evaluation of Recomposed Groups of Supervisors and the Immediately Preceding Regular Groups from Which Members Came*

	Mean Difference in Orientation			
		(Recomposed Group)		
Postmeeting Evaluation	Self (Blue)	Interaction (Brown)	Task (Purple)	Residual (Orange)
1. Quality of group	−.5[a]*	1.0	−.9*	−1.2
2. Clarity of group's goals	.4	1.1*	−1.8*	−.6
3. Worked hard at task	.5	1.3**	−1.5*	−.8
4. Practical, realistic discussion	−.4	1.3*	−2.1**	−.5
5. Discussion about ourselves	−1.9	2.0*	1.1	−.6
6. Members out to win own points	−.3	−.9	−1.8	2.2**
7. Group worked at developing itself	−.4	.6	−1.2*	−1.2
8. I leveled with others	−.5	.8	.5	−1.0
9. I felt joined up	−.6	.8*	.2	−1.1
10. Tolerated different views	.5	.4	−.9*	−.8
11. Received help from others	−.5	.5	−.9	−.6
12. Group concerned with content rather than process	−1.5*	1.4*	.2	−2.8*

[a] A positive value indicates response higher for recomposed group; negative value indicates higher rating of regular group.

* $p < .05$, $df = 6$.

** $p < .01$, $df = 6$.

recomposed group than the group they had been meeting with for the past three days.

On the other hand, self-oriented members (the Blue group) tended to rate more favorably the regular training group from which each had come, significantly more so, on the first and last of the twelve items.

Some of the differences in reaction between self-oriented and interaction-oriented subjects may be due to the fact that interaction-oriented individuals seem to be much less interested in examining the "whys" and "wherefores" of discussion process than self-oriented persons who are much more reflective and introverted concerning the process about them. In sensitivity training groups, efforts are made to get the group members to focus in a sophisticated way on the process of their interaction. Interaction-oriented subjects paradoxically seem desirous of avoiding looking deeply into the very phenomena from which they seem to get the greatest enjoyment. Their opinion is often verbalized as: "people around here are trying to kill the discussion in order to dissect the corpse." The twelfth item illustrates the differences between interaction and self-oriented groups. In comparison to the regular groups from which they had come, self-oriented supervisors reported their Blue group to be 1.5 lower in concern with content rather than process. In opposite fashion, interaction-oriented subjects noted that their Brown group was 1.4 higher in concern with content rather than process.

As seen in Table 2, like self-oriented subjects, task-oriented subjects also felt less favorably about their recomposed Purple group of only task-oriented members. They judged it was less adequate a group, had less clear goals, worked less hard, yielded a less practical and less realistic discussion. Furthermore, they felt that their recomposed group did not progress in its own development and was more intolerant of different views than the "back-home" regular training group from which each of the members had come.

The "residual" Orange group lived up to its mixed composition. Much more conflict appeared in its discussion according to its members' negative value on Item 6, "members were out to win own points." The residual members also felt that their recomposed group was much more content oriented than the regular training group from which they had come (Item 12).

Supervisors' Critique: Before announcing the actual basis upon which the groups had been recomposed, a critique was held in an assembly of all 32 subjects after the recomposition experience. Each of the recomposed groups was asked to summarize the content and process of its discussion. Illustrative of the effects of homogeneous grouping was the comment of the spokesman for the recomposed group of highly interaction oriented members (Brown group):

> . . . In reflecting on our postdiscussion ratings of our group, we felt that they would likely be at the highest level in comparison to what we had been going through during the past two or three days. . . . This gave us a very interesting feeling and we thought you in the laboratory did a remarkable job [in com-

posing our Brown group]. . . . There wasn't a single excuse, argument or a difference of opinion and we all reached the same conclusions.

Secretary Analyses: After meeting in recomposed groups, the secretaries, unlike the supervisors, had not been filling out postmeeting questionnaires after each meeting. So after meeting in the recomposed groups homogeneous in orientation, each secretary completed a single five-item questionnaire. For each question she compared the recomposed with her regular training group on a nine-point scale coded +4 to −4. As in Table 2, a positive mean score indicated choice of the recomposed group, while a negative mean score indicated that the item was more true about the regular group. However, the measurement procedure was not directly comparable with the supervisors' ratings. With 5 or 6 *df*, a value ±.5 generally was likely to be significantly different from 0.

Table 3 *Differences in Evaluation of Recomposed Groups of Secretaries and the Regular Groups from Which Members Came*

	Mean Difference in Orientation (Recomposed Group)		
Comparative Evaluation	Self	Interaction	Task
1. Quality of group	1.1[a]	1.3	.9
2. Worked hard at task	−.2	1.0	.3
3. Would rather return	.1	1.7	−.1
4. Common interests felt	.8	.9	.1
5. Much conflict	−1.9	−1.3	−.3

[a] A positive value indicates a higher rating of the recomposed group; a negative value indicates a higher rating of the regular group.

Results

Contrary to expectations, all three groups tended to be more favorable in response to their recomposed group, as can be seen by the high proportion of positive responding to Items 1, 2, 3, and 4 of Table 3 concerning group quality, drive, attractiveness, and mutual interest. The recomposed groups were smaller (7 or 8) in comparison to the regular groups of 11 to 13 members, so direct comparisons may be less important than the relative contrasts between the three homogeneous, recomposed groups. Once again, the interaction-oriented secretaries, like the interaction-oriented supervisors, were most favorably inclined to their newly recomposed group. They felt their recomposed group to be best in comparison to their regular group; they felt it had worked hardest, they preferred the most to return to it rather than their regular group, and felt most compatible.

As before, the group of self-oriented subjects felt relatively more compatible in interests than the comparable assemblage of task-oriented subjects, for relatively more conflict was perceived in recomposed groups homogeneous in task orientation. However, as indicated by the negative values, all subjects saw more conflict in regular, than recomposed groups.

Secretaries Critique: Again, in general session, participants were asked to describe their meeting.

The task and interaction groups spent a large portion of their time discussing aspects of the previous weeks' discussions involving the goals of development group training, while the self-oriented group utilized a great proportion of their available time introducing one another and discussing themselves. Also, the task group spent effort examining the possibility of applying knowledge derived from the laboratory to the working situation. Some individuals seemed aware that each group contained members homogeneous in something, but none could verbalize just what these similarities were.

PART IV

Orientation of the Most Influential Member of the Recomposed Group of Members All High in a Particular Orientation

It is fairly well recognized that the traits of the successful leader depend upon the particular traits of those he leads (Bass, 1960, pp. 174–177). Where physical prowess is valued by the group, the leader tends to be above the average in this trait of those he leads; where criminal tendencies are commonplace in the group, the leader is often an archcriminal; where the group is highly frustrated and resentful, the most vocally aggressive individuals are likely to come to the fore.

A working hypothesis was formulated that in a group composed solely of task-oriented members, the most influential member would tend to be outstanding in task orientation relative to the others in his group; in a group of highly interaction-oriented members, the most outstanding member in interaction orientation would tend to be most influential in the group; and in a group of self-oriented members, the most influential member would tend to be most extreme in self-orientation.

The six recomposed groups of supervisors and secretaries provided data for examining the hypothesis. Parallel findings emerged from the two samples of men and women when each subject ranked every other in his recomposed group in influencing the group. The discussant with the highest assigned mean rank by his peers was identified as successful leader of the group.

RESULTS

In the task-oriented group of seven secretaries, the leader was the highest in the group in task orientation, exactly as predicted. In the task-oriented group of eight supervisors, the leader was third highest. Similarly, the most influential secretary among interaction-oriented secretaries and the most influential supervisor among interaction-oriented supervisors were both next-to-highest in interaction orientation in their respective recomposed groups.

A complete reversal (which made sense, after discovery) occurred in parallel fashion for both secretaries and supervisors when the self-oriented discussants were analyzed. The leader of self-oriented secretaries was next-to-lowest in self-orientation while the leader of the self-oriented supervisors was tied for lowest score in self-orientation.

Further Analyses

As reported earlier, task orientation had been found to correlate .43 and .44 with influence in regular discussion groups. (Self- and interaction orientation were negatively correlated with influence in their regular discussion groups, but not significantly so.) The increased homogeneity of the recomposed groups compared to regular training groups was expected to, and did, reduce these correlations substantially. For example, the correlation in the recomposed group of eight supervisors between task orientation and influence in the recomposed group of task-oriented supervisors reduced to .24, while the correlation between task orientation and influence among groups composed of self-oriented or interaction-oriented members remained low negative. No correlation was found between previous influence in his regular group and successful influence in groups composed of self-oriented or interaction-oriented members. However, a correlation of .53 was obtained between leadership in one's regular groups and influence among task-oriented members.

Partial Effects: A corrected measure was calculated of how much influence in a recomposed group was associated with high scores on the particular scale used to compose the group, subtracting the effects of the same scale score on influence in one's regular group. The emerging partial correlations were consistent with inferences based on the single most successful leader of each recomposed group. The partial correlation between interaction orientation and influence among members high in interaction orientation (corrected for their respective influences back in their own regular group) was .42. The corresponding partial correlation between task orientation and influence among highly task-oriented members in a recomposed group was .13 while the corresponding partial correlation between self-orientation scores and influence in a recomposed group of self-oriented members was only −.01.

Placing a highly interaction-oriented subject among like-minded subjects increases his success as a leader. Since most task-oriented subjects tend to lead regular training groups, when placed with other task-oriented subjects, high task orientation, per se, reduces in importance in determining influence patterns. In groups of self-oriented, no relation remains between leadership and orientation after previous behavior in regular groups is discounted.

DISCUSSION AND CONCLUSION

Modifications in Conceptualization

The interaction-oriented member is now seen as considerably more superficial in his overall approach to group affairs. His concern with maintaining happy, harmonious relations makes it difficult for him to contribute to the group's progress (unless everyone in the group is interaction oriented). The interaction-oriented member's interest in group activities is at a nonfunctional level as far as the group's progress is concerned. Results here fit with unpublished learning data collected by Leo Postman suggesting that in comparison to other subjects, interaction-oriented subjects "speak before they think" in that they have a relatively high error rate coupled with the fastest attainment of an easy criterion of nine out of twelve correction responses. In comparison, the task-oriented member is ready to examine all facets of group activities including the way members need to relate to each other in order to accomplish the purposes of their group. Despite his concern with the task, the task-oriented member works hard within the group to make it as productive as possible. It is the task-oriented member who is likely to be rated as most helpful to the group and its constituent members—although among women, derogatory feelings may be aroused because of the initiative displayed.

But why did the pooling of only task-oriented members fail to achieve an effective hard-working group? Task-oriented supervisors and secretaries seemed to be relatively less favorable to homogeneous groupings. Several unrelated factors may be involved. First, the task-oriented subject participated the most in his regular group and therefore probably had developed more of a commitment to it. He may have felt the arbitrary recomposition of membership, suddenly imposed by the training staff, to be an intrusion interrupting the work of his regular group to which he was contributing more than other members. Second, assuming that successful leadership is rewarding, the task-oriented member had relatively less opportunity for such reward once placed among other task-oriented subjects. Third, it was suggested in the critique that task-oriented subjects were more inclined to bring into their new recomposed group the particular norms and standards developed in their regular group (which they, no doubt, had been most instrumental in developing). The result was more difficulty in reaching agreement on how to proceed in the recomposed group.

While the task-oriented member emerges as the hero of the training group, as seen in our recomposed groups, for reasons indicated, it by no means leads to the extrapolation that the best group contains only task-oriented members. In addition to the specific situation just discussed, it must be reiterated that while we suggest that some subjects are generally and consistently more task oriented than others over many situations, there are various conditions when the usually task-oriented subject becomes least concerned with the task. Thus, task-oriented subjects are most likely to become apathetic when faced with a dull, irrelevant group chore not providing them a sense of accomplishment, while interaction-oriented subjects might remain content just to have the opportunity to keep interacting. For example, when dyads of subjects of varying combinations of self-, interaction, and task orientation were asked to judge photos during a regular class hour instead of doing classwork, it was interaction-oriented subjects, not the task oriented, who were most favored as partners (Campbell, 1961). Yet, when the task for the dyads involved midterm examinations, interaction-oriented subjects proved themselves least agreeable and caused their partners to feel more conflict in two-man discussions about the right answers to the examinations.

As a combination of several factors including the need to dominate as well as to introspect, the self-oriented member is most likely to be rejected by others as well as to be unresponsive to the needs of his group. His concerns with himself are detrimental to his evaluation as a group member by his associates and to his likelihood of modifying his behavior in response to the group's needs in comparison to his own extrinsic demands unrelated to the task at hand. An understanding of his performance may be found in the fact that when given control of a two-way communication system, the self-oriented discussant "turns off" disagreeing partners, and "turns on" agreeing ones, behaving in the Hull-Spence tradition, increasing what is immediately rewarding and avoiding what is immediately unpleasant. The behavior of interaction- and task-oriented subjects follows more dynamic theory. Their talking is positively reinforced by agreeable partners. When they can control the systems, they talk more and listen less to agreement; they talk less and listen more to disagreeing partners (Kanfer & Bass, in press). The lack of receptivity of self-oriented subjects is illustrated by a study in progress by Jerry Mendelsohn where he finds in simulated counseling that the more self-oriented the counselor or counselee, the less either agrees on what they talked about during counseling, but the more valuable they thought the counseling session. Lack of modifiability among the self-oriented seems reflected in their tendency to shift their opinions less. Rejection by peers of the self-oriented supervisors and secretaries seems consistent with the tendencies of self-oriented subjects to indicate more defense feelings under ego threat than matched interaction- or task-oriented subjects (Bass, in press) and with their greater tendency to show up as maladjusted clients at counseling centers or in institutions for juvenile delinquents.

Results of these analyses also appear consistent with a most direct exploration by Frye (1961) of the proposition developed by Bass (1960, pp. 153–157) of how orientation affects attempts to lead under various conditions of success and effectiveness as a leader. Frye studied 48 quartets homogeneous in one orientation or another as they discussed the solutions to a series of nine problems. After each trial, subjects were fed back false information concerning the effectiveness of the group solution as well as their success or failure in influencing others.

First, Frye found that regardless of treatment, interaction-oriented subjects spent significantly more time in discussion than subjects of other orientations, while task-oriented subjects were most attracted to these problem-solving groups after nine trials of experience. Self-oriented subjects talked the least and were least attracted to their groups at the conclusion of the experiment. However, in opposition to what had been suggested by Bass (1960), when a subject was told he was influential but the resulting group solution was ineffective, he was significantly more likely to increase his attempts to lead if he was task oriented, and significantly more likely to reduce his attempts to lead if he was self-oriented. Continued failure at the task spurred the task oriented who saw himself as influential, while it deterred the self-oriented. The interaction-oriented subject was most stimulated into increasing his attempts to lead when told that the group was achieving effective decisions, but that he was not successfully influencing the group.

Minimally, it seems warranted to conclude that identifying group members in advance as self-, interaction, or task oriented is a profitable discrimination that correlates consistently with patterns of leadership and other aspects of group behavior.

SUMMARY

To further the theoretical expectation that orientation would be associated with leadership and related group behavior, the Bass Orientation Inventory was correlated with rated performance in sensitivity training groups of 32 male supervisors and 25 female secretaries, in groups of 48 candidates for supervisory positions undergoing three days of assessment, and in reformed groups homogeneous in orientation. Task-oriented *S*s, particularly among men, were judged most favorably and interaction-oriented *S*s least favorably both by peers and outside assessors. However, homogeneous groupings for sensitivity training were most satisfying to interaction-oriented *S*s, whose leaders were most highly interaction oriented. Task-oriented group leaders were highly task oriented, but leaders of self-oriented groups were relatively low in self-orientation.

REFERENCES

Bass, B. M. *Leadership, psychology and organizational behavior.* New York: Harper, 1960.

Bass, B. M. *Orientation Inventory.* Palo Alto: Consulting Psychologists Press, 1962.

Bass, B. M. Defensiveness and susceptibility to coercion as a function of self, interaction and task-orientation. *J. Soc. Psychol.*, in press.

Bass, B. M., Frye, R., Dunteman, G., Vidulich, R., & Wambach, H. Orientation

Inventory scores associated with overt behavior and personal factors. *Educ. Psychol. Measmt.*, 1963, **23**, 101–116.

Campbell, O. H. Objective behavior in dyads of self, interaction and task-oriented members. Unpublished master's thesis, Louisiana State University, 1961.

Dunteman, G., & Bass, B. M. Supervisory success and engineering assignment associated with Orientation Inventory scores. *Personnel Psychol.*, 1963, **16**, 13–21.

Frye, R. L. The effect of feedback of success and effectiveness on self, task, and interaction-oriented group members. Unpublished doctoral dissertation, Louisiana State University, 1961.

Kanfer, F., & Bass, B. M. Dyadic speech patterns, orientation and social reinforcement. *J. Consult. Psychol.*, in press.

Vernon, P. E. The validation of civil service selection board procedures. *Occup. Psychol.*, 1950, **24**, 75–95.

10.4 CONTROL, PERFORMANCE, AND SATISFACTION: AN ANALYSIS OF STRUCTURAL AND INDIVIDUAL EFFECTS

Jerald G. Bachman
Clagett G. Smith
Jonathan A. Slesinger

The present investigation is concerned with the relationship between organizational effectiveness and social control in organizations. In particular, it is designed to explore two aspects of control: the *distribution* of control among organizational levels, and the *bases* for this control.

In many discussions of organizational life there appears to be a serious dilemma concerning control. On the one hand, hierarchical control is said to be necessary to insure efficient administration and coordination of effort. On the other hand, decentralization of control and decision making is said to lead to higher rank-and-file motivation. Recent research has suggested that this may not really be a dilemma. It has been argued that increased control at the lower levels need not, and should not, involve any sort of proportionate

Source: This article was written as part of a program of research on organizations under a grant from the Carnegie Corporation of New York to the Survey Research Center, Institute of Social Research, University of Michigan. Reprinted with slight abridgment from the *Journal of Personality and Social Psychology*, 1966, **4**, 127–137, with permission of the authors and the American Psychological Association, Inc., copyright holder. This article, and others dealing with related topics, also appears in *Control in Organizations*, edited by Arnold S. Tannenbaum, New York: McGraw-Hill, 1968.

decrease in control at some other level. A number of studies indicate that relatively high amounts of control exercised by members at *all* organizational echelons is associated with higher performance and increased satisfaction (Bowers, 1964; Smith & Tannenbaum, 1963; Tannenbaum, 1962). Tannenbaum (1961) and Likert (1961) have argued that this pattern of high total control is successful because it involves members at all levels of the organization, leading to more effective decisions and also to higher motivation.

A related question concerns the bases of control in organizations, and how these may be associated with performance, satisfaction, and total amount of control. French and Raven (1960) describe five bases for the social power which an agent, O, can exert over a person, P:

> (a) Reward power, based on P's perception that O has the ability to mediate rewards for him; (b) coercive power, based on P's perception that O has the ability to mediate punishments for him; (c) legitimate power, based on the perception by P that O has a legitimate right to prescribe behavior for him; (d) referent power, based on P's identification with O; (e) expert power, based on the perception that O has some special knowledge or expertness [pp. 612–613].

In the present research we have attempted to measure these five bases of power (or social control) and relate them to the total amount of control as well as to performance and satisfaction.

Likert (1961) and Tannenbaum (1962) have suggested that the processes underlying a system of high total control and its effects derive essentially from the satisfaction of the ego motives of the individuals, such as the desire for status, achievement, and acceptance. If their interpretation is correct, then we would expect reward, referent, and expert power to be the more important bases underlying total control and its implications. In contrast, if the more traditional Weberian view is indeed correct, then the more important bases of control and its effects would be legitimate authority and the manipulation of rewards and sanctions.

The setting for the present study has certain features which make it especially attractive for our purposes. It involves subjects in responsible positions, with fairly high levels of skill and income. Thus we have an opportunity to see whether earlier findings obtained largely from rank-and-file workers can be generalized to persons at higher organizational levels. Another important advantage is the availability of accurate individual performance data, which permits us to study factors affecting performance at individual as well as group levels.

Finally, the subjects are located in 36 branch offices, each under the supervision of an office manager. We are thus able to study a fairly large number of distinct organizational units, each with basically the same tasks and the same criteria of success.

SOME METHODOLOGICAL CONSIDERATIONS

Frequently, quantitative studies of organizations depend upon members' perceptions to provide measures of organizational characteristics, particularly administrative characteristics. Indeed, most of the research mentioned above falls into this category. The traditional procedure for handling such data is to characterize each organizational unit in terms of average ratings by all respondents in that unit. Thus, for example, if a researcher found that organizational units with high mean ratings of total amount of control also have relatively high mean satisfaction ratings, he might well conclude that total control and satisfaction are positively related at the organizational level. More specifically, he might view the pattern of influence as a part of the objective *structure* of the organizational environment which has real-life consequences for its members.

While organizational studies using this traditional form of analysis have been valuable, they continue to be subject to a serious weakness: what appears to be an objective structural effect may in fact be spurious—merely a reflection of purely individual-level relationship (Blau, 1957, 1960; Davis, Spaeth, & Huson, 1961; Tannenbaum & Bachman, 1964). Returning to our example, a positive correlation between mean satisfaction and mean ratings of total control might indicate only that persons who *perceive* a high degree of total control tend also to be satisfied persons. Such as individual-level relationship would be consistent with a *phenomenological* interpretation of the control-satisfaction findings. March and Simon (1958) illustrate this point of view as follows:

> . . . most students of the subject agree that (providing the deception is successful) the perception of individual participation in goal setting is equivalent in many respects to actual participation [p. 54].

Tannenbaum and Smith (1964) studied the problem of structural versus phenomenological effects using several analytic techniques in addition to the correlation of group mean data. They concluded that both types of effect occurred in their study, depending upon the criterion used to measure organizational effectiveness. When the criterion was the amount of time spent in organizational affairs, a structural relationship with patterns of control was observed. But in the case of loyalty, a more subjective dimension, a phenomenological effect appeared.

The analysis strategy used in the present study, following the same basic approach as Tannenbaum and Smith (1964), makes an operational distinction between office-level effects (including structural effects) and individual-level effects (including phenomenological effects). We assume that the criterion scores (performance and satisfaction) *for each individual* are influenced in part by aspects of the organizational environment which are common to most or all of his office colleagues, and we refer to these influences as *office-level effects.* Such effects include, but are by no means limited to, the impact of administrative characteristics such as control and bases of power.[1] We assume that the criterion scores are also influenced by a host of idiosyncratic factors which differ from person to person, and we refer to these influences as *individual-level effects.* This definition includes so-called phenomenological effects, but it also includes such spurious relationships as halo effects and simple response biases. (Indeed, while the present study deals only with the correlates of perceptions, our definition of individual-level effects encompasses the effects of all individual differences—ability, motivation, etc.) Note that the same *individual* criterion scores are used to assess both office-level and individual-level effects; we are thus exploring the extent to which each subject's performance and satisfaction are affected by office-level versus individual-level variables.

Ideally, of course, office-level variables should be manipulated experimentally, measured by observers, or assessed through other methods which are independent of the persons directly involved. In the present study, however, it was necessary to rely on the subjects' own perceptions. Nevertheless, we have been able to maintain the distinction between office-level and individual-level effects in the analysis of our results. Our basic strategy is to partial out the individual's own perception of office characteristics and compare his performance and satisfaction with the perceptual measures of the other group members. And we consider this distinction to be an important advance over the traditional correlation of group mean data.

[1] The term office level is somewhat specific to the present study. We might speak more broadly of these relationships as group-level effects, since the analysis could equally well be applied to any group or organization that provides some sort of common climate for most or all members.

METHOD

Research Site

The data used in the present study were obtained in 36 branch offices of a national firm selling intangibles. Each branch office is managed by a single office manager, who has sole responsibility for the conduct of his office. His functions include supervision, on-the-job training of employees, and enforcement of home-office policies.

Directly under each office manager are a number of salesmen. The salesman's functions include soliciting and opening new accounts, and servicing existing accounts; he may also serve as the client's main source of information and expertise for decisions leading to sales. Since the firm derives its income largely from commissions on the sale of intangibles, the salesman is the basic producer in any branch office. The salaries of salesmen are indirectly related to individual productivity; most are within a range from $10,000 to $25,000 per year.

The remaining employees in each branch office serve in essentially a supporting or staff capacity. They provide necessary technical information, secretarial and clerical services, and the like, which help the salesmen provide service to their clients. In the present study we will not deal directly with these staff functions; instead, we will concentrate upon the line side of the branch office: the office manager and his salesmen.

The branch offices used in the analysis were divided into two groups for separate analysis. The 18 offices in Group A are all located in areas judged to have high business potential, and yet they vary widely in actual office performance. Offices in Group B are all located in areas rated as having lower business potential, and yet some are high on actual performance, others relatively low. Ratings of business potential were derived from the pooled judgment of ten high-level members of the home-office staff who had personal knowledge of the business conditions. The eighteen offices in Group A were selected from among those offices which at least eight of the ten raters placed in the top quartile for business potential. The eighteen offices in Group B were selected from among those offices which at least eight raters placed *below* the top quartile. Thus in terms of business potential, the Group A offices may be more homogeneous than the Group B offices.

In order to restrict the sample to those offices having continuity of operations and leadership, no office was included which had been established within the five-year period preceding the study, or which had experienced a change of manager within the two years preceding the study.

Measures

The data for this study consist of sales performance measures and salesmen's questionnaire responses. The number of salesmen in Group A offices ranged from 10 to 35, with a mean of 23.4 and median of 22.5. In Group B the number ranged from 8 to 17, with a mean of 13.1 and median of 14. The total number of respondents was 656, with 421 in Group A offices and 235 in Group B offices.

Virtually every salesman in each of the 36 offices filled out an extensive questionnaire dealing with many aspects of his work and his adjustment to it.[2] The administrative variables of interest in the present study include control, and the bases of the office manager's power. The criterion variables consist of salesmen's performance, and their satisfaction with their office manager.

Control: Two closely related measures of control were used. They have been treated separately because they involved somewhat different "influence receivers." The measures of *control over the office* dealt with the general amount of influence over the way the office is run. The *interpersonal control* measures dealt strictly with influence patterns between the office manager and his salesmen (with respect to office-relevant matters).

The following questionnaire item was used as a measure of the office manager's control over the office: "In general, how much say or influence do you feel [the office manager] has on how your office is run?" The extent of salesmen's control over the office was measured by a similar item: "In general, how much say or influence do you feel [the salesmen as a group] have on how your office is run?" Response categories for both items ranged from 1, "little or no influence," to 5, "a great deal of influence." A measure of *total control over the office* was derived by combining the responses to these two items.

The following items were used to measure the amount of inter-

[2] Since it was necessary to identify respondents, conditions of complete anonymity could not be maintained; however, respondents were assured that the information they provided would be kept in strictest confidence, and would be available only to the research team.

personal control between the office manager and his salesmen: "How much say or influence does your office manager have with [the salesmen in your office] when it comes to activities and decisions that affect the performance of your office? Now, thinking in the other direction, how much say or influence [do the salesmen] in your office have on your office manager when it comes to his activities and decisions that affect the performance of your office?" Both items used response categories ranging from 1, "no influence at all," to 5, "a great deal of influence." A measure of *total interpersonal control* was derived by adding the responses to the two items.

Bases of Power: A single questionnaire item was used to assess five bases of the office manager's power or influence over the salesman respondent: referent, expert, reward, coercive, and legitimate power.

Listed below are five reasons generally given by people when they are asked *why* they do the things their superiors suggest or want them to do. Please read all five carefully. Then number them according to their importance to you as reasons for doing the things your office manager suggests or wants you to do. *Give rank "1" to the most important factor, "2" to the next, etc.* "I do the things my office manager suggests or wants me to do because:

A. "I admire him for his personal qualities, and want to act in a way that merits his respect and admiration;

B. "I respect his competence and good judgment about things with which he is more experienced than I;

C. "He can give special help and benefits to those who cooperate with him;

D. "He can apply pressure or penalize those who do not cooperate;

E. "He has a legitimate right, considering his position, to expect that his suggestions will be carried out."

In order to simplify analysis and interpretation of results, the rank values for this item were later reversed so that a value of 5 indicates maximum importance, 1 indicates minimum importance. The measures of the five bases of power are not independent, because of the ranking procedure involved; in a sense, any single base of power can be given prominence only at the expense of the other bases.[3]

Satisfaction with Office Manager: Each salesman's satisfaction with

[3] The ranking procedure has the advantage of forcing the respondent to discriminate among all of the bases of power, rather than giving prominence to only one or two. Moreover, it may in this case help the respondent to avoid confusing the *extent* to which he does what the office manager asks and the *reason* for doing so.

his office manager was assessed by the following item: "All things considered, how satisfied are you with the way your office manager is doing his job?" Response categories ranged from 1, "very dissatisfied," to 5, "very satisfied."

Standardized Salesman Performance: The measure of salesmen's performance was designed to rule out the effects of length of service upon dollar productivity, thus permitting a fair comparison of younger men with more experienced men. This was accomplished by separating salesmen into the following subgrouping based on years of experience: less than 1 year, 1–2 years, 2–3 years, 3–4 years, 4–5 years, 5–10 years, and more than 10 years. Within each of these subgroups, the distribution of dollar productivity was sharply skewed toward the high end. A logarithmic transformation applied to the dimension of dollar productivity yielded distributions that were approximately normal. Moreover, although the means of each of the seven subgroups were different, the standard deviations of the transformed distributions were almost identical. Each salesman was assigned a score corresponding to his position within the transformed productivity distribution for his subgroup. The standard performance scores which resulted from these operations were independent of length of service and approximated the normal distribution. (To facilitate computation, this distribution was given a mean value of 50, with a standard deviation of 10.)

Significance Level: Because many of the relationships examined in this study were not specifically predicted in advance, two-tailed tests were used with the .05 minimum criterion for significance. (Although all subjects completed questionnaires, a small proportion of nonresponses occurred for some questions. Accordingly, a consistent 10 per cent nonresponse rate was assumed for each pair of variables when computing degrees of freedom. This was slightly conservative; the actual frequency of nonresponse was usually smaller.)

RESULTS

Because of the differences between Group A and Group B offices outlined above, it seemed appropriate to carry out separate analyses for the two groups of offices, thereby controlling most effects of differences in business potential. The separate analyses produced very similar results, thus indicating a high degree of reliability for the data. It then appeared that reporting these findings separately would be an unnecessary duplication; therefore, the data were combined, and weighted means of Group A and Group B findings were used throughout the present paper.[4]

Statistical Analysis and Rationale

Our analysis explores the effects of several administrative characteristics upon two criterion variables, performance and satisfaction. The mean responses and standard deviations for all measures are presented in Table 1. Tables 2, 3, and 4 present the results of several types of correlational analyses, as described below.

We make the assumption that the best available estimate of organizational structure in our data is a composite of perceptions within a given organizational unit. Thus our measure of each administrative characteristic consists of the mean rating by all salesmen in a given office. These mean ratings are correlated with performance and satisfaction at two distinct levels of analysis: office mean criterion scores and individual criterion scores.

Office Mean Criterion Scores: The first level of analysis involves what we have called the traditional comparison of office mean data. The correlations between administrative characteristics and office mean criterion scores are presented in Table 2.[5] This form of analysis often highlights office-level effects, since many kinds of individual-level effects may be canceled by the use of mean criterion data. We noted earlier, however, that *systematic* individual-level effects, including some phenomenological effects, are not canceled, and the danger that they will be misinterpreted as genuine office-level effects remains a major weakness of the traditional method. Thus the analysis in Table 2 cannot stand alone as a demonstration of office-level effects; further evidence is necessary.

Individual Criterion Scores: The second level of analysis deals with individual salesmen; Table 3 presents correlations computed between

[4] When the office was the unit of analysis (see Table 2) results for Group A ($N =$ 18 offices) and Group B ($N = 18$ offices) were weighted equally. When the unit of analysis was the individual, the results for Group A ($N = 421$ salesmen) received proportionately more weight than those for Group B ($N = 235$ salesmen). Mean correlations were obtained using the z transformation procedure described in Table 4 (Johnson, 1949).

[5] The correlations in Table 2 are based upon office mean scores, with each office weighted equally. An alternative procedure weighting each office according to its number of salesmen produced almost identical results. As a further check, Spearman rank correlations were computed for all relationships shown in the table. The results were essentially the same as the product-moment correlations.

Table 1 *Administrative and Criterion Variables: Means and Standard Deviations*

	M Rating[a]	*SD* among Individuals	*SD* among Offices
Control over office			
Exercised by office manager	4.57	0.81	0.36
Exercised by salesmen	3.01	1.05	0.45
Total control	7.58	1.40	0.63
Interpersonal control			
Office manager's influence on salesmen	4.30	0.91	0.43
Salesmen's influence on office manager	3.00	1.03	0.42
Total interpersonal control	7.30	1.55	0.72
Bases of office manager's power			
Referent	2.93	1.30	0.57
Expert	3.46	1.35	0.61
Reward	2.70	1.09	0.42
Coercive	1.90	1.23	0.48
Legitimate	4.02	1.11	0.39
Criterion variables			
Standardized performance	50.43	9.70	2.78
Satisfaction with office manager	3.78	1.09	0.58

[a] Possible scores range from 1.0 (lowest) to 5.0 (highest), except for total control measures (ranging from 2.0 to 10.0), and standardized performance (described in text).

administrative characteristics (still based on office mean perceptions) and the individual criterion ratings ($N = 656$ salesmen).[6] This form of analysis deals with the question: Given the many causes of an individual's performance and satisfaction, what is the relative importance of administrative characteristics such as the distribution and bases of control? It is clear at a glance that the correlations in Table 3 are, on the whole, much smaller than those in Table 2. The office administrative characteristics have a sort of monopoly in Table 2, whereas in Table 3 their impact is shared with the many causes that may

[6] These correlations were obtained by simply treating the office mean perceptions as if they were individual data. Each salesman was characterized by the administrative ratings for his office (based on mean perceptions), as well as his own personal criterion scores; then these two kinds of variables were correlated for all salesmen.

Table 2 *Administrative Characteristics Correlated with Office Mean Criterion Scores (N = 36 Offices)*

Office Mean Ratings	Office Mean Criterion Scores: Standardized Performance	Office Mean Criterion Scores: Satisfaction with Office Manager
Control over office		
Exercised by office manager	.22	.60**
Exercised by salesmen	.39*	.60**
Total control	.39*	.79**
Interpersonal control		
Office manager's influence over salesmen	.35*	.82**
Salesmen's influence over office manager	.39*	.75**
Total interpersonal control	.41*	.88**
Bases of office manager's power		
Referent	.40*	.75**
Expert	.36*	.69**
Reward	−.55**	−.51**
Coercive	−.31	−.71**
Legitimate	−.17	−.57**

Note: Cell entries are product-moment correlations.
* $p < .05$, two-tailed.
** $p < .01$, two-tailed.

be different for each individual, another instance of aggregate correlations showing higher values than individual correlations.

Isolation of Office-Level Effects: The individual level of analysis has an additional advantage; it can tell us something about the *way* in which administrative characteristics have their influence on individual performance and satisfaction. Early in this paper we raised the question: Is it merely the *perception* of these characteristics which affects the criterion variables (or perhaps vice versa)? In order to deal with this issue, the relationships in Table 3 are presented in two forms: zero-order correlations and partial correlations. The partial correlations rule out the effects of each salesman's own perception of the office administrative characteristics, thereby removing that portion of the relationships which might be attributed to individual-level effects. The relationships that remain are office-level effects. (For a further discussion of the background and rationale for this form of analysis, see Tannenbaum & Bachman, 1964.) We interpret these

Table 3 *Administrative Characteristics Correlated with Individual Criterion Scores (N = 656 Salesmen)*

Office Mean Ratings	Individual Criterion Scores: Standardized Performance	Individual Criterion Scores: Satisfaction with Office Manager
Control over office		
Exercised by office manager	.06	.31**
	.07	**.19****
Exercised by salesmen	.11**	.28**
	.13**	**.14****
Total control	.11**	.38**
	.12**	**.21****
Interpersonal control		
Office manager's influence over salesmen	.06	.41**
	.10*	**.25****
Salesmen's influence over office manager	.10*	.33**
	.12**	**.22****
Total interpersonal control	.11**	.43**
	.14**	**.25****
Bases of office manager's power		
Referent	.11**	.36**
	.09*	**.22****
Expert	.10*	.33**
	.13**	**.17****
Reward	−.14**	−.25**
	−.12**	**−.16****
Coercive	−.09*	−.33**
	−.09*	**−.19****
Legitimate	−.07	−.31**
	−.08	**−.24****

Note: The upper entry in each cell presents the zero-order product-moment correlation, r_{Ab}; the lower boldface entry presents the partial correlation, $r_{Ab.a}$; where A = office mean ratings of administrative characteristics, b = individual criterion scores, a = individual ratings of administrative characteristics.

* $p < .05$, two-tailed.

** $p < .01$, two-tailed.

Table 4 Intraoffice Correlations between Individual Ratings of Administrative Characteristics and Individual Criterion Scores

	Individual Criterion Scores	
Individual Ratings	Standardized Performance	Satisfaction with Office Manager
Control over office		
Exercised by office manager	−.03	.21**
Exercised by salesmen	−.06	.36**
Total control	−.07	.42**
Interpersonal control		
Office manager's influence over salesmen	−.05	.33**
Salesmen's influence over office manager	−.06	.38**
Total interpersonal control	−.07	.46**
Bases of office manager's power		
Referent	.02	.41**
Expert	−.08	.40**
Reward	−.01	−.30**
Coercive	.02	−.40**
Legitimate	.02	−.21**

Note: Cell entries present the weighted means of 36 intraoffice product-moment correlations. The weighted means were obtained by using the z transformation ($z = \tan h^{-1} r$) in the following formula (Johnson, 1949, pp. 52–53):

$$\bar{z} = \frac{(n_1 - 3)z_1 + (n_2 - 3)z_2 + \ldots}{(n_1 - 3) + (n_2 - 3) + \ldots}$$

$\bar{z}$ values were then transformed to the $\bar{r}$ values which appear in the table.

** $p < .01$, two-tailed.

office-level relationships as being specific structural effects of control and bases of power, since these are the office-level variables we have attempted to measure. It must be noted, however, that this particular interpretation does not follow necessarily from the logic of our analysis. It is possible, for example, that our measures have actually tapped some cultural stereotype common to the office as a whole, rather than the actual behaviors assumed to be associated with control and bases of power.

Effects of Office Administrative Characteristics

Control: Measures of control over the office and interpersonal control correlated positively with both criterion measures (Tables 2 and

3). These positive relationships appeared no matter who exercised the control—the office manager, the salesmen, or both. Moreover, there is a strong positive relationship between the amount of interpersonal control exercised by the office manager and that exercised by the salesmen ($N = 36$ offices, $r = .50$, $p < .01$, two-tailed). These findings seem inconsistent with the position that the total amount of control in any situation remains a fixed quantity; on the contrary, they support the view that the total amount of control or influence is variable.

Bases of Power: For the average salesman, the most important basis of the office manager's control was legitimate power (Table 1); nevertheless, in offices relatively high on this dimension, respondents indicated significantly less satisfaction with their office manager, and there was a tendency for performance to be lower (Tables 2 and 3).

The second and third most important dimensions were expert and referent power. Offices in which the office manager was rated relatively high on these bases of power were also high on performance and satisfaction with the office manager.

Reward and coercive power were rated the least important reasons for complying with the office manager's wishes, and both were negatively related to the criterion variables.

It is important to note that the five bases of power related to the overall amount of control in much the same way as they related to performance and satisfaction: Correlations with total control were .66 and .58 for expert and referent power; −.48, −.49, and −.58 for legitimate, reward, and coercive power, respectively. Nearly identical correlations were obtained with the measure of total interpersonal control. (All were product-moment correlations, $p \leq .01$, two-tailed.)

Some caution must be exercised in interpreting correlations with the bases of power. The ranking method used in obtaining the data makes it impossible for all five bases of power to be correlated in the same direction with any single criterion variable. Thus, it may be that positive correlations with expert and referent power are responsible for negative correlations with the other bases of power, or vice versa.

Office-Level versus Individual-Level Effects

A comparison of the zero-order and partial correlations in Table 3 indicates the presence of office-level relationships between the administrative characteristics and both criterion variables. When the effects of the individual's perception of administrative characteristics are removed, the small but significant correlations with performance are not reduced. On the other hand, the same partial correlation procedure does lead to a substantial reduction in the correlations between administrative characteristics and satisfaction with the office manager. This suggests that a portion of the zero-order relationship with satisfaction is attributable to individual-level effects.

Isolation of Individual Effects: In order to isolate individual-level effects, it is necessary to reverse the strategy employed earlier; we now rule out any possibility of an office-level effect, thus leaving only those relationships which we have defined as individual effects. This is accomplished by treating each office separately, and correlating individual perceptions of administrative characteristics with individual criterion scores. Since we are considering objective administrative characteristics to be identical for all persons within a given office, these intraoffice correlations provide a measure of pure individual-level effects.

Table 4 presents the means of the intraoffice correlations, weighted according to the number of respondents in each office. The pattern of relationships is clear and highly consistent. Individual performance is unrelated to individual perceptions of office administrative characteristics. On the other hand, an individual salesman's satisfaction with his office manager is significantly related to his personal appraisal of administrative characteristics in his office, and the pattern of individual-level relationships parallels very closely the pattern of office-level effects isolated earlier.[7]

Relationship between Performance and Satisfaction: On the whole, our criterion variables—performance and satisfaction with the office manager—have shown fairly similar patterns of correlation with administrative characteristics. This finding might indicate that high performance causes a salesman to be satisfied with his office manager; or perhaps such satisfaction is a cause of high performance. If either of these explanations were correct, we should find that an *individual's* performance is correlated with his personal satisfaction with the manager. But in fact, when the possibility of office-level effects is removed, no such relationship is evident; the mean intraoffice correlation between performance and satisfaction is −.02 (using the procedures described in Table 4). However, the correlation between office

[7] The mean intraoffice variance is, of course, smaller than the variance for all individuals grouped together. But the reduction is too small to have much effect on Table 4. (For most variables, including performance and satisfaction, the mean intraoffice *SD* is only about 10 per cent smaller than the *SD* among individuals shown in Table 1.)

mean performance and office mean satisfaction is .35, $p < .05$ (using the procedures described in Table 2). In other words, our criterion measures covary at the office mean level of analysis, but are entirely independent at the intraoffice level, and these findings are fully consistent with the view that performance and satisfaction are subject to similar but separate *structural* relationships with the administrative characteristics under study.

DISCUSSION

The present findings again illustrate the importance of total control as a factor in organizational effectiveness: the overall amount of influence in the organization correlated substantially with performance and satisfaction. Moreover, the generality of this relationship has been extended to include highly skilled persons performing a variety of complex tasks. It may be that the branch offices under study are especially conducive to the patterns of influence and power reported above. An office manager's success is largely dependent upon the performance of the salesmen in his office; thus he has a strong incentive toward management practices which support and encourage high productivity.

It is of particular interest to note that the degree of control exercised by an office manager over his subordinates was positively related to the control they exercise over him. These findings clearly imply that control at one level is not exercised at the expense of another level.[8] On the contrary, the data indicate that any increase in control—by office manager, subordinates, or both—should be associated with higher satisfaction and performance.

The comparison of bases of power further illuminates the processes which underlie a pattern of high total control. Total control, performance, and satisfaction with the office manager were all relatively high for the office manager whose leadership was perceived as resting largely upon his skill and expertise (expert power) and upon his personal attractiveness (referent power). Conversely, the less effective office manager was one who appeared to rely more heavily upon the use of rewards and sanctions (reward power and coercive power) and upon the formal authority of his position (legitimate power)—as a

[8] Although the data have not been reported in the present paper, it should be noted that an index of *relative* control (derived by subtracting the office manager's control from that exercised by his subordinates) showed no clear relationship with criteria of satisfaction or performance.

formal description of his role might indicate. At the level of inter-office comparison, this overall relationship was substantial and highly consistent (see Table 2).

The negative relationship between the use of reward power and our measures of effectiveness requires further explanation. We stated earlier that reward power might be associated with supportive or ego-enhancing practices of management (Likert, 1961). However, it may well be that many employees are ambivalent about the use of reward power by their superiors. It may be well to reward someone for a job well done, but rewards may also be perceived as bribes, payoffs, favoritism, and the like. The phrase used in the present study, "He can give special help and benefits to those who cooperate with him," may have implied the latter type of reward.

The relationships between control, bases of power, satisfaction, and performance are still far from clear; nevertheless, the present findings suggest two tentative conclusions. First, it appears that the most effective offices can be characterized by the following high total control syndrome: high levels of interpersonal control, and control over the office, by both office manager and salesmen; relatively greater reliance by the office manager on expert and referent power (as opposed to legitimate, reward, and coercive power); and high mean levels of performance and satisfaction with the office manager. Second, since an individual salesman's satisfaction with his office manager is not correlated with his performance (at the intraoffice level of analysis), it seems clear in the present setting that neither variable is the direct cause of the other. A more likely explanation is that they are both caused in part by the high total control syndrome.

The present comparison of office-level versus individual-level effects yielded results largely consistent with those of Tannenbaum and Smith (1964). Satisfaction with the office manager was associated to a considerable degree with each salesman's personal perception of the office administrative pattern, but after this relationship was removed, an individual's satisfaction was also substantially related to a more objective measure of administration—the mean of all perceptions by those in his office. Performance, on the other hand, was not at all related to individual perceptions of control and bases of power, but it did show small correlations with the more objective office mean perceptions. We interpret these findings as indicating that satisfaction was subject to both structural and individual-level effects, whereas performance was subject only to structural effects.

It is of interest that administrative characteristics proved to be weak predictors of individual performance (Table 3), yet fairly good predictors of performance on the average (Table 2). This relationship, which may be a very common phenomenon in organizations, would have gone entirely unnoticed had we limited our analysis to the traditional correlations among office means (as in Table 2). This observation highlights the differences between grouped data and individual data, and it points to the importance of both forms of analysis in studying the impact of organizations upon their members.[9]

One final conclusion is in order. This paper has stressed very strongly the distinction between office-level and individual-level effects. We have noted the difficulties that attend the use of perceptual measures, particularly when the analysis is limited to the usual practice of correlating mean data. Our strategy of partialing out the individual's own perceptions eliminates the possibility of a halo effect, since a halo must exist in individuals rather than in groups. We have no guarantee that our measures tapped exactly the structural dimensions we intended, but the evidence is clear that they tapped something that exists in the organization—something that influences an individual's performance and satisfaction, quite apart from his perception of it.

SUMMARY

Measures of control, bases of power, satisfaction, and performance were obtained from 656 salesmen in 36 branch offices of a national firm selling intangibles. The most effective offices were characterized by the following high total control syndrome: high levels of interpersonal control, and control over the office, by both office manager and salesmen; relatively greater reliance by the office manager on expert and referent power, as opposed to legitimate, reward, and coercive power; high satisfaction with the office manager; and above average performance by salesmen. The analysis isolated group structural effects between office administrative characteristics and the performance and satisfaction criteria by partialing out individual

[9] It is worth mentioning that for "practical" purposes the small relationship with individual performance shown in Table 3 would be fully as useful as the larger correlation with mean performance in Table 2; in either case a change in office characteristics would lead to essentially the same overall *predicted effect* (using ordinary regression equations).

relationships. At the individual level, relationships were found between referent and expert power and satisfaction but not with performance.

REFERENCES

Blau, P. M. Formal organization: Dimensions of analysis. *Am. J. Sociol.*, 1957, **63,** 58–69.

Blau, P. M. Structural effects. *Am. Sociol. Rev.*, 1960, **25,** 178–193.

Bowers, D. G. Organizational control in an insurance company. *Sociometry*, 1964, **27,** 230–244.

Davis, J. A., Spaeth, J. L., & Huson, C. A technique for analyzing the effects of group composition. *Am. Sociol. Rev.*, 1961, **26,** 215–225.

French, J. R. P., Jr., & Raven, B. The bases of social power. In D. Cartwright & A. Zander (Eds.), *Group dynamics: Research and theory*, 2nd ed. Evanston, Ill.: Row, Peterson, 1960. Pp. 607–623.

Johnson, P. O. *Statistical methods in research*. Englewood Cliffs, N.J.: Prentice-Hall, 1949.

Likert, R. *New patterns of management*. New York: McGraw-Hill, 1961.

March, J., & Simon, H. *Organizations*. New York: Wiley, 1958.

Smith, C. G., & Tannenbaum, A. S. Organizational control structure: A comparative analysis. *Hum. Relat.*, 1963, **16,** 299–316.

Tannenbaum, A. S. Control and effectiveness in a voluntary organization. *Am. J. Sociol.*, 1961, **67,** 33–46.

Tannenbaum, A. S. Control in organizations: Individual adjustment and organizational performance. *Admin. Sci. Quart.*, 1962, **7,** 236–257.

Tannenbaum, A. S., & Bachman, J. G. Structural versus individual effects. *Am. J. Sociol.*, 1964, **69,** 585–595.

Tannenbaum, A. S., & Smith, C. G. The effects of member influence in an organization. *J. Abnorm. Soc. Psychol.*, 1964, **69,** 401–410.

10.5 THE EXPERIMENTAL CHANGE OF A MAJOR ORGANIZATIONAL VARIABLE

Nancy C. Morse
Everett Reimer

This experiment is one in a series of studies of social behavior in large-scale organizations undertaken by the Human Relations Program of the Survey Research Center. Its primarily aim is to investigate the relationship between the allocation of decision-making processes in a large hierarchical organization and (*a*) the individual satisfactions of the members of the organization, (*b*) the productivity of the organization.

The results of several previous studies suggested that the individual's role in decision-making might affect his satisfaction and productivity. The effectiveness of decision-making in small groups shown by Lewin, Lippitt, and others (4, 5) and the successful application of small-group decision-making to method changes in an industrial setting by Coch and French (1) both indicated the possibilities for enlarging the role of the rank and file in the ongoing decision-making of an organization. The practical experience of Sears, Roebuck and Co. with a "flat," administratively decentralized structure, described by Worthy (8), pointed in the same direction, as did the survey findings by Katz, Maccoby, and Morse (2) that supervisors delegating greater authority had more productive work groups. The logical next step seemed to be the controlled testing of hypotheses concerning the relationship between role in organizational decision-making and two aspects of organizational effectiveness: satisfaction and productivity. Two broad hypotheses were formulated:

Hypothesis I: An increased role in the decision-making processes for rank-and-file groups increases their satisfaction (while a decreased role in decision-making reduces satisfaction).

Source: This is a short description of an experiment done while the authors were on the staff of the Human Relations Program of the Survey Research Center, University of Michigan. Financial support for field work and analysis of data came from the Rockefeller Foundation, the Office of Naval Research, and the company in which the research was done. Reprinted with slight abridgment from the *Journal of Abnormal and Social Psychology*, 1956, 52, 120–129, with permission of Dr. Nancy M. Samelson (née Morse) and the American Psychological Association, Inc., copyright holder.

Hypothesis II: An increased role in decision-making for rank-and-file groups increases their productivity (while a decreased role in decision-making decreases productivity).

Both these hypotheses deal with the effects on the rank and file of different hierarchical allocations of the decision-making processes of the organization. The rationale for the satisfaction hypothesis (I) predicts different and more need-satisfying decisions when the rank and file has decision-making power than when the upper echelons of the hierarchy have that power. Furthermore, the process of decision-making itself is expected to be satisfying to the majority of people brought up in American traditions. Underlying the productivity hypothesis (II) was the consideration that local unit policy-making would increase motivation to produce and thus productivity. Motivation should rise when productivity becomes a path for greater need satisfaction. The productivity hypothesis predicts a higher degree of need satisfaction (as does Hypothesis I) *and* an increase in the degree of dependence of satisfactions upon productivity under conditions of greater rank-and-file decision-making. It is expected that when rank-and-file members work out and put into effect their own rules and regulations, their maintenance in the organization (and thus their satisfactions) will depend much more directly upon their performance.

PROCEDURE

The experiment was conducted in one department of a nonunionized industrial organization which had four parallel divisions engaged in relatively routine clerical work. The design involved increasing rank-and-file decision-making in two of the divisions and increasing upper-level decision-making in the other two divisions. The time span was one and one-half years: a before measurement, one-half year of training of supervisors to create the experimental conditions, one year under the experimental conditions, and then remeasurement. The two pairs of two divisions each were comparable on relevant variables such as initial allocation of the decision-making processes, satisfaction and productivity, as well as on such background factors as type of work, type of personnel, and type of supervisory structure.

The rank-and-file employees were women, mostly young and unmarried, with high school education. The usual clerk's plans were for marriage and a family rather than a career. The population used in the analysis except where noted is a subgroup of the clerks, the "matched" population. These clerks were present throughout the one and one-half year period, and their before and after questionnaires were individually matched. While they comprise somewhat less than half of the clerks present in these divisions at any one time, they are comparable to the total group, except on such expected variables as length of time in the division, in the work section, and on the job.

One aspect of the work situation should be mentioned, as it bears on the adequacy of the setting for a test of the productivity hypothesis. The amount of work done by the divisions was completely dependent upon the flow of work to them, i.e., the total number of units to be done was not within the control of the divisions. With volume fixed, productivity depends upon the number of clerks needed to do the work, and increased productivity can be achieved only by out-placement of clerks or by foregoing replacement of clerks who leave for other reasons.

The Development of the Experimental Conditions

Creating the experimental programs included three steps: (*a*) planning by research staff and company officials; (*b*) introducing the programs to the division supervisory personnel and training of the supervisors for their new roles; and (*c*) introduction to the clerks and operation under the experimental conditions.

The experiment was carried out within the larger framework of company operations. The introduction, training, and operations were in the hands of company personnel. The experimental changes were not made through personnel shifts; the changes were in what people did in their jobs with respect to the decision-making processes of the organization.

Two main change processes were used in both the Autonomy program, designed to increase rank-and-file decision-making, and in the Hierarchically controlled program, designed to increase the upper management role in the decision-making processes. First, there were formal structural changes to create a new organizational environment for the divisions in each program. In both programs the hierarchical legitimization of new roles preceded the taking of the new roles.[1] In the Autonomy program authority was delegated by

[1] Weber and others have used the word "legitimization" to refer to the acceptance by subordinates of the authority of superiors. We are using the word in quite a different sense. By hierarchical legitimization we mean the formal delegation of authority by superiors to subordinates. This delegation *legitimizes* the subordinates' utilization of this authority.

upper management to lower levels in the hierarchy with the understanding that they would redelegate it to the clerical work groups. In the Hierarchically controlled program, authority was given to the higher line officials to increase their role in the running of the divisions and to the staff officials to increase their power to institute changes within the two divisions in that program. Second, there were training programs for the supervisors of the divisions to ensure that the formal changes would result in actual changes in relations between people. (For a longer description of the change programs see Reimer [6].)

Measurement

The results of the changes were gauged through before and after measurements and through continuing measurements during the experimental period. The major emphasis was on the attitudes and perceptions of the clerks as reflected in extensive questionnaires. In addition, the training programs and the operations phase of the experiment were observed. Before and after interviews were conducted with the supervisory personnel of the division. Data from company records such as productivity rates, turnover figures, etc., were also included.

The data reported here will be confined to material most pertinent to the testing of the two hypotheses. For other related aspects of the experiment, see Tannenbaum's study of the relationship of personality characteristics and adjustment to the two programs (7), Kaye's study of organizational goal achievement under the Autonomy program (3), as well as forthcoming publications.

RESULTS[2]

Success of Experimental Manipulation

The first question was to discover whether or not the change programs were successful in creating the conditions under which the hypotheses could be tested. Two types of data are pertinent. The first is descriptive data concerning the actual operations of the two

[2] For the statistical tests used in this section, we have assumed that the individuals were randomly chosen, while the selection of individuals by divisions undoubtedly results in some clustering effect. The levels of significance should, therefore, be considered as general guides rather than in any absolute sense.

programs. The second is perceptual data from the clerical employees themselves indicating the degree to which they saw changes in their role in organizational decisions.

The operations of the divisions in fact changed in the direction expected. In the Autonomy program the clerical work groups came to make group decisions about many of the things which affected them and which were important to them. The range of the decisions was very great, including work methods and processes, and personnel matters, such as recess periods, the handling of tardiness, etc. Probably the most important area in which the clerks were not able to make decisions was the area of salary. Some of the work groups were more active in the decision-making process than others, but all made a very great variety of decisions in areas important to them. In the Hierarchically controlled program the changes decreased the degree to which the employees could control and regulate their own activities. One of the main ways in which this greater limitation was manifested was through the individual work standards that staff officials developed for the various jobs. Also the greater role of upper line and staff officials in the operation of the divisions meant that the indirect influence which the clerks could have on decisions when they were made by division managers and section supervisors was reduced.

The clerks were operating under different conditions in the two programs as the result of the experimental changes, but did they perceive these changes? The method of measuring the perception of changes in decision-making was by asking clerks about their part and about the part of people above their rank in decisions with respect to a wide variety of areas of company operations, or company systems. The following questions were asked about each major area of company operations or system: "To what degree do company officers or any employees of a higher rank than yours decide how the——— System is set up and decide the policies, rules, procedures or methods of the———Systems?" (followed by a line with the landmark statements: not at all, to a slight degree, to some degree, to a fairly high degree and to a very high degree) and, "To what degree do you and the girls in your section decide how the———System is set up and decide the policies, rules, procedures or methods of the——— System?" (followed by a line with the same landmark statements as the first question).

The extreme degree of perceived hierarchical control of the decision-making processes would be shown by the clerks answering that employees of a higher rank than theirs made the decisions, "to a very high degree" and the clerks made them "not at all." Table 1[3] shows the number of systems where there are half or more of the clerks endorsing these two statements for the before situation and for the two experimental situations. (The Autonomy program is designated in Table 1 and thereafter as Program I and the Hierarchically controlled program as Program II.) Questions were asked for 27 company systems in the "before" measurement and 24 systems in the "after" measurement.

Table 1 shows that the clerks perceived the decision-making processes for most of the company operations measured as located at hierarchical levels above their own, prior to the introduction of the experimental changes. The experimental changes in the Autonomy program divisions resulted in their seeing decision-making activities as much less exclusively confined to levels above theirs. The changes in the Hierarchically controlled program were less striking but they resulted in the clerks judging that all of the systems about which they were asked in the "after" situation had their policies molded to a very high degree by people above their level.

The relative role of the hierarchy compared to the rank and file as perceived by the clerks was measured by assigning scores from 1 to 9 for the landmark positions on the scales for the two questions and then dividing the score for upper-level decision-making by the score for rank-and-file decision-making. The theoretical range for the resulting index is from 9.0 to 0, with numbers less than 1 indicating greater local control than upper-level control. Table 2 includes the average index scores for the systems from the before and after measurements calculated by division.

Table 2 indicates the change in the divisions in the Autonomy program toward greater perceived rank-and-file role in decision-making, but also shows that the upper levels are seen as still having the major role in the after situation. (The downward shift in perceived decision-making control in the Autonomy program is significant above the 1 per cent level by the Student's t test for paired data. A statistically significant, but slight, change toward greater upper-level control took place in the Hierarchically controlled program.)

Both Tables 1 and 2 show that the clerks in the Autonomy program perceive as predicted a significant shift away from upper-level control when their before-after answers are compared, and that the

[3] Table 1 has been omitted for purposes of brevity.

Table 2 *Effect of Change Programs on Perception of Decision-Making Allocation*

Experimental Groups	Index of Perceived Decision-Making Allocation				
	Mean Before	Mean After	Diff.	*SE* Diff.	*N*
Program I					
Div. A	5.69	4.39	−1.30**	.24	61
Div. B	6.49	4.08	−2.41**	.26	57
Average	6.08	4.24	−1.84**	.18	118
Program II					
Div. C	6.15	6.87	+ .72**	.22	44
Div. D	6.78	7.13	+ .35	.26	44
Average	6.41	7.00	+ .59**	.17	88

Note: Higher values correspond to perception of predominance of upper levels of organization in decision-making.
** Significant at the 1 per cent level.

clerks in the Hierarchically controlled program see some increase in upper-level control over policy-making, even though it was already perceived as highly controlled from above before the experiment.

These measures of successful experimental manipulation suggest that the conditions in the two programs are sufficiently different to permit tests of the experimental hypotheses.

Hypothesis I

This hypothesis states that an increase in the decision-making role of individuals results in increased satisfactions, while a decrease in opportunity for decision-making is followed by decreased satisfaction. The general hypothesis was tested for a variety of specific areas of satisfaction. The attitudinal areas to be reported include: (*a*) self-actualization and growth, (*b*) satisfaction with supervisors, (*c*) liking for working for the company, (*d*) job satisfaction, (*e*) liking for program. Student's one-tailed t test for paired data was used for tests of significance. Results reaching the 5 per cent level or above are considered significant.

Self-actualization: One of the hypotheses of the study was that greater opportunity for regulating and controlling their own activities within the company structure would increase the degree to which individuals could express their various and diverse needs and could move in the direction of fully exploiting their potentialities. An increase in upper-management control on the other hand was predicted to decrease the opportunities for employee self-actualization and growth.

Table 3 *Effect of Change Programs on Feelings of Self-actualization on Job*

	Index of Perceived Self-actualization				
Experimental Groups	Mean Before	Mean After	Diff.	*SE* Diff.	*N*
Program I					
Div. A	2.67	2.74	+.07	.09	52
Div. B	2.18	2.39	+.21*	.11	47
Average	2.43	2.57	+.14*	.07	99
Program II					
Div. C	2.43	2.24	−.19	.14	43
Div. D	2.30	2.23	−.07	.10	38
Average	2.37	2.24	−.13*	.07	81

Note: Scale runs from 1, low degree of self-actualization to 5, a high degree.
* Significant at the 5 per cent level, one-tailed t test for paired data.

Five questions were used to measure this area: (1) Is your job a real challenge to what you think you can do? (2) How much chance does your job give you to learn things you're interested in? (3) Are the things you're learning in your job helping to train you for a better job in the company? (4) How much chance do you have to try out your ideas on the job? (5) How much does your job give you a chance to do the things you're best at? These five items, which were answered by checking one position on a five-point scale, were intercorrelated and then combined to form an index.[4] Table 3 shows the means for the four divisions and two groups on the self-actualization and growth index.

While both groups of clerks indicated that their jobs throughout the course of the experiment did not give them a very high degree of self-actualization, the experimental programs produced significant changes. In the Autonomy program, self-actualization increased significantly from before to after, and a corresponding decrease was

[4] The items were intercorrelated by the tetrachoric method. When these correlations were converted to z scores the average intercorrelation was .62, corrected for length of test, a reliability index of .89 was obtained.

shown in the Hierarchically controlled program. At the end of the experimental period, the Autonomy program is significantly higher on this variable than the Hierarchically controlled program.

Satisfaction with Supervision: A variety of indices were developed in order to test the hypothesis that the Autonomy program would improve satisfactions with supervisors and that the Hierarchically controlled program would reduce such satisfactions. Two general types of attitudes were separately measured: (*a*) satisfaction with relations with supervisors and (*b*) satisfaction with supervisors as a representative. These two types of attitudes were studied before and after the experimental period with respect to three levels of supervision: the first-line supervisor, the assistant manager of the division, and the manager of the division. The following three questions were asked for each of these levels in order to tap the clerks' degree of satisfaction with relations with supervisors:

1. How good is your supervisor (assistant manager, manager) at handling people?
2. Can you count on having good relations with your supervisor (assistant manager, manager) under all circumstances?
3. In general, how well do you like your supervisor (assistant manager, manager) as a person to work with?

These three questions were combined to form indices of satisfaction with relations with supervisors, assistant manager, and manager. (The items were intercorrelated for the satisfaction with relations with supervisor index. Through converting to z scores, the average intercorrelation of items is found to be .78. Correcting for length of test, i.e., using three items to form the index rather than one, for reliability index is .91 with an N of 360.)

Table 4[5] shows that in general there was a shift toward greater satisfaction with supervisors in the Autonomy program and toward less satisfaction with supervisors in the Hierarchically controlled program. The divisions, however, show certain characteristic differences in satisfaction at the outset and shift in the expected direction to different degrees.

Both divisions in the Hierarchically controlled program show a decrease in satisfaction with the first-line supervisor, although the changes are not statistically significant. The after differences between

[5] Table 4 has been omitted for purposes of brevity. Interested readers are referred to the original article.

the Autonomy and the Hierarchically controlled programs are, however, significant.

Satisfaction with relations with both the assistant manager and the manager increased significantly in the Autonomy program and decreased significantly in the Hierarchically controlled program. Each of the divisions within the groups likewise shifted in the hypothesized directions for the two managerial indices. In the Autonomy program the assistant manager index shifted in the right direction for both divisions, but the changes were not statistically significant when each division was tested separately.

Thus while the employees were generally quite satisfied with their relations with their different supervisors, the experimental programs did have the expected effects of increasing the satisfactions of those in the Autonomy program and decreasing the satisfaction of those in the Hierarchically controlled program. The effects of the programs appear to be most evident in attitudes toward the managerial level and least marked in attitudes toward the first-line supervisors, probably because the managers occupy the key or pivotal positions in the structure (see Kaye, [3]).

The second type of attitude toward supervisors measured was satisfaction with the supervisors as representatives of the employees. Three questions were asked employees as a measure of this type of satisfaction:

1. How much does your supervisor (assistant manager, manager) go out of her (his) way to help get things for the girls in the section?
2. How effective is she (he) in helping you and the other girls get what you want in your jobs?
3. How much does your supervisor (assistant manager, manager) try to help people in your section get ahead in the company?

These three items were intercorrelated for the attitudes toward the supervisor as a representative index and the average intercorrelation was .83 with a corrected reliability of .94 (*N* of 340).

The findings for the three levels of supervision on the satisfaction with supervisors as representatives index are shown in Table 5.[6]

The employees' attitudes toward their supervisors as effective representatives of their interests show significant changes in the predicted directions in the two programs. Those in the Autonomy program

[6] Table 5 has been omitted for reasons of brevity, and interested readers are referred to the original article.

became more satisfied than they had been previously, while those in the Hierarchically controlled program became less satisfied. On satisfaction with the first-line supervisor as a representative both Division B in the Autonomy program and Division D in the Hierarchically controlled program shifted significantly in the hypothesized directions, although the other two divisions did not shift significantly. The two program groups were not matched on degree of satisfaction with manager and assistant manager as a representative at the beginning of the experiment, as there was significantly more satisfaction in the Autonomy program divisions than there was in Program II. However the changes for both groups of divisions were statistically significant and in the predicted direction. For attitude toward manager all of the division differences are in the predicted direction and all except Division D are statistically significant.

Satisfaction with the Company: One general question was used to measure company satisfaction: "Taking things as a whole, how do you like working for——— (the name of the company)?"

Table 6[7] indicates an increase in favorableness toward the company under the Autonomy program and a decrease under the Hierarchically controlled program.

All of the changes are significant in the predicted direction, except for the before-after difference in Division B which is only at the 10 per cent level of significance.

Job Satisfaction: Three questions were used as an index of job satisfaction:

1. Does your job ever get monotonous?
2. How important do you feel your job is compared with other jobs at (the company)?
3. In general, how well do you like the sort of work you're doing in your job?

These three questions showed an average intercorrelation of .47 with a corrected reliability of .73 (N of 369). The results on this index are reported in Table 7.[8]

While the trend for the changes in job satisfaction are in the direction predicted, the differences are not sufficiently great to be statistically significant except for Division C. The lack of change in job satisfaction in the Autonomy program may be due to the fact

[7] Table 6 has been omitted for reasons of brevity.

[8] Table 7 has been omitted for purposes of brevity.

that the job content remained about the same. It is also possible that the increases in complexity and variety of their total work were offset by a rise in their level of aspiration, so that they expected more interesting and varied work.

Satisfaction with the Program: In the after measurement additional questions were asked concerning attitudes toward the programs. Most of these questions were open-ended and required the employee to write her response in her own words. Although less than half of the clerks taking the after measurement filled them out, the results on questions relevant to the satisfaction hypothesis deserve brief mention. The clerks in the Autonomy program typically: wanted their program to last indefinitely, did not like the other program, felt that the clerks were one of the groups gaining the most from the program and described both positive and negative changes in interpersonal relations among the girls. The clerks in the Hierarchically controlled program, on the other hand, most frequently: wanted their program to end immediately, liked the other program and felt that the company gained the most from their program. Not one single person in the Hierarchically controlled program mentioned an improvement in interpersonal relations as a result of this program. All of the noted changes were for the worse, with increases in friction and tension being most frequently mentioned.

Taking all of these results on the attitudinal questions together, the first hypothesis would appear to be verified. Increasing local decision-making increased satisfaction, while decreasing the role of rank-and-file members of the organization in the decision-making decreased it.

Hypothesis II

This hypothesis predicts a direct relationship between degree of rank-and-file decision-making and productivity. Thus, in order for the hypothesis to be verified, productivity should increase significantly in the Autonomy program, and should decrease significantly in the Hierarchically controlled program.

We have previously described the problems of assuming a direct relationship between motivation to produce and productivity in a situation in which volume is not controllable by employees and level of productivity depends upon the number of people doing a fixed amount of work. The Autonomy program was handicapped by both the fact that increasing productivity required reducing the size of their own work group and the fact that the upper management staff and line costs were not included in the measure of costs per volume of work.

The measure of productivity, then, is a measure of clerical costs. The results for this measure are shown in Table 8.[9]

The clerical costs have gone down in each division and thus productivity has increased. All these increases in productivity are statistically significant (by *t* tests). In addition, the productivity increase in the Hierarchically controlled program is significantly greater than that in the Autonomy program. These increases in productivity do not seem to be accounted for by a general rise in productivity throughout the company, since the divisions outside the experimental groups which were most comparable to them showed no significant gain in productivity during this period. The rise in productivity appears to be the result of the experimental treatments. The two divisions initially low in productivity showed the greatest differential change. Division D increased its productivity the most of the four while Division A increased the least.

A second measure of the organizational costs of the two programs is the degree of turnover which could be attributed to on-the-job factors. A method of control and regulation which reduces clerical costs, but which produces the hidden costs of training new employees is of greater cost to the organization than would at first appear evident. In this company turnover, however, is not high and much of the turnover that does occur is due to personal reasons (marriage, pregnancy, etc.) rather than on-the-job reasons. Out of the 54 employees who left the company from the four divisions during the time of the experiment, only nine resigned for other jobs or because of dissatisfaction. Out of these nine, however, all but one were in the Hierarchically controlled program. In the exit interviews conducted by the company personnel department 23 of the girls leaving made unfavorable comments about pressure, work standards, etc. Nineteen of these girls were from the Hierarchically controlled program.

These results indicate that the productivity hypothesis is clearly not verified in terms of direct clerical costs, since the Hierarchically controlled program decreased these costs more than the Autonomy program, contrary to the prediction. The indirect costs for the Hierarchically controlled program are probably somewhat greater. But even when this is considered the evidence does not support the hypothesis.

[9] Table 8 has been omitted for reasons of brevity.

DISCUSSION

The results on productivity might suggest a "Hawthorne effect" if it were not for the satisfaction findings. The increase in satisfaction under the Autonomy program and the decrease under the Hierarchically controlled program make an explanation of productivity changes in terms of a common attention effect unlikely.[10]

The Hierarchically controlled program reduced staff costs by ordering reductions in the number of employees assigned to the tasks. Increases in productivity for Divisions C and D were brought about as simply as that. This temporary increase in one measure of productivity is not surprising and is traditional history in industry. In the Autonomy program, decrease in costs was more complex but can be simply stated as follows. The Autonomy program increased the motivation of the employees to produce and thus they did not feel the need for replacing the staff members who left the section. In addition, they were willing to make an effort to try to outplace some of their members in other jobs which they might like. The reductions in staff in the two programs came about in different ways. Those occurring by order in the Hierarchically controlled program surpassed in number those occurring by group decision in the Autonomy program, but it is not clear how long the superiority of the Hierarchically controlled program would have lasted.

The results of the experiment need to be placed in a larger theoretical framework in order to contribute to the understanding of the functioning of large-scale organizations. We shall first consider briefly the role and function of the social control processes, as it is these processes which were changed by the experimental manipulations.

The high degree of rationality which is characteristic of the institutional behavior of man is achieved through a complex system for controlling and regulating human behavior. Hierarchy is a requirement because human beings must be fitted to a rational model. There are essentially two functions which the usual hierarchy serves: a *binding-in* function and a *binding-between* function. By *binding-in* we mean insuring that there will be individuals present to fill the necessary

[10] It is unlikely that even in the Hawthorne experiment the results were due to attention. There were a number of changes in addition to an increase in attention, including relaxation of rules, better supervisors, no change in piece rates despite raises in productivity—to name a few.

roles. The role behavior required by the organization must be a path to individual goals. Money is the most important means used for binding-in, but all ways to motivate a person to enter and remain in the system are means of binding-in. By *binding-between* we mean the insurance of the rationality of action, that is, the setting up and continuation of institutional processes which will accomplish the ends for which the organization is designed. The role behavior of individuals must be integrated into a pattern to produce interrelated action directed toward the goals of the organization. The development of assignments, work charts, job specifications, etc., are but a few examples of the many means used by organizations for binding-between.

Any means for controlling and regulating human behavior in a large organizational setting, then, needs to serve these two functions. The experiment shows that the allocation of decision-making processes to the upper hierarchy results in a greater emphasis on the binding-between function, while the function of binding-in is handled by an external reward system. Such a direct stress on the binding-between function was shown in the Hierarchically controlled program and resulted in the increase in productivity (an indication of binding-between) and a decrease in employee satisfaction (an indication of degree of binding-in) and some increase in turnover (another indication of binding-in).

The greater allocation of the decision-making processes to the rank-and-file employees in the Autonomy program resulted in an emphasis on both the binding-between and the binding-in functions. Thus there was both an increase in productivity and an increase in satisfaction. While the program is addressed primarily to the binding-in function, in such a context the binding-between function is also served.

The problems of the Hierarchically controlled system are maintaining the employee effectively "bound-in" to the organization and continuing favorable relations between the supervisory personnel who have involvement in the organization and the rank and file who must do the work. Indications of these problems are dissatisfaction, distortions in communications up the hierarchy, the tendency to "goof off" and cut corners in the work, and the greater turnover.

The Autonomy program is an integrated means of handling both the binding-between and the binding-in functions, but it requires in the long run that the organization be willing to grant employee decision-making in the key areas of binding-in such as pay and promotions. The granting of "safe" areas of decision-making and the withholding of "hot" ones is not likely to work for long. It is necessary for the rank and file to be sufficiently bound in to the organization for them to want to make decisions which are rational for the system. But the rationality of their decisions will also depend upon the orientation of the key supervisors whose values they will interiorize. (Thus the clerks in Division B were more organizationally oriented than those in Division A—see Kaye [3].)

SUMMARY

A field experiment in an industrial setting was conducted in order to test hypotheses concerning the relationship between the means by which organizational decisions are made and (*a*) individual satisfaction, and (*b*) productivity.

Using four parallel divisions of the clerical operations of an organization, two programs of changes were introduced. One program, the Autonomy program involving two of the divisions, was designed to increase the role of the rank-and-file employees in the decision-making processes of the organization. The other two divisions received a program designed to increase the role of upper management in the decision-making processes (the Hierarchically controlled program). The phases of the experiment included: (*a*) before measurement, (*b*) training programs for supervisory personnel lasting approximately six months, (*c*) an operations period of a year for the two experimental programs, and (*d*) after measurement. In addition, certain measurements were taken during the training and operational phases of the experiment. Findings are reported on the question of the experimental "take" and on the general hypotheses on individual satisfactions and productivity. Briefly, it was found that:

1. The experimental programs produced changes in decision-making allocations in the direction required for the testing of the hypotheses.
2. The individual satisfactions of the members of the work groups increased significantly in the Autonomous program and decreased significantly in the Hierarchically controlled program.
3. Using one measure of productivity, both decision-making systems increased productivity, with the Hierarchically controlled program resulting in a greater increase.

The relationship of the findings to the so-called "Hawthorne effect" is examined and the experimental programs and their results are considered in the light of a theoretical description of the role of the control and regulation processes of large organizations.

REFERENCES

1. Coch, L., & French, J. R. P., Jr. Overcoming resistance to change. *Hum. Relat.*, 1948, **1**, 512–532.
2. Katz, D., Maccoby, N., & Morse, Nancy. *Productivity, supervision and morale in an office situation.* Ann Arbor: Survey Res. Center, Univ. of Michigan, 1950.
3. Kaye, Carol. *The effect on organizational goal achievement of a change in the structure of roles.* Ann Arbor: Survey Res. Center, 1954 (mimeographed).
4. Lewin, K. Group decisions and social change. In G. E. Swanson, T. M. Newcomb, & E. L. Hartley (Eds.), *Readings in social psychology*, 2nd ed. New York: Holt, 1952. Pp. 459–473.
5. Lippitt, R., & White, R. K. An experimental study of leadership and group life. In G. E. Swanson, T. M. Newcomb, & E. L. Hartley (Eds.), *Readings in social psychology*, 2nd ed. New York: Holt, 1952. Pp. 340–354.
6. Reimer, E. *Creating experimental social change in an organization.* Ann Arbor: Survey Res. Center, 1954 (mimeographed).
7. Tannenbaum, A. *The relationship between personality variables and adjustment to contrasting types of social structure.* Ann Arbor: Survey Res. Center, 1954 (mimeographed).
8. Worthy, J. C. Factors influencing employee morale. *Harvard Bus. Rev.*, 1950, **28**, 61–73.

§ 11 AGGRESSION AND ITS MANAGEMENT

Aggression, in its several forms, may be the most serious problem faced by man, but the resarch conducted by Stanley Milgram shows that it is not a simple one. For one thing, Milgram's results show that a great many of us are more capable of aggressive acts than we are ordinarily aware. Milgram's subjects were persuaded by group consensus to administer high voltages of what they thought was electric shock, even though the "victim" could be heard to complain bitterly. The subjects were free to reduce the amount of "shock" or to leave the situation, yet a surprising percentage of them yielded to the suggestion of the experimenter's confederates and administered ever higher levels of shock.

In real life, many acts of institutionalized aggression are perpetrated by individuals who are relatively unmotivated by hostility, but who act out of a sense of duty, or a feeling of obligation to an institution or to society. It is quite likely that Milgram's subjects fall into this category. Ordinarily, however, aggression is preceded or accompanied by feelings of hostility. Aggression of this type is typically perceived as antisocial and is the object of widespread concern. The paper by Leonard Berkowitz consists of a review of research on hostility and is concerned both with its reduction, as well as its causes.

The recent increase in urban riots and other forms of group aggression has led Magoroh Maruyama to write the paper that we have included as the third selection in this section. The views that Maruyama, a cultural anthropologist, expresses in this report are based on first-hand experiences and interviews with members of subcultural groups living in the slums of the San Francisco Bay area. His thesis is that the only middle-class individuals with whom slum Negroes come in contact are those who exploit and harass them. They are unaware that these oppressors are not typical of the white-collar class as a whole and, as a consequence, they direct their resentment against the entire middle-class establishment.

A somewhat different perspective on antisocial aggression is provided by a study conducted by McCord, McCord, and Howard, who undertook an analysis of the experiences during childhood and adolescence of men who had been convicted for larceny, breaking and entering, assault, or sex crimes. These early experiences were then compared with those of men who had grown up in the same deteriorated neighborhood, but who did not have criminal records. The fathers of those who became criminals were more likely to have been socially deviant and aggressive, to have administered physical punishment, and to have openly displayed hostile feelings toward their sons. The research results strongly suggest, in short, that the hostile-aggressive behavior of the men studied by the researchers had been learned from the adult male models who were most readily available to them: their fathers.

11.1 GROUP PRESSURE AND ACTION AGAINST A PERSON

Stanley Milgram

A great many variations of a paradigm provided by Asch (1951) show that there is an intelligible relationship between several features of the social environment and the degree to which a person will rely on others for his public judgments. Because it possesses merits of simplicity, clarity, and reconstructs in the laboratory powerful and socially relevant psychological processes, this paradigm has gained widespread acceptance as a basic technique of research on influence processes.

One feature that has been kept constant through the variations on Asch's work is that verbal judgment has been retained as the end product and basic index of conformity. More generally, a *signal*

Source: This research was supported by the National Science Foundation. Reprinted with slight abridgment from the *Journal of Abnormal and Social Psychology*, 1964, **69**, 137–143, with permission of the author and the American Psychological Association, Inc.

offered by the subject as representing his judgment has been the focus of study. Most often the signal has taken the form of a verbal pronouncement (Asch, 1956; Milgram, 1961), though mechanical devices which the subject uses to signal his judgment have also been employed (Crutchfield, 1955; Tuddenham & MacBride, 1959).

A distinction can be made between *signal conformity* and *action conformity* in that the immediate consequence of the former is purely informational; the subject states his opinion or reports on his perception of some feature of the environment. Action conformity, on the other hand, produces an immediate effect or alteration in the milieu that goes beyond a contribution of information. It refers to the elicitation of a *deed* by group forces, the induction of an act that is more than communicative in its effect. The act may be directed toward the well being of another person (e.g., a man is induced by group pressure to share bread with a beggar) or it may be oriented toward nonsocial parts of the environment (a delinquent is induced by gang pressure to throw a rock at a shop window).

There is little reason to assume a priori that observations made with regard to verbal conformity are automatically applicable to action. A person may pay lip service to the norms of a group and then be quite unwilling to carry out the kinds of behavior the group norms imply. Furthermore, an individual may accept and even promulgate a group standard at the verbal level, and yet find himself *unable* to translate the belief into deeds. Here we refer not to the distinction between overt compliance and private acceptance, but of the relationship between a genuinely accepted belief and its transformation into behavior.

The main point of the present experiment is to see if a person will perform acts under group pressure that he would not have performed in the absence of social inducement. There are many particular forms of action that can be inserted into a general group-pressure experimental design. One could study sorting IBM cards, or making paper cutouts, or eating crackers. Convenience makes them attractive, and in several valuable experiments investigators have used these tasks to good advantage (Frank, 1944; French, Morrison, & Levinger, 1960; Raven & French, 1958). But eventually social psychology must come to grips with significant behavior contents, contents that are of interest in their own right and are not simply trivial substitutes for psychologically meaningful forms of behavior. Guided by this consideration, a relatively potent form of action was selected for shaping by group pressure. We asked: Can a group induce a person to deliver punishment of increasing severity to a protesting individual? Whereas Asch and others have shown in what manner group pressure can cause a person to pronounce judgments that contradict his thinking, the present study examines whether group pressure causes a person to engage in acts at variance with his uninfluenced behavior.

METHOD

The details of subject recruitment, subject composition, experimenter's introductory patter, apparatus, and learning task have been described elsewhere (Milgram, 1963) and need only be sketched here.

Subjects consisted of 80 male adults, ranging in age from 20 to 50 years, and distributed in equal numbers, ages, and occupational statuses in the experimental and control conditions.

Procedure for Experimental Condition

General: The basic experimental situation is one in which a team of three persons (including two confederates) tests a fourth person on a paired-associate learning task. Whenever the fourth party makes a mistake the team punishes him with an electric shock. The two confederates suggest increasingly higher shock levels; the experimenter observes in what degree the third member of the team (a naive subject) goes along with or resists the confederates' pressure to increase the voltage levels.

Details: Four adults arrive at a campus laboratory to participate in a study of memory and learning. On arrival each subject is paid $4.50. The experimenter explains that a variety of roles must be performed in the experiment, and that to make role assignments fairly, subjects are to draw printed slips from a hat, each slip designating a particular experimental role. Actually, three of the adults are confederates, and only one naive subject is tested each hour. The drawing is rigged so that the naive subject is always assigned the position, Teacher 3, and Confederate B is always the Learner. The role assignments, which the subjects read from the drawn slips, are as follows:

Role title	*Participant*	*Task*
Teacher 1	Confederate C	First, you will read word pairs to the learner. Then you will read a stimulus word along with four possible answers.
Teacher 2	Confederate A	When the learner gives his answer, your task is to indicate whether he is correct or

Role title	*Participant*	*Task*
		incorrect. When he has erred you will provide him with the correct answer.
Teacher 3	Naive subject	Whenever the learner gives an incorrect answer, you will administer punishment by activating a shock generator.
Learner	Confederate B	Your task will be to learn a list of word pairs read to you by Teacher 1.

The experimenter explains that the purpose of the experiment is to study the effects of punishment on memory in a context of "collective teaching." Confederate B is taken to an adjoining room and in full view of the others is strapped into an electric-chair apparatus. The experimenter explains the nature of the learning task to the Learner and, passing over a remark made by the Learner concerning a mild heart condition, takes the three teachers to the main experimental room.

They are seated before an imposing shock generator whose essential feature is a horizontal line of 30 lever switches, labeled 15–450 volts, in 15-volt increments. Verbal designations are spread along the line of switches reading: Slight Shock, Moderate Shock, Strong Shock, Very Strong Shock, Intense Shock, Extreme Intensity Shock, and Danger: Severe Shock.

The experimenter restates that the Learner is to be tested on a paired-associate learning task (see Milgram, 1963, for details). Teachers are told that the Learner must be shocked each time he errs in the learning task. The experimenter explains how the level of shock is to be determined:

> Now the amount of punishment given on any trial is decided by the teachers themselves. Each of you will suggest a shock level. And the shock actually administered will be the lowest level suggested by any of the three teachers. In order to keep the experiment running smoothly, give suggested levels in this order: Teacher 1, submit your bid first; Teacher 2, submit your bid second; and Teacher 3, submit your bid third. Remember you can stick to one level or raise or lower your level as you desire, but on any trial, the punishment administered will be the lowest level suggested by any teacher on that trial.

Thus the naive subject finds himself in a position in which, on any trial, he can effectively control the maximum shock administered to the Learner, e.g., the ground rules of the experiment would permit him to hold the shock level down to 15 volts throughout the laboratory session. On the other hand he may go along with or move in the direction of the group choice. It is the naive subject who actually administers the shock by depressing the appropriate lever on the generator (i.e., he always emerges from the rigged drawing as Teacher 3).

The three teachers each have their roles spelled out for them again, and there remains only the task of giving each a sample shock from the generator before the experiment gets under way.

Behavior of Teachers 1 and 2 (Confederates): According to a prearranged schedule the two confederates at the shock generator call for a one-step increase in the shock level each time the Learner errs. On the first error they both call for Shock Level 1 (15 volts); on the twentieth error they both call for Shock Level 20 (300 volts), and so forth. Their constant unanimity is rendered credible by having Teacher 1 play a somewhat domineering, and Teacher 2 a somewhat submissive type. The confederates, played by adult actors, appear indifferent to the complaints of the Learner.

Behavior of the Learner: According to a prearranged schedule the Learner responds to the learning task by providing answers in the proportion of three wrong answers to each correct one. There are a total of 40 trials, 30 of them being critical (occasions when the Learner answers incorrectly).

The Learner's responses are not limited to providing answers. As the shocks administered to him become stronger, he grunts, protests, and demands to be let out of the experiment. Each complaint of the Learner is, in fact, prerecorded on magnetic tape, and is coordinated to a specific shock level. The protests and expressions of discomfort follow spontaneously the administration of an electric shock.

The Learner indicates no discomfort until the 75-volt shock is administered, at which time there is a slight grunt in response to the punishment. Similar reactions follow the 90- and 105-volt shocks, and at 120 volts the Learner shouts to the experimenter that the shocks are becoming painful. Painful groans are heard on the administration of the 135-volt shock, and at 150 volts the Learner cries out that he wants to be released from the experiment, complaining of a heart disturbance. Cries of this type continue with generally rising intensity, so that at 180 volts, the Learner cries out "I can't stand the pain," and by 285 volts his response to the shock is clearly an agonized scream. At 300 volts the victim shouts in desperation that he will no longer provide answers to the memory test, and so forth through 450 volts. In other words, increases in shock level are met by increasingly severe reactions from the person being punished.

It is to be remembered that this is merely a *potential* series of responses. If a shock no higher than the 75-volt level is administered, only a grunt is heard. As a point of procedure, protests were not repeated at the same shock level, e.g., after the first grunt was used in response to Shock Level 75, no further complaints were introduced until and if a higher shock level were used.

Experimental Measures: The principal experimental measure, therefore, is the level of shock administered by the subject on each of the 30 critical trials. The shock levels were automatically recorded by an Esterline-Angus event recorder wired directly into the shock generator, providing us with a permanent record of each subject's performance.

Postexperimental Session: An interview and debriefing session were held immediately after each subject's performance. A variety of background measures was obtained, as well as qualitative reactions to the experimental situation.

Control Condition

The purpose of the control condition is to determine the level of shock the naive subject administers to the Learner in the absence of group influence. One naive subject and one confederate (the Learner) perform in each session. The procedure is identical to that in the experimental condition, except that the tasks of Confederates A and C are collapsed into one role handled by the naive subject. References to collective teaching are omitted.

The naive subject is instructed to administer a shock each time the Learner errs, and the naive subject is told that as teacher he is free to select any shock level on any of the trials. In all other respects the control and experimental procedures are identical.

RESULTS

Figure 1 shows the mean shock levels for each critical trial in the experimental and control conditions. It also shows a diagonal representing the stooge-group's suggested shock level on each critical trial. The degree to which the experimental function moves away from the control level and toward the stooge-group diagonal represents the effects of group influence. Inspection indicates that the confederates

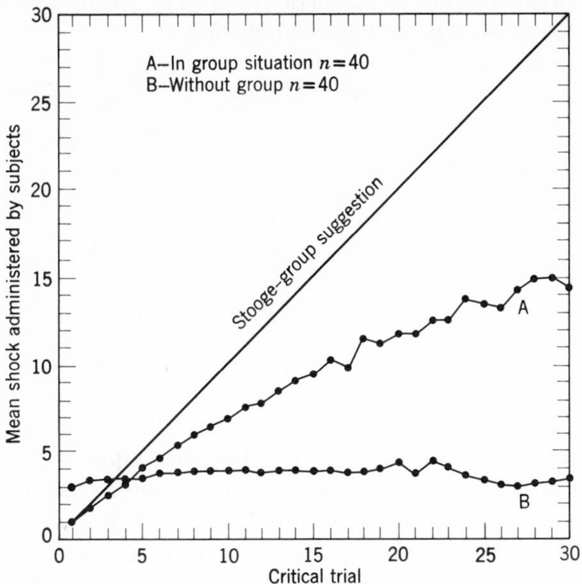

Figure 1. Mean shock levels in experimental and control conditions over 30 critical trials.

substantially influenced the level of shock administered to the Learner. The results will now be considered in detail.

In the experimental condition the standard deviation of shock levels rose regularly from trial to trial, and roughly in proportion to the rising mean shock level. However, in the control condition the standard deviation did not vary systematically with the mean through the 30 trials. Representative mean shock levels and standard deviations for the two conditions are shown in Table 1. Hartley's test for homogeneity of variance confirmed that the variances in the two conditions were significantly different. Therefore a reciprocal-of-the-square root transformation was performed before an analysis of variance was carried out.

As summarized in Table 2,[1] the analysis of variance showed that the overall mean shock level in the experimental condition was significantly higher than that in the control condition ($p < .001$). This

[1] Table 2 has been omitted in the interests of brevity.

Table 1 *Representative Mean Shock Levels and Standard Deviations in the Experimental and Control Conditions*

	Experimental Condition		Control Condition	
Trial	Mean Shock Level	*SD*	Mean Shock Level	*SD*
5	4.03	1.19	3.35	2.39
10	6.78	2.63	3.48	3.03
15	9.20	4.28	3.68	3.58
20	11.45	6.32	4.13	4.90
25	13.55	8.40	3.55	3.85
30	14.13	9.59	3.38	1.89

is less interesting, however, than the differing slopes in the two conditions, which show the group effects through the course of the experimental session.[2] The analysis of variance test for trend confirmed that the slopes for the two conditions differed significantly ($p < .001$).

Examinations of the standard deviations in the experimental condition shows that there are large individual differences in response to group pressure, some subjects following the group closely, others resisting effectively. Subjects were ranked according to their total deviation from the confederates' shock choices. On the thirtieth critical trial the most conforming quartile had a mean shock level of 27.6, while the mean shock level of the least conforming quartile was 4.8. Background characteristics of the experimental subjects were noted: age, marital status, occupation, military experience, political preference, religious affiliation, birth-order information, and educational history. Less educated subjects (high school degree or less) tended to yield more than those who possess a college degree ($\chi^2_{df=1} = 2.85$, $p < .10$). Roman Catholic subjects tended to yield more than Protestant subjects ($\chi^2_{df=1} = 2.96$, $p < .10$). No other background variable measured in the study was associated with amount of yield-

[2] On the first four trials the control group has a higher mean shock than the experimental group; this is an artifact due to the provision that in the experimental condition the shock actually administered and recorded was the lowest suggested by any member of the group; when the subject called for a shock level higher than that suggested by the confederates, it was not reflected in the data. (This situation arose only during the first few critical trials.) By the fifth critical trial the group pressure begins to show its effect in elevating the mean shock level of the naive subjects.

ing, though the number of subjects employed was too small for definite conclusions.

The shock data may also be examined in terms of the *maximum* shock administered by subjects in the experimental and control conditions, i.e., the highest single shock administered by a subject throughout the 30 critical trials. The information is presented in Table 3. Only 2 control subjects administered shocks beyond the tenth voltage level (at this point the Learner makes his first truly vehement protest), while 27 experimental subjects went beyond this point. A median test showed that the maximum shocks administered by experimental subjects were higher than those administered by control subjects ($\chi^2_{df=1} = 39.2$, $p < .001$).

The main effect, then, is that in the experimental condition subjects were substantially influenced by group pressure. When viewed in terms of the mean shock level over the 30 critical trials, as in Figure 1, the experimental function appears as a vector more or less bisecting the angle formed by the confederates' diagonal and control slopes. Thus one might be tempted to say that the subject's action in the experimental situation had two major sources: it was partly determined by the level the subject would have chosen in the control condition, and partly by the confederates' choice. Neither one nor the other entirely dominates the average behavior of subjects in the experimental condition. There are very great individual differences in regard to the more dominant force.

DISCUSSION

The substantive contribution of the present study lies in the demonstration that group influence can shape behavior in a domain that might have been thought highly resistant to such effects. Subjects are induced by the group to inflict pain on another person at a level that goes well beyond levels chosen in the absence of social pressure. Hurting a man is an action that for most people carries considerable psychological significance; it is closely tied to questions of conscience and ethical judgment. It might have been thought that the protests of the victim and inner prohibitions against hurting others would have operated effectively to curtail the subject's compliance. While the experiment yields wide variation in performance, a substantial number of subjects submitted readily to pressure applied to them by the confederates.

The significance of yielding in Asch's situation is sometimes ques-

Table 3 *Maximum Shock Levels Administered in Experimental and Control Conditions*

Verbal Designation and Voltage Indication	Number of Subjects for Whom This Was Maximum Shock	
	Experimental	Control
Slight shock		
15	1	3
30	2	6
45	0	7
60	0	7
Moderate shock		
75	1	5
90	0	4
105	1	1
120	1	1
Strong shock		
135	2	3
150	5	1
165	2	0
180	0	0
Very strong shock		
195	1	0
210	2	0
225	2	0
240	1	0
Intense shock		
255	2	0
270	0	0
285	1	0
300	1	0
Extreme intensity shock		
315	2	0
330	0	0
345	1	0
360	2	0
Danger: severe shock		
375	0	1
390	0	0
405	1	0
420	2	0
XXX		
435	0	0
450	7	1

tioned because the discriminative task is not an issue of self-evident importance for many subjects (Bronowski).[3] The criticism is not easily extended to the present study. Here the subject does not merely feign agreement with a group on a perceptual task of undefined importance; and he is unable to dismiss his action by relegating it to the status of a trivial gesture, for a person's suffering and discomfort are at stake.

The behavior observed here occurred within the framework of a laboratory study presided over by an experimenter. In some degree his authority stands behind the group. In his initial instructions the experimenter clearly legitimized the use of any shock level on the console. Insofar as he does not object to the shocks administered in the course of the experiment, his assent is implied. Thus, even though the effects of group pressure have been clearly established by a comparison of the experimental and control conditions, the effects occurred within the context of authoritative sanction. This point becomes critical in any attempt to assess the relative effectiveness of *conformity* versus *obedience* as means of inducing contravalent behavior (Milgram, 1963). If the experimenter had not approved the use of all shock levels on the generator, and if he had departed from the laboratory at an early stage, thus eliminating any sign of authoritative assent during the course of the experiment, would the group have had as powerful an effect on the naive subject?

There are many points of difference between Asch's investigation and the procedure of the present study that can only be touched upon here.

1. While in Asch's study the *adequate* response is anchored to an external stimulus event, in the present study we are dealing with an internal, unbound standard.

2. A misspoken judgment can, in principle, be withdrawn, but here we are dealing with action that has an immediate and unalterable consequence. Its irreversibility stems not from constraints extrinsic to the action, but from the content of the action itself: once the Learner is shocked, he cannot be unshocked.

3. In the present experiment, despite the several sources of opinion, there can be but a single shock level on each trial. There is, therefore, a competition for outcome that was not present in the Asch situation.

4. While in the Asch study the focus of pressure is directed toward the subject's judgment, with distortion of public response but an intermediary stage of influence, here the focus of pressure is directed toward performance

[3] J. Bronowski, personal communication, January 10, 1962.

of action itself. Asch's yielding subject may secretly harbor the true judgment; but when the performance of an action becomes the object of social pressure, there is no comparable recourse to a covert form. The subject who performed the act demanded by the group has yielded exhaustively.

5. In the Asch situation a yielding subject engages in a covert violation of his obligations to the experimenter. He has agreed to report to the experimenter what he sees, and insofar as he goes along with the group, he breaks this agreement. In contrast, in the present experiment the yielding subject acts within the terms of the "subject-experimenter contract." In going along with the two confederates the subject may violate his own inner standards, and the rights of the Learner, but his relationship with the experimenter remains intact at both the manifest and private levels. Subjects in the two experiments are faced with different patterns of social pressure and violate different relationships through social submission.

SUMMARY

A distinction is made between action conformity and signal conformity; the former refers to group-induced behavior that has more than an informational impact on the environment. A study of action conformity is described in which the effects of group pressure are measured by comparing the amount of electric shock administered by a naive *S* to a person, under experimental and control conditions. In the experimental condition the *S* performs in the midst of two confederates who call for increasingly more powerful shocks against a victim. The naive *S* has control over the level of shock and can hold down the punishment or yield to group influence. In the course of 30 critical trials the mean shock levels rise in response to the confederates' pressure. The structure of the experimental situation is examined by a comparison with Asch's study of verbal compliance.

REFERENCES

Asch, S. E. Effects of group pressure upon the modification and distortion of judgment. In H. Guetzkow (Ed.), *Groups, leadership, and men.* Pittsburgh: Carnegie Press, 1951.

Asch, S. E. Studies of independence and conformity: I. A minority of one against a unanimous majority. *Psychol. Monogr.,* 1956, **70**,(9, Whole No. 416).

Crutchfield, R. S. Conformity and character. *Am. Psychol.,* 1955, **10,** 191–198.

Frank, J. D. Experimental studies of personal pressure and resistance. *J. Genet. Psychol.,* 1944, **30,** 23–64.

French, J. R. P., Jr., Morrison, H. W., & Levinger, G. Coercive power and forces affecting conformity. *J. Abnorm. Soc. Psychol.,* 1960, **61,** 93–101.

Milgram, S. Nationality and conformity. *Sci. Am.*, 1961, **205**, 45–51.
Milgram, S. Behavioral study of obedience. *J. Abnorm. Soc. Psychol.*, 1963, **67**, 371–378.
Raven, B. H., & French, J. R. P. Legitimate power, coercive power, and observability in social influence. *Sociometry*, 1958, **21**, 83–97.
Tuddenham, R. D., & MacBride, P. The yielding experiment from the subject's point of view. *J. Pers.*, 1959, **27**, 259–271.

11.2 THE EXPRESSION AND REDUCTION OF HOSTILITY

Leonard Berkowitz

The publication of *Frustration and Aggression* by Dollard, Doob, Miller, Mowrer, and Sears (17) in 1939 represents a milestone in the application of the methods and concepts of experimental psychology to important social problems. Perhaps stimulated by the early phases of World War II, the authors sought to translate clinical and sociological observations concerning hostile behavior into the operationally definable language of the laboratory. These men must be given credit for the attempt, whatever the merit of their hypotheses. In the tradition of science's continuing search for unifying principles, they showed that many apparently different phenomena could be "explained" employing only a relatively small number of theoretical variables and, in contrast to earlier writers, formulated their propositions in a relatively precise manner.

In addition, *Frustration and Aggression* also provides a systematic foundation for further research on aggressive behavior. The present paper is a review of studies reported after 1939 within the general theoretical framework utilized by Dollard and his associates. Inevitably, in the course of this review our attention will focus upon the question of the adequacy of this framework for the study of human hostility. Three groups of factors will be discussed: (*a*) those governing the occurrence of overt aggression, (*b*) those determining the nature and object of the aggressive act, and (*c*) those related to the reduction of the instigation to aggression.

Source: This review was supported by a grant from the National Institute of Mental Health. Reprinted from the *Psychological Bulletin*, 1958, **55**, 257–283, with permission of the author and the American Psychological Association, Inc.

CONDITIONS AROUSING OVERT AGGRESSION

Theoretical Principles

The fundamental hypothesis in *Frustration and Aggression* was first expressed formally in Sigmund Freud's earlier writings. He has suggested that aggression was the "primordial reaction" to the frustration occurring "whenever pleasure-seeking or pain-avoiding behavior was blocked" (17, p. 21). Acknowledging their indebtedness to Freud, the authors presented a sweeping generalization as their basic postulate: ". . . the proposition is that the occurrence of aggressive behavior always presupposes the existence of frustration and, contrariwise, that *the existence of frustration always leads to some form of aggression*"[1] [*italics mine*] (17, p. 1). Needless to say, the second phrase drew the fire of many critics (e.g., 6, 26, 41).

In a symposium on the frustration-aggression hypothesis appearing two years later, Miller (49) admitted that this phrase "was unclear and misleading" for two principal reasons:

> In the first place it suggests, though it by no means logically demands, that frustration has no consequences other than aggression. This suggestion seems to have been strong enough to override statements appearing later in the text which specifically rule out any such implications (cf. pp. 8–9, 19, 58, 101–102). A second objection to the assertion in question is that it fails to distinguish between instigation to aggression and the actual occurrence of aggression. Thus it omits the possibility that other responses may be dominant and inhibit the occurrence of acts of aggression. In this respect it is inconsistent

[1] A "frustration" is defined by the F-A psychologists as "an interference with the occurrence of an instigated goal-response at its proper time in the behavior sequence" (17, p. 7). This is the usage adopted in the present paper. It should be noted that other writers (e.g., 9) utilize the term to refer to the emotional state created by such an interference.

Dollard, Doob, et al. define "aggression" as any "sequence of behavior, the goal-response to which is the injury of the person toward whom it is directed" (17, p. 9). The authors explicitly state that they are not referring to "instrumental" aggression: "aggression is that response which follows frustration, reduces only the secondary, frustration-produced instigation, and leaves the strength of the original instigation unaffected" (17, p. 11). Allport discusses various kinds of acts that have been labeled "aggressiveness" (1, pp. 355–356).

The term "instigation to aggression," as used here, denotes an aggressive drive, or more generally, a state of readiness to make aggressive responses, and *not* the frustrating event.

with later portions of the exposition which make a distinction between the instigation to a response and the actual presence of that response. . . .

Both of these unfortunate aspects of the former statement may be avoided by the following rephrasing: Frustration produces instigations to a number of different types of response, one of which is an instigation to some form of aggression (49, p. 338).

Dollard et al. hypothesize that the strength of the instigation to aggression varies directly with at least three factors: "(1) the strength of instigation to the frustrated response, (2) the degree of interference with the frustrated response, and (3) the number of frustrated response-sequences" (17, p. 28). A subsequent section adds the anticipation of punishment for aggressive behavior to the list of variables affecting the likelihood of an overtly hostile response to frustration; specific aggressive acts will be inhibited to the extent that punishment is anticipated to be a consequence of these acts (17, p. 33).

This list obviously is not complete; nothing is said of persistent individual characteristics, and the Frustration-Aggression group, with two slight exceptions, tends to neglect this class of factors in their psychological principles. One exception is found on p. 37. Discussing Allport's theory of trait structure, they suggest that individuals may have "generalized habits" of responding to frustrating situations with either overt or nonovert aggression. For the second exception, it is stated: "As a result of his life history any given person will carry into adult life a high or low ability to 'tolerate' frustrations and will stand at some point on a dimension of 'readiness to be aggressive' in frustrating situations" (17, p. 88).

Miller's 1941 article presents a further elaboration of the role possibly played by persistent response tendencies in the frustration-aggression sequence. "Instigation to aggression may occupy any one of a number of positions in the hierarchy of instigations aroused . . . [by a frustration]" (49, p. 338). Therefore, if, for a given individual, the instigation to aggression is lower in this hierarchy than instigations to other responses incompatible with aggression, he is not likely to demonstrate hostile behavior when confronted with a frustration situation. It is clear, then, that relatively stable individual characteristics, including the strength of the instigation to aggression relative to the strength of other frustration-produced instigations, should be considered among the factors affecting the likelihood of an overt hostile act.

The following section will review studies having some bearing upon the above list of factors presumably affecting the occurrence of a hostile act. Generally consistent with the theoretical expectations of Dollard and his colleagues, these results frequently add needed details to their somewhat overly general hypotheses.

Empirical Investigations

Strength of Instigation to the Frustrated Response: An experiment and two questionnaire studies are cited as evidence for the hypothesis that the strength of the instigation to aggression is directly related to the strength of the frustrated drive. Sears and Sears measured the latency of a crying response to the withdrawal of a bottle from the mouth of a five-month-old infant with the strength of his hunger drive manipulated by varying the amount of milk that the baby was permitted to take. Assuming that crying was an aggressive reaction, their "figures indicate that as the child became more nearly satiated, i.e., as the strength of instigation decreased, frustration induced a less and less immediate aggressive response" (17, p. 29).[2] In the first questionnaire study, college students queried by Doob and Sears indicated that they were more likely to react aggressively in frustrating situations the stronger the drive whose goal-responses had suffered interference (17, p. 29). Somewhat similar results were obtained by Miller with a list of "annoyances" presented to college students (17, p. 30). For further studies along this latter line, an investigator might care to make use of the list of anger situations reported by Anastasi et al. (2) based upon "controlled diaries" kept by 38 college women.

Getting away from the dangers inherent in the use of questionnaires, two experiments make use of the familiar Hullian principle that drive strength increases the closer the organism is to making the appropriate goal response. Seward (73) paired six rats in a number of different combinations after 21 hours of food deprivation. He found that the animal in possession of the food pellet, and therefore, who was closer to eating, showed reliably more aggression than the one without it. Presumably, the hunger drive whose goal responses were blocked by the behavior of the other animal was stronger in the rat possessing the food pellet. The second of these studies, carried out by Haner and Brown (25), provides additional support for the hypoth-

[2] Sears may no longer regard the child's cry as an aggressive response. In his most recent book, he distinguishes between rage or anger, on the one hand, and the desire to hurt on the other (71, pp. 221–222), a distinction similar to that proposed by McClelland (44, p. 513). The cry is an indication of rage and not aggression, as this latter response is defined by Dollard, Doob, et al.

esis of a positive relationship between closeness to the goal and drive strength. Thirty elementary school children individually played a game in which marbles had to be inserted into holes. The *E* terminated the trials at various distances from the goal of game completion, with each termination causing a buzzer to be sounded until *S* pushed a plunger to stop it. The investigators assume that the pressure exerted in pushing the plunger is a direct function of the strength of *S*'s instigation to aggression, and show that this pressure generally tends to increase the closer *S* is to task-completion. Apparently, then, the greater the strength of the drive frustrated the greater the resultant aggression—if the pressure against the plunger is indeed a hostile act and not a manifestation of something else, such as a frustration-induced tendency to exert more vigorous responses in general (40).

Degree of Interference with the Frustrated Response: The second hypothesis posits a direct relationship between strength of the aggressive drive and the degree of interference with the frustrated response. The evidence utilized by Dollard et al. in support of this principle comes from two correlational studies. First, in Miller's study of annoyances already referred to, *S*s "reported that they felt much more irritated at being completely 'off form' in their favorite sport than at being only slightly 'off form.' The critical ratio of this difference was 5.5" (17, p. 31). Somewhat more unsatisfactory is the second investigation by Hovland and Sears (17, p. 31). Reasoning that bad economic conditions should produce "a greater interference with customary goal-responses" than good business conditions, they employed the per acre value of cotton as "an index of the severity of interference with economic actions." For 14 Southern states for the years 1882 to 1930 the correlation between this index and the number of lynchings was −.67; "i.e., the number of lynchings (aggression) increased when the amount of interference increased." Mintz (51), however, questions the magnitude of the reported correlation. He claims the true correlation is much lower than that given by the F-A (Frustration-Aggression) psychologists.

Three more recent investigations can be cited as evidence for the present principle if we first assume that the degree to which some drive possessed by *S*, such as for self-enhancement, is blocked is a positive function of the strength of a hostile act directed against *S*. Explicitly making this assumption (24, p. 518), Graham, Charwat, Honig, and Weltz presented 50 incomplete statements to 106 adolescents. The statements described five types of hostile actions that various instigators had taken against a person, with these actions ranging from a physical blow to not liking the person. The *S*s had to indicate what they thought would be the "most likely way for a person to act in such a situation." If a very hostile act directed against the individual can be considered as producing greater blocking of his goal responses than a less hostile act,[3] the present hypothesis is confirmed: "When the instigation to aggression is itself a form of aggression, the strength of the aggressive response will vary as a function of the strength of the instigation" (24, p. 514). In the second experiment, by McClelland and Apicella (42), similar results were obtained. There was a significant increase in the number of aggressive responses made in the frustrating situation when *E* increased the intensity of the derogatory remarks made to *S*. Consistent with this, French (22) employed 10 groups of *S*s working on three problems, and found that there was a general tendency for those individuals who received most aggression to initiate most aggression. As French notes, "Presumably those who receive aggression from others perceive these aggressors as interfering agents . . ." (22, p. 286).

French also compared the number of aggressive responses made during a task involving high member interdependence with the number elicited in the two low interdependence tasks. Although no quantitative data are given, French suggests that "the comments of both the observers and the subjects prove that a member suffers more interference by the others" on the former problem. He reports more aggression per minute directed against other members of the group in this problem than in the low interdependence. A statistical analysis is given (22, pp. 286–287), however, that adds further corroboration to the present hypothesis.

Number of Frustrated Response-Sequences: The third hypothesis maintains that the total strength of the instigation to aggression is a positive function of the number of frustrated response-sequences. The only evidence for this principle given in *Frustration and Aggression* is of an anecdotal nature. Thus, in an experiment by Sears, Hovland, and Miller, it was observed that "a man who had previously been a willing subject for several arduous experiments complained vigorously at having to give free associations to fifty stimulus words" (17, p. 32). Apparently the minor frustrations he had suffered had combined to produce a hostile response of greater strength than would ordinarily

[3] An alternative interpretation also utilized by Graham et al. is reported below in the section, Opposing Hypotheses.

be expected from the immediate frustrating situation alone. Incidental support for the present hypothesis is found in a more recent experiment by Thibaut and Coules (79). In one part of the investigation two conditions were established after all *S*s had been angered by notes supposedly written by a fellow college student. In one of these conditions *S*s were interrupted by *E* after the instigation for about three minutes, while the remaining *S*s were allowed to write one note to the instigator before this informal interruption occurred. Then, *S*s in both treatments continued communication with the instigator. There was a significantly greater volume of aggression communicated to their fellow student by the former *S*s, even though the experimenter rather than this person was responsible for the interruption.

Several points may be noted here if we assume, as seems likely, that there was little cathartic reduction of hostility in the writing of the single note. First, the interference with the aggressive responses apparently was in itself frustrating, as Dollard et al. have hypothesized (17, p. 40), and this seems to have led to increased hostility. Second, since the insulting notes probably had made all *S*s angry (in the absence of a control group in the present case it is impossible to demonstrate this unequivocally), the hostility produced by the interference to the aggression presumably had added to the hostility created by the faked notes.

Miller's 1941 paper (49) contains an hypothesis that is closely related to the present problem. He proposes that frustration-induced instigations to responses other than aggression weaken as the frustration persists. Since the earlier statement maintains that the aggressive effects of a number of interferences summate, both hypotheses yield the same prediction: there is a greater probability of overt aggressive acts with repeated frustrations.

Otis and McCandless (56) attempted to test Miller's newer hypothesis in an experiment with 63 preschool children placed in an eight-trial frustration task. The *S*s showed significant increases in "aggressive-dominant" behavior scores from the first four to the last four frustration trials, and showed reliable decreases in a class of behavior found to be incompatible with aggression, "submissive-complaisant" behavior. In contrast to this support for the present hypothesis, McClelland and Apicella (42) obtained negative results in an experiment employing college students on only two frustration trials.

Inhibition of Aggression: Basically, according to the F-A group, "the strength of the inhibition of any act of aggression varies positively with the amount of punishment anticipated to be a consequence of that act" (17, p. 33). The evidence presented for this proposition stems from the above mentioned questionnaire study by Doob and Sears (17, p. 35). When asked to indicate how they had responded to frustrating situations they had actually experienced, the 185 college students were more likely to report an overtly hostile act when the satisfaction obtained from making this response was greater than the anticipated punishment, while the smallest frequency of overt aggression occurred when the anticipated punishment was greater than the anticipated satisfaction.

On the basis of records of actual experiences kept by 120 adults, McKellar (47) reports that acts of aggression tend to be directed against an object from which retaliation is unlikely. The most direct recent support for the hypothesis dealing with the effects of punishment comes from an investigation conducted by Chasdi and Lawrence (10). Twenty-three preschool children were divided into two groups: 12 in an experimentally punished group and the remainder in a control group. Both groups had four sessions of doll play with the experimental group receiving punishment for the expression of aggression in Session II. There were significant differences between the two groups on both the frequency and intensity of aggression in Session III. The difference was still in the predicted direction during Session IV, but it is no longer significant. According to the experimenters, this latter change "is consistent with a session to session increase in aggression resulting from a decrease in aggression anxiety due to the reinstatement of permissiveness" (10, p. 522).

In this study, as well as others employing doll play measures of hostile tendencies (e.g., 4, 37, 84), there was a significant increase in aggressive manifestations from the first to the last sessions for all groups, presumably because the children learned they would not be punished for displaying hostility in the play situation. Somewhat in accord with this last hypothesis, Feshbach (19) found that boys initially low in aggressiveness tended to increase in their display of overt hostility following a series of permissive free play experiences. This increase was not obtained with the girl *S*s.

Seward's studies of aggressive behavior in rats also illustrate the inhibitory effects of punishment. In one experiment (74), he observed that the day after a fight the average loser made fewer aggressions or advances than before not only against the winner but also against others rats. Seward attempts to show how stable dominance-submission relationships can develop through the conditioning of the fear drive in one animal to the presence of another (72).

Something analogous to this probably is involved in the class of dominance-subordination relationships we term social status. For one thing, human beings undoubtedly learn they will be punished by the dominant, high-status figures in their social groupings if they aggress against them. Thus, it is not surprising to see *S*s express less hostility toward frustrators vested with power and authority by society than toward lower-status instigators (13, 24, 33, 80).

Social groups may not only teach the individual to anticipate punishment for disapproved actions, they also may influence the reaction to these anticipations. One of the first studies to demonstrate this was carried out by Wright (82). Pairs of nursery school children, grouped in terms of whether they were "strong" or "weak" friends, were frustrated by the adult *E*. The pairs of strong friends were more likely to express aggression, including direct physical attacks, against the experimenter than the pairs of weak friends. An experiment by Pepitone and Reichling (58) suggests that the variable probably largely accounting for this type of effect is the liking of the group members for each other. After they had been treated in an unjust and arbitrary manner by an instigator who then left the room, male college student members of experimentally produced high liking (high cohesive) groups expressed significantly more hostility toward the instigator than did the members of the low cohesive groups. The former *S*s apparently felt fewer restraints in attacking *E* and the experiment.

Conceivably, the lowering of restraints accompanying high liking among the group members also can result in a greater volume of intragroup overt hostility. French, in the experiment described earlier (22), studied two types of groups working under conditions in which the members were likely to see each other as frustrators. In one type of group the members had known each other for some time, while the *S*s in the remaining groups did not have this history of previous contact. The observers recorded significantly more overt aggression directed toward other group members in the former groups, supposedly because the higher liking resulting from the greater degree of acquaintance had lowered the members' inhibitions.

Levin and Turgeon (37) also have shown that the presence of a familiar person is associated with a relatively great release of overt aggression, but the reason for this finding in their experiment is not clear. They found that aggressive doll play behavior significantly increased when a child's mother was present, and tended to decrease (nonsignificantly) when an adult female stranger watched the child's play. The reduction in hostile behavior in the presence of the stranger cannot be traced to a general inhibition of activity in this condition, and the authors speculate that the decrease is "a reflection of the child's training in 'company manners,' to behave well in front of strangers." In opposition to the hypothesis that the mother's presence served to weaken the inhibitions against the expression of aggression, there are suggestive, but nonsignificant, indications that the mother's presence actually instigated such actions, particularly in the case of the boys.

As will be discussed more fully later, the F-A psychologists propose that the inhibition of direct acts of aggression increases the likelihood of either: (*a*) indirect acts of aggression against the instigator (only the form of the aggression is changed, not the target) or (*b*) displaced aggression in which a target other than the frustrator is attacked. A third inhibitory reaction to internal feelings of anger also has been described (55): withdrawal from communication with the instigator. Although the withdrawal, in its effect, may be an indirect attack, as in the case of "snubbing," it is likely that the break in communication is motivated by: (*a*) inhibition of direct hostile attacks against the instigator and (*b*) the unpleasant effects within the individual created by the frustration of the instigation to aggression. Thibaut and Coules (79) have shown that interference with the occurrence of aggressive responses can become a source of discomfort. Whatever the reason for the withdrawal reaction, Newcomb (55) points out that hostile attitudes often persist because they lead to a breakdown in communication with the object of the hostility. Thibaut and Coules also report findings partially supporting this hypothesis. On the basis of each *S*'s initial attitudes toward his assigned co-worker, the sample was divided into those initially hostile and those initially friendly toward their partners. (These were attitudes that the *S*s had brought into the experiment.) The initially hostile *S*s produced a significantly smaller volume of communications to their partners prior to the experimental instigation to aggression.

Characteristic Individual Differences: There can be little doubt that individuals differ reliably in the readiness with which they display hostile behavior. Documentation for this point, if it is needed, can be found, for example, in a study conducted by Yarrow (84). Based on a sample of 60 preschool children, indices of aggression computed from the first doll play session were found to be significantly related to the indices obtained in the second session following a frustration. The Pearson product-moment *r*'s ranged from .38 to .77 for the entire group. Instead of demonstrating that these individual differences exist, therefore, the more important research problem is to isolate the classes of relatively stable characteristics that affect the probability of an aggressive reaction to a given frustration.

One factor warranting further investigation involves apparent differences in the characteristic strength of the instigation to aggression. Research findings in this area point to a number of complexities that may have to be unraveled before personality tests can be used to predict the probability of hostile behavior at a satisfactory level of confidence. For example, there is an apparently paradoxical result of the Thibaut and Coules experiment. After receiving the insulting notes, the initially hostile *S*s communicated a significantly *smaller* amount of aggression to the supposed insulter than the initially friendly *S*s. A similar difference, obtained in another experiment, suggests that this may be a reliable pattern. Hokanson and Gordon (27) classified their *S*s, 40 male college students, as either high- or low-hostility expressers on the basis of their responses to a scale of "manifest hostility." The *S*s scoring at the extreme ends of this scale were placed in either a situation designed to arouse relatively strong hostility, or in a low-arousal situation, and then allowed to express aggression in fantasy (to TAT pictures), and in overt behavior. Relative to the comparable *S*s in the low-arousal condition, there was a significant tendency for the "strongly aroused" *S*s with low manifest hostility scores to express more hostility on the TAT, while the similarly "aroused" high manifest hostility *S*s gave fewer aggressive responses. No significant relationships were found in the overt behavior situation.

There is no unequivocal explanation for the above findings. It may be, as Hokanson and Gordon assumed, and as Feshbach suggests (19, p. 452), that the initially "friendlier" *S*s in these studies were low in overt aggressiveness more because of high inhibition in the original (or test-taking) situation than because of low drive strength. As was mentioned earlier, Feshbach (19) obtained results somewhat in accord with this interpretation. Similarly, Bach (4) found a tendency, though nonsignificant, for 12 preschool children previously rated by their teachers as showing "little destructive aggression" to have higher doll play aggression in the last of four permissive play sessions than the 14 children previously rated characteristically high in aggression. According to this view, then, the permissive experimental situation lowered the inhibitions felt by the *S*s ostensibly low in characteristic aggression. As a result, their stronger instigation to aggression led to stronger aggressive responses.

Another possibility is suggested by Miller's "approach-avoidance" conflict model (50). The *S*s with high initial hostility scores may have had a truly stronger aggressive drive, or perhaps a stronger readiness to respond aggressively to an instigation, than the *S*s with low scores. The effect of the hostility instigation, then, was to produce greater anger in the former *S*s. However, as a consequence of this hostility arousal, the *S*s also were likely to have stronger guilt feelings, or aggression-anxiety, when they became aware of their hostility. In reaction to this emotion, these *S*s then suppressed the overt manifestations of aggression. Instead of stating that anxiety inhibits aggression only prior to the experimental situation, as the first hypothesis maintains, this latter hypothesis suggests that it inhibits the expression of aggression during the experiment.

There is some support for this alternative explanation in an experiment by Clark (12) dealing with another drive that also is often socially disapproved, sex. Clark found that male college students, whose sex drive presumably was heightened as a result of seeing pictures of nude women, expressed significantly lower "manifest sex" to TAT cards than the *S*s in the nonaroused group (*S*s not shown these pictures and therefore presumably having a low drive level). It was not until the *S*s were placed in a highly permissive situation (with their superegos "dissolved in alcohol") that the sexually aroused group had higher manifest sex scores. Thus, when the arousal of the socially disapproved drive was likely to produce guilt feelings, the aroused *S*s overtly displayed a lower level of this drive than the nonarousal *S*s.

Interestingly enough, Clark also found that the sexually aroused *S*s under nonalcohol conditions gave significantly fewer aggressive responses to the TAT cards than the control *S*s. Evidence is presented suggesting that the former group "was not only anxious about expressing manifest sex, but also was anxious about expressing manifest aggression . . ." (12, p. 56).

The present data do not permit us to choose between the above alternatives, and indeed, both may be correct. The first possibility may account for the increase in overt aggression for *S*s characteristically low in this mode of behavior, the second for the decrease shown by the supposedly "hostile" *S*s. But whatever the explanation, the results obtained by Thibaut and Coules and Hokanson and Gordon add further documentation to a point made by many writers (e.g., 17): the amount of overt aggression typically displayed by an individual is not necessarily a direct function of the strength of the instigation to aggression within him.

Two hypotheses may be formulated which relate characteristic overt hostility to the strength of the individual's instigation to aggression by extending the F-A propositions regarding anticipation of punishment. The first hypothesis maintains that an individual's characteristic level of overt aggression is more likely to coincide with the strength of his aggressive drive the more his important socializing agents (e.g., parents) have permitted or encouraged aggressive behavior.

There is support for this hypothesis in two recent investigations. Lesser (35) obtained a significant +.43 product-moment correlation between fantasy aggression scores and reputation among peers for overt aggression for 23 elementary school boys whose mothers, when interviewed, indicated they were relatively supportive of aggression. The correlation was negative (−.41) in the case of 21 boys whose mothers said they discouraged aggression. Similarly, contending that lower-class culture often encourages aggression, Mussen and Naylor (54) found a significantly positive association between ratings of overt aggression and number of aggressive TAT themes for a sample of 24 lower-class juvenile delinquent boys. In both of these studies, therefore, the results suggest that the level of the individual's fantasy aggression is likely to approach the level of his overt aggression when important figures who can either reward or punish his hostile behavior tend to reinforce this type of response. Although investigations mentioned earlier (10, 12, 27, 37) indicate that fantasy aggression is not always directly proportional to the strength of the instigation to aggression, this direct relationship is plausible in the case of the present two studies. The agents primarily involved in the socialization of the Lesser and Mussen and Naylor *S*s presumably punished aggressive behavior, including the kind of indirect hostility involved in the fantasy tests, relatively infrequently. Sears, Maccoby, and Levin also show that characteristic overt aggression is associated positively with the socializing agents' permissiveness for aggression (71, pp. 258–259).

The second hypothesis, relating characteristic hostile behavior to the level of the aggressive drive, states: Frequent punishment for the expression of aggression increases the strength of the instigation to aggression. This obviously is consistent with the F-A principle, previously mentioned, that "interference with direct aggression constitutes in itself an additional frustration" (17, p. 40). A variation of this hypothesis, first postulated by Whiting, is employed by Sears and his colleagues. They argue that frequent punishment for hostile behavior produces aggression anxiety which interferes with the occurrence of aggressive acts. Therefore, the greater the aggression anxiety, the greater the frustration, and consequently, the stronger the resulting instigation to aggression (70, p. 218).

Two recent studies conducted by Sears and his associates have results generally consistent with this reasoning. In the first of these (70), the mothers' statements of how punitive they were with regard to aggression correlated +.50 with teachers' ratings of the aggressiveness of 21 nursery school boys, and +.60 with the observed frequency of this behavior in 16 15-minute nursery school time samples. These correlations were in the opposite direction for the 19 girls in the group, −.04 and −.41 respectively. To account for the sex difference, the investigators suggest that girls are more likely to identify with their mothers than boys, and therefore, a given amount of punishment by the mother is felt more strongly by the girls. As a consequence of the strong aggression anxiety, the highly punished girls exhibit a stronger tendency to inhibit direct overt aggression (70, p. 219). When the children's activity level was taken into consideration, "the more severely punished girls were relatively [but not reliably] more aggressive than the less severely punished" (70, p. 216).

The second study, reported more recently by Sears, Maccoby, and Levin, does not show sex differences in reactions to maternal punitiveness. For both boys and girls, mothers who indicated that they punished their children's aggressiveness severely tended to describe their children as highly aggressive (71, p. 259). While admitting the possibility that maternal punishment was a response to the child's aggressiveness, the authors argue that this punishment also is likely to have bred counteraggression in the children.

To summarize, the extent to which important socializing agents either reinforce or punish the individual's aggressive behavior appear to be important determinants of the degree to which the level of his overt hostility coincides with the strength of his aggressive drive. Evidence indicates that there is a positive association between these two variables if the socializing agents permit or encourage the expression of hostile behavior. Punishment of this behavior, on the other hand, seems to increase the strength of the instigation to aggression, although, particularly if it is intense enough, inhibiting direct overt aggression.

Past learning experiences apparently can also modify the relative dominance of the instigation to aggression in the hierarchy of frustration-produced instigations by reinforcing other modes of response. Experiments suggest that it is possible to teach nursery school (32) and elementary school (14) children to react "constructively" to frustrating situations.

Several writers, when describing characteristic modes of behavior, refer to constructive frustration reactions as a manifestation of a high "frustration tolerance" (e.g., 61, p. 385), while others (e.g., 7) prefer to employ the construct, "strong ego control." In the last-mentioned paper, Block and Martin show, in an extension of the classic Barker, Dembo, and Lewin (5) study, that "ego-control capacity" defined independently in terms of ability to delay gratification and low cosatiation,[4] is predictive of individual differences in reactions to frustration. In a sample of 22 preschool children, those with low "ego-control" responded to a frustration with less constructive play behavior and acted aggressively more frequently than the other children. Consistent with this finding, Livson and Mussen (39) report that in a sample of 36 nursery school children the above two measures of ego control were negatively related to indices of aggressive behavior obtained in a two-week observation period (the correlation was significant only for the cosatiation measure).

Other individual characteristics apparently affecting reactions to frustration have been described as well. Rosenzweig found that *S*s are most likely to react aggressively to frustration experiences when they possess relatively great confidence and ability (60). According to Zander (85) extroverted *S*s tend to show more aggression against the frustrating experimenter than introverted *S*s. Lindzey indicates that *S*s high in minority group prejudice are more likely to react emotionally to frustrations but not necessarily with aggression (38). The sex of the *S* has frequently been found to be a determinant of response to frustration, with males usually reported as displaying more aggression than females (65; 71, p. 264; 72; 84). Social class membership often is said to be related to the extent to which aggression is a characteristic frustration-reaction (e.g., 46, 64), but this has not always been confirmed (e.g., 71, p. 265).

[4] Cosatiation is the satiation of one drive resulting from the satiation of another drive.

Finally, there is suggestive evidence concerning the home environments that affect the learning of persistently hostile behavior. Allinsmith found that middle-class (but not lower-class) males are most likely to feel guilty about their aggressive death wishes when their mothers have employed psychological rather than physical discipline (48, p. 155). Sears, Maccoby, and Levin (71) show that mothers who characteristically employ physical punishment and/or who are relatively cold in their affectional interaction with their children also tend to describe their children as highly aggressive. (The *r*'s are very low but still significant.) Bornston and Coleman (8) have somewhat similar results with regard to maternal coldness. After administering the Rosenzweig P-F Study to 56 college students and a parent attitude survey to the students' mothers, they found that the frequency of aggressive (extrapunitive plus intrapunitive) responses on the personality test was significantly positively related to both maternal domineering and ignoring attitudes toward the child. The Sears group also reports that the prolonged absence of the father from the home produces a relatively low level of fantasy aggression in preschool boys, but not girls (65, 69). Other studies along these lines are cited by Child (11, pp. 669–672). In conclusion, both Sears, Maccoby, and Levin (71, p. 266) and Child (11, p. 670) offer suggestions as to how parents should respond to a child's aggressiveness if they want to avoid producing a characteristically hostile child.

Opposing Hypotheses

Most of the attacks upon the *Frustration and Aggression* hypotheses concentrate on the basic postulate. As was indicated earlier, many writers have disputed the contention that frustration always leads to some form of aggression, and their objections are not necessarily overcome by Miller's 1941 revision (49). This later statement still proposes that an instigation to some form of aggression is an invariant product of frustration, even though other instigations may be stronger, while the critics usually suggest that only certain classes of frustrations give rise to hostility. Substantially in agreement with one another, they maintain that aggression is a reaction only to threatening frustrations or attacks, and does not occur in response to sheer deprivations (e.g., 41, 61).

However, these critics have not satisfactorily overcome the major difficulty inherent in this alternative formulation: the a priori specification of the operations distinguishing "threat" or "attack" from "deprivation." It obviously is not enough to state that the former involves the security of the organism while the latter does not; for example, even minor deprivations can provoke aggression at times (17, p. 31), suggesting either that this alternative hypothesis is incorrect, or that deprivations can become threats depending upon changing conditions of the organism. Those arguing for the latter point of view can easily find themselves holding a circular definition of "threat." Taking a somewhat different approach, McClelland hypothesizes that an individual is most likely to display defensive behavior, including aggression, when he is faced by an unknown danger and has no problem-solving response readily available (44, pp. 504–505).

Clearly, as Sears has pointed out in the 1941 symposium on the *Frustration-Aggression* hypotheses, one of the major problems in the study of hostile behavior has to do with "the determination of the specific factors which cause one kind of frustration-reaction rather than another to occur" (66, p. 345), and the question of whether qualitatively different classes of frustrations produce different reactions must be included as one of the more important aspects of this problem. It also is clear that an unequivocal answer to this question will come only from carefully controlled experiments rather than from questionnaire investigations posing hypothetical situations to which *S*s are asked to respond.

Three papers appearing in the last several years illustrate the difficulties in obtaining answers to this question. Graham et al. (24) state that an aggressive act directed against *S* can be interpreted not only as an interference with some drive such as self-esteem, (this is the interpretation employed in our earlier citation of this study) but also as an attack (or threat). In order to demonstrate that only the latter produce aggressive reactions, it is necessary to establish independent operational definitions of "degree-of-blocking" and "strength of attack."

While such a distinction conceivably could be made in a questionnaire investigation this type of procedure is particularly susceptible to the intrusion of *S*s' own hypotheses. They may be more likely to respond in terms of what they *believe* is, or should be, the case when presented with questionnaire descriptions of hypothetical situations that when actually confronted with a frustrating event. Pastore (57), for example, has argued that the frustrating situations referred to by Doob and Sears in their questionnaire study (17, p. 29), evoked hostile reactions primarily because these frustrations were unreasonable or arbitrary in nature. Employing a similar procedure, he showed that *S*s are significantly more likely to indicate they would react aggressively when given hypothetical arbitrary frustrations than when the frustrations appear "reasonable." (Cohen (13) has obtained identical results with the "arbitrary—reasonable frustration" variable utilizing the same procedure.) However, Pastore acknowledges that the *S*s could have inhibited aggressive responses when the frustrations were not arbitrary because hostility was "unreasonable." If this is the case, we might also speculate that this inhibition is more evident in a questionnaire investigation than in an actual experiment.

Pastore also proposes another explanation of his results that is similar to an hypothesis advanced by several writers (e.g., 85). He suggests that the arbitrary frustration involves the frustration of an expectancy (e.g., and *S* had expected to get on a bus; when it suddenly passed him by, this expectancy was frustrated). According to this view, then, aggressive reactions are most likely when the expected attainment of a goal is blocked. Bateson presents an essentially similar hypothesis in his discussion of cultural factors affecting the frustration-aggression relationship (6). Because of continual frustration, particularly at the hands of their mothers, the Balinese presumably do not learn to expect strong satisfaction, and therefore, Bateson argues, "they are infinitely willing to suffer interruption" (6, p. 353).

THE NATURE AND TARGET OF THE AGGRESSIVE RESPONSE

Theoretical Principles

The F-A discussion of factors affecting the nature and target of the aggressive response, particularly as elaborated by later theoretical papers (e.g., 50), must be considered among the prime examples of the benefits to be derived from the wedding of learning theory and psychoanalysis. The concept of generalization, developed largely through laboratory investigations of learning, is integrated in a highly fruitful manner with the often rich insights provided by psychoanalysis.

The first specific hypothesis listed by Dollard and his associates has to do with the strength of various hostile tendencies. "The strongest instigation, aroused by a frustration, is to acts of aggression directed against the agent perceived to be the source of the frustration and progressively weaker instigations are aroused to progressively less direct acts of aggression" (17, p. 39). The second half of this hypothesis appears to be based upon the notion of response generalization; "the more direct acts of aggression will be those which are more similar . . . to the act of most direct aggression" (17, p. 39). Indirect evidence supporting the first part of the hypothesis is reported in the previously cited study by Doob and Sears. Their *S*s indicated that acts of direct aggression were more satisfying to them than other, more indirect, forms of aggression.

In an interesting extension of the principle that aggression is directed against the object perceived to be the source of the frustration, Dollard, Doob, et al. hypothesize that self-aggression results when the self is seen as the frustrating agent. Therefore, "self-restraint of an act of aggression should instigate aggression against the self" (17, p. 48).

Since the interference with a directly aggressive response is an additional frustration adding to the total strength of the instigation to aggression (17, p. 40), as has been shown earlier, another hypothesis is derived: "The greater the degree of inhibition specific to a more direct act of aggression, the more probable will be the occurrence of less direct acts of aggression" (17, p. 40).

Similarly, if acts of aggression directed against a given object are prevented there will be a tendency for the individual to attack other objects. In a later paper (50), Miller shows that this phenomenon, labeled "displacement" by psychoanalytic theory, can be understood as a case of stimulus generalization. He also points out the importance of determining whether the direct act of aggression is prevented by the absence of the perceived instigating object or by conflict (produced by anticipation of punishment for aggression or by aggression-anxiety). If it is the former, displaced responses will occur to other similar objects and the strongest hostile response will occur to the most similar object present. If there is conflict, however, on the assumption that the gradient of generalization of the interfering responses is steeper than that of the aggressive responses they inhibit, it is predicted that the strongest displaced hostile act will occur to stimulus objects which have an intermediate degree of similarity to the original object. Increasing the relative strength of the inhibitory response serves to shift the displacement to a less similar target, while a more similar target will be attacked the greater the relative strength of the instigation to aggression. Increasing the aggressive drive also raises the likelihood that increasingly dissimilar objects will be capable of evoking responses.

Three studies are reported by the authors of *Frustration and Aggression* in support of the principle of displacement. First, it was shown that rats who had been trained to strike at another rat would attack a celluloid doll when no other rat was present (17, p. 42). Second, in a study carried out by Miller and Bugelski, experimentally frustrated *S*s tended to rate their friends (who had not been responsible for the frustration) lower on a personality scale than did control *S*s who had not been subjected to these frustrations (17, pp. 42–43). The last experiment, also conducted by Miller and Bugelski, is frequently cited by proponents of the "scapegoat" theory of prejudice. Boys in a CCC camp displayed less favorable attitudes toward Mexicans and Japanese after a frustration (17, pp. 43–44).

Empirical Investigations

French's previously mentioned study of "organized" and "unorganized" groups contains observations supporting the view that aggression tends to be directed against the agent perceived to be the source of the frustration (22, p. 286). Pepitone and Reichling (59) also report corroborating observations: over all groups in their experiment the major target for hostility (in terms of mean seconds of expression) was the insulting *E*, rather than Psychology, the experiment, or the physical setting.

McClelland presents suggestive evidence for the proposition that self-restraint of an act of aggression leads to self-aggression (44, p. 516). Utilizing the results of a study by MacKinnon, he argues that intropunitives (those who tend to blame themselves for a frustration, i.e. who are high in self-aggression) had been restrained from aggression and other antisocial acts as children by the development of internal standards of conscience. "Consequently these internal restraints would more often be perceived as frustrators by them and aggression should consequently be more often directed against the self for imposing them. . . ." On the basis of a significant negative correlation between intensity of overt aggression and self-aggression, Thibaut and Riecken (80) consider acts of aggression toward the self to be a "sensitive symptom of strength of inhibition of aggression."

French (22) also reports findings in support of the hypothesis that indirect acts of aggression are more likely to result the greater the inhibition of direct aggression. The "organized groups" in his study exhibited less social restraint than the "unorganized" groups, presumably because the members of the former groups had known each other longer. Thus, where there were 61 instances of direct aggression (physical attacks, verbal hostility) in the organized groups, the inhibiting social restraints in the unorganized groups apparently produced only indirect acts of hostility (blaming, dominating others, arguing, hostile jokes). Explicitly employing the concept of response generalization, Dinwiddie (15) showed that *S*s with high scores on a scale of "social anxiety" exhibit reliably more indirect aggression responses to the Rosenzweig P-F Study than the *S*s low on this anxiety measure with hostility level (as assessed by a manifest hostility scale) held constant statistically. The "social anxiety" is assumed to serve as an aggression-inhibitor.

In contrast to the previously mentioned experiments demonstrating a shift in the target of aggression (i.e., displacement) when direct attacks are prevented, several studies have yielded negative results (e.g., 21, 38, 76). The lack of displaced aggression in two of these investigations (38, 76) is regarded by some writers as limiting the generality of the displaced hostility—"scapegoat" theory of prejudice. Thus, Allport comments, "It is not true that a defenseless minority is always chosen for displacement purposes" (1, p. 351).[5]

However, Miller's conflict model (50) proposes that displacement should occur only in situations resembling but yet psychologically distant (in terms of either time, space or similarity) from the situation originally eliciting the inhibited aggressive responses. A given stimulus object will not be attacked solely because it is available if it is either too close to or too far removed from the original instigating situation on some appropriate stimulus-generalization gradient. Doll play investigations of hostility can provide relevant data. Since fantasy activities in a nursery school setting probably are sufficiently removed from the instigating home environment, aggressive tendencies that are punished in the home situation, and therefore, that are inhibited, should become manifest in doll play. Several studies, employing doll play measures of aggression, demonstrate that children who are severely punished at home for aggressiveness exhibit greater fantasy aggression than less severely punished children (10, 36, 70, also discussed in 67, 68).

Two recent correlational investigations also support Miller's analysis of displacement. Murney (53) asked judges to rank 20 figures taken from Schneidman's Make-A-Picture-Story Test on the basis of a "global impression" of their similarity to the figure of an army officer also taken from this test. An agreed-upon similarity continuum was constructed employing 10 of the figures. The *E* then told a story to each of 90 male patients at a VA center in which an army officer

[5] Feshbach and Singer (20) recently have obtained results consistent with the displaced hostility—"scapegoat" theory of prejudice.

arbitrarily frustrated a private, and they were asked to describe what the private would do. They were encouraged to give an aggressive response and could choose any of the 11 figures (including the officer) as the object of aggression. Aggression drive and anxiety scores for each *S* were derived from TAT responses. The stronger *S*'s instigation to aggression the more similar the figure chosen as the aggressive target was to the instigator ($r = .82$ with anxiety held constant). The object for the target of displaced hostility shifted in the direction of greater dissimilarity with increased anxiety ($r = -.72$ with the aggressive drive measure partialed out).

Wright (81) analyzed 12 folk tales from each of 33 societies for signs of displaced aggression and related these to a measure of aggression anxiety based upon ratings of the extent to which children were punished for aggression. The greater the aggression anxiety the less similar both the object and the agent of the aggression was to the hero of the folk tale. Wright also found that the intensity of the fantasy aggression increased reliably with the severity of the punishment for aggression.

CATHARSIS

Theoretical Principles

As described by Dollard and his associates, there are many points of similarity between obviously physiological drives, such as hunger and sex, and the instigation to aggression. This assumed similarity is nowhere seen more clearly than in their discussion of catharsis. When an organism makes an appropriate goal response, such as eating, the strength of the relevant physiological drive (in this case, hunger) is reduced. Causing injury to another, particularly the frustrating agent, is held to be the aggressive drive's goal response, and therefore, the occurrence of an act of aggression supposedly reduces the instigation to aggression (17, p. 50).

Their discussion of catharsis also includes a reference to an important implication of the joint operation of catharsis and displacement: "With the level of frustration held roughly constant, there should be an inverse relationship between the occurrence of different forms of aggression" (17, p. 51). Just as displacement to other forms of aggression follows the inhibition of any aggressive response, the cathartic effect resulting from the expression of a hostile act should reduce the instigation to other aggressive behaviors.

Two admittedly "slender threads of evidence" are presented for this derivation (17, p. 52). First, in a sleep-deprivation experiment involving six male college students, the *S* who expressed the most overt aggression injured himself least in a self-administered algesimeter test. Conversely, the *S* rated as expressing the least overt aggression inflicted the most injurious pressure upon himself. Second, in an experiment by Miller and Bugelski, *S*s who gave their frustrating partners relatively low ratings "did not drop so markedly in their own ratings of themselves, the correlation between the ratings of partner and self being −.3 (S.E.2= ± .1)." In both experiments, therefore, aggression directed against others presumably reduced the intensity of self-directed aggression, and/or vice versa.

It is important to note that this chapter also suggests two limiting conditions (unfortunately relegated to a footnote on p. 50); (*a*) the cathartic reduction of hostility may only be temporary if the original frustration persists, and (*b*) "repetition of a mode of release may presumably produce learning of it." A third condition possibly limiting the generality of the catharsis hypothesis is pointed to by Morlan (52). Dollard earlier (16) had shown how an aggressive act committed by an individual might stimulate him to further aggression. Aggressive responses (either overt or covert) can provoke a fear of retaliation which, in turn, increases the instigation to aggression (presumably because the fear of retaliation, in itself, is a frustration). In sumamry, according to the F-A group, the occurrence of an aggressive act reduces the instigation to aggression, unless (*a*) the frustration persists, adding further strength to the aggressive drive, (*b*) the aggressive behavior becomes a learned response, or (*c*) implicit verbal responses are aroused or aggression-anxiety is produced which lead to further frustrations.

The following section is a review of studies having relevance to the catharsis hypothesis. As will be shown, the results tend to be equivocal for two main reasons. They either fail to take cognizance of the above mentioned limiting conditions (e.g., not controlling the frustrations suffered by the *S*s), or they fail to distinguish between aggressive responses and the instigation to aggression. Obviously, this latter failure means the investigator cannot demonstrate clearly that the decrease in hostile behavior is due to drive reduction and not to response inhibition.

Empirical Investigations

The studies can be organized in terms of the types of situations in which *S*s express aggression. Several investigations attempt to assess the strength of the instigation to aggression in children following a series of experiences in which aggressive behavior is permitted or encouraged (3, 4, 19, 34). Some measure the drive strength in young adults after athletic contests (29, 30, 77), while others deal with experimentally aroused hostility and then seek to determine the level of the residual aggression after the occurrence of aggressive responses (18, 22, 58, 74, 78, 79).

To discuss these in order, two studies deserve special comment because of the widespread interest in play therapy as a psychotherapeutic technique. Kenny (34) provided an experimental group of 15 first-grade children with two "catharsis" situations utilizing a play therapy technique. A matched group of 15 children in the control condition spent an equal time playing on the swings or with a jigsaw puzzle. Using the first five episodes of the Korner Incomplete Story Test for the assessment of initial aggressive drive strength, and the last five episodes of this test for the final hostility measure, it was found that the *control* group showed a decrease in total aggression scores which was significantly greater than the slight decrease in the experimental group. Feshbach (19) also found no evidence of a cathartic reduction of hostility as a function of the usual play therapy. As was mentioned earlier, he observed that boys initially low in aggressive behavior increased significantly in overt aggression after a series of permissive free play experiences, contrary to the tendency noted by Kenny. There was no significant effect for the girl *S*s. Feshbach points out that the *S*s in this experiment were not protected from continuing sources of frustration so that the catharsis hypothesis cannot be discarded. However, he also found that play with aggressive toys seemed to promote more inappropriate later aggression than play with neutral toys.

While these investigations appear to threaten several important assumptions involved in the use of play experiences as a therapeutic technique, they do not seriously attack the F-A catharsis hypothesis. There are a number of obvious flaws in their design: (*a*) the *S*s in these studies were not isolated from continuing frustration; (*b*) the amount of frustration provided by the experimental tasks was not controlled; (Kenny's *S*s given the "cathartic play" situation may have been more interested in the swings or jigsaw puzzles so that they actually were angered more than the control *S*s); and (*c*) there is no information as to the amount of aggressive behavior expressed in the various conditions prior to the administration of the residual hostility instrument; (thus, the *S*s playing on the swings may have made many more aggressive responses than the experimental *S*s).

Appel (3), obtained results consistent with the catharsis hypothesis, but alternative explanations are available in this case as well. Children who had been in a nursery school that permitted fighting showed less hostility later in kindergarten than children coming from a nursery school that discouraged fighting. However, as Morlan notes, the former children may have fought less because their greater experience with quarrels had led them to develop better techniques of dealing with one another (52, pp. 3–4).

The studies of individuals engaged in combative sport illustrate the necessity of distinguishing between aggressive drive strength and response inhibition. Johnson and Hutton (30) administered the H-T-P test to eight collegiate wrestlers under three conditions: (*a*) before the wrestling season; (*b*) four to five hours before the first intercollegiate match of the season; and (*c*) the morning after the match. They report that aggressive feelings increased prior to the wrestling match, supporting Dollard's self-stimulation hypothesis, and then decreased considerably ("in most cases to a level below condition A") following the match. However, the reliability of these differences is not known since no statistical data are presented. Nor is it stated whether the psychologist who scored the protocols knew the conditions under which they were obtained. This type of research obviously requires some control over the intrusion of the projective test scorer's own hypotheses. In another inadequately reported study (although some statistical data are given), Husman (29) obtained the responses of collegiate boxers, wrestlers, cross-country runners and a group of non-athletes to three projective tests, including the TAT. Statistically significant differences were found among the various groups employing the TAT measures of aggression, with the boxers showing considerably less aggression than the others. However, the boxers also were rated on the Rosenzweig P-F Study administered shortly after a match as "possessing more superego" than the control group. Husman believes this increase in "superego" is to be expected. The boxers aggressive behavior in athletic contests presumably made them feel guilty even though this aggression is socially sanctioned. After the boxing season their mean rating on Rosenzweig's "superego" trait tended to decrease (nonsignificantly) approaching that of a normal population. Husman does not report any significant differences for wrestlers.

Stone (77) also obtained indications of inhibited hostility following a socially sanctioned athletic contest. The TAT was given to football players both during and after the athletic season, and their responses were compared with the responses of a matched control group. There was no difference between the two groups in fantasy aggression during the football season, but the football players showed significantly less manifest aggression on the TAT following the completion of the season. Interestingly enough, however, the aggression that the football players did display tended to be of a "projective" nature, i.e., it was attributed to an impersonal source. Stone argues that this aggression was projected from the self onto an impersonal source because of *S*'s aggression-anxiety. Clark (12), in a study reported earlier, also obtained a high proportion of "projective hostility" TAT responses and relatively few manifest aggression themes in an experimental condition presumably arousing guilt.

Thus, there is reason to believe that sanctioned overt aggression may lead to a reduction in the display of hostility, but not necessarily because of catharsis. The present studies suggest that aggression-anxiety frequently results (at least in middle class college students) from aggressive actions, even in situations where aggression is encouraged or permitted, and this anxiety may inhibit subsequent aggressive responses. Therefore, before an investigator can demonstrate catharsis unequivocally, it is necessary for him to show that any decrease in overt hostility is not due to the arousal of aggression-anxiety.

While the above studies have all the advantages inherent in dealing with "real-life" situations, they typically also suffer from inadequate controls. Ultimately, then, the crucial tests of the catharsis hypothesis must come from laboratory investigations utilizing experimentally aroused hostility. Several studies carried out under relatively controlled conditions have obtained results which, on the surface at least, are consistent with the notion of catharsis (18, 22, 58, 74, 78). However, there are plausible alternative explanations in all of these cases.

Thus, in the experiment by Pepitone and Reichling (58) mentioned earlier, the investigators angered all *S*s and then created conditions either facilitating or inhibiting the occurrence of overt aggression, i.e., high or low liking among the group members. The 13 two-man high-liking groups at first expressed relatively strong hostility toward the instigator and then showed a steady decline in open aggression toward him. The 13 low-liking groups, in contrast, did not show this decline. Furthermore, in accord with the catharsis hypothesis, the high-liking groups, which had expressed a reliably greater total volume of aggression toward the instigator, rated him significantly more favorably at the conclusion of the experiment than the low-liking groups. Here again it is possible that the relatively strong hostility expressed by the members of the high-liking groups had evoked strong guilt feelings (or aggression-anxiety). These feelings could have (*a*) inhibited the later aggressive responses and (*b*) produced the favorable ratings of the instigator. In addition, as Pepitone and Reichling suggest on the basis of (already cited) findings by Thibaut and Coules (79), the restraints against aggressive behavior felt by the members of the low-liking groups could have added to the hostility-producing frustration. Guilt or aggression-anxiety can also account for French's observation that the groups that had previously expressed the most aggression tended to be the least aggressive in the next situation (22, p. 288).

Somewhat similar explanations, plus others, may be offered for Thibaut's results (78). After frustrating the status aspirations of 18 five- or six-person groups, he succeeded in having these *S*s direct some aggression against the high-status teams. Nine of the low-status teams then won high status while the other nine remained low in status. Since the frustration does not persist in the former groups, they are the only ones who should demonstrate a cathartic reduction of hostility. For these teams the correlation between pre- and postupward mobility overt aggression is $-.69$ ($p = .05$). For the persistently frustrated teams remaining in the low-status position this r is only $-.22$.

This difference in correlations can be interpreted either according to the catharsis formulation or in terms of a quite different process discussed more recently by Thibaut and his colleagues (80, pp. 95–97). They have shown that the instigation to aggression is reduced when an individual's hostile action appears to further his ends. Thus, the decrease in aggressive behavior observed in the successfully upward-mobile low-status teams could have resulted from the *S*'s judgment that this behavior had been at least partly responsible for their rise in status. It also is possible that the group members who previously had expressed a good deal of hostility had developed guilt feelings about this when their frustration was shown to be only temporary (i.e., when they were elevated to the high-status position).

These guilt feelings then could have produced the decline in overt hostility as well as the second catharsis-like finding noted by Thibaut; the successfully upward-mobile low-status teams did not give less favorable sociometric ratings to the other, high-status teams in the second part of the experiments (after their status rise) as did the persistently low-status groups. The former groups could have rated the teams they displaced relatively more favorably because of guilt created by their previous aggression.

In one of the most recent investigations of catharsis, Feshbach (18) tested the hypothesis that the instigation to aggression could be reduced through symbolic satisfactions. Two experimental treatments were applied to introductory psychology classes angered by an insulting lecturer: (*a*) interpolation of fantasy activity (administration of four TAT cards) before having the *S*s respond to the two main aggression measures—a brief questionnaire assessing attitudes toward the experiment, and the Sentence Completion Test; and (*b*) interpolation of nonfantasy activity before the *S*s responded to these forms. A control group of *S*s was given the interpolated fantasy task without the insult treatment. Both aggression instruments proved to be sensitive to aggression arousal, with the insulted fantasy group scoring significantly lower on these measures than the insulted nonfantasy group. The insulted fantasy group also expressed significantly more total aggression to the TAT cards than the noninsulted fantasy group. Further support for the catharsis hypothesis is found in the significant negative r between TAT aggression and aggression on the questionnaire ($r = -.25$, $p = .01$) in the insulted group. Feshbach presents some inconclusive evidence suggesting that the lowered aggression in the insulted fantasy group was not due to guilt arousal (his guilt measures had not been validated), and that the greater aggression in the control groups was not due to the frustrating qualities of the interpolated neutral task.

However, the previously mentioned findings reported by Thibaut and Coules (79) cast some doubt on Feshbach's last contention. These writers have shown that the type of interference with the occurrence of aggressive responses brought about by the administration of the neutral task could have increased the aggressive drive. McClelland, maintaining his previously expressed (43) views against the notion of drive satisfaction through implicit symbolic responses, also questions Feshbach's interpretations (45, p. 53). He suggests that the instructions for the TAT ("feel free to write whatever you like . . .") reduced *S*s' irritation with the insulting *E*. Along these lines, the present writer has observed that frustrated *S*s may find the comparatively novel TAT test sufficiently enjoyable to overcome much of their frustration-produced annoyance.[6]

Evaluation

The catharsis hypothesis is not accepted by all personality theorists (e.g., 1, 44). Allport (1), for example, disputes the concept, implicit in many discussions of catharsis, of a "reservoir" of hostility that may be "drained off" in any number of different ways. In opposition to this "drainage theory," he cites studies (e.g., 75) reporting positive correlations among different modes of aggression instead of the negative correlations explicity predicted by Dollard, Doob, et al. (17, p. 51). In general, Allport suggests, "All this evidence is hard on the theory that free-floating aggression may be 'drained off' from one object to another. . . . It simply is not true that a given quantum of free-floating aggression can be used up in this, that, or the other way" (1, p. 359).

Dollard and his colleagues were aware of findings similar to that reported by Allport (but discuss them only in a footnote to p. 52):

> It appears that there are positive correlations between the occurrence of various forms of overt aggression and between various forms of non-overt aggression. The reciprocal relationship is probably between overt and non-overt on the one hand and between self-directed and object-directed on the other and may not appear at all if the amount of frustration is not held constant.

There is evidence both for and against aspects of this hypothesized negative relationship between different modes of aggression. McClelland cast some doubt on the expectation of an inverse relation between overt and covert hostility (44, pp. 516–517). He notes that in Stone's study of sanctioned overt aggression (77) there were many cases of football players who exhibited high aggression both overtly on the field and, covertly, in response to the TAT, or who were low in both. The previously cited results obtained by Lesser (35) and Mussen and Naylor (54) are in accord with this observation. However, there also are recent experimental findings (80, p. 113) showing that angered *S*s who attack others tend reliably not to demonstrate

[6] Feshbach did not have equal sex ratios in all conditions. Preliminary evidence collected by the present writer suggests that men "get over" their anger much more quickly than women after working on interpolated tasks.

self-aggression, supporting the "slender thread of evidence" reported by the Yale psychologist in defense of their hypothesis (17, p. 52).

Again, the above evidence is inconclusive with regard either to the confirmation or rejection of the catharsis hypothesis. The reported positive correlations among various modes of aggression could well stem from generalized habits. Studies of social prejudice have shown repeatedly that hostility is a broadly generalized response for the prejudiced individual. Strangers, minority group members, foreigners, and all who are "different," tend to be equated as potentially dangerous stimulus objects and all arouse aggressive responses within him. Thus, the person who is consistently aggressive, overtly and covertly, might well have learned to tie many objectively different kinds of situations together on a single stimulus generalization gradient. All of these situations for example, might be labeled by him as threatening, with an instigation to aggression resulting from the labeling response.

In general, then, a major difficulty with these studies, regardless of whether they show positive or negative relationships among various modes of aggression, is that they are correlational in nature. To use the negative relationship cited above as an illustration, we cannot prove that the self-aggression subsequently reduced the instigation to other-aggression and/or vice versa. The negative correlation may be due to some common process acting upon both types of responses. Self-aggression and other-aggression may be relatively stable and incompatible response patterns through past learning so that any given individual is likely either to attack himself or another when frustrated. This suggestion, of course, is the basis of Rosenzweig's frustration-response typology (61).

Experimental investigations can overcome this type of difficulty if designed properly, i.e., if there is cognizance of the conditions limiting the generality of the catharsis hypothesis. As was pointed out earlier, an adequate test of this hypothesis must: (*a*) determine whether there is inhibited aggression and, if possible, eliminate aggression-anxiety, (*b*) protect the *S*s from continuing frustration, (*c*) demonstrate that a greater volume of aggressive behavior was expressed in the "cathartic" condition than in the control condition, and (*d*) analyze separately the results for the *S*s who have a "habit" of behaving aggressively when faced by frustration (and, consequently, who would persist in this type of response long after other *S*s have ceased acting in a hostile manner).

The term "catharsis" also has been applied to a phenomenon

somewhat different from that discussed by the F-A psychologists. McClelland and Apicella (42), for example, differentiate between anger and aggression, and they propose that the emotion anger has "some tension-reducing capacity of its own *prior* to the discovery of some object against which it may be directed" (cited in 44, p. 513). Sears, Maccoby, and Levin refer to a similar process when they suggest that "adults often experience this relief of tension after they have lost their tempers—they speak of 'letting off steam'. . . ." (71, p. 225). However, they believe the emotional tension results from the approach-avoidance conflict of wanting to injure but being afraid or reluctant to do so. Whatever the source of this tension, this usage (reduction of discomfort) is not identical with the hypothesis formulated by Dollard, Doob, et al. (which involves a decrease in the aggressive drive).

Recent experimental evidence provided by Worchel (83) indicates that the expression of aggression can reduce performance-interfering tension. After aggressing against the frustrating experimenter either directly to him or indirectly to his assistant, college students performed significantly better on a digit-symbol test than the insulted *S*s not given this opportunity for "catharsis." Worchel assumes that the performance of the latter *S*s was disrupted by their anxiety and aggression, while these interfering emotional states were dispelled in the cathartic treatment. Along these lines, we might speculate whether the blocking of aggressive responses in the noncatharsis conditions was one of the frustrations interfering with effective performance. If so, the performance difference might be due to this latter type of frustration predominantly. At any rate, the reduction of performance-disruptive emotional states following the expression of hostility does not necessarily mean that the instigation to aggression also was reduced.

REFERENCES

1. Allport, G. W. *The nature of prejudice.* Cambridge, Mass.: Addison-Wesley, 1954.
2. Anastasi, Anne, Cohen, Nadis, & Spatz, Dorothy. A study of fear and anger in college students through the controlled diary method. *J. Genet. Psychol.*, 1948, **73**, 243–249.
3. Appel, M. H. Aggressive behavior of nursery school children and adult procedures in dealing with such children. *J. Exptl. Educ.*, 1942, **2**, 195–199.
4. Bach, G. R. Young children's play fantasies. *Psychol. Monogr.*, 1945, **59**, No. 2 (Whole No. 272).

5. Barker, R. G., Dembo, Tamara, & Lewin, K. Frustration and regression: an experiment with young children. *Univ. Iowa Stud. Child Welf.*, 1941, **18**, 1-314.
6. Bateson, G. The frustration-aggression hypothesis and culture. *Psychol. Rev.*, 1941, **48**, 350–355.
7. Block, Jeanne, & Martin, B. C. Predicting the behavior of children under frustration. *J. Abnorm. Soc. Psychol.*, 1955, **51**, 281–285.
8. Bornston, Frieda L., & Coleman, J. C. The relationship between certain parents' attitudes toward child rearing and the direction of aggression of their young adult offspring. *J. Clin. Psychol.*, 1956, **12**, 41–44.
9. Brown, J. S., & Farber, I. E. Emotions conceptualized as intervening variables—with suggestions toward a theory of frustration. *Psychol. Bull.*, 1951, **48**, 465–495.
10. Chasdi, Eleanor H., & Lawrence, Margaret S. Some antecedents of aggression and effects of frustration in doll play. In D. McClelland (Ed.), *Studies in motivation.* New York: Appleton-Century-Crofts, 1955.
11. Child, I. L. Socialization. In G. Lindzey (Ed.), *Handbook of social psychology*, Vol. 2, Ch. 18. Cambridge, Mass.: Addison-Wesley, 1954.
12. Clark, R. A. The effect of sexual motivation on phantasy. In D. McClelland (Ed.), *Studies in motivation.* New York: Appleton-Century-Crofts, 1955.
13. Cohen, A. R. Social norms, arbitrariness of frustration, and status of the agent of frustration in the frustration–aggression hypothesis. *J. Abnorm. Soc. Psychol.*, 1955, **51**, 222–226.
14. Davitz, J. R. The effects of previous training on postfrustration behavior. *J. Abnorm. Soc. Psychol.*, 1954, **47**, 309–315.
15. Dinwiddie, F. M. *An application of the principle of response generalization to the prediction of displacement of aggressive responses.* Washington: Catholic Univ. of America Press, 1955.
16. Dollard, J. Hostility and fear in social life. *Soc. Forces*, 1938, **17**, 15–25.
17. Dollard, J., Doob, L. W., Miller, N. E., Mowrer, O. H., & Sears, R. R. *Frustration and aggression.* New Haven: Yale Univ. Press, 1939.
18. Feshbach, S. The drive-reducing function of fantasy behavior. *J. Abnorm. Soc. Psychol.*, 1955, **50**, 3–11.
19. Feshbach, S. The catharsis hypothesis and some consequences of interaction with aggressive and neutral play objects. *J. Pers.*, 1956, **24**, 449–462.
20. Feshbach, S., & Singer, R. The effects of personal and shared threats upon social prejudice. *J. Abnorm. Soc. Psychol.*, 1957, **54**, 411–416.
21. Frederiksen, N. The effects of frustration on negative behavior of young children. *J. Genet. Psychol.*, 1942, **61**, 203–226.
22. French, J. R. P. Organized and unorganized groups under fear and frustration. In K. Lewin, C. E. Meyers, J. Kalhorn, & M. L. Farber (Eds.), *Authority and frustration. Univ. Iowa Stud. Child Welf.* Iowa City: Univ. of Iowa Press, 1944.
23. Gatling, F. P. Frustration reactions of delinquents using Rosenzweig's classification system. *J. Abnorm. Soc. Psychol.*, 1950, **45**, 749–752.
24. Graham, F. K., Charwat, W. A., Honig, A. S., & Weltz, P. C. Aggression as a function of the attack and the attacker. *J. Abnorm. Soc. Psychol.*, 1951, **46**, 512–520.
25. Haner, C. F., & Brown, P. A. Clarification of the instigation to action concept in the frustration-aggression hypothesis. *J. Abnorm. Soc. Psychol.*, 1955, **51**, 204–206.
26. Himmelweit, Hilde. Frustration and aggression: A review of recent experimental

work. In T. H. Pear (Ed.), *Psychological factors of peace and war.* New York: Philosophical Library, 1950.

27. Hokanson, J. E., & Gordon, J. E. The expression and inhibition of hostility in imaginative and overt behavior. *J. Abnorm. Soc. Psychol.*, 1958, **57**, 327–333.
28. Holzberg, J. D., Bursten, B., & Santiccioli, A. The reporting of aggression as an indication of aggressive tension. *J. Abnorm. Soc. Psychol.*, 1955, **50**, 12–18.
29. Husman, B. F. Aggression in boxers and wrestlers as measured by projective techniques. *Res. Quart. Am. Assn. Hlth. Phys. Educ.*, 1955, **26**, 421–425.
30. Johnson, W. R., & Hutton, D C. Effects of a combative sport upon personality dynamics as measured by a projective test. *Res. Quart. Am. Assn. Hlth. Phys. Educ.*, 1955, **26**, 49–53.
31. Kagan, J. The measurement of overt aggression from fantasy. *J. Abnorm. Soc. Psychol.*, 1956, **52**, 390–393.
32. Keister, M. E., & Updegraff, R. The behavior of young children in failure: an experimental attempt to discover and to modify undesirable responses of preschool children to failure. *Univ. Iowa Stud. Child Welf.*, 1938, **14**, 27–82.
33. Kelley, H. H. Communication in experimentally created hierarchies. *Hum. Relat.*, 1951, **4**, 39–56.
34. Kenny, D. T. *An experimental test of the catharsis theory of aggression.* Ann Arbor: Univ. Microfilms, 1953.
35. Lesser, G. S. The relationship between overt and fantasy aggression as a function of maternal response to aggression. *J. Abnorm. Soc. Psychol.*, 1957, **55**, 218–221.
36. Levin, H., & Sears, R. R. Identification with parents as a determinant of doll play aggression. *Child Develpm.*, 1956, **27**, 135–153.
37. Levin, H., & Turgeon, Valerie F. The influence of mother's presence on children's doll play aggression. *J. Abnorm. Soc. Psychol.*, 1957, **55**, 304–308.
38. Lindzey, G. An experimental examination of the scapegoat theory of prejudice. *J. Abnorm. Soc. Psychol.*, 1950, **45**, 296–309.
39. Livson, N., & Mussen, P. H. The relation of ego control to overt aggression and dependency. *J. Abnorm. Soc. Psychol.*, 1957, **55**, 66–71.
40. Marx, M. H. Some relations between frustration and drive. In M. R. Jones (Ed.), *Nebraska symposium on motivation, 1956.* Lincoln, Neb.: Univ. of Nebraska Press, 1956.
41. Maslow, A. H. Deprivation, threat and frustration. *Psychol. Rev.*, 1941, **48**, 364–366.
42. McClelland, D. C., & Apicella, F. S. A functional classification of verbal reactions to experimentally induced failure. *J. Abnorm. Soc. Psychol.*, 1945, **40**, 376–390.
43. McClelland, D. C., Clark, R. A., Roby, T. B., & Atkinson, J. W. The projective expression of needs: IV. The effect of need for achievement on thematic apperception. *J. Exptl. Psychol.*, 1949, **39**, 242–255.
44. McClelland, D. C. *Personality.* New York: Dryden, 1951.
45. McClelland, D. C. Personality. In P. R. Farnsworth, & Q. McNamar (Eds.), *Ann. Rev. Psychol.*, Vol. 7. Stanford: Annual Reviews, 1956.
46. McKee, J. P., & Leader, Florence, B. The relationship of socioeconomic status and aggression to the competitive behavior of pre-school children. *Child Develpm.*, 1955, **26**, 135–142.
47. McKellar, P. The emotion of anger in the expression of human aggressiveness. *Brit. J. Psychol.*, 1949, **39**, 148–155.
48. Miller, D. R., & Swanson, G. E. The study of conflict. In M. R. Jones (Ed.),

Nebraska symposium on motivation, 1956. Lincoln, Neb.: Univ. of Nebraska Press, 1956.

49. Miller, N. E. The frustration-aggression hypothesis. *Psychol. Rev.*, 1941, **48**, 337–342.
50. Miller, N. E. Theory and experiment relating psychoanalytic displacement to stimulus-response generalization. *J. Abnorm. Soc. Psychol.*, 1948, **43**, 155–178.
51. Mintz, A. A re-examination of correlations between lynchings and economic indices. *J. Abnorm. Soc. Psychol.*, 1946, **41**, 154–160.
52. Morlan, G. K. A note on the frustration-aggression theories of Dollard and his associates. *Psychol. Rev.*, 1949, **56**, 1–8.
53. Murney, R. G. *An application of the principle of stimulus generalization to the prediction of object displacement*, Washington, D.C.: Catholic Univ. of America Press, 1955.
54. Mussen, P. H., & Naylor, H. K. The relationships between overt and fantasy aggression. *J. Abnorm. Soc. Psychol.*, 1954, **49**, 235–240.
55. Newcomb, T. M. Autistic hostility and social reality. *Hum. Relat.*, 1947, **1**, 3–20.
56. Otis, N. B., & McCandless, B. Responses to repeated frustrations of young children differentiated according to need area. *J. Abnorm. Soc. Psychol.*, 1955, **50**, 349–353.
57. Pastore, N. The role of arbitrariness in the frustration-aggression hypothesis. *J. Abnorm. Soc. Psychol.*, 1952, **47**, 738–731.
58. Pepitone, A., & Reichling, G. Group cohesiveness and the expression of hostility. *Hum. Relat.*, 1955, **8**, 327–337.
59. Pepitone, A., & Kleiner, R. The effect of threat and frustration on group cohesiveness. *J. Abnorm. Soc. Psychol.*, 1957, **54**, 192–199.
60. Rosenzweig, S. The experimental measurement of types of reactions to frustration. In Murray, H. A. (Ed.), *Explorations in personality*. New York: Oxford Press, 1939.
61. Rosenzweig, S. An outline of frustration theory. In J. McV. Hunt (Ed.), *Personality and the behavior disorders*. New York: Ronald, 1944.
62. Rosenzweig, S., & Rosenzweig, L. Aggression in problem children and normals as evaluated by the Rosenzweig P-F study. *J. Abnorm. Soc. Psychol.*, 1952, **47**, 683–687.
63. Rotter, J. B., & Wickens, D. D. The consistency and generality of ratings of "social aggressiveness" made from observation of role playing situations. *Am. Psychol.*, 1947, **2**, 333.
64. Sargent, S. S. Reaction to frustration—a critique and hypothesis. *Psychol. Rev.*, 1948, **55**, 108–114.
65. Sears, Pauline S. Doll play aggression in normal young children: Influence of sex, age, sibling status, father's absence. *Psychol. Monogr.*, 1951, **65**, No. 6 (Whole No. 323).
66. Sears, R. R. Non-aggressive reactions to frustration. *Psychol. Rev.*, 1941, **48**, 343–346.
67. Sears, R. R. Effects of frustration and anxiety on fantasy aggression. *Am. J. Orthopsychiat.*, 1951, **21**, 498–505.
68. Sears, R. R. A theoretical framework for personality and social behavior. *Am. Psychol.*, 1951, **6**, 476–483.
69. Sears, R. R., Pintler, Margaret H., & Sears, Pauline S. Effect of father separation on preschool children's doll play aggression. *Child Develpm.*, 1946, **17**, 219–243.

70. Sears, R. R., Whiting, J. W. M., Nowlis, V., & Sears, Pauline S. Some child-rearing antecedents of aggression and dependency in young children. *Genet. Psychol. Monogr.*, 1953, **47**, 135–234.
71. Sears, R. R., Maccoby, Eleanor S., & Levin, H. *Patterns of child rearing*, Evanston, Ill.: Row, Peterson, 1957.
72. Seward, J. P. Aggressive behavior in the rat: I. General characteristics; age and sex differences. *J. Comp. Psychol.*, 1945, **38**, 175–197.
73. Seward, J. P. Aggressive behavior in the rat: III. The role of frustration. *J. Comp. Psychol.*, 1945, **38**, 225–238.
74. Seward, J. P. Aggressive behavior in the rat: IV. Submission as determined by conditioning, extinction and disuse. *J. Comp. Psychol.*, 1946, **39**, 51–76.
75. Stagner, R. Studies of aggressive social attitudes: I. Measurement and interrelation of selected attitudes. *J. Soc. Psychol.*, 1944, **20**, 109–120.
76. Stagner, R., & Congdon, C. S. Another failure to demonstrate displacement of aggression. *J. Abnorm. Soc. Psychol.*, 1955, **51**, 695–696.
77. Stone, A. A. *The effect of sanctioned overt aggression on total instigation to aggressive responses.* Unpublished honors thesis, Harvard Univ., 1950.
78. Thibaut, J. An experimental study of the cohesiveness of underpriviliged groups. *Hum. Relat.*, 1950, **3**, 251–278.
79. Thibaut, J., & Coules, J. The role of communication in the reduction of interpersonal hostility. *J. Abnorm. Soc. Psychol.*, 1952, **47**, 770–777.
80. Thibaut, J., & Riecken, H. Authoritarianism, status, and the communication of aggression. *Hum. Relat.*, 1955, **8**, 95–120.
81. Wright, G. O. Projection and displacement: a cross-cultural study of folk-tale aggression. *J. Abnorm. Soc. Psychol.*, 1954, **49**, 523–528.
82. Wright, M. E. The influence of frustration upon the social relations of young children. *Character and Pers.*, 1943, **12**, 111–122.
83. Worchel, P. Catharsis and the relief of hostility. *J. Abnorm. Soc. Psychol.*, 1957, **55**, 238–243.
84. Yarrow, L. J. The effect of antecedent frustration on projective play. *Psychol. Monogr.*, 1948, **62**, No. 6 (Whole No. 293).
85. Zander, A. F. A study of experimental frustration. *Psychol. Monogr.*, 1944, **56**, No. 3 (Whole No. 256).

11.3 THE GHETTO LOGIC

Magoroh Maruyama

It may seem that the current racial unrest is a conflict between the ghetto and the middle class. This view is oversimplified. It bypasses the immediate, more specific source of frictions that is invisible to the middle class. We need to understand the significance of a third, very thin social layer which acts as a buffer between the ghetto and the middle class. This is the layer of the "immediate oppressors" of the ghetto.

The immediate oppressor has two faces, or rather he has only one face but he looks different depending on who sees his face. To the ghetto, he appears to be an agent appointed by the whole middle class to exploit, harass, and abuse the ghetto. To the middle class, he is practically unknown. But if he ever comes into contact with middle-class people, he is indistinguishable from any law-abiding, dutiful, middle-class citizen. But the truth of the matter is that he operates behind the back of the honest portion of the middle class. He is a cheater and a social parasite in a double sense. First, he manipulates his legal power against the legally powerless in the ghetto in order to suck the economic blood out of the ghetto. Second, he corrodes the middle-class sense of justice and fairness while taking advantage of his connections with the middle class. He exists in spite of and thanks to, but generally not because of, the middle class.

The ghetto is powerless against the immediate oppressor. Therefore the task of discovering and eliminating the immediate oppressors falls squarely on the shoulders of the middle class. There are some middle-class citizens who knowingly or unknowingly support the immediate oppressors. But even those who have nothing to do with the immediate oppressors are nevertheless responsible for letting the immediate oppressors exploit the ghetto.

Source: English version of an article scheduled for the June 1968 issue of the *Revue de psychologie des peuples*. Reprinted with permission of the author and of the editor of the *Revue de psychologie des peuples*.

Today's tragedy lies in a twofold misunderstanding. The major portion of the middle class is unaware or incredulous of the abuse and the exploitation taking place in the ghetto. The ghetto, on the other hand, identifies the middle class with the immediate oppressors and attacks the entire middle class. The middle class, perplexed, retaliates back against the ghetto. This confirms the ghetto's belief that the whole middle class is against the ghetto. A vicious circle of self-fulfilling prophecy is at work.

The middle class is not a homogeneous entity. It consists of several components: (1) downright bigots; (2) those who exploit anybody, regardless of race; (3) those who are uninformed or incredulous of the abuse and the exploitation in the ghetto, and are therefore unsympathetic toward the ghetto uprising; (4) those who are against the abuse and the exploitation but do not know how to go about eliminating them.

Fortunately the first two are not the majority. The majority consists of the third category. This is the category of people who believe in hard work, honesty, and lawful order, and who cannot imagine that there are legally powerless people against whom the law can be misused. They are against the ghetto because they believe that the ghetto residents are lawless. But the very nature of their philosophy will make them support the goal of the ghetto if they realize that the ghetto is protesting against the immediate oppressors' misuse of legal power and, in many cases, legalized exploitation. The fourth category, obviously, is supportive of the goal of the ghetto.

Our current social situation, therefore, is not a conflict between the ghetto and the whole middle class. At least it need not and should not be. The ghetto and the middle class can gain mutually by uniting to eliminate the immediate oppressors and their supporters instead of fighting each other.

The immediate oppressors of the ghetto may be divided into economic oppressors and legal oppressors, even though economic oppressors need legal power, and legal oppressors manipulate and are manipulated by money. The economic oppressors consist of pawn shop owners, liquor store and grocery store operators, slum lords, finance companies, banks, and the like. The legal oppressors consist of some of the low-echelon policemen, court employees, parole officers, and social workers. What most of the middle class does not realize is that there are two kinds of store owners, two kinds of clerks, two kinds of policemen. The kind the middle class knows is courteous, fair, and helpful. The kind the ghetto knows is exploitative, unjust, and abusive. The policemen the ghetto resents are not the same policemen who serve the middle class in a praiseworthy manner. The immediate oppressors are like a crafty child who attacks smaller children three blocks away and never tells his parents about it. They abuse the legally powerless and never tell the civic authorities or the public about it. They get away with incredible degrees of injustice.

In order to understand how an immediate oppressor operates in the ghetto, put yourself in the shoes of a ghetto youth. You are just standing on the street. A police car comes by and slows down. You know you are going to be picked on for harassment. The officer steps out from his car, orders you to stand against a wall with your hands up, and searches your pockets. You happened to have $130 you have just earned from your job. You obtained your job by falsifying your name because you have a previous arrest record and the employer did not want anybody with a police record. The officer finds $130 and tells you: "Punk, I know you couldn't have gotten this much unless you stole it. Well, I'll let you get away easy this time. I'll give you $20 back. Make sure you keep your black mouth shut."

You know the policeman will keep the $110 to himself. But what can you do? If you tried to file a complaint, the court would not accept it. Even if the court would listen, you are afraid of losing your job if your real name becomes known. Still worse, you will become a target of retaliation by policemen.

Or you may be quietly chatting in your apartment with your sisters who are visiting you from another city. A policeman knocks on the door, comes in, searches around, and makes remarks insinuating that the girls are prostitutes you are pimping.

These are harassments that occur many times daily in the ghetto. The policemen do not have to exercise physical brutality to be resented. Naturally an abusive policeman will not report his harassments to his superior. The police chief hears nothing about it. If he does, he "knows nothing" about it. Certainly he will not report it to the mayor, and the mayor can rest in his clear conscience.

Not all policemen in the ghetto are abusive. But the abusive ones become conspicuous and create the stereotyped image of the police. In most cities the police department tends to protect abusive policemen from complaints. This is a self-defeating strategy. It only serves to generalize the ghetto's resentment onto the whole police department instead of confining it onto specific policemen. This is unfair to fair policemen. The ghetto youths may throw bricks at any policeman, even at the one who arrives to save the life of a man dying from a serious injury.

The ghetto knows nothing but exploitation. The social workers may practice favoritism in exchange for sex. The stores may raise prices on the day the welfare checks are distributed. The banks may charge higher interests and fees to ghetto residents. The slum lords and the car-financing companies may manipulate laws to exploit the legally powerless. If you are a ghetto resident, you cannot expect law-enforcement officers to protect you because many of them assume from the beginning that you are wrong. The ghetto residents do not receive the service the middle class receives from the police. In fact, if you are a ghetto resident and you call the police because someone has broken into your apartment, the police may ignore you or show up with much delay, or may decide that the burglary was caused by your negligence.

The middle class lives in security. This includes not only financial security but also legal security. If someone cheats you, mistreats you, or is unfair to you, you can always take legal action against him. The legal machinery protects you. From this legal security you derive a tremendous sense of psychological security. In the ghetto, the same legal apparatus is abused by the immediate oppressors to cause financial, legal, and psychological insecurity in the population.

The middle-class people may complain about a stomach ulcer caused by an internal revenue audit. But try to imagine the physical and mental stress if policemen insulted you every other day, gave you traffic citations for far-fetched reasons, searched your car for no reason, assuming that everything he finds in it is what you stole from somebody, provoked you into physical fights, and the court would not listen to you because it arbitrarily decided that you are an inferior human being. Harassed on the streets, you may try to seek refuge at your home. But your home also is a dangerous place. The fire department will not answer your fire alarm. The police will not protect your home from burglars. The insurance company will cancel your policy because you are a high risk. You lose your job because you are put in jail for not paying a heavy traffic fine which you believe you did not deserve and which exceeds your monthly salary. Well, what would become of you? A nervous breakdown? A physical wreck? An alcoholic? A drug addict? A murderer?

I have heard many middle-class people say: "Why do Negroes resort to violence? Why don't they solve their problems by nonviolent means?" The fact is that the nonviolent means that are available for the middle class are not open to the ghetto Afro-Americans. (They prefer to call themselves "Black" or "Afro-Americans." This does not necessarily mean they are Black Muslims. They consider "Negro" a label tagged by whites.) The whites within reach are immediate oppressors, including policemen. The Blacks cannot bring their complaints to the immediate oppressors. If the Blacks try to bypass the immediate oppressors and appeal to higher administration, it will not listen because it is unaware of the reality of the immediate oppressors. In fact, the administration will refer the matter back to the immediate oppressors who then retaliate by increasing their oppression. The vicious circle worsens until massive violence erupts.

The only solution lies in the civic administration's taking up the responsibility of eliminating the practice of the immediate oppressors. The administration has to go beyond job training, fair employment, better housing, and improved recreation facilities. It has to tackle the very basic problem: the legal feudalism in the ghetto in which there is no channel of complaint against injustice. The civic administration needs direct feedback from the very bottom, not filtered through several layers of bureaucratic hierarchy. It also needs executive power independent from police, welfare, and employment agencies to rectify the injustice. The feedback channel has to have accessible input tentacles right in the ghetto, manned by ghetto people themselves who walk on the streets, hang around in pool halls, bars, and beauty salons to talk with people, check store prices and loan interest rates, and monitor and report exploitation and abuse. The tentacles have to reach out into the most voiceless, hidden corners of the ghetto and actively seek out information, instead of sitting in an office to passively receive complaints. Preferably the mayor himself should act from time to time as one of the tentacles, walking in the ghetto, unaccompanied by immediate oppressors, possibly incognito, to talk with ordinary individuals on a person-to-person basis, not with official "organizers" or in organized meetings. If this is impracticable, the mayor should have one of his closest workers to perform that function for him. There should be no more than one person standing between the bottom corner of the ghetto and the mayor.

The honesty of the information the tentacles can obtain depends on the rapport and the mutual trust between the tentacles and the ghetto residents. The ghetto is filled with harassment and abuse. Personal information may become a tool for manipulation. Information gatherers may be suspected as agents of the immediate oppressors. Even if the information gatherers have a good intention, they may be naive enough to pass information onto "wrong" persons without realizing it. Ghetto residents are skilled at giving "phony" answers which satisfy the information gatherers.

The only way to gain trust in the ghetto is to prove yourself by action. The information givers have to be protected by confidentiality and anonymity from the immediate oppressors. The information obtained has to produce positive, visible results. The administration has to demonstrate its sincerity by promptly rectifying the reported injustice and by preventing retaliation resulting from the rectification.

This may be too difficult a task for a local civic administration. The federal government may be in a more independent and stronger position to operate such an injustice-rectifying loop. Whether run by the local or the federal government, such an injustice-rectifying device will be much less costly than riots.

The voices of the ordinary ghetto residents are seldom heard. The Negro voices the middle class hears come mostly from middle-class Negro intellectuals or from political extremists. The Black ghetto resents the Negro bourgeoisie as people who have gone into the white man's "system" and have turned against their own race. Conversely, many of the middle-class Negroes look down upon the ghetto Blacks as inferiors. They resent the ghetto Blacks as damaging the Negro's social acceptance by whites. For this reason the middle-class Negroes tend to discard the ghetto problems as someone else's problems. Often middle-class Negroes become policemen or other authority figures to act as immediate oppressors.

The Negro bourgeoisie not only may exploit the Black ghetto but also may use the pretext of helping the Black ghetto in order to advance its own cause which is irrelevant for the Black ghetto. Racial discrimination in real estate transactions, home loan interest, or hotel accommodation is a middle-class problem. The Black ghetto is worried about today's bread and immediate oppressors.

Most of the Negro organizations and organizers whom whites consider as "leaders" of the Black community are promoters of the interests of the middle-class Negroes. They have no power over the Black community and are resented by it. The civic administration cannot solve the ghetto problems by negotiating with the middle-class Negro "leaders" or by appointing middle-class Negroes to civic positions. It needs to communicate directly with the Black ghetto residents.

The ghetto life has a logic of its own. It cannot be understood with the middle-class logic. Take the case of a man who has accumulated a few hundred dollars in unpaid traffic citations because of his defective car which he has to drive to his work. His low salary delayed his payment of the fines, and this delay made his fines multiply. He has just started on a steady job. One day he sees a policeman approach him on the street. He fears being arrested and given a short prison term, which will result in loss of his job and collapse of his future which has just begun to open up. Hoping to get away, he stabs the policeman. The abstract term "murder" would not explain his act. You have to understand the despair of being trapped in the vicious circle of punitive chain and the dilemma of striving in it for any future at all.

Take another example. Two boys had a knife fight. It started as a matter of face-saving. They did not intend to kill each other. They staged the fight to display enough courage in front of their friends. But suddenly a policeman appeared and blew his whistle. One of the boys stabbed the other three times in the belly and the chest, and the victim died. Psychological analysis of this case showed that there were three reasons for this mortal act. First, the boy displaced his hostility toward the policeman to his innocent victim. He knew he could not fight the policeman who had a pistol. Therefore he stabbed his friend instead. Second, he knew he would be given a severe punishment, and wanted to "make up" for the punishment in advance. Third, now that the policeman appeared and blew his whistle, the knife fight became a reason for arrest. The friend therefore would be an indirect cause of the arrest. The boy wanted to "revenge" against his friend in advance for the anticipated punishment.

In these examples the aggressors acted with a certain logic because there was no way out for them. Like these two aggressors, the whole ghetto is caught in a blind alley. Increased oppression will result in increased violence.

Man acts with purpose. The relation between the purpose and the action is determined by the logic of the environment. Many ghetto women turn to prostitution. Some of them do so in order to earn easy money. But there are also many who become prostitutes because they want to be financially independent instead of depending on welfare checks. When opportunities for legitimate jobs are denied, prostitution becomes one of the few ways of self-assertion, financial independence, and self-respect. Prostitution is also a way to exploit white men's money, as in some areas most of the clients are whites.

In the middle-class logic, prostitution means degeneration. In the ghetto logic, prostitution sometimes can be motivated by the desire for financial independence and self-respect, for which the middle-class people also strive. The point I want to make is not that prostitution is a virtue in the ghetto, but that the ghetto people also strive for financial independence and self-respect, using the only means available to them.

The same goes for the pimps who run prostitutes. The middle-class male attains his self-image in this work and derives his sense of worth from it. The Black ghetto male lacks this source of self-image. Traditionally, Black women, who worked as housemaids, seamstresses, prostitutes, and mistresses, had an income and social status higher than Black men who worked as seasonal laborers. As a result the Black men lacked the means to assert their manhood. As they consider themselves worthless, their children lack a father image, and their wives lack a husband image. To be a pimp running prostitutes is an opportunity for a Black man to assert his manhood and to act as a father image to his girls. He may also gain a sense of victory over the white men from whom his girls take money.

These are some examples of the ghetto logic. The ghetto logic has developed as a result of the life under a peculiar pressure. The pressure comes from concrete individuals who exploit the ghetto. They are the immediate oppressors. The ghetto identifies the immediate oppressors with the entire middle class.

A large portion of the middle class is puzzled by the ghetto riots because it is unaware of the existence of the immediate oppressors. The immediate oppressors are our social disgrace. Our society is responsible for letting the immediate oppressors flourish. The middle class and the ghetto have a common cause: elimination of immediate oppressors. But of the two social strata, only the middle class possesses legal and nonviolent means. The ghetto is legally powerless. Its only means of expression is violence. Riots are a message to the middle class: "Why don't you people in power do something to eliminate our immediate oppressors?" So, let us do it. We can do it by extending our tentacles directly into the ghetto to monitor activities of the immediate oppressors, legally rectifying their abusive practices, and opening up nonabusive facilities to drive the abusive manipulators out of business.

11.4 FAMILY INTERACTION AS ANTECEDENT TO THE DIRECTION OF MALE AGGRESSIVENESS

Joan McCord
William McCord
Alan Howard

The development of aggressiveness has been the focus of much recent research in social science. Attacks on the problem have been from two directions: studies of antisocial behavior (Bandura & Walters, 1959; Glueck & Glueck, 1950; McCord & McCord, 1959) concerned with delinquents, and studies of general aggressiveness (McCord, McCord, & Howard, 1961; Sears, Maccoby, & Levin, 1957; Sears, Whiting, Nowlis, & Sears, 1953) based on samples of nondelinquents or predelinquents. The two approaches have yielded generally similar findings—of rejection, punitiveness, inconsistency—in the backgrounds of delinquents and of aggressive boys. This apparent similarity in environment and the fact that the majority of delinquents participate in aggressive behavior has created a tendency to translate the results of delinquency studies into conclusions about aggression and vice versa.[1] Yet, one of the few attempts to measure the relation between socialized and antisocial aggression, reported by Robert Sears,[2] gives no support for this tendency. Sears, in a study of 76 boys and 34 girls, found no positive relationship between antisocial aggression and other forms of aggressiveness (prosocial, aggression anxiety, projected aggression, or self-aggression), as measured by self-report scales of aggressiveness. Despite the difficulties inherent in use of self-report techniques to measure aggressiveness, it seems reasonable to reassess the

[1] One notes, for example, that *Adolescent Aggression* (Bandura & Walters, 1959) is a study of delinquent adolescents—although the focus of the book is on the development of aggression.

[2] Unpublished mimeographed report, "Relation of Early Socialization Experiences to Aggression in Middle Childhood," by Robert Sears.

Source: This research was supported by the Ella Lyman Cabot Foundation, the Harvard Laboratory of Social Relations, and the National Institute of Mental Health. Reprinted from the *Journal of Abnormal and Social Psychology*, 1963, **66,** 239–242, with permission of the authors and the American Psychological Association, Inc.

assumption that socialized and antisocial aggression have similar roots within the family circle.

Since most previous work on the etiology of delinquency has utilized control groups of nonaggressive boys or boys who, at the minimum, were presumably less aggressive than the delinquents, and many studies of nondelinquent aggressiveness have been carried out without distinguishing predelinquents from nondelinquents, the possibility arises that the two types of studies may have been confusing the origins of aggression with the origins of criminality. Both theoretically and practically—for some parents would like to see their children become "aggressive," though few would wish them to be criminals—the distinction seems to have importance. Thus, the question remains: In what ways do the family backgrounds of aggressive delinquent boys differ from aggressive nondelinquent boys? Or, somewhat differently stated, "What family environments tend to produce antisocial as opposed to socialized aggressiveness?"

There are, of course, many ways to define "antisocial" and aggressive. Some of these overlap in such a way that, by definition, the aggressive child is antisocial and vice versa. In order to inquire into the difference between forms of aggression which are considered acceptable by society and those which are condemned as criminal, definitions must be used which will make the two forms of behavior distinguishable. For the present study, an outgrowth of the Cambridge-Somerville Youth Study (Powers & Witmer, 1950), it was possible to use a longitudinal approach employing behavioral measures of both aggressiveness (in childhood and early adolescence) and antisocial behavior (in late adolescence and adulthood).

METHOD

The Cambridge-Somerville Youth Study took place between 1939 and 1945, during which time 255 boys living in deteriorated areas surrounding Boston, Massachusetts, between (on the average) ages 10 and 15, were observed at home, at school, and at play. Teachers and social workers who visited the families approximately every other week recorded their observations of the behavior of parents as well as children after each visit. The social workers appeared unannounced and with a frequency which enabled a variety of types of observations—at meals, in the midst of crises, and performing daily routines. In 1956 and 1957, trained researchers, reading these running records, classified each boy and his parents on variables ranging from occupation and religion to affectional interaction.[3] Interrater agreement, tested on a random sample, was high and the categorized ratings yielded strong relationships to completely independent measures of social deviance among the subjects when they had become adults (McCord & McCord, 1960).

To measure aggressiveness, the raters utilized reports made by teachers, camp counselors, and psychologists in addition to those of the home visitors. Those boys who reacted aggressively to most forms of frustration (they were involved in fist fights, bullying, or destructive behavior) were designated as "highly aggressive." The boys who, although they occasionally reacted aggressively, were generally realistic in response to frustration, were classified as "assertive." And those who rarely, if ever, exhibited aggression were considered "nonaggressive." Interrater reliability on this measure was .867.

To ascertain antisocial behavior, in 1955 the names of the 255 boys in the study were checked for court records. Those who had been convicted for larceny, breaking and entering, assault, or sex crimes were classified as "antisocial."[4]

Using these measures of aggressiveness and antisocial behavior, we found that adolescent aggressiveness was strongly related to antisocial behavior. Yet half of the aggressive adolescents had no records of antisocial behavior, and approximately two-thirds of the criminals had not been highly aggressive in adolescence. In order to concentrate upon the differentiating factors among aggressive boys, three groups were selected for comparison: the 26 men who, during early adolescence, had manifested extreme aggressiveness and had criminal records as adults (aggressive-antisocial men); the 25 men who, despite showing extreme aggressiveness during the earlier period of study, had not developed criminal records (aggressive-socialized men); and the 52 men who were neither aggressive nor criminal (nonaggressive men). Use of these three groups permitted differentiation among presumed causal conditions which contributed to antisocial aggressiveness and to socialized aggressiveness—for the two aggressive groups had exhibited similar behavior in childhood. Those conditions which differentiated the aggressive-antisocial from the aggressive-socialized men may be presumed to promote antisocial aggression; those which distinguished

[3] See McCord and McCord (1960) for a complete description of the ratings.

[4] This definition of "antisociality" is admittedly one which accepts society's definition of what is opposed to its interest. We recognize, of course, the numerous alternative definitions which might be employed with different results.

the aggressive from the nonaggressive—but failed to differentiate between the socialized and antisocial—may be presumed relevant only to a general syndrome of aggressiveness.

Table 1 *Family Background and Level of Aggression*

The Parents:	Percentage of Non-aggressive	Percentage of Aggressive-Socialized	Percentage of Aggressive-Antisocial
Were in conflict	($N = 43$) 12	($N = 21$) 38	($N = 21$) 57
Provided little supervision	($N = 52$) 25	($N = 25$) 48	($N = 26$) 77
Used extreme threats	($N = 41$) 32	($N = 22$) 64	($N = 23$) 87
Rejected the boy	($N = 42$) 10	($N = 19$) 21	($N = 23$) 87
Used inconsistent discipline	($N = 52$) 48	($N = 25$) 72	($N = 26$) 81
Held low expectations for boy	($N = 51$) 55	($N = 25$) 84	($N = 26$) 81
Provided no religious training	($N = 50$) 52	($N = 24$) 79	($N = 26$) 62

Note: The N reflects the number of subjects for whom there was sufficient information for a rating to be made for the category.

RESULTS

Even more than their socialized counterparts, the aggressive-antisocial men had experienced family discord, neglect, and parental attacks. Slightly more than half the aggressive-antisocial men had been reared by parents who were in almost constant conflict. Seventy-seven per cent had had no adult supervision during childhood. The parents of 87 per cent of the aggressive-antisocial men had frequently used extreme threats (e.g., of castration or of turning out of the house) in their child rearing. Seventy-seven per cent of their mothers (compared to 56 per cent of the aggressive-socialized and 42 per cent of the nonaggressive) rarely expressed, verbally or nonverbally, approval of or pleasure in their children. The fathers of 61 per cent of the aggressive-antisocial men (compared to 45 per cent of the aggressive-socialized and 23 per cent of the nonaggressive) openly displayed dislike of their offspring.

Other influences which are related to the level of aggression among socialized men (cf. McCord et al., 1961)—inconsistency in mother's discipline, low expectations, and absence of religious training[5]—were

[5] A mother who attended church or Mass once a week was assumed to provide religious training.

not found with greater frequency in the backgrounds of aggressive-antisocial than of aggressive-socialized men.

In addition to those conditions which also produced a relatively high proportion of aggressive-socialized men, the aggressive-antisocial men had been subjected to greater parental punitiveness. Parental discipline was judged on the basis of direct observation. Physical punishment (ranging from spanking to brutal beatings) was considered "punitive" and was opposed, for purposes of categorization, to such techniques as withdrawal of privileges, scoldings, or isolation. A significantly higher proportion of the aggressive-antisocial men than of the aggressive-socialized men had received punitive discipline from both their parents ($p < .01$).[6]

Table 2 *Punitiveness and Direction of Aggression*

Punitiveness by:	Percentage of Non-aggressive	Percentage of Aggressive-Socialized	Percentage of Aggressive-Antisocial
Both parents	20	22	70
One parent	35	61	26
Neither parent	45	17	4
Total	($N = 40$) 100	($N = 18$) 100	($N = 23$) 100

Note: The *N* reflects the number of subjects for whom there was sufficient information for a rating to be made for both parents.

Among single factors, the greatest direct influence on antisocial aggression, seems to come from the nature of the paternal model. Fathers were considered deviant if they were criminals or alcoholics; their aggressiveness was rated on the same scale as was that of their sons. A significantly higher proportion of the aggressive-antisocial men than of the aggressive-socialized men had been reared by deviant and aggressive fathers ($p < .05$). The fathers of 38 per cent of the aggressive-antisocial men, 12 per cent of the aggressive-socialized men, and 8 per cent of the nonaggressive men had been deviant and aggressive.

The measures of family interaction cannot be presumed to be independent, for a rejecting family was more likely to be punitive, a deviant father was more likely to be aggressive and rejecting. When,

[6] The chi-square test, two-tailed, was used to test for the significance of obtained differences.

as frequently occurred, these characteristics appeared in combination, the result was most likely to be an aggressive-antisocial son.

Other variables—intelligence, religious affiliation, neighborhood, father's birthplace—were tested and found to have no significant relationship either to antisocial aggressiveness or to socialized aggressiveness within our sample.

Table 3 *Summary: Differentiating Backgrounds*

	Percentage of Non-aggressive	Percentage of Aggressive-Socialized	Percentage of Aggressive-Antisocial
High drive production and:			
Deviant model	4	0	42
Nondeviant model	2	8	8
Moderate drive production and:			
Deviant model and high controls	6	8	35
Nondeviant model and high controls	19	12	0
Low controls	4	52	8
Low drive production and:			
Low controls	17	12	7
High controls	48	8	0
	$(N = 52)$ 100	$(N = 25)$ 100	$(N = 26)$ 100

Note: The absence of "perfect" relationships may be attributed to failures in measurement, incompleteness of the theory, or to potential freedom in behavior. See McCord and McCord (1960) for a discussion of this issue.

By combining various background conditions, it is possible to illustrate the different influences which relate to socialized and to antisocial aggressiveness. Rejection, punitiveness, and use of threats, we presumed, would tend to increase aggressive drive. By counting the mother and father separately for rejection and punitiveness, we obtained a drive producing scale ranging from zero to five—with scores of zero and one considered "low," two and three as "moderate," four and five as "high." We assumed that supervision, parental agreement, consistent discipline, high expectations, and religious training would tend to produce a controlled environment. A family providing two to five of these conditions was considered to have relatively high controls; families providing none or only one were considered to have low controls. The combinations of high drive production with deviant model (regardless of controls) and moderate drive production combined with deviant model and high controls tended to produce aggressive-antisocial men ($p < .001$). Moderate drive production with low controls (regardless of the model) tended to result in aggressive-socialized men ($p < .001$). Low drive production and high controls (regardless of model) tended to produce nonaggressive men ($p < .001$).

SUMMARY

In a longitudinal study of antisocial aggressiveness in males, reports on direct observation of behavior in childhood and early adolescence were used to rate general level of aggressiveness. Criminal records were used to ascertain antisocial behavior during adolescence and adulthood. To distinguish between conditions which contribute to socialized aggressiveness and those which direct aggression into antisocial channels, the family backgrounds of men who had been equally aggressive in childhood were compared. The results suggest that extreme neglect and punitiveness, coupled with a deviant-aggressive paternal model, produces antisocial aggressiveness. In contrast (though not contradiction), moderate neglect, moderate punitiveness, and ineffective controls produce socialized aggressiveness.

REFERENCES

Bandura, A., & Walters, R. *Adolescent aggression*. New York: Ronald, 1959.

Glueck, S., & Glueck, Eleanor. *Unraveling juvenile delinquency*. New York: Commonwealth Fund, 1950.

McCord, W., & McCord, Joan. *Origins of crime*. New York: Columbia Univ. Press, 1959.

McCord, W., & McCord, Joan. *Origins of alcoholism*. Stanford: Stanford Univ. Press, 1960.

McCord, W., McCord, Joan, & Howard, A. Familial correlates of aggression in nondelinquent male children. *J. Abnorm. Soc. Psychol.*, 1961, **62**, 79–93.

Powers, E., & Witmer, Helen. *An experiment in the prevention of delinquency*. New York: Columbia Univ. Press, 1950.

Sears, R., Maccoby, Eleanor E., & Levin, H. *Patterns of child rearing*. Evanston, Ill.: Row, Peterson, 1957.

Sears, R., Whiting, J. W. M., Nowlis, V., & Sears, Pauline S. Some child-rearing antecedents of aggression and dependency in young children. *Genet Psychol. Monogr.*, 1953, **47**, 135–234.

INDEX

Abegglen, J. G., 215, 233
Abernethy, E. M., 374, 382
Abrahams, Darcy, 38, 53–69
Acculturation, of American Indians, 422–432
Achenbach, T., 351–354, 359, 363–366
Achieve, need to, 255–261, 262–270
Adams, J. S., 137, 210–234
Ader, R., 147–148, 153
Adler, A., 381, 382
Adorno, T. W., 247, 254
Affiliation, need for, 262, 268–270
Affiliative behavior, 39–53
Aggression, and its management, 580–642
  antisocial, 636–642
  and childhood experiences, 636–642
  inhibition of, 599–608
  overt, 594–610
  as reduced by catharsis, 614–623
  as a result of group pressure, 581–592
  as resulting from frustration, 593–627
Alexander, S., 475, 477
Allee, W. C., 144–145, 153
Allport, F. H., 3, 145–146, 152, 153
Allport, G. W., 594, 613, 621, 623
Alpenfels, E. J., 332, 338
Alpert, R., 394, 397
Altrocchi, J., 351, 364, 366
Altus, W. D., 350, 374–382
Anastasi, Anne, 333, 338, 596, 623
Anderson, H. H., 391
Anderson, J. E., 286
Anxiety, capacity for, 364
Apicella, F. S., 598, 599, 623, 625
Appel, M. H., 616, 617, 623
Aronfreed, J., 103, 104, 105, 106, 110
Aronson, E., 40, 53, 203, 204
Aronson, Vera, 38, 53–69
Arousal, from presence of others, 149–152
Arrowood, A. J., 229, 233
Asch, S. E., 154, 165, 166, 179, 581, 582, 591, 592
Atkinson, J. W., 256, 259–263, 269, 271
Attitude change, 9–21, 179–205
Attitudes, 246–271
  effect of role changes on, 317–331
  parental, 247–255
  similarity in, 85–100
Attraction, social, 38–101
Attractiveness, physical, in dating, 53–69
Audience, role in communication, 399–412
Audience effects, in social facilitation, 138–141
Authoritarianism, 247–255
Avoidance learning, 147–149
Axelrod, H., 466, 477

Bach, G. R., 339, 348, 600, 603, 616, 623
Bachman, J. G., 511, 544–562
Baer, D. M., 104, 108, 109, 110
Bales, R. F., 294, 443, 451, 521, 527
Bandura, A., 102, 110–126, 133, 134, 135, 166, 179, 636, 642
Bank clerks, status inequity among, 212
Banta, T. J., 70, 84
Barker, C. H., 167, 179

Barker, R. G., 607, 624
Bass, B. M., 510, 527–544
Bateson, G., 610, 624
Bauer, R. A., 398, 399–412
Bayer, E., 141, 153
Bechtel, R. B., 247, 261–271
Beegle, J. A., 23, 36
Beier, E. G., 70, 84
Bell, C. B., 512, 518
Beller, E. K., 341, 348
Bem, D. J., 500, 509
Bender, I. E., 374, 375, 382
Bendix, R., 274, 282
Berdie, R. F., 66, 69
Berelson, B., 400, 405, 412
Berger, E. M., 57, 69
Bergum, B. O., 139, 153
Berkowitz, L., 580, 593–627
Berkun, M., 85, 100
Bieri, J., 368, 369, 372, 373
Birth order, 39, 40, 43, 44, 49, 52, 374–382
Bishop, D. W., 433, 466–477
Bixenstine, V. E., 478, 488
Blau, P. M., 546, 562
Blaylock, Barbara, 82, 84, 250, 254
Bliss, E. L., 149, 153
Block, Jeanne, 248, 254, 607, 624
Blomfield, J. M., 333, 338
Board, F., 149, 153
Bogart, L., 405, 411
Borgatta, E. F., 82, 84, 513, 518
Bornston, Frieda L., 608, 624
Bovard, E. W., 151, 152, 153
Bowerman, C. E., 69–70, 84
Bowers, D. G., 545, 562
Brady, J. V., 149–150, 153
Breed, Warren, 22–37
Brehm, J. W., 9, 182, 186, 204
Bronfenbrenner, U., 285, 286, 293, 294
Bronowski, J., 591
Brown, D. G., 341, 348
Brown, J. S., 594, 624
Brown, P. A., 596, 624
Brownfain, J. J., 351, 363, 367
Bruce, P., 364, 367
Bruner, J., 167, 179
Brunswik, E., 420, 421
Bugelski, B. R., 612, 615
Burgess, E. W., 82, 84
Burlingham, D. T., 347, 348
Buss, A. H., 469, 477
Byrne, D., 82, 84, 85–101, 246, 247–255

Campbell, D. T., 38, 69–85, 163, 165
Campbell, O. H., 541, 544
Capra, P. C., 378, 382
Carlsmith, J. M., 137, 166, 179–205
Carroll, E. E., 284
Casey, R. D., 400, 412
Catharsis, in reduction of aggression, 614–623
Cattell, J. M., 375, 382
Cattell, R. B., 444, 451
Cattell, R. S., 41, 52
Chance, June E., 393, 397
Chapanis, A., 205, 210
Chapanis, Natalia P., 205, 210
Charwat, W. A., 597, 598, 601, 609, 624
Chasdi, Eleanor H., 600, 605, 613, 624
Chen, S. C., 142–144, 153
Chicago, 24
Child, I. L., 608, 624
Child-parent relations among Hawaiians, 392–397
Christensen, C. R., 211, 224, 234
Christie, R., 251–252, 254
Civil rights, opinions about, 412–422
Clark, J. V., 215, 225–227, 233
Clark, K. B., 431, 432
Clark, R. A., 256, 259, 260, 261, 271, 604, 605, 618, 624
Clelland, C. C., 354, 363, 367
Clerical workers, pay inequity among, 224–225
Clinard, M., 23, 36
Co-action effects, in social facilitation, 141–147
Coch, L., 563, 579
Coelho, G. V., 391
Cognitive dissonance, 7–21, 179–205, 205–210
Cohen, A. R., 182, 186, 204, 408, 412, 601, 610, 624
Cohen, J., 333, 338
Cohen, Nadis, 596, 623
Coleman, J. C., 407, 412, 608, 624
Collins, B. E., 38, 39–53, 137, 179–205, 349
Collins, Mary E., 86, 100
Commins, W. D., 70, 85

Communication, 398–432
as a transactional process, 399–412
Compatibility, expectations for, 261–271
Competition, among groups, therapeutic effect of, 466–477
in groups, 452–466
Complementarity, and friendship, 69–85
Conformity, and reinforcement schedules, 154–165
Congdon, C. S., 613, 627
Conger, J. J., 332, 338
Congruity, 5
principle of, 234–245
Cooper, M., 24, 37
Coopersmith, S., 354, 363, 364, 367
Corsini, R., 70, 84
Coules, J., 599, 602, 603, 605, 619, 620, 627
Cox, D. F., 408–409, 412
Crandall, V. J., 333, 338
Crossley, A., 400
Crozier, M., 107
Crutchfield, R. S., 154, 156, 165, 582, 592
Csikszentmihalyi, M., 392

Dahlstrom, W. G., 66, 69
Danielson, W., 407
Darley, J. M., 40, 53
Das, J. P., 242, 244
Dashiell, J. F., 139, 145, 153
Dating behavior, 53–69
Davids, A., 368, 373
Davis, E. E., 413, 414, 421
Davis, J. A., 546, 562
Davison, W. P., 399–400, 404, 412
Davitz, J. R., 152, 153, 607, 625
Day, Barbara R., 70, 84
Day, C. R., 228, 233
Decision making, in business organizations, 563–579
Defensiveness, and role expectations, 443–452
Delinquency, and childhood experiences, 636–642
Dembo, Tamara, 54–69, 607, 624
Deprivation, social, 103–110
Deutsch, M., 86, 100, 167, 179, 452–454, 466, 477
DeVinney, L. C., 211, 214, 234, 317, 331
Dexter, L. A., 404, 412
Diab, L. N., 248, 254
Diaz-Guerrero, R., 383, 391, 392
Dickoff, H., 351, 364, 366
Dinwiddie, F. M., 613, 624
Dissonance theory, 179–210
Distler, L., 340, 348
Dittes, J. E., 378, 382
Dodge, Joan S., 469, 477
Doll, R., 392
Dollard, J., 593–623, 624
Doob, L. W., 593–623, 624
Dorwart, W., 102, 103–110
Douglas, J. W. B., 333, 338
Douvan, Elizabeth, 273, 282
Drucker, E. H., 475, 477
Dubois, Maria Eugenia, 392
Duffy, Elizabeth, 141, 153
Dunham, H. W., 24, 36
Dunn, R. E., 433, 434, 452–466
Dunteman, G., 510, 527–544
Durkheim, E., 3, 23, 26, 36
Durkin, D., 123, 125
Duvall, Evelyn M., 288
Dymond, Rosalind, 350–351, 363, 366, 367

Eber, H. W., 41, 52
Edmonson, M. S., 33, 34, 36
Edwards, A. L., 446, 448, 449, 451
Edwards, W., 334, 337, 338
Electric shock, simulated, 581–592
Elkin, A. P., 282
Ellis, H., 375, 382
Elms, A., 183, 197, 204
Endler, N. S., 136, 154–165
Engel, Mary, 354, 367, 368, 373
English, quality of spoken, 412–422
Erickson, Marilyn T., 108, 109, 110
Erikson, E. H., 110, 125
Ethical behavior, and group discussion, 500–509
Ethnocentrism, 304–305
Evans, R. I., 86, 95, 100
Expectancy-value theories, 261
Ezerman, R., 102, 103–110

Family, in Mexican-American culture, 298–299
Farber, J. E., 594, 624
Faris, R. E. L., 24, 36
Farrell, F. M., 434, 489–500
Fathers, effects of absence on sons, 339–348

Faust, W. L., 445, 452
Fear, 39–53
of failure, 261, 270
of rejection, 262–270
Feld, Sheila C., 263, 271
Ferson, Jean E., 87, 100
Feshbach, S., 253, 255, 600, 603, 613, 616, 618, 620, 624
Festinger, L., 8, 39–40, 53, 54, 69, 155, 163, 165, 166, 179, 180, 181–188, 197, 204, 211, 214, 219, 220, 233, 405, 406
Fiedler, F. E., 433, 466–477, 519, 520, 527
Field, P. B., 41, 53
Firstborn, advantages in college, 374–382
Fishbein, M., 416, 422
Fiske, D. F., 76, 77, 84
Foot-in-the-door technique, 165–179
Formica, R., 39, 53
Frank, J. D., 582, 592
Franklin, S. S., 263, 271
Fraser, S. C., 136, 165–179
Fredericksen, N., 613, 624
Freedman, J. L., 136, 165–179, 203, 204
Freedman, R., 24, 36
French, J. R. P., Jr., 545, 562, 563, 574, 582, 592, 598, 601, 612, 618, 619, 624
French, R. L., 512, 518
Frenkel-Brunswik, Else, 247, 254
Freud, Anna, 347, 348
Freud, S., 3, 110, 125, 594
Friendship, and leadership, 511–519
Friendship choice, 69–85
Frustration, as leading to aggression, 593–627
Frye, R., 528, 542, 543

Galliani, C., 392
Gallimore, R., 350, 392–397
Gallo, P., 434, 478–488
Gallup, G. H., 400
Game behavior, strategies in, 478–488
Gardener, D. H., 365, 367
Garfield, R. L., 70, 84
Garfield, S. L., 398, 422–432
Gates, M. J., 144–145, 153
Gaudet, H., 400, 412
Gengel, R. W., 234, 236, 239, 244, 245
Gerard, H. B., 39, 53, 167, 179
Gesell, A., 110, 125, 287
Gewirtz, J. L., 104, 108, 109, 110
"Ghetto" logic, 628–635
Gibb, J. R., 446, 451
Gibbs, J. P., 34, 36
Gilmore, J. B., 180, 182–183, 203, 204
Glucksberg, S., 70, 84
Glueck, Eleanor, 636, 642
Glueck, S., 636, 642
Goffman, E., 53, 69
Goldberg, M. H., 433, 435–443
Goldman, M., 433, 434, 452–466
Gordon, J. E., 603, 605, 625
Gough, H. G., 253, 254
Graham, F. K., 597, 598, 601, 609, 624
"Grasshopper" experiment, 10–14
Groesbeck, B. L., 269, 271
Grossack, M. M., 372, 373
Group discussion, and risk taking, 500–509
Group formation, and children's performance, 434–443
Group pressure, and aggression, 581–592
Group processes, 433–509
Group productivity, and leadership, 519–527
and role expectations, 443–452
Groups, competition within and among, 452–466
feeling within, 452–466
friendship and leadership in, 511–519
members' behavior in, 527–544
members' control within, 544–562
performance within, 544–562
problem solving by, 489–500
satisfaction within, 544–562
structure in, 489–500
Grusec, Joan, 102, 126–134, 246
Gurin, G., 263, 271
Gurnee, H., 149, 153
Gynther, M. D., 349, 353, 367, 368–373

Haaland, G. A., 155, 165
Haefner, D., 466, 467
Hagenah, T., 66, 69
Hall, Eleanor R., 416, 422
Hamburg, D. A., 149, 153
Hammond, L. K., 452, 465
Haner, C. F., 596, 624
Hanlon, T. E., 364, 367
Hansel, M., 333, 338

Harlow, H. F., 141–142, 153
Harris, D. B., 253, 254
Harrison, A. A., 434, 478–488
Hart, I., 248, 254
Hartley, E. L., 424, 432
Hartley, Ruth E., 424, 432
Harvey, O. J., 466, 477
Havel, Joan, 247, 254
Havighurst, R. J., 392
Havron, M. D., 471, 477
Hawaiians, independence training among, 392–397
"Hawthorne effect," 578
Hawthorne study, 576
Hayes, A. B., 332, 338
Hayes, S. P., 374–375, 382
Heard, W. G., 242, 244
Hebb, D., 364, 367
Heider, F., 8, 405
Helmreich, R. L., 38, 39–53, 137, 179–205
Helper, M. M., 398, 422–432
Henry, W. E., 405, 412
Herzog, Herta, 405, 412
Hetherington, E. Mavis, 70, 84, 273, 339–348
Heyns, R. W., 154, 165, 262, 271
Hill, W. F., 103, 110
Hillson, J. S., 351, 364, 367
Himmelweit, H., 594, 624
Hoffman, R. I., 70, 84
Hofstaetter, P. R., 364, 367
Hokanson, J. E., 603, 605, 625
Hollander, E. P., 155, 165
Holtzman, W. H., 87, 100
Homans, G. C., 211, 224–225, 233
Homme, L. E., 520, 527
Honig, A. S., 597, 598, 601, 609, 624
Horowitz, Frances D., 368, 373
Hostility, 580–642
expression and reduction of, 593–627
and frustration, 593–627
Hovland, C. I., 166, 179, 203, 204, 401, 412, 597
Howard, A., 305, 392–397, 581, 636–642
Hoyt, D. P., 469, 477
Huffman, Phyllis E., 248, 249, 250, 254
Hull, C., 596
Hurwitz, J. I., 512, 518
Husband, R. W., 140, 153
Husman, B. F., 617, 625
Huson, C., 546, 562
Huston, A. C., 112, 126, 133, 135
Hutchins, E. G., 469, 477
Hutton, D. C., 617, 625
Hyman, H. H., 263, 271, 274, 282, 290, 401, 412
Hymovitch, B., 512, 518

Ichheiser, G., 279, 282
Ideal self, 351–367
Ideal-self descriptions, 368–373
Ilg, Frances L., 110–125
Indians (American), acculturation of, 422–432
Inkeles, A., 288, 406, 407, 412
Intelligence, and self-concept in children, 352–366
Interaction orientation, and behavior in groups, 527–544
Interpersonal attitudes, 412–422
"Instant coffee" experiment, 17–20
"Irradiated meat" experiment, 14–17
Irvine, L. V., 253, 254
Izard, E. C., 70, 84

James, W. T., 142, 153
Janis, I. L., 40, 41, 53, 180, 182, 197, 203, 204, 408, 412
Jaques, E., 211, 217, 233
Jeffrey, T. E., 211, 233
Johnson, P. O., 556, 562
Johnson, W. R., 617, 625
Jones, E. E., 154, 165
Jones, L. V., 211, 233
Jordan, Cathie, 350, 392–397
Julian, J. W., 155, 165, 433, 466, 477

Kagan, J., 259, 260, 332, 338, 340, 348
Kahl, J. A., 273, 282
Kanfer, F., 542, 544
Karal, Pearl, 108, 110
Kardiner, A., 340, 348
Karon, B. P., 340, 348
Kass, N,, 333, 338
Kates, S. L., 248, 254
Katz, D., 2–5, 563, 579
Katz, E., 407, 412
Katz, F. M., 272, 273–282
Katz, I., 70, 84
Katz, Phyllis, 349, 351–367

Kaye, Carol, 566, 572, 578, 579
Keister, M. E., 607, 625
Keller, Helen, 112, 125
Kelley, H. H., 485, 488, 601, 625
Kelly, E. L., 70, 84
Kelly, J. G., 87, 100
Kelman, H. C., 155, 165, 166, 179, 181, 204
Kennedy, W. A., 425, 432
Kenny, D. T., 616, 625
Kimball, P., 405, 412
Kipnis, D., 8
Kitt, Alice S., 214, 233
Klapper, J., 402, 404, 412
Klaus, D. J., 520, 527
Klausner, S. J., 368, 372, 373
Klopfer, P. H., 144, 153
Kluckhohn, C., 283
Koch, Helen L., 85, 100
Kogan, N., 500, 501, 509
Kohn, M. L., 272, 282–296
Krauss, R., 70, 84
Krawitz, Rhoda N., 263, 271
Ktsanes, T., 69, 85
Ktsanes, Virginia, 69, 85

LaForge, R., 368, 369, 373
Lana, R. E., 510, 511–519
Langham, P., 466, 477
Lanzetta, J. T., 466, 477
Lasagna, L., 150, 153
Laswell, H. D., 400, 412
Lawrence, Margaret S., 600, 605, 613, 624
Lawton, Marcia J., 368, 373
Layton, W. L., 66, 69
Lazarsfeld, P. F., 400, 412
Leacock, Eleanor, 23, 36
Leader, F. B., 607, 625
Leader, influence of, 9–10
Leadership, 510–544
  and friendship, 511–519
  and group productivity, 519–527
  and least-preferred co-worker (LPC), 519–527
  and personal orientation, 532–533
Leary, T., 370
Least-preferred co-worker (LPC), 519–527
Leat, M., 134, 135
Lee, E. S., 23, 26, 36
Lehr, D. J., 139, 153
Leiderman, P. H., 150, 151, 153
Lemkau, P., 24, 37
Lesser, G. S., 263, 271, 605, 621, 625
Lev, J., 89, 101
Levin, H., 285, 394, 397, 600, 601, 605–608, 623, 625, 636, 642
Levin, Leslie A., 398, 413–422
Levinger, G., 582, 592
Levinson, D. J., 247, 248, 249, 250, 254
Levitt, E. E., 248, 252, 254
Lewin, K., 3, 8, 54–55, 69, 281, 282, 401, 563, 579, 607, 624
Lewis, M., 102, 103–106, 110
Lieberman, S., 273, 317–331
Light, C. S., 365, 367
Likert, R., 545, 562
Lincoln, J. F., 333, 338
Lindquist, E., 355, 357
Lindzey, G., 82, 84, 513, 518, 607, 613, 625
Linton, R., 274, 282
Lippitt, R., 563, 579
Lipset, S. M., 274, 282, 291
Lipsitt, L. P., 364, 367, 368, 373
Littman, R. A., 285
Litwin, G. H., 256, 260
Livson, N., 607, 625
Lobeck, R., 368, 369, 372, 373
Loh, W. D., 398, 413–422
Lonergan, B. G., 500, 509
Lott, A. J., 86, 100
Lowell, E. L., 256, 259, 260, 261, 271
Lubetsky, J., 70–71, 84
Luchins, A. S., 155, 165
Luchins, E. H., 155, 165
Lumsdaine, A. A., 203, 204, 401, 412
Lutzker, D., 478, 482, 488
Lyle, W. H., 248, 254
Lynn, D. B., 339, 348
Lysgaard, S., 370, 373

MacBride, P., 582, 592
Maccoby, Eleanor E., 127, 133, 135, 285, 394, 397, 405, 412, 433, 435–443, 606, 607, 608, 623, 627, 636, 642
Maccoby, N., 405, 412, 563, 579
MacGregor, G., 422, 424, 431, 432
MacKinnon, D. W., 612
Maclay, H., 422, 432
Magoon, T. M., 469, 477
Mahrer, A. R., 117, 125

Malof, M., 86, 100
Malzberg, B., 23, 26, 36
Management, assessment of, 544, 562
Mandler, G., 263, 271
Mann, J. H., 85, 100
March, J., 546, 562
Martin, B. C., 607, 624
Martin, W. E., 253, 254
Martin, W. T., 34, 36
Maruyama, M., 580, 628–635
Marx, M. H., 597, 625
Maslow, A. H., 594, 608, 625
Mason, J. W., 149–150, 153
Mason, L. J., 152, 153
Mason, R., 10
Masure, R. H., 144, 153
Mausner, B., 155, 165
Maxwell, J., 327, 382
McAfee, R. O., 354, 363, 367
McCandless, B. R., 363–365, 367, 599, 626
McCann, W. P., 150, 153
McClelland, D. C., 246, 255–261, 271, 596, 598, 599, 609, 612, 620, 621, 623, 625
McClintock, C. G., 434, 478–488, 500, 509
McCord, Joan, 339, 348, 581, 636–642
McCord, W., 339, 348, 581, 636–642
McDonald, F. J., 102, 110–126
McDonald, R. D., 87, 100
McDonald, R. I., 349, 368–373
McDonald, R. L., 353, 367
McGinnies, E., 510, 511–519
McGrath, J. E., 471, 477
McGraw, C., 85–101
McKee, J. P., 607, 625
McKellar, P., 600, 625
McNemar, Q., 335, 338
Mead, G. H., 307, 316
Meeland, T., 85, 100
Mendelsohn, J., 542
Menzel, H., 407, 412
Merton, R. K., 213–214, 233, 274, 282
Merwin, J. C., 66, 69
Mexican youth, value systems of, 383–392
Meyer, H. H., 256, 260
Mezei, L., 134, 135
Middle class and the "ghetto," 628–635
Migrants, suicide among, 22–36
Milgram, S., 580, 581–592
Miller, D. R., 292, 608, 625
Miller, N. E., 38, 39, 53, 69–85, 268, 271, 593–623, 624, 626
Mintz, A., 435, 443, 597, 626
Mischel, W., 102, 126–135, 246
Mitnick, L. L., 512, 518
Models, influence on children's behavior, 110–126
Moore, H. E., 34, 36
Moore, R. C. A., 285
Moral judgments, by children, 110–126
Morlan, G. K., 615, 617, 626
Morrison, H. W., 582, 592
Morse, Nancy C., 511, 563–579
Morton, A., 82, 84
Mosher, D. L., 253, 254
Moss, H. A., 259, 260, 340, 348
Mowrer, E. R., 23, 36
Mowrer, O. H., 103, 110, 593–623, 624
Murney, R. G., 613, 625
Murstein, B. I., 70, 84
Mussen, P. H., 332, 338, 340, 348, 605, 607, 621, 626
Myers, A. E., 466, 471, 477

Nanda, P. C., 242, 244
National character, 386
Naylor, H. K., 605, 621, 626
Need achievement (n Ach), 255–261, 262–270
Negroes, in "ghetto," 628–635
  conflicts between lower- and middle-class, 633
  interpersonal attraction toward, 85–101
  interpersonal reaction to, 413–422
  suicide among, 33–36
Nelson, D. H., 149, 153
Newcomb, T. M., 70, 85, 100, 250, 254, 269, 271, 317, 331, 405, 602, 626
New Orleans, 22–36
Nichols, R. C., 380, 382
Nicol, Elizabeth H., 434, 489–500
Nieuwenhuyse, B., 141, 153
North African immigrants to Israel, 306–316
Nowlis, H., 341, 348
Nowlis, V., 606, 613, 627, 636, 642
Nuttin, J. M., 184–185, 204

O'Connell, E. J., 38, 69–85
O'Connor, J. P., 364, 367

Oltean, Mary, 248, 255
Organizational behavior, 510–579
Organizational structure, participating vs. centralized, 563–579
Osgood, C. E., 8, 234, 238, 244, 405, 413, 421, 422, 423, 432, 470, 477
Otis, N. B., 599, 626
Ovesey, L., 340, 348

Packard, Rita, 263, 271
Palmore, E. B., 86, 100
Parent-child relationships, and social class, 282–296
Paris, 23
Parsons, O. A., 351, 364, 366
Parsons, T., 294, 317, 331, 404, 412
Pasamanick, B., 502, 503, 509
Pastore, N., 609–610, 626
Patchen, M., 211, 214, 221, 224, 234
Paterson, T. T., 466, 477
Patterson, C. H., 419, 421
Peck, R. F., 350, 383–392
Pepitone, A., 601, 612, 618, 619, 626
Perkins, C. W., 354, 363, 367
Persky, H., 149, 153
Peryam, D. R., 12
Pessin, J., 139–140, 153
Phillips, L., 351, 367
Piaget, J., 102, 110, 112, 113, 114, 116, 118, 121, 125, 351, 352, 367
Pierce-Jones, J., 285
Pilgrim, F. J., 12
Pilliner, A. E., 377, 382
Pintler, Margaret H., 339, 348, 608, 626
Pool, I., 407, 411
Porterfield, A. L., 24, 36
Postman, L., 540
Potash, H. M., 478, 488
Powers, E., 637, 642
Powers, J. H., 333, 338
Prejudice, racial, 85–100
Prisoner's Dilemma game, 478–488
Pritzker, H. A., 166, 179

Quinn, M. J., 108, 110

Rabbie, J. M., 39, 53
Rabinovitch, M. S., 351, 367
Rabson, A., 333, 338
Race, and interpersonal attitudes, 413-422
Racial differences, in paternal absence on boys, 339–348
and self-concept, 368–373
Rasmussen, E., 147, 153
Rau, Lucy, 394, 397
Raven, B. H., 545, 562, 582, 592
Rawson, H. E., 503, 509
Ray, E., 108, 110
Reichling, G., 601, 612, 618, 619, 626
Reilly, Mary St. A., 70, 85
Reimer, E., 511, 563-579
Reinforcement, 103-110
Reinforcement, and conformity, 154–165
Rettig, S., 434, 500–509
Rewards, within groups, 544–562
Ricciuti, H. N., 257, 261
Richardson, H. M., 82, 85
Rickard, T. E., 419, 421
Riecken, H., 601, 612, 619, 621, 627
Riesman, D., 329, 331
Riley, J. W., Jr., 404
Riley, Matilda W., 404
Risk taking, ethical, 500–509
sex differences in, 332–338
Roby, T. B., 434, 489–500
Roethlisberger, F. J., 211, 224, 234
Rogers, C., 350–351, 363, 366, 367
Rohrer, J. H., 33, 34, 36
Rokeach, M., 86, 95, 100
Role, 272–348
Role expectations, clear and unclear 443–452
Roles, effect of changes in, 317–331
Roper, E., 400
Rosen, B. C., 273, 282
Rosen, E., 422, 432
Rosenbaum, W. B., 227–229, 233
Rosenberg, M. J., 180, 205
Rosenfield, H. M., 53, 69, 247, 261–271
Rosenhan, D., 102, 103–110
Rosenthal, R., 186, 205
Rosenzweig, S., 607, 608, 622, 626
Ross, Dorothea, 112, 125, 126, 133, 134, 135, 166, 179
Ross, Sheila A., 112, 125, 126, 133, 134, 135, 166, 179
Rossi, A. M., 70, 84
Roth, Chaya H., 104, 110
Rottman, L., 38, 53–69
Ruebush, B., 364, 367

Russell, P. N., 137, 205–210

Sadacca, R., 257, 261
Samelson, Nancy M., 563
Sample, J. A., 510, 519–527
Samuels, L. T., 149, 153
Sandberg, A. A., 149, 153
Sanford, R. N., 247, 254
Sarason, S. B., 263, 271
Sarbin, T. R., 443, 451
Sargent, S. S., 607, 626
Sawrey, W. L., 339, 348
Schachter, S., 39–40, 51, 52, 53, 374, 375, 379, 380, 382
Schaefer, E. S., 294
Scheier, I., 167, 179
Schein, E. H., 154, 165, 167, 179
Schertzer, A. L., 333, 338
Schizophrenia, 24
Schmid, C. F., 25, 35, 36
Schneider, L., 370, 373
Schooley, Mary, 250, 254
Schramm, W., 407
Schroeder, J. W., 23, 37
Schulman, S., 301
Scodel, A., 253, 254
Scollon, R. W., 9–10
Scott, W., 351, 367
Sears, Pauline S., 54, 69, 339, 341, 348, 596, 606, 607, 608, 613, 626
Sears, R. R., 103, 110, 285, 339, 341, 348, 394, 397, 593, 623, 624, 626, 627, 636, 642
Seidenfeld, M. A., 403, 412
Self-concepts, and sex, race, and social class, 368–373
Self-image disparity, effects of, 351–367
Self-orientation, and behavior in groups, 527–544
Self-rejection, among immigrants to Israel, 306–316
Selye, H., 149, 153
Semantic differential, 422–432
Seward, J. P., 596, 600–601, 607, 618, 627
Sex differences, 332–338
  and self concept, 368–373
Shannon, D. T., 354, 363, 367
Shapiro, D., 150, 151, 153
Sheatsley, P. B., 401, 412
Sheffield, F. D., 203, 204, 401, 412
Sherif, Carolyn W., 466, 477
Sherif, M., 154, 165, 466, 477
Shuval, Judith T., 273, 306–316
Sidman, M., 149–150, 153
Siegel, S. M., 106, 110, 253, 255, 446, 452
Similarity, and attraction, 85–100
  as factor in friendship, 69–85
Simon, H. A., 489, 500, 546, 562
Singer, R. D., 253, 255, 613, 624
Sinha, J. B., 502, 509
Skinner, B. F., 110, 112, 126
Slesinger, J. A., 511, 544–562
Slovic, P., 273, 332–338
Slum culture, 628–635
Smith, B. L., 400, 412
Smith, C., 512, 519
Smith, C. G., 511, 544–562
Smith, E. E., 1, 7–21, 433, 443–452
Smith, F. T., 86, 100
Smith, Patricia W., 86, 95, 100
Social acceptance, expectations for, 261–271
Social class, and self concept, 368–373
Social class, meaning of success in, 273–281
  and parent-child relations, 282–296
Social deprivation, 103–110
Social-drive theory, 108–109
Social facilitation, 138–153
Social influence, 136–245
Social learning, and model characteristics, 126–135
Social motives, 246–271
Social psychology, present status of, 2–5
  research methodology in, 2–3
Social reinforcement, 103–110, 110–126
Social self, 351, 357–358
Sociometry, 511–519
Soviet refugees, 406
Spaeth, J. L., 546, 562
Spanish-speaking migrants, 297–306
Spatz, Dorothy, 596, 623
Spence, K. W., 141, 149, 153
Spock, B., 287
Staats, A. W., 242, 244
Staats, Carolyn K., 242, 244
Stagner, R., 613, 627
Star, Shirley A., 211, 214, 234, 317, 331
Status, 272–348
  and quality of speech, 412–422
Status discrepancy, 261–271
Stefic, E. C., 70, 85

Steinberg, Alma G. B., 391
Stereotypes, regarding immigrants to Israel, 310–312
Stewart, Mary, 378–379, 382
Stolz, Lois M., 339, 348
Stone, A. A., 618, 627
Stouffer, S. A., 211, 214, 234, 317, 331
Strand, Susan, 478, 488
Strategies, in game behavior, 478–488
Stress, effect on affiliative behavior, 39–53
Structure, in groups, 489–500
Success, meaning of, 273–281
Suchman, E. A., 211, 214, 234, 317, 331, 333, 338
Suci, G. J., 238, 244, 413, 421, 422, 423, 470, 477
Suczek, R. F., 368, 369, 373
Suicide, 22–36
Sullivan, H. S., 110, 126
Supermarket clerks, status inequity among, 225–227
Svehla, G., 250, 254
Swanson, E. O., 66, 69
Swanson, G. E., 292, 608, 625
Swineford, F., 332–333, 338

Takezawa, S. I., 413, 421
Tannenbaum, A. S., 544–547, 554, 562, 566, 579
Tannenbaum, P. H., 8, 137, 234–245, 405, 413, 421, 423, 432, 470, 477
Task orientation, and behavior in groups, 527–544
Tatum, R., 147–148, 153
Taylor, D. W., 445, 452
Taylor, Janet A., 469, 477
Terman, L. M., 65, 69, 374–375, 380, 382
Tharp, R. G., 69, 85
Thibaut, J. W., 485, 488, 599, 601, 602, 603, 605, 612, 618–621, 627
Thiessen, D. D., 150, 153
Thurber, E., 339, 348
Tietze, C., 24, 37
Tiller, P. O., 339, 348
Tolman, C. W., 141, 153
Torrance, E. P., 10, 13, 21, 444, 452
Torrey, R., 154, 165
Travis, L. E., 138–139, 140, 146, 153
Triandis, H. C., 95, 101, 398, 413–422, 432
Triandis, Leigh M., 413, 416, 422
Triplett, N., 138, 153
Tuddenham, R. D., 332, 338, 582, 592
Turgeon, V. F., 600, 601, 605, 625
Turner, E. A., 203, 205
Twedt, Helen, 38, 69–85

Ulibarri, H., 272, 297–306
Updegraff, R., 607, 625

Values, cross-cultural study of, 383–392
Van Arsdol, M. F., 34, 36
Van DeRiet, V., 425, 432
Vaughan, W., 510, 511–519
Veldman, D., 384
Vernon, P. E., 532, 544
Veroff, J., 262, 263, 271
Vidulich, R., 528, 543

Walker, E. L., 154, 165
Walker, Helen M., 89, 101
Walker, N. B., 256, 260
Wall, A. M., 103–106, 110
Wallach, M. A., 500, 501, 509
Wallin, P., 82, 84
Walster, Elaine, 38, 53–69
Walters, R. H., 108, 110, 134, 135, 636, 642
Wambach, H., 528, 543
Ware, E. E., 422, 432
Warner, W. L., 405, 412
Weber, M., 3
Weiss, W., 243, 245
Wells, H. H., 154, 165
Welsh, G. S., 66, 69
Welty, J. C., 149, 153
Weltz, P. C., 597, 598, 601, 609, 624
Werner, H., 351
White, D. M., 404, 412
White, J. C., 425, 532
White, M. S., 286
White, R. K., 563, 579
Whiting, J. W. M., 341, 348, 606, 613, 627, 636, 642
Williams, R. M., Jr., 211, 214, 234, 283, 284, 317, 331
Wilson, G. T., 141, 153
Wilson, K. V., 478, 488
Wilson, P. R., 137, 205–210
Wilson, T. R., 510, 519–527
Winch, R. F., 69, 85

Winer, B. J., 49, 53, 207, 210, 239, 245
Winick, C., 405, 412
Winterbottom, Marian R., 393, 397
Witmer, Helen, 637, 642
Wong, T. J., 85, 86, 88, 92, 93, 99, 101
Worchel, P., 351, 364, 367, 623, 627
Worthy, J. C., 563, 579
Wright, C., 404, 412
Wright, G. O., 614, 627
Wright, J. C., 203, 205
Wright, M. E., 601, 627
Wrightsman, L., 40, 53
Wylie, Ruth, 350, 353, 367, 368, 369, 372, 373

Yarrow, L. J., 600, 602, 627

Zajonc, R. B., 136, 138–153
Zaleznik, A., 211, 224, 234
Zander, A. F., 512, 518, 607, 627
Zax, M., 365, 367
Zigler, E., 349, 351–367
Zimbardo, P. G., 9, 39, 53
Zimmerman, Claire, 407, 410, 412
Zuckerman, M., 248, 255